Bridges Not Walls

A Book About Interpersonal Communication

TENTH EDITION

John Stewart
University of Dubuque

 **Higher Education**

Boston Burr Ridge, IL Dubuque, IA New York San Francisco St. Louis
Bangkok Bogotá Caracas Kuala Lumpur Lisbon London Madrid Mexico City
Milan Montreal New Delhi Santiago Seoul Singapore Sydney Taipei Toronto

 **Higher Education**

Published by McGraw-Hill, an imprint of The McGraw-Hill Companies, Inc., 1221 Avenue of the Americas, New York, NY 10020. Copyright © 2009, 2006, 2002, 1999, 1995, 1990, 1986, 1982, 1977, 1973. All rights reserved. No part of this publication may be reproduced or distributed in any form or by any means, or stored in a database or retrieval system, without the prior written consent of The McGraw-Hill Companies, Inc., including, but not limited to, in any network or other electronic storage or transmission, or broadcast for distance learning.

This book is printed on acid-free paper.

1 2 3 4 5 6 7 8 9 0 DOC/DOC 0 9 8

ISBN: 978-0-07-338499-3
MHID: 0-07-338499-2

Editor in Chief: *Michael Ryan*
Publisher: *Frank Mortimer*
Executive Editor: *Katie Stevens*
Executive Marketing Manager: *Leslie Oberhuber*
Developmental Editor: *Marley Magaziner*
Editorial Assistant: *Erika Lake*
Production Editor: *Karol Jurado*
Production Service: *Melanie Field, Strawberry Field Publishing*
Manuscript Editor: *Tom Briggs*
Cover Designer: *Allister Fein*
Senior Production Supervisor: *Richard DeVitto*
Permissions Coordinator: *Karyn Morrison*
Composition: *10/12 Palatino by Aptara*
Printing: *45# New Era Matte Plus, R. R. Donnelley & Sons*

Credits: The credits section for this book begins on page 585 and is considered an extension of the copyright page.

Library of Congress Cataloging-in-Publication Data

Bridges not walls : a book about interpersonal communication / [edited by] John Stewart.—10th ed.
   p. cm.
   Includes bibliographical references and index.
   ISBN-13: 978-0-07-338499-3 (alk. paper)
   ISBN-10: 0-07-338499-2 (alk. paper)
1. Interpersonal communication. I. Stewart, John Robert.
BF637.C45B74 2009
158.2—dc22

                           2008009212

The Internet addresses listed in the text were accurate at the time of publication. The inclusion of a Web site does not indicate an endorsement by the authors or McGraw-Hill, and McGraw-Hill does not guarantee the accuracy of the information presented at these sites.

www.mhhe.com

For Rima

About the Editor

JOHN STEWART taught interpersonal communication at the University of Washington from 1969 to 2001. He attended Centralia Community College and Pacific Lutheran University, then earned his M.A. at Northwestern University and completed his Ph.D. at the University of Southern California in 1970. In 2001 John moved to the University of Dubuque in northeast Iowa, where he is Vice President for Academic Affairs and Dean of the Graduate School. He continues to teach interpersonal communication at UD. He has three children and two grandchildren.

Books and People

Imagine yourself in a situation where you are alone, wholly alone on earth, and you are offered one of the two, books or [people]. I often hear [speakers] prizing their solitude, but that is only because there are still [people] somewhere on earth, even though in the far distance. I knew nothing of books when I came forth from the womb of my mother, and I shall die without books, with another human hand in my own. I do, indeed, close my door at times and surrender myself to a book, but only because I can open the door again and see a human being looking at me.

—Martin Buber

Contents

Part Four
BRIDGES NOT WALLS

Preface

This tenth edition of *Bridges Not Walls* maintains the approach and most of the basic format of the previous nine editions. The book's major divisions parallel those of most interpersonal communication books—foundations are first, followed by treatments of inhaling and exhaling (making meaning together), relationships, and building bridges not walls (difficult communication, conflict, cultural differences, dialogue). I have kept almost the same chapter sequence and the articles that reviewers appreciated, but I have updated several chapters to reflect current communication concerns and directions of current research and teaching. For example, Malcolm R. Parks' research and analysis significantly expands and enriches the discussion of the relationship between quality of communication and quality of life in Chapter 2. The chapter on communication and identities now includes a treatment of deafness. The listening chapter contains an analysis of mindful/mindlessness. Deborah Tannen discusses family metamessages and mother-daughter communication in Chapter 7. Robert Hopper and Malcolm R. Parks treat gender and ethnic similarities and differences in Chapter 8. A team of communication researchers discuss bullying in Chapter 9. The "Bridging Cultural Differences" chapter includes a Muslim-Christian discussion by Akbar Ahmed and an article about communicating with persons with disabilities by Dawn and Chuck Braithwaite. Daniel Yankelovich, Rabbi Jonathan Sacks, and the founders of the Public Conversations Project significantly enrich the final chapter, on dialogue.

Bridges Not Walls is still designed primarily for college students enrolled in interpersonal communication classes, but the readings discuss topics also included in social work, humanities, counseling, and sociology courses. A majority of the readings are authored by communication scholars and teachers, but there are also materials from authors in a range of disciplines, including education, organizational development, clinical and social psychology, cultural and media studies, international relations, and philosophy.

Since the first edition of *Bridges*, published in 1973, the approach to communication that has guided this collection of readings has been a relational one that focuses on the quality of contact that people create *together*. In other words, as the first two chapters explain, "communication" is understood basically as the term humans use for our collaborative processes of meaning making. To say that humans are "social animals" is to say that we make sense of things *with others*, and "communication" is the general label for these processes. When I call these processes "collaborative," I obviously do not mean that humans always agree as we make meanings together, but only that we "co-labor," or work out meanings in response to one another. All this implies that communication is not simply an activity that one person performs or does "to" another but is a process that happens *between* people. For those with theoretical interests, these basic ideas can be found in primary works by Mikhail Bakhtin, Martin Buber, Martin Heidegger, Alfred Schutz, and Hans-Georg Gadamer, and in works by social construction theorists and practitioners.

Interpersonal communication is a subset of communication, a type or kind of contact that happens when the people involved talk and listen in ways that maximize the presence of the personal. This approach to interpersonal communication emphasizes the prominence of culture, it highlights the ways communication affects social and personal identities, and it emphasizes the close connection between quality of communication and quality of life. In other words, although communication clearly can be expressive and instrumental, this approach emphasizes that it is also person building, which is to say that *who humans are* gets worked out in our verbal/nonverbal contact. Virtually all of the authors represented here acknowledge these features of communication, and many comment directly on them.

This is a book for people who want practical suggestions and skills that will help them communicate more effectively with their friends, partners, spouses, family, and coworkers. But unlike much of the self-help literature, *Bridges* resists the tendency to gloss over conceptual issues and to reduce interpersonal effectiveness to techniques or formulas. The authors of these readings recognize that there is much more to effective communication than simply "being open and honest." For example, there are thought-provoking discussions of the nature of interpersonal contact, the inseparability of verbal and nonverbal cues, identity management and social intelligence, listening, deception and betrayal, interpersonal ethics, family intimacy, cultural diversity, and dialogue. *Bridges* also includes systematic treatments of self-awareness, functions of nonverbal behavior, social perception, listening, disclosure, gender patterns, hurtful messages, and defensiveness. But no reading claims to offer the definitive "6 steps" or "12 easy techniques" for guaranteed success. The authors emphasize that the unique situation, the constancy of change, and especially the element of human choice all make it impossible to design and execute a purely technical approach to *human* relationships.

   This point is rooted in the book's definition of its subject matter, which I've already sketched. *Bridges* does not define interpersonal communication as something that happens only in face-to-face settings, during discussions of weighty topics, or in long-term, intimate relationships. Instead, the term "interpersonal" designates a kind or quality of contact that emerges between people whenever they are willing and able to highlight in their speaking and listening aspects of what makes them human. My introduction in Chapter 1 and the first essay in Chapter 2 explain this definition, and subsequent readings extend and develop it. Throughout the book, the point is also made that different kinds or qualities of contact are appropriate in different situations. "More" interpersonal communicating is *not* always better. There is much more to it than that, as the readings in Chapters 9–11 especially demonstrate. At the same time, materials in several chapters clarify how most people's personal, educational, and work lives could profit from increased interpersonal contact.

   Many readings also emphasize the point made earlier that communication is more than just a way to get things done, because it affects who we are—that is, our identities. I introduce this idea at the beginning of the book; Stuart Sigman, Harold Barrett, Daniel Goleman, Karen Zediker and Saskia Witteborn and I, Donal Carbaugh, Lawrence B. Rosenfeld and Jack M. Richman, Deborah Tannen, Julia T. Wood, and Marsha Houston develop and extend the discussion of identity; and the person-building dimension of communication is a profound part of Martin Buber's essay that concludes Chapter 2.

   These theoretical and conceptual commitments are complemented by my desire to make the book as readable as possible. This is the main reason why few research articles from scholarly journals are included. As in all earlier editions, I have tried to select substantive materials that speak directly to the student reader. I continue to search for authors who "write with their ears," or talk with their readers. Selections from past editions, by Susan Scott, Virginia Satir, Julia Wood, Susan Campbell, and Hugh and Gayle Prather, are included in this edition partly because they do this so well. I have also found this accessibility in some new authors, especially Maggie Herzig and Laura Chasin, and Akbar Ahmed.

New Features

People familiar with earlier editions will notice that Part Five, "Approaches to Interpersonal Communication," is missing from this edition. Reviewers told me that they seldom had the class time to assign those readings, especially in an introductory course. I did keep Martin Buber's "Elements of the Interhuman" essay, placing it in Chapter 2 to emphasize how thoroughly his philosophy underlies everything in the other chapters.

   Each time *Bridges Not Walls* is reviewed, I get some complaints that Buber is "too dense," "too hard to read," and "too heavy," to say nothing of the sometimes archaic and sexist language. Happily, I also hear and see what happens when students in my classes—and in classes I observe being taught by graduate teaching assistants—actually begin to connect with Buber and his ideas. When teacher and student are patient and diligent, they often find that Buber can significantly deepen their understanding of interpersonal communicating. This experience frequently motivates them to apply these ideas, even in the face of hardships and challenges. All this continues to make teaching Buber rewarding for me and for many of the people I work with.

Another emphasis that is new to this edition appears especially in the readings by Akbar Ahmed (Chapter 11), Maggie Herzig and Laura Chasin (Chapter 12), and Jonathan Sacks (Chapter 12). These materials push this book's approach to interpersonal communication into the public arena. Ahmed is a distinguished professor of international relations who believes that dialogue can ameliorate the Christian-Muslim tensions that are at the root of much that is labeled "terrorist," including the War on Terror. Maggie Herzig and Laura Chasin founded the Public Conversations Project to foster dialogue across such divides as those between pro-life and pro-choice forces, Red and Blue states, and GLBT proponents and anti-GLBT advocates. Rabbi Jonathan Sacks argues persuasively that the three Abrahamic faiths that are currently fueling worldwide unrest are the very systems that can effectively restore peace, but only if they can return to their shared roots. I hope that teachers and students will find these conceptual and practical extensions to be edifying.

Reviewers urged me to keep many features of the book that have been maintained. They strongly recommended that I bring back Jack Gibb's classic treatment of defensiveness, and I have. They asked that I reduce the number of articles that consisted mainly of lists, and I have attempted to comply. They expressed appreciation for the diversity of voices, which I have attempted to maintain. Twenty-seven of the authors are women; there are discussions of nontraditional families and gay, lesbian, and bisexual friends; several authors treat gender differences; and I include descriptions of aspects of deaf, Blackfeet, online, Black, Muslim, and Jewish cultures.

Other Features

As in earlier editions, my introduction shows how *Bridges Not Walls* is different from the standard, faceless, "objective" college textbook. I want readers to consider the potential for, as well as the limits of, interpersonal communicating between writer and reader. I also want them to remember that a book or essay is always somebody's point of view. I'd like readers to respond to what's here not as "true because it's printed in black and white" but as the thoughtful speech of the person addressing them. In the Introduction, I tell readers a little about myself, give a rationale for the way the book is put together, and argue for the link between quality of communication and quality of life.

Two sets of questions follow each reading. The first, "Review Questions," are designed to prompt the reader's recall of key ideas. If the student can respond to these, there is some clear indication that he or she understands what's in the reading. Then "Probes" ask the reader to take some additional steps by extending, criticizing, or applying the author's ideas. Some "Probes" also explore links among readings in various chapters.

Many of the readings include extensive bibliographies or references. There are lengthy lists of additional sources, for example, accompanying the readings that discuss the book's approach, personal relationships and health, verbal and nonverbal dimensions of talk, nonverbal messages, perception, listening, gender and ethnic similarities and differences, hurtful messages, identity management, and communication with people with disabilities. A detailed index also locates and provides cross-references to authors and key ideas.

As before, I want to remind readers that this book *about* interpersonal communicating cannot substitute for direct contact between persons in the concrete, everyday world. This is why I've once again begun the book with Buber's comment about "Books and People" and ended with Hugh Prather's reflections on the world of ideas and the world of "messy mortals."

Acknowledgments

This book would not be possible without the cooperation of the authors and publishers of material reprinted here. Thanks to all of them for their permissions.

I am also grateful to reviewers of the earlier edition. The following people offered insightful comments that guided the revision process this time:

> Heather M. Crandall, Whitworth College
> John Douglas Lepter, Trevecca Nazarene University
> Keith Forrest, Atlantic Cape Community College
> Anntarie Lanita Sims, The College of New Jersey
> Krista Longtin, Indiana University Purdue University Indianapolis
> Mark T. Morman, Baylor University

Many people I am fortunate enough to contact regularly have also contributed in direct and indirect ways to what's here. I appreciate many interpersonal communication teachers in the program at the University of Washington, including Milt Thomas, Lyall Crawford, Kathy Hendrix, Jeff Kerssen-Griep, Lisa Coutu, Roberta Gray, Laura Manning, Tasha Souza, Amanda Graham, Laura Black, Jodi Koenig Kellas, Andi Hamilton Zamora, and Aimee Carillo Rowe. I also deeply appreciate past contacts with colleagues who have supported and challenged my ideas, including Gerry Philipsen, Mac Parks, Barbara Warnick, Valerie Manusov, Jody Nyquist, Ken Cissna, Ron Arnett, Kim and Barnett Pearce, John Shotter, and, since 2001, new colleagues at the University of Dubuque, including Jeff Bullock, Paula Carlson, Bob Reid, Peter Smith, Brad Longfield, Henry Pitman, and Gail Hodge. I continue to notice how both the greatest tests and the most solid confirmations of what's in this book emerge in my most important living relationships with Lincoln, Marcia, Lisa, Jamie, Josh, Barbara, Dorothy, Gary, and other family members.

Two things that still have not changed through all ten editions of *Bridges Not Walls* are my awareness of the difficulty and the necessity of interpersonal communicating and my excitement about the challenge of working toward achieving it. I hope that some of this excitement will rub off on you.

John Stewart
Dubuque, IA 2008

PART ONE

Foundations of Interpersonal Communication

CHAPTER 1

Introduction to the Editor and to This Book

Writing about interpersonal communication, especially in a book that's used mainly as a text, is difficult because it's almost impossible to practice what you preach. Like many other text authors and editors, I could think of you as just "reader" or "student" and of myself as just "editor" or "teacher" and proceed to tell you what I want you to know. But if I did, we'd have something a lot closer to *impersonal* rather than *interpersonal* communication.

Why? Because, if I write simply as "teacher," and address you simply as "student" or "reader," and if you respond the same way, we will be relating to each other only in terms of our social roles, not in terms of who we are *as persons*. If I use the vocabulary introduced in the next chapter, this kind of contact would connect us as interchangeable parts.

But there's more to it than that. Both you and I are *non*interchangeable, multidimensional persons with distinctive ideas, convictions, wants, and needs. For my part, my name is John Stewart, I've been teaching college for over 40 years, I am now serving as a college administrator, and I like almost everything about my job. For the past 15 years I've been in the exciting, demanding, and rewarding position of being a 50-plus-year-old parent. This is my second time around as a dad. My daughters, who were born shortly after I finished high school, are in their mid-40s, the grandkids are 22 and 20, and our son Lincoln is 15. So Lincoln is an uncle to a niece and nephew older than he, and is also one of the younger members of a large extended family of aunts, uncles, and cousins.

I'm a native of the northwestern United States who moved in 2001 to northeast Iowa. I love the smell of saltwater and the fizz it makes behind a quiet boat; the exhilaration of biking and downhill skiing; the dazzling brightness of a winter sun on Midwest snow; the babble of a crowded family gathering; and the opportunity to leave home each day to respond to a calling, rather than just to do a job. I dislike phony smiles, grandiose flattery or apologies, pretentious academicians, rules that are vaguely stated but rigidly enforced, oysters, and machinery that runs roughly. I also get impatient with people who have trouble saying what they mean and meaning what they say. I was raised in a small town in Washington State and now live on the Mississippi, right at the point where Iowa, Illinois, and Wisconsin meet. I like the challenges of helping people in my classes learn new and old ideas, mentoring young faculty, and helping our small college live into its mission. I feel very fortunate to have my occupation, family, and health.

The longer I study and teach interpersonal communication, the more I'm struck by how much the person I am today has been molded by the relationships I've experienced. Some of the most important people in my life are no longer alive: for example, my dad and mom; my first real "boss," Marc Burdick; college teachers Peter Ristuben and "Prof" Karl; and Allen Clark, the friend who introduced me to Martin Buber's writings. Some others I've almost completely lost contact with, like high school and college teachers, coworkers in the pea cannery, and graduate school classmates. But many other relationships continue to teach and mold me, including those I have with Lincoln, my sister Barbara, cousins Jim and Carol, and close friends Karen Zediker, Tim Milander, John Campbell, David Kendell, Father Ralph Carskadden, Henry Pitman, Gail Hodge, and Jeff Bullock. I've also been affected by relationships with many authors who have made themselves available in their writing, especially Martin Buber, Hans-Georg Gadamer, Mikhail Bakhtin, John Shotter, Eric Voegelin, Martin Heidegger, Parker Palmer, and Carl Rogers. Contacts with all these persons have helped shape me. At the same time, I sense the presence of a continuous "me" who's never static but who's firmly anchored in values, understandings, weaknesses, and strengths that make me who I am.

If I stuck to being just "writer" or "teacher," I could also skip the fact that I am almost as grateful and excited about doing this tenth edition of *Bridges Not Walls* as I was about the first edition, and that I continue to be a little amazed that this book speaks to so many different people. Each mention of the book by a student who has read it or a teacher who has used it is a delight, and I especially like hearing from the communication graduate students and teachers who tell me that this was their introduction to the field. It's a gift to be able to share some ideas and feelings about interpersonal communication in this way, and I'm pleased that readers continue to allow me to talk relatively personally rather than just in the safe, sterile, and distant style of some "educational materials."

The impersonal approach I mentioned would also get in the way of the contact between you and me, because *you* are not simply "reader" or "student." Where were you born and raised, and how has that affected you? Are you reading this book because you want to or because somebody required it? If you're reading it as part of a college course, how do you expect the course to turn out? Challenging? Boring? Threatening? Useful? Inhibiting? Exciting? How do you generally feel about required texts? About going to school? What groups have you been in or are you a part of? A sports team? A neighborhood gang? A band? Campfire or Scouts? Natural Helpers? A church group? A sorority or fraternity? Alateen? What important choices have you made recently? To end a relationship? Move? Change majors? Quit work? Make a new commitment?

I'm not saying that you have to pry into the intimate details of somebody's life before you can communicate with him or her, but I am saying that interpersonal communication happens between *persons*, not between roles, masks, or stereotypes. Interpersonal communication can happen between you and me only to the degree that each of us makes available some of what makes us a person *and* at the same time is aware of some of what makes the other a person, too.

One way to conceptualize what I'm saying is to think about what could be called your Contact Quotient, or CQ. Your CQ is a measure of how you connect with another person. It's the quotient that expresses the ratio between the quality of contact you experience and the quality of contact that's possible. In other words,

$$\frac{\text{Richness or quality of contact achieved}}{\text{Richness or quality of contact possible}}$$

A husband and wife who have been married for 40 years have a huge CQ denominator (the figure below the line)—let's say 10,000. When one is giving the other the silent treatment, their numerator (the figure above the line) is painfully small—maybe 15. So their CQ in this instance would be 15/10,000—pretty low. But when they spend an afternoon and evening together in conversation, mutually enjoyed activities, and lovemaking, their numerator is very high—perhaps 9,500—and their CQ approaches 10,000/10,000. You and I, on the other hand, have a pretty small denominator. This means that the absolute quality of contact we can achieve by way of this book is relatively low. But we can still work toward a CQ of unity—maybe 100/100—and this is one of my goals in this introduction and the other materials I've written for this book.

It's going to be difficult, though, to maximize the CQ between you and me. I can continue to tell you some of who I am, but I don't know whether what I write is what you need in order to know me as me. In addition, I know almost nothing about what makes you a person—nothing about your choices, feelings, hopes, fears, insights, or blind spots—your individuality. This is why *writing* about interpersonal communication can sometimes be frustrating. Interpersonal communication can be discussed in print, but not much of it can happen here.

More can happen, though, than usually does with a textbook. Our relationship can be at least a little closer to interpersonal than it often is. I will work toward this end by continuing to share some of what I'm thinking and feeling in my introductions to the readings, in the Review Questions and Probes at the end of each selection, and in the essays I've authored or co-authored. I hope you'll be willing to make yourself available by becoming involved enough in this book to recognize clearly which ideas and skills are worthwhile for you and which are not. I also hope you'll be willing and able to make yourself available to other persons reading this book, so they can benefit from your insights and you can benefit from theirs.

WHY APPROACH INTERPERSONAL COMMUNICATION THIS WAY?

Before we begin breaking human communication down into manageable parts, I want to talk about a couple of beliefs that guide my selection and organization of the materials in this book. I believe that when you know something about this book's rationale, it'll be easier for you to understand what's being said about each topic, and you'll be in a better position to accept what works for you, while leaving aside the rest.

Quality of Communication and Quality of Life

One of my basic assumptions is that *there's a direct link between the quality of your communication and the quality of your life.* I can best explain this idea with a little bit more of my history.

After high school, I attended a community college for two years and then transferred to a four-year college to finish my degree. I took a basic speech communication course at both schools and noticed that in each something was missing. The teachers emphasized how to inform others and persuade them to do what you want. They showed our classes how to research and outline ideas, how to move and gesture effectively, and how to use vocal variety to keep our listeners' attention. Students were required to write papers and give speeches to demonstrate that they'd mastered these skills. But the courses seemed to overlook something important. Neither the textbooks nor the instructors said anything about the connection between the quality of your communication and the quality of your life.

Other texts and teachers did. In my literature and anthropology classes, I read that "no human is an island" and that "the human is a social animal." Psychology books reported studies of infants who suffered profoundly when they were deprived of touch, talk, or other kinds of contact. A philosophy text made the same point in these words: "communication means life or death to persons.... Both the individual and society derive their basic meaning from the relations that exist between [persons]. It is through dialogue that [humans] accomplish the miracle of personhood and community."[1]

The speech texts and teachers promised that they could help students learn to make ideas clear, be entertaining, and persuade others to agree with them. But they seemed to miss the communication impact of the point being made in literature, anthropology, psychology, and philosophy. If humans really are social beings, then *communication is where humanness happens.* In other words, although communication is definitely a way to express ideas, get things done, and entertain, convince, and persuade others, it's also more than that. It's the process that defines who we are. As a result, *if we experience mainly distant, objective, impersonal communicating, we're liable to grow up pretty one-sided, but if we experience our share of close, supportive, interpersonal communicating, we're likely to develop more of our human potential.* This is how the quality of your communication affects the quality of your life.

One reason I started teaching interpersonal communication is that I figured out the truth of this idea, and this same point has motivated me to edit this book. I've also been impressed with some research that supports this reason for studying interpersonal communication. Malcolm Parks reviews this research in the next chapter.

As Parks notes, medical doctors have done some of the most impressive studies. James J. Lynch was co-director of the Psychophysiological Clinic and Laboratories at the University of Maryland School of Medicine when he introduced one of his books with these words:

> As we shall see, study after study reveals that human dialogue not only affects our hearts significantly but can even alter the biochemistry of individual tissues at the farthest extremities of the body. Since blood flows through every human tissue, the entire body is influenced by dialogue.[2]

In other words, Lynch is saying that the quality of your communication affects the *physical* quality of your life. One of his important discoveries was that blood pressure changes much more rapidly and frequently than people used to believe, and that some of the most significant blood pressure changes occur when people speak and are spoken to. Computerized instruments permitted Lynch and other researchers to monitor blood pressure constantly and to map the effects of a person's entering the room, engaging in nonverbal contact, reading aloud, and conversing. Speech appears to directly affect blood pressure; in one study, the mean arterial pressure of healthy nurses went from 92 when they were quiet to 100 when they "talked calmly."[3] Listening has the opposite effect. Rather than just returning to baseline when a person stops speaking, blood pressure actually drops below baseline when one concentrates on the other person.[4] And this happens only when we talk with people; "conversation" with pets does not produce the same result.[5]

In an earlier book, Lynch discussed some of the more global effects of essentially the same phenomenon. There he reported the results of hundreds of medical studies that correlate loneliness and poor health. For example, people with few interpersonal relationships tend to die before their counterparts who enjoy a network of family and friends.[6] In fact, a study of identical twins found that smoking habits, obesity, and cholesterol levels of the twins who had heart attacks were not significantly different from the twins with healthier hearts. But there were some other important differences, one of which was what the doctors called "poor childhood and adult interpersonal relationships."[7]

What conclusions can be drawn from evidence like this? Lynch put it this way:

> Human companionship does affect our heart, and . . . there is reflected in our hearts a biological basis for our need for loving human relationships, which we fail to fulfill at our peril. . . . The ultimate decision is simple: we must either learn to live together or increase our chances of prematurely dying alone.[8]

In other words, if you view quality of life physically, it becomes apparent that there's more to it than ample food, warm clothing, shelter, education, and modern conveniences. The quality of your existence is linked directly to the quality of your communication.

If you go beyond physical quality of life, the same point can be made even more strongly. In fact, nonmedical people have been talking about the link between the quality of your communication and the quality of your life for many years. For example, to paraphrase the philosopher Martin Buber:

> The unique thing about the human world is that something is continually happening between one person and another, something that never happens in the animal or plant world. . . . *Humans are made human by that happening.* . . . This special event begins by one human turning to another, seeing him or her as this particular other being, and offering to communicate with the other in a mutual way, building from the individual world each person experiences to a world they share together.[9]

Jesuit psychologist John Powell put the same idea in simpler terms: "What I am, at any given moment in the process of my becoming a person, will be determined by my relationships with those who love me or refuse to love me, with those I love or refuse to love."[10]

"Okay," you might be saying, "I don't disagree with the lofty ideals expressed by all these people, and I can see how quality of life and quality of communication are related, but let's be a little practical. It's not always *possible* to treat everybody as a personal friend, and more importantly, it's not always *wise*. So you can't realistically expect your communication always to be friendly and supportive. Impersonal communication happens all the time, and often it's exactly the right kind of communication to have."

I agree. And this is an important point. Many factors make interpersonal communication difficult or even impossible. Role definitions, status relationships, cultural differences, physical surroundings, and even the amount of time available can all be obstacles to interpersonal contact. Lack of awareness and lack of skills can also affect your CQ. One person may want to connect interpersonally with someone else but may simply not know how to do it.

In other situations, it may be possible but, as you point out, it may not be wise. The power relationships or amount of hostility may make it too risky. Everyday communication also includes a great deal of deception. One study concluded that 62 percent of statements made in conversations could be classified as deceptive, and in two other large surveys, more than one-third of the respondents admitted to lying to close friends about important topics.[11] I know a man who used to teach interpersonal communication as part of a Living Skills program in a prison work-release facility. Eric also worked there as a guard. His power as a guard—he had the authority to send people back to the county jail—drastically affected what he could accomplish as an interpersonal communication teacher. Some people in his classes responded openly to his efforts to connect with them. Others were so hardened by their years in various prisons that they could think only about maintaining their own power in the convict hierarchy and getting out as soon as possible—legally or otherwise. It simply didn't make good sense for Eric to try to communicate with all the persons in his class in consistently interpersonal ways. The bottom line is that all of our contacts certainly cannot be interpersonal, but in most cases, more of them could be. And if they were, the quality of our lives would be enhanced.

Human Being Results from Human Contact

The second, closely related basic assumption behind the materials in this book is that *there is a basic movement in the human world, and it is toward relation, not division.* This might sound a little vague, but I think it'll get clearer if you bear with me for a couple of paragraphs. First, I believe that human life is a process and that the general kind of process we humans are engaged in is growing into fully developed persons. So far, no big deal, right?

Second, humans are relational, not solitary, beings. We fundamentally need contact with other persons. If you could combine a human egg and sperm in a completely impersonal environment, what you'd end up with would not be a person. This is different from cloning. I'm thinking about an artificial womb, machine-assisted birth, mechanical feeding and changing, and so on. Why wouldn't the being that was created this way be a person? Because in order to become a person, the human needs to experience relationships with other persons. This point can't be proved experimentally, of course, because it would be unethical to treat any human organism that way. But some empirical evidence supports this claim; I'm thinking of studies of "feral," or "wild," children—children discovered after they'd been raised for a time by wolves or other animals. One book tells about the Wild Boy of Aveyron, a "remarkable creature" who came out of the woods near a small village in southern France on January 9, 1800, and was captured while digging for vegetables in a village garden. According to the people who knew him, the creature

> was human in bodily form and walked erect. Everything else about him suggested an animal. He was naked except for the tatters of a shirt and showed no modesty, no awareness of himself as a human person related in any way to the people who had captured him. He could not speak and made only weird, meaningless cries. Though very short, he appeared to be a boy of about eleven or twelve.[12]

The creature was taken to a distinguished physician named Dr. Pinel, one of the founders of psychiatry. The doctor was unable to help, partly because "the boy had no human sense of being in the world. He had no sense of himself as a person related to other persons."[13] The "savage of Aveyron" made progress toward becoming human only after he was taken on as a project by another medical doctor named Jean-Marc Gaspard Itard. Itard's first move was to place the boy in a foster family, in the care of a mature, loving mother, Mme. Guerin. In this household, the boy was able to learn to "use his own chamber pot," dress himself, come when he was called, and even associate some letters of the alphabet with some pictures.

Itard's first report about his year of efforts to socialize the wild boy emphasized the importance of human contact in becoming a person. Itard described in detail events that demonstrate the significance of "the feeling of friendship" between him and the boy and especially between the boy and Mme. Guerin: "Perhaps I shall be understood if people remember the major influence on a child of those endless cooings and caresses, those kindly nothings which come naturally from a mother's heart and which bring forth the first smiles and joys in a human life."[14] Without this contact, the young human organism was a creature, a savage. With contact, he began to develop into a person.

Accounts like this one help make the point that *human being results from human contact*. Our genes give us the potential to develop into humans, but without contact, this potential cannot be realized. People definitely are affected by solitude, meditation, and quiet reflection, but mostly because those individualized activities happen in the context of ongoing relationships. As many writers have pointed out, we are molded by our contacts with nature, our contacts with other humans, and our contacts with whatever supreme being, higher power, or god we believe in. This book focuses on the second kind—our contacts with people.

This is *why* there is a direct connection between the quality of your communication and the quality of your life. This is also why I encourage you to think about your communicating in terms of its Contact Quotient. You certainly cannot have the same quality of contact with everybody you meet, in every situation. But you can recognize the quality of contact that's possible between you and the other person(s) and work toward a CQ of 1/1.

Again, I'm not saying that if everybody just holds hands, smiles, and stares at the sunset, all conflict will disappear and the world will be a happy place. I'm not that naïve. But the kind of communicating discussed in this book is not just a trendy, pop-psychology, Western, white, middle-class exercise in narcissism or New Age good feeling. It's grounded in some basic beliefs about who human beings are and what communication means in human life—regardless of ethnicity, gender, class, or age. In the first reading of Chapter 2, I say more about this point. When you read those pages, you might want to refer to the two assumptions I just described.

PREVIEW OF THE BOOK

So far I've tried to say that for me, interpersonal communication differs from impersonal communication in that it consists of *contact between (inter) persons*. This means that for interpersonal communication to happen, each participant has to be willing and able to talk and listen in ways that maximize the presence of the personal. This willingness and ability will happen only when the people involved (1) are familiar with the foundations of interpersonal communication, (2) are willing and able to accurately perceive and listen to themselves and others, and to make themselves and their ideas available to others, (3) recognize how the basic communication processes work in various relationships, and (4) have some resources to deal with communication difficulties.

This is why I've organized *Bridges Not Walls* into four sections, or parts; the readings in each part are designed to do what I've just outlined. So the next three chapters, which complete Part One, explore the rest of the foundations—your overall view of the communication process (Chapter 2), the communicative or social nature of who we are (Chapter 3), and the verbal and nonverbal parts of the process (Chapter 4). Part Two is organized around the metaphor "inhaling-exhaling." I explain the reasons for this metaphor in the introduction to Chapter 5. Basically, I use the term *inhaling* to highlight the perception and listening parts of the communication process and *exhaling* to focus attention on the messages that are expressed. The allusion to breathing emphasizes the impossibility, in actual practice, of separating these two processes.

Chapter 5 treats various parts of inhaling, including person perception and listening. Chapter 6 is made up of articles discussing self-expression and self-disclosure. Together, Parts One and Two lay out the general communication process and specific information about each of its main subparts.

The last two sections of this book focus solidly on application. The two chapters of Part Three discuss applications to relationships. There are four readings about family and friend relationships in Chapter 7, and four treatments of communication between intimate partners in Chapter 8. Next are the four chapters that make up Part Four, "Bridges Not Walls," where 31 different authors grapple with some of the most difficult situations where communication knowledge and skills are applied. Chapter 9 focuses on some of the kinds of communication that generate walls: hurtful messages, deception, betrayal, aggression, defensiveness, power, and bullying. Then in Chapter 10, eight authors offer suggestions about how to manage conflict by turning walls like these into bridges. This is followed by a chapter that focuses on the special difficulties that often emerge in contacts between members of different cultures—ethnic groups, genders, ages, and so on. Finally, Chapter 12 describes dialogue, a kind of communicating that, at the beginning of the 21st century, many people are offering as the best way to build bridges not walls.

Before each reading, some introductory comments pinpoint what I think are the key ideas that appear there. At the end of each reading, I've also included two kinds of questions. Review Questions prompt your recall of key ideas. Probes are questions intended to provoke your thinking and discussion, especially about how the ideas in the reading relate (1) to your own life experience and (2) to ideas in other readings.

One final note: A few of the essays that I have reprinted here were written before people learned about the destructive potential of the historical male bias in the English language. As a result, when these authors mean "humanity," "humans," or "humankind," they write *man* or *mankind*. And when they are using a pronoun to refer to a person in the abstract, it's always *he* rather than *she* or *he and she*. In some cases, I've tried to delete offensive uses or to substitute terms in brackets. In other cases, that kind of editing would make the essay very awkward and difficult to read. This is especially a problem in the reading by Martin Buber (Chapter 12). I hope in this case that you'll be able to read beyond the sexist language for the important ideas.

I also hope that you can have some fun with at least parts of what's ahead. Sometimes the topics are serious, and occasionally the concepts are complex. But this book is about familiar activities that all of us engage in just about all the time. By the time you're finished with it, you should be an even more effective communicator than you already are. This kind of learning can be exciting!

NOTES

1. Reuel Howe, *The Miracle of Dialogue* (New York: Seabury, 1963), cited in *The Human Dialogue*, ed. F. W. Matson and A. Montagu (New York: Free Press, 1968), pp. 148–49.
2. James J. Lynch, *The Language of the Heart: The Body's Response to Human Dialogue* (New York: Basic Books, 1985), p. 3.

3. Lynch, pp. 123–24.
4. Lynch, pp. 160ff.
5. Lynch, pp. 150–55.
6. James J. Lynch, *The Broken Heart: The Medical Consequences of Loneliness* (New York: Basic Books, 1977), pp. 42–51.
7. E. A. Liljefors and R. H. Rahe, "Psychosocial Characteristics of Subjects with Myocardial Infarction in Stockholm," in *Life Stress Illness,* ed. E. K. Gunderson and R. H. Rahe (Springfield, IL: Charles C Thomas, 1974), pp. 90–104.
8. Lynch, *The Broken Heart,* p. 14.
9. Paraphrased from Martin Buber, *Between Man and Man* (New York: Macmillan, 1965), p. 203.
10. John Powell, *Why Am I Afraid to Tell You Who I Am?* (Chicago: Argus Communications, 1969), p. 43.
11. H. Dan O'Hair and Michael J. Cody, "Deception," in *The Dark Side of Interpersonal Communication,* ed. W. R. Cupach and B. H. Spitzberg (Hillsdale, NJ: Lawrence Erlbaum, 1994), pp. 183–84.
12. Roger Shattuck, *The Forbidden Experiment: The Story of the Wild Boy of Aveyron* (New York: Farrar Straus Giroux, 1980), p. 5.
13. Shattuck, p. 37.
14. Shattuck, p. 119.

CHAPTER 2

Communication and Interpersonal Communication

Communicating and Interpersonal Communicating

John Stewart

One of the best courses I took during my first year of college was Introduction to Philosophy. Part of the appeal was the teacher. He knew his topic, and he loved to teach it. But as I discovered a few years later, I also enjoyed the course because I liked the kind of thinking that was going on in the materials we read and the discussions we had. As I continued through college, I supplemented my communication courses with other work in philosophy. The topics I talk about in this essay reflect this dual interest.

One definition of philosophy is "the systematic critique of presuppositions." This means that philosophers are interested in first principles, basic understandings, and underlying assumptions. If you've read much philosophy, you may have the impression that it can be stuffy or even nitpicky to the point of irrelevance. But it can also be exciting and important, because the philosopher says something like, "Hold it! Before you go off to spin a complicated web of explanations about something important—like how people should treat each other, principles of economics and business, or how people communicate—try to get clear about some *basic* things. When you're talking about human communication, for example, what are you assuming about what actually gets passed between people as they communicate? Ideas? Meanings? Or just light and sound waves?" The philosopher might say, "Since meanings are internal, and all that gets exchanged are light and sound, one person can communicate only with *his or her perceptions of* another person. This means I can *never* communicate directly with you. All I can do, when it comes right down to it, is communicate with myself!"

Basic issues like these intrigue me, mainly because they have so many practical effects. Our assumptions about things "leak" out in everything we do. For example, do you know somebody who fundamentally believes that it's a dog-eat-dog world? Watch him or her walk. Listen to the way that person answers the phone. Look at his or her typical facial expression. People's everyday choices about both big and small beliefs and actions grow out of their assumptions—about what's right, what's important, what's honorable, what will provide the best income, or whatever.

So it's important to think about these assumptions and to change them when they aren't working well. I know that many potentially exciting conversations have been squelched by someone's dogmatic insistence that all participants "define their terms." But I also know that a great deal of fuzziness can be cleared up and many unhealthy choices can be revised when a conversation starts with some shared understandings about the assumptions behind and definitions of what's being discussed.

In the following essay, I describe my definition of the topic of this book—interpersonal communication. I begin with a six-part description of communication in general that includes a practical implication of each of the six parts. Then I discuss interpersonal communication as a subset of the more general term.

As you'll notice, the views of communication and interpersonal communication that I develop here extend the point I made in Chapter 1 about quality of communication and quality of life. One of the most important things I want to emphasize throughout this book is that communication functions partly to negotiate identities, or selves. In other words, who we are emerges in our listening and talking. This is why the reading begins with an extended explanation of how human worlds or realities are collaboratively constructed (built, modified, torn down, rebuilt) in communication. And the definition of interpersonal communication grows out of this point. In brief, as I put it, interpersonal communication happens when the people involved talk and listen in ways that maximize the presence of the personal.

The reading is a little long, and I apologize for that. But I'm using it to frame just about everything that follows in this book.

Communication is an intriguing topic to study because, on the one hand, you and I have been doing it since at least the day we were born, so we have some claim to being "experts," and on the other hand, many of the difficulties that people experience are communication difficulties, which suggests that we all have a lot to learn. If your communication life is trouble-free, this book and the course it is probably a part of might not be for you. But if your experience is anything like mine, you might be interested in some help. After over 40 years of communication study and teaching, I still experience plenty of misunderstandings, but I've found that some basic insights about what communication is and how it works can smooth many of the rough spots. That's why this introduction describes the general subject matter of communication and this book's specific focus, interpersonal communication. I don't want to make too much out of "defining our terms," but as I think you'll discover, there are some common ways of thinking about these topics that can actually make things harder rather than easier. And there are some important features of communication and interpersonal communication that significantly affect how they work.

COMMUNICATING[1]

In the most general sense, the terms "communication" and "communicating" label *the continuous, complex, collaborative process of verbal and nonverbal meaning-making*. When somebody says, "She's a good communicator" or "We communicate well," it basically means that contacts with these persons tend to go smoothly and that there aren't many confusions or misunderstandings, which is to say that the meanings the people build together generally work okay. By the same token, people talk about "poor communication" when they experience confusing, ambiguous, frustrating, disrespectful, or incomplete meanings.

The word "continuous" in the definition reminds us that communication was going on when we were born and it will continue well after we're dead. "Complex" means that there are many elements or dimensions of every commu-nicative event, including facial expression, tone of voice, choice of words, past history, and social roles, among dozens of other factors. The words "verbal and nonverbal" highlight the two basic codes that humans work with. And the term "collaborative" just means that we co-labor, or work together on the meanings we make. Even when two parties are in the midst of a violent disagreement, they are still co-constructing their meanings of anger, hostility, fairness, and respect. So whether you're talking about written or spoken communication, face-to-face or computer-mediated, conflict or cooperation, the process basically involves humans making meaning together.

Meaning is what makes the human world different from the spaces inhabited by other living beings—worms, dogs and cats, and even, so far as we now know, chimpanzees, whales, and dolphins. Since humans live in worlds of meaning— rather than worlds made up of only objects or things—communication is a major part of human living.

To clarify this idea that humans live in worlds of meaning, consider the part of your world that's your "home." If someone asked you to describe your home, you probably wouldn't just talk about how many square feet it has, how tall it is, how far it is from your home to some prominent landmark, or what color the bedroom walls are (objective features). Instead, you'd talk about what it *means* to live in a place this small or this big, what you think and feel about the wall color, and what it *means* to live where your home is located. Similarly, the transportation part of your world is significant not simply because you travel by bike or on a bus, in your own old or new SUV or convertible, or on foot or on a motorcycle, but because of what it *means* in your family, group of friends, and culture to get around this way. And the meanings of all these parts of our worlds get built up (constructed) and changed in communication—the written and oral, verbal and nonverbal contact people have with each other.

When each of us was born, this process of meaning-making was going on all around us, and we entered it kind of like a chunk of potato when it's plopped into a pot of simmering soup. The soup was there before we were born, it will be simmering all the time we're alive, and these communication processes will continue after we die. As individuals and groups, we certainly affect our worlds a whole lot more than a chunk of potato affects a pot of soup. But each of us is also a participant in an ongoing process that we do not completely control, a process as old and as vast as the history of humanity. All the time, everywhere, in all the contacts that make us social animals, humans are constructing meaning together, and "communication" is the name of this ongoing process.

Interpersonal communication is a subset of this general process, a particular kind or type of communication. I'll describe what it is later. But first I want to explain six important features of all kinds of communication, the first of which I've already introduced, and an important implication or practical application of each of the six:

1. **Meaning:** Humans live in worlds of meaning, and communication is the process of collaboratively making these meanings.

Implication 1: No one person can completely control a communication event, and no single person or action causes—or can be blamed for—a communication outcome.

2. **Choice:** All communication involves choices, some of which we actively consider, and others that follow cultural norms and seem almost automatic.
   Implication 2: The choices communicators make reveal their ethical standards and commitments.

3. **Culture:** Culture and communication are intertwined. Ethnicity, gender, age, social class, sexual orientation, and other cultural features always affect communication and are affected by it.
   Implication 3: Your cultures, and mine, affect what I say about communication in this book and how you respond to it.

4. **Identities:** Some of the most important meanings people collaboratively construct are identities; all communicating involves negotiating identities, or selves.
   Implication 4: Identity messages are always in play.

5. **Conversation:** The most influential communication events are conversations.
   Implication 5: The most ordinary communication events are generally the most significant.

6. **Nexting:** The most important single communication skill is "nexting."
   Implication 6: Whenever you face a communication challenge or problem, the most useful question you can ask yourself is, "What can I help to happen next?"

1. Meaning: Humans Live in Worlds of Meaning, and Communication Is the Process of Collaboratively Making These Meanings

When I introduced this idea, you might have thought it was kind of strange. Most people don't give much thought to their definition of *communication*, and if pressed, a person who's new to this subject matter might just say that communication basically means "getting your ideas across," or "sending and receiving messages." In fact, there's a widespread belief in many cultures that communication

- Begins when a sender gets an idea he or she wants to communicate
- Works by having the sender translate the idea into words or some other kind of message
- Requires the receiver to perceive the message and retranslate it into an idea
- Can be evaluated in terms of the match, fit, or, fidelity between message sent and message received
- Can be analyzed by figuring out who *caused* its successes or failures (who's responsible, who gets the credit, who's at fault or to blame)

According to this definition, the general process of communication can be diagrammed this way:

$$\text{Idea}_1 \rightarrow \text{Message Sent} \rightarrow \text{Message Received} \rightarrow \text{Idea}_2$$

When idea_2 is the same as idea_1, then communication is successful. When the two ideas don't match, there's a misunderstanding that's somebody's "fault."

This might sound like a fairly reasonable, even accurate, understanding of communication. **But all these common beliefs about communication are misleading, and if you act on them, you're likely to have problems.**

Let's consider each briefly.

Communication Consists Mainly of "Getting Your Ideas Across"   This belief focuses attention on the topic or content of the communication—the ideas people talk about. And it's reasonable to believe that idea transmission or information sharing is the most important function of communication. But to test this belief, look for a minute at an excerpt from an actual conversation:

JOHN: So what do you THINK about the bicycles on campus?
JUDY: I think they're terrible.
JOHN: Sure is about a MILLION of 'em.
JUDY: Eh, heh.
JOHN: (Overlapping Judy) Duzit SEEM to you ... there's a lot more people this year?
JUDY: The re-yeah, for sure.
JOHN: (Overlapping) Go-GOD, there seems to be a mILLion people.
JUDY: Yeah. (brief pause) YEah, there's way too many. I can't ... at TIMES the bicycles get so bad I just get off mine and ... hhh ... give up.
JOHN: (Overlapping) Oh, really ...
JOHN: I dunno, when I DODGE one then I have to DODGE another one, 'n it's an endless cycle.
JUDY: Yeah (brief pause), oh they're TERrible.
JOHN: 'S so many people.
JUDY: Um hmm.[2]

The content of this conversation—bicycles on campus—is only a small part of what's going on here. John and Judy are college students who have just met, and they are using the topic of bicycles in part to figure out who they are to and for each other. In fact, the most important parts of this conversation are probably not John's and Judy's ideas about bicycles, but the commonality that their similar opinions creates, combined with the subtle power relationship that's constructed when John defines the topic and overlaps Judy's talk, and Judy is willing to go along with this slightly one-up/one-down relationship. In other words, especially if you remember that John and Judy don't know each other well, you'd probably agree that the most important features of this conversation are what communication researchers call the *identity messages* or *relationship messages*. These are the verbal and nonverbal indicators of how John defines himself, how he views Judy, and what he thinks Judy thinks of him, along with Judy's verbal and nonverbal ways of defining herself, what she thinks of John, and what she thinks John thinks of her. These messages about the identities, or selves, of the persons involved and their relationships with each other are at least as important as the idea content, and often more so. So the first part of the common definition of communication is misleading because human communication always involves more than simply getting ideas across.

Communication Works by Having the Sender Translate the Idea into Words or Some Other Kind of Message   This belief assumes that speech happens when a speaker changes a mental idea into spoken words. But this conversation didn't just "start" when John got a nonverbal idea about bicycles in his head. He's encountering Judy in a particular context—in this case, they're both volunteer subjects in a communication experiment. Their social, political, and religious cultures help define how similar-age men and women strangers relate to one another, and they're probably each looking for ways to make the encounter as comfortable as possible. So the topic of bicycles emerges out of a context much broader than John's mind. In addition, before John spoke, there was probably no clearly identifiable, singular piece of mental content (an idea) located somewhere in his brain. The phenomena called "ideas" are complex and always changing; they're made up not simply of synapse patterns or cognitions but of words, intonations, stresses, pauses, and facial expressions; and they change as they are being uttered. This means that there is no unitary, identifiable thing inside a person's head (an idea) that gets translated or encoded into spoken words.

Communication Requires the Receiver to Perceive the Message and Retranslate It into an Idea   This belief suggests that listeners are doing the same things that speakers are, only in reverse. But again, human communication is not this simple. First, notice that neither John nor Judy is simply "sender" or "receiver" at any point in this exchange; in fact, they're both sending and receiving at every moment. *As she speaks*, Judy is noticing John's response (she is receiving) and is modifying what she says and how she says it. John is doing the same thing. *As he listens*, he's "saying" things to Judy with his face and body. And this goes on all the time. Human communicators are always sending and receiving simultaneously. As a result, each communicator has the opportunity to change how things are going at any time in the process. When this excerpt of the conversation ends, John and Judy are at a point of potential change, and the next utterance may move them closer together or further apart. John could pick up on Judy's disclosure that she is a cyclist, for example, or Judy could introduce a new topic that's more important to her than this one. The point is, much more is going on here than back-and-forth translation and retranslation of individual ideas.

Communication Can Be Evaluated in Terms of the Match, Fit, or Fidelity between Message Sent and Message Received   This belief suggests that you could isolate and define John's and Judy's mental contents (ideas) so you could figure out how well they match or fit. But since ideas are so fluid and dynamic, and since communication happens as much in talk as in people's heads, the fidelity model doesn't fit living conversation very well. In order to apply this notion of matching or fitting, you'd have to slow down and distort the exchange to the point where it wouldn't be anything like what actually happened. Communication success has more to do with the people's ability to continue relating smoothly with each other than with matching mental contents.

Communication Problems Can Be Analyzed by Identifying Fault and Blame
To say that a problem is somebody's "fault" is to say that she or he *caused* it, just as a temperature below 0°C causes water to freeze, or pushing down on one end of a lever causes the other end to rise. In other words, this belief assumes that human communication is governed by laws of cause and effect. But is it? If Judy noticed the one-up/one-down power relationship with John, she might believe that it's John's fault because he asserted power by taking on the roles of topic definer and overlapping speaker.[3] John, on the other hand, might think that any power imbalance between them is due to Judy's initial silence or to her willingness to go along with his topic choice. Who's right? Whose fault is it, really? Who's really to blame?

One problem with questions like these is that they require somebody to identify where the exchange *started*, so they can determine what's "cause" and what's "effect." But as I've already noted, some of what's going on in a conversation is as old as the participants themselves, or older. And this is literally always true. Every single thing the participants say and do may be understood as a *response* to what preceded it in their lives. No living human is the original Adam or Eve, the first one to disturb the cosmic silence of the universe. An enormous amount of communication precedes everything all of us communicate.[4] Even the first "hi" in a relationship can be understood as a response to a smile, the situation, or a lesson your parents taught you about being polite. In John and Judy's conversation, some of what's said can be traced back to the gender definitions that each of them developed when they were growing up. And these influences could be traced back to John's and Judy's parents' definitions of themselves, which came in part from *their* parents, and so on. This is the kind of complex mess a search for original causes can suck you into. And for the sake of argument, let's assume that John and Judy finally agree on just where the exchange started and whose fault some part of it was. What then? Will the resulting guilt feelings or an apology from the accused party fix the problem? Not usually. Even when people agree on fault and blame, that agreement doesn't usually improve things much. The reason is that human communication is much too complex to be profitably analyzed into simple cause-effect, fault-blame sequences.

In short, two things can be learned from this brief example:

- Some of the most common understandings or definitions of human communication are plausible but misleading.
- Since the way you think about or define something determines what you experience, and what you experience determines the responses you make (in other words, assumptions, as I said before, "leak" out in all our beliefs and behaviors), it's important to have a workable definition of human communication so you can respond in ways that help you communicate effectively.

The main reason that this common definition of communication is misleading is that it's oversimplified.

Communication Is the Continuous, Complex, Collaborative Process of Verbal and Nonverbal Meaning-Making   As I mentioned before, it's *continuous* because humans are always making meaning—figuring out, making sense of, or interpreting what's happening. It's *complex* because it involves not just words and ideas but also intonation, facial expression, eye contact, touch, and several other nonverbal elements, and it always includes identity and relationship messages, culture and gender cues, more or less hidden agendas, unspoken expectations, and literally dozens of other features that usually become apparent only when they create problems. It's *collaborative*, because we do it with other people; we don't communicate alone.[5] "Co-labor-ating" just means working together, and collaboration can be as anonymous as obeying traffic laws and speaking the local language, or as intimate as attending to your partner's lovemaking preferences.

Implication 1: No One Person Can Completely Control a Communication Event, and No Single Person or Action Causes—or Can Be Blamed for—a Communication Outcome   Many people come to communication classes or workshops wanting to learn how to "do it right." They want to know how to *solve* the communication problems they experience—get their parents off their backs; eliminate misunderstandings with roommates, co-workers, or dating partners; deal with a critical and complaining boss; end a painful relationship; become a masterful salesperson. Some of these people want to learn the surefire techniques that will give them control over their communication lives. These people are disappointed, and some are even angry, when they learn that it isn't that simple. They are even more uncomfortable when they learn that it's an illusion to believe that surefire techniques of human communication even exist! As philosopher William Barrett put it over 30 years ago in his book *The Illusion of Technique,* "Technical thinking cannot deal with our human problems."[6]

I don't mean that technical thinking is hopeless or that there's nothing to be gained from scientific and social scientific experiments. But one direct implication of the recognition that communication is a *collaborative* process is that no one person can completely control any communication event and no technique or set of communication moves can definitely determine its outcome.

Regardless of how clearly I write or speak, you may still interpret me in a variety of ways. Regardless of how carefully I plan a meeting, one or more people are likely to have agendas very different from mine. Even a successful dictator whose orders are consistently followed can't control how people understand or feel about his or her demands. And as I mentioned, even though I've been working on my communication for years, I still experience difficulties that I cannot completely predict or control in relationships with family members, friends, co-workers, and acquaintances.

I believe that your skill as a communicator will be enhanced if you try to manage your expectations about control and perfection. The more you understand how communication works and the more communication skills you develop, the more effective and competent you will be. It is possible to learn how to give and get criticism gracefully, to manage conflict effectively, and to develop relationships smoothly. But not 100 percent of the time.

Cause-effect, fault-blame thinking is one of the oversimplifications people often fall into. I won't repeat what I said in the discussion of John and Judy's communication, but I do want to reemphasize it in this context. Problems obviously happen in communication, and the choices of the people involved help create, maintain, worsen, and solve these problems. But when you understand that communication is *continuous, complex,* and *collaborative,* you cannot coherently blame one person or one set of actions for whatever you might see as problematic. For one thing, fault and blame ignore the continuousness of communication. In order to say someone is at fault, you need to assume that whatever happened *began with the guilty person's action.* But all the people involved have been engaged in communication literally since they were born and have developed and reinforced each other's ways of speaking, listening, and interpreting since at least the time they met. So the person whom you say is at fault because he didn't call you back to confirm the meeting may be remembering your complaints about "getting all those annoying calls" and your insistence that it's only necessary to call if meeting plans change.

Fault and blame also ignore the fact that communication is collaborative. When directions are unclear, for example, it's due to both the direction-giver and the direction-receiver. Did the receiver ask about what confused her? Did the giver check the receiver's understanding? It may have seemed perfectly legitimate to one person to assume that everybody understood that the meeting was at 8:00 P.M. and not 8:00 A.M., for example, or that the family would gather for the holiday dinner just like they had in the past. But others might have radically different assumptions that lead to significantly different interpretations.

Does this mean that when there are problems, nobody's responsible? Does this idea eliminate any possibility of accountability? No, not at all. Individual responses still make a difference, and some are definitely more ethical, appropriate, or humane than others. But I'm trying to replace the oversimplified and distorted notions of fault and blame with a broader focus on both or all "sides" of the communication process. I do not mean to replace "It's his fault" with "It's her fault," "It's both of their faults," or "It's nobody's fault." Instead,

I encourage you to give up the notion of fault altogether, at least when you're thinking or talking about human communication.

Another way to put this point is to say that this view of communication redefines what responsibility means. Traditionally, being responsible means that you *caused* something to happen, that it was your fault. But from the perspective I'm developing here, responsibility means *ability to respond*, not fault, blame, or credit. It means *"response-able."* You are response-able when you have the willingness and the ability to contribute in some way to how things are unfolding, rather than ignoring what's going on or dropping out of the event. "Irresponsible" people are not responsive; they act without taking into account what else is going on or how their actions may influence others. Responsible (response-able) actions consider the larger wholes that they help make up. This idea is related to the basic skill of "nexting" that's discussed in feature 6.

2. Choice: All Communication Involves Choices, Some of Which People Actively Consider, and Others That Follow Cultural Norms and Seem Almost Automatic

Human meanings are inherently ethical because they involve choices. Individually and collectively, humans create and abide by guidelines for evaluating actions as right or wrong, good or bad, and appropriate or inappropriate. These ethical standards influence people's actions but do not always determine them. Interpersonal communication, as I'll explain, involves reflective and responsive choices.

Some of the choices people make don't feel much like choices. For example, shaking hands and bowing are two culturally influenced actions that one may choose to engage in when meeting another person for a business lunch. Although decisions about how long and how firmly to shake a hand or how deep to bow may be something you actively consider, the initial behavior of shaking or bowing may not be. You may not actively choose the tone of voice you use with your sibling in the same way you may consider how to talk with your best friend, because the norms for interaction in your family culture may be taken for granted, but not in your friendship.

Implication 2: The Choices Communicators Make Reveal Their Ethical Standards and Commitments   Consider the issue of shoplifting food from a grocery store, for example. Many people admit to stealing a candy bar as a kid, a choice made for the thrill, as a response to peer pressure, or just because they wanted one and didn't have the money at the time. They might have had an ethical standard that stealing was wrong and another, competing standard that the adrenaline rush, fitting in with friends, or immediate gratification was good. They had to choose between competing standards, and in this case, the stealing-is-wrong ethic carried less weight. Other people cannot understand how anyone could ever decide to steal. For these people, the stealing-is-wrong ethical standard is more heavily weighted, perhaps in response to explicit lessons from family, teachers, or a religious community. But whether you would or would not steal something from a grocery store, how would you evaluate an individual who had been involuntarily unemployed for months, exhausted the limited resources of the local food bank, and had decided that the only way members of her family would eat today would be if she took a loaf of bread and a jar of peanut butter without paying for them? In this case, is the stealing right or wrong? A good or bad choice? An appropriate or inappropriate action?

The point is that there are always competing forces in human lives and that part of what it means to be human is to make meaningful choices among them. If communication is a collaboratively constructed process, no one individual has complete control over its outcome. All of our choices are made within the context of our personal experience and are evaluated in relation to cultural norms and expectations. Standards for evaluation can differ from person to person, family to family, and culture to culture over time.

3. Culture: Culture and Communication Are Intertwined. Ethnicity, Gender, Age, Social Class, Sexual Orientation, and Other Cultural Features Always Affect Communication and Are Affected by It

When many people think about culture, they envision a group's customs, cooking, and clothing, but there's much more to it than that. In a very general sense, culture provides you with ways to make meaning. One way to talk about culture is to say that *culture means shared norms, values, and beliefs related to how people live and how people communicate.* These shared values, norms, and beliefs influence every part of people's lives.

Dating, for example, is one context in which the interaction of culture and communication can be observed. In some cultures, dating is a means to an end—a way to select a life partner, and whom you date is your business. In other cultures, it would be inappropriate to bring someone home to meet the folks, because "the folks" (parents, community members, or tribal leaders) will already have made arrangements for marriage.

When you think about culture this way, you'll realize that it involves much more than just national identity. People who share ways of living and speaking—who belong to "the same culture"—can be members of different ethnic groups. Even two members of the same family (a heterosexual brother and his lesbian sister) inhabit different cultures.

Especially today, with the increasing globalization of sports, music, media, business, education, and religion; with the explosion of international communication via the Internet and the Web; and with the growing recognition in education and business that diversity in organizations is a strength rather than a threat, culture is on almost everybody's minds. This is partly why I say that culture figures prominently in communication.

But there is a more basic reason: Culture becomes concrete in communication. What it *means* to belong to a culture is to communicate in certain ways—to use certain expressions that members of other cultures don't use, to prefer certain kinds of meetings, to honor certain styles of speaking, to maintain certain distances, to touch in certain ways, and so on. This means that your culture is present in your communicating and other people's cultures are present in their communicating, too.

Implication 3: Your Cultures—and Mine—Affect What I Say About Communication in This Book and How You Respond to It   Importantly for each author in this book—and for you as reader—*our* cultures are present in our communicating, too. I consider myself to be culturally Western, Anglo, middle class, late middle-aged, heterosexual, gendered, a parent, and a teacher-scholar. This means that my communication content and style in this book will embody these cultural features (and probably others I am not aware of). You'll get cultural information about some of the other authors in this book, and none about other authors. If you do *not* identify yourself culturally with an author, you may legitimately ask, "How are this person's ideas relevant to me? If culture and communication are so intertwined, what can I—an African-American, perhaps, or Latino, 20-year-old, gay or lesbian, engineering or chemistry student—learn from writings by this person?"

Enough, I hope, to keep you reading. This book offers some knowledge and skills about communication that are supported by evidence from a variety of cultures, and its authors speak from positions in cultures with fairly large memberships and fairly wide ranges of influence. If you are not a member of one or more of the cultures an author belongs to, this material can still be useful to you in at least two ways: (1) You can test generalizations against your experience in your own cultures to determine which apply and which don't, and (2) when an author's ideas don't apply in one or more of your cultures, you can use them to enhance your ability to communicate with people in the cultures the author inhabits.

For example, my first three claims about human communication are that humans live in worlds of meaning that are constructed in communicating, that choices embody ethical standards, and that culture figures prominently in all communication. I believe that there is ample evidence to demonstrate that these points are true about all people in all cultures, *not* just Western, Anglo, middle-class, late middle-aged, heterosexual, gendered, parent, and teacher-scholar cultures. Do you? I encourage you to test these generalizations against your own experience and to discuss the results with your instructor and classmates. On the other hand, as just one example, this book's readings about nonverbal communication may contain some generalizations about space or eye contact that don't ring true for one or more of your cultures. If so, you can combine your understanding of your own culture with what the author says about hers or his and then use this knowledge about space or eye contact in the author's culture to enhance your ability to communicate outside your own culture, with people in the culture the author inhabits.

And notice that you can do this without being co-opted. If you feel culturally different from some of the writers in this book, you don't have to give up your distinctiveness to profit from what's here. You can operate like a global businessperson. People who have to serve customers or work with producers outside their own cultures routinely learn how to adapt to these other cultures, but from their own position of strength—as representatives of their cultures. These people want to do business in another culture, so their adaptation is based on that foundation; it doesn't mean that their values or morals are co-opted. Regardless of the culture you enter or the adaptations you may choose to make, you can do so from a comparable position of strength.

4. Identities: Some of the Most Important Meanings People Collaboratively Create Are Identities; All Communicating Involves Negotiating Identities, or Selves

Communication theorist and teacher John Shotter emphasizes this point when he says that our "ways of being, our 'selves,' are produced in our … ways of interrelating ourselves to each other—these are the terms in which we are socially accountable in our society—and these 'traditional' or 'basic' (dominant) ways of talking are productive of our 'traditional' or 'basic' psychological and social [identities]."[7] In other words, who we are—our identities—is built in our communicating. People come to each encounter with an identifiable "self," built through past interactions, and *as we talk,* we adapt ourselves to fit the topic we're discussing and the people we're talking with, and we are changed by what happens to us as we communicate.

The way communication and identity are closely related became especially apparent in a conversation I had with a friend who was going through a painful divorce. "Mary Kay is not the person she used to be," Dale said. "Sometimes I hardly know her. I wish we could communicate and enjoy each other like we did when we were first married."

The times Dale was remembering were before Mary Kay was a mother, before she completed medical school, before she suffered through her residency in an urban hospital 2,000 miles from home, before she joined a prestigious medical clinic, and before she became a full-fledged practicing physician. They were also before Dale was a dad, before he started his import-export business, before he became active in his state professional association, and before he began attending church regularly. Dale was forgetting that Mary Kay could not possibly still be "the person she used to be." Neither could he. Both of them had experienced many relationships that changed them decisively. Mary Kay had been treated like a medical student—required to cram scientific information into her head and spout it on command—and like a first-year resident—forced to go without sleep, stand up to authoritarian doctors, and cope with hospital administrators. Now nurses obey her, many patients highly respect her for her skills, and prestigious doctors treat her like an equal. And she's treated as a mom by her son. Dale has also experienced many different relationships, and he's changed, too. He's treated as a boss by his employees and as "a respected American businessman" by his Japanese customers. Because of the contacts both have experienced, each is a different person. And the process continues as both Mary Kay and Dale continue to be changed by their communication.

Obviously, these identity changes are limited. Most people don't change their gender, ethnicity, or family of origin. But some changes are inevitable over time, and others can happen in the short term. For example, a woman can communicate in ways that say she is more feminine—or more masculine—than her conversation partner and as a person with greater or less authority or power than her conversation partner has. The other person's responses will contribute to the identity as it's negotiated verbally and nonverbally.

Consider the difference, for example, between "Shut the door, stupid!" and "Please close the door." The command projects the identity of a superior speaking to a subordinate. On the other hand, the request identifies the speaker as an equal to the person being addressed. The person who's told to "Shut the door, stupid!" may silently comply, in which case he or she is reinforcing part of the identities of superior and subordinate. Or the person may respond, "Shut it yourself!" which is a negotiation move that says, in effect, "You're not my superior; we're equals."

Implication 4: Identity Messages Are Always in Play   The point is that *identity negotiation, or the collaborative construction of selves, is going on whenever people communicate.* It definitely is not the *only* thing that's happening, but it's one of the very important processes, and it often gets overlooked. When it does, troubles usually result. By contrast, people who are aware of identity negotiation processes can communicate more effectively and successfully in many different situations. So whenever you communicate—on the telephone, via e-mail, face-to-face, in meetings, even in front of the television—part of what is happening is identity negotiation.

Communication content is important, too, and sometimes problems can be solved only when the parties involved have more or better information. Policies may be out of date, data may be incomplete, and people may have misread or misheard key instructions. In these cases, the people involved may need to complete, refine, or recalibrate the information they're working with.

But as I noted, effective communicators understand and manage what they're verbally and nonverbally "saying" about *who they are* to the people they're communicating with. Identities are communicated in many different ways. Topic choice and vocabulary are important. Grooming and dress also contribute to this process, as people offer definitions of themselves using nose rings and other body piercing, tatoos, starched white shirts or blouses, and conservative business suits. Tone of voice is similarly identity-defining. Some people foster misunderstanding by unknowingly sounding like they're skeptical, hostile, or bored, and other tones of voice can help their listeners feel genuinely appreciated and supported. Facial expressions also help define a person as attentive, careful, positive, or their opposites.

Especially when you're troubleshooting—or just trying to live through—a disagreement or conflict, it usually works best to start by understanding the identities that are in play. Who might be getting defined as inattentive, insensitive, or incompetent? What communication moves make one person appear more important, trustworthy, moral, or thorough than the other? Does everybody involved feel able to influence the ways they're viewed by the others? Or are identities being treated as unchangable? By the time you've worked through this book, you should have a wealth of ideas and practical skills for constructively managing how you define yourself and how others define you.

5. Conversation: The Most Influential Communication Events Are Conversations

If you had to identify one event that humans all over the world engage in characteristically—because they're humans—routinely, naturally, and almost constantly, what would it be? We all breathe, but so do other animals. We eat and drink, but not constantly, and again, other animals do too. The one activity that marks us as human and that occupies a large part of our personal and occupational lives is conversation, verbal and nonverbal exchange in real time, either face-to-face or mediated by some electronic medium (e.g., a computer or cell phone).

For a long time, people who studied communication and language tended to overlook this point. Language scholars focused on rules of grammar and syntax, dictionary definitions, and other features of writing, and speech research and teaching paid primary attention to public speaking and deliberation in law courts and legislatures. But in the last third of the 20th century, an increasing number of scholars and teachers have shown how written and formal kinds of communicating are derived from the most basic human activity, informal conversation. For example, two well-known psychologists from Stanford University began a report of their National Science Foundation–supported research with these words:

> Conversation is the fundamental site of language use. For many people, even for whole societies, it is the only site, and it is the primary one for children acquiring language. From this perspective other arenas of language use—novels, newspapers, lectures, street signs, rituals—are derivative or secondary.[8]

Another respected scholar puts it more simply. "Conversation," he writes, "is sociological bedrock,"[9] the absolute foundation or base for everything humans do as social beings. This explains the sense of the title of one of communication theorist John Shotter's books, *Conversational Realities: Constructing Life through Language*.[10] Shotter's book explains in detail how human realities get constructed in communication—my point 1—and emphasizes that the most characteristic form of this communication is *conversation*.

Implication 5: The Most Ordinary Communication Events Are the Most Significant   The reason I highlight this idea as one of the six main points about human communication is that it justifies paying close attention to something common and ordinary. The fact that humans engage in conversation so constantly, and so often almost without thinking, is part of what makes the process so important. As organizational theorist and trainer Peter Senge puts it, effective conversation is "the single greatest learning tool in your organization—more important than computers or sophisticated research."[11] Whether in a living group, a family-run shop, a small work team, or a multinational corporation, the real organizational structure and rules—as contrasted with what's on the organizational chart—get defined in the subtleties of verbal and nonverbal conversation. (Susan Scott makes this point later in this chapter.) Superior and subordinate status get negotiated in face-to-face contacts. Key decisions are heavily influenced by brief informal contacts in the bathrooms and halls as much as they are by formal presentations in meetings. And when the organization needs to change and there are feelings about rights or two worthwhile principles in conflict, the only realistic options are some form of authoritarianism or some form of problem-solving conversation. Similarly, conversation is the primary way families have of making decisions and negotiating differences. And children become effective participants in play groups, classrooms, sports teams, and their own families by learning how to converse well.

This means that one very important way to improve your communication competence is to pay close attention to the most common and everyday kind of communicating—conversation. When you do, you'll discover that you already have a great deal of experience with many of the concepts and skills this book discusses. This means that you have a solid foundation to build on. Even if you don't believe you're very good at conversation, you've done it often and well enough, and it's going on around you so much, that you can build on the experiences you have. One way is with point 6.

6. Nexting: The Most Important Single Communication Skill Is "Nexting"

Nexting is a strange term, I admit. But it's the best one I've come up with for this skill. If, as you read this section, you come up with a better one, please let me know. You can email me at jstewart@dbq.edu.

By "nexting" I mean *doing something helpful next, responding fruitfully to what's just happened, taking an additional step in the communication process.* If you've grasped how I've described communication so far, this is the most important single skill you can build on this understanding. Here's why:

Since you realize that communication is complex, continuous, and collaborative, you'll always recognize that, no matter what's happened before and no matter how bad things currently look, you always have the option to try a *next* step. No matter how many times the same insult has been repeated, the next response can be creative rather than retaliatory. No matter how long the parties have not been speaking to each other, the next time they meet, one of them could speak. No matter how ingrained and toxic the pattern is that two groups are caught in, the next move one side makes could be positive. No matter how much you feel "thrown" by what the other person just said and did, if you give yourself a little time to regroup, you can make a next move that could help get the relationship back on track. No matter how little power the system gives you, your next communication choice can maximize the power you have. Even when it is very difficult not to strike back, your next comment could conceivably be helpful rather than abusive.

When you understand that communication is continuous and collaborative, you'll recognize the potential value of what you do next. Why? Because since no one person determines all the outcomes of a communication event, you can help determine some outcomes, even if you feel almost powerless. Since no one person is 100 percent to blame or at fault, and all parties share response-ability, your next contribution can affect what's happening. Since all communication is collaborative—remember, even prizefighters are co-labor-ating—your next communication move can make a change in the situation, or at least keep the conversation going.

Implication 6: Whenever You Face a Communication Challenge or Problem, the Most Useful Question You Can Ask Yourself Is, "What Can I Help to Happen Next?"   You can apply the skill of nexting by remembering that no human system is ever completely determined or cast in stone. Regardless of how well or badly things are going between you and someone else, remember that what you do next will help maintain or destroy this quality. It almost goes without saying that in some cases you may not *want* to try to improve a bad situation or to maintain a good one. You may have tried to make positive contributions and have been continually rebuffed, and you may be out of patience, resources, or caring. You may in this particular case decide not to make a positive, supportive, or conciliatory move. You may also decide to let silence remain, to keep your distance, or to let the hostility fester. But if you understand the world-constructing nature of human communication, you can understand these options for what they are—*responses*, choices, decisions about what you are going to do *next*. They have their benefits and their consequences, just as other responses would.

To put it simply, people who understand communication to be the kind of process I've outlined so far are not generally thrown off balance by communication difficulties. They understand that the most important thing to consider is what they are going to do *next*.

INTERPERSONAL COMMUNICATING

As I said at the start of this chapter, interpersonal communication is a subset of communication in general. This means that collaboration, choices, culture, identities, conversation, and nexting are all parts of interpersonal communicating, too. The kind of communication I'm calling "interpersonal" doesn't happen all the time, but it can take place in families, between friends, during an argument, in business situations, and in the classroom. It can also happen on the telephone, online, among jurors, at a party, across a bargaining table, and even during public speeches or presentations. The main characteristic of interpersonal communication is that the people involved are contacting each other *as persons*. This might sound pretty simple, but again, there's a little more to it than you might think.

For one thing, as you and I move through our daily family, work, social, and school lives, we tend to relate with others in two different ways. Sometimes we treat others and are treated by them *impersonally* as role-fillers (bank teller, receptionist, employer, bus driver, etc.). And sometimes we connect with others *personally*, as a unique individual (not just role-filler or cultural representative). I don't mean that there are sharp divisions; sometimes we move back and forth between impersonal and interpersonal contact. But these two terms can anchor a sliding scale or continuum that models the qualities or kinds of communication that people experience.

QUALITIES OF COMMUNICATION
Impersonal ————————————————————— Interpersonal

The left side of the continuum, the impersonal side, is characterized by communication that is based on social roles and exchanges that minimize the presence of the communicators' personal identities. Impersonal communication is the label I use to describe your typical experiences at the bank, convenience store, and fast-food restaurant, and in front of the television. In these situations, people usually connect in ways that emphasize their social roles—teller/customer, buyer/seller, server/diner, and so on. Even though human beings are obviously involved, they all function pretty much like interchangeable parts of an automobile or computer. So long as the teller, buyer, or server knows his or her job (social role), and so long as the customer, seller, or diner remains in his or her role, it doesn't matter much who they are as individuals. I call this quality of communication *impersonal* because it's the most generic kind of human contact. There is human association but little or no close human contact.

Often, of course, this is exactly the best kind of communicating to have. For one thing, it's efficient. Nobody wants to wait in line while the Burger King cashier has a personal chat with each customer. It's also often the most appropriate kind of communicating. We don't ordinarily approach bank tellers, ticket sellers, or driver's license clerks expecting or wanting to have a deep conversation.

However, not all impersonal communicating takes place with people we hardly know. It is not unusual to engage in efficient, issue-centered communication with people we know well and care about. We also engage in generic greeting rituals with our best friends and family members as well as strangers. It's not uncommon to hear parents involve role-based communication patterns with their children (e.g., "Because I'm the mom, that's why!"). The important point is that impersonal communicating is a common, normal, useful, and often very appropriate way of relating.

But some of almost every day's communicating also fits near the right-hand end of the scale. During a committee meeting or team activity, you may contact another person as a unique individual, and you may get treated that way by him or her. The same kind of communicating can happen in your conversations with a dating partner, a parent, a sibling, your roommate, co-workers, or close friends.

No one's communication life can be packaged into neat boxes; that's why the model is a sliding scale. At one moment you may be contacting someone impersonally, and at the next moment your communication may become interpersonal. But what I've said so far clarifies what I mean when I define interpersonal communication, the main topic of this book, as *the type or kind of communication that happens when the people involved talk and listen in ways that maximize the presence of the personal.*

Notice that this definition is not based on the number of people involved or whether they are in the same place. I believe that it is possible to communicate interpersonally in groups and even through phone lines or email. When communication emphasizes the persons involved rather than just their roles or stereotypical characteristics, interpersonal communication is happening.

Features of the Personal

So what do I mean by "the personal"? Many philosophers, anthropologists, and communication scholars have defined what it means to be a person and how persons differ from other kinds of animals. One widely recognized description was created by a philosopher of communication named Martin Buber. (Buber was born in 1878; lived in Austria, Germany, and Israel; visited the United States a couple of times; and died in 1965.) He suggested that there are five qualities, or characteristics, that distinguish persons across many—though perhaps not all—cultures: uniqueness, measurability, responsiveness, reflectiveness, and addressability.[12] These five define what I mean by "the personal," and I will use the five and their opposites to distinguish *impersonal* from *interpersonal* communicating.

Unique Uniqueness means noninterchangeability. We, as persons, can be treated as if we were interchangeable parts, but each of us can also be thought of as unique in a couple of ways, genetically and experientially. The main reason that genetic cloning experiments are controversial is that they threaten this quality. Unless they are cloned or are identical twins, the probability that two persons would have the same genetic materials is 1 in 10 to the ten-thousandth power. That's less than one chance in a billion trillion!

But cloning wouldn't really threaten uniqueness, because even when persons have the same biological raw material, each experiences the world differently. For example, recall identical twins you've known. Both twins might see the same film in the same theater on the same night at the same time, sitting next to each other. Both might leave the theater at the same time and say exactly the same words about it: "I liked that film." At a superficial level, someone might suggest that the experiences of the two are, in this situation, interchangeable. But additional talk will show that they aren't. Did both twins like the film for the same reasons? Did they recall the same experiences as they interpreted the film? Will the film have the same effect on both of them? Will both remember the same things about it? If you asked the twins these questions, you'd get different answers, and you'd discover what you probably knew before you began the process: Each human is unique.

When people are communicating with each other impersonally, they're overlooking most of this uniqueness and focusing on the similarities among all those who play a given social role. All of us naturally and constantly fill many different roles—student, daughter or son, sibling, employee, and so on. And role relationships are an inescapable part of communicating. But the sliding scale emphasizes that people can move from impersonal communication to interpersonal contact.

So the first feature that distinguishes *persons* is experiential and, in most cases, genetic uniqueness. Some cultures downplay this feature, but most Western cultures emphasize it. The more present this feature is in your communicating, the farther your communication is toward the right-hand side of the impersonal-interpersonal continuum.

Unmeasurable   Objects are measurable; they fit within boundaries. An event is of a certain duration; it lasts a measurable amount of time. Even extremely complex objects, such as sophisticated supercomputers, 70-story buildings, and space vehicles, can be completely described in space-and-time terms. This is what blueprints do. They record all the measurements necessary to re-create the object—length, height, width, mass, specific gravity, amperage, voltage, velocity, circumference, hardness, ductility, malleability, conductivity, and so on. Although it's difficult to measure some things directly—the temperature of a kiss, the velocity of a photon, the duration of an explosion—no object or event has any parts that are unmeasurable, in theory at least.

It's different with persons. Even if your physician accurately identifies your height, weight, temperature, blood pressure, serum cholesterol level, hemoglobin count, and all your other data right down to the electric potential in your seventh cranial nerve, the doctor still will not have exhaustively accounted for the person you are, because there are parts of you that can't be measured. Many scientists, social scientists, philosophers, and theologians have made this point. Some cognitive scientists, for example, include in their model of the person components they call "schematas," or "cognitive patterns" that don't have any space-and-time (measurable) existence, but that can be inferred from observations of behavior. Others call the unmeasurable elements of a person the "human spirit," "psyche," or "soul." But whatever you call it, it's there.

Emotions or feelings are the clearest observable evidence of this unmeasurable part. Although instruments can measure things related to feelings—brain waves, sweaty palms, heart rate, paper-and-pencil responses—what the measurements record is a long way from the feelings themselves. "Pulse 110, respiration 72, Likert rating 5.39, palmar conductivity 0.036 ohms" may be accurate, but it doesn't quite capture what's going on inside when you encounter somebody you can't stand or greet somebody you love.

One other thing: These emotions or feelings are *always* a part of what we are experiencing. Psychologists and educators agree that it's unrealistic to try to separate the intellectual or objective aspect of a person or a subject matter from the affective or emotional parts. This is because humans are always thinking *and* feeling. As one writer puts it, "It should be apparent that there is no intellectual learning without some sort of feeling and there are no feelings without the mind's somehow being involved."[13]

Even though feelings are always present, some communication acknowledges them and some communication doesn't. The cashier who's dedicated to her social role will greet people with a smile and wish them a "nice day" even if she feels lousy. Servers in a restaurant are taught not to bring their feelings to work. Two persons who are in a minority may share similar feelings of isolation or exclusion, but they may or may not talk about them. On the other hand, when people are communicating interpersonally, some of their feelings are in play. This does not mean that you have to wear your heart on your sleeve to communicate interpersonally. It just means that when people are making interpersonal contact, some feelings are appropriately acknowledged and shared.

Responsive   Humans are thoroughly and uniquely responsive beings. Objects can only react; they cannot respond. They cannot choose what to do next. Automatic pilots, photoelectric switches, personal and industrial robots, thermostats, and computers can sometimes seem to operate on their own or turn themselves off and on, but they too are dependent on actions initiated outside them. The computers and robots have to be programmed, the thermostat reacts to temperature, which reacts to the sun's rays, which are affected by the earth's rotation, and so on. Similarly, a ball can go only where it's kicked, and if you were good enough at physics calculations, you could figure out how far and where it would go, on the basis of weight, velocity, aerodynamics, the shape of your shoe, atmospheric conditions, and so on.

But what if you were to kick a person? It's an entirely different kind of activity, and you cannot accurately predict what will happen. The reason you can't is that when persons are involved, the outcome depends on *response*, not simply *reaction*. If you tap my knee, you may cause a reflex jerk, but the feelings that occur are not completely predictable, and the behavior or actions that accompany my reflex may be anything from giggles to a slap in the face.

The range of responses is limited, of course. We can't instantly change sex, become three years younger, or memorize the contents of Wikipedia. But we can decide whether to use a conventional word or an obscene one; we can choose how to prioritize our time commitments; and, as will be discussed in later chapters, choice is even a part of the feelings we experience.

In fact, the more you realize your freedom and power to respond rather than simply react, the more of a person you can be. Sometimes it's easy to get out of touch with this freedom and power. You feel like saying, "I *had* to shout back; he was making me look silly!" or "I just *couldn't* say anything!" These statements make it sound like you don't have any choice, like what you do is completely *caused* by what another person does. But as the discussion of fault and blame noted, even when circumstances are exerting pressure, persons still have some freedom and power to choose how to respond. It may mean resisting a culturally rooted preference or breaking some well-established habit patterns, and it may take lots of practice, but it's possible to become aware of your responses and, when you want to, to change them. The reason it's important to learn this skill is that when you believe you're just reacting, you've lost touch with part of what it means to be a person. So, all communication involves choices because persons are responsive, and the more you remember and act on this feature, the more interpersonal your communicating can become.

Reflective   A fourth distinguishing characteristic is that persons are reflective. Being reflective means not only that we are aware of what's around us but also that we can be aware of our awareness. As one author puts it, "No matter how much of yourself you are able to objectify and examine, the quintessential, living part of yourself will always elude you, i.e., the part of you that is conducting the examination,"[14] the reflective part. Wrenches, rocks, and rowboats aren't aware at all. Dogs, cats, armadillos, and giraffes are all aware of their environments, but we don't have any evidence that they are aware of their awareness. So far as we know, only humans compose and save histories of their lives, elaborately bury their dead, explore their extrasensory powers, question the meaning of life, and speculate about the past and future. And only humans are aware that we do all these things.

Reflection is not a process that affects only philosophers and people who know that they don't have long to live. Healthy, "ordinary" people reflect, too. I wonder from time to time whether I'm spending my work time wisely and whether I'm making the right parenting decisions. Sometimes you probably wonder what you'll be doing five years from now. Before you make an important decision, you ask questions of yourself and others about priorities and probable consequences. On clear days, you may notice the beauty of the landscape around you and reflect on how fortunate you are to live where you do. Like all persons, you ask questions and reflect.

When people ignore the fact that persons are reflective, their communication usually shows it. For example, you may stick with superficial topics—the weather, recent news items, gossip. On the other hand, when you're aware of your own and others' reflectiveness, you can respond to more of what's going on as you communicate. Questions can be a clear indicator that a person is reflecting. Often people who express their opinions with absolute certainty have forgotten to reflect, to ask what they might be unsure of and what they might not have thought about. But the reflective person will often explicitly express appropriate reservations and qualifications— "I think this is the right thing to do, but I'm not absolutely sure," or "I know I don't want to lie to him, but I'm not sure how or when to tell him."

Addressable   Beings who are addressable can recognize when they are addressed, that is, when they are called or spoken to in language, and can also respond in language. Addressability is what makes the difference between talking *to* and talking *with*. Neither baseball bats nor dogs and cats are addressable, because you can talk to them, but not with them. You can call them, curse them, scold them, and praise them, but you cannot carry on a mutual conversation, even with an "almost human" pet.

One student described what addressability meant to her by recounting her experience as a child with her imaginary playmate, Sharla. Mary said that Sharla went everywhere with her and was always dressed appropriately. Sharla was also (in Mary's mind) always sympathetic to what Mary was doing and feeling. Mary would talk *to* Sharla constantly, telling her how she felt, complaining about her parents and older sister, and sometimes making elaborate plans. Occasionally, Mary would talk *about* Sharla to her friends or her mother. But of course Sharla never responded out loud. She never talked back. Mary could talk *to* and *about* Sharla, but not *with* her. Sharla was not addressable; she wasn't a person.

Communication theorist John Shotter talks about this feature of human communication under the heading of "addressivity," which he defines as "the quality of being directed toward someone."[15] "Addressed" speech is directed or "aimed" speech, and one characteristic of persons is that they can recognize address and respond in kind. So, for example, as you sit in an audience of several hundred, the speaker can single you out for immediate contact: "Holly Tartar? Are you here? Your question is about job programs, and I want to try to answer it now." Or even more commonly and more directly, you may sit across from a friend and know from the friend's eyes, the touch of his hand, and his voice that he means *you;* he's *present* with you; you are being addressed.

Definition of Interpersonal Communication

Remember that communicators are always both talking and listening, sending and receiving, giving off cues and taking them in—Part Two of this book calls it "exhaling" and "inhaling." These five features—unique, unmeasurable, responsive, reflective, and addressable—can be used to describe how communicators engage in these exhaling and inhaling processes. That is, these five can describe what people are giving out (exhaling) and what they are taking in (inhaling). And, as I noted a few paragraphs earlier, **the term *interpersonal* labels the kind of communication that happens when the people involved talk and listen in ways that maximize the presence of the personal.** When communicators give and receive or talk and listen in ways that emphasize their uniqueness, unmeasureability, responsiveness, reflectiveness, and addressability, then the communication between them is interpersonal. When they listen and talk in ways that highlight the opposites of these five features—interchangeability, measurable aspects, reactivity, unreflectiveness—and imperviousness—their communicating fits on the impersonal end of the sliding scale.

Interpersonal communication is easiest when there are only two of you and you already know and trust each other. But it can also occur early in a relationship—even at first meeting—and, as I've already mentioned, it can occur over the telephone, during an argument, on the job, in group meetings, and even in public speaking or presentation situations. The important thing is not how many people there are or where they're located, but the people's willingness and ability to choose personal over impersonal communication attitudes and behaviors.

Importantly, the terms *impersonal* and *interpersonal* are *descriptive*, not *prescriptive*. Interpersonal communication can be appropriate, effective, or "good" in some situations, and "bad" in others, and the same goes for impersonal contact. The point of this simple model is to give you some control over where your communication is on the impersonal-interpersonal scale.

So the basic definition of interpersonal communication is pretty simple. It's the counterpart of impersonal communication. But as you'll see, I base this book's entire approach on this simple definition. As I've already explained in Chapter 1, each major division of the book, each chapter, and each reading extend a part of the approach to communication, and to interpersonal communication, that I've outlined here. So although this book contains writings by 58 different people, we all view interpersonal communication in similar ways. As a result, by the time you're finished with the book, you ought to have developed not only a deeper understanding of interpersonal communication but also a more powerful and effective sense of how to help make it happen when you want to.

REVIEW QUESTIONS

1. According to this reading, what is the main distinction between the world inhabited by a dog, cat, chimpanzee, or dolphin and the world inhabited by a human?
2. Why is it misleading to think about human communication in terms of senders and receivers?
3. Complete the sentence: Communication is the c_____, c_____, c_____ process of verbal and _____ meaning-making.
4. According to this reading, what's the difference between responsibility and response-ability?
5. List three qualities in addition to ethnicity that make up a person's culture.
6. True or false: Identity negotiation is the only process that's occurring when humans communicate. Explain.

7. Define *nexting,* and give an example of it from your own communication experience.
8. What is the clearest example of the unmeasurable part of persons?
9. What's the difference between a reaction and a response?
10. The presence of questions in one's communicating is a clear example of which of the following: uniqueness, unmeasurability, responsiveness, reflectiveness, or addressability?
11. Complete the following: This reading defines *interpersonal communication* as the kind of _____ that happens when the people involved _____ and _____ in ways that _____ the presence of the _____.

PROBES

1. At the start of this reading, I outline five common but misleading ideas about communication: that it happens between sender and receiver, that it starts when an idea is translated into a message, that it continues when a message is retranslated into another idea, that it can be evaluated in terms of fidelity, and that it can be understood in terms of cause and effect. Which of these five are part(s) of your understanding of communication? Which are you least willing to give up or change?
2. How often does your communication focus on issues of fault and blame? How productive are these discussions? What alternative do you hear me proposing here?
3. Paraphrase the point I make when I say that collaboration doesn't necessarily mean agreement.
4. Implication 1 says, "No one person can completely control a communication event, and no single person or action causes—or can be blamed for—a communication outcome." How do you respond to this claim?
5. How would you describe the greatest cultural distance between you and the author of this reading? Where are you and this author culturally closest?
6. Describe the identity that you understand me (the author of this reading and the editor of this book) to be trying to develop so far in this book.
7. Without reading ahead to Chapter 3, which do you believe are more important in the identity negotiation process, verbal or nonverbal cues?
8. Which of the five features of the personal—uniqueness, unmeasurability, responsiveness, reflectiveness, or addressability—do you believe is most important in interpersonal communicating?

NOTES

1. "Communica*tion*" or "communica*ting?*" I started with the "-ion" form because it's a little more familiar. But many "-ion" words, like *education, expression, persuasion,* and *sensation,* call to mind the finished product

rather than the ongoing process. Education, for example, is something I get at school and expression is something that comes from my voice or body. "Educat*ing*," on the other hand, calls to mind events, occurrences, and processes, just like such terms as *singing, laughing, arguing,* and *making love.* It's helpful to remember that the topics of this reading are processes. This is why the reading title and main headings use the "-ing" forms.

2. Adapted from an example in Douglas W. Maynard, "Perspective-Display Sequences in Conversation," *Western Journal of Speech Communication* 53 (1989), p. 107.

3. Interruptions, or overlapping speech, can manifest a variety of power relationships between conversation partners. Sometimes overlaps can be supportive, and at other times they are denigrating. See, for example, Deborah Tannen, *Talking from 9 to 5* (New York: Morrow, 1994), pp. 232–34.

4. Russian communication theorist Mikhail Bakhtin put it this way: "Any concrete utterance is a link in the chain of speech communication of a particular sphere.... Each utterance is filled with echoes and reverberation of other utterances to which it is related by the communality of the sphere of speech communication.... The speaker is not Adam, and therefore the subject of his speech itself inevitably becomes the arena where his opinions meet those of his partners." *Speech Genres and Other Essays,* trans. Vern W. McGee, ed. Caryl Emerson and Michael Holquist (Austin: Univ. of Texas Press, 1986), pp. 91, 94.

5. Some people call talking to yourself or thinking out loud "intrapersonal communication," or communication "within" one person. I prefer to reserve the term *communication* for what happens between two or more people. The main reason is that *common* or *commune* is the root of *communication,* and you can't make something common that's not divided or separated. While any one person obviously has various "parts" or "sides," I think it's most useful to understand the human as a whole, a unity captured by such terms as *I, me,* or *the person.* Talking to yourself and thinking out loud are important processes, but they are fundamentally different from connecting with an *other,* someone who is not you. In addition, I want to emphasize that humans are, first and foremost, "social animals," relational beings. Humans become who we are in our contacts with others, not mainly as a result of thinking and talking to ourselves.

6. William Barrett, *The Illusion of Technique: A Search for Meaning in a Technological Civilization* (Garden City, NY: Anchor Doubleday), 1978, p. xx.

7. John Shotter, "Epilogue," *Conversational Realities: Constructing Life through Language* (London: Sage, 1993), p. 180.

8. Herbert H. Clark and Deanna Wilkes-Gibbs, "Referring as a Collaborative Process," *Cognition* 22 (1986), p. 1.

9. Emanuel A. Schegloff, "Discourse as an Interactional Achievement III: The Omnirelevance of Action," *Research on Language and Social Interaction* 28 (1995), pp. 186–87.

10. Shotter, 1993.
11. Peter M. Senge, Art Kleiner, Charlotte Roberts, Richard B. Ross, and Bryan J. Smith, *The Fifth Discipline Fieldbook: Strategies and Tools for Building a Learning Organization* (New York: Doubleday, 1994), p. 14.
12. Buber was an international citizen whose major book has been translated into over 20 languages. So he believed that his definition of the person applied across cultures. Many people agree, but others argue that his view of the person is in some ways more Western than Eastern. Some people in cultures that emphasize group identity (Japan, e.g.) believe that Buber's emphasis on the individual was misleading. But most people in Western cultures think that his description fits their experience pretty well. What do you think? See Martin Buber, *I and Thou*, trans. Walter Kaufmann (New York: Scribners, 1970).
13. For a discussion of this point, see George Isaac Brown, *Human Teaching for Human Learning: An Introduction to Confluent Education* (New York: Viking Press, 1971).
14. Fredrick Buechner, *Wishful Thinking: A Theological ABC* (New York: Harper Collins, 1973), p. 64.
15. John Shotter, *Cultural Politics of Everyday Life: Social Constructionism, Rhetoric and Knowing of the Third Kind* (Toronto: Univ. of Toronto Press, 1993), p. 176.

Personal Relationships and Health

Malcolm Parks

Mac Parks is a communication researcher whose research and teaching have substantially increased our understanding of how personal networks affect interpersonal relationships. In this excerpt from his 2007 book, he greatly expands my point that there is a strong and important relationship between the quality of your communication and the quality of your life.

Parks reviews extensive research that connects interpersonal communication with five aspects of mental and physical health: social skill deficits, violence and suicide, cardiovascular difficulties, immune system malfunctions, and risky health practices.

In each case, he summarizes findings from social scientific research, which means that the list of references at the end of this reading could support a detailed research paper. But the connections he draws are even more impressive than the references.

Parents' communication, for example, can cripple the chances of their children to succeed. Sexual abuse may be a precursor to eating disorders. Violent spouses tend to raise children who create violent marriages. Divorce can be a precursor of violence and abuse in young adults' romantic relationships. Suicide is often linked to the absence of lasting interpersonal relationships. Disruptions in significant relationships can lead to disruptions in the body's immune system. And poor interpersonal relationships can promote, or at least fail to discourage, risky and destructive behavior such as smoking, careless driving, and unsafe sex.

The point of this reading is not to scare you but to underscore the close connection between the quality of your communication and the quality of your life. This article focuses on physiological and psychological aspects of your life. As Parks concludes, "personal relationships, then, are much more than private arrangements. They are linked to the physical and mental health of their participants ..."

The articles at the end of this book, in Chapters 11 and 12, extend this point to apply to our lives as cultural members and our lives as world citizens. Remember Parks' essay when you read about the life-destroying relationships between Christians and Muslims, Shiites and Sunnis, Hamas and Fatah, and Jews and Palestinians in later chapters. At all levels, for all persons, the relationships between quality of communication and quality of life are profound.

Inadequate or disordered interpersonal relationships can kill, sometimes slowly, sometimes swiftly. Although the idea that physical and mental well-being are linked to the quality of social life dates from antiquity, the connection has been demonstrated in convincing fashion by research in the life and social sciences over the last 40 years. Classic works, such as Alexander's (1950) *Psychosomatic Medicine,* perpetuated the idea that specific psychological conflicts were associated with specific diseases. Although this view is still influential in the popular press, researchers have now moved beyond this rather mechanical model. In fact the entire concept of a *psychosomatic disease* may be misleading because it implies that some diseases have psychological components while others do not (Plaut & Friedman, 1981). It is more accurate to think of interpersonal and psychological factors as altering the person's susceptibility to illness or injury in general rather than as causing specific types of disease.

By the late 1980s, research evidence on the dangers of inadequate or disordered personal relationships was as strong as the evidence against cigarette smoking was when the United States government issued its first warnings in 1964 (J. House, Landis & Umberson, 1988). But even this comparison is probably conservative. More linkages come into view when we fully liberate ourselves from the biomedical and psychosomatic models.

I believe that there are at least five interrelated pathways linking the quality of our personal relationships with our physical and mental health. Disrupted or inadequate personal relationships are associated with: (a) social skill deficits, (b) violence and suicide, (c) stress-induced illnesses of the cardiovascular system, (d) malfunctions in the immune system, and (e) risky health practices.

SOCIAL SKILL DEFICITS

As social animals, we are born with a strong foundation for the acquisition of social skills. Yet additional learning and practice are required for nearly all of the social skills needed to manage complex interactions—perspective-taking, turn-taking, regulating emotional expression, constructing persuasive strategies, managing conflict, and so on. Interactions with family and peers in childhood and adolescence are among the most important arenas in which we develop these skills. When these early relationships are disordered, then important learning opportunities are lost or distorted and a variety of illnesses may result. This means that many illnesses, particularly mental illnesses may result. This means that many illnesses, particularly mental illnesses, can properly be thought of as interpersonal illnesses (Segrin, 2001).

The damaging effects of interactions with those with poor social skills can be found all across the literature on mental illness. Children who are rejected by their parents, for example, are more likely to have difficulty regulating their own emotional expression and engaging in interaction (Cohn, Campbell, Matias, & Hopkins, 1990). Similarly, parents who are simultaneously highly controlling and yet unable to express affection toward their children may be setting their children up for lifelong deficits in social skills that manifest themselves in a wide range of mental health and relational problems (Hudson & Rapee, 2000). Adolescents with a history of negative interactions with parents, for example, are more likely to behave coercively and abusively with dating partners years later (K. J. Kim, Conger, Lorenz, & Elder, 2001).

This is not to suggest that people are necessarily victims of their early relationships. Early relationships matter, but critics have rightly faulted approaches to mental illnesses that place too much importance on childhood relationships (e.g., Coyne, 1999). Regardless of when they occur, interpersonal relationships serve as arenas for developing or damaging social skills. They are "rolling laboratories" in which the level of skills found in relationships at one point in life help determine the level of skills in relationships at the next point. Social skill deficits can thus be self-perpetuating.

In some cases, it is not merely the lack of positive models that leads to mental and physical illness, but the presence of negative models. Sexual abuse, for instance, is thought to be a precursor to eating disorders partly because it reduces its victims' sense of social competency (Mallinckrodt, McCreary, & Robertson, 1995). It is no wonder, then, that physical and sexual abuse in childhood are strongly linked to mental and physical illnesses across the adult life cycle (Dinwiddie et al., 2000).

VIOLENCE AND SUICIDE

Violence and abuse in personal relationships pose profound problems for society (for a survey, see Harvey & Weber, 2002). Those with inadequate or dysfunctional personal relationships are particularly susceptible to violence, either by their own hand or the hands of others. Some simply carry violent patterns from previous relationships. Violence in dating relationships, for example, is linked both to a history of family violence and to having friends who treat their dating partners abusively (Arriaga & Foshee, 2004). Similarly, spouses in violent marriages frequently grew up in families with a history of violence and abuse (Bergman & Brismar, 1993). Even nonviolent families may fail to provide positive models of conflict management. Parental neglect and divorce are also precursors of violence and abuse in young adults' romantic relationships (Billingham & Notebaert, 1993; Straus & Savage, 2005). People in dysfunctional relationships are themselves more likely to be victims of violence. They may have more people mad at them, but they may also just be more vulnerable and isolated. For example, school children who do not have a reciprocated friendship are more likely to be bullied by their classmates (Boulton Trueman, Chau, Whitehand, & Amatya, 1999). More generally, data both from the United States and other countries indicates that people who are divorced or separated are far more likely to be homicide victims than people who are married (Lynch, 1977; M. Wilson & Daly, 1993).

Over a century ago Durkheim (1897/1951) hypothesized that people committed suicide because they were no longer integrated into the larger social institutions that give their lives meaning. Although we now consider suicide from a number of different perspectives, it is clear that being or feeling disconnected from friends and family contributes to suicide. Some of the most disturbing evidence comes from counselors who report that suicidal behavior among elementary school children is frequently a response to the divorce, illness, or death of parents or other significant relatives (D. E. Matter & R. M. Matter, 1984). In her study of people whom the police had rescued from suicide in Vienna, Margarethe von Andics (1947) painted the attempted suicide as a person who was either unable to form lasting relationships or unable to recover from their loss. More broadly based studies also support the link between suicide and inadequate or disordered personal relationships (Beautrais, Joyce, & Mulder, 1996; Trout, 1980). Demographic data reveals that divorced people have consistently had higher suicide rates over the last 25 years than people who are married, despite the fact that divorce has become more socially acceptable during that time (Stack, 1990).

CARDIOVASCULAR DISEASE

Poor personal relationships break people's hearts—literally. A large and varied body of evidence testifies to the effects of dysfunctional, inadequate personal relationships on cardiovascular disease. The conflict-laden, aggressive, unsupportive, and unsupportable "Type A" personality was formally recognized as a risk factor in coronary disease by the National Blood, Heart, and Lung Institute in the early 1980s. Global personality types, however, are crude measures because they are so far removed from social interaction itself. And indeed, the evidence linking Type A behavior to cardiovascular disease is far from consistent (Suls & Wan, 1993).

More powerful predictors of cardiovascular disease emerge when we look at the give and take of the social support process. Cardiovascular activity appears to be quite sensitive to changes in the nature of interpersonal communication (Lynch, 1985). Blood pressure changes less in reaction to stress, for example, in children whose family communication patterns are open and emotionally expressive, than in families where interpersonal communication is closed (L. B. Wright et al., 1993). Adult men reported less angina pectoris (severe pain radiating from the heart area to the left shoulder and arm) when they perceived their wives as supportive than when they perceived their wives as unsupportive (Medalie & Goldbourt, 1976).

All this implies that death from cardiovascular disease should be more common among those with disrupted or inadequate personal relationships. And indeed it is. Studies in a number of countries consistently reveal that cardiovascular disease is both more common and more likely to be fatal among people who experience high levels of family conflict, are divorced, separated, have few friends, and/or who have little involvement in informal and formal groups (Ebrahim, Wannamethee, McCallum, Walker, & Shaper, 1995; Orth-Gomer et al., 2000; Rosengren et al., 2004). These are not small risk factors. High psychosocial stress poses risks as great as high blood pressure and obesity....

IMMUNE SYSTEM MALFUNCTIONS

The immune system is our body's private physician, curing and protecting us from a host of diseases (Desowitz, 1987). Although the complex interplay of the immune system's components is far from understood, research over the last 40 years demonstrates convincingly that disruptions in significant relationships cause significant disruptions in the immune system. This effect takes at least two forms: immunosuppression and autoimmune disease.

In everyday language, we would say that a person experiencing immunosuppression has a low resistance to disease. The ability to form an immune response to foreign cells or toxins entering the body is reduced. This occurs in large part because of disruptions in the various neuropeptides, neurotransmitters, and neuroendocrines that regulate immune responses (Fleshner & Laudenslager, 2004). People are simply more likely to get sick during periods of interpersonal stress because their immune systems are not as effective at warding off and recovering from disease. This was illustrated quite clearly in an early study by Meyer and Haggerty (1962), who tracked respiratory infections in 16 families over the course of a year. They found that respiratory illnesses were four times more common during periods of stressful family interaction than during less stressful periods.

Studies conducted over the past 30 years have consistently shown that chronic stress reduces immunity (Segerstrom & G. E. Miller, 2004). Immunosuppression has been associated with a variety of interpersonal and psychological conditions including depression, loneliness, family conflict, role conflict, separation from family and peers, divorce, and bereavement (Kaplan, 1991).

Moreover, the consequences of this immunosuppression can be fatal. Divorced people are, for example, are far more likely to die of pneumonia than married people (Lynch, 1977).

The second major effect of interpersonal factors on the immune system is to stimulate autoimmune disease. In these diseases the body attacks itself. The immune system fails to distinguish properly between what is self and what is foreign. Consequently, the immune system produces antibodies that mistakenly injure the body's own tissue. The onset and severity of autoimmune diseases appears to vary with interpersonal events. Rheumatoid arthritis, for instance, progresses more rapidly and is more disabling among people who experience high levels of anger, depression, or stress (Latman & Walls, 1996; Solomon, 1985). These emotional disturbances may be caused by a variety of factors, of course, but the most common stressor identified in the literature is disrupted relationships with spouses or parents. Conversely, the presence of supportive relationships, especially ones in which the interaction helps the sufferer feel in greater control of his or her disease, is associated with better coping and less severe episodes (e.g., Evers, Kraaimaat, Geene, Jacobs, & Bijlsma, 2003; Holtzman, Newth, & Delongis, 2004).

Just as a lack of support worsens autoimmune disease, the disease itself limits social participation. Thus people with rheumatoid arthritis report significant reductions across the entire range of their social activities (P. P. Katz, 1995). For some, the net result is a vicious cycle of increasing social isolation and worsening disease.

RISKY HEALTH PRACTICES

Poor interpersonal relationships promote, or at least fail to discourage, risky and plainly destructive behavior. Failure to seek needed health care or to follow treatment regimens are common forms. People whose friends and family are unsupportive, for example, are less successful when it comes to smoking cessation, taking high blood pressure medication, maintaining control over diabetes, and losing weight (Gorin et al., 2005; Hanson, De Guire, Schinkel, & Kolterman, 1995; Umberson, 1987).

People may also be more prone to engage in risky activities or to engage in activities in unsafe ways if they lack commitments to positive personal relationships. For example, recently separated or divorced people are nearly three times more likely than married people to be involved in a traffic accident (Lagarde et al., 2004). Divorced parents or parents who are distracted by relational problems may provide less supervision and instruction to their children, making their children more susceptible to accidents, injury, or unsafe sexual practices. Teenagers who come from families with poor supervision and cohesiveness, for example, are more likely to drink and drive than teenagers whose parents provide better supervision (Augustyn & Simons-Morton, 1995). Another study found that a greater proportion of 12- to 14-year-olds from recently divorced families had engaged in sexual intercourse than from intact or stepparent families (Flewelling & Bauman, 1990). Even in intact families, poor mother-daughter communication is among the most powerful predictors of teenage pregnancy (Adolph, Ramos, Linton, & Grimes, 1995; Silva & Ross, 2002).

Death from drug and alcohol abuse is far more common among people with disordered personal relationships (Risser, Bonsch, & Schneider, 1996). Disordered relationships are both the product and cause of drug and alcohol abuse. Certainly some people do cope with their relational inadequacies and losses by turning to drugs and alcohol. Compared to children from intact families, children from divorced families are more likely to try drugs and alcohol, to have drug and alcohol problems, and perhaps worst of all, to perpetuate the entire cycle by having greater difficulty forming stable relationships of their own (Flewelling & Bauman, 1990; Jeynes, 2001; Needle, Su, & Doherty, 1990).

The cycle continues when these people become parents themselves. The children of parents who abuse alcohol or drugs are at far greater risk for accidents and injuries. A study of house fires in Scotland between 1980 and 1990, for instance, indicated that parental alcohol abuse was a significant contributor to the death of children (Squires & Busuttil, 1995). Another study in the United States reported that children whose mothers were problem drinkers were over twice as likely to have serious accidents and injuries as children whose mothers are not problem drinkers. The risks were even higher when both parents were problem drinkers or when the problem drinker was also a single mother (Bijur, Kurzon, Overpeck, & Scheidt, 1992).

These findings remind us that negative social and health outcomes typically appear together—drinking, school problems, violence, suicide, psychological disorders, and so on. Yet to the extent that these problems are the consequence of low interpersonal skills and poor social relationships, all can be addressed by interventions that build communicative skills and provide a social support network. Indeed, programs that focus on exactly these factors have proven successful in enhancing self-esteem, improving school performance, decreasing drug use, and reducing suicide potential among adolescents (e.g., Eggert, Thompson, Herting, Nicholas, & Dicker, 1994; E. A. Thompson, Eggert, Randell, & Pike, 2001).

Personal relationships, then, are much more than private arrangements. They are linked to the physical and mental health of their participants and, by virtue of the social and economic roles they play, to the vitality of society as a whole. This recognition has grown slowly as the study of personal relationships has evolved over the past 100 years.

REVIEW QUESTIONS

1. The lack of positive models of interpersonal communication can promote illness, as well as the presence of what?
2. What relationship does Parks suggest between bullying (see Chapter 9) and childhood friendships?

3. What is the relationship between disrupted or inadequate personal relationships and cardiovascular disease?
4. How can family stress affect family members' respiratory illnesses?
5. What are some other illnesses that are worsened by stress?

PROBES

1. If you were to base a "Family Communication" workshop on the content of this reading, what topics would you address in your workshop?
2. In the "Social Skill Deficits" section, Parks notes that "people are [not] necessarily victims of their early relationships." What point is he making here about causality (fault and blame) in interpersonal relationships?
3. Summarize the evidence in this essay about the possible effects of divorce.
4. What are the implications of this essay for the importance of premarital counseling and education?
5. What connections do you see between the quality of your communication and the quality of your life?

REFERENCES

Adolph, C., Ramos, D. E., Linton, K. L., & Grimes, D. A. (1995). Pregnancy among Hispanic teenagers: Is good parental communication a deterrent? *Contraception, 51*(5), 303–306.

Alexander, F. (1950). *Psychosomatic medicine.* New York: Norton.

Arriaga, X. B., & Foshee, V. A. (2004). Adolescent dating violence: Do adolescents follow in their friends', or their parents', footsteps? *Journal of Interpersonal Violence, 19,* 162–184.

Augustyn, M., & Simons-Morton, B. G. (1995). Adolescent drinking and driving: Etiology and interpretation. *Journal of Drug Education, 25,* 41–59.

Beautrais, A. L., Joyce, P. R., & Mulder, R. T. (1996). Risk factors for serious suicide attempts among youths aged 13 through 24 years. *Journal of the American Academy of Child and Adolescent Psychiatry, 35,* 1174–1182.

Bergman, B., & Brismar, B. (1993). Assailants and victims: A comparative study of male wife-beaters and battered males. *Journal of Addictive Diseases, 12*(4), 1–10.

Bijur, P. E., Kurzon, M., Overpeck, M. D., & Scheidt, P. C. (1992). Parental alcohol use, problem drinking, and children's injuries. *Journal of the American Medical Association, 267,* 3166–3171.

Billingham, R. E., & Notebaert, N. L. (1993). Divorce and dating violence revisited: Multivariate analyses using Straus's conflict tactics subscores. *Psychological Reports, 73,* 679–684.

Boulton, M. J., Trueman, M., Chau, C., Whitehand, C., & Amatya, K. (1999). Concurrent and longitudinal links between friendship and peer victimization: Implications for befriending interventions. *Journal of Adolescence, 22,* 461–466.

Cohn, J. F., Campbell, S. B., Matias, R., & Hopkins, J. (1990). Face-to-face interactions of postpartum depressed and nondepressed mother-infant pairs at 2 months. *Developmental Psychology, 26,* 15–23.

Coyne, J. C. (1999). Thinking interactionally about depression: A radical restatement. In T. Joiner & J. C. Coyne (Eds.), *The interactional nature of depression* (pp. 365–392). Washington, DC: American Psychological Association.

Desowitz, R. S. (1987). *The thorn in the starfish: How the human immune system works.* New York: Norton.

Dinwiddie, S. H., Heath, A. C., Dunne, M. P., Bucholz, K. K., Madden, P. A. F., Slutske, W. S., et al. (2000). Early sexual abuse and lifetime psychopathology: A co-twin-control study. *Psychological Medicine, 30,* 41–52.

Durkheim, E. (1951). *Suicide.* New York: Free Press. (Original work published 1897).

Ebrahim, S., Wannamethee, G., McCallum, A., Walker, M., & Shaper, A. G. (1995). Marital status, change in marital status, and mortality in middle-aged British men. *American Journal of Epidemiology, 142,* 834–842.

Eggert, L. L., Thompson, E. A., Herting, J. R., Nicolas, L. J., & Dicker, B. G. (1994). Preventing adolescent drug abuse and high school dropout through an intensive school-based social network development program. *American Journal of Health Promotion, 8,* 202–215.

Evers, A., Kraaimaat, F. W., Greene, R., Jacobs, J., & Bijlsma, J. (2003). Pain coping and social support as predictors of long-term functional disability and pain in early rheumatoid arthritis. *Behaviour Research & Therapy, 41,* 1295–1310.

Fleshner, M., & Laudenslager, M. L. (2004). Psychoneuroimmunology: Then and now. *Behavioral & Cognitive Neuroscience Reviews, 3*(2), 114–130.

Flewelling, R. L., & Bauman, K. E. (1990). Family structure as a predictor of initial substance use and sexual intercourse in early adolescence. *Journal of Marriage and the Family, 52,* 171–181.

Gorin, A., Phelan, S., Tate, D., Sherwood, N., Jeffery, R., & Wing, R. (2005). Involving support partners in obesity treatment. *Journal of Consulting and Clinical Psychology, 73,* 341–343.

Hanson, C. L., De Guire, M. J., Schinkel, A. M., & Kolterman, O. G. (1995). Empirical validation for a family-centered model of care. *Diabetes Care, 18*(10), 1347–1356.

Harvey, J. H., & Weber, A. L. (2002). *Odyssey of the heart: Close relationships in the 21st century* (2nd ed.). Mahwah, NJ: Lawrence Erlbaum Associates.

Holtzman, S., Newth, S., & Delongis, A. (2004). The role of social support in coping with daily pain among patients with rheumatoid arthritis. *Journal of Health Psychology, 9,* 677–695.

House, J., Landis, K., & Umberson, D. (1988). Social relationships and health. *Science, 241*(4865), 540–545.

Hudson, J. L., & Rapee, R. M. (2000). The origins of social phobia. *Behavior Modification, 24*(1), 102–129.

Jeynes, W. H. (2001). The effects of recent parental divorce on their children's consumption of marijuana and cocaine. *Journal of Divorce and Remarriage, 35*(3–4), 43–65.

Kaplan, H. B. (1991). Social psychology of the immune system: A conceptual framework and review of the literature. *Social Science and Medicine, 33*, 909–923.

Katz, P. P. (1995). The impact of rheumatoid arthritis on life activities. *Arthritis Care and Research, 8*, 272–278.

Kim, K. J., Conger, R., Lorenz, F. O., & Elder, G. H. (2001). Parent-adolescent reciprocity in negative affect and its relation to early adult social development. *Developmental Psychology, 37*, 775–790.

Lagarde, E., Chastang, J. F., Gueguen, A., Coeuret-Pellicer, M., Chiron, M., & Lafont, S. (2004). Emotional stress and traffic accidents: The impact of separation and divorce. *Epidemiology, 15*, 762–766.

Latman, N. S., & Walls, R. (1996). Personality and stress: An exploratory comparison of rheumatoid arthritis and osteoarthritis. *Archives of Physical and Medical Rehabilitation, 77*, 796–800.

Lynch, J. J. (1977). *The broken heart: The medical consequences of loneliness.* New York: Basic Books.

Lynch, J. J. (1985). *The language of the heart.* New York: Basic Books.

Mallinckrodt, B., McCreary, B. A., & Robertson, A. K. (1995). Co-occurrence of eating disorders and incest: The role of attachment, family environment, and social competencies. *Journal of Counseling Psychology, 42*, 178–186.

Matter, D. E., & Matter, R. M. (1984). Suicide among elementary school children: A serious concern for counselors. *Elementary School Guidance and Counseling, 18*, 260–267.

Medalie, J. H., & Goldbourt, U. (1976). Angina pectoris among 10,000 men. II. Psychosocial and other risk factors as evidenced by a multivariate analysis of a five-year incidence study. *American Journal of Medicine, 60*, 910–921.

Meyer, R. J., & Haggerty, R. J. (1962). Streptococcal infections in families. Factors altering individual susceptibility. *Pediatrics, 29*, 536–549.

Needle, R. H., Su, S. S., & Doherty, W. J. (1990). Divorce, remarriage, and adolescent substance use: A prospective longitudinal study. *Journal of Marriage and the Family, 52*, 157–169.

Orth-Gomer, K., Wamala, S. P., Horsten, M., Schenck-Gustafsson, K., Schneiderman, N., & Mittleman, M. A. (2000). Marital stress worsens prognosis in women with coronary heart disease: The Stockholm Female Coronary Risk Study. *Journal of the American Medical Association, 284*, 3008–3014.

Plaut, S. M., & Friedman, S. B. (1981). Psychosocial factors in infectious disease. In R. Ader (Ed.), *Psychoneuroimmunolgy* (pp. 3–30). New York: Academic Press.

Risser, D., Bonsch, A., & Schneider, B. (1996). Family background of drug-related deaths: A descriptive study based on interviews with relatives of deceased drug users. *Journal of Forensic Science, 41,* 960–962.

Rosengren, A., Hawken, S., Ôunpuu, S., Silwa, K., Zubain, M., Almahmeed, W. A., et al. (2004). Association of psychosocial risk factors with risk of acute myocardial infarction in 11,119 cases and 13,648 controls from 52 countries (the Interheart Study): Case-control study. *Lancet, 364,* 953–962.

Segerstrom, S. C., & Miller, G. E. (2004). Psychological stress and the human immune system: A meta-analytic study of 30 years of inquiry. *Psychological Bulletin, 130,* 601–630.

Segrin, C. (2001). *Interpersonal processes in psychological problems.* New York: Guilford Press.

Silva, M., & Ross, I. (2002). Association of perceived parental attitudes towards premarital sex with initiation of sexual intercourse in adolescence. *Psychological Reports, 91*(3, Pt. 1), 781–784.

Solomon, G. F. (1985). The emerging field of psychoneuroimmunology: With a special note on AIDS. *Advances, 2,* 6–19.

Squires, T., & Busuttil, A. (1995). Child fatalities in Scottish house fires 1980–1990: A case of child neglect? *Child Abuse and Neglect, 19,* 865–873.

Stack, S. (1990). New micro-level data on the impact of divorce on suicide, 1959–1980: A test of two theories. *Journal of Marriage and the Family, 52,* 119–127.

Straus, M. A., & Savage, S. A. (2005). Neglectful behavior by parents in the life history of university students in 17 countries and its relation to violence against dating partners. *Child Maltreatment: Journal of the American Professional Society on the Abuse of Children, 10*(2), 124–135.

Suls, J., & Wan, C. K. (1993). The relationship between trait hostility and cardiovascular reactivity: A quantitative review and analysis. *Psychophysiology, 30,* 615–626.

Thompson, E. A., Eggert, L. L., Randell, B. P., & Pike, K. C. (2001). Evaluation of indicated suicide risk prevention approaches for potential high school dropouts. *American Journal of Public Health, 91,* 742–752.

Trout, D. L. (1980). The role of social isolation in suicide. *Suicide and Life-Threatening Behavior, 10,* 10–23.

Umberson, D. (1987). Family status and health behaviors: Social control as a dimension of social integration. *Journal of Health & Social Behavior, 28,* 306–319.

Von Andics, M. (1947). *Suicide and the meaning of life.* London: W. Hodge.

Wilson, M., & Daly, M. (1993). Spousal homicide risk and estrangement. *Violence and Victims, 8,* 3–16.

Wright, L. B., Treiber, F. A., Davis, H., Strong, W. B., Levy, M., Van Huss, E., et al. (1993). Relationship between family environment and children's hemodynamic responses to stress: A longitudinal evaluation. *Behavioral Medicine, 19,* 115–121.

Toward Study of the Consequentiality (Not Consequences) of Communication

Stuart J. Sigman

This brief reading responds to the question, "Why should I study communication?"

Some people believe that, since we've all been communicating since at least the day we were born, we don't need to study it. Others claim that if you study something as normal and everyday as communication, you turn it into something mechanical and artificial. Still others argue that human communication is so complex and changeable that it is impossible to generalize about it without distorting what actually occurs.

Communication scholar and teacher Stuart Sigman argues here that we should study communication because it "matters." It matters because it affects the kinds of lives people lead. And importantly, this impact is more due to the *ways* people communicate than to *what* they say. Process is more important than content.

You will hear this idea developed in several of the following chapters. By the time you're finished with the readings in this book, you should be able to talk in some detail about how and why communication *matters.*

Communication matters. It matters whether a word is spoken with a certain inflection, a gesture is displayed at a particular body height and with a particular intensity, an article of clothing is donned, or a bodily incision is endured at just some moment in an activity sequence. *What* persons do when constructing messages with others has an impact on the kinds of lives they lead, the kinds of institutions and organizations they find themselves inhabiting, and the kinds of connections with other persons they make—separated across space, time, and rank.

Thus, this book is concerned with the idea that the communication process is consequential in and to people's lives. This consequentiality cannot be explained by primary recourse to cultural, psychological, or sociological variables and theorizing, however. It is the ebb and flow of the communication process itself that must be studied, and a theory of communication consequentiality apart from anthropological, psychological, or sociological theory that must be developed.

As detailed later, *consequentiality of communication* means that *what* transpires during, within, and as part of persons' interactive dealings with each other has consequences for those persons. Those consequences come from the communication process, not the structure of language or the mediation of particular personality characteristics or social structures. Communication is consequential both in the sense that it is the primary process engendering and constituting sociocultural reality, and in the sense that, as it transpires, constraints on and affordances to people's behavior momentarily emerge. In this view, communication is not a neutral vehicle by which an external reality is communicated about, and by which factors of psychology, social structure, cultural norms, and the like are transmitted or are influential. The communication process: (a) exerts a role in the personal identities and self-concepts experienced by persons; (b) shapes the range of permissible and impermissible relationships between persons, and so produces a social structure; and (c) represents the process through which cultural values, beliefs, goals, and the like are formulated and lived.

Thus, to study the consequentiality of communication is to envision a world composed of a continuous process of meaning production, rather than conditions antecedent and subsequent to this production. To study the consequentiality of communication is to take seriously—for purposes of description and analysis—a world sustained by persons behaving, engaged in the negotiation and renegotiation of messages, not a world of a priori (or a posteriori) cognitive states, cultural rules, social roles, or the like.

REVIEW QUESTIONS

1. When Sigman says communication "matters," what does he mean?
2. Explain what it means to say that the process of communication often has more impact than the content.

PROBES

1. What is the relationship between this short reading and my essay that begins this chapter?
2. Assume that you are a communication major and that you've decided to focus your undergraduate studies on communication. At a family gathering, an aunt or uncle asks you what you're studying and why. Using the readings in this chapter, respond to your aunt or uncle.

Fierce Conversations
Susan Scott

Susan Scott is an executive educator who has helped clients around the world transform the cultures of their organizations. In this excerpt from her best-selling book, she explains how, as I noted earlier in the chapter, conversations are the most important communication events people experience. As she puts it, "our work, our relationships, and, in fact, our very lives succeed or fail gradually, then suddenly, *one conversation at a time.*"

Although Scott's primary audience is businesspeople rather than college students, her main points apply to everyone. Regardless of your station in life, when you face an important challenge, your first step should be to resist what she calls the "accountability shuffle" of blaming others, and your second should be to "identify the conversations out there with your name on them and resolve to have them with all the courage, grace, and vulnerability they require." If life is good, you can also realize that you got here "gradually, then suddenly, one *successful* conversation at a time." And her advice applies as much to experiences at home as it does to experiences at work.

Scott reinforces what other authors in this chapter have also said: Relationships exist in the conversations that make them up. Whether you're thinking about a dating relationship, a marriage relationship, a work relationship, or a family relationship, "the conversation is the relationship." Relationship problems begin in specific conversations, negative spirals can be tracked through conversations, and improvement can occur when conversations change.

By "fierce conversation," Scott explains that she means intense, strong, powerful, passionate, eager, and robust conversation. "Fierce" does not mean angry or hostile; it emphasizes the importance of being genuinely present and authentic in as many as possible of the conversations you experience. Scott urges her readers to embrace the possibility that fierce conversations are opportunities to be known, seen, and changed.

Near the end of this reading, Scott tells her story of discovering the importance of conversation while working with business leaders on issues that undercut their effectiveness. As she explains, her brief and superficial explanation of what she did for a living was "I ran think tanks for corporate leaders and worked with them one-to-one." But "what I really did was extend an intimate invitation to my clients, that of conversation." And most clients experienced significant improvement in their effectiveness and their job satisfaction.

This reading ends with a challenge for you to begin working to make more of your conversations genuinely authentic or "fierce." The rest of Scott's 290-page book effectively details how to do this. But as a contribution to the second chapter of this book, I hope her words emphasize how crucially important it is for you to pay attention to the communication events that most define your reality and determine your success and happiness: conversations.

O ver ten thousand hours of one-to-one conversations with industry leaders, as well as workshops with men and women from all walks of life confronting issues of relationship and life direction, have convinced me that our work, our relationships, and, in fact, our very lives succeed or fail gradually, then suddenly, *one conversation at a time.*

Equally provocative has been my realization that while no single conversation is guaranteed to change the trajectory of a business, a career, a marriage, or a life, any single conversation *can.* . . .

Whether you intend to maintain positive results in your life or turn things around, considering all of the conversations you need to have could feel a bit discouraging, so let's take the curse off the somewhat daunting field of "communications." I'd like you to simply take it *one conversation at a time*, beginning with the person who next stands in front of you. Perhaps there are very few conversations in between you and what you desire.

... Once you get the hang of it, once you master the courage and the skills and, more important, enjoy the benefits of fierce conversations, there will be no going back. It could change the world. It will certainly change *your* world.

When *Here* Is Troubling

Be patient with yourself. You got here—wherever "here" is—one conversation at a time. Allow the changes needed at home or at work to reveal themselves one conversation at a time.

Sometimes *here* just happens. Following the high-tech carnage, crashing economies, corporate layoffs, and terrorist attacks of 2001, which altered our individual and collective realities in a heartbeat, it would be easy to conclude that life has grown too unpredictable, that there's nothing to do but hang on and muddle through as best you can.

Perhaps you received a major wake-up call. You lost your biggest customer—the one that counted for 40 percent of your net profit. Or you lost your most valued employee. Or you lost your job, and it wasn't due to a layoff. You lost the loyalty of your team. You lost your eighteen-year marriage, or the cohesiveness of your family.

Perhaps your company is experiencing turnover, turf wars, rumors, departments not cooperating with one another, long overdue reports and projects, strategic plans that still aren't off the ground, and lots of very good reasons and excuses why things can't be any different or better.

To experience what happens for many individuals and organizations facing challenges, put your right arm out and point your finger, then visualize pointing it at someone who is the bane of your professional or personal life right now. That's called the *accountability shuffle*. He did it, she did it, they did it to me.

Blame isn't the answer, nor is cocooning in the perceived safety of your home. Once you reflect on the path that led you to a disappointing or difficult point and place in time, you may remember, often in vivid detail, the conversation that set things in motion, ensuring that you would end up exactly where you find yourself today. It is very likely that you arrived at this destination one *failed* conversation at a time.

Ask yourself, "How did I get *here*? How is it that I find myself in a company, a role, a relationship, or a life from which I've absented my spirit? How did I lose my way?"

So many times I've heard people say, "We never addressed the real issue, never came to terms with reality." Or, "We never stated our needs. We never told each other what we were really thinking and feeling. In the end, there were so many things we needed to talk about, the wheels came off the cart."

In February 2002, Robert Kaiser and David Ottaway wrote an article for the *Washington Post* about the fragility of U.S.-Saudi ties. Brent Scowcroft, national security adviser to the first President Bush, is quoted as saying, "Have we [the United States and Saudi Arabia] understood each other particularly well? ... Probably not. And I think, in a sense, we probably avoid talking about the things that are the real problems between us because it's a very polite relationship. We don't get all that much below the surface."

Take your finger and touch your nose. This is where the resolution begins. This is the accountable position. If you want to make progress toward a better "here" in your professional or personal life, identify the conversations out there with your name on them and resolve to have them with all the courage, grace, and vulnerability they require.

When *Here* Is Wonderful

And on the positive side, you finally landed that huge customer, the one your competition would kill for. Or you successfully recruited a valuable new employee. Or you discovered that your team is committed to you at the deepest level. Or you just received a promotion. Or you enjoy a deeply fulfilling relationship. You are clear and passionate about your life.

You got to this good place in your life, this satisfying career path, this terrific relationship, gradually, then suddenly, one *successful* conversation at a time. Perhaps one marvelously *fierce* conversation at a time. And now you are determined to ensure the quality of your ongoing conversations with the people central to your success and happiness.

If you want better results at home or at work, you've come to the right place. After reading this, gathering your courage, and working with the tools we'll explore together, you will return to your colleagues at work, to your partner at home, and, most important, to your *self*, prepared to engage in ongoing, groundbreaking conversations that will profoundly transform your life.

While it was tempting to give in to suggestions that I write two books—*Fierce Conversations in the Workplace* and *Fierce Conversations at Home*—breaking this material into two books would have been a mistake. Perhaps you've bought into the premise that we respond differently depending on whom we are with, that our work and home personas are really quite different. Perhaps you pay fierce attention to conversations at work but slip into a conversational coma at home, convinced there's nothing new, interesting, or energizing to discuss, preferring the company of the remote control. Perhaps you leave your warmth, playfulness, and authenticity at home and prop up an automaton at your desk at work, afraid to let your authentic self show up lest you be judged as poor fodder for the corporate feast. Perhaps you've told yourself that conversations at work are unavoidably and substantially different from conversations at home. That that's just the way it has to be. This is not true.

Each of us must discard the notion that we respond differently depending on whom we're with and that our work and home conversations are really quite different.

When you squeeze an orange, what comes out of it? Orange juice. Why? Because that's what's inside it. The orange doesn't care whether it's on a boardroom table or beside the kitchen sink. It doesn't leak orange juice at home and tomato juice at work.

When we get squeezed—*when things aren't going well for us*—what comes out of us? Whatever's inside us. To pretend that what's going on in our personal lives can be boxed, taped shut, and left in the garage while we are at work is hogwash. It seeps in everywhere. Who we are is who we are, all over the place. So if your conversations at work are yielding disappointing results, I'd be willing to bet you're getting similar results at home. The principles and skills needed to engage in conversations that produce mind-blowing, world-class results in the workplace are exactly the same principles and skills that produce mind-blowing, world-class results at home.

The Conversation Is the Relationship

Going hand in hand with the discovery that our lives succeed or fail one conversation at a time is a second insight, courtesy of poet and author David Whyte. During a keynote speech at TEC International's annual conference several years ago, David suggested that in the typical marriage, the young man, newly married, is often frustrated that this person with whom he intends to enjoy the rest of his life seemingly needs to talk, yet again, about the same thing they talked about last weekend. And it often has something to do with their relationship. He wonders, Why are we talking about this again? I thought we settled this. Couldn't we just have one huge conversation about our relationship and then coast for a year or two?

Apparently not, because here she is again. Eventually, if he is paying attention, it occurs to him, Whyte suggests, that "this ongoing, robust conversation he has been having with his wife is not about the relationship. The conversation *is* the relationship."

The conversation is the relationship. If the conversation stops, all of the possibilities for the relationship become smaller and all of the possibilities for the individuals in the relationship become smaller, until one day we overhear ourselves in midsentence, making *ourselves* smaller in every encounter, behaving as if we are just the space around our shoes, engaged in yet another three-minute conversation so empty of meaning it crackles.

Incremental degradation—if we compromise at work or at home; if we lower the standards about how often we talk, what we talk about, and, most important, what degree of authenticity we bring to our conversations—it's a slow and deadly slide. One company president has been known to stop candid input in its tracks with the pronouncement "Howard, I do not consider that a career-enhancing response."

Fortunately, few leaders exhibit such exaggerated violations of the general rules of communication. However, many work teams as well as couples have a list of undiscussables, issues they avoid broaching at all costs in order to preserve a modicum of peace, to preserve the relationship. In reality, the relationship steadily deteriorates for lack of the very conversations they so carefully avoid. It's difficult to raise the level if the slide has lasted over a period of years, and that's what keeps many of us stuck.

In our significant relationships, in the workplace, and in our conversations with ourselves, we'd like to tell the truth. We'd like to be able to successfully tackle the topic that's keeping us stuck or apart, but the task is too hard, we don't know how to avoid the all-too-familiar outcome of talks gone south, and besides, we've learned to live with it. Why wreck another meeting with our colleagues, another weekend with our life partner, trying to resolve the tough issues or answer the big questions? We're tired and we just want peace in the land.

The problem is, whether you are running an organization or your life, you are required to be responsive to your world. And that response often requires change. We effect change by engaging in robust conversations with ourselves and others.

Each conversation we have with our coworkers, customers, significant others, and children either enhances those relationships, flatlines them, or takes them down. Given this, what words and what level of attention do you wish to bring to your conversations with the people most important to you? Throughout the book we will explore principles and practices that will help you engage in conversations that enrich relationships, no matter how sensitive or challenging the topic.

What Is a "Fierce" Conversation?

But a "fierce" conversation? Doesn't "fierce" suggest menacing, cruel, barbarous, threatening? Sounds like raised voices, frowns, blood on the floor, no fun at all. In *Roget's Thesaurus*, however, the word *fierce* has the following synonyms: robust, intense, strong, powerful, passionate, eager, unbridled, uncurbed, untamed. In its simplest form, *a fierce conversation is one in which we come out from behind ourselves into the conversation and make it real.*

While many are afraid of "real," it is the unreal conversation that should scare us to death. Whoever said talk is cheap was mistaken. Unreal conversations are incredibly expensive for organizations and for individuals. Every organization wants to feel it's having a real conversation with its employees, its customers, its territory, and with the unknown future that is emerging around it. Each individual wants to have conversations that are somehow building his or her world of meaning.

If you are a leader, your job is to accomplish the goals of the organization. How will you do that in today's workplace? In large part, by making every conversation you have as real as possible. Today's employees consider themselves owners and investors. They own their time, their energy, and their expertise. They are willing to invest these things in support of the individuals, ideals, and goals in which they believe. Give them something real in which to believe.

What I've witnessed over and over is that when the conversation is real, the change occurs before the conversation has even ended.

Being real is not the risk. The real risk is that:

> *I will be known.*
>
> *I will be seen.*
>
> *I will be changed.*

Think about it. What are the conversations you've been unable or unwilling to have—with your boss, colleague, employee, customer; with your husband, wife, parent, child; or with *yourself*—that, if you *were* able to have, might change everything?

My Own Journey

For thirteen years, I worked with corporate leaders through the auspices of TEC International, an organization dedicated to increasing the effectiveness and enhancing the lives of CEOs. Thousands of CEOs in eighteen countries meet for monthly one-to-one conversations with someone like myself to focus on their businesses and lives—from budgets, strategies, acquisitions, personnel, and profitability (or the lack thereof) to faltering marriages, health issues, or kids who are upside down.

Twelve conversations over the course of a year with each CEO. Since time is a CEO's most precious commodity, it seemed essential that our time together be qualitatively different from time spent with others. Each conversation needed to accomplish something useful. My success, and that of my peers, depended on our ability to engage leaders in conversations that provoked significant change.

In the beginning, a fair number of my conversations were less than fierce. They were somewhat useful, but we remained in relatively familiar, safe territory. Some, I confess, were pathetic. No guts, no glory. I wimped out. Either I didn't have it in me that day, or I looked at the expression on my TEC member's face and took pity. I don't remember those conversations. They had no lasting impact. And I am certain my TEC members would say the same.

The fierce conversations I remember. The topics, the emotions, the expressions on our faces. It was as if, together, we created a force field by asking the questions, by saying the words out loud. Things happened as a result of those conversations.

When people asked me what I did, I told them that I ran think tanks for corporate leaders and worked with them one-to-one. That was the elevator speech. What I really did was extend an intimate invitation to my clients, that of conversation. And my job was to make each conversation as real as possible.

As my practice of robust conversations became increasingly compelling to me, I imagined that I was turning into a conversational cartographer, mapping a way toward deepening authenticity for myself and for those who wanted to join me. The CEOs with whom I worked became increasingly candid, and with that candor came a growing sense of personal freedom, vitality, and effectiveness. The most successful leaders invariably determined to engage in an ongoing, robust conversation with themselves, paying fierce attention to their work and lives, resulting in a high level of personal authenticity, ferocious integrity, emotional honesty, and a greater capacity to hold true to their vision and enroll others in it.

My colleagues worldwide asked me to conduct workshops on what I was doing, to pass along the skills needed for these conversations about which I had become so passionate. This required me to articulate for myself the approach I was developing. I led my first workshop in 1990.

In January 1999, I ran a redesigned, incredibly "fierce" workshop attended by sixteen extraordinary individuals from seven countries. In my workshops there is no role-play. No one pretends to be someone else. No one works on imaginary issues. It's all *real* play. All the participants engage in conversations as themselves, using real, current, significant issues as the focus for our practice sessions. Following one of the exercises, a colleague from Newcastle on Tyne, England, had tears in his eyes.

"I've longed for conversations like this all my life," he said, "but I didn't know they were possible. I don't think I can settle for anything less going forward."

Attendees e-mailed others about the impact of the workshop, about how they were applying the principles and using the tools they had learned, and about the results they were enjoying with their colleagues and family members. Word spread and the demand grew. Each subsequent workshop had a waiting list and each workshop went deeper. Corporate clients invited me to work with their key executives to foster courageous dialogue within their companies.

In November 2001, I recognized that my travel schedule had gotten out of hand when I sat down in my seat at the Sydney Opera House and reached for my seat belt. But my work with clients has been worth it. Over time I recognized that we were exploring core principles, which, when embraced, dramatically changed lives... one conversation at a time. Fierce conversations are about moral courage, clear requests, and taking action. *Fierce* is an attitude. A way of conducting business. A way of leading. A way of life.

Many times I hear words to this effect: "Your work has profoundly improved our leadership team's ability to tackle and resolve tough challenges. The practical tools allow leaders to become fierce agents for positive change." Or this: "You've helped me engage my workforce in moving the company to a position of competitive superiority!" Or this: "A fierce conversation is like the first parachute jump from an airplane. In anticipation, you perspire and your mouth goes dry.

Once you've left the plane, it's an adrenaline rush that is indescribable." Or this: "This weekend my wife and I had the best conversation we've had in ten years. It feels like falling in love all over again.". . .

Getting Started

Here is what I'd like you to do. Begin listening to yourself as you've never listened before.

Begin to overhear yourself avoiding the topic, changing the subject, holding back, telling little lies (and big ones), being imprecise in your language, being uninteresting even to yourself. And at least once *today*, when something inside you says, "This is an opportunity to be fierce," stop for a moment, take a deep breath, then come out from behind yourself into the conversation and make it real. Say something that is true for you. For example, my friend Ed Brown sometimes stops in midsentence and says, "What I just said isn't quite right. Let me see if I can get closer to what I really want to say." I listen intently to the next words he speaks.

When you come out from behind yourself into the conversation and make it real, whatever happens from there will happen. It could go well or it could be a little bumpy, but at least you will have taken the plunge. You will have said at least one real thing today, one thing that was real for you. And something will have been set in motion, and you will have grown from that moment. . . .

REVIEW QUESTIONS

1. What is the "accountability shuffle"? Why is it ineffective?
2. What does it mean to say, "the conversation is the relationship"?
3. Explain Scott's notion of "fierce" conversation.
4. According to Scott, what does it take to make a conversation "real"?

PROBES

1. Scott argues that similar successes and problems occur in conversations at work and conversations at home. Do you agree? If you do, what are some implications of this fact for your communicating?
2. What does Scott say about the risks of being known, being seen, and being changed? How do you respond to what she says?
3. How can the job of "mak[ing] each conversation as real as possible" actually be meaningful and productive?

———

Elements of the Interhuman
Martin Buber

This book's approach to interpersonal communication is based primarily on the life work of Martin Buber, the author of this next essay. Even though his writings are challenging, I have included one here, because Buber is the primary source for almost everything in this book.

Buber was a Jewish philosopher and teacher who was born and raised in Austria and Germany and who died in 1965 in Israel. In many ways, he was very different from me, and he was probably also very different from you. He was a 19th-century European, a Jew who fled the Holocaust to Israel, and a world-renowned writer and speaker. His native language was German, and his writings in German, I am told, are difficult even for other German speakers to understand. But Buber recognized something about human life that has resonated with literally millions of people since he first expressed it in the early 1920s. His main book, *I and Thou,* has been translated into over 20 languages, and for many years, it sold more copies worldwide than any books other than the Bible and the Quràn.

The idea that impressed so many people is that humans are born with the ability to connect with what's around us in two very different ways. Buber called them "I-It" and "I-Thou," and I call them "impersonally" and "interpersonally." Each is important. But, as Buber wrote late in his life, he was born into a world where "I-It" relating predominated, so he dedicated his creative and communicative energies to describing and encouraging the other alternative. This is where each of us can connect with Buber. If your experience is anything like mine, I-It relating predominates for you, too. And more I-Thou relating could enrich your life. This is why it can be worth it to read Buber carefully.

As I mentioned, because he was raised by his grandparents in Europe during the late-19th and early-20th centuries (Buber's parents were divorced), lived through both world wars, was active in several political movements, and was a well-known, even famous, citizen of Israel, his life experiences are different in many ways from yours and mine. But for me, Buber's peculiar genius is that he can sense the part of his experience that is universal and can project that universal knowledge about human meetings through his European heritage and his "foreign" native language in such a way that he talks to me directly. In other words, even though he is in many ways very different from me, he says, "This is my experience; reflect on it a little and you might find that it's your experience, too." Sometimes I stumble over Buber's language, the way he puts things. For example, like some other older authors in this book, Buber uses "man" when he means "human." But when I listen to him and do what he asks, I discover that he's right. It *is* my experience, only now I understand it better than I did before.

I don't know whether this one excerpt from Buber's writing will work this way for you. But the possibility is there if you open yourself to hear him.[1] That's one thing about Buber's writings. Although he's a philosopher, some scholars criticize him because he doesn't state philosophical propositions and then try to verify and validate them with "proof." Instead, Buber insists that his reader try to meet him in a *conversation,* a dialogue. The main thing

"Elements of the Interhuman," by Martin Buber from *The Knowledge of Man* edited by Maurice Friedman and translated by Maurice Friedman and Ronald Gregor Smith. Copyright © 1965. Reprinted by permission of The Balkin Agency.

is for the reader to see whether his or her life experiences resonate with Buber's. This resonance is the main "proof" of the validity of Buber's ideas.

In almost all his writing, Buber begins by observing that each of us lives a twofold reality. One "fold" is made up of our interaction with objects—human and otherwise—in the world. In this model of living, we merely need to develop and maintain our ability to be "objective," to explain ourselves and the world with accurate theories and valid cause-and-effect formulations. But the other "fold" occurs when we become fully human *persons* in genuine relationships with others, when we meet another and "make the other present as a whole and as a unique being, as the person that he is."

The genuine relationship Buber talks about is the "highest form" of what I've been calling interpersonal communication. Buber's term for it is an "*I-Thou* relationship."[2] According to Buber, the individual lives always in the world of *I-It;* the person can enter the world of *I-Thou.* Both worlds are necessary. You can't expect to communicate interpersonally with everyone in every situation. But you can only become a fully human person by sharing genuine interpersonal relationships with others. As Buber puts it, without *It,* the person cannot live. But he (or she) who lives with *It* alone is not a person.

This article is taken from a talk Buber gave when he visited the United States in 1957. It's especially useful because it is a kind of summary of much of what he had written in the first 79 years of his life (he died when he was 87).

I've outlined the article to simplify it and to show how clearly organized it actually is. As you can see from the outline, Buber's subject is interpersonal relationships, which he calls "man's personal dealings with one another," or "the interhuman." Like the rest of this book, Buber's article doesn't deal with some mystical spirit world in which we all become one. Rather, he's writing about communication between today's teachers and students, politicians and voters, dating partners, and you and me. First, he explains some attitudes and actions that keep people from achieving "genuine dialogue." Then he describes the characteristics of this dialogue, or *I-Thou* relationship. In the outline, I've paraphrased each point that he makes.

A reminder about his language: I pointed out in the Introduction that a few of the readings in *Bridges Not Walls* were written before we had learned about the destructive potential of the male bias in the English language. This is one of these readings. When I paraphrase Buber, I remove this bias, and I have tried to soft-pedal it when I quote him. But it's still part of his writing, at least as it is now translated. Given what he believed about human beings—and given the strong intellectual influence his wife, Paula, had on him—I am sure that Buber would have been quick to correct the gender bias in his language if he had lived long enough to have the opportunity. I hope you can overlook this part of his writing and can hear his insights about *persons.*

OUTLINE OF MARTIN BUBER'S "ELEMENTS OF THE INTERHUMAN"

I.   Interhuman relationships are not the same as "social relationships."
   A. Social relationships can be very close, but no *existential* or person-to-person relation is necessarily involved.
   B. This is because the collective or social suppresses individual persons.

C. But in the interhuman, person meets person. In other words, "the only thing that matters is that for each of the two [persons] the other happens as the particular other, that each becomes aware of the other and is thus related to him in such a way that he does not regard and use him as his object, but as his partner in a living event, even if it is no more than a boxing match."

D. In short, "the sphere of the interhuman is one in which a person is confronted by the other. We [i.e., Buber] call its unfolding the dialogical."

II. There are three problems that get in the way of dialogue.

A. The first problem is the duality of *being* and *seeming*. Dialogue won't happen if the people involved are only "seeming." They need to try to practice "being."

   1. "Seeming" in a relationship involves being concerned with your image, or front—with how you wish to appear.

   2. "Being" involves the spontaneous and unreserved presentation of what you really are in your personal dealings with the other.

   3. These two are generally found mixed together. The most we can do is distinguish between persons in whose essential attitude one or the other (being or seeming) predominates.

   4. When seeming reigns, real interpersonal communication is impossible: "Whatever the meaning of the word 'truth' may be in other realms, in the interhuman realm it means that [people] communicate themselves to one another as what they are."

   5. The tendency toward seeming, however, is understandable.
      a. We *essentially* need personal confirmation—that is, we can't live without being confirmed by other people.
      b. Seeming often appears to help us get the confirmation we need.
      c. Consequently, "to yield to seeming is [the human's] essential cowardice, to resist it is his [or her] essential courage."

   6. This view indicates that there is no such thing as "bad being," but rather people who are habitually content to "seem" and afraid to "be." "I have never known a young person who seemed to me irretrievably bad."

B. The second problem involves the way we perceive others.

   1. Many fatalist thinkers, such as Jean-Paul Sartre, believe that we can ultimately know *only* ourselves, that "man has directly to do only with himself and his own affairs."

   2. But the main prerequisite for dialogue is that you get in direct touch with the other, "that each person should regard his partner as the very one he is."
      a. This means becoming aware of the other person as an essentially unique being. "To be aware of a [person]... means in particular to perceive his wholeness as a person determined by the spirit: it means to perceive the dynamic centre which stamps his

every utterance, action, and attitude with the recognizable sign of uniqueness."
   b. But this kind of awareness is impossible so long as I objectify the other.
3. Perceiving the other in this way is contrary to everything in our world that is scientifically analytic or reductive.
   a. This is not to say that the sciences are wrong, only that they are severely limited.
   b. What's dangerous is the extension of the scientific, analytic method to all of life, because it is very difficult for science to remain aware of the essential uniqueness of persons.
4. This kind of perception is called "personal making present." What enables us to do it is our capacity for "imagining the real" of the other.
   a. Imagining the real "is not a looking at the other but a bold swinging—demanding the most intensive stirring of one's being—into the life of the other."
   b. When I *imagine* what the other person is *really* thinking and feeling, I can make direct contact with him or her.
C. The third problem that impedes the growth of dialogue is the tendency toward imposition instead of unfolding.
   1. One way to affect a person is to impose yourself on him or her.
   2. Another way is to "find and further in the soul of the other the disposition toward" that which you have recognized in yourself as right.
      a. Unfolding is not simply "teaching," but rather *meeting*.
      b. It requires believing in the other person.
      c. It means working as a helper of the growth processes already going on in the other.
   3. The propagandist is the typical "imposer"; the teacher *can* be the correspondingly typical "unfolder."
   4. The ethic implied here is similar to Immanuel Kant's; that is, persons should never be treated as means to an end, but only as ends in themselves.
      a. The only difference is that Buber stresses that persons exist not in isolation but in the interhuman.
      b. For the interhuman to occur, there must be:
         (1) as little seeming as possible.
         (2) genuine perceiving ("personal making present") of the other.
         (3) as little imposing as possible.

III. Here is a summary of the characteristics of genuine dialogue:
   A. Each person must turn toward and be open to the other, a "turning of the being."
   B. Each must make present the other by imagining the real.
   C. Each confirms the other's being; however, confirmation does not necessarily mean approval.

D. Each must be authentically him or herself.
    1. Each must say whatever she or he "has to say."
    2. Each cannot be ruled by thoughts of his or her own effect or effective-
        ness as a speaker.
E. Where dialogue becomes genuine, "there is brought into being a memo-
    rable common fruitlessness which is to be found nowhere else."
F. Speaking is not always essential; silence can be very important.
G. Finally, all participants must be committed to dialogue; otherwise, it will
    fail.

Again, Buber's language sometimes can get in the way of understanding
him. But if you listen carefully, I think at least some of what he says will resonate
with you.

THE SOCIAL AND THE INTERHUMAN

It is usual to ascribe what takes place between men to the social realm, thereby
blurring a basically important line of division between two essentially different
areas of human life. I myself, when I began nearly fifty years ago to find my own
bearings in the knowledge of society, making use of the then unknown concept
of the interhuman, made the same error. From that time it became increasingly
clear to me that we have to do here with a separate category of our existence,
even a separate dimension, to use a mathematical term, and one with which we
are so familiar that its peculiarity has hitherto almost escaped us. Yet insight
into its peculiarity is extremely important not only for our thinking but also for
our living.

We may speak of social phenomena wherever the life of a number of men,
lived with one another, bound up together, brings in its train shared experiences
and reactions. But to be thus bound up together means only that each individual
existence is enclosed and contained in a group existence. It does not mean that
between one member and another of the group there exists any kind of personal
relation. They do feel that they belong together in a way that is, so to speak,
fundamentally different from every possible belonging together with someone
outside the group. And there do arise, especially in the life of smaller groups, contacts which frequently favour the birth of individual relations, but, on the other
hand, frequently make it more difficult. In no case, however, does membership
in a group necessarily involve an existential relation between one member and
another. It is true that there have been groups in history which included highly
sensitive and intimate relations between two of their members—as, for instance, in
the homosexual relations among the Japanese samurai or among Doric warriors—
and these were countenanced for the sake of the stricter cohesion of the group. But
in general it must be said that the leading elements in groups, especially in the
later course of human history, have rather been inclined to suppress the personal
relation in favour of the purely collective element. Where this latter element reigns

alone or is predominant, men feel themselves to be carried by the collectivity, which lifts them out of loneliness and fear of the world and lostness. When this happens—and for modern man it is an essential happening—the life between person and person seems to retreat more and more before the advance of the collective. The collective aims at holding in check the inclination to personal life. It is as though those who are bound together in groups should in the main be concerned only with the work of the group and should turn to the personal partners, who are tolerated by the group, only in secondary meetings.

The difference between the two realms became very palpable to me on one occasion when I had joined the procession through a large town of a movement to which I did not belong. I did it out of sympathy for the tragic development which I sensed was at hand in the destiny of a friend who was one of the leaders of the movement. While the procession was forming, I conversed with him and with another, a good-hearted "wild man," who also had the mark of death upon him. At that moment I still felt that the two men really were there, over against me, each of them a man near to me, near even in what was most remote from me; so different from me that my soul continually suffered from this difference, yet by virtue of this very difference confronting me with authentic being. Then the formations started off, and after a short time I was lifted out of all confrontation, drawn into the procession, falling in with its aimless step; and it was obviously the very same for the two with whom I had just exchanged human words. After a while we passed a café where I had been sitting the previous day with a musician whom I knew only slightly. The very moment we passed it the door opened, the musician stood on the threshold, saw me, apparently saw me alone, and waved to me. Straightway it seemed to me as though I were taken out of the procession and of the presence of my marching friends, and set there, confronting the musician. I forgot that I was walking along with the same step; I felt that I was standing over there by the man who had called out to me, and without a word, with a smile of understanding, was answering him. When consciousness of the facts returned to me, the procession, with my companions and myself at its head, had left the café behind.

The realm of the interhuman goes far beyond that of sympathy. Such simple happenings can be part of it as, for instance, when two strangers exchange glances in a crowded streetcar, at once to sink back again into the convenient state of wishing to know nothing about each other. But also every casual encounter between opponents belong to this realm, when it affects the opponent's attitude—that is, when something, however imperceptible, happens between the two, no matter whether it is marked at the time by any feeling or not. The only thing that matters is that for each of the two men the other happens as the particular other, that each becomes aware of the other and is thus related to him in such a way that he does not regard and use him as his object, but as his partner in a living event, even if it is no more than a boxing match. It is well known that some existentialists assert that the basic factor between men is that one is an object for the other. But so far as this is actually the case, the special reality of the interhuman, the fact of the contact, has been largely eliminated. It cannot indeed be entirely eliminated. As a crude example, take two men who are observing one another. The essential thing is not that the one makes the other his object, but the fact that he is not fully able to do so and the reason for his failure. We have in common with all existing things that we can be made objects of observation. But it is my privilege as man that by the hidden activity of my being I can establish an impassable barrier to objectification. Only in partnership can my being be perceived as an existing whole.

The sociologist may object to any separation of the social and the interhuman on the ground that society is actually built upon human relations, and the theory of these relations is therefore to be regarded as the very foundation of sociology. But here an ambiguity in the concept "relation" becomes evident. We speak, for instance, of a comradely relation between two men in their work, and do not merely mean what happens between them as comrades, but also a lasting disposition which is actualized in those happenings and which even includes purely psychological events such as the recollection of the absent comrade. But by the sphere of the interhuman I mean solely actual happenings between men, whether wholly mutual or tending to grow into mutual relations. For the participation of both partners is in principle indispensable. The sphere of the interhuman is one in which a person is confronted by the other. We call its unfolding the dialogical.

In accordance with this, it is basically erroneous to try to understand the interhuman phenomena as psychological. When two men converse together, the psychological is certainly an important part of the situation, as each listens and each prepares to speak. Yet this is only the hidden accompaniment to the conversation itself, the phonetic event fraught with meaning, whose meaning is to be found neither in one of the two partners nor in both together, but only in their dialogue itself, in this "between" which they live together.

BEING AND SEEMING

The essential problem of the sphere of the interhuman is the duality of being and seeming. Although it is a familiar fact that men are often troubled about the impression they make on others, this has been much more discussed in moral philosophy than in anthropology. Yet this is one of the most important subjects for anthropological study.

We may distinguish between two different types of human existence. The one proceeds from what one really is, the other from what one wishes to seem. In general, the two are found mixed together. There have probably been few men who were entirely independent of the impression they made on others, while there has scarcely existed one who was exclusively determined by the impression made by him. We must be content to distinguish between men in whose essential attitude the one or the other predominates.

This distinction is most powerfully at work, as its nature indicates, in the interhuman realm—that is, in men's personal dealings with one another.

Take as the simplest and yet quite clear example the situation in which two persons look at one another—the first belonging to the first type, the second to the second. The one who lives from his being looks at the other just as one looks at someone with whom he has personal dealings. His look is "spontaneous," "without reserve"; of course, he is not uninfluenced by the desire to make himself understood by the other, but he is uninfluenced by any thought of the idea of himself which he can or should awaken in the person whom he is looking at. His opposite is different. Since he is concerned with the image which his appearance, and especially his look or glance, produces in the other, he "makes" this look. With the help of the capacity, in greater or lesser degree peculiar to man, to make a definite element of his being appear in his look, he produces a look which is meant to have, and often enough does have, the effect of a spontaneous utterance—not only the utterance of a physical event supposed to be taking place at that very moment, but also, as it were, the reflection of a personal life of such-and-such a kind.

This must, however, be carefully distinguished from another area of seeming whose ontological legitimacy cannot be doubted. I mean the realm of "genuine seeming," where a lad, for instance, imitates his heroic model and while he is doing so is seized by the actuality of heroism, or a man plays the part of a destiny and conjures up authentic destiny. In this situation there is nothing false; the imitation is genuine imitation and the part played is genuine; the mask, too, is a mask and no deceit. But where the semblance originates from the lie and is permeate by it, the interhuman is threatened in its very existence. It is not that someone utters a lie, falsifies some account. The lie I mean does not take place in relation to particular facts, but in relation to existence itself, and it attacks interhuman existence as such. There are times when a man, to satisfy some stale conceit, forfeits the great chance of a true happening between I and Thou.

Let us now imagine two men, whose life is dominated by appearance, sitting and talking together. Call them Peter and Paul. Let us list the different configurations which are involved. First, there is Peter as he wishes to appear to Paul, and Paul as he wishes to appear to Peter. Then there is Peter as he really appears to Paul, that is, Paul's image of Peter, which in general does not in the least coincide with what Peter wishes Paul to see; and similarly there is the reverse situation. Further, there is Peter as he appears to himself, and Paul as he appears to himself. Lastly, there are the bodily Peter and the bodily Paul. Two living beings and six ghostly appearances, which mingle in many ways in the conversation between the two. Where is there room for any genuine interhuman life?

Whatever the meaning of the word "truth" may be in other realms, in the interhuman realm it means that men communicate themselves to one another as what they are. It does not depend on one saying to the other everything that occurs to him, but only on his letting no seeming creep in between himself and the other. It does not depend on one letting himself go before another, but on his granting to the man to whom he communicates himself a share in his being. This is a question of the authenticity of the interhuman, and where this is not to be found, neither is the human element itself authentic.

Therefore, as we begin to recognize the crisis of man as the crisis of what is between man and man, we must free the concept of uprightness from the thin moralistic tones which cling to it, and let it take its tone from the concept of bodily uprightness. If a presupposition of human life in primeval times is given in man's walking upright, the fulfillment of human life can only come through the soul's walking upright, through the great uprightness which is not tempted by any seeming because it has conquered all semblance.

But, one may ask, what if a man by his nature makes his life subservient to the images which he produces in others? Can he, in such a case, still become a man living from his being, can he escape from his nature?

The widespread tendency to live from the recurrent impression one makes instead of from the steadiness of one's being is not a "nature." It originates, in fact, on the other side of interhuman life itself, in men's dependence upon one another. It is no light thing to be confirmed in one's being by others, and seeming deceptively offers itself as a help in this. To yield to seeming is man's essential cowardice, to resist it is his essential courage. But this is not an inexorable state of affairs which is as it is and must so remain. One can struggle to come to oneself—that is, to come to confidence in being. One struggles, now more successfully, now less, but never in vain, even when one thinks he is defeated. One must at times pay dearly for life lived from the being; but it is never too dear. Yet is there not bad being, do weeds not grow everywhere? I have never known a young person who seemed to me irretrievably bad. Later indeed it becomes more and more difficult to penetrate the increasingly tough layer which has settled down on a man's being. Thus there arises the false perspective of the seemingly fixed "nature" which cannot be overcome. It is false; the foreground is deceitful; man as man can be redeemed.

Again we see Peter and Paul before us surrounded by the ghosts of the semblances. A ghost can be exorcized. Let us imagine that these two find it more and more repellent to be represented by ghosts. In each of them the will is stirred and strengthened to be confirmed in their being as what they really are and nothing else. We see the forces of real life at work as they drive out the ghosts, till the semblance vanishes and the depths of personal life call to one another.

PERSONAL MAKING PRESENT

By far the greater part of what is today called conversation among men would be more properly and precisely described as speechifying. In general, people do not really speak to one another, but each, although turned to the other, really speaks to a fictitious court of appeal whose life consists of nothing but listening to him. Chekhov has given poetic expression to this state of affairs in *The Cherry Orchard,* where the only use the members of a family make of their being together is to talk past one another. But it is Sartre who has raised to a principle of existence what in Chekhov still appears as the deficiency of a person who is shut up in himself. Sartre regards the walls between the partners in a conversation as simply impassable. For him it is inevitable human destiny that a man has directly to do only with himself and his own affairs. The inner existence of the other is his own concern, not mine; there is no direct relation with the other, nor can there be. This is perhaps the clearest expression of the wretched fatalism of modern man, which regards degeneration as the unchangeable nature of *Homo sapiens* and the misfortune of having run into a blind alley as his primal fate, and which brands every thought of a breakthrough as reactionary romanticism. He who really knows how far our generation has lost the way of true freedom, of free giving between I and Thou, must himself, by virtue of the demand implicit in every great knowledge of this kind, practice directness—even if he were the only man on earth who did it—and not depart from it until scoffers are struck with fear and hear in his voice the voice of their own suppressed longing.

The chief presupposition for the rise of genuine dialogue is that each should regard his partner as the very one he is. I become aware of him, aware that he is different, essentially different from myself, in the definite, unique way which is peculiar to him, and I accept whom I thus see, so that in full earnestness I can direct what I say to him as the person he is. Perhaps from time to time I must offer strict opposition to his view about the subject of our conversation. But I accept this person, the personal bearer of a conviction, in his definite being out of which his conviction has grown—even though I must try to show, bit by bit, the wrongness of this very conviction. I affirm the person I struggle with: I struggle with him as his partner, I confirm him as creature and as creation, I confirm him who is opposed to me as him who is over against me. It is true that it now depends on the other whether genuine dialogue, mutuality in speech arises between us. But if I thus give to the other who confronts me his legitimate standing as a man with whom I am ready to enter into dialogue, then I may trust him and suppose him to be also ready to deal with me as his partner.

But what does it mean to be "aware" of a man in the exact sense in which I use the word? To be aware of a thing or a being means, in quite general terms, to experience it as a whole and yet at the same time without reduction or abstraction, in all its concreteness. But a man, although he exists as a living being among living beings and even as a thing among things, is nevertheless something categorically different from all things and all beings. A man cannot really be grasped except on the basis of the gift of the spirit which belongs to man alone among all things, the spirit as sharing decisively in the personal life of the living man, that is, the spirit which determines the person. To be aware of a man, therefore, means in particular to perceive his wholeness as a person determined by the spirit; it means to perceive the dynamic centre which stamps his every utterance, action, and attitude with the recognizable sign of uniqueness. Such an awareness is impossible, however, if and so long as the other is the separated object of my contemplation or even observation, for this wholeness and its centre do not let themselves be known to contemplation or observation. It is only possible when I step into an elemental relation with the other, that is, when he becomes present to me. Hence I designate awareness in this special sense as "personal making present."

The perception of one's fellow man as a whole, as a unity, and as unique—even if his wholeness, unity, and uniqueness are only partly developed, as is usually the case—is opposed in our time by almost everything that is commonly understood as specifically modern. In our time there predominates an analytical, reductive, and deriving look between man and man. This look is analytical, or rather pseudo analytical, since it treats the whole being as put together and therefore able to be taken apart—not only the so-called unconscious which is accessible to relative objectification, but also the psychic stream itself, which can never, in fact, be grasped as an object. This look is a reductive one because it tries to contract the manifold person, who is nourished by the microcosmic richness of the possible, to some schematically surveyable and recurrent structures. And this look is a deriving one because it supposes it can grasp what a man has become, or even is becoming, in genetic formulae, and it thinks that even the dynamic central principle of the individual in this becoming can be represented by a general concept. An effort is being made today radically to destroy the mystery between man and man. The personal life, the ever-near mystery, once the source of the stillest enthusiasms, is levelled down.

What I have just said is not an attack on the analytical method of the human sciences, a method which is indispensable wherever it furthers knowledge of a phenomenon without impairing the essentially different knowledge of its uniqueness that transcends the valid circle of the method. The science of man that makes use of the analytical method must accordingly always keep in view the boundary of such a contemplation, which stretches like a horizon around it. This duty makes the transportation of the method into life dubious; for it is excessively difficult to see where the boundary is in life.

If we want to do today's work and prepare tomorrow's with clear sight, then we must develop in ourselves and in the next generation a gift which lives in man's inwardness as a Cinderella, one day to be a princess. Some call it intuition, but that is not a wholly unambiguous concept. I prefer the name "imagining the real," for in its essential being this gift is not a looking at the other, but a bold swinging—demanding the most intensive stirring of one's being—into the life of the other. This is the nature of all genuine imagining, only that here the realm of my action is not the all-possible, but the particular real person who confronts me, whom I can attempt to make present to myself just in this way, and not otherwise, in his wholeness, unity, and uniqueness, and with his dynamic centre which realizes all these things ever anew.

Let it be said again that all this can only take place in a living partnership, that is, when I stand in a common situation with the other and expose myself vitally to his share in the situation as really his share. It is true that my basic attitude can remain unanswered, and the dialogue can die in seed. But if mutuality stirs, then the interhuman blossoms into genuine dialogue.

IMPOSITION AND UNFOLDING

I have referred to two things which impede the growth of life between men: the invasion of seeming, and the inadequacy of perception. We are now faced with a third, plainer than the others, and in this critical hour more powerful and more dangerous than ever.

There are two basic ways of affecting men in their views and their attitude to life. In the first a man tries to impose himself, his opinion and his attitude, on the other in such a way that the latter feels the psychical result of the action to be his own insight, which has only been freed by the influence. In the second basic way of affecting others, as man wishes to find and to further in the soul of the other the disposition toward what he has recognized in himself as the right. Because it is the right, it must also be alive in the microcosm of the other, as one possibility. The other need only be opened out in this potentiality of his; moreover, this opening out takes place not essentially by teaching, but by meeting, by existential communication between someone that is in actual being and someone that is in a process of becoming. The first way has been most powerfully developed in the realm of propaganda, the second in that of education.

The propagandist I have in mind, who imposes himself, is not in the least concerned with the person whom he desires to influence, as a person; various individual qualities are of importance only in so far as he can exploit them to win the other and must get to know them for this purpose. In his indifference to everything personal the propagandist goes a substantial distance beyond the party for which he works. For the party, persons in their difference are of significance because each can be used according to his special qualities in a particular function. It is true that the personal is considered only in respect of the specific use to which it can be put, but within these limits it is recognized in practice. To propaganda as such, on the other hand, individual qualities are rather looked on as a burden, for propaganda is concerned simply with *more*—more members, more adherents, an increasing extent of support. Political methods, where they rule in an extreme form, as here, simply mean winning power over the other by depersonalizing him. This kind of propaganda enters upon different relations with force; it supplements it or replaces it, according to the need or the prospects, but it is in the last analysis nothing but sublimated violence, which has become imperceptible as such. It places men's souls under a pressure which allows the illusion of autonomy. Political methods at their height mean the effective abolition of the human factor.

The educator whom I have in mind lives in a world of individuals, a certain number of whom are always at any one time committed to his care. He sees each of these individuals as in a position to become a unique, single person, and thus the bearer of a special task of existence which can be fulfilled through him and through him alone. He sees every personal life as engaged in such a process of actualization, and he knows from his own experience that the forces making for actualization are all the time involved in a microcosmic struggle with counterforces. He has come to see himself as a helper of the actualizing forces. He knows these forces; they have shaped and they still shape him. Now he puts this person shaped by them at their disposal for a new struggle and a new work. He cannot wish to impose himself, for he believes in the effect of the actualizing forces, that is, he believes that in every man what is right is established in a single and uniquely personal way. No other way may be imposed on a man, but another way, that of the educator, may and must unfold what is right, as in this case it struggles for achievement, and help it to develop.

The propagandist, who imposes himself, does not really believe in his own cause, for he does not trust it to attain its effect of its own power without his special methods, whose symbols are the loudspeaker and the television advertisement. The educator who unfolds what is there believes in the primal power which has scattered itself, and still scatters itself, in all human beings in order that it may grow up in each man in the special form of that man. He is confident that this growth needs at each moment only that help which is given in meeting and that he is called to supply that help.

I have illustrated the character of the two basic attitudes and their relation to one another by means of two extremely antithetical examples. But wherever men have dealings with one another, one or the other attitude is to be found to be in more or less degree.

These two principles of imposing oneself on someone and helping someone to unfold should not be confused with concepts such as arrogance and humility. A man can be arrogant without wishing to impose himself on others, and it is not enough to be humble in order to help another unfold. Arrogance and humility are dispositions of the soul, psychological facts with a moral accent, while imposition and helping to unfold are events between men, anthropological facts which point to an ontology, the ontology of the interhuman.

In the moral realm Kant expressed the essential principle that one's fellow man must never be thought of and treated merely as a means, but always at the same time as an independent end. The principle is expressed as an "ought" which is sustained by the idea of human dignity. My point of view, which is near to Kant's in its essential features, has another source and goal. It is concerned with the presuppositions of the interhuman. Man exists anthropologically not in his isolation, but in the completeness of the relation between man and man; what humanity is can be properly grasped only in vital reciprocity. For the proper existence of the interhuman it is necessary, as I have shown, that the semblance does not intervene to spoil the relation of personal being to personal being. It is further necessary, as I have also shown, that each one means and makes present the other in his personal being. That neither should wish to impose himself on the other is the third basic presupposition of the interhuman. These presuppositions do not include the demand that one should influence the other in his unfolding; that is, however, an element that is suited to lead to a higher stage of the interhuman.

That there resides in every man the possibility of attaining authentic human existence in the special way peculiar to him can be grasped in the Aristotelian

image of entelechy, innate self-realization; but one must note that it is an entelechy of the work of creation. It would be mistaken to speak here of individuation alone. Individuation is only the indispensable personal stamp of all
realization of human existence. The self as such is not ultimately the essential,
but the meaning of human existence given in creation again and again fulfills
itself as self. The help that men give each other in becoming a self leads the life
between men to its height. The dynamic glory of the being of man is first bodily
present in the relation between two men each of whom in meaning the other also
means the highest to which this person is called, and serves the self-realization
of this human life as one true to creation without wishing to impose on the other
anything of his own realization.

GENUINE DIALOGUE

We must now summarize and clarify the marks of genuine dialogue.

In genuine dialogue the turning to the partner takes place in all truth, that
is, it is a turning of the being. Every speaker "means" the partner of partners to
whom he turns as this personal existence. To "mean" someone in this connection
is at the same time to exercise that degree of making present which is possible to
the speaker at that moment. The experiencing senses and the imagining of the real
which completes the findings of the senses work together to make the other present as a whole and as a unique being, as the person that he is. But the speaker does
not merely perceive the one who is present to him in this way; he receives him as
his partner, and that means that he confirms this other being, so far as it is for him
to confirm. The true turning of his person to the other includes this confirmation,
this acceptance. Of course, such a confirmation does not mean approval; but no
matter in what I am against the other, by accepting him as my partner in genuine
dialogue I have affirmed him as a person.

Further, if genuine dialogue is to arise, everyone who takes part in it must
bring himself into it. And that also means that he must be willing on each occasion to say what is really in his mind about the subject of the conversation. And
that means further that on each occasion he makes the contribution of his spirit
without reduction and without shifting his ground. Even men of great integrity
are under the illusion that they are not bound to say everything "they have to
say." But in the great faithfulness which is the climate of genuine dialogue, what
I have to say at any one time already has in me the character of something that
wishes to be uttered, and I must not keep it back, keep it in myself. It bears for
me the unmistakable sign which indicates that it belongs to the common life of
the word. Where the dialogical word genuinely exists, it must be given its right
by keeping nothing back. To keep nothing back is the exact opposite of unreserved speech. Everything depends on the legitimacy of "what I have to say."
And of course I must also be intent to raise into an inner word and then into a
spoken word what I have to say at this moment but do not yet possess as speech.
To speak is both nature and work, something that grows and something that is

made, and where it appears dialogically, in the climate of great faithfulness, it has to fulfill ever anew the unity of the two.

Associated with this is that overcoming of semblance to which I have referred. In the atmosphere of genuine dialogue, he who is ruled by the thought of his own effect as the speaker of what he has to speak has a destructive effect. If, instead of what has to be said, I try to bring attention to my *I*, I have irrevocably miscarried what I had to say; it enters the dialogue as a failure and the dialogue is a failure. Because genuine dialogue is an ontological sphere which is constituted by the authenticity of being, every invasion of semblance must damage it.

But where the dialogue is fulfilled in its being, between partners who have turned to one another in truth, who express themselves without reserve and are free of the desire for semblance, there is brought into being a memorable common fruitfulness which is to be found nowhere else. At such times, at each such time, the word arises in a substantial way between men who have been seized in their depths and opened out by the dynamic of an elemental togetherness. The interhuman opens out what otherwise remains unopened.

This phenomenon is indeed well known in dialogue between two persons; but I have also sometimes experienced it in a dialogue in which several have taken part.

About Easter of 1914 there met a group consisting of representatives of several European nations for a three-day discussion that was intended to be preliminary to further talks. We wanted to discuss together how the catastrophe, which we all believed was imminent, could be avoided. Without our having agreed beforehand on any sort of modalities for our talk, all the presuppositions of genuine dialogue were fulfilled. From the first hour immediacy reigned between all of us, some of whom had just got to know one another; everyone spoke with an unheard-of unreserve, and clearly not a single one of the participants was in bondage to semblance. In respect of its purpose the meeting must be described as a failure (though even now in my heart it is still not a certainty that it had to be a failure); the irony of the situation was that we arranged the final discussion for the middle of August, and in the course of events the group was soon broken up. Nevertheless, in the time that followed, not one of the participants doubted that he shared in a triumph of the interhuman.

One more point must be noted. Of course it is not necessary for all who are joined in a genuine dialogue actually to speak; those who keep silent can on occasion be especially important. But each must be determined not to withdraw when the course of the conversation makes it proper for him to say what he has to say. No one, of course, can know in advance what it is that he has to say; genuine dialogue cannot be arranged beforehand. It has indeed its basic order in itself from the beginning, but nothing can be determined, the course is of the spirit, and some discover what they have to say only when they catch the call of the spirit.

But it is also a matter of course that all the participants, without exception, must be of such nature that they are capable of satisfying the presuppositions of genuine dialogue and are ready to do so. The genuineness of the dialogue is called in question as soon as even a small number of those present are felt by themselves and by the others as not being expected to take any active part. Such a state of affairs can lead to very serious problems.

I had a friend whom I account one of the most considerable men of our age. He was a master of conversation, and he loved it: his genuineness as a speaker was evident. But once it happened that he was sitting with two friends and with the three wives, and a conversation arose in which by its nature the women were clearly not joining, although their presence in fact had a great influence. The conversation among the men soon developed into a duel between two of them (I was the third). The other "duelist," also a friend of mine, was of a noble nature; he too was a man of true conversation, but given more to objective fairness than to the play of the intellect, and a stranger to any controversy. The friend whom I have called a master of conversation did not speak with his usual composure and strength, but he scintillated, he fought, he triumphed. The dialogue was destroyed.

REVIEW QUESTIONS

1. What distinction does Buber make between the social and the interhuman?
2. What feature of interpersonal contact does Buber say can characterize even "a boxing match"?
3. What does Buber mean when he says that "it is basically erroneous to try to understand the interhuman phenomena as psychological"?
4. Does Buber say that a person can practice "being" consistently, all the time? Explain.
5. Paraphrase the last sentence in the first paragraph under the heading "Personal Making Present." What is Buber challenging readers to do here?
6. Identify three possible things that a person who is imposing could impose on his or her conversational partner. In other words, what is (are) imposed when a person is imposing? What is unfolded when a person is unfolding?
7. What does Buber mean when he says that "to keep nothing back is the exact opposite of unreserved speech"?

PROBES

1. What does it mean to you when Buber says that social contacts don't involve an existential relation, but that interhuman contacts do?
2. For Buber, does "being" mean total honesty? Is "seeming" lying?
3. What circumstances make it difficult for you to "be"? How can you best help others to "be" instead of "seem"?
4. How do Buber's comments about the way we perceive others relate to the discussion of person perception in Chapter 5?
5. It sounds as if Buber is saying that science *cannot* be used to study human life. Is he saying that? Do you agree with him? Why or why not?
6. How is Buber's discussion of "imagining the real" related to what Stewart, Zediker, and Witteborn (Chapter 5) say about empathy?

7. Which teacher that you've had has functioned most as an "imposer"? Which teacher has been most consistently an "unfolder"?
8. What does "personal making present" mean to you? What do you need to do in order to perceive someone that way?
9. Have you ever experienced a silent "dialogue" of the kind Buber mentions here? What happened?

NOTES

1. You might also be interested in other things written by or about Buber. For starters I recommend Aubrey Hodes, *Martin Buber: An Intimate Portrait* (New York: Viking Press, 1971), or Hilary Evans Bender, *Monarch Notes: The Philosophy of Martin Buber* (New York: Monarch, 1974). Maurice Friedman has written the definitive Buber biography, and I'd especially recommend the third volume, *Martin Buber's Life and Work: The Later Years, 1945–1965* (New York: Dutton, 1983). Buber's most important and influential book is *I and Thou*, trans. Walter Kaufmann (New York: Scribner, 1970).
2. Buber's translators always point out that this "thou" is not the religious term of formal address. It is a translation of the German *Du*, the familiar form of the pronoun "you." As Walter Kaufmann, one of Buber's translators, explains, "German lovers say *Du* to one another and so do friends. Du is spontaneous and unpretentious, remote from formality, pomp, and dignity."

CHAPTER 3

Communication Building Identities

Constructing Identities

John Stewart, Karen E. Zediker, and Saskia Witteborn

Now that we've defined communication and interpersonal communication, the next step is to think about the people who engage in it. For most of the past 300 years, westerners have understood people to be individuals—separate, singular selves. But in the last half of the 20th century, some European and American researchers rediscovered an idea that had been clear to our Greek forebears and to most members of Eastern cultures for a long time: Humans are more than singular individuals. We are relational beings, unique selves mixed from many ingredients. The readings in this chapter develop this understanding of humans *as communicators.*

I introduced this idea in the first reading of Chapter 2 when I said that communication always involves negotiating identities or selves. Every time you or I communicate with anybody, one thing we're doing is mutually working out who we are for and with each other. Identities are always in play.

One way to talk about this identity negotiation or identity management part of communication is to use the vocabulary of "co-constructing selves," which is what Karen Zediker, Saskia Witteborn, and I do in this reading. This essay comes from a basic interpersonal communication text that the three of us wrote together. We begin with some examples of how this co-construction process operates to demonstrate that it's going on all the time. We point out that, since it is a continuous process, nobody always does it perfectly or poorly. As we emphasize, there is no one best or worst way to participate in this process. There are just outcomes of how you do it, results that people may or may not want. We also make the point that this process goes on in every culture, wherever humans communicate. And the reason it's important to understand this process is that when you want to influence where your communicating is on the impersonal-interpersonal continuum explained in Chapter 2, you need to pay attention to how you're co-constructing selves.

We define identity or self as a constellation of features or labels that establish social expectations that we have of ourselves and others. Then we contrast old and new views of identities. We point out that the individualistic, Western view is very narrow and that increasing numbers of researchers and teachers are recognizing that identities are relational and multidimensional. They get built in the contacts we experience with others, and they are made up of many different elements.

This multidimensionality is part of the first of the four characteristics of identities or selves that we discuss. The second is that selves are responders. No human starts behaving from ground zero, so that everything we do can be understood to be in reply or answer to something else. The third feature is that identities are developed in past and present relationships. The families we are raised in significantly affect who we are, and our identities are also shaped by friends, dating partners, and work relationships. The fourth characteristic is that identities can be both avowed and ascribed. This means that we can verbally and/or nonverbally "assert" an identity—avowal—and that others can ascribe identity features to us. This is one reason why it is important to be reflective about your communicating—because in every conversation you're not only expressing your ideas but also defining who you are.

This essay and the other readings in Chapter 3 will flesh out this basic understanding of how selves—who people are—get co-constructed in people's communicating.

WHAT IS IDENTITY OR SELF?

Notice what happens in the following conversation:

ALIA: Hi, just wanted to introduce myself. I'm Alia. I'm your new roommate. Just switched universities. Kind of sucks to move in your senior year, but well …

CHERYL: Cool. I'm Cheryl. Nice to meet you, finally. I just knew that a girl named Alia—how do you pronounce your name?—would be my new roommate, that's all. Anyways, good to meet you. Any preference in terms of where you wanna sleep?

ALIA: Not really.

CHERYL: I'm just asking because I just got back from Germany. Exchange student, you know? I was sleeping in a dorm there and was glad that my roommate let me sleep by the window. I'm kind of claustrophobic. Ha-ha. Don't worry; otherwise I'm pretty much together. Let me guess where you're from. Honestly, you don't quite look as if you were from around here.

ALIA: Well, whatdaya think?

CHERYL: Greece. Oh no, Italy.

ALIA: Naaa.

CHERYL: Spain or South America?

ALIA: Wrong again. Born in Chicago, my parents are from Iraq. Where are you from?

CHERYL: Born in Detroit and raised in Oregon.

ALIA: So you are American, too?

CHERYL: Absolutely, although it's not that important to me, really. No kidding. Could have sworn you were from Greece. My best friend in Germany looks like you, and she's Greek. Well, I feel stupid to ask this, but … aren't you supposed to wear a scarf?

ALIA: Guess what? I am a Christian, Chaldean to be exact. Not all Arabs are Muslims, and not all Muslims are Arabs. Islam's the biggest religion in the Arab world, but there're also lots of Christians.

CHERYL: Wow. Let's talk more about that. That's exciting. I'm living with an Iraqi woman.

ALIA: Iraqi American is better. I was born here. Chicago, remember?

CHERYL: You're right, I'm sorry I went off on this cultural thing. I'm really, really glad to finally live with someone who is from another culture. I'm still in a kind of culture shock, coming back to the States from Germany. That's why I'm so glad about you.

ALIA: Sure, but first, if you don't mind, could you show me around here? I need to register before classes start.

CHERYL: Yep, no problem. I'm sorry if I talked too much. Let's start with the library.

Cheryl and Alia are constructing themselves together. At first, Cheryl gives Alia a national identity that Alia does not identify with. Cheryl does this mainly because of how Alia looks. For a minute Cheryl restricts Alia's self to her nationality and religion. Alia is the "Iraqi woman," even though she would probably have liked to be the *person* Alia first, or the senior who is new to the university. Cheryl, on the other hand, constructs herself as a curious and outspoken young woman, a student, and someone who has been exposed to different cultures.

This conversation shows how identities or selves are outcomes of conversations and something that we do, rather than are. Cheryl and Alia move from negotiating their student identities when they talk about being a senior and an exchange student, to negotiating their national and ethnic identities, and back to negotiating their student selves again. Alia does not want to be known only as an Iraqi and an Arab. She wants Cheryl to recognize her multiple identities as a woman, a student, a Chaldean Christian, and an Iraqi American. Cheryl also emphasizes that her national identity is not that important to her. At that moment, she wants to be perceived as a knowledgeable and open person and a possible friend, and not just as an American. As you can see, identities are fluid, not static. No one wants to be put in an ethnic, national, or gender box, especially at the beginning of a relationship.

Here is another example of how identities are constructed in verbal and nonverbal talk:

Conversation 2:

JAN: Hey, how's it goin'?
HEATHER: (Silence and a scowl)
JAN: What's the matter?
HEATHER: Nothing. Forget it.
JAN: What are you so pissed about?
HEATHER: Forget it! Just drop it.
JAN: Well, all right! Pout! I don't give a damn!

Here, even though Jan and Heather are not talking about any specific object, issue, or event, they are definitely constructing identities together. In this conversation Heather's definition of herself and of Jan goes something like this:

> Right now I identify myself as independent of you (Silence. "Nothing. Forget it."). You're butting into my space, and you probably think I'm antisocial. But I've got good reasons for my anger.

On the other hand, Jan's definition of herself and of Heather is something like this:

> Right now I identify myself as friendly and concerned ("Hey, how's it goin'?" "What's the matter?"). I'm willing to stick my neck out a little, but you're obviously not interested in being civil. So there's a limit to how long I'll *stay* friendly and concerned ("Well, all right! Pout! I don't give a damn!").

We want to emphasize that nobody in these conversations is constructing identities perfectly or poorly, right or wrong. In one sense, there is no right or wrong way to participate in this process. There are just *outcomes* of how you do it, *results* that you may or may not want.

We also want to emphasize that none of the people in these conversations could avoid constructing selves. It's a process that happens whenever people communicate. Some of the most important meanings we collaboratively construct are our identities, and all communicating involves constructing identities or selves. No matter how brief or extended the contact, whether it's written or oral, mediated or face-to-face, impersonal or interpersonal, the people involved will be directly or indirectly constructing definitions of themselves and responding to the definitions offered by others. Radio talk show hosts and television newscasters are continually building identities. The person who writes a letter longhand on colorful stationery is defining him- or herself differently from the person who writes the same letter on a word processor. The person who answers the telephone, "Yeah?" is defining him- or herself differently from the one who answers, "Good morning. May I help you?"

Research on intercultural communication shows how identity construction occurs in different cultures. For instance, Bailey (2000) shows how young Dominican Americans negotiate their cultural identities by switching between Spanish and English. Speaking in Spanish indicates solidarity with their peers who are similar in cultural background. In another study, Hegde (1998) shows how immigrants from India navigate between their Indian identity and their new American identity. Saskia has also studied Arab identities and has found that people of Arab descent enact multiple national and religious identities and feel more or less strongly Arab at various times, but it really depends on the context. For instance, some people say that they call themselves Arab American mostly when they have to fill out official forms, and that they feel Arab rather than Arab American when they talk about families because family is so important in the Arab world. As Scotton (1983) summarizes, in various cultural contexts, speakers use language choices "imaginatively … a range of options is open to them within a normative framework, and … taking one option rather than another is the *negotiation of identities*."

So two reasons why it's important to understand the process of identity construction are (1) that you're doing it whenever you communicate—and everybody else is, too—and (2) that the process affects who you are in relation to others. The third reason why it's important is that *your negotiation responses also affect where your communication is on the impersonal-interpersonal continuum.*… Some responses just about guarantee that your communication will be impersonal. Others lead to more interpersonal communicating. So if you want to help change the quality of your contacts with your dating partner, employer, roommate, sister, or parent in either direction on the continuum, you'll probably want to learn as much as you can about this process.

Definition of Identity

As identity or self is made up of interlocking features that mark how we behave and respond to others, identities are constellations of labels that establish social expectations that we have of ourselves and others. These social expectations can include roles that we want or have to play in specific situations and the languages or dialects we speak and expect others to speak. When you enter a classroom in the United States, you expect your instructor to talk and behave in certain ways. For instance, most North Americans expect that a person enacting the identity of an "instructor" should normally stand in front of the class, speak in a loud and intelligible voice, have control in the classroom, and, unless it's a foreign language class, express him- or herself in some form of English. And in order to enact the role of instructor, this person needs students who enact their role. Notice how we say "enact." This is another way of emphasizing that identities are something that we *do* rather than what we *are* (Collier and Thomas 1988; Hecht, Jackson, and Ribeau 2003). You are not born to be a student for all of your life, but you are socialized into this identity, and it becomes salient in different times and places.

Old versus Current Views of Identity

It may sound weird to you to say that identities or selves are co-constructed in verbal and nonverbal talk. You might think of your *self* as fairly stable, identifiable, and clearly bounded. If so, you're not alone. Most people in Western cultures have been taught to think of their selves as individual containers that enclose their unique essence. As one book puts it,

> There is an individualist mode of thought, distinctive of modern Western cultures, which, though we may criticize it in part or in whole, we cannot escape. … This inescapable cultural vise has given us—or, at least, the dominant social groups in the West—a sense of themselves as distinctive, independent agents who own themselves and have relatively clear boundaries to protect in order to ensure their integrity and permit them to function more effectively in the world. (Sampson 1993, 31)

Most members of dominant social groups in the Western world think of the boundary of the individual as the same as the boundary of the body, and that the body houses or contains the self. Common metaphors reflect this view, as when people say that a person is *"filled* with anger," "unable to *contain* her joy," *"brimming* with laughter," or "trying to get anger *out of our system"* (Lakoff 1987, 383). Some theories of psychology reinforce this view of identity or the self. Psychologists influenced by the famous therapist Sigmund Freud, for example, think of society as made up of individual selves who are each working out their inner tensions. One Freudian insisted that a student revolt against university administrators was caused by the students' unresolved conflicts with their fathers. In his view,

> protestors were taking out their inner conflicts with parental authority by acting against the authority represented by the University. It was as though there

were no legitimate problems with the University; it only symbolized protestors' unresolved Oedipal conflicts with the real source of their troubles, their fathers. (Sampson 1993, 44)

For this psychologist, selves were individual and internal.

But in the last decades of the twentieth century, the development of space travel, satellite television, and the World Wide Web; the globalization of music and business; and the end of the Cold War have all helped westerners understand that this view of the person as a bounded individual is, as one anthropologist puts it, rather "peculiar" (Geertz 1979, 229). For centuries, people in many cultures outside the West have not been thinking this way. For example, if a North American is asked to explain why someone financially cheated another person, the North American's tendency will be to locate the cause in "the kind of person she is." A Hindu, by contrast, is more likely to offer a social explanation—"The man is unemployed. He is not in a position to give that money" (Miller 1984, 968). This is because many members of the Hindu culture don't think of identity or the self as individual, but as social or communal. For them, identity is a function of cultural or group memberships. Or, to take another example, in a study of U.S. and Samoan child care workers, U.S. preschool teachers tended to help children socialize by developing their individuality, whereas Samoan caregivers' efforts "were directed towards helping the children learn how better to fit into their in-group" (Ochs 1988, 199). In their broader culture, Samoans in this study also recognized the central role of other people in events that were deemed worthy of praise or compliments. So one researcher reported that when a Samoan passenger complimented a driver with language that translates, "Well done the driving," the driver typically responded, "Well done the support." "In this Samoan view, if a performance went well, it is the supporters' merit as much as the performer's" (Ochs 1988, 200). Many Japanese understand the person in a similar way. In Japan, one author notes, "The concept of a self completely independent from the environment is very foreign" (Kojima 1984, 972). Rather, Japanese think of individuals in terms of the social context they fit into—their family, work group, and so on. The United States, Canada, Australia, Great Britain, and some other Western cultures have a strong belief in the individual self, but many European countries (e.g., Spain, Austria, and Finland) and most Asian and Latin American cultures understand identities or selves as social, relational, or group-oriented (Hofstede 1980).

It's easier to understand how identity construction works—and how to manage your own identity constructing—if you adopt what has historically been a more Eastern perspective. This doesn't mean that you have to change cultures or religions, or to pretend to be somebody you're not. In fact, this understanding is being accepted by communication scholars, psychologists, anthropologists, and other students of human behavior all over the world. Especially in the final decade of the twentieth century, many of these scholars and teachers recognized that selves or identities are relational from birth, or maybe even before. They began taking seriously what Lev Vygotsky and George Herbert Mead, two very influential human development researchers, said several decades ago: namely, that infants are first *social* beings and only later in life learn to see themselves as *individuals*. As psychologist Edward Sampson explains,

> Both Vygotsky and Mead clearly emphasize the necessary social bases of human thinking, cognition, and mindedness. Indeed, rather than viewing the individual's mind as setting forth the terms for the social order, the reverse describes the actual event: the social process—namely, dialogue and conversation—precedes, and is the foundation for, any subsequent psychological processes that emerge. (Sampson 1993, 103)

In short, the English terms *self* and *identity* and their meanings are only about 300 years old. Studies of history and of other cultures illustrate that the Western definition developed over the last 275 of these 300 years is very narrow. Today, this idea that selves are individual containers is being revised as communication scholars and psychologists are recognizing how much our selves are developed in communication with others. Westerners increasingly recognize that identities or selves are multidimensional and that they change in response to the people and institutions we connect with. Each of our identities has athletic, artistic, ethnic, gendered, occupational, scientific, political, economic, and religious dimensions, and all of these shift in content and importance as we move from situation to situation.

FOUR CHARACTERISTICS OF IDENTITIES OR SELVES

This understanding of identities or selves can be summarized in four primary characteristics.

1. Identities Are Multidimensional and Changing

One feature of selves is that we're complex. On the one hand, each of us is characterized by some stabilities or patterns. A person's genetic makeup is stable, and your ethnic identity also probably hasn't changed and probably won't. Someone who's known you all your life can probably identify some features you had when you were 4 or 5 years old that you still have, and as you look at old photographs of yourself, you might recognize how the identity of the person in the picture is in some ways "the same" as who you are today.

On the other hand, you are different in at least as many ways as you are the same. Think, for example, of who you were at age 9 or 10 and who you were at age 14 or 15. Adolescence is a time of *significant* change in our selves. Or, if it fits you, think of yourself before you were married and after, or your identity before and after you had children.

Some researchers broadly classify identities or selves into personal, relational, and communal features (Hecht, Jackson, and Ribeau 2003). *Personal* identity is all the characteristics that you think make you a unique person, such as being friendly, helpful, disciplined, hard working, beautiful, and so forth. *Relational* identities are based on relationships you have with others, such as mother-daughter, teacher-student, or employer-employee. *Communal* identities are usually related to larger groups, such as ethnicities, race, religion, gender, or nationality.

2. Selves Are Responders

I've already introduced this second feature of selves in Chapter 2 when we said that responsiveness is one of the five features that makes each of us a person. Our main point there was to contrast responding with simply reacting. Now we want to build the meaning of this idea by noting that responding implies both *choice* (not just reacting) and *connection* with what's already happened.

To say that selves are responders is to say that we grow out of and fit into a context of actions and events that we behave-in-relation-to. On the one hand, this is just another way of saying that selves are relational or social. Remember how Alia responded to Cheryl's question about where she is from and how they both constructed their student and ethnic/national identities? They responded to each other. In one instance, Cheryl might be regarded as just reacting when she asks about Alia's absent scarf. However, in most instances, both women are responding to each other, which includes reflecting about what the other person just said. Responding means that all human action is joint action. No human starts behaving from ground zero, so that everything we do, from the very beginning, is in reply or answer to something else.

Humans begin responding from the first moment we develop any awareness, which, as we noted earlier, probably happens before birth. Every baby is born into a world of verbal and nonverbal talk, family relationships, gender patterns, ongoing activities, and social and political events. This is the sense in which no person is, "after all, the first speaker, the one who disturbs the eternal silence of the universe." Since none of us is Adam or Eve, all of our actions more or less effectively connect with or fit into the activities and language systems that surround us (Bakhtin, 1986, 69).

3. Identities Are Developed in Past and Present Relationships

The reason selves change over time is that we develop who we are in relationships with the people around us. Some of the most important parts of each person's identity are established in one's family of origin, the people with whom you spend the first five to seven years of your life. One of your parents may have consistently introduced you to new people from the time you were old enough to talk, and today you may still find it easy to make acquaintances. Or you may have moved around a lot when you were young, and today you feel secure only when you have your own "place" and you prefer to spend holidays close to home. You may treasure a wonderful relationship with your dad, or you may have had the opposite kind of experience. Your family is the role model for many types of relational, religious, or ethnic identities. For instance, you learn what it means to be a good friend or a good neighbor, a good brother or sister or mother or father, or perhaps not such a good one:

> My father is an alcoholic. He has never admitted to that fact. He and my mom used to get in lots of fights when I lived at home. The six of us kids were used as pawns in their war games. I always wondered whether or not I was responsible for his drinking. When the fights were going on, I always retreated to my room. There I felt secure. Now, I am 22, and have been married for two years. I have this affliction that, whenever the slightest thing happens, I always say I am so sorry. I am sorry when the milk is not cold, sorry that the wet towel was left in the gym bag. I just want to take the blame for everything, even things I have no control over. (Black 1982, 9)

Many current studies about dysfunctional families emphasize how people with addictions to alcohol, cocaine, prescription drugs, and other chemicals developed the communication patterns that reinforce these addictions in their families of origin (Fuller et al., 2003). Other research focuses on how addictions affect the children or other family members of addicted persons. One review of studies about adult children of alcoholics concludes that, regardless of gender, socioeconomic group, or ethnic identity, these people develop 13 common features. For example, many adult children of alcoholics "have difficulty following a project through from beginning to end," "lie when it would be just as easy to tell the truth," "judge themselves without mercy," "take themselves very seriously," "constantly seek approval and affirmation," and "are extremely loyal, even in the face of evidence that the loyalty is undeserved" (Beatty, 1989). These books and articles illustrate how much our family of origin contributes to the response patterns that we follow in identity construction.... Past relationships contribute a great deal to the patterns that help make up our present selves.

Present relationships are also important. When you realize that a new friend really likes you, it can do great things for your self-definition. Getting a top grade from a teacher you respect can affect how you see yourself. At work, a positive performance evaluation from your supervisor or a raise can improve not only your mood and your bank account but also your perception of yourself. And again, the reverse can obviously also happen. The point is, genetic makeup does not determine your identity, and we call the communication process that produces these identities *identity construction*.

4. Identities Can Be Avowed and Ascribed

Finally, identities or selves can be ascribed and avowed. *Ascribed* means that others assign you an identity that you may or may not agree with; *avowed* means that you personally assign yourself an identity and act it out. People also try to negotiate this avowal and ascription process. Remember the conversation between Cheryl and Alia? Cheryl ascribed to Alia a somewhat stereotyped national and religious identity that Alia did not accept as her main identity in that particular situation. During the conversation they both put their student and cultural identities on the table (being from Detroit and growing up in Oregon can imply two different regional identities) and reached somewhat of an alignment on how they wanted to be perceived in this initial encounter. However, sometimes when people stereotype, they rigidly stick with their opinions about people and make them one dimensional. For instance, sometimes people talk slower when they realize that English is Saskia's second language or start immediately to talk about beer when they hear that Saskia is from Germany. It can be entertaining for a while, but then Saskia wants to be perceived as Saskia or a woman or an instructor and not only as German. Rigid ascription of identities can become a problem for the person who is ascribed the identity. This is also true for many African Americans, Latinas, or Asian Americans. People are often judged on their looks and language and not who else they are or want to be. The question of ascription and avowal will come up again when we talk about response options.

REVIEW QUESTIONS

1. Fill in the blank: " _____ appear and are constructed or worked out in verbal and nonverbal talk."
2. Identify three plausible features of the identity being offered by the person who answers the telephone with a loud "Yeah?" What are three plausible features of the identity of the person who answers the telephone, "Good morning. May I help you?"
3. What is the difference between a reaction and a response?
4. Describe one feature of your *personal* identity. Label one feature of your *relational* identity. Describe one feature of your *communal* identity.

PROBES

1. The old view of selves is that individuality comes first, and then individuals interact to form social groups. The new view reverses this sequence. Explain how.
2. Since no person is Adam or Eve, and we are all responding to what happens around us, (a) what does this say about the claim, "He started it!" and (b) what's the most accurate way to define "creativity"?
3. What can a person do about the parts of his or her identity that were formed in past relationships? If you're the child of an alcoholic, for example, what can you do about the parts of your self that were formed by that set of experiences?
4. Does the ethnicity or culture that you primarily identify with generally view selves as individualistic or relational? How does this affect your own sense of self?

5. What past relationships most affected the development of your self? Which present relationships are having the most impact on the current development of your self?
6. If you are mainly a product of your relationships, what happens to your individual integrity?

REFERENCES

Bach, G. R., and Wyden, P. 1968. *The Intimate Enemy: How to Fight Fair in Love and Marriage*. New York: Avon Books.

Bailey, B. 2000. "Language and Negotiation of Ethnic/Racial Identity among Dominican Americans." *Language in Society*, 29: 555–582.

Bakhtin, M. M. 1986. *Speech Genres and Other Late Essays*. (Translated by V. W. McGee). Austin: University of Texas Press. (Originally published 1953.)

Beatty, M. 1989. *Beyond Codependency*. New York: Harper/Hazelden.

Black, C. 1982. *'It Will Never Happen to Me!' Children of Alcoholics as Youngsters—Adolescents—Adults*. Denver: M.A.C.

Cissna, K. N. L., and Sieburg, E. 1981. "Patterns of Interactional Confirmation and Disconfirmation." In C. Wilder-Mott and J. H. Weakland (eds.), *Rigor and Imagination: Essays from the Legacy of Gregory Bateson*. New York: Praeger. Pages 230–239.

Collier, M. J., and Thomas, M. 1988. "Cultural Identity: An Interpretive Perspective." In Y. Y. Kim and W. B. Gudykunst (eds.), *Theories of Intercultural Communication*. Newbury Park, CA: Sage. Pages 99–120.

Fuller, B. E., Chermack, S. T., Cruise, K. A., Kirsch, E., Fitzgerald, H. E., and Zucker, R. A. 2003. "Predictors of Aggression across Three Generations among Sons of Alcoholics: Relationships Involving Grandparental and Parental Alcoholism, Child Aggression, Marital Aggression and Parenting Practices." *Journal of Studies on Alcohol*, 64: 472–484.

Geertz, C. 1979. "From the Native's Point of View: On the Nature of Anthropological Understanding." In P. Rabinow and W. M. Sullivan (eds.), *Interpretive Social Science*. Berkeley: University of California Press. Pages 225–246.

Hall, B. J. 2002. *Among Cultures: The Challenge of Communication*. New York: Harcourt College Publishers.

Hecht, M. L., Jackson II, R. L., and Ribeau, S. A. 2003. *African American Communication: Exploring Identity and Culture*. 2nd ed. Mahwah, NJ: Erlbaum.

Hegde, R. S. 1998. "A View from Elsewhere: Locating Difference and the Politics of Representation from a Transnational Feminist Perspective." *Communication Theory*, 8: 271–297.

Hofstede, G. 1980. *Culture's Consequences: International Differences in Work-Related Values*. Beverly Hills, CA: Sage.

Kojima, H. 1984. "A Significant Stride toward the Comparative Study of Control." *American Psychologist*, 39: 972–973.

Laing, R. D. 1961. *The Self and Others*. New York: Pantheon.
———. 1969. *The Self and Others*. Baltimore: Penguin Books.
Lakoff, G. 1987. *Women, Fire, and Dangerous Things*. Chicago: University of Chicago Press.
Miller, J. G. 1984. *The Development of Women's Sense of Self*. Work in Progress, No. 12. Wellesley, MA: Stone Center Working Paper Series.
Ochs, E. 1988. *Culture and Language Development: Language Acquisition and Language Socialization in a Samoan Village*. Cambridge: Cambridge University Press.
Rogers, C. R. 1965. "Dialogue between Martin Buber and Carl R. Rogers." In M. Friedman and R. G. Smith (eds.), *The Knowledge of Man*. London: Allen and Unwin.
Sampson, E. E. 1993. *Celebrating the Other: A Dialogic Account of Human Nature*. Boulder, CO: Westview.
Scotton, C. M. 1983. "The Negotiation of Identities in Conversation: A Theory of Markedness and Code Choice." *International Journal of Sociological Linguistics*, 44: 119–125.

———

Maintaining the Self in Communication
Harold Barrett

Harold Barrett is an award-winning professor of communication at California State University, Hayward. This reading is taken from his book, which approaches interpersonal communication from what he argues is the normal, natural, and pervasive human tendency to protect the self. As he puts it early in the reading, "our persistent and compelling need in communication is to give an account of ourselves." Barrett offers some specific ways to overcome the detrimental effects of defensiveness.

Barrett begins from the idea that, whenever we communicate, we want to influence our listeners—he calls them "audiences"—favorably about ourselves. Yet we can never be sure of their attitude toward us or of our capability to relate to their attitude. So we adopt a more or less rigid posture of defensiveness. Barrett anchors his analysis in the neo-Freudian explanation of the human self put forward by a psychologist named Heinz Kohut. Kohut argued that unless a person had just about completely perfect parents and was raised in a perfect network of relationships, he or she carries some "shame," some feelings of "emptiness, unfulfillment, and deficiency." So from this perspective shame is not necessarily bad; it's just part of what each human experiences. And this experience leads us "to invent modes of maintaining the self," some of which work positively and some of which work negatively.

One tension that arises in this situation is that "rewards of individualism increasingly come into conflict with rewards of community affiliation." That is, people can get caught

"Maintaining the Self in Communication" by Harold Barrett from *Maintaining the Self in Communication*. Alpha & Omega Book Publishers, 1998.

between the "rock" of individual integrity and the "hard place" of getting along with others. Culture, especially ethnicity, helps determine how we cope with these tensions. But regardless of culture or ethnicity, Barrett writes, we're all struggling with similar issues. In short, regardless of who you are, says Barrett, "the great commandment is to maintain the self." And interpersonal contacts are the ones that both pose the greatest threats to the self and provide the most maintenance of it. This means that selves are "in play" in every interpersonal encounter—as Barrett puts it, in "every conversation, public speech, interview, and discussion." But there are also at least eight specific self-maintenance resources available to every communicator, and the last major section of this reading explains these eight resources—Barrett uses the term *topoi*—that people use to maintain their threatened selves.

Barrett begins by talking about how control can help maintain your sense of self. Then he discusses achievement, which can also help, so long as you avoid its extreme, which is perfectionism. The third resource, or *topos,* is opposition, which means "standing up for oneself." The fourth is attribution, or identifying responsibility. Anger, denial, withdrawal, and lying are the final four resources, or *topoi.* The last part of the reading encourages you to reflect on which resources you draw on in various situations.

I put this reading into this chapter in order to offer the opportunity to reflect on how the natural tendency to "protect your own ego" affects your interpersonal communicating. If Barrett and the scholars he cites are right, defensiveness is a normal and always-present human tendency. It can be helpful to think and talk about how this dynamic operates in our own communicating.

LOOKING AFTER THE SELF

Interpersonal security is currently a common topic in the media. An example is a recent interview with Harvard political scientist Robert D. Putnam. Putnam believes that Americans have lost much of their willingness to trust. A generation ago, when asked if they trusted other people, two-thirds said yes; now two-thirds say no. Americans are untrusting because they don't know each other, Putnam says. Today they are less connected to each other—and less happy.[1]

One result of this lack of connection and trust is a greater dedication to self-protection in communicating with others. Given a condition of insecurity, the solution is predictable: purposeful effort to look after and justify the self. Insecurity and protectiveness have always been a part of human interaction; the issue of the moment is about their increase....

Self-maintenance behavior arises from some sense of uncertainty with others, from a perception of danger to the self—whether negligible or great, obscure or obvious. Thus we have defense mechanisms, as they are called. Theorist Karl E. Scheibe holds that *defense* mechanisms are so named in psychoanalytic theory because "the ego is considered to be under a more or less constant state of siege."[2] And, I would add, the communicator's response to the siege is *constant.*

It's easy to find testimony to the pervasiveness of insecurity and consequent safeguarding. Psychoanalytic theorist Marshall Edelson holds that defensiveness is "a ubiquitous aspect of human action." (Indeed, *any* use of language is defensive, he believes.)[3] Just yesterday I heard down at my little post office, "Why is everyone so damned defensive these days?"

A FUNCTION OF COMMUNICATION

Gregory Rochlin ... offers this truth on the self (and self-esteem): "Its defense may bring the highest honors and justify the lowest violence."[4] Defending and thus maintaining the self, an ordinary function of communication, has both good and bad dimensions. Moreover, no mode of conduct is more fascinating in the drama of human interaction, as is apparent in the life stories of communicators, including those whose deeds we celebrate: Washington and Lincoln, Churchill and Roosevelt, Joan of Arc and Susan B. Anthony, Martin Luther and Martin Luther King, Jr.—as well as in those whose deeds we deplore: Joseph Stalin, Richard III, Adolf Hitler, and Joseph McCarthy. All of these notable figures were self-defenders in their communicating. Sigmund Freud said that defenses of the self direct the daily functioning of humankind. That's true, for better or worse.

There's high adventure and peril in communication, a fact that all of us seem to feel. Using athletic talk about teams playing defense ("D"), we can say that in the risky interactive game called communication, we play "D" at every moment. Knowing our ways, advisers urge, "Don't explain, don't complain!" ("Don't be defensive!") That's appealing advice, yet asking us not to look after ourselves is like asking us to give up being human.

Every Communicator's Story

Plots of every communicator's story are built around self-maintenance. Why so? Because self-worth is always at issue in communication; it hurts to be disrespected, dismissed, or disregarded. This may explain why **our persistent and compelling need in communication is to give an account of ourselves.** Intense or minimal, our motivation will never cease; protective messages will continue, whether as simple explanations, subtle excuses, hostile retorts, or anxious retreats. Such is our uneasiness about personal status and safety—apparent now more than ever before. A generation ago, Dean C. Barnlund saw signs of increasing interpersonal vulnerability— if not danger—and noted that a common use of communication is to act on our own behalf: "Communication arises out of the need to reduce uncertainty, to act effectively, to defend or strengthen the ego."[5] Thus, in studying the act of communication, we must include the fundamental needs of self as sources of motivation.

Now, before expanding the discussion, I want to present some concepts in communication that will be basic from this point on.

A Rhetorical Perspective

In this exploration of ordinary human interaction, I am guided by a rhetorical perspective on communication: that we *choose* ways to be with others, always with *purpose*, always seeking to be *effective* with them. That's what it means to be rhetorical in communication. Whether succeeding or failing, our aim is to use self-sustaining methods that will help us be effective. Psychologist Guy E. Swanson, in his scientific study of defenses, holds that defensive strategies of daily life, grounded in social interaction and interdependence, "are justifications tailored to social relations that are in danger and need of preservation." In other words, the goal is to adapt to others and maintain connections to them. In this, the choices are "likely to be determined by the nature of the social relationship concerned."[6] What's useful in maintaining one relationship may not be useful in another.

Characterized by strategic choice in the exchange of messages, the interactive function of communication is rhetorical. **To be rhetorical is to make choices for success.** Consequently, I will always use the word *communication* in a rhetorical sense, i.e., to refer to the symbolic interactions of people *exercising options* in saying things and pursuing their respective *purposes*. The rhetorical function is at the heart of communication, for participants put messages together to secure responses from each other. . . .

In terms of rhetorical theory, those with whom we relate and communicate are our "audiences." Moreover, as audience-conscious communicators, we're never innocent in our efforts to get a response, for our intent is to "get something"; most fundamentally, it is to secure confirmation of the person we believe we are—or want to be. That's why mindfulness of *self*-status is foremost in communication—*always*, regardless of the occasion or apparent meaning of the message. **We can never be sure of ourselves, especially of the other's attitude toward us or of our capability to relate to that.** Possessed of a vulnerable self and being rhetorically aware, we involve ourselves inventively with relevant ideas and feelings, dealing with issues of the moment, seeking to be successful: we want to identify with audiences and be confirmed by them. . . .

The Rhetorical Imperative   **Our strategies of interaction arise from a powerful rhetorical imperative: to affect audiences favorably about ourselves.** Most of our self-sustaining measures work fairly well most of the time and with most audiences. Swanson found that defenses "enable us to go on acting in a coherent fashion," promising to "afford us whatever gratification seems possible. In that sense they are adequate—sometimes ingeniously so."[7] Stories of brilliant accomplishment can be traced to this very ingenuity: for example, the eloquence of Winston Churchill.[8] Yet, other stories tell of inadequate self-maintenance strategy: stories of personal failure, strained relations, and communicative disaster.

And remember our internal messages, those we send to ourselves. In an in*tra*personal sense, excuses, denials, rationalizations, and other kinds of validating messages to ourselves about ourselves can help us to feel good with ourselves and to accept ourselves. Being comfortable with ourselves is basic to acting comfortably with others.

SHAME

For a psychological grounding on the nature of the social threat to the self, we can do no better than to consult Heinz Kohut, founder of the school of self psychology. Kohut's study of human behavior led to an important challenge to classical Freudian psychoanalytic thought. Departing from classical theory on the conflict of drives as fundamental to human behavior, Kohut centered instead on humankind's sense of self-defectiveness. In arguing his theory, he contrasted the family environment of Freud's time with that of subsequent generations, finding great differences in influences on child development. He contrasted the close household involvements and constant family stimulation of Freud's Victorian era with conditions of more recent decades. Families now have looser ties. There's much greater emotional distance among members, and one result is understimulation.

In Freudian theory, the *neurosis* is the common psychological complaint; it's tied to guilt and overstimulation from the persistent presence of family members, particularly parents. Guilt results from felt transgression, e.g., in violation of parental or social rule. But more recently, reflecting shame from felt neglect or deprivation, particularly parental, it is *narcissism* that is the common condition.

Shame results from a sense of felt defectiveness. In the absence of optimal parental or social constraint, the self is inadequately responded to, resulting in the narcissistic feelings of emptiness, unfulfillment, and deficiency. Thus, Kohut concluded, this is "the era of the endangered self."[9] The prime motivator of our time is shame. As we strive to protect ourselves against shame, our communicating is affected....

To counter the shame of personal deficit (felt inadequacy), humans invent modes of maintaining the self: some facilitative, others maladaptive. Of course, shame has always been with us, and the response to it is not a new behavioral act. But now the incidence is much higher, leading to a higher incidence of corrective activity to protect and justify ourselves. Of course guilt continues, but given increased narcissistic injury, e.g., from neglect, shame has become the master emotion. We live in an age of diminished parental presence and authority and in a general culture marked by increased social disregard. Consequently, we are provided with less feedback on connectedness and worth—or less constructive feedback. We are more on our own and more likely to question our adequacy, experience social endangerment, and respond self-protectively. The results—good and bad, hardly noticeable or blatant—appear in all daily communication: at home, on the job, at school—everywhere....

ON CULTURE AND SOCIALIZATION

Consider the following premise and implications for communication: **Rewards of individualism increasingly come into conflict with rewards of community affiliation.** "I want to be *me*, but I need *you*" expresses this personal-interpersonal conflict of our time: Or "It's great to be a person apart from others, but I need things from them." Issues of the conflict can be set out in various subjective terms:

- being gloriously alone and independent versus being safely associated and interdependent
- magnifying personal differences versus acknowledging kinship with others
- keeping distance versus seeking intimacy
- suffering the pain of separation versus enjoying the compensations of communication

The communicator's dilemma is about wanting to rely on self-confirmation versus needing the confirmation of others. It's a question of *intra*personal (individual) versus *inter*personal (social) satisfaction. It's an old story but with numerous postmodern twists and significant connections to other conditions of this age.[10] The dilemma is basic to the study of maintaining the self in communication.

East and West

At the outset, let's recognize the fact of cultural diversity in communication patterns. For example, in the United States, there is variance from culture to culture in strategies of self-maintenance—and from family to family, gender to gender, and from region to region. Communicators and students of communication should be aware that differences exist, and should be attentive to specific instances, some of which may influence the character of a moment of communication.

Thus we take the workings of socialization into account when studying variations in communication methods. And though anthropologists occasionally point to an isolated culture in which constraints on infant behavior appear to be minimal, apparently all cultures impose a socialization process on their children, one that moderates expression of their natural and normal narcissism. Certain differences in self-perception observed among Western and Eastern cultures can be traced to variations in the tightness of socialization processes that are imposed, primarily during the first two years or so of life. In some cultures, the social framing of the self is keen, and narcissism is actively suppressed, i.e., expressions of self and self-fulfillment are discouraged. The most familiar examples are collectivistic cultures like those of Asia. In others, such as the traditionally individualistic cultures of North America, greater encouragement is given to development of a self and related behaviors.

We know that in East Asian cultures, shame is a product of ardent socialization and group association. But in North American cultures … individuals value independence, and they feel shame when they sense personal inadequacy. Thus they seek some kind of exoneration or justification when they perceive themselves to be in violation of their self-concept. Pride, respect, trust, specific kinds of prowess, and other personal mandates are among the major issues. East

Asians feel shame when they violate group norms, when their behavior hurts the group.

But note the common property. While forces of socialization differ in intensity, people of every culture and background possess a self that is subject to threat and injury. And all are influenced by a concept of self. For instance, the pain that East Asians feel in bringing discredit to the group comes from knowing that they have violated their concept on group allegiance. Defending against that shame—maintaining or saving face—is necessary because self-worth and continuation of benefits of membership are in the balance....

When interpersonally uncertain or threatened, people on all continents respond protectively. Thus **the great commandment is to maintain the self....**

Of the Highest Order

Self-maintenance activity is more than mere habit; it pursues a major goal and is carried on with structures that have become integral to one's total being. Looking after the self has a place of the highest order in everyone's life.

... First of all, each of us has a self-concept: a demanding and assertive personal view of who we are and how we want to be seen and taken, of the kind of person we feel ourselves to be or the kind of person we think we *ought* to be. Specific reflections of this insistent self-concept appear in our attitudes, values and ideals, ways of doing, and positions on just about anything that is important to us.

Second, each of us needs to be treated as a worthy person and cared about—at least, to be taken seriously and respected. We need others to support and confirm us in who we are. In a word, self-esteem is a critical personal factor in communicating; it has to do with how you pay attention to my *self* needs and I to yours. **Climates of mutual support—and nonsupport—are created by the two of us together, as we bring our needy and sensitive selves to each other.**

... Effort to uphold and justify the self arises from threat to individual well-being—and it appears most obviously in *interpersonal* communication, as we put ourselves in association with others. And the fear of being hurt, offended, disqualified, or diminished in some way can be very strong....

The All-Powerful Self-Concept

What do the incidents below suggest about the self-concept and the need to be regarded well? Note the variety of motivating circumstances and how the individuals met ordinary human challenges. The circumstances are in italics.

Offended and wanting revenge, he vowed, "I'm gonna tell everyone what I know about her!"

Pleased with acknowledgment and praise, he modestly admitted, "Well, yes, I was the one who assisted him with CPR."

Unwilling to accept an almost unbearable feeling of defeat, she proclaimed, "I feel great! No problem! None whatever!"

Stinging from a felt attack on her religion, she never said another word during the entire evening.

Jolted by a sudden and loud command to leave the room, she cringed and murmured submissively, "Yes, ma'am."

Consumed with jealousy, he held her shoulders tightly and demanded, "Where in hell were you when I called seventeen times last night?"

Add to these instances all those messages communicated by persons who feel *slighted, put down, praised only faintly, unfairly compared, ridiculed,* or *passed over.* There's pain in *feeling unwanted and rejected, "out of one's element," unappreciated and misunderstood, incompetent*—and *believing oneself to be an imposter, a victim, weak link, traitor to the cause, ugly duckling,* or *an outsider.*

What about You?

Then there's you. Are you ever defensive or anxious to prove your worth? Say "Yes," because I know you are. Like the rest of us, you have a vulnerable self. It's disturbing to you to feel neglected or perceived as less than you think you ought to be. You have pride but also occasional feelings of inadequacy; you need recognition and approval. Feeling insecure at times about your place in life or your status at home, work, or school, you try harder—you're anxious to do better, to feel good about yourself or show that you're somebody. Much of such effort to achieve is beneficial, but it doesn't always come off smoothly. Sometimes there's distracting anger and hostility, criticism of self and others, backing off, and hiding out.

Try This   Recall a recent intense urge to protect yourself: when you felt that "call to action," to justify your background, explain your sexual orientation, stand behind your family, or vindicate your profession or political party or favorite music group. Or think back to how you felt down deep when you sensed that someone was trying to

- manipulate you or boss you around. What was your response to this felt abuse?
- lord it over you, acting in a superior manner. How did you handle that interpersonal wrong?
- impose on you a rigid and unacceptable point of view. What did you do about that?
- be noncommittal with you, remaining adamantly silent and evasive. How did you meet that?

On such occasions, how did you react? With a self-maintenance strategy? Quite likely. If so, what form did it take?

HOW PREVALENT IS THIS BEHAVIOR?

Self-maintenance strategies in communication appear in all relationships and interpersonal events: in friendships, romantic relationships, family systems, professional situations, church organizations, political entities, all school groups, and so forth....

Who can begin to calculate the vast amount of communicative energy spent in ordinary self-maintenance by one ordinary person in one ordinary day? That's a good question, for it suggests a fact: **A degree of uncertainty about one's social safety or status operates in every message sent: in every conversation, public speech, interview, and discussion.** And it's a part of every display of "attitude," as we call some kinds of scornful behavior or insolence.

Human uncertainty is one of the staple elements of television situation comedies. It's prominent in the lives of characters in novels, stage plays, movies, and comic strips. One of the most lovable insecure comic strip people is Cathy; her self-maintenance strategies are quite true to life. Without conditions of self-doubt and unpredictability on personal status, communication in the Doonesbury and Dilbert strips would be literally unreal. The conditions of characters would be false and the stories unappealing. Can you identify any important character in any well-written piece of fiction who is fully secure? I can't. The characters of *good* fiction are *real* in their self-maintenance activity.

Now, when talking about proving the self, justifying, and so forth, we must acknowledge (and be grateful for) the good results that often occur. Worthy accomplishment, professional success, and good works all have beginnings related to self-maintenance needs, in that all are associated with requirements of security and support—and of choices made to meet those requirements. Thus there are two possible consequences: Our self-protective ways *do* find positive and useful expression, but sometimes they function negatively against our best interests: for example, when they take the shape of neglectfulness or some kind of abuse. It follows that communicative interaction, energized with goals of self-maintenance, ranges from stimulating and constructive dialogue and rewarding interpersonal communication to personal attack and counter-attack. Whether obvious or indistinct, strategies of self-care are ever-present in communication....

SELF-MAINTENANCE IN COMMUNICATION:
EIGHT *TOPOI*

Is there a useful way to categorize self-maintenance resources available for communication? Classically, we have the psychological nomenclature called "defense mechanisms." Remember those? They have names like rationalization, repression, regression, projection, introjection, sublimation, and so forth.

But rather than adopt a list of mental "mechanisms" and end up with nothing but an outline of abstractions, we must find categories that will reflect a sense of the behavioral dynamics of communicative *interaction*. Any practical study of self-maintenance strategies will take account of the potent energy involved, while emphasizing the interactive give-and-take and ever-present fact of personal purpose. Consequently, we need action terms to depict what goes on, to give meaning to the justifying, qualifying, rationalizing, asserting, confronting, bragging, avoiding, excusing, soft-pedaling, soothing, supporting, and so forth of ordinary communicating. To this end, I have identified eight strategic groupings. They are expressed as common purposes: to control, achieve, oppose, attribute, express anger, deny, withdraw, and prevaricate.[11] Each of the eight *topoi* is a package, a collection of related options. Incidentally, *topoi* is a Greek word for topics. Aristotle used it. I like the word because it conveys the idea of *purposeful action* and connotes *strategic choice in interaction* and *variety of choice and opportunity in interaction....* As you look over the eight categories, note those that seem to have appeared in your recent communications with others. You hear and see them every day.

1. Control

Needs of security and certainty move communicators to regulate events, to find strategies for making things happen favorably. The need to control may be compelling or casual, and specific behaviors are numerous. Aims relate to ordinary communicative effectiveness, e.g., in being ready to handle unwelcome surprises or shocks as they might arise. But the goal may extend beyond seeking ordinary communicative control and effectiveness. For example, contrast the simple act of a person's choosing appropriate telephone language in placing a catalog order (necessarily exercising some control) to the extreme of a parent's determination to regulate an adult child's social activities. Likewise, at work, one employee may be rather easygoing, getting the routine communicative jobs done without excessive exertion (though there's always *some* management of events in communication), while another person will act to gain complete personal dominance of all functions related to on-the-job interactions. The latter mode might be considered "more defensive" than the former. Yet another example is the individualistic, iron-handed executive who seems unable to delegate authority to others or make use of cooperative problem-solving methods.

2. Achievement

Achievement needs frequently lie behind acts like self-justification. Related strategies often operate at a sensible and relaxed level: for example, that of doing a job adequately and feeling good about it. But contrast that with a level of functioning that is tremendously intense—when the communicator is determined to be absolutely right or brilliant or unchallengeable—anxious to stand out over others. Behavior of this extreme type is commonly called "perfectionism."

An example of the extreme is the vice president whose quarterly reports consistently and unnecessarily double the length of other vps' reports. This person's fervent drive to achieve—and get credit for it—requires great expenditure of time and energy.

3. Opposition

Protection of the self is a purpose of messages using the *topos* of *Opposition*. In this instance, a communicator assumes a contrary stance in communication with others, e.g., in "standing up for oneself." It may be expressed in some cases as disagreement or disapproval and in other cases as abject repugnance or contempt. *Opposition,* whether taken as ordinary dissent, rebuttal, stubbornness, resistance, challenge, nonconformity, derision, obstinacy, negativity, or scorn—whether seen as spirited support of one's position or as fierce denunciation or counteraction—is prevalent in all quarters of daily life.

4. Attribution

Attribution is common in communication to maintain the self. Communicators frequently face "How did this happen?" issues and matters of cause, responsibility, fault, or blame. In "getting to the bottom of things," one may name someone responsible—or oneself. Whether the communicator's spirit is constructive or malicious, the motivation is often one of self-protection, from a need to ascribe blame or accountability, and so forth. In this way the communicator attempts to maintain personal equilibrium and satisfactory communication.

Examples include the employee who realizes his computation error and consequently accepts responsibility; an older brother who blames his little sister when he trips on the stairs; the baseball batter whose habit is to scowl at the umpire when he takes a called third strike; the well-intentioned soul who needs to know whom to *absolve,* and the person who is motivated to solve "Who dunnit?" puzzles of relationships, whether concerned with a minor disagreement or a serious interpersonal conflict. . . .

5. Anger

If or when one is inclined toward sustaining the self through *Anger,* one will express strong displeasure or perhaps resort to violent verbal attacks. Like all *topoi, Anger* may be either beneficial or harmful. Others may view the behavior as useful passion, righteous indignation, bad temper, sullenness, belligerence, wrath, resentment, or great furor.

One example is two drivers' heated exchange after racing to occupy that empty space in the parking lot. What's at the root of such expression? Fairness is an issue, as is self-worth. Thus do self-maintenance needs of these communicators enter in: They feel a need to stand up for themselves and protect their "rights." That's one reason why some businesses install a "Take-a-Number" system to facilitate fair turn-taking at the counter. Customers who become preoccupied with protecting themselves may be less likely to return than customers who feel secure.

6. Denial

When choosing *Denial* as a method of self-care, one seeks to dodge an unpleasant or threatening reality, whether with a customary strategy or a spur-of-the-moment choice. Such communication involves inventing a method to protect against facing the "truth" or the "facts." In refusing to perceive something that's psychologically menacing, the communicator attempts to insulate the self from it by negating reality.

For example, a person may deny the fact of someone's death and thus provide cushioning against loss. Another example is the middle-aged woman who prefers teenage-style clothes, thereby revealing both her self-perception and her protective regression. Then there's the father who, unwilling to accept his son's rather ordinary athletic ability, criticizes the coach for not nominating his boy to the all-star team.

7. Withdrawal

If maintaining the self through *Withdrawal*, one will shun a certain event or individual, retreat from a threatening scene, maintain silence and mental distance, assume a passive posture, repress thoughts or feelings, resist disclosure of feelings, or in any number of other ways protect against the dangers and discomforts of social participation or judgment.

8. Prevarication

Prevarication is self-protection involving falsehood, excuse-making, justification of personal beliefs or actions, inhibition, deceptive statement, evasion, and so forth. As with all *topoi*, the strategic aim is to uphold the self: the self-concept, self-esteem, or sense of worth. Other modes of *Prevarication* are equivocation, euphemizing, use of passive voice, and "waffling."

An example of *Prevarication* is the socially useful "white lie." Another is shown in the case of the project coordinator who when asked for a progress report responded evasively, "Everybody's working real hard on this one, Chief—yes sir. I'll have more to tell you at mid-week." In this case, what needs of the self is the communicator seeking to care for?

Selecting Useful *Topoi*

In the process of communication, one isn't restricted to drawing from only one of the eight *topoi*.[12] Some of us find ourselves using them all at various times. Also interesting is the view that choice of *topos* may depend on personality type. For instance, extroverts may favor expressions of *Anger*, while introverts may favor *Withdrawal*.[13] But our social consciousness dictates that our choice of *topos* will be influenced by our perception of the situation and conditions. Audience characteristics are particularly significant in communication. That is, we fashion our messages in accord with the likely reactions of others. Why? Because we humans are *rhetorical* creatures: practical, purposeful, and adaptable. That's a point not to be forgotten by communicators! ...

Try This   From the twenty-five OCCASIONS FOR SELF-MAINTENANCE COMMUNICATION listed below, select one that relates to an experience you've had. Recall the occasion, and do the following:

1. Tell how in an insecure moment you came to perceive an exigence (some condition that required a response).
2. From which of the eight *topoi* did you draw for a strategic response? Was it one of the eight that I have discussed above? If not, what's your name for it?
3. Briefly stated, what message did you want to send? To whom did you send the message? What kinds of inward—intrapersonal—messages were a part of the process? Distinguish between verbal and nonverbal elements of the message. What result and feedback (response) did you want?

Occasions for Self-Maintenance Communication

When you ...

- respond to the charge of damaging another's property
- are embarrassed after making a social error
- try to handle the boss's dissatisfaction with a job you've done
- seek satisfaction after an acquaintance spreads a false story
- feel hurt in not being invited to the party
- sense public criticism of your behavior
- take a comment as threatening to your self-image
- feel shunned by a friend
- feel slighted in a group activity
- don't want to face the facts or your true feelings
- hear a comment that seems to be critical of your race, religion, sex, family, or school
- are jolted by a loud command of a coach, parent, or other
- feel down deep that you do not believe yourself to be qualified, e.g., to be in college or a given profession ("I'm just an imposter.")
- feel apprehensive about a surprising change in company policy or a relationship
- have a feeling of not belonging in a certain group
- are jealous
- are unsure of your personal status with someone or some group
- feel socially awkward in a specific situation
- fear speaking up in class
- are denied an expected honor or reward
- sense diminishment of your reputation in the family or other group
- feel wronged by a boyfriend or girlfriend
- feel that you deserve better treatment from someone on whom you depend for confirmation
- feel incompetent as a writer, athlete, cook, mother, etc.
- feel lacking in good looks

REVIEW QUESTIONS

1. According to Barrett, what is a defense mechanism?
2. Barrett says he is "guided by a rhetorical perspective on communication." What does this mean?
3. Define *shame* as Barrett discusses it.
4. Explain the individual versus social-cultural tension that Barrett describes.
5. What's the difference between an individualistic and a collectivistic culture?
6. What's narcissism?
7. What's the difference between the first two *topoi*—control and achievement?

PROBES

1. I can imagine people agreeing with Barrett about the significance of defensiveness and appreciating the increased self-awareness that comes from reading this selection. And I can also imagine some people rejecting Barrett's analysis as too obscurely Freudian, negative and pessimistic, and ultimately not very productive. If we imagine a sliding scale between these two positions, where on the scale would you put your response to this reading?
2. Barrett argues that every single time we communicate we are partly engaged in defending our selves. Do you agree or disagree? Explain.
3. Which type of culture that Barrett discusses do you identify with—individualistic or collectivistic? How does this affect your communicating?
4. "Are you ever defensive or anxious to prove your worth?" Barrett asks. "Say 'Yes,' because I know you are. Like the rest of us, you have a vulnerable self." How do you respond to that part of the reading?
5. Compare and contrast Barrett's discussion of attribution and my discussion of fault and blame in Chapter 2.
6. What did you learn from the list of "occasions for self-maintenance communication" at the end of this selection?

NOTES

1. "Social Insecurity," *America West Airlines Magazine*, April 1996: 74, 76–77, 79–80.
2. "Historical Perspectives on the Presented Self," *The Self and Social Life*, ed. Barry R. Schlenker (New York: McGraw-Hill, 1985), pp. 33–64.
3. "Two Questions about Psychoanalysis and Poetry," *The Literary Freud: Mechanisms of Defense and the Poetic Will*, ed. Joseph H. Smith (New Haven: Yale UP, 1980), pp. 113–18. To demonstrate the ubiquity or prevalence of the defensiveness that Edelson notes, I can't resist quoting a line from a recent film version of *Shadowlands* (a story about the relationship of C. S. Lewis and Joy Davidman): "People read to know they're not alone." The

quotation suggests that to be alone is to be unprotected, an unacceptable condition, and to read is to guard against that.

4. *Man's Aggression: The Defense of the Self* (Boston: Gambit, 1973), p. 216.
5. "Toward a Meaning-Centered Philosophy of Communication," *Journal of Communication* 12 (1962): 197–211.
6. *Ego Defenses and the Legitimation of Behavior* (Cambridge: Cambridge UP, 1988), p. 2.
7. *Ego Defenses*, p. 24.
8. See Heinz Kohut, *The Analysis of the Self* (London: Hogarth Press, 1971), pp. 108–9 and Kohut, *Self Psychology and the Humanities: Reflections on a New Psychoanalytic Approach*, ed. Charles B. Strozier (New York: Norton, 1985), pp. 12–13, 110, 198–99.
9. *The Restoration of the Self* (New York: International Universities Press, 1977), p. 290. For an important comment on Kohut's belief on shame as the central affect in narcissism, see Andrew P. Morrison, "Shame and the Psychology of the Self," *Kohut's Legacy: Contributions to Self Psychology*, ed. Paul E. Stepansky and Arnold Goldberg (Hillsdale: The Analytic Press, 1984).
10. In this regard, I recommend David Zarefsky's thoughtful (and rhetorical) exploration of the problem relating to the current conflict in the United States on diversity and community interests: *The Roots of American Community* (Boston: Allyn and Bacon, 1996).
11. Besides relying on my catalogue of extensive observations of human interaction and responses of focus groups, I have found two books particularly useful as sources for developing the eight *topoi:* Merle A. Fossum and Marilyn J. Mason, *Facing Shame: Families in Recovery* (New York: Norton, 1986) and Gershen Kaufman, *Shame: The Power of Caring,* 2nd ed. rev. (Cambridge, MA: Schenkman, 1985).
12. On the topic of choice in selecting maintenance strategies, defenses in particular, turn to George Vaillant, *The Wisdom of the Ego* (Cambridge: Harvard UP, 1993).
13. See Gershen Kaufman, *Shame*, p. 71.

The Rudiments of Social Intelligence

Daniel Goleman

This next reading helps show how human selves are fundamentally communicative by defining the counterpart of IQ (Intelligence Quotient), as EQ (Emotional Quotient), which is basically the willingness and ability to connect effectively with others. For a long time, at least in the Western world, people have trusted IQ tests as the best measure of a person's "smarts." For many decades, IQ tests have been given to schoolchildren, and IQ scores have been used to define people as "gifted," "special needs," or "genius." Daniel Goleman argues that these tests are fundamentally flawed because they measure only part of what it means to be intelligent. There is a very important, complementary set of human competencies that he calls "emotional intelligence," and these are embodied in our ways of relating with others.

In other words, emotional intelligence is basically interpersonal intelligence. It is made up of four main abilities: organizing groups, negotiating solutions, personal connection, and social analysis. Each is significantly different from the kinds of intelligence that standard IQ tests measure.

The first involves "initiating and coordinating the efforts of a network of people." The second is the talent of a mediator—resolving conflicts. The third kind of emotional intelligence is the capacity for empathy—reading emotions and responding appropriately to them. And the fourth consists of being able to "detect and have insights about people's feelings, motives, and concerns."

Goleman briefly describes how these abilities are related to other kinds of emotional intelligence. For example, the person who is empathic is also able to notice his or her own emotions, to fine-tune them to fit the situation, and to adjust them flexibly. He also cites research about self-monitoring to make the point that it's important to have a balance of the emotional capabilities of empathy and the awareness of your *own* needs and feelings.

In a section of the reading called "The Making of a Social Incompetent," Goleman discusses some of the experiences that help shape individual emotional intelligence. He quotes a psychologist who emphasizes that children need to be taught "to speak directly to others when spoken to; to initiate social contact, not always wait for others; to carry on a conversation, not simply fall back on yes or no or other one-word replies; to express gratitude toward others, ... to thank others, to say 'please,' to share," and so on. Young children learn these capabilities—or fail to learn them—in countless informal contacts with family members, schoolmates, and friends, and this fact underscores the significance, in the early years, of these everyday, mundane activities. Goleman notes that psychologists have coined the term *dyssemia* to label people who haven't learned to read the nonverbal messages that primarily communicate emotions. He also points out that this difficulty affects not only a child's interpersonal life but also his or her academic success.

One of the primary tests of a young child's emotional intelligence is being on the edge of a group that the child wants to join. Some research indicates that even popular second- and third-graders are rejected almost a quarter of the time they attempt to join in such groups. And as each of us can probably remember, young children can be brutally candid in this situation. Researchers observe these events in classrooms and on playgrounds in order to assess individual abilities and clarify the features of emotional intelligence.

The selection ends with a description of an event of "emotional brilliance" that a friend of Goleman's observed on a train outside Tokyo. This story, along with the rest of this reading, should enable you to evaluate your own emotional or interpersonal intelligence and to recognize how this kind of knowledge affects your perceptions of people, relationships, and social situations.

It's recess at a preschool, and a band of boys is running across the grass. Reggie trips, hurts his knee, and starts crying, but the other boys keep right on running—save for Roger, who stops. As Reggie's sobs subside Roger reaches down and rubs his own knee, calling out, "I hurt my knee, too!"

Roger is cited as having exemplary interpersonal intelligence by Thomas Hatch, a colleague of Howard Gardner at Spectrum, the school based on the concept of multiple intelligences.[1] Roger, it seems, is unusually adept at recognizing the feelings of his playmates and making rapid, smooth connections with them. It was only Roger who noticed Reggie's plight and pain, and only Roger who tried to provide some solace, even if all he could offer was rubbing his own knee. This small gesture bespeaks a talent for rapport, an emotional skill essential for the preservation of close relationships, whether in a marriage, a friendship, or a business partnership. Such skills in preschoolers are the buds of talents that ripen through life.

Roger's talent represents one of four separate abilities that Hatch and Gardner identify as components of interpersonal intelligence:

- *Organizing groups*—the essential skill of the leader, this involves initiating and coordinating the efforts of a network of people. This is the talent seen in theater directors or producers, in military officers, and in effective heads of organizations and units of all kinds. On the playground, this is the child who takes the lead in deciding what everyone will play, or becomes team captain.
- *Negotiating solutions*—the talent of the mediator, preventing conflicts or resolving those that flare up. People who have this ability excel in deal-making, in arbitrating or mediating disputes; they might have a career in diplomacy, in arbitration or law, or as middlemen or managers of takeovers. These are the kids who settle arguments on the playing field.
- *Personal connection*—Roger's talent, that of empathy and connecting. This makes it easy to enter into an encounter or to recognize and respond fittingly to people's feelings and concerns—the art of relationship. Such people make good "team players," dependable spouses, good friends or business partners; in the business world they do well as salespeople or managers, or can be excellent teachers. Children like Roger get along well with virtually everyone else, easily enter into playing with them, and are happy doing so. These children tend to be best at reading emotions from facial expressions and are most liked by their classmates.
- *Social analysis*—being able to detect and have insights about people's feelings, motives, and concerns. This knowledge of how others feel can lead to an easy intimacy or sense of rapport. At its best, this ability makes one a competent therapist or counselor—or, if combined with some literary talent, a gifted novelist or dramatist.

Taken together, these skills are the stuff of interpersonal polish, the necessary ingredients for charm, social success, even charisma. Those who are adept in social intelligence can connect with people quite smoothly, be astute in reading their reactions and feelings, lead and organize, and handle the disputes that are bound to flare up in any human activity. They are the natural leaders, the people who can express the unspoken collective sentiment and articulate it so as to guide a group toward its goals. They are the kind of people others like to be with because they are emotionally nourishing—they leave other people in a good mood, and evoke the comment, "What a pleasure to be around someone like that."

These interpersonal abilities build on other emotional intelligences. People who make an excellent social impression, for example, are adept at monitoring their own expression of emotion, are keenly attuned to the ways others are reacting, and so are able to continually fine-tune their social performance, adjusting it to make sure they are having the desired effect. In that sense, they are like skilled actors.

However, if these interpersonal abilities are not balanced by an astute sense of one's own needs and feelings and how to fulfill them, they can lead to a hollow social success—a popularity won at the cost of one's true satisfaction. Such is the argument of Mark Snyder, a University of Minnesota psychologist who has studied people whose social skills make them first-rate social chameleons, champions at making a good impression.[2] Their psychological credo might well be a remark by W. H. Auden, who said that his private image of himself "is very different from the image which I try to create in the minds of others in order that they may love me." That trade-off can be made if social skills outstrip the ability to know and honor one's own feelings: in order to be loved—or at least liked—the social chameleon will seem to be whatever those he [or she] is with seem to want. The sign that someone falls into this pattern, Snyder finds, is that they make an excellent impression, yet have few stable or satisfying intimate relationships. A more healthy pattern, of course, is to balance being true to oneself with social skills, using them with integrity.

Social chameleons, though, don't mind in the least saying one thing and doing another, if that will win them social approval. They simply live with the discrepancy between their public face and their private reality. Helena Deutsch, a psychoanalyst, called such people the "as-if personality," shifting personas with remarkable plasticity as they pick up signals from those around them. "For some people," Snyder told me, "the public and private person meshes well, while for others there seems to be only a kaleidoscope of changing appearances. They are like Woody Allen's character Zelig, madly trying to fit in with whomever they are with."

Such people try to scan someone for a hint as to what is wanted from them before they make a response, rather than simply saying what they truly feel. To get along and be liked, they are willing to make people they dislike think they are friendly with them. And they use their social abilities to mold their actions as disparate social situations demand, so that they may act like very different people depending on whom they are with, swinging from bubbly sociability, say, to reserved withdrawal. To be sure, to the extent that these traits lead to effective impression management, they are highly prized in certain professions, notably acting, trial law, sales, diplomacy, and politics.

Another, perhaps more crucial kind of self-monitoring seems to make the difference between those who end up as anchorless social chameleons, trying to impress everyone, and those who can use their social polish more in keeping with their true feelings. That is the capacity to be true, as the saying has it, "to thine own self," which allows acting in accord with one's deepest feelings and values no matter what the social consequences. Such emotional integrity could well lead to, say, deliberately provoking a confrontation in order to cut through duplicity or denial—a clearing of the air that a social chameleon would never attempt.

THE MAKING OF A SOCIAL INCOMPETENT

There was no doubt Cecil was bright; he was a college-trained expert in foreign languages, superb at translating. But there were crucial ways in which he was completely inept. Cecil seemed to lack the simplest social skills. He would muff a casual conversation over coffee, and fumble when having to pass the time of day; in short, he seemed incapable of the most routine social exchange. Because his lack of social grace was most profound when he was around women, Cecil came to therapy wondering if perhaps he had "homosexual tendencies of an underlying nature," as he put it, though he had no such fantasies.

The real problem, Cecil confided to his therapist, was that he feared that nothing he could say would be of any interest to anybody. This underlying fear only compounded a profound paucity of social graces. His nervousness during encounters led him to snicker and laugh at the most awkward moments, even though he failed to laugh when someone said something genuinely funny. Cecil's awkwardness, he confided to his therapist, went back to childhood; all his life he had felt socially at ease only when he was with his older brother, who somehow helped ease things for him. But once he left home, his ineptitude was overwhelming; he was socially paralyzed.

The tale is told by Lakin Phillips, a psychologist at George Washington University, who proposes that Cecil's plight stems from a failure to learn in childhood the most elementary lessons of social interaction:

> What could Cecil have been taught earlier? To speak directly to others when spoken to; to initiate social contact, not always wait for others; to carry on a conversation, not simply fall back on yes or no or other one-word replies; to express gratitude toward others, to let another person walk before one in passing through a door; to wait until one is served something … to thank others, to say "please," to share, and all the other elementary interactions we begin to teach children from age 2 onward.[3]

Whether Cecil's deficiency was due to another's failure to teach him such rudiments of social civility or to his own inability to learn is unclear. But whatever its roots, Cecil's story is instructive because it points up the crucial nature of the countless lessons children get in interaction synchrony and the unspoken rules of social harmony. The net effect of failing to follow these rules is to create waves, to make those around us uncomfortable. The function of these rules, of course, is to keep everyone involved in a social exchange at ease; awkwardness spawns anxiety. People who lack these skills are inept not just at social niceties, but at handling the emotions of those they encounter; they inevitably leave disturbance in their wake.

We all have known Cecils, people with an annoying lack of social graces—people who don't seem to know when to end a conversation or phone call and who keep on talking, oblivious to all cues and hints to say good-bye; people whose conversation centers on themselves all the time, without the least interest in anyone else, and who ignore tentative attempts to refocus on another topic; people who intrude or ask "nosy" questions. These derailments of a smooth social trajectory all bespeak a deficit in the rudimentary building blocks of interaction.

Psychologists have coined the term *dyssemia* (from the Greek *dys-* for "difficulty" and *semes* for "signal") for what amounts to a learning disability in the realm of nonverbal messages; about one in ten children has one or more problems in this realm.[4] The problem can be in a poor sense of personal space, so that a child stands too close while talking or spreads their belongings into other people's territory; in interpreting or using body language poorly; in misinterpreting or misusing facial expressions by, say, failing to make eye contact; or in a poor sense of prosody, the emotional quality of speech, so that they talk too shrilly or flatly.

Much research has focused on spotting children who show signs of social deficiency, children whose awkwardness makes them neglected or rejected by their playmates. Apart from children who are spurned because they are bullies, those whom other children avoid are invariably deficient in the rudiments of face-to-face interaction, particularly the unspoken rules that govern encounters. If children do poorly in language, people assume they are not very bright or poorly educated; but when they do poorly in the nonverbal rules of interaction, people—especially playmates—see them as "strange," and avoid them. These are the children who don't know how to join a game gracefully, who touch others in ways that make for discomfort rather than camaraderie—in short, who are "off." They are children who have failed to master the silent language of emotion, and who unwittingly send messages that create uneasiness.

As Stephen Nowicki, an Emory University psychologist who studies children's nonverbal abilities, put it, "Children who can't read or express emotions well constantly feel frustrated. In essence, they don't understand what's going on. This kind of communication is a constant subtext of everything you do; you can't stop showing your facial expression or posture, or hide your tone of voice. If you make mistakes in what emotional messages you send, you constantly experience that people react to you in funny ways—you get rebuffed and don't know why. If you're thinking you're acting happy but actually seem too hyper or angry, you find other kids getting angry at you in turn, and you don't realize why. Such kids end up feeling no sense of control over how other people treat them, that their actions have no impact on what happens to them. It leaves them feeling powerless, depressed, and apathetic."

Apart from becoming social isolates, such children also suffer academically. The classroom, of course, is as much a social situation as an academic one; the socially awkward child is as likely to misread and misrespond to a teacher as to another child. The resulting anxiety and bewilderment can themselves interfere with their ability to learn effectively. Indeed, as tests of children's nonverbal sensitivity have shown, those who misread emotional cues tend to do poorly in school compared to their academic potential as reflected in IQ tests.[5]

"WE HATE YOU": AT THE THRESHOLD

Social ineptitude is perhaps most painful and explicit when it comes to one of the more perilous moments in the life of a young child: being on the edge of a group at play you want to join. It is a moment of peril, one when being liked or hated, belonging or not, is made all too public. For that reason that crucial moment has been the subject of intense scrutiny by students of child development, revealing a stark contrast in approach strategies used by popular children and by social outcasts. The findings highlight just how crucial it is for social competence to notice, interpret, and respond to emotional and interpersonal cues. While it is poignant to see a child hover on the edge of others at play, wanting to join in but being left out, it is a universal predicament. Even the most popular children are sometimes rejected—a study of second and third graders found that 26 percent of the time the most well liked children were rebuffed when they tried to enter a group already at play.

Young children are brutally candid about the emotional judgment implicit in such rejections. Witness the following dialogue from four-year-olds in a preschool.[6] Linda wants to join Barbara, Nancy, and Bill, who are playing with toy animals and building blocks. She watches for a minute, then makes her approach, sitting next to Barbara and starting to play with the animals. Barbara turns to her and says, "You can't play!"

"Yes, I can," Linda counters. "I can have some animals, too."

"No, you can't," Barbara says bluntly. "We don't like you today."

When Bill protests on Linda's behalf, Nancy joins the attack: "We hate her today."

Because of the danger of being told, either explicitly or implicitly, "We hate you," all children are understandably cautious on the threshold of approaching a group. That anxiety, of course, is probably not much different from that felt by a grown-up at a cocktail party with strangers who hangs back from a happily chatting group who seem to be intimate friends. Because this moment at the threshold of a group is so momentous for a child, it is also, as one researcher put it, "highly diagnostic ... quickly revealing differences in social skillfulness."[7]

Typically, newcomers simply watch for a time, then join in very tentatively at first, being more assertive only in very cautious steps. What matters most for whether a child is accepted or not is how well he or she is able to enter into the group's frame of reference, sensing what kind of play is in flow, what's out of place.

The two cardinal sins that almost always lead to rejection are trying to take the lead too soon and being out of synch with the frame of reference. But this is exactly what unpopular children tend to do: they push their way into a group, trying to change the subject too abruptly or too soon, or offering their own opinions, or simply disagreeing with the others right away—all apparent attempts to draw attention to themselves. Paradoxically, this results in their being ignored or rejected. By contrast, popular children spend time observing the group to understand what's going on before entering in, and then do something that shows they accept it; they wait to have their status in the group confirmed before taking initiative in suggesting what the group should do.

Let's return to Roger, the four-year-old whom Thomas Hatch spotted exhibiting a high level of interpersonal intelligence.[8] Roger's tactic for entering a group was first to observe, then to imitate what another child was doing, and finally to talk to the child and fully join the activity—a winning strategy. Roger's skill was shown, for instance, when he and Warren were playing at putting "bombs" (actually pebbles) in their socks. Warren asks Roger if he wants to be in a helicopter or an airplane. Roger asks, before committing himself, "Are you in a helicopter?"

This seemingly innocuous moment reveals sensitivity to others' concerns, and the ability to act on that knowledge in a way that maintains the connection. Hatch comments about Roger, "He 'checks in' with his playmate so that they and their play remain connected. I have watched many other children who simply get in their own helicopters or planes and, literally and figuratively, fly away from each other."

EMOTIONAL BRILLIANCE: A CASE REPORT

If the test of social skill is the ability to calm distressing emotions in others, then handling someone at the peak of rage is perhaps the ultimate measure of mastery. The data on self-regulation of anger and emotional contagion suggest that one effective strategy might be to distract the angry person, empathize with his feelings and perspective, and then draw him into an alternative focus, one that attunes him with a more positive range of feeling—a kind of emotional judo.

Such refined skill in the fine art of emotional influence is perhaps best exemplified by a story told by an old friend, the late Terry Dobson, who in the 1950s was one of the first Americans ever to study the martial art aikido in Japan. One afternoon he was riding home on a suburban Tokyo train when a huge, bellicose, and very drunk and begrimed laborer got on. The man, staggering, began terrorizing the passengers: screaming curses, he took a swing at a woman holding a baby, sending her sprawling in the laps of an elderly couple, who then jumped up and joined a stampede to the other end of the car. The drunk, taking a few other swings (and, in his rage, missing), grabbed the metal pole in the middle of the car with a roar and tried to tear it out of its socket.

At that point Terry, who was in peak physical condition from daily eight-hour aikido workouts, felt called upon to intervene, lest someone get seriously hurt. But he recalled the words of his teacher: "Aikido is the art of reconciliation. Whoever has the mind to fight has broken his connection with the universe. If you try to dominate people you are already defeated. We study how to resolve conflict, not how to start it."

Indeed, Terry had agreed upon beginning lessons with his teacher never to pick a fight, and to use his martial-arts skills only in defense. Now, at last, he saw his chance to test his aikido abilities in real life, in what was clearly a legitimate opportunity. So, as all the other passengers sat frozen in their seats, Terry stood up, slowly and with deliberation.

Seeing him, the drunk roared, "Aha! A foreigner! You need a lesson in Japanese manners!" and began gathering himself to take on Terry.

But just as the drunk was on the verge of making his move, someone gave an earsplitting, oddly joyous shout: "Hey!"

The shout had the cheery tone of someone who has suddenly come upon a fond friend. The drunk, surprised, spun around to see a tiny Japanese man, probably in his seventies, sitting there in a kimono. The old man beamed with delight at the drunk, and beckoned him over with a light wave of his hand and a lilting "C'mere."

The drunk strode over with a belligerent, "Why the hell should I talk to you?" Meanwhile, Terry was ready to fell the drunk in a moment if he made the least violent move.

"What'cha been drinking?" the old man asked, his eyes beaming at the drunken laborer.

"I been drinking sake, and it's none of your business," the drunk bellowed.

"Oh, that's wonderful, absolutely wonderful," the old man replied in a warm tone. "You see, I love sake, too. Every night, me and my wife (she's seventy-six, you know), we warm up a little bottle of sake and take it out into the garden, and we sit on an old wooden bench . . ." He continued on about the persimmon tree in his backyard, the fortunes of his garden, enjoying sake in the evening.

The drunk's face began to soften as he listened to the old man; his fists un-clenched. "Yeah . . . I love persimmons, too . . . ," he said, his voice trailing off. "Yes," the old man replied in a sprightly voice, "and I'm sure you have a wonderful wife."

"No," said the laborer. "My wife died. . . ." Sobbing, he launched into a sad tale of losing his wife, his home, his job, of being ashamed of himself.

Just then the train came to Terry's stop, and as he was getting off he turned to hear the old man invite the drunk to join him and tell him all about it, and to see the drunk sprawl along the seat, his head in the old man's lap.

That is emotional brilliance.

REVIEW QUESTIONS

1. What's the difference between ability 3, "personal connection," and ability 4, "social analysis"?
2. What does Goleman mean when he says that emotionally intelligent people are "nourishing" to others?
3. What's *dyssemia*, and what is its relevance to this reading?
4. Goleman says that "the two cardinal sins that almost always lead to rejection" are (a) trying to _____ too soon and (b) being _____ the frame of reference."
5. How did the old man on the train outside Tokyo demonstrate a key principle of aikido?

PROBES

1. Explain the balance that Goleman emphasizes is necessary between emotional intelligence and "an astute sense of one's own needs and feelings and how to fulfill them."
2. In this selection, Goleman does not describe in detail *how* emotional intelligence can result in using one's social polish in keeping with one's true feelings, rather than becoming an "anchorless social chameleon." What do you believe it takes to do this?
3. It's relatively easy to describe what Cecil in Goleman's example failed to learn—"to speak directly to others when spoken to; … to carry on a conversation, not simply fall back on yes or no … replies," and so on. But it's more difficult to describe what parents (and other caregivers) need *to do* to be sure their children learn all these things. What do you believe are the most important ways to help young children learn emotional intelligence?
4. How does Goleman's focus on *nonverbal* communication support or challenge what's said about nonverbal communication in the last two readings in Chapter 4?
5. Young children can be brutally candid in their rejection of would-be playmates. Do adults communicate these same messages in other ways? Or is rejection less common among adults? Discuss.
6. Goleman discusses a child named Roger who shows his emotional intelligence by checking with his playmate before committing himself "to be in a helicopter or an airplane." Describe an adult version of this same communication move.

NOTES

1. Thomas Hatch, "Social Intelligence in Young Children," paper delivered at the annual meeting of the American Psychological Association (1990).

2. Social chameleons: Mark Snyder, "Impression Management: The Self in Social Interaction," in L. S. Wrightsman and K. Deaux, *Social Psychology in the '80s* (Monterey, CA: Brooks/Cole, 1981).
3. E. Lakin Phillips, *The Social Skills Basis of Psychopathology* (New York: Grune and Stratton, 1978), p. 140.
4. Nonverbal learning disorders: Stephen Nowicki and Marshall Duke, *Helping the Child Who Doesn't Fit In* (Atlanta: Peachtree Publishers, 1992). See also Byron Rourke, *Nonverbal Learning Disabilities* (New York: Guilford Press, 1989).
5. Nowicki and Duke, *Helping the Child Who Doesn't Fit In.*
6. This vignette, and the review of research on entering a group, is from Martha Putallaz and Aviva Wasserman, "Children's Entry Behavior," in Steven Asher and John Coie, eds., *Peer Rejection in Childhood* (New York: Cambridge University Press, 1990).
7. Putallaz and Wasserman, "Children's Entry Behavior."
8. Hatch, "Social Intelligence in Young Children."

———

Forming Online Identities

Andrew F. Wood and Matthew J. Smith

Computer-mediated communication (CMC), which includes not only e-mail, chat rooms, listserv, and multiuser domains (MUDs) but also instant messaging (IM), changes so rapidly that most of the published writing about it is out of date by the time it appears. But in this essay, Andrew Wood and Matthew Smith discuss an aspect of CMC that will probably never change: the ways participants construct and alter their online identities.

After defining what they mean by "identity," the authors discuss how CMC participants perform multiple roles. As they note, this is an extension of what the prominent sociologist Erving Goffman called "face-work." As in the rest of our lives, sometimes we consciously manage our identity to "put the best foot forward," and other times we experiment with projecting an identity that we cannot successfully portray in real life. Not only can this be interesting and fun, but identity projection can also generate the experience of empathy, a glimpse into the experiences of others.

As with face-to-face communication, online identities are affected by both what is said and how it is communicated. Writing style, signature attachment, nicknames, photographs and other graphics, and avatars can all contribute to CMC identity management.

In the last section of the essay, the authors distinguish among anonymity, pseudonymity, and identity. They propose a "principle of truth in the nature of naming" that could

From *Online Communication: Linking Technology, Identity & Culture,* 2nd Edition by Andrew F. Wood and Matthew J. Smith. Mahwah, NJ: Lawrence Erlbaum Associates, 2008. Reprinted by permission.

benefit much of the communication that happens on some blogs. They also discuss the advantages and disadvantages of the use of pseudonyms.

A main benefit of this essay is that it highlights how prominent identity management is in CMC. It will help increase your awareness of the identities you and your conversation partners construct via e-mail, game involvement, and IM.

> *Looking at the proliferation of personal Web pages on the Net, it looks like very soon everyone on Earth will have 15 megabytes of fame.*

> —M. G. Siriam

For 3 years, women who participated in a CompuServe discussion group grew closer and closer to a woman they knew as Julie Graham. During that time, Julie posted messages that disclosed increasingly intimate details of her life, including the fact that she was a mute, paraplegic victim of a car crash who had wrested with suicidal depression. Her plight so moved her fellow participants that after a number of months of interacting with her online, one well-intentioned woman set out to find Julie and offer her face-to-face comfort and support. Much to this woman's surprise, "Julie Graham" turned out to be a fiction, and the facts behind the person creating her were quite contrary to what the woman and others had read. First of all, Julie wasn't a mute paraplegic. Second, she wasn't housebound, but a full-time professional psychologist. Third, she wasn't a she, but a man who had created the online persona of Julie to delve deeper into the female psyche by impersonating one. When the sleuthing woman reported her discovery to the rest of the bulletin board's participants, outraged contributors condemned the experiment, remarking that in impersonating one of them, the psychologist had violated their privacy (Stone, 1991).

Why were the women upset with "Julie's" deception? After all, how could these women feel betrayed by someone with whom they had never met face-to-face? Despite the intuitive conclusion of those outside the context that these were "just words," the self that this psychologist presented and the one that his conversation partners perceived seemed quite authentic. CMC [computer-mediated communication] contexts, like no other person-to-person media before them, offer communicators the ability to manipulate their personal identities in ways that call info question assumptions about what is possible and what is appropriate in the presentation of self.

Professor Sherry Turkle has been particulary helpful in illuminating just how computing technologies have challenged us to reevaluate how we think about ourselves. Turkle has thus labeled the computer an evocative object, that is, an object to think with (Rheingold, n.d.). As we review shortly, computers have been helpful in showing us just how multifaceted our lives are. Whereas popular conceptions of psychological health have considered an unfragmented, unitary self the ideal, Turkle suggests that the ability to move from one aspect, or self, to another and to do so with an understanding of the process is a more healthy conception of who we are. Computers, with their ability to multitask various jobs simultaneously, serve as a metaphor for our own lives in which we are called on to fill more than one role, oftentimes simultaneously. The computer's communication applications, those in which we practice CMC, are just some that allow us to practice, to explore, and ultimately to reflect on the nature of who we are in terms of not just one self, but our many selves.

Thus, this [essay] explores several key issues dedicated to questions of identity in communicating through mediating technologies. An **identity** is a complex personal and social construct, consisting in part of who we think ourselves to be, how we wish others to perceive us, and how they actually perceive us. In particular, CMC research has looked at the second of these fragments: how we wish others to perceive us. The process of setting forth an image we want others to perceive is known as *self-presentation*.

PERFORMING IDENTITY ON THE INTERNET

… Perhaps you have acquaintances who do not leave messages on telephone answering machines, declaring, "I don't like those machines." Such individuals are probably a bit self-conscious about what they say or how they sound on tape. This kind of self-awareness is but another manifestation of humanity's long struggle with identity. Again, an important aspect of identity is how we present ourselves to others. To some degree, we can control what others know of us by making some choices in life, yet certain qualities of our identities are predetermined for us. In face-to-face interactions, people infer qualities of our identities based on our gender, race, clothing, and other nonverbal characteristics. Because many of these cues are invisible online, Internet technologies offer us the possibility of controlling more aspects of our identity for public consideration than has been possible before…. Consider the process you undergo in the morning when deciding what clothes to wear. Do you purposefully choose a professional outfit because you have to go to work or make a presentation for a class? Or do you throw on the first thing you trip over on your floor? If you know you have to work or make a presentation, would it be inappropriate to show up in baggy sweat pants and a T-shirt? Certainly, just as it would be inappropriate to show up for a touch football game in a blazer. Most of us are aware that costuming is an important aspect of the parts we play and the self we choose to present at one time or another.

Casting Call: Performing Multiple Roles

Communication scholars have long pulled on the works of noted sociologist Erving Goffman, who wrote extensively on how people work to present themselves in everyday life. Goffman would have agreed with Shakespeare, who wrote:

> All the world's a stage,
> And all the men and women merely players.
> They have their exits and their entrances;
> And one man in his time plays many parts. (*As You Like It*, Act II, Scene 7)

It was Goffman's (1959) contention that everyday life was a performance of sorts, and that our behaviors and attitudes could be explained in terms of a theatrical metaphor. Accordingly, Goffman wrote of how people adopted particular roles when they were in public view by putting on a face. The effort people invest in "staying in character," as it were, Goffman calls *face-work*, noting that people are persistently attending to the requirements of a particular face lest they break the image of their role. Over the years, Goffman's work has been instrumental in advancing the understanding of how elements of performance contribute to what and how people communicate. More recent researchers have echoed Goffman's fascination with the theatrical metaphor and have invoked similar language in attempting to explain how people construct identities online.

Pulling on another theatrical term, Amy Bruckman (1992) dubs text-based forums like MUDs [multiuse domains] "identity workshops." A workshop in theatrical training presents an opportunity for actors to experiment with various roles. An actor in training might take on the role of a vocal football coach one moment and then change over to a portrayal of a sidewalk mime the next, all to exercise the range of his or her acting ability. In like manner, then, an identity workshop presents people with a chance to display different manifestations of themselves. One could very well maintain an identity as a rough-and-tough sailor in one MUD but portray a sensitive artist in another chat room.

Turkle (1995) confirms the notion that the computer enables users to explore multiple roles. Turkle says, "In ... computer-mediated worlds, the self is multiple, fluid and constituted in interaction with machine connections; it is made and transformed by language" (p. 15). This view of the self as multiple and fluid ... rather than singular and static is further explored in Turkle's writings by drawing a comparison to the multiple tasks one can accomplish in a windows-based environment. Current software allows users to change from using a word-processing program to author a research paper, to sending e-mail to one's boss, to participating in an MUD, all by merely clicking from window to window. Thus, one can quite readily switch roles from student, to employee, to fantasy figure. Certainly, this is a manifestation of the concept of multiphrenia. However, Turkle clearly suggested that people control the multiple roles rather than suffer from the burden of having to negotiate among them.

Why do people engage in such role-playing then? Turkle (1995) suggests that one reason is that people can experience an identity they could not successfully portray in real life. A benefit of such role-playing is that individuals can gain a new perspective on their world and their place in it. Borrowing from anthropology, Turkle uses the term *dépaysement* to describe the experience of seeing the familiar through unfamiliar eyes. In interviews with people who adopted identities distinctly different from their own for their online personas, most notably those who changed their genders, Turkle found that the experience of living a life unlike their own opened them up to the struggles and pleasures that come along with living with another gender, race, class, or other distinction.

A good example of how role-playing might promote better understanding comes from the simulations conducted by Andrew Vincent of Macquarie

University in Sydney, Australia (Vincent & Shepherd, 1998). Coming to the simulations, Vincent's students tend to have limited comprehension of the political
problems facing the Middle East, which is unsurprising given the distance that
the conflict is from most of his students' experiences and the complexity of the
issues involved. Following a format similar to that of a model United Nations
program, Vincent assigns both students in his course and those at a cooperating institution to roles of various contemporary figures in the conflict (e.g., the
leader of the Palestinians, the prime minister of Israel). Through several weeks
of Internet-based exchanges, the role-players try to come to some agreements.
By the end of the simulation, students begin to understand more about the
Middle East situation, for, as one of Vincent's students explained it:

> Putting yourself in someone else's shoes—you may get the role of particular
> character but you don't necessarily agree with them but you have to try to
> develop their mindset. It's interesting. Right in there at the moment we've got a
> girl with leanings towards the Palestinians playing Benjamin Netanyahu [then
> Israeli prime minister], so it's a complete turn-around for her. It's imperative
> to be able to see other points of view and realise that they're just as valuable as
> yours. (Vincent & Shepherd, 1998)

That kind of insight is educational, indeed.

Another reason for role-playing might reside in the increased control people
experience over their online identities. In real life, one can adopt a limited
number of roles, given that one's gender, race, age, accent, and other nonverbal
determinants influence people's perceptions of how well one functions in a
given role. For instance, a middle-aged, Euro-American man might decide he
wants to experiment with a female identity. With the appropriate costuming and
mannerisms, he might be successful in appearing to be a female to someone he
has not previously met, but if he wants to know what it is like to be an African
American, he is less likely to be able to pull off such a charade. However, in an
online forum, he can more readily adopt and enact a change in his gender, race,
or any other characteristic he chooses.

In whatever identity he selects, he can exert greater control over his identity
in the online environment than in face-to-face interaction. In face-to-face
interactions, we communicate not only through our words but also through our
appearance. For example, in real life, someone might decide to discount your
opinion because of your age, because he or she perceives that you are either
too young or too old to know much about a topic. But in online forums, what
people know about others is based on the disclosure of information that one
wishes others to know (Cutler, 1996). If one's age is not relevant to the persona
one wishes to have others perceive, then one needs merely not to reveal this
information to prevent skewing others' perceptions one way or another.

In fact, research from John Bargh, Katelyn McKenna, and Grainne Fitzsimons
(2002) shows that people are better able to express and have others perceive
their "true self" online than off. In their experiment, participants were asked to
disclose components of their inner, nonpublic selves before logging into a chat

room. Their conversation partners were then asked to rate qualities about these people after their chat. Compared to a similar group of face-to-face conversants, those online were more accurately perceived. That is, their faceless conversation partners were better able to match their descriptors of the participants with the descriptors that the participants themselves had offered. Bargh et al. theorize that the qualities of the medium itself help to ease one's tensions about disclosing details that might be otherwise socially taboo. As we see shortly, the ability to be heard, but not seen, can be quite liberating. Let us consider first the role that language plays in text-only media such as chat rooms.

Learning One's Lines: Performing through Language

In the presentation of self in text-only media, one is not recognized by one's physical appearance, but through one's verbal behaviors. Obviously, one might offer a description of one's persona or disclose personal characteristics that contribute to others' impression formations. Yet according to Mark Giese (1998), there is another way that people come to identify an individual as participants interact with one another. "In a sense I am 'recognized' by a host of personal markers that include my writing style, my .sig [signature attachment], the way I conduct myself with various members of the groups and my contribution to the cooperative narrative." In short, both what people say about themselves and how they behave with others contribute to a perception of personal identity online. The use of language is consequently of immense importance in cyberspace, for it is through the use of language that people construct their identities.

Language is thus the primary vehicle for establishing one's own and perceiving another's online persona. A term for such figures originated among fantasy game-players and embraced among CMC practitioners is *avatar*. An avatar is a representation of oneself in a virtual environment, in other words, one's alter ego or persona. If you've ever used Instant Messenger icons on America Online or created a signature file to attach to your outgoing e-mail messages, then you are already somewhat familiar with the process of employing an avatar online.

The selection of a rather unusual term to express the relationships between identity and cyberspace is perhaps justified by the unusual nature of the medium itself. As with all mediated environments, one does not have a body in the nonspace of cyberspace, only a representation of oneself, wholly constructed by individual choices. Even in the case of a handwritten letter, which is seemingly devoid of many nonverbal cues, readers (like handwriting experts) infer qualities about the person on the other end based on something (loops in letters, dotting of letters) other than the content of what is written. Only in cyberspace is the proverbial playing field leveled of such biasing cues, suggesting that a new type of representation is occurring in this context.

Of course, the practice of representing oneself through language and controlled cues (as in Web pages that offer photographs or sound bites) is not above suspicion. People tend to mistrust what they cannot verify through other sources. We all know that lies are constructs of language. Even telling someone to "put it in writing" does not preclude deception. Socrates, whose philosophical treatises formed the foundations for Western thought, never committed a word to paper. (What we know of the insights attributed to him were set down by his pupil, Plato.) Socrates was suspicious of writing, fearing that someone could just as easily misquote him as quote him. The persistent fear that language does not provide an accurate depiction of reality is revisited in the construction of avatars. How are we to know that what we read is what we get? Contributing to a lack of ease is dealing with people only through their online presentations is the much-touted practice of gender-swapping.

Gender-Swapping: Performing in Virtual Drag

The opening vignette of this essay illustrates one well-known case in which gender-swapping was not favorably received. *Gender-swapping* occurs when an individual of one gender self-presents as a member of another gender. As you probably know, gender is a social construct that provides guidelines for how we expect people of a certain biological sex to behave. For example, men are expected to be masculine and thus strong and women to be feminine and thus compassionate. Such expectations are reinforced throughout our lives, so when we encounter someone who seemingly violates these stereotypes, we can be frustrated by the inconsistency. Several years ago, *Saturday Night Live* featured a character called Pat, and the confusion over whether Pat's name and behaviors were indicative of a man or a woman revealed how obsessed we are with gender (Bruckman, 1996).

Research has indicated that when people gender-swap (and more typically than not it is men portraying women), they tend to adopt the same rigid gender roles that their culture has come to expect (Bornstein, 1994). As such, masculine avatars devote a great deal of attention to, and will eagerly come to the aid of, female avatars (Bruckman, 1996). The perpetuation of stereotypical responses to gender such as this may explain why when someone is exposed for gender-swapping, others can respond with disbelief, confusion, or anger.

Reports of gender-swapping, and the anxieties that accompany it and other forms of misrepresentation, may yet prove to be overly exaggerated. According to research reported by Diane Schiano (1999), most people in online forums act as idealized versions of themselves (rather than markedly distinct individuals), and the majority of MUD participants maintain only one character. In fact, she found that participants experienced "an awareness of social pressure to maintain the authenticity and accountability afforded by a single primary identity." Such a finding corroborates survey results among people making presentations of self through personal Web sites. Approximately 67% of those responding to the survey reported that they do not feel it is appropriate for anyone to misrepresent themselves online (Buten, 1996). Interestingly, 91% agreed that they accurately represented themselves on their own home pages. Such research clearly suggests that although experimentation with identity is possible, it is neither encouraged nor the norm for the presentation of self.

ANONYMITY, PSEUDONYMITY, AND IDENTITY

When people enter chat rooms, contribute to bulletin boards, or participate in MUDs, they can exercise control over elements of their self-presentation. In choosing names, signature files, or personal descriptions, they make conscious decisions about how they wish to be perceived by others. The range of possible selves one might elect to present could be considered along a continuum of identification (Marx, 1999). At one end of this continuum would be the nearly emptied state of anonymity. Along the continuum would be differing levels of an invented self-representing pseudonymity. At the opposite end, then, would be the identity presented in real life (or as close as one could get to it through the limited stimuli of mediating technologies). In the section that follows, we look at the manipulation of identity along this continuum.

Anonymity

Although most Americans would consider being "up-front" with people to be a common value, the fact is that in many instances we value privacy even more than frankness. There are certain legitimate circumstances in which our safety is protected by issuing our messages anonymously. In mediated contexts, *anonymity* is a state of communicating where the identity of the communicator is not readily apparent. People use anonymity to solicit dates in newspaper and magazine advertisements, to report knowledge of criminal activities on police tip lines, to engage in whistle blowing activities that draw media or legal attention to corporate misdoing, and to seek shelter when involved in abusive relationships (Wayner, 1999). In such circumstances, not being obliged to disclose one's true identity, and thus risk one's personal security, may well encourage important messages that might not otherwise be communicated.

The ability to communicate anonymously has been a particularly thorny issue in CMC. Although anonymity can function to protect people from reprisals it can also distance them from accountability, that is, taking responsibility for what they say.... Some people misuse the anonymity that online communication technologies afford to commit crimes. According to Gia Lee (1996), the debates over online anonymity have centered on three key issues. The first issue has to do with the informative aspect of identity. Knowing the reputation of the person issuing a statement is a double-edged sword. On one hand, knowing who has said something suggests the credibility that person has to speak on that topic. For example, having information about a source's expertise on a given topic influences how much one will trust the source's position. On the other hand, knowing characteristics like the sender's gender, race, and social standing could lead to an unfair hearing based on receiver's personal biases and stereotypes. The second issue concerning anonymity deals with group pressures. One side of this argument suggests that people who must be associated with their ideas will only express things they truly believe. Knowing that others will judge them by what they say serves to minimize blind attacks. The other side of this argument suggests that anonymity allows others to express unpopular opinions or question conventional wisdom. Such statements can function as agents of change when those who issue them are not suffocated by group pressures to remain silent. The third issue involves the enforcement of existing legal restrictions on speech. Without knowing who has issued them, it is impossible for law enforcement agents to prosecute those who commit libel, obscenity, or copyright infringement.

Although there are no quick fixes to these debates, scholars and legal experts have suggested that a compromise would be to enact "a principle of truth in the nature of naming" (Marx, 1999). As such, either the people issuing anonymous messages or the ISP facilitating them would indicate that their statements were anonymous. Such "visible anonymity" (Lee, 1996) would still protect the interests of the source while signaling to the receiver that the source has, for whatever reason, chosen not to associate with the message.

Pseudonymity

If anonymity lies at one end of the identity continuum and one's real-life identity lies at the other, then pseudonymity covers a good deal of the area in between. *Pseudonym* comes from the Latin words for "false" and "name," and it provides an audience with the ability to attribute statements and actions to a common source. Like an anonym, a pseudonym provides its owner with some degree of protection. But unlike an anonym, a pseudonym allows one to contribute to the fashioning of one's own image. Authors and performers have long recognized such a virtue. In the 19th century, Samuel L. Clemens recognized that the river pilot's call, "Mark twain!" reflected his desire to be an author associated with life on the Mississippi River. A century later, would-be actor Bernard Schwartz realized that Tony Curtis was a much more glamorous name for earning recognition in Hollywood.

Although celebrities have popularized adopting pseudonyms, the practice of renaming oneself in different communication contexts is by no means inaccessible to common people. In fact, pseudonyms were quite popular among people who communicated on a medium that could be considered the predecessor to the Internet, CB radio. As we noted earlier, CB enthusiasts adopted *handles* to identify themselves when broadcasting messages over the airwaves. Because these messages were in the public arena, many people chose to participate in public discussions without giving out their real names (and some security) by using their handles instead. They also chose handles that allowed them to fashion some perception of their unique identities. As CB radio grew increasingly popular throughout the 1970s, participants adopted identities like "Stargazer" and "Midnight Delight," each of which conjures up distinct images of what the person behind them might be like. One researcher found that women users in particular tended to adopt handles that suggested either the temptress imagery of an Eve figure or the loyalty and purity of a Mary figure, depending on what type of image they wanted to project (Kalcik, 1985). The precedent established by CB users to choose a pseudonym that reflects some aspect of their personal disposition was paralleled by Internet communicators in the decades that followed.

Haya Bechar-Israeli (1995) investigated the function and personal importance of pseudonyms among IRC participants. Not surprisingly, Bechar-Israeli concluded that pseudonyms, or *nicks*, as these nicknames are known among IRCers, served as attempts to present the self in a single line of text.... The most frequently selected pseudonyms were referential of some quality of one's identity. Nearly one-half of these participants chose to disclose something about their character <shydude>, profession <medoctor>, state <sleepless>, or appearance <handsom> through their nick. Though very few people chose to use their actual names in this setting, a clear majority tended to share qualities about their identities that they wanted others to perceive through their choice of pseudonym.

The ownership of one's pseudonym is something fiercely guarded in these contexts. As Bechar-Israeli observed, when a participant discovers his or her nick in use by another, the original owner reacts with hostility toward the perceived identity thief. Hence, even though play with identity is possible in such environments, consistency of presentation is practiced, even valued, among participants.

This same sense of perpetuated and consistent identity is found among personal Web sites. Unlike text-only channels like MUDs and chat rooms, Web sites allow the transmission of text, pictures, animation, and sounds to convey an online identity. However, the inclusion of any of these additional sources of information is still under the control of the author, allowing the individual to determine what identity will be presented. Daniel Chandler (1997) pointed out that the ubiquitous "under construction" sign found on so many personal Web sites is indicative of a process of creating identity. People are building a representation of themselves for the consideration and approval of others.

Certainly, electing pseudonymity can produce an advantageous effect for those behind the false names, especially in opening channels to those who might be reticent to interact if their true names were known. In particular, research has indicated that working with pseudonyms can be a liberating experience for students. Andrea Chester and Gillian Gwynne (1998) conducted a class in which they and their students interacted exclusively online. Fully two thirds of their students later reported that they participated more in the online environment, where "there was no pressure to adhere to the scripts normally governing classroom behavior." The use of a pseudonym, one of the prerequisites for the course, allowed the participants to choose when and how they would disclose things like their gender, race, and other social demographics.

The veneer of the Internet allows us to determine how much of an identity we wish to front in online presentations. These images can range from a vague silhouette to a detailed snapshot. Whatever the degree of identity presented, however, it appears that control and empowerment are benefits for users of these communication technologies.

SUMMARY

… Establishing our own identities as well as determining the identities of others is surrounded by a host of issues, ranging from the metaphysical to the mundane. Although technology has introduced them into a new context, many of the questions about identity that we confront are as old as humanity's search for knowledge: Who am I? How can I get others to understand me? Can I accept that these people are who and what they claim to be? Certainly, we have not answered theses enduring questions…, but we have reviewed concepts that have cast these queries into new light. As Turkle has suggested, we are made to think about the nature of identity through these technologies. By examining points about telepresence, performance, and pseudonymity, we have indicated directions that people are following in pursuit of answers to these questions in this electronic era.

REVIEW QUESTIONS

1. List all the kinds of CMC and MUDs you are aware of.
2. According to this essay, why do Internet technologies "offer us the possibility of controlling more aspects of our identity for public consideration than has been possible before"?
3. Why do some people who study CMC call MUDs "identity workshops"?
4. Explain what an avatar is and how it functions.
5. What is the relationship between anonymity and pseudonymity online?

PROBES

1. Is what Erving Goffman calls "face-work" a process of being phony and artificial, or can face-work be authentic and sincere?
2. What are the disadvantages of engaging online in an "identity workshop"? What are some of the advantages?
3. The authors cite research that concludes that 91 percent of the people surveyed reported that they accurately represented themselves online. Do you believe this figure is correct for MySpace and Facebook entries? Discuss.
4. Agree or disagree and explain your position: Anonymous contributors to blogs are much more reckless and irresponsible in their postings than people who sign their contributions.

REFERENCES

Bargh, J. A., McKenna, K. Y. A., & Fitzsimons, G. M. (2002). Can you see the real me? Activation and expression of the "true self" on the internet. *Journal of Social Issues, 58,* 33–48.

Bechar-Israeli, H. (1995). From <Bonehead> to <cLoNehEAd>: Nicknames, play, and identity on Internet relay chat. *Journal of Computer-Mediated Communication, 1.* Retrieved January 22, 1998, from http:www.ascusc.org/jcmc/vol1/issue2/bechar.html

Bornstein, K. (1994). *Gender outlaw: On men, women, and the rest of us.* New York: Vintage Books.

Bruckman, A. (1992). *Identity workshop: Emergent social and psychological phenomena in text-based virtual reality.* Retrieved January 22, 1998, from ftp://ftp.lambda.moo.mud.org/pub/MOO/papers

Bruckman, A. S. (1996). Gender-swapping on the Internet. In P. Ludlow (Ed.), *High noon on the electronic frontier: Conceptual issues in cyberspace* (pp. 317–325). Cambridge, MA: MIT Press.

Buten, J. (1996). *The personal home page institute.* Retrieved, January 22, 1998, from http://www.asc.upenn.edu/usr/sbuten/survey/htm#top

Chandler, D. (1997). *Writing oneself in cyberspace.* Retrieved January 22, 1998, from http://www.aber.ac.uk/~dgc/hompgid.html

Chester, A., & Gwynne, G. (1998). Online teaching: Encouraging collaboration through anonymity. *Journal of Computer-Mediated Communication, 4.* Retrieved January 10, 2000, from http://www.ascusc.org/jcmc/vol4/issue2/chester.html

Cutler, R. H. (1996). Technologies, relations, and selves. In L. Strate, R. Jacobson, & S. B. Gibson (Eds.), *Communication and cyberspace: Social interaction in an electronic environment* (pp. 317–333). Cresskill, NJ: Hampton Press.

Giese, M. (1998). Self without body: Textual self-presentation in an electronic community. *First Monday, 3.* Retrieved January 10, 2000, from http://www.firstmonday.dk/issues/issue3_4/giese/index.html

Goffman, E. (1959). *The presentation of self in everyday life.* Garden City, NY: Anchor.

Lee, G. B. (1996). Addressing anonymous messages in cyberspace. *Journal of Computer Mediated Communication, 2.* Retrieved January 10, 2000, from http://www.ascusc.org/jcmc/vol2/issue1/anon.html

Marx, G. T. (1999). What's in a name? Some reflections on the sociology of anonymity. *Information Society, 15,* 99–112.

Rheingold, H. (n.d.). *Mind to mind with Sherry Turkle. Brainstorms.* Retrieved July 2, 2003, from http://www.well.com/user/hlr/texts/mindtomind/turkle/html

Schiano, D. J. (1999). Lessons from LambdaMOO: A social, text-based virtual environment. *Presence: Teleoperators & Virtual Environments, 8*(2), 127–140.

Stone, A. R. (1991). Will the real body please stand up? Boundary stories about virtual cultures. In M. Benedikt (Ed.), *Cyberspace: First steps* (pp. 81–118). Cambridge, MA: MIT Press.

Turkle, S. (1995). *Life on the screen: Identity in the age of the Internet.* New York: Simon & Schuster.

Vincent, A., & Shepherd, J. (1998). Experiences in teaching Middle East politics via internet-based role-play simulations. *Journal of Interactive Media in Education.* Retrieved July 1, 2003, from http://www-jime.open. ac.uk/98/11/vincent-98-11-01.html

Wayner, P. (1999). Technology for anonymity: Names by other nyms. *The Information Society, 15,* 91–97.

————

Deafness and the Riddle of Identity
Lennard J. Davis

Since at least the mid-1980s, it has been clear that, for many deaf and hearing people, deafness is a cultural marker. This article from *The Chronicle of Higher Education* begins with a reference to the 2006 demonstrations at Gallaudet University, the premier university serving deaf students and culture, about their (now ex-) president, Jane K. Fernandes. The point of the reference is to highlight the criticism of Fernandes that prompted demonstrations and eventually led to her resignation: that she was not "deaf enough."

As the author points out, deaf activists and scholars have used the civil rights movement as a model for the struggle to form a deaf identity. One step was to establish American Sign Language (ASL) as a genuine language, not just a set of gestures or pantomime. Native speakers of ASL have been considered to be the most complete and legitimate members of deaf culture.

But the author of this essay criticizes this way of defining this culture because "you have to patrol the fire wall between the deaf and nondeaf in very rigid ways." And attempts to define deafness in terms of ethnicity also don't hold up. Both efforts end up excluding people and creating marginalized communities.

In the end, this essay is an argument against defining any social group in terms of ethnicity, minority status, or national *identity.* The author seriously questions such labels as "black," "Latino," "Asian," "disabled," and "aged," all of which, like "deaf," construct groups of people as if they were surrounded by unclear and often unfair borders.

I have included this essay to encourage you to think about "identity politics." On the one hand, it is undeniable that identity negotiation is a part of interpersonal communication that is going on all the time. On the other hand, identity itself is a problematic construct. Perhaps, as this author argues, we should not try "to force the foot into a glass slipper" of defined identity but should "make a variety of new shoes that actually fit."

The recent demonstrations at Gallaudet University did more to launch deafness and deaf culture onto the national scene than any event since the release of the 1986 film *Children of a Lesser God*. Media reports of hour-by-hour dramas unfolding on the campus, culminating in a shutdown of the university, evoked in many people's minds the student revolution of the 60s. But in the hearing world, from blogosphere to op-ed page, observers expressed confusion about what the issues really were and why there was so much turmoil and anger over the mere choosing of an upperlevel administrator.

That administrator, Jane K. Fernandes, selected to be president, was quoted widely as saying that one of the reasons she was such a lightning rod for criticism was that deaf students and faculty members perceived her as "not deaf enough." That charge was quickly rebutted by many within the deaf community, who said that their opposition to Fernandes was based not on her degree of deafness but on her leadership style, decisions she had made in the past, irregularities in the selection process, and her inability to quell the agitation at Gallaudet.

But the "not deaf enough" issue is alive and well among deaf scholars, students, and activists. Even though Fernandes may have exaggerated that accusation to bolster her own position, and even though her detractors denied its relevance, the charge formed at least part of the subtext of students' anger and is a topic of debate within the deaf community. Now that passions have been spent and an interim president, Robert R. Davila, appointed, it might be useful to examine what deaf identity might be and how that identity fits in with current notions of other identities based on race, gender, sexual orientation, and so on. Even with all the recent hoopla about deaf issues, most people probably aren't paying a lot of attention to what goes on within the deaf community. But the discussions there can point the way to a new and better understanding of identity in our postmodern world.

What does it mean to be "not deaf enough"? In Fernandes's case, the accusation meant that she was not a native signer of American Sign Language (ASL). Fernandes learned to sign later in life; she is best described as a user of Pidgin Signed English (PSE), a blend of English and ASL. So she cannot speak with the "accentless" signs that would read, to a native signer, as the most elegant ASL. In effect, she would be speaking sign language the way that Henry Kissinger, Arnold Schwarzenegger, or perhaps Borat speak English.

Many hearing people would deem any prejudice against someone because of his or her accent shocking and unethical. To understand the issue, you have to know that ASL has become the armature on which the figure of deaf identity has been built. Until relatively recently, deafness was seen as simply a physical impairment: the absence of hearing. In the past, much discrimination against deaf people was based on the assumption that they were in fact people without language—that is, dumb. And "dumb" carried the sense of being not only mute but also stupid, as in a "dumb" animal.

But over the past 30 or so years, the status of deaf people has changed in important ways, as deaf activists and scholars have reshaped *the idea* of deafness, using the civil-rights movement as a model for the struggle to form a deaf identity. Deaf people came to be seen not just as hearing-impaired, but as a linguistic minority, isolated from the dominant culture because that culture didn't recognize or use ASL.

Important scholarship formed the foundation for this new construction of deafness as a sociological phenomenon rather than a physical impairment. That view of deafness became possible only after linguists like William C. Stockoe Jr. established ASL as a genuine language (in the late 50s and early 60s), not just a set of gestures or pantomime, as had been thought. Later, in 1993, Harlan Lane, a professor of psychology and linguistics at Northeastern University (and the winner of a 1991 MacArthur "genius award"), drew on the ideas of Edward Said and Michel Foucault to suggest that the deaf were like a colonized people. Lane was instrumental in defining deaf identity based on the notion that deaf people were a linguistic and even an ethnic minority, since they not only shared a common language (ASL) and, by this time, a common culture, but also were seen by others as a separate group.

Other deaf-studies scholars who solidified the concept of the deaf as a minority group include Carol Padden, Tom Humphries, Jack R. Gannon, John Vickrey Van Cleve, Benjamin J. Bahan, Paddy Ladd, and MJ Bienvenu.

The definition of the deaf as a colonized, ethnic, linguistic minority has in turn been widely accepted in deaf circles and taught for more than a decade in deaf-studies programs and at institutions like Gallaudet and the National Technical Institute for the Deaf. It was that definition of deaf identity that fueled some of the student animosity toward Fernandes and the protests at Gallaudet. (Fernandes was also seen as lacking other characterisitics, besides classic ASL proficiency, that deaf "insiders" consider crucial to "pure" deafness: a physical warmth and directness that is intense and intimate; pride in being deaf; and a certain attitude, both amused and cynical, toward the hearing world that results from a shared set of experiences. Fernandes was seen as not having those traits and experiences, and as being cold, aloof, detached from those markers—in sum, "not deaf enough.")

The construct of the deaf as a linguistic, ethnic minority is attractive, but flawed. Yes, it has removed the biological stigma of deafness; for the most part, the deaf are no longer viewed as " handicapped" or "disabled." Deaf people get to be a sociological group, a "community." But there is a negative side: The idea of an ethnic group or minority is tinged with the brutal history of racial politics. There is a sense in which slavery, apartheid, miscegenation laws, and medical experiments have forged the apartness of the racialized minority and in which the oppressor group has created the oppressed. Is that the best model on which deafness should base its existence? Furthermore, a re-examination of identity politics is under way in this country that questions even the concept of group identity. Postmodernism combined with globalization has undermined traditional notions of individual and community. It's hard enough to say what it is to be an "American" now, let alone a member of a minority in the United States. It seems to me the minority model of deaf identity is too crude, too rigid, too limiting.

The central problem with defining deaf people as a linguistic group is that to do so, you have to patrol the fire wall between the deaf and nondeaf in very rigid ways. If deaf people are defined as only those who are native users of ASL, you have to define all nonusers of ASL as "other." That excludes, or at least marginalizes, deaf people who are orally trained—that is, who were taught to eschew ASL for speech alone; have cochlear implants; or never had the chance to learn sign language. Many people who grew up in non-ASL settings in the 1950s and 1960s and who have quite happily thought of themselves as deaf would have to reassign themselves to some other camp. Likewise, the strict linguistic-group definition expels hard-of-hearing people who have not learned ASL. Ironically, the model also stigmatizes those who have been educated orally; they are seen as victims of oral education rather than as victims of audism. Since it is hearing parents who usually make the decision to educate their deaf children orally, rather than with ASL, or to give them cochlear implants, it doesn't seem fair to define those children as not deaf. The other flaw in the model is that it defines hearing, signing children of deaf adults (CODA's) as deaf, since they are native sign-language speakers. One could argue that CODA's aren't discriminated against by the hearing world, but if one takes that tack, then one has to abandon the idea that language is the key defining term. And that brings us back to some notion of deafness as a biological impairment.

Defining deafness in terms of ethnicity doesn't hold up any better than linguistic definitions. While it is true that many deaf people share a common culture, history, language, and social behavior, with the advent of the Internet, the mainstreaming of deaf students into regular classrooms, the decline of residential schooling for the deaf, and the demise of deaf clubs (where deaf people in large cities gathered regularly to socialize), it is harder to argue that the deaf are significantly different from the nondeaf. There is less of a *there* there. Changes in the overall culture have to some degree erased the sense of "otherness" that the deaf historically have held on to as a way of defining themselves. That is why places like Gallaudet have come to be seen nostalgically as the "home" of deaf people and deaf culture: They continue to define the deaf as a separate cultural group. (Naturally the choice of an overseer of such a safe house would be seen as crucial, since that person would be a kind of keeper of the flame.)

The argument that the deaf are an ethnic minority also presupposes a "pure" deaf person, imitating the worst aspects of racial profiling. In this ethnic-group model, just as in the linguistic model, there is an in-group and an out-group. Those most "in" are deaf-on-deaf people, that very small percentage (perhaps only 5 percent of all those born deaf) who come from a deaf family—that is, whose parents were born deaf. The elite also includes those who have been lucky enough to have attended Gallaudet, the National Technical Institute for the Deaf, and other deaf institutions of higher education. Excluded are the hard of hearing, those who learned to lip-read and speak instead of sign, hearing children of deaf adults, those who never had a chance to learn sign language (because they were too poor, or the facilities weren't available), and deaf people with limb impairments or spinal injuries that make it impossible for them to sign.

Further complicating definitions of deafness are all things digital. Deafness "disappears" in cyberspace. While using the Internet or pagers, for example, deaf people do not use language much differently from anyone else. In the blogosphere, we are all bloggers, whether we are deaf or not.

And is a deaf person excluded from his ethnic identity of deafness if he or she chooses not to act deaf? Some deaf people have lip-reading and speaking skills that might allow them to pass for hearing. Others might choose to avoid the more obvious deaf markers—such as colloquial ASL, physical warmth, and intensity—that I've already mentioned. African-Americans who speak standard English and do not code-switch are sometimes accused of being "Oreos"—black on the outside and white on the inside. Do we really want to go down the road of thinking of some people as deaf "Oreos"? (Or would the comparative term be "cochleos"?)

The ethnic model is also dubious because of the current association between ethnic groups and violence. Regionalism, tribalism, and ethnicity have recently led to wars in Darfur, Bosnia, and the Middle East. Is the model of ethnic pride really more desirable than a cosmopolitan internationalism?

One of the key notions of an *ethnos,* a people, is the idea of an extended kinship system. People within an ethnic group are related not only by language, history, and culture, but also by a family structure that passes along a genetic inheritance. But the vast majority of deaf people do not come from deaf families. According to a widely cited statistic, well over 90 percent of deaf people are born to hearing families. The deaf, hearing children of deaf adults, people with disabilities, and queer folk are, as the deaf-studies scholar Robert J. Hoffmeister has written, only "one generation thick," having parents and children most likely different from them. In that sense, those four groups have more in common with each other than with any ethnic group. One can argue that deaf people pass along their culture through a nonkinship system, but then you are talking about a different kind of social organization than an ethnic group.

Related to this point is a strategic issue. Are legal protections for ethnic groups used as effectively to redress problems related to disability as those in the Americans With Disabilities Act? Does one want to choose the category of ethnic group as the regnant defining term and then seek legal protection or redress under that status? Or is it better to allow legal rights and protections to apply under the statutes that cover disability? People with disabilities have fought hard and revised our notion of civil rights. Why should deaf people adhere to a problematic notion of ethnicity when their rights are more clearly protected under the rubric of disability?

The concept "deaf world" or "deaf culture" (indicated by ASL signs) is compelling for many deaf people. It does not have any associations with biological deficiency or race. The problem with the terms is that they are too general and too elastic. If you start defining what you mean by either, you immediately fall back into categorical generalizations of the kind we have been discussing. Who is deaf? Who belongs in the "deaf world"? How do you get into it? Who are the gatekeepers? What makes "deaf culture" different from any other culture? If one were to substitute "white world," "black world," "Jewish world," or "non-Jewish

world" for "deaf world," would one be happy to celebrate and analyze the meaning of those terms? What if we said "ASL-users-only world," or "40-percent- to
100-percent-hearing-loss world"?

The problem with such concepts is that they exclude people, reduce their
rights, and create marginalized communities. And then there is the question
of who gets to set up the barriers and checkpoints. In the past, it was hearing
people who did; now segments of the deaf community have declared themselves the gatekeepers, by defining deafness in the narrowest possible terms.
Of course no group of people can exist without some kind of cultural and social
distinctions. But in thinking through, in the best theoretical sense, new directions for deafness, we have to look at the problems and the solutions with a high
degree of rigor.

Deaf people aren't the only ones struggling to define themselves in this new
age of post-identity. They don't have to go it alone. What brings together all the
social injustices of the past 200 years is the idea that people with various bodily
traits have been discriminated against because of those traits. Rather than *defining* people according to those traits, a newer, more-inclusive concept of identity
holds that you can't base your full and complex identity on those putative
bodily traits because you can't justify their existence as markers anymore. The
grand categories of race, gender, and so on are no longer valid because they
no longer contain rigid fire walls. Who is black and who is white, who is a
man and who is a woman are questions whose answers are murkier than ever.
Likewise, deafness as a category can exist only if you rely on comparably rigid
fire walls. If you let go of the idea of rigid boundaries, then you have to face a
more continuous line of possibilities, including the hearing-impaired, hard of
hearing, partially deaf, profoundly deaf, and so on. You also have to deal with
people with varying degrees of both oral and ASL abilities, including a range
of ASL usage among children of deaf adults. So the concept of deafness can get
very messy, unless you perform a kind of "common sense" purifying of the
category—which might work, but has the same pitfalls as "common sense" racial categories, for example. Common sense in this context is really just socially
constructed truisms that are never really common at all.

I am arguing that defining the deaf or any other social group in terms of
ethnicity, minority status, and nationhood (including "deaf world" and "deaf
culture") is outdated, outmoded, imprecise, and strategically risky. We would
be better off expanding our current notions of identity by being less Procrustean
and more flexible. Rather than trying to force the foot into a glass slipper, why
not make a variety of new shoes that actually fit?

In that scenario, for example, people who are "one generation thick" could
find commonality. So people with disabilities, deaf people, gay people, and
children of deaf adults could say: We represent one potential way out of the
dead end of identity politics. We are social groups that are not defined solely by
bodily characteristics, genetic qualities, or inherited traits. We are not defined by
a single linguistic practice. We need not be defined in advance by an oppressor.
We choose to unite ourselves for new purposes. We are not an ethnic or minority

group, but something new and different, emerging from the smoke of identity politics and rising like a phoenix of the postmodern age.

REVIEW QUESTIONS

1. Describe in your own words some of the problems that arose when Gallaudet president Jane Fernandes was criticized for being "not deaf enough."
2. Explain the two ways of defining a culture that this author discusses—using linguistic markers or defining deafness in terms of ethnicity.
3. What point does the author make about deafness in cyberspace?

PROBES

1. How does the author, Lennard J. Davis, connect the dispute over deaf identity with identities based on race, gender, sexual orientation, and so on?
2. Review the description of why Fernandes was criticized—she was not proficient enough in ASL, she lacked a certain variety of physical warmth and directness, and so on. How is this definition of what it "means" to be "deaf" similar to the definition of what it "means" to be "gay," "lesbian," "black," or "Latino"?
3. Explain the question the author raises about the advantages and disadvantages of deaf people defining themselves in terms of civil rights versus people with disabilities.
4. The author seems to be arguing against all group identity labels. Is it practical to treat people always as individuals?

CHAPTER 4

Verbal and Nonverbal Contact

Verbal and Nonverbal Dimensions of Talk

John Stewart and Carole Logan

This next reading starts with its own introduction and is longer than most, so I'll make this short. These pages come from the 1998 edition of an interpersonal communication text that I co-authored with Carole Logan, a colleague who teaches communication at the University of San Diego. As you can tell from the title, the reading reverses the popular tendency to discuss verbal and nonverbal communicating in separate chapters. We explain why at the start.

This selection is broad enough in coverage to give you a fairly comprehensive introduction to both language and most nonverbal cues. We resist the "verbal/nonverbal" dichotomy by locating the main communication building blocks on a continuum or sliding scale that runs from primarily verbal (written words), to mixed (vocal pacing, pause, loudness, pitch, and silence), to primarily nonverbal (gestures, eye gaze, facial expression, touch, and space). Our goal is to encourage you to view these aspects of your communicating as holistically as you can and to notice the ways the various kinds of cues affect each other.

We briefly review the three main ways language has been discussed—as a system of symbols, an activity, and what we call a "soup." Then we discuss some features of mixed and primarily nonverbal cues. If you read both this introductory overview and the three other readings in this chapter, I think you'll have a pretty decent understanding of these parts of communication's basic ingredients.

Interpersonal communication texts typically devote one chapter to verbal codes and a separate one to nonverbal communication. This practice began in the late 1960s when communication researchers and teachers first discovered the importance of the nonverbal parts of communicating— eye contact, body movement, facial expression, tone of voice, touch, silence, and so on. For about 30 years, most textbooks treated each subject as significant and distinct.

But now research is focusing more and more closely on conversations as people actually experience them, and it has become obvious that you can't really separate the verbal and nonverbal parts. In the words of two researchers, "It is impossible to study either verbal or nonverbal communication as isolated structures. Rather, these systems should be regarded as a unified communication construct."[1] And as teacher and theorist Wendy Leeds-Hurwitz puts it, "In discussing communication as consisting of verbal and nonverbal modes ... we leave ourselves open to the impression that the two are somehow distinct and should be studied separately. This is not at all the case, and there is now a current body of literature devoted to rejoining the two."[2]

Interestingly, almost this same point was made at the beginning of the twentieth century by Ferdinand de Saussure, one of the founders of linguistics. Saussure said that language is like a sheet of paper, where sound makes up one side of the page and the concepts or thoughts make up the other. You can't pick up one side of the paper without picking up the other, and you can't cut one side without cutting the other. So it's best to think of them together.[3] We think the same way about the verbal and the nonverbal parts of communication; they're like the two sides of one sheet of paper.

This is actually the way they occur in human experience. For example, consider this conversation:

SCOTT: *(Smiling and nodding)* Hi, John Paul. Howzit goin'?

JOHN PAUL: *(Excited look)* Scott! *(Shaking hands)* It's good to see you! I heard you'd moved. Where've you *been*?

SCOTT: *(Smiling knowingly)* Nowhere, really. I've just been working and going to school. But Heather and I have been hanging out together quite a bit.

JOHN PAUL: *(Teasing)* Yeah, I heard that. What's the story with you two anyway?

SCOTT: *(Playful but cagey)* What do you mean "What's the story"? We just like each other, and we spend a lot of time together.

JOHN PAUL: *(Still teasing)* Yeah, like all weekend. And every afternoon. And most of the rest of the time.

SCOTT: *(Turning the tables)* Well, what about you and Bill? I've heard you two are a duo ... partners ... an item.

JOHN PAUL: *(A little shy)* Where'd you hear that? Yeah, it's pretty true. *(Brighter)* And it's kind of neat, actually. It's the first time I've felt like part of *a couple.* We might even get an apartment together. But he's got to get a job that pays more. I can't support both of us.

SCOTT: *(Friendly)* Sounds like you've got the same questions Heather and I have. But her folks are also a problem.

JOHN PAUL: *(Serious)* My mom and dad are fine. But Bill's parents don't know anything about us, and I'm trying to get him to change that. In fact, I was thinking that I'd like to talk to you about that. I also wonder how you and Heather plan to actually set up living together. But I've got to get to work now. Give me your cell number so I can give you a call, okay?

John Paul and Scott build this conversation together by using verbal and nonverbal aspects of language simultaneously. There is never a point in the talk where these two parts of communicating are separate. When Scott's intent is to be "playful," he communicates this verbally and nonverbally to John Paul. When the tone of the conversation turns "serious," John Paul communicates this through posture, facial expression, and tone of voice, as well as through the words he chooses.

This chapter emphasizes the fact that people engaged in conversation construct all verbal and nonverbal aspects of talk together. To put it in researchers' terms, utterance meaning and nonverbal meaning are not discrete and independent.[4] This is true even of words written on a page. What you might consider to be "purely verbal" written words appear in a designed typeface, on a certain weight and color of paper, and surrounded by more or less white space. All of these nonverbal elements affect how people interpret the written words of any language. Similarly, even purely nonverbal behaviors, such as gestures or eye behavior, occur in the context of some spoken or written words. One way to sort out the verbal and nonverbal aspects of language is to think in terms of a continuum or sliding scale like the following.

Primarily Verbal _____	**Mixed** _____	**Primarily Nonverbal**
written words	vocal pacing, pause, loudness, pitch, silence	gestures, eye gaze, facial expression, touch, space

Written words are classified as primarily verbal for the reasons we just gave. They appear in a nonverbal typeface surrounded by nonverbal space, but readers interpret or make meaning primarily on the basis of the words' verbal content. To the degree that you can isolate the words speakers use, they might be considered primarily verbal, too. But spoken words always come with vocal pacing, pause, loudness, pitch, and silence, and as a result these are labeled mixed. Gestures, facial expression, and so on are labeled primarily nonverbal because they can occur without words, but they are usually interpreted in the context of spoken words.

It would be possible to highlight some of the verbal parts of Scott and John Paul's conversation. Scott says, "Howzit going'?" rather than "How is it going?" or the even more formal "It's good to see you again." He uses the general phrase "spending a lot of time together" rather than a more specific description of his and Heather's activities. For John Paul, the word "couple" is significant. The two share an understanding of what it means, in this context, to say that parents are a "problem."

We could also pinpoint some nonverbal aspects of the conversation. For example, Scott's initial tone of voice is pretty low-key, but John Paul sounds excited to see him. They touch briefly as they shake hands. Their smiles "say" several different things—"It's good to see you." "I like you." "I'm teasing." "I'm teasing back." "We've got something in common." Since they're friends, they stand fairly close together.

In order to focus on the exclusively verbal or exclusively nonverbal parts, however, we'd have to distort what actually happens in Scott and John Paul's conversation. As we've said, the verbal and nonverbal aspects of the conversation are as inseparable as the two sides of a piece of paper. So in this reading:

We describe three approaches to *primarily verbal* cues ("language") that help clarify our reasons for combining verbal and nonverbal communication.

We discuss how several *mixed* cues affect meaning-making and how facial expression and gestures work together with words.

We describe the five most influential *primarily nonverbal* cues—facial expression, eye contact and gaze, space, touch, and body movement and gesture.

THREE APPROACHES TO STUDYING PRIMARILY VERBAL CUES (LANGUAGE)

1. Language Is a System of Symbols

Historically, this is the oldest point of view. From this perspective, language is a system made up of different kinds of words and the rules governing their combinations. Your grade-school teachers emphasized the systematic features of language when they helped you learn the differences among nouns, verbs, adjectives, and adverbs and the rules for making grammatical sentences. When you think of German, Mandarin Chinese, or Spanish as a "language," you're thinking of it as a language *system*. Dictionaries record a part of a language system and provide a record of, for example, word histories and new words like ROM, uplink, and downsize.

Those who study language as a system emphasize that it is a system of symbols. They develop a point made about 2,500 years ago when the Greek philosopher Aristotle began one of his major works on language this way: "Spoken words are the symbols of mental experience and written words are the symbols of spoken words."[5] As a contemporary linguist explains, "This criterion implies that for anything to be a language it must function so as to *symbolize* (represent for the organism) the not-necessarily-*here* and not-necessarily-*now*."[6] In brief, since a symbol is something that stands for something else, this approach emphasizes that units of language—words, usually—represent, or stand for, chunks or pieces of nonlinguistic reality. In the simplest terms, the word "cat" stands for the furry, purring, tail-twitching animal sitting in the corner.

One of the features of symbols that this approach also highlights is that they're _arbitrary_. This means that there is no necessary relationship between the word and the thing it symbolizes. Even though the word *five* is physically smaller than the word *three,* the quantity that *five* symbolizes is larger. So there's no necessary relationship between word (in this case, its size) and meaning. Or consider the words that people from different language communities use to symbolize a dwelling where someone lives: *casa* in Spanish, *maison* in French, and *Haus* in German. This couldn't happen unless the relationship between the word and its meaning were arbitrary.

A classic book, first published in 1923, elaborated just this point. Its authors, C. K. Ogden and I. A. Richards, diagrammed this insight with their famous "triangle of meaning" (see Figure 4-1). Ogden and Richards' triangle is meant to

FIGURE 4-1 Ogden and Richards' triangle of meaning.

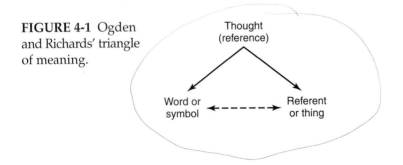

illustrate how words are related to both thoughts and things. The word-thought relationship is direct—that's why the line is solid. For Aristotle, words stood for thoughts. The relationship between thought and thing was also more or less direct. But the word-thing relationship is arbitrary; there is no necessary relationship between the word and its referent. The dotted line across the bottom of the triangle emphasizes this point.

The main advantage of viewing language as a system of arbitrary symbols is that it alerts us to the dangers of abstractions and of the assumptions people make about what words mean by emphasizing that the *thought* or meaning associated with a word may or may not be directly related to the *thing* the word symbolizes. The clearest, most easily understood words are those that are easiest to connect with concrete reality: "this car," "my CD collection," "his blue hair." But from Ogden and Richards' point of view, people should be careful with abstract words like "safety," "style," "love," and "honesty," because the thoughts that they call up may or may not be linked to concrete realities that they symbolize. One person's writing or talk about safety may be connected with safety pins, bank vaults, or a seat belt, and because of the dotted-line relationship in the triangle, the individual to whom the person is writing or talking may not be able to tell the difference. We can also learn from this perspective that, since the relationship between words and meanings is arbitrary, we should never assume that another person means exactly what we do, even when he or she uses the same words. What does "early" mean, for example, when your mom or dad tells you to "get home early"? When your teacher says you should "get started early on your papers"? When the person you're dating feels it's too early in the relationship for sex? When you tell your roommate you want to get up early? Assumptions about identical word meaning often create communication problems.

This view of language is also drastically oversimplified, however. The triangle of meaning makes it appear that language is essentially made up of concrete nouns, labels for things in the world. It doesn't take much reflection to realize that language is much more complicated than that. Often the topic you're discussing and the ideas you want to express require abstract words, such as "love," "pride," and "homelessness." The advice to avoid these kinds of words because there are no "things" or "referents" to which they are even arbitrarily related is not very practical. And what about words like "and," "whether," "however," and "larger"? It can be really confusing to try to figure out what things these words symbolize. Even more important, we don't usually experience language as individual words, but as statements, utterances, messages, or parts of a conversation. So an approach that tries to explain living language by focusing on individual words has to be limited. All this is why it's partly true to say that language is a system of symbols, but there's much more to it than that.

2. Language Is an Activity

A second, more recent approach to the study of language views it as an activity. The most influential version of this approach began in the 1950s when several researchers showed how many utterances actually perform actions. They called these utterances "speech acts." For example, the words "I will" or "I do" in a marriage ceremony are not just symbolizing or referring to getting married. Rather, they are an important part of the activity of marrying itself. If they're not said at the right time by the right people, the marriage hasn't happened. Similarly, the words "I agree" or "Okay, it's a deal" can perform the activity of buying, selling, or contracting for work. And "Howzitgoin'?" is not about a greeting; it is the activity of greeting itself. A group of researchers called conversation analysts have shown how to extend and apply this insight about the action-performing function of language.

Conversation analysts, for instance, have identified the crucial features of many of the speech acts that people typically perform, such as promise, request, threat, offer, command, compliment, and greeting.[8] Each of these terms labels what certain utterances *do* rather than what they symbolize or say. And, these researchers point out, a given utterance won't perform this action unless it has certain features. For example, a *request* requires the speaker to ask for a preferred future behavior from the hearer, and the person who hasn't done this has not competently performed a request. A *promise* is also about a preferred future behavior, but it identifies what the speaker rather than the hearer will do.

If you understand the building blocks of each speech act, you can see why some *indirect* requests and promises will work and others won't. For example, "Are you taking your car to the game tonight?" could function as a *request* for a ride to the game, even though it does not actually identify a preferred future behavior. But it can only work as a request when the context allows both speaker and hearer to fill in the parts that the words themselves leave out. This explains how problems arise when one person fills in the blanks and another doesn't, or when one person means or hears a promise even though the crucial parts of the speech act are absent. For example, when Reggie and Kevin were discussing the game they both wanted to attend, Reggie heard Kevin's "Yeah, I'll be driving" as a *promise* to give him a ride. But Kevin meant it only as a response to Reggie's direct question. So he was surprised and a little angry when Reggie called to confirm the ride he'd "promised."

Conversation analysts have also studied several ways in which people collaborate to mutually construct some speech acts. For example, greetings, goodbyes, invitations, apologies, offers, and congratulations are all speech acts that almost always require two or more conversational moves rather than just one. If one conversation partner greets the other, the expectation is that the other will respond with another greeting. If this doesn't happen, the speech act of "greeting" has only partly occurred. The same thing happens with goodbyes; it takes both one person's "goodbye" *and* the other person's response. This requirement can create problems when one person means to be leaving and the other doesn't pick up on it. Similarly, an invitation is expected to be followed by an acceptance, questioning, or rejection of the invitation; an apology is expected to be followed by an acceptance or rejection, and so on. As one conversation analyst puts it:

As we shall see, when one of these first actions has been produced, participants orient to the presence or absence of the relevant second action. There is an expectation by participants that the second action should be produced, and when it does not occur, participants behave as if it should have.[9]

Many insights into language use have been generated by people viewing it as an activity that people carry out by following certain sets of conversational rules. At the same time, the more researchers have studied communication as people actually experience it, the more they've recognized that although a great deal can be learned about the individual moves conversation partners make with their various speech acts, natural conversations almost always include unpredictable events or surprises. People improvise as much as they follow conversational rules. In other words, there is a structure to conversation, but it is less like the repetitive pattern followed by a supermarket checkout clerk and more like the loose and varied collaboration of five good musicians getting together to jam.

In summary, conversation analysts have demonstrated the value of studying language as an activity. They have shown that every time we say something, we're also doing something—that speech is a kind of action. They have catalogued many of the actions that people perform by talking and have also shown that some of these actions are produced collaboratively. But they have only been able to consider a few of the important nonverbal elements of conversation, and they have had to admit that there is almost as much improvisation as rule following. Every day people engage in greetings, goodbyes, promises, threats, compliments, offers, commands, requests, and dozens of other conversation acts. But we also improvise and modify expected patterns. Finally, conversation analysts have very little to say about the crucial identity-constructing function of communication.... We believe that the most helpful approach to language is the one that includes a focus on identities.

3. Language Is a Soup

This may sound a little weird, but stay with us for a few paragraphs. This approach does include identities.

Especially in the last 30 years, many scholars have recognized the limitations of both the system and action views of language. Both of these views treat language as a tool that humans manipulate, either to arbitrarily stand for some referent or to perform an action. As we have explained, there's some truth to these views, and they can teach us some important things about language. But language is more than a tool. If it were just a tool, we could lay it aside when we didn't need it and pick up some other tool, just as we can lay aside a screwdriver and pick up a hammer. But we can't do that. As humans, we're immersed in language, like a fish is immersed in water. And this quality is what the "soup" metaphor is meant to highlight. As one writer puts it:

> In all our knowledge of ourselves and in all knowledge of the world, we are always already encompassed by the language that is our own. We grow up,

and we become acquainted with [people] and in the last analysis with ourselves when we learn to speak. Learning to speak does not mean learning to use a preexistent tool for designating a world already somehow familiar to us; it means acquiring a familiarity and acquaintance with the world itself and how it confronts us.[10]

This is what it means to say that language is a soup. We're immersed in it from birth to death, just as a fish is immersed in the water in which it lives.

In fact, language experience may begin even before birth. As soon as 20 weeks after conception, the human fetus has functioning ears and is beginning to respond to sounds.[11] Its mother's voice is clearly one sound the fetus learns to identify.[12] Some pregnant couples talk to and play music for their unborn child. When the infant is born, it typically enters an environment of exclamations and greetings. Then verbal and nonverbal communication experiences fill the infant's life. Touch, eye contact, smiles, and a great deal of talk are directed to him or her. As infants develop, parents and other caregivers invite them into conversations or exclude them from conversations by providing a context for talk, by encouraging them with positive attitudes toward talk or discouraging them with negative attitudes, and by interpreting, modeling, and extending talk.[13] This process continues right up to the last tearful goodbyes a person hears at death. In between, humans live more or less like nutritious morsels in a broth of language. This soup includes all the verbal and nonverbal parts of our communicative life. In fact, the theorists and researchers who treat language as a soup have begun to mean by "language" what used to be called "communication"—all the verbal and nonverbal, oral and nonoral, ways that humans make meaning together. As you might be assuming, this view of language fits most comfortably with the approach to communication outlined in Chapter 2.

Language and Perception   If this notion of language as a soup sounds a little abstract, consider one important practical implication of the fact that language is all-encompassing: Because we are immersed in language all our lives, language and perception are thoroughly interrelated. . . . When we perceive, we select, organize, and make meaning out of the things and events we see, hear, touch, taste, and smell. The point that language and perception are thoroughly interrelated means that everything we perceive, all the things that make up our world, is affected by the language in which we live. In the early 20th century, one version of this insight about language and perception was called the SapirWhorf hypothesis, for the two people who originally wrote about it, Edward Sapir and Benjamin Lee Whorf. It was summarized by Whorf in these words:

> The background linguistic system (in other words, the grammar) of each language is not merely a reproducing instrument for voicing ideas but rather is itself the shaper of ideas, the program and guide for the individual's mental activity, for his [or her] analysis of impressions. . . . We dissect nature along lines laid down by our native language.[14]

Thus, if you have spent enough time on boats and around the water to learn a dozen different words for water conditions, you will perceive more differences in the water than will the person who was born and raised in Cheyenne, Oklahoma City, or Calgary. That person might distinguish between *waves* and *smooth water,* but you will see and feel differences between *cats' paws, ripples, chop,* and *swells* that he or she probably won't even notice.[15] Or if you have learned important meanings for *latex, natural, lubricated,* and *spermicidal,* you can make distinctions among condoms that were impossible for the high school graduate of the 1970s or early 1980s.

A Chinese-American woman, Mandy Lam, made the point that she felt "similar to the fish that lives in an area of water where the river mixes with the ocean. I have only to travel a little further in either direction to experience the extremes." Her grandparents speak only Chinese, and she relates to them, and often to her parents and other elders, in Chinese ways. But all her premed classes are in English, and she lives in an almost completely English world at school.

As the two of us try in this [essay] to write about communication as a continuous, complex, collaborative meaning-making process, we especially notice two particular ways in which our native language limits our perceptions. The first has to do with the ways that the English language affects how people understand ongoing processes. Unlike some languages, English maintains clear distinctions between noun subjects and verb predicates, causes and effects, beginnings and ends, and this affects how native English speakers perceive communication. A surprising number of other language systems do not do this. According to one researcher, for example, Navajo speakers characteristically talk in terms of processes—uncaused, ongoing, incomplete, dynamic happenings. The word that Navajos use for wagon, for example, translates roughly as "wood rolls about hooplike."[16] The Navajo words that we would translate as "He begins to carry a stone" mean not that the actor produces an action, but that the person is simply linked with a given round object and with an already existing, continuous movement of all round objects in the universe. The English language, by contrast, requires its users to talk in terms of present, past, future, cause and effect, beginning and end. Problems arise when some things that English speakers would like to discuss just can't be expressed in these terms. To continue our example, we would like to be able to talk more clearly about the emergent, ongoing nature of communication.... But, especially since communication doesn't always obey the rules of cause and effect, the noun-plus-verb-plus-object structure of the English language makes it difficult to do this. For this topic, Navajo would probably work better than English.

The second way in which we notice that the English language affects our discussion of communication has to do with the ways English speakers perceive gender differences. One accomplishment of research encouraged by the feminist movement of the 1960s and 1970s is that people now recognize how the male bias of standard American English has contributed to the ways in which English-speaking cultures perceive women and men. The fact that, until recently, there were no female firefighters was not caused simply by the existence of the word fire*man*. It's not that simple. But research indicates that gender-biased words affect perceptions in at least three ways. They shape people's attitudes about careers that are "appropriate" for one sex but not for the other, they lead some women to believe that certain jobs and roles aren't attainable, and they contribute to the belief that men deserve higher status in society than do women.[17] This is why changes in job titles have helped open several occupations to more equal male-female participation. Consider, for example, *parking checker* instead of *metermaid, chair* or *chairperson* instead of *chairman, salesperson* instead of *salesman,* and *server* instead of *waiter* or *waitress.* We have also just about stopped referring to female physicians as woman doctors and female attorneys as lady lawyers, and it is more than a coincidence that these changes have been accompanied by significant increases in the numbers of women in these two professions.

Since the mid-1990s, both scholarly and popular books have emphasized this point about gender, language, and perception by highlighting the differences between the language worlds into which men and women are socialized in North America. Sociolinguist Deborah Tannen's book *You Just Don't Understand: Women and Men in Communication*[18] was on the best-seller list for months, and John Gray has sold millions of copies of *Men Are from Mars, Women Are from Venus*[19] and *Mars and Venus in Love.*[20] All of these books describe the ways in which women's communication differs from men's and explain how many problems between genders are influenced by these differences. Some people complain that the books reinforce the very stereotypes they're trying to reduce by generalizing about "women's communication" and "men's communication." Despite the very real danger of this oversimplification, however, there is considerable research evidence to indicate that most North American, English-speaking women and most of their male counterparts do communicate differently. In other words, carefully controlled observations of how these men and women actually talk found that there are important gender-linked patterns.

The women observed in these studies generally use communication as a primary way to establish and maintain relationships with others, whereas the men generally talk to exert control, preserve independence, and enhance status. More specifically, most of these women's communicating is characterized by seven features that are not generally found in the men's talk: an emphasis on equality, support, attention to the relationship, inclusivity, concreteness, and tentativeness, and a preference for collaborative meaning-making. Men's communicating is described in this same research as functioning to exhibit knowledge or skill, accomplish goals, assert dominance, avoid tentativeness, stay abstract rather than concrete, and minimize relationship responsiveness.[21]...

To summarize, from the point of view of this soup or fish-in-water idea, language is more than a *system* we use or an *activity* we perform. It is larger than any of us; it happens to us and we are subject to it as much as we manipulate or use it.... When studied from this third perspective, language has both verbal and nonverbal aspects. Language researchers and teachers have become increasingly aware that languaging as people actually live it is less of a system or action and more of a mutual event or collaborative process. "Language" is the term these researchers and teachers use for the communicating that, as [was] said in Chapter 2, makes us who we are.

MIXED CUES: VOICE, SILENCE, FACE AND WORDS, GESTURES AND WORDS

The first section of this reading was about the primarily verbal parts of communication—the parts that are often called "language." By now, you know that language includes both verbal and nonverbal elements, but that it can still be distinguished from the "mixed" parts, which include the rate, pitch, volume, and quality of the voice; silence; facial expressions accompanying words; and gestures that accompany words. Let's consider next how these mixed cues operate.

Voice

Sometimes people overlook the fact that spoken language includes many different nonverbal vocal elements. The technical term for these cues is *paralinguistics,* and they include rate of speech, pitch variation, volume, and vocal quality. If you think about your perceptions of someone who speaks really rapidly or v-e-r-r-r-y s-l-o-o-o-w-l-y, you have a sense of how rate affects communicating. Listeners and conversation partners also make inferences about how monotone or melodic speech is, how softly or loudly someone speaks, and whether a speaker's vocal quality is resonant, squeaky, nasal, or breathy. Sometimes people manipulate these four dimensions of their voice to assist listeners in interpreting what they're saying, whether they're emphasizing various words or phrases, expressing feelings, or indicating when they're serious and when they're sarcastic or joking. In other cases, speakers don't mean to manipulate any of the four; they're "just talking normally" when people hear them as too fast, as too soft, as a monotone, or as too loud.

As these examples suggest, one of the ways people interpret others' vocal cues is to make stereotyped judgments about the speakers' personalities. It's not a good idea, but we do it nonetheless. For example, a male with a breathy voice is likely to be stereotyped as gay, or at least as young and artistic, whereas a female with the same vocal quality is usually thought of as "more feminine, prettier, more petite, more effervescent, more high-strung, and shallower."[22] Nasal voices are heard as undesirable for both males and females, and low, deep voices are perceived as being more sophisticated, more appealing, and sexier than are higher-pitched voices. People also use vocal cues to draw conclusions about the age, sex, and ethnicity of speakers they hear. What can you conclude from the fact that we use voices this way? According to Mark Knapp:

> You should be quick to challenge the cliché that vocal cues only concern how something is said—frequently they are what is said. What is said might be an attitude ("I like you" or "I'm superior to you"), it might be an emotion ... or it might be the presentation of some aspect of your personality, background, or physical features. Vocal cues will, depending on the situation and the communicators, carry a great deal of information....[23]

Silence

> With silence we express the most varied and conflicting states, sentiments, thoughts and desires. Silence is meaningful. There is the silence of fear and terror, of wonder and stupor, of pain and joy.... "Dumb silence" is a contradictory expression. Instead of describing the same thing the two terms exclude each other; silence is not dumb and whatever is dumb is not silent. Silence is a form of communication ... dumbness, on the other hand, isolates and excludes us from all communication.[24]

The reason we classify silence as a mixed cue is that it most often becomes significant in the context of talk. As one author puts it, "A discourse without pauses [is] incomprehensible. Silence is not an interval ... but the bridge that unites sounds."[25] In other words, silence is usually noticed because of the way it relates to speaking. Examples include the failure or refusal to respond to a question, and the pregnant pause. Even the silence of the forest, prairie, mountain, lake, or bayou is most meaningful because of the way it contrasts with the noises of city crowds.

Silence is one of the least understood nonverbal behaviors, partly because people use and interpret it in so many different ways. Silence can be interpreted to mean apathy, patience, boredom, fear, sadness, love, intimacy, anger, or intimidation. We have talked with married couples who use silence as a weapon. One husband, who knew his wife hated it when he didn't talk out a problem, sometimes would refuse to talk to her for two or three days. His wife said she found this "devastating." When there are prolonged silences in group meetings, people start shifting nervously and making inferences, such as "nobody is interested," "people don't like this group," and "nobody really cares what we're doing."

But silence also works in positive ways. Beginning teachers, for example, have to learn that the silence that sometimes comes after they ask their students a question can be very fruitful. A group's silence can mean that there's a lot of thinking going on. Two close friends may also say nothing to each other just so they can share the experience of the moment. Or in an interview, silence can be a welcome opportunity for the interviewee to elaborate, return to a topic discussed earlier, or simply reorganize her or his thoughts. A friend of ours reported that the long silences he and his mother shared during the last two days of her life were some of the richest times they had spent together. Love, warmth, and sympathy are sometimes best expressed through silent facial and body movements and touch.

Facial Expression and Words

[Later in] this reading, we'll discuss facial expression as a primarily nonverbal cue. But peoples' faces also connect with words when they help to regulate utterance "turns" in conversations, and when they do, they can be considered mixed cues. The next time you're in a conversation, notice how you know when it's your turn to talk. The other person's face and eyes will almost always "tell" you. People also use faces and eyes to tell someone who approaches them either that they are welcoming the person into conversation or that they would rather be left alone.

Eye behavior is an important part of facial expression, and people use specific forms of eye behavior to accomplish several general goals in most conversations. First, we look away when we're having difficulty putting our thoughts into words. The amount of information we seem to be getting from another's eyes can be intense enough to be distracting, so if we're having trouble saying what we want to say, we look away to reduce the amount of input.

We also use eye contact to monitor feedback, to check the other's responses to the conversation. If we notice that the person is looking at us, we infer that she or he is paying attention; if we see that the person is staring into space, or over our shoulder to something or someone behind us, we draw the opposite conclusion. This phenomenon often helps make "cocktail party" conversation uncomfortably superficial. Neither conversation partner wants to be left standing alone, so both are as concerned about the next conversation as they are about the current one. As a result, both divide their looking between eye contact with the other and the search for the next partner.

Visual contact is also a primary way to indicate whose turn it is to talk. When a person tries to "catch the eye" of a server in a restaurant, the point is to open the channel, to initiate talk. And the same thing happens in conversation; I can "tell" you that it's your turn to talk by making eye contact with you. One communication researcher summarizes the typical conversation pattern in this way: "As the speaker comes to the end of an utterance or thought unit, gazing at the listener will continue as the listener assumes the speaking role; the listener will maintain gaze until the speaking role is assumed when he or she will look away. When the speaker does not yield a speaking turn by glancing at the other, the listener will probably delay a response or fail to respond.... "[26] Of course, this description is accurate for some cultures and not for others. Like other nonverbal cues, the facial expressions that accompany words vary among ethnic groups, genders, social classes, and sexual preferences. Eye contact and facial expressions are so critical to regulating conversations that a speaker's elimination of either one will seriously affect the responses of the listener.

Gestures and Words

Researcher David McNeill emphasizes why gestures can be considered mixed cues by examining their connection to spoken words. In one of McNeill's articles, "So You Think Gestures Are Nonverbal?" he explains how they are not just nonverbal, because gestures and speech are part of the same language structure. As he puts it, certain "gestures are verbal. They are the overt products of the same internal processes that produce the other overt product, speech." He goes on to point out that this is another reason we have to change what we mean by "language." He writes, "We tend to consider linguistic what we can write down, and nonlinguistic, everything else...."[27] However, he says, we now know better. Language is made up of both verbal and nonverbal aspects. This is "contrary to the idea of body language, that is, a separate system of body movement and postural signals that is thought to obey its own laws and convey its own ... meanings."[28] It's misleading to talk of body language, McNeill argues, because posture and gesture are too intimately connected with the other part of language—words....

Communication researcher Janet Bavelas and her colleagues have extended McNeill's work by studying what they call interactive gestures. These are movements that are related not to the content of the conversation, but to the relationship between or among the people communicating. Interactive gestures include the listener and thus "act to maintain the conversation as a social system."[29] For example, Bavelas describes how one speaker was discussing the summer job options that would contribute the most to his career goal.

> The listener had suggested earlier that working for Canada Customs would be a good idea; the speaker, after listing several other possibilities, adds "and Customs is DEFINITELY career-oriented." As he said "Customs," the speaker moved his hand up and toward the other person (almost as if tossing something to him), with palm up, fingers slightly curled, and thumb pointing directly at the other at the peak of the movement. Our translation of this gesture is "which YOU suggested," that is, the speaker credits the other person with the idea.[30]

Other interactive gestures were translated as "Do you get what I mean?" "Would you give me the answer?" and "No, no, I'll get it myself." All of these gestures are connected not to the conversational topic, but to the other speaker. Thus, they add important social content to the conversation, content separate from what is contributed verbally. In this way, they take on part of the work of mutual meaning constructing that is normally thought to be done only by words. So these so-called nonverbal gestures are actually functioning exactly as words do to add substance to the conversation.

Bavelas and her colleagues explain the importance of this added substance when they write:

> An interesting, intrinsic problem in dialogue is that, while both partners must remain involved, only one person can talk at once. Whenever a speaker has the floor, there exists the possibility that the conversation could veer off into monologue. One solution to the problem ... is for the speaker to involve the listener regularly. To a certain extent, the speaker can do this by verbal statements, such as "You know," "As you said," "As you know," "I'm sure you agree," etc. However, the frequent use of verbal interjections and addenda would constantly disrupt the flow of content, so nonverbal means of seeking or maintaining involvement are well suited to this function....

We propose that interactive gestures, for all their many specific forms and translations, form a class with the common function of including the listener and thereby counteracting the beginning of a drift toward monologue that is necessarily created every time one person has the floor.[31]

In summary, vocal rate, pitch, volume, and quality affect how people collaboratively construct meaning in communication; this is why they can be thought of as mixed cues. Silence is another influential mixed building block. In addition, many facial expressions, much eye behavior, and even many gestures work so intimately with spoken words that they should also be thought of as mixed.

PRIMARILY NONVERBAL CUES: FACE, EYE CONTACT AND GAZE, SPACE, TOUCH, MOVEMENT AND GESTURE

Although we're not going to present an exhaustive list of primarily nonverbal cues (for example, we omit appearance and dress, smells, time, and colors), we think that the following five categories will give you a broad sense of the most influential primarily nonverbal parts of your communicating.

Facial Expression

Your face is probably the most expressive part of your body and one of the most important focal points for nonverbal communicating. Most of the time, people are unaware of how much they rely on faces to give and get information. But a little reflection—or reading some of the research—can change your level of awareness. Consider, for example, how important the face is in expressing emotion. An extensive program of research has demonstrated that certain basic emotions are facially expressed in similar ways across cultures.[32] Every culture studied so far has been found to include some conventional facial expressions that people use to communicate joy or happiness, sadness, surprise, fear, anger, and disgust. There are some culture-specific rules for the display of these emotions, but they are expressed in very similar ways in most cultures.

Researchers have discovered these similarities by showing photographs of North American faces, for example, to Japanese or preliterate New Guinean observers, and then showing photographs of Japanese and New Guineans to North Americans. In most cases, members of one culture were able to identify accurately the emotions being expressed by the faces of persons from the other cultures.[33] They recognized, for example, that surprise is consistently communicated by a face with widened eyes, head tilted up, raised brow, and open mouth. Disgust is communicated with brows pulled down, wrinkled nose, and a mouth with raised upper lip and downturned corners.

Although the facial expression of emotions is similar across cultures, there are important differences in facial displays, for example, between Japanese and North Americans. Historically, Japanese have been taught to mask negative facial expressions with smiles and laughter and to display less facial emotion overall.[34] There are a number of competing ideas about why these differences exist, but regardless of the origins, differences in expression have contributed to misunderstandings between Japanese and North American businesspeople. Many Japanese still appear to be some of the least facially expressive of all cultural groups, and persons from other cultures are learning to adapt to this difference.

Eye Contact and Gaze

Although eyes are obviously a part of facial expression, gaze and eye contact are important enough to discuss separately. Eye contact appears to be one of the first behaviors that infants develop. Within a few days of birth, infants seem to recognize and attend to the caregiver's eyes. In the weeks immediately after birth, researchers have observed that simply seeing the eyes of the caregiver is enough to produce a smiling reaction.[35] Eye contact also significantly affects development. Infants who lack mutual gaze do not appear to mature perceptually and socially as rapidly as those who experience regular eye contact.[36]

If you doubt the importance of eye contact, consider the inferences you make about someone who doesn't look you in the eye "enough." What "enough" means varies from person to person, and certainly from culture to culture, but most Caucasians in the U.S. infer that the person with too little eye contact is insincere, is disinterested, lacks confidence, is trying to avoid contact, or is lying. There aren't many other possibilities. And all these inferences are negative. Generally, there are *no* positive messages conveyed by too little eye contact in white U.S. cultures....

One important function of eye gaze is to enhance the intimacy of the relationship. Especially when it is accompanied by forward lean, direct body orientation, and more gesturing, it can help promote closeness.[37] Some intimacy research has studied not sexual contact, but the kind of intimacy that increases the desire to help. Gaze has been found to increase the probability that a bystander will help a person with a medical problem or someone who has fallen.[38] But this phenomenon seems to characterize female-female contacts more than it does those involving males. As Judee Burgoon and her colleagues summarize, "Under some circumstances, prolonged gaze may serve as an affiliative cue in the form of a plea for help, while in other cases it may be seen as overly forward or aggressive behavior."[39]

Another primary function of eye behavior is to express emotions. Some of the same people who studied facial expressions have also researched how people use eyes and eyebrows to interpret the six common emotions. Generally eyes are used more than brows/forehead or lower face for the accurate perception of fear, but eyes help less for the accurate perception of anger and disgust.[40]

Feelings about others are also communicated visually. For example, if you perceive a person as being of significantly lower status than you are, the tendency will be for you to maintain considerable eye contact. On the other hand, communicators tend to look much less at high-status people. Generally, we also look more at people we like and at those who believe as we do. The obvious reason, as Albert Mehrabian explains, is that eye contact is a kind of approach behavior, and approach behaviors are connected with liking.[41] So one response to someone who is appealing is to approach by looking, and one way to avoid a person we dislike is to look away.

We also use gaze and eye behavior to make and influence credibility judgments. Several studies on persuasive effectiveness and willingness to hire a job applicant have underscored the importance of normal or nearly continuous gaze. It appears that gaze avoidance is interpreted negatively, as we mentioned above, and that it can significantly affect your chances of being perceived as credible.[42] This is why those who teach or coach people for public speaking or interview situations emphasize that speakers and interviewees should generally try to maintain eye contact 50 to 70 percent of the time. As we mentioned earlier, cultural identities affect this formula, but it is a reliable basic guideline for many North American communication situations.

The bottom line is that people give considerable weight to eye behavior and eye contact, because they apparently believe that the eyes are indeed the "windows of the soul." Especially in Western cultures, people are confident that they can spot even the most practiced liar if they can just "look the person in the eye"[43] (although detecting deception is more complicated than this, as we explain below). People are also generally impressed by the confidence and overall effectiveness of a speaker with good eye contact. But since different cultures have different estimates of what constitutes "good" eye contact, it's important not to oversimplify gaze and eye behavior and to remember that, especially because this category of nonverbal cues is given so much credence, it's important to become aware of and to learn to manage your own eye behavior.

Proximity or Space

You have probably noticed that you often feel possessive about some spaces—perhaps your room, yard, or car—and that you sometimes sit or stand very close to people with whom you're talking and at other times feel more comfortable several feet away. These feelings are related to what is known as *proxemics*, the study of the communicative effects of space or distance.

As [was] said in Chapter 2, space is one of the basic dimensions of every human's world, and the primary tension that describes this dimension is near-far. Because we all have basic human needs both for privacy (distance) and to be interdependent (nearness), one way we manage this tension is by defining and defending a *territory*. A territory is an identifiable geographic area that is occupied, controlled, and often defended by a person or group as an exclusive domain.[44] For example, for many North Americans, one's bedroom, or a particular space in a shared room, is yours whether you're in it or not, and one of the reasons you guard your right to keep it in your preferred state of neatness or disorder is to underscore the point that it's your territory. In a library, cafeteria, or other public space, people use overcoats, briefcases, newspapers, food trays, dishes, and utensils to establish a claim over "their" space, even though it's temporary.

A number of studies have identified differences between ways women and men use territory. For example, in most cultures, women are allowed less territory than are men. As Judy Pearson notes, "Few women have a particular and unviolated room in their homes while many men have dens, studies, or work areas which are off limits to others. Similarly, it appears that more men than women have particular chairs reserved for their use."[45]

Each of us also lives in our own personal space, a smaller, invisible, portable, and adjustable "bubble," which we maintain to protect ourselves from physical and emotional threats. The size of this bubble varies; how far away we sit or stand depends on our family and cultural memberships, the relationship we have with the other person, the situation or the context, and how we are feeling toward the other person at the time. Anthropologist Edward Hall says it this way:

> Some individuals never develop the public phase of their personalities and, therefore, cannot fill public spaces; they make very poor speakers or moderators. As many psychiatrists know, other people have trouble with the intimate and personal zones and cannot endure closeness to others.[46]

Within these limitations, Hall identifies four distances he observed among middle-class adults in the northeastern United States. Although the limits of each zone differ from culture to culture, something like these four types of space exist in many cultures.

Intimate Distance (Contact to 18 Inches)   This zone begins with skin contact and ranges to about a foot and a half. People usually reserve this distance for those to whom they feel emotionally close, and for comforting, protecting, caressing, or lovemaking. When forced into intimate distance with strangers— as on an elevator, for example—people tend to use other nonverbal cues to reestablish separateness. So we avoid eye contact, fold our arms, or perhaps hold a briefcase or purse in front of our body. Allowing someone to enter this zone is a sign of trust; it says we have willingly lowered our defenses. At this distance, not only touch, but also smells, body temperature, and the feel and smell of breath can be part of what we experience. Voices are usually kept at a low level to emphasize the "closed circle" established by intimates.

Personal Distance (1.5 to 4 Feet)   This is the distance preferred by most conversation partners in a public setting. Typically, subjects of personal interest and moderate involvement can be discussed at this distance. Touch is still possible, but it is limited to brief pats for emphasis and reassurance. Finer details of the other's skin, hair, eyes, and teeth are visible, but one can't discern body temperature or feel the breath.

The far range of this distance is just beyond where you can comfortably touch the other. Hall calls it the distance we can use to keep someone "at arm's length." John sometimes works as a communication consultant training people to do information-gathering interviews. In that context, he encourages the people he's training to try to work within this zone. It appears that three to four feet is far enough away not to threaten the other and yet close enough to encourage the kind of relatively candid responses that make the interviews most successful.

Social Distance (4 to 12 Feet)   More impersonal business generally is carried out at this distance. People who work together or who are attending a social gathering tend to use the closer ranges of social distance. Salespeople and customers typically are comfortable within the four- to seven-foot zone. Most people feel uncomfortable if a salesperson approaches within three feet, but five or six feet nonverbally "says," "I'm here to help but I don't want to be pushy."

At the farther ranges of this distance, eye contact becomes especially important. When a person is 10 or 11 feet away, it's easy to be uncertain about who the person is talking with until you can determine where the person is looking. This is also the distance we often use with people of significantly higher or lower status. Sitting at this distance from a superior will tend to create a much more formal conversation than might take place if one or both persons moved their chairs much closer. As a result, it can be more effective to reprimand using social distance and less effective to give praise in this zone.

Public Distance (12 to 25 Feet)   The closer range of this distance is the one commonly used by instructors and managers addressing work groups. The farthest end of this zone is usually reserved for public speeches. When communicating at this distance, voices need to be loud or electronically amplified. At the farther ranges of this distance, facial expression, movements, and gestures also need to be exaggerated in order to be meaningful.

Like many other general observations about human communication, these four distances need to be taken with a grain of salt. Several studies have shown, for example, that females sit and stand closer together than do males, and that mixed-sex pairs consistently adopt closer distances than do male-male pairs.[47] Interpersonal distance also generally increases with age from preschool and grade school through the teen years to adulthood, but this tendency is mitigated somewhat by the fact that people also tend to adopt closer distances with age peers than with those who are younger or older.[48] So people's interpretations of distance and closeness may depend not only on their cultural identity, but also on their gender and age and on the gender and age of the person with whom they're conversing.

Space is usually interpreted in the context of other nonverbal cues. For example, a Chinese-American student reported:

> [My grandfather] commands his presence with silence, limited facial expressions and lots of space between himself and others. I have never thought of jumping into his lap like Ol' St. Nick or even felt comfortable talking to him at any great length. When I do scrounge up the courage to speak to him, it is almost always to greet him or ask him to come to dinner. The speech used would have to be laden with respectful words.[49]

Touch

Touch is the most direct way that humans establish the contact that makes us who we are. "It is well documented that touch is essential to the physical, emotional, and psychological well-being of human infants and to their intellectual, social, and communication development."[50] Touch is equally important for adults, although taboos in many Western cultures make it much more difficult to accomplish. That's why some scholars believe that these cultures are "touch-starved."

Touch plays a part in just about every activity of our waking day—not just with other humans but also with objects. You may not be aware of the feel of your clothes; the chair, couch, or floor on which you're sitting, standing, or lying; or the feel of the book you're holding, the pencil or pen you're grasping, or the shoes you're wearing. But you couldn't write, walk, make a fist, smile, or comb your hair without the sense of touch. In addition, the ways in which we hold and handle such things as books, pencils, cups or glasses, and purses or briefcases can affect another person's responses to us.

Touch between persons is even more complex. Stan Jones and Elaine Yarbrough, two speech communication researchers, found that people touch to indicate positive feelings, to play, to control, as part of a greeting or departure ritual, to help accomplish a task, to combine greeting or departure with affection, and accidentally.[51] In their studies, control touches occurred most frequently, touches that were primarily interpreted to mean a request for compliance or attention getting. A spot touch with the hand to a nonvulnerable body part—hands, arms, shoulders, or upper back—frequently accompanies and emphasizes such statements as, "Move over," "Hurry up," "Stay here," "Be serious," and "Do it." A similar touch reinforces such messages as, "Listen to this," "Look at that," and "I want your attention." These touches are almost always accompanied by verbalization, and both sexes initiate these touches with almost equal frequency.

Positive affect touches were the second most frequent kind of touch Jones and Yarbrough observed. The highest number of these touches were expressions of affection. As you would expect, these occur predominantly in close relationships and include hugs, kisses, and often contacts with "vulnerable body parts"—head, neck, torso, lower back, buttocks, legs, or feet. But affection can also be communicated by touch in some business settings. Long-term work teams sometimes engage in spontaneous brief touches among team members that are interpreted as positive and supportive. On the other hand, ... sexual harassment in the workplace often consists in part of inappropriate or manipulative positive affect touching.

Research such as that of Jones and Yarbrough is important because it helps us comprehend a poorly understood, and sometimes even feared, aspect of our communicating. As Mark Knapp says:

> Some people grow up learning "not to touch" a multitude of animate and inanimate objects; they are told not to touch their own body and later not to touch the body of their dating partner; care is taken so children do not see their parents "touch" one another intimately; some parents demonstrate a noncontact

norm through the use of twin beds; touching is associated with admonitions of "not nice" or "bad" and is punished accordingly—and frequent touching between father and son is thought to be something less than masculine.[52]

We know that touch is an enormously powerful kind of nonverbal communication; a very small amount of it can say a great deal. We can harness this power by becoming aware of how touch affects where our communication is on the social-cultural-interpersonal scale.

Body Movement and Gestures

The technical term for the study of movement and gesture is *kinesics*, from the Greek word for "motion." Some kinesic behaviors mean virtually the same thing whether they're performed by men or women, young or old people, and in the United States, Latin America, Europe, Australia, or Japan. For example, the head nod for agreement, shaking a fist in anger, clapping hands for approval, raising a hand for attention, yawning in boredom, rubbing hands to indicate coldness, and the thumbs-down gesture for disapproval are all interpreted similarly in at least several western hemisphere cultures.

Movements and gestures can also reflect the type of relationship that exists between partners or spouses. Communication researcher Mary Anne Fitzpatrick has distinguished among three general couple types who are identifiable in part by their patterns of movement and gesture. Traditionals accept conventional beliefs about relational roles, for example, about which are "the husband's" duties and which are "the wife's."[53] They value stability over spontaneity and affirm the traditional community customs that a woman should take her husband's last name when she marries, and the belief that infidelity is always inexcusable. Independent couples are at the opposite end of the ideological scale. They believe that one's relationship should not limit her or his individual freedom in any way. "The independent maintains a high level of companionship and sharing in marriage, but ... [he or she] maintains separate physical spaces to control accessibility." Separates are conventional regarding marital and family issues but also support independent values. "They may espouse one set [of values] publicly while believing another privately. The separates have significantly less companionship and sharing in their marriage."[54] One of the ways to distinguish among the three couple types is to observe their movements and gestures when they are together.

Traditionals engage in a high number of meshed movements and actions. Each partner facilitates the other partner's actions. If the woman moves toward the door, for example, the man will typically move to open it for her. Separates, on the other hand, engage in very few meshed action sequences. They are disengaged from one another. However, even though their gestures and movements don't interconnect, they are often parallel. For example, one may move toward the door while the other moves to get his or her coat. Finally, the gestures and movements of independents clash more often than they are parallel. If one moves toward the door, the other may sit down or even try to keep the door closed.

People also communicate dominance and submission posturally. A male may hook his thumbs in his belt and both females and males may stand with hands on hips in the akimbo position. When a seated person leans back with hands clasped behind her or his head, this is typically another dominance posture. When a conversational group of three is approached by a fourth person, they typically rotate their bodies out to encourage the fourth to join them or in to discourage him or her.

Forward lean is commonly interpreted as more involved and usually more positive, while "seated male and female communicators both perceived a person leaning backward and away from them as having a more negative attitude than one who was leaning forward."[55] A direct vis-à-vis posture, movement toward the other, affirmative head nods, expressive hand gestures, and stretching are all rated as "warm" behaviors, while moving away, picking one's teeth, shaking the head, and playing with hair are rated as "cold."[56] All of these descriptions illustrate how body movement and gesture make up still another important category of nonverbal behaviors.

REVIEW QUESTIONS

1. To check your understanding of the relationship between verbal and non-verbal cues, itemize six nonverbal features of the words you find in this book.
2. Explain what it means to say that words are "arbitrary symbols."
3. What's the problem with an explanation of language based on an analysis of concrete nouns?
4. What's missing, according to Stewart and Logan, from the account of language as an activity?
5. Explain the Sapir-Whorf hypothesis in your own words.
6. Give an example from your own experience of gendered (masculine/feminine) language affecting your perception of someone or something.
7. What are paralinguistics?
8. Especially in conversation, silence, this reading argues, is much more than the absence of noise. Explain.
9. Why is facial expression discussed in two separate places in this reading?
10. What are interactive gestures?
11. What makes eye behavior so important in conversations?
12. Stewart and Logan make the point that a very small amount of touch can "say" a great deal. Which other mixed and primarily nonverbal cues are similarly high in potency—where a little can go a long way?

PROBES

1. Carole and I explain some disadvantages of separate discussions of verbal and nonverbal cues. What are some advantages?

2. When does it most seem as if language is a "system"? When does this label seem least appropriate?
3. One famous author expressed something very close to the "language is a soup" idea in these words: "The limits of my language are the limits of my world." With the "soup" metaphor in mind, explain what you believe that means.
4. Carole and I repeat the claims about the differences between masculine and feminine communication styles that have been popularized by some authors. The readings in Chapter 8 challenge these claims. Flip forward in the book to Chapter 8, and make a note there to discuss whether you agree with this reading or those.
5. In your experience, which kinds of mixed and primarily nonverbal cues vary the most between or among cultures? Which kinds of cues from other cultures are the most different from your preferred patterns?
6. Give an example from your own experience of gender differences in spatial nonverbal cues.
7. Summarize three pieces of advice about your own verbal and nonverbal communicating that you drew from this reading. If you are to take seriously what's here, what three changes might you make?

NOTES

1. D. J. Higginbotham and D. E. Yoder, "Communication within Natural Conversational Interaction: Implications for Severe Communicatively Impaired Persons." *Topics in Language Disorders* 2 (1982): 4.
2. Wendy Leeds-Hurwitz, *Communication in Everyday Life* (Norwood, NJ: Ablex, 1989), p. 102.
3. Ferdinand de Saussure, *Course in General Linguistics*, ed. Charles Bally and Albert Sechehaye, trans. Roy Harris (LaSalle, IL: Open Court, 1986), pp. 66–70. After making this point, de Saussure focused his attention on the *system* of language, in order to make linguistics a "science."
4. Robert E. Sanders, "The Interconnection of Utterances and Nonverbal Displays." *Research on Language and Social Interaction* 20 (1987): 141.
5. Aristotle, De Interpretatione, trans. E. M. Edgehill in The Basic Works of Aristotle, ed. Richard McKeon (New York: Random House, 1941), p. 20.
6. Charles E. Osgood, "What Is a Language?" in I. Rauch and G. F. Carr (eds.), *The Signifying Animal* (Bloomington, IN: Indiana University Press, 1980), p. 12.
7. C. K. Ogden and I. A. Richards, *The Meaning of Meaning,* 8th ed. (New York: Harcourt Brace, 1986), p. 11. If you're interested in reading more about this view of language and its problems, see John Stewart, *Language as Articulate Contact: Toward a Post-Semiotic Philosophy of Communication* (Albany, NY: State University of New York Press, 1995); and John Stewart (ed.), *Beyond the Symbol Model: Reflections on the Representational Nature of Language* (Albany, NY: State University of New York Press, 1996).

8. Robert E. Nofsinger, *Everyday Conversation* (Newbury Park, CA: Sage, 1991), pp. 19–26.

9. Nofsinger, p. 51.

10. Hans-Georg Gadamer, "Man and Language," in David E. Linge (ed.), *Philosophical Hermeneutics* (Berkeley, CA: University of California Press, 1976), pp. 62–63.

11. D. B. Chamberlain, "Consciousness at Birth: The Range of Empirical Evidence," in T. R. Verney (ed.), *Pre- and Perinatal Psychology: An Introduction* (New York: Human Sciences, 1987), pp. 70–86.

12. A. Tomatis, "Ontogenesis of the Faculty of Listening," in Verney (ed.), pp. 23–35.

13. Beth Haslett, "Acquiring Conversational Competence." *Western Journal of Speech Communication* 48 (1984): 120.

14. John B. Carroll (ed.), *Language; Thought and Reality: Selected Writings of Benjamin Lee Whorf* (New York: Wiley, 1956), pp. 212–213.

15. For over 50 years, linguistics, anthropology, and communication textbooks have used the example of Eskimo words for snow to illustrate how language and perception are interrelated. According to this account, the importance of snow in Eskimo culture is reflected in the many terms they have for "falling snow," "drifting snow," "snow on the ground," "slushy snow," and so on. Earlier editions of this text repeated this myth. But we now know it isn't true. The myth began in 1911 when an anthropologist working in Alaska compared the different Eskimo root words for "snow on the ground," "falling snow," "drifting snow," and "a snow drift" with different English root words for a variety of forms of water (liquid, lake, river, brook, rain, dew, wave, foam, and so on). The anthropologist's comment was popularized in a 1940 article and then found its way into literally hundreds of publications that confidently asserted that Eskimos had 9, 23, 50, and even 100 words for snow. But they don't. The best available source, *A Dictionary of the West Greenlandic Eskimo Language,* gives just two: *quanik,* meaning "snow in the air," and *aput,* meaning "snow on the ground." So if you hear or read of the Eskimo-words-for-snow example, feel free to correct it. Or at least don't repeat it. See Geoffrey Pullum, "The Great Eskimo Vocabulary Hoax." *Lingua Franca* 14 (June 1990): 28–29.

16. Harry Hoijer, "Cultural Implications of Some Navajo Linguistic Categories." *Language* 27 (1951): 117.

17. J. Birere and C. Lanktree, "Sex-Role Related Effects of Sex Bias in Language." *Sex Roles* 9 (1980): 625–632; D. K. Ivy, "Who's the Boss? He, He/She, or They?" Unpublished paper, 1986; cited in D. K. Ivy and Phil Backlund, *Exploring Gender Speak: Personal Effectiveness in Gender Communication* (New York: McGraw-Hill, 1994), p. 75.

18. Deborah Tannen, *You Just Don't Understand: Women and Men in Communication* (New York: Morrow, 1990).

19. John Gray, *Men Are from Mars, Women Are from Venus* (New York: HarperCollins, 1992).

20. John Gray, *Mars and Venus in Love* (New York: HarperCollins, 1996).

21. Julia T. Wood reviews this research in *Gendered Lives: Communication, Gender, and Culture* (Belmont, CA: Wadsworth, 1994), pp. 141–145.

22. D. W. Addington, "The Relationship of Selected Vocal Characteristics to Personality Perception." *Speech Monographs* 35 (1968): 492–503.

23. Mark L. Knapp, *Essentials of Nonverbal Communication* (New York: Holt, 1980), p. 361.

24. M. F. Sciacca, *Come Si Vinci a Waterloo* (Milan: Marzorati, 1963), p. 129; quoted in Gemma Corradi Fiumara, *The Other Side of Language: A Philosophy of Listening* (London: Routledge, 1990), p. 101.

25. Sciacca, p. 26, quoted in Corradi Fiumara, p. 102.

26. Knapp, p. 298.

27. D. McNeill, "So You Think Gestures Are Nonverbal." *Psychological Review* 92 (1985): 350–371.

28. McNeill, p. 350.

29. Janet Beavin Bavelas, Nicole Chovil, Douglas A. Lawrie, and Allan Wade, "Interactive Gestures." Paper presented at the annual meeting of International Communication Association, Chicago, 1991, p. 2.

30. Bavelas, Chovil, Lawrie, and Wade, p. 7.

31. Bavelas, Chovil, Lawrie, and Wade, pp. 10–11.

32. See, for example, Paul Ekman, "Universal and Cultural Differences in Facial Expressions of Emotions," in *Nebraska Symposium on Motivation,* Vol. 19, ed. J. K. Cole (Lincoln, NE: University of Nebraska Press, 1971), pp. 207–283; C. E. Izard, *Human Emotions* (New York: Plenum, 1977).

33. Paul Ekman, W. V. Friesen, and S. Ancoli, "Facial Signs of Emotional Experience." *Journal of Personality and Social Psychology* 39 (1980): 1125–1134; Paul Ekman and W. V. Friesen, *Unmasking the Face* (Englewood Cliffs, NJ: Prentice-Hall, 1975).

34. R. A. Miller, *Japan's Modern Myth: The Language and Beyond* (Tokyo: Weatherhill, 1982).

35. Michael Argyle and M. Cook, *Gaze and Mutual Gaze* (Cambridge, England: Cambridge University Press, 1976).

36. Janis Andersen, Peter Andersen, and J. Landgraf, "The Development of Nonverbal Communication Competence in Childhood." Paper presented at the annual meeting of the International Communication Association, Honolulu, May 1985.

37. Judee K. Burgoon, David B. Buller, and W. Gill Woodall, *Nonverbal Communication: The Unspoken Dialogue* (New York: Harper & Row, 1989), p. 438.

38. R. L. Shotland and M. P. Johnson, "Bystander Behavior and Kinesics: The Interaction between the Helper and Victim." *Environmental Psychology and Nonverbal Behavior* 2 (1978): 181–190.

39. Burgoon, Buller, and Goodall, p. 438.

40. Ekman and Friesen, *Unmasking the Face,* pp. 40–46.

41. Albert Mehrabian, *Silent Messages: Implicit Communication of Emotion and Attitudes,* 2nd ed. (New York: Random House, 1981), pp. 23–25.

42. See, for example, J. K. Burgoon, V. Manusov, P. Mineo, and J. L. Hale, "Effects of Eye Gaze on Hiring Credibility, Attraction, and Relational Message Interpretation." *Journal of Nonverbal Behavior* 9 (1985): 133–146.

43. We elaborate on the process of deception in Chapter 8. Closely related to the work on deception is research on equivocal communication. See, for example, Janet Beavin Bavelas, Alex Black, Nicole Chovil, and Jennifer Mullet, "Truths, Lies, and Equivocation," in *Equivocal Communication* (Newbury Park, CA: Sage, 1990), pp. 170–207.

44. Burgoon, Buller, and Woodall, p. 81.

45. Judy C. Pearson, *Communication in the Family* (New York: Harper & Row, 1989), p. 78.

46. Edward T. Hall, *The Hidden Dimension* (Garden City, NY: Doubleday, 1966), p. 115.

47. For example, N. M. Sussman and H. M. Rosenfeld, "Influence of Culture, Language, and Sex on Conversational Distance." *Journal of Personality and Social Psychology* 42 (1982): 66–74.

48. Burgoon, Buller, and Woodall, p. 110.

49. Mandy Lam, *Interpersonal Communication Journal*, October 19, 1996. Used with permission.

50. Burgoon, Buller, and Woodall, p. 75.

51. Unless otherwise noted, the material on touch is from Stanley E. Jones and A. Elaine Yarbrough, "A Naturalistic Study of the Meanings of Touch." *Communication Monographs* 52 (1985): 19–56.

52. Knapp, pp. 108–109.

53. Mary Anne Fitzpatrick, *Between Husbands and Wives* (Newbury Park, CA: Sage, 1988), p. 76.

54. Fitzpatrick, pp. 218–219.

55. Knapp, p. 224.

56. G. L. Clore, N. H. Wiggins, and S. Itkin, "Judging Attraction from Nonverbal Behavior: The Gain Phenomenon." *Journal of Consulting and Clinical Psychology* 43 (1975): 491–497.

Paying Attention to Words

Virginia Satir

Virginia Satir was a family counselor who spent over 40 years helping parents and children communicate. Her small book, *Making Contact,* is her response to the many persons who asked her to write down the ideas and suggestions that she shared in workshops and seminars. As she said in the introduction, "The framework of this book is the BARE BONES of the possible, which I believe applies to *all* human beings. You, the reader, can flesh out the framework to fit you."

I like the simple, straightforward, no-nonsense way she talks about words, and I think that she's pinpointed several insights that can help all of us communicate better. If we did, as she suggests, pay more attention to the ways we use the 10 key words she discusses, I'm convinced that we'd experience considerably less conflict, misunderstanding, and frustration. See if you agree.

Words are important tools for contact. They are used more consciously than any other form of contact. I think it is important to learn how to use words well in the service of our communication.

Words cannot be separated from sights, sounds, movements, and touch of the person using them. They are one package.

However, for the moment, let's consider only words. Using words is literally the outcome of a whole lot of processes that go on in the body. All the senses, the nervous system, brain, vocal chords, throat, lungs, and all parts of the mouth are involved. This means that physiologically, talking is a very complicated process....

If you think of your brain as a computer, storing all your experiences on tapes, then the words you pick will have to come from those tapes. Those tapes represent all our past experiences, accumulated knowledge, rules, and guides. There is nothing else there until new tapes are added. I hope that what you are reading will help you to add new tapes out of getting new experiences.

The words we use have an effect on our health. They definitely influence emotional relationships between people and how people can work together.

WORDS HAVE POWER

Listen to what you say and see if you are really saying what you mean. Nine people out of ten can't remember what they said sixty seconds ago; others remember.

There are ten English words that it is well to pay close attention to, to use with caution and with loving care: *I, You, They, It, But, Yes, No, Always, Never, Should.*

If you were able to use these special words carefully it would already solve many contact problems created by misunderstanding.

I

Many people avoid the use of the word *I* because they feel they are trying to bring attention to themselves. They think they are being selfish. Shades of childhood, when you shouldn't show off, and who wants to be selfish? The most important thing is that using "I" clearly means that you are taking responsibility for what you say. Many people mix this up by starting off with saying "you." I have heard people say "You can't do that." This is often heard as a "put-down," whereas "I think you can't do that" makes a more equal relationship between the two. It gives the same information without the put-down.

"I" is the pronoun that clearly states "me" when I am talking so it is important to say it. If you want to be clear when you are talking, no matter what you say, it is important to state clearly your ownership of *your* statement.

> "I am saying that the moon is made of red cheese."
> (*This is clearly your picture*)

instead of saying ...

> "The moon is made of red cheese."
> (*This is a new law*)

Being aware of your clear use of "I" is particularly crucial when people are already in crisis. It is more clear to say "It is my picture that ..." (which is an ownership statement). Whoever has the presence of mind to do this can begin to alter an escalating situation. When "I" is not clear, it is easy for the hearer to get a "you" message, which very often is interpreted as a "put-down."

You

The use of the word *you* is also tricky. It can be felt as an accusation when only reporting or sharing is intended.

"You are making things worse" can sound quite different if the words "I think" are added. "I think you are making things worse...."

When used in clear commands or directions, it is not so easily misunderstood. For example, "I want you to ..." or "You are the one I wanted to speak to."

They

The use of *they* is often an indirect way of talking about "you." It is also often a loose way of spreading gossip.

> "They say ..."

"They" can also be some kind of smorgasbord that refers to our negative fantasies. This is especially true in a situation where people are assessing blame. If we know who "they" are we can say so.

How many times do we hear "They won't let me." "They will be upset." "They don't like what I am doing." "They say ..."

If someone else uses it, we can ask "Who is your *they?*"

The important part of this is to have clear who "they" are so that inaccurate information is not passed on and it is clear exactly who is being referred to. Being clear in this way seems to add to everyone's security. Information becomes concrete, which one can get hold of, instead of being nebulous and perhaps posing some kind of threat.

It

It is a word that can easily be misunderstood because it often isn't clear what "it" refers to. "It" is a word that has to be used with care.

The more clear your "it" is, the less the hearer fills it in with his [or her] own meaning. Sometimes "it" is related to a hidden "I" message. One way to better understand your "it" is to substitute "I" and see what happens. "It isn't clear" changed to "I am not clear" could make things more accurate and therefore easier to respond to.

"It often happens to people" is a statement that when said straight could be a comfort message that says, "The thing you are talking about has happened to me. I know how feeling humiliated feels."

To be more sure that we are understood, it might be wiser to fill in the details.

But

Next is the word *but.*

"But" is often a way of saying "yes" and "no" in the same sentence.

"I love you *but* I wish you would change your underwear more often."

This kind of use can easily end up with the other person feeling very uncomfortable, uneasy, and frequently confused.

Try substituting the word "and" for "but," which will clarify the situation. Your body will even feel different.

By using "but" the speaker is often linking two different thoughts together, which is what causes the difficulty.

Thus "I love you, but I wish you would change your underwear more often" could be two expressions.

"I love you," and "I wish you would change your underwear more often."

It could also represent someone's best, although fearful, attempt to make an uncomfortable demand by couching the demand in a love context, hoping the other person would not feel hurt.

If this is the case, what would happen if the person were to say "I want to ask something of you that I feel very uncomfortable about. I would like you to change your underwear more often."

Yes, No

A clear "yes" and "no" are important. Too many people say "yes, but" or "yes, maybe" or "no" just to be on the safe side, especially if they are in a position of power.

When "yes" or "no" are said clearly, and they mean NOW and not forever, and it is further clear "yes" and "no" relate to an issue rather than a person's value, then "yes" and "no" are very helpful words in making contact.

People can get away with much misuse of words when trust and good feeling have been established and when the freedom to comment is around. However, so often people feel so unsure about themselves that the lack of clarity leaves a lot of room for misunderstanding and consequent bad feelings. It is easy to build up these bad feelings once they are started.

"No" is a word that we all need and need to be able to use when it fits. So often when people feel "no," they say "maybe" or "yes" to avoid meeting the issue. This is justified on the basis of sparing the other's feelings. It is a form of lying and usually invites distrust, which, of course, is death to making contact.

When the "no" isn't clear, the "yes" can also be mistrusted. Have you ever heard "He said yes, but he doesn't really mean it"?

Always, Never

Always is the positive form of a global word. *Never* is the negative form. For example:

> *Always* clean up your plate.
> *Never* leave anything on your plate.

The literal meaning of these words is seldom accurate and the directions seldom applicable to life situations. There are few cases in life where something is always *or* never. Therefore to try to follow these demands in all situations will surely end up in failure like the rules I described earlier.

Often the use of these words is a way to make emotional emphasis, like ...

> "You *always* make me mad."

meaning really ...

> "I am NOW very mad at you."

If the situation were as the speaker states, the adrenals would wear out.

Sometimes the words *always* and *never* hide ignorance. For example, someone has spent just five minutes with a person and announces,

> "He is always bright."

In most cases the literal use of these two words could not be followed in all times, places and situations. Furthermore, they are frequently untrue. For the most part they become emotionally laden words that harm rather than nurture or enlighten the situation.

I find that these words are often used without any meaning in any literal sense....

Should

"Ought" and "should" are other trap words from which it is easy to imply that there is something wrong with you—you have failed somehow to measure up.

Often the use of these words implies stupidity on someone's part ...

"You should have known better."

This is frequently heard as an accusation. Sometimes it merely represents some friendly advice. When people use the words "ought" and "should," often they are trying to indicate a dilemma in which they have more than one direction to go at a time—one may be pulling harder than the rest although the others are equally important ...

"I like this, but I should get that."

When your words are these, your body often feels tight. There are no easy answers to the pulls which "ought" and "should" represent. Biologically we really can go in only one direction at a time.

When your body feels tight your brain often freezes right along with your tight body, and so your thinking becomes limited as well.

Hearing yourself use the words "ought" and "should" can be a tip-off to you that you are engaged in a struggle. Perhaps instead of trying to deal with these opposing parts as one, you can separate them and make two parts.

"I like this ..." (one part)
"But I should get that"

translated into ...

"I also need that ..." (a second part).

Such a separation may be helpful in considering each piece separately and then considering them together.

When you do this your body has a chance to become a little looser, thus freeing some energy to negotiate a bit better.

When I am in this spot, I can help myself by asking whether I will literally die in either situation. If the answer is no, then I have a different perspective, and I can more easily play around with alternatives, since I am now out of a win-loss feeling in myself. I won't die. I may be only a little deprived or inconvenienced at most.

Start paying attention to the words you use.

Who is your *they?*
What is your *it?*
What does your *no* mean?
What does your *yes* mean?
Is your *I* clear?

Are you saying *never* and *always* when you mean sometimes and when you want to make emotional emphasis?

How are you using *ought* and *should?*

REVIEW QUESTIONS

1. What reasons do people give for *not* using the word *I?*
2. What is similar about the problems Satir finds with the words *they* and *it?*
3. Does Satir suggest that we should not use the words *but, yes,* and *no?* What is she saying about these words?
4. How does a person's use of the words *ought* and *should* reflect his or her value system?

PROBES

1. When you're in a conversation, can you recall what you said 60 seconds earlier? Try it. What do you notice?
2. Notice how, as Virginia Satir says, *it* and *they* both often work to hide the fact that some *I* is actually talking. When do you hear yourself using *it* and *they* that way?
3. What happens when you substitute *and* for *but?*
4. Do you experience your body responding, as Satir describes, to the words *ought* and *should?*

———

Nonverbal Communication: Basic Perspectives

Mark L. Knapp and Judith A. Hall

Knapp and Hall begin this next reading with a point made before: The line separating verbal from nonverbal communication is not distinct. Both are virtually always found together, and the main—perhaps the only—benefit of separating them is to make it a little easier to study them.

In this excerpt from their book *Nonverbal Communication in Human Interaction,* Knapp and Hall divide nonverbal cues into three general categories: the communication environment, the communicators' physical characteristics, and body movement and position. Then they discuss some ways that nonverbal communication works in the overall communication process. When they turn to everyday life, their examples involve nonverbal elements of the criminal justice system, nonverbal cues in televised politics, nonverbal aspects of classroom behavior, and nonverbal courtship behavior.

Their comments about the physical environment should sensitize you to the ways that furniture, lighting conditions, colors, and music or environmental noise affect interpersonal communicating. They also sketch effects of *proxemics,* the study of the impact of space.

Their brief comments about communicators' physical characteristics are meant to remind their readers of the potential impact body shape, skin color, and body or breath odors can have on communication. Artifacts such as clothes, hairpieces, jewelry, and accessories such as purses or portable electronic devices—cell phones, PDAs, and so on—can also affect how people communicate.

The section on body movement and position is divided into six topics: gesture, posture, touch, facial expression, eye behavior, and vocal behavior. Knapp and Hall do not attempt to cover any of these topics thoroughly. They say just enough about each to remind readers of the potential impact of each category of cue. For example, forward-leaning posture, they note, has been associated with higher involvement, more liking, and lower status. Touching others is a highly ambiguous form of communicating that takes its meaning from the context, the nature of the relationship, and the way the touching is done, rather than the type of touch, per se. Eye behavior can significantly affect judgments of credibility and attraction. And such elements of vocal behavior as rate, loudness, precise versus slurred articulation, laughing, swallowing, and moaning can all be understood to be significant.

The second major section of the reading reasserts the point that since verbal and nonverbal signals are virtually always inseparable, it is difficult to distinguish between the primary functions of either. Nonetheless, some research has emphasized the importance of non-verbal cues in (1) expressing emotion, (2) conveying interpersonal like/dislike, dominance/submission, and so on, (3) presenting one's personality to others, and (4) accompanying speech for the purposes of managing turn taking, feedback, attention, and so on. Another researcher emphasized the importance of nonverbal cues in the communication of immediacy, status, and responsiveness.

The final part of the reading illustrates the pervasive importance of nonverbal communication in everyday life by highlighting some ways these cues function in four contexts. In the criminal justice system, some researchers have tried to associate facial features or styles of appearance and movement with "criminal type" people. These efforts have been debunked, but contemporary nonverbal studies do generate advice, for example, about how to walk on a crowded street in order to minimize your vulnerability. Courtroom studies also provide material for lawyers and their consultants to aid in the process of jury selection.

Everyone who's viewed political campaigning on television is aware of the importance of appearance, dress, and location or context in politics. Handlers or managers place their candidates in locations that emphasize aspects of their verbal messages—the factory gate to discuss labor-management legislation, the national park to discuss environmental politics, in front of Congress or the White House to emphasize national credibility. Studies of televised debates have attributed success and failure to facial expressions, eye gaze, and even dress.

As you know first-hand, classroom communication also includes important nonverbal elements. Students learn where to sit to reinforce their self-definition as "involved" or "laid back." They develop subtle and powerful rhythms of eye behavior to avoid being called on or to present themselves as interested and engaged. Professors announce that they make time for students and then contradict themselves by habitually glancing at their watches. And U-shaped or circular arrangement of chairs can facilitate interaction and make "hiding at the back of the room" more difficult. With respect to online learning, Knapp and Hall note that "the influence of nonverbal behavior that communicates warmth and closeness in conventional classrooms promises to be even more important to the success of distance education."

Their final topic is courtship behavior, and all of us have experienced the importance of nonverbal cues in this context. The authors note that research has not yet systematized or quantified the powerful elements that contribute to attractiveness and signal availability or its opposite. They review results of some research on flirtation behavior between men and women in bars that you might usefully test against your own experience. Knapp and Hall also summarize some studies of the sequence of steps in courtship behavior, both generally—approach, a turn toward the other, nonintimate touch, increased eye gaze, and so on—and in specific nonverbal courtship behaviors—eye to body, eye to eye, hand to hand, and so on.

An entire course—or more—could be dedicated to the study of the nonverbal aspects of interpersonal communicating. This reading and the one that follows are designed to provide an overview of these processes and the ways they function. I hope that this reading will sensitize you to the many different ways you communicate nonverbally and to the many nonverbal cues you interpret.

To most people, the phrase *nonverbal communication* refers to *communication effected by means other than words* (assuming words are the verbal element). Like most definitions, this one is generally useful, but it does not account adequately for the complexity of this phenomenon. As long as we understand and appreciate its limitations, this broad definition should serve us well.

We need to understand that separating verbal and nonverbal behavior into two separate and distinct categories is virtually impossible. Consider, for example, the hand movements that make up American Sign Language (a language of the deaf). These gesticulations are mostly linguistic (verbal), yet hand gestures are often considered behavior that is "other than words." McNeill (1992) has demonstrated the linguistic qualities of some gestures by noting that different kinds of gestures disappear with different kinds of aphasia, namely, those gestures with linguistic functions similar to the specific verbal loss. Conversely, not all spoken words are clearly or singularly verbal—as, for example, onomatopoeic words such as *buzz* or *murmur* and nonpropositional speech used by auctioneers and some aphasics. . . .

Another way of defining nonverbal communication is to look at the things people study. The theory and research associated with nonverbal communication focus on three primary units: the environmental structures and conditions within which communication takes place, the physical characteristics of the communicators themselves, and the various behaviors manifested by the communicators. A detailed breakdown of these three features follows.

THE COMMUNICATION ENVIRONMENT

Physical Environment

Although most of the emphasis in nonverbal research is on the appearance and behavior of the persons communicating, increasing attention is being given to the influence of nonhuman factors on human transactions. People change environments to help them accomplish their communicative goals; conversely, environments can affect our moods, choices of words, and actions. Thus this category concerns those elements that impinge on the human relationship but are not directly a part of it. Environmental factors include the furniture, architectural style, interior decorating, lighting conditions, colors, temperature, additional noises or music, and the like, amid which the interaction occurs. Variations in arrangements, materials, shapes, or surfaces of objects in the interacting environment can be extremely influential on the outcome of an interpersonal relationship. This category also includes what might be called *traces of action.* For instance, as you observe cigarette butts, orange peels, and wastepaper left by the person you will soon interact with, you form an impression that will eventually influence your meeting. Perceptions of time and timing comprise another important part of the communicative environment. When something occurs, how frequently it occurs, and the tempo or rhythm of actions are clearly a part of the communicative world even though they are not a part of the physical environment per se.

Spatial Environment

Proxemics is the study of the use and perception of social and personal space. Under this heading is a body of work called *small group ecology,* which concerns itself with how people use and respond to spatial relationships in formal and informal group settings. Such studies deal with seating and spatial arrangements as related to leadership, communication flow, and the task at hand. On an even broader level, some attention has been given to spatial relationships in crowds and densely populated situations. Personal space orientation is sometimes studied in the context of conversation distance and how it varies according to sex, status, roles, cultural orientation, and so forth. The term *territoriality* is also used frequently in the study of proxemics to denote the human tendency to stake out personal territory (or untouchable space) much as wild animals and birds do.

THE COMMUNICATORS' PHYSICAL CHARACTERISTICS

This category covers things that remain relatively unchanged during the period of interaction. They are influential nonverbal cues that are not visibly movement bound. Included are physique or body shape, general attractiveness, height, weight, hair, skin color or tone, and so forth. Odors (body or breath) associated with the person are normally considered part of a person's physical appearance. Further, objects associated with the interactants also may affect their physical appearance. These are called *artifacts* and include things such as clothes, lipstick, eyeglasses, wigs and other hairpieces, false eyelashes, jewelry, and accessories such as attaché cases.

BODY MOVEMENT AND POSITION

Body movement and position typically includes gestures, movements of the body (limbs, hands, head, feet, and legs), facial expressions (smiles), eye behavior (blinking, direction and length of gaze, and pupil dilation), and posture. The furrow of the brow, the slump of a shoulder, and the tilt of a head are all considered body movements and positions. Specifically, the major areas are gestures, posture, touching behavior, facial expressions, and eye behavior.

Gestures

There are many different types of gestures (and variations of these types), but the most frequently studied are the following:

1. **Speech independent.** These gestures are not tied to speech, but they have a direct verbal translation or dictionary definition, usually consisting of a word or two or a phrase. There is high agreement among members of a culture or subculture on the verbal "translation" of these signals. The gestures used to represent "A-OK" or "Peace" (also known as the "V-for-Victory" sign) are examples of speech-independent gestures for large segments of U.S. culture.
2. **Speech related.** These gestures are directly tied to, or accompany, speech— often serving to illustrate what is being said verbally. These movements may accent or emphasize a word or phrase, sketch a path of thought, point to present objects, depict a spatial relationship, depict the rhythm or pacing of an event, draw a picture of a referent, depict a bodily action, or serve as commentary on the regulation and organization of the interactive process.

Posture

Posture is normally studied in conjunction with other nonverbal signals to determine the degree of attention or involvement, the degree of status relative to the other interactive partner, or the degree of liking for the other interactant. A forward-leaning posture, for example, has been associated with higher involvement, more liking, and lower status in studies where the interactants did not know each other very well. Posture is also a key indicator of the intensity of some emotional states, for example, the dropping posture associated with sadness or the rigid, tense posture associated with anger. The extent to which the communicators mirror each other's posture may also reflect rapport or an attempt to build rapport.

Touching Behavior

Touching may be self-focused or other focused. Self-focused manipulations, not usually made for purposes of communicating, may reflect a person's particular state or a habit. Many are commonly called *nervous mannerisms*. Some of these actions are relics from an earlier time in life—times when we first learn how to manage our emotions, develop social contacts, or perform some instructional task. Sometimes we perform these manipulations as we adapt to such learning experiences, and they stay with us when we face similar situations later in life, often as only part of the original movement. Some refer to these types of self-focused manipulation as *adaptors*. These adaptors may involve various manipulations of one's own body such as licking, picking, holding, pinching, and scratching. Object adaptors are manipulations practiced in conjunction with an object, as when a reformed male cigarette smoker reaches toward his breast pocket for the nonexistent package of cigarettes. Of course, not all behaviors that reflect habitual actions or an anxious disposition can be traced to earlier adaptations, but they do represent a part of the overall pattern of bodily action.

One of the most potent forms of nonverbal communication occurs when two people touch. Touch can be virtually electric, but it also can irritate, condescend, or comfort.

Touch is a highly ambiguous form of behavior whose meaning often takes more from the context, the nature of the relationship, and the manner of execution than from the configuration of the touch per se. Some researchers are concerned with touching behavior as an important factor in the child's early development; some are concerned with adult touching behavior. Subcategories include stroking, hitting, greetings and farewells, holding, and guiding another's movements.

Facial Expressions

Most studies of the face are concerned with the configurations that display various emotional states. The six primary affects receiving the most study are anger, sadness, surprise, happiness, fear, and disgust. Facial expressions also can function as regulatory gestures, providing feedback and managing the flow of interaction. In fact, some researchers believe the primary function of the face is to communicate, not to express emotions.

Eye Behavior

Where we look, when we look, and how long we look during interaction are the primary foci for studies of gazing. *Gaze* refers to the eye movement we make in the general direction of another's face. *Mutual gaze* occurs when interactants look into each other's eyes. The dilation and constriction of our pupils also has interest to those who study nonverbal communication because it is sometimes an indicator of interest, attention, or involvement.

Vocal Behavior

Vocal behavior deals with *how* something is said, not what is said. It deals with the range of nonverbal vocal cues surrounding common speech behavior. Generally, a distinction is made between two types of sounds:

1. The sound variations made with the vocal cords during talk that are a function of changes in pitch, duration, loudness, and silence
2. Sounds that result primarily from physiological mechanisms other than the vocal cords, for example, the pharyngeal, oral, or nasal cavities

Most of the research on vocal behavior and its effects on human interaction has focused on pitch level and variability; the duration of sounds (clipped or drawn out); pauses within the speech stream and the latency of response during turn exchanges; loudness level and variability; resonance; precise or slurred articulation; rate; rhythm; and intruding sound during speech such as "uh" or "um." The study of vocal signals encompasses a broad range of interests, from questions focusing on stereotypes associated with certain voices to questions about the effects of vocal behavior on comprehension and persuasion. Thus even specialized sounds such as laughing, belching, yawning, swallowing, moaning, and the like may be of interest to the extent that they may affect the outcome of interaction.

NONVERBAL COMMUNICATION IN THE TOTAL COMMUNICATION PROCESS

[A close examination of these varied cues reveals] the inseparable nature of verbal and nonverbal signals. Ray Birdwhistell, a pioneer in nonverbal research, reportedly said that studying only *nonverbal* communication is like studying *noncardiac* physiology. His point is well taken. It is not easy to dissect human interaction and make one diagnosis that concerns only verbal behavior and another that concerns only nonverbal behavior. The verbal dimension is so intimately woven and subtly represented in so much of what has been previously labeled *non*verbal that the term does not always adequately describe the behavior under study. Some of the most noteworthy scholars associated with nonverbal study refuse to segregate words from gestures and hence work under the broader terms of *communication* or *face-to-face interaction* (McNeill, 2000).... Because verbal and nonverbal systems operate together as part of the larger communication process, efforts to distinguish clearly between the two have not been very successful. One common misconception, for example, assumes nonverbal behavior is used solely to communicate emotional messages, whereas verbal behavior is for conveying ideas. Words can carry much emotion—we can talk explicitly about emotions, and we also communicate emotion between the lines in verbal nuances. Conversely, nonverbal cues are often used for purposes other than showing emotion; as examples, people in conversation use eye movements to help tell each other when it is time to switch speaking turns, and people commonly use hand gestures while talking to help convey their ideas (McNeill, 2000).

Argyle (1988) has identified the following primary functions of nonverbal behavior in human communication as follows:

1. Expressing emotion
2. Conveying interpersonal attitudes (like/dislike, dominance/submission, etc.)
3. Presenting one's personality to others
4. Accompanying speech for the purposes of managing turn taking, feedback, attention, and so on.

Argyle also notes that nonverbal behaviors are important in many rituals, such as greeting. Notice that none of these functions of nonverbal behavior is limited to nonverbal behavior alone; that is, we can express emotions and attitudes, present ourselves in a particular light, and manage the interaction using verbal cues, too. This does not suggest, however, that in any given situation we might not rely more heavily on verbal behavior for some purposes and on nonverbal for others.

We also need to recognize that the ways we attribute meanings to verbal and nonverbal behavior are not all that different either. Nonverbal actions, like verbal ones, may communicate more than one message at a time—for example, the way you nonverbally make it clear to another person that you want to keep talking may simultaneously express your need for dominance over that person and, perhaps, your emotional state. When you grip a child's shoulder during a reprimand, you may increase comprehension and recall, but you may also elicit such a negative reaction that the child fails to obey. A smile can be a part of an emotional expression, an attitudinal message, part of a self-presentation, or a listener response to manage the interaction. And, like verbal behavior, the meanings attributed to nonverbal behavior may be stereotyped, idiomatic, or ambiguous. Furthermore, the same nonverbal behavior performed in different contexts may, like words, receive different attributions of meaning. For example, looking down at the floor may reflect sadness in one situation and submissiveness or lack of involvement in another. Finally, in an effort to identify the fundamental categories of meaning associated with nonverbal behavior, Mehrabian (1970, 1981) identified a threefold perspective resulting from his extensive testing:

1. **Immediacy.** Sometimes we react to things by evaluating them—positive or negative, good or bad, like or dislike.
2. **Status.** Sometimes we enact or perceive behaviors that indicate various aspects of status to us—strong or weak, superior or subordinate.
3. **Responsiveness.** This third category refers to our perceptions of activity—slow or fast, active or passive.

In various verbal and nonverbal studies over the past three decades, dimensions similar to Mehrabian's have been reported consistently by investigators from diverse fields studying diverse phenomena. It is reasonable to conclude, therefore, that these three dimensions are basic responses to our environment and are reflected in the way we assign meaning to both verbal and nonverbal behavior. Most of this work, however, depends on subjects translating their reactions to a nonverbal act into one identified by verbal descriptors. This issue has already been addressed in our discussion of the way the brain processes different pieces of information. In general, then, nonverbal signals, like words, can and do have multiple uses and meanings; like words, nonverbal signals have denotative and connotative meanings; and like words, nonverbal signals play an active role in communicating liking, power, and responsiveness....

NONVERBAL COMMUNICATION IN EVERYDAY LIFE

Clearly nonverbal signals are a critical part of all our communicative endeavors. Sometimes nonverbal signals are the most important part of our message. Understanding and effectively using nonverbal behavior is crucial in virtually every sector of our society.

Consider the role of nonverbal signals in therapeutic situations. Therapists use nonverbal behavior to build rapport with clients (Tickle-Degnen & Rosenthal, 1994). Their ability to read nonverbal signals associated with client problems surely assists in diagnosis and treatment. A slight change in tone of voice or a glance away from the patient at the wrong time and a physician may communicate a message very different from intended (Buller & Street, 1992). In situations where verbal communication is often constrained, as in nurse-physician interaction during an operation, effective nonverbal communication is literally the difference between life and death. The significance of nonverbal cues in the arts—dance, theatrical performances, music, films, photography, and so on—is obvious. The nonverbal symbolism of various ceremonies and rituals (e.g., the trappings of the marriage ceremony, Christmas decorations, religious rituals, funerals, and so forth) creates important and necessary responses in the participants. Certainly, an understanding of nonverbal signals prepares us for communicating across cultures, classes, or age groups and with different ethnic groups within our culture (Lee, Matumoto, Kobayashi, Krupp, Maniatis, & Roberts, 1992). Nonverbal messages not only help determine how well you do in a job interview, but also play an integral part in your job performance—whether it involves public relations, customer service, marketing, advertising, supervision, or leadership (DePaulo, 1992; Hecker & Stewart, 1988). Diplomats often prefer implicit accommodation rather than explicit, thereby using and relying heavily on nonverbal signals.

A list of all the situations where nonverbal communication plays an important role would be interminable—especially if we included our everyday activities involving forming impressions of other people and building, maintaining, and ending relationships. Therefore, we limit our discussion in this chapter to four areas that touch all our lives: crime and punishment, televised politics, classroom behavior, and courtship behavior. . . .

Crime and Punishment

The desire to identify criminal types has been a subject of study for centuries. Because it is unlikely that a person will tell you that he or she is a criminal or potential criminal, nonverbal indicators become especially important. At one time, some people thought criminals could be identified by their facial features or the pattern of bumps on their head. In recent years, scientists have used a knowledge of nonverbal behavior to examine both criminal acts and the arena for assessing guilt or innocence, the courtroom.

One study analyzed the appearance and movements of people who walked through one of the highest assault areas in New York City (Grayson & Stein, 1981). Then, prisoners who had knowledge of such matters were asked to view the films of the potential victims and indicate the likelihood of assault. In addition to finding that older people are a prime target, the researchers also found that potential victims tended to move differently. They tended to take long or short strides (not medium); and their body parts did not seem to move in synchrony; that is, they seemed less graceful and fluid in their movement. Other studies have tried to identify nonverbal characteristics that rapists use to select their victims. Some rapists look for women who exhibit passivity, a lack of confidence, and vulnerability; others prefer the exact opposite, wishing to "put an uppity woman in her place." The conclusion seems to recommend a public nonverbal demeanor that is confident yet not aggressive (Myers, Templer, & Brown, 1984).

Another study that assessed potentially aggressive acts focused on mothers who abused their children (Givens, 1978). It was noted that even while playing with their children, these mothers communicated their dislike (turning away, not smiling, etc.) by their nonverbal behavior. Just as abusive and nonabusive mothers differ in their behavior, the children of abusive parents and nonabusive parents differ in their nonverbal behavior (Hecht, Foster, Dunn, Williams, Anderson, & Pulbratek, 1986). . . .

Because of the important implications of decisions made in courtrooms and the desire to maintain impartial communication, almost every facet of the courtroom process is being analyzed. Judges are cautioned to minimize possible signs of partiality in their voice and positioning. Research suggests that judges' attitudes and nonverbal cues may indeed influence the outcome of a trial (Blanck & Rosenthal, 1992). . . . In some cases, attorneys and witnesses have been videotaped in pretrial practice sessions to determine whether they are conveying nonverbally any messages they want to avoid. The study of nonverbal behavior is also important to the process of jury selection. Although this attention to nonverbal signals emanating from prospective jurors may indicate a degree of sensitivity that did not previously exist, we need not worry that attorneys or social scientists will become so skilled they can rig juries (Saks, 1976).

Televised Politics

Politicians have long recognized the important role of nonverbal behavior.... The tired, overweight, physically unappealing political bosses of yesteryear have been replaced by younger, good-looking, vigorous candidates who can capture the public's vote with an assist from their nonverbal attraction. The average American currently watches between 30 and 40 hours of television each week. Television has certainly helped to structure some of our nonverbal perceptions, and more and more political candidates recognize the tremendous influence these perceptions may have on the eventual election outcome. Television seems especially well suited to nonverbal signals that express positive relationship messages (e.g., facial expressions that communicate sincerity, body positions that suggest immediacy, or vocal tones that are perceived as caring). Television requires what Jamieson (1988) calls "a new eloquence—a softer, warmer style of communication." This in no way minimizes the necessity of a candidate also displaying nonverbal signals that would help to communicate assertiveness and energy. How have our presidential candidates fared? ...

An analysis of the 1976 Carter-Ford presidential debates argues that Gerald Ford's "loss" was attributable to less eye gaze with the camera, grimmer facial expressions, and less favorable camera angles (Tiemens, 1978). Subsequently, Jimmy Carter's loss to Ronald Reagan in the 1980 debate was attributed to Carter's visible tension and his inability to "coordinate his nonverbal behavior with his verbal message" (Ritter & Henry, 1990). Effective leaders are often seen as people who confidently take stock of a situation, perform smoothly, and put those around them at ease. Many saw Reagan's nonverbal behavior this way. In 1984 Reagan's expressiveness and physical attractiveness were evident, whereas his opponent, Walter Mondale, was perceived as low in expressiveness and attractiveness (Patterson, Churchill, Burger, & Powell, 1992). Expressions of fear may be the biggest turnoff for voters. Looking down, hesitating, making rapid, jerky movements or seeming to freeze as Dan Quayle did when Lloyd Bentsen told him in the 1988 vice presidential debate, "You're no Jack Kennedy." Some even associated Walter Mondale's tense smile with a fear grimace (Masters, 1989; Sullivan et al., 1991).

Fortunately, media experts do not control all the variables—not the least of which is the public's increasing knowledge of how political images can be molded through television. One of Richard Nixon's image-makers in 1968, Roger Ailes, offered the following perspective 15 years later: "The TV public is very smart in the sense that somewhere, somehow, they make a judgment about the candidates they see. Anybody who claims he can figure out that process is full of it."

Classroom Behavior

Whether it takes place in the classroom itself or not, the teaching/learning process is a gold mine for discovering the richness and importance of nonverbal behavior (Andersen & Andersen, 1982; Babad, 1992; Philippot, Feldman, & McGee, 1992; Woolfolk & Brooks, 1983).

Acceptance and understanding of ideas and feelings by both teacher and student, encouraging and criticizing, silence, and questioning all involve nonverbal elements. Consider the following instances as representative of the variety of classroom nonverbal cues:

1. The frantic hand-waver who is sure he or she has the correct answer
2. The student who is sure she or he does not know the answer and tries to avoid eye contact with the teacher
3. The effects of student dress, hair length, and adornment on teacher-student interaction
4. The glowering facial expressions, threatening gestures, and critical tone of voice frequently used for discipline in elementary schools
5. Teachers who request student questioning and criticism, but whose nonverbal actions make it clear they will not be receptive
6. The way arrangement of seating and monitoring behavior during examinations reveal a teacher's degree of trust in students
7. Professors who announce they have plenty of time for student conferences, but whose fidgeting and glancing at a watch suggest otherwise
8. Teachers who try to assess visual feedback to determine student comprehension
9. The ways different classroom designs (wall colors, space between seats, windows) influence student participation and learning
10. The nonverbal cues that signal student-teacher closeness or distance

Subtle nonverbal influence in the classroom can sometimes have dramatic results, as Rosenthal and Jacobson (1968) found. Intelligence quotient (IQ) tests were given to elementary school pupils prior to their entering for the fall term. Randomly (that is, not according to scores), some students were labeled as high scorers on an "intellectual blooming test" indicating they would show unusual intellectual development in the following year. Teachers were given this information. These students showed a sharp rise on IQ tests given at the end of the year, which experimenters attributed to teacher expectations and to the way these students were treated.

> To summarize our speculations, we may say that by what she said, by how and when she said it, by her facial expressions, postures, and perhaps by her touch, the teacher may have communicated to the children of the experimental group that she expected improved intellectual performance. Such communications together with possible changes in teaching techniques may have helped the child learn by changing his self-concept, his expectations of his own behavior, and his motivation, as well as his cognitive style and skills. (p. 180)

The influence of nonverbal behavior in the classroom can be a two-way street. Teachers who are perceived by their students as establishing physical and psychological closeness through nonverbal behavior produce positive learning outcomes. Furthermore, students whose nonverbal behavior is perceived by teachers as establishing this kind of immediacy seem more likely to elicit positive expressions from their teachers (Baringer & McCroskey, 2000). The influence of nonverbal behavior that communicates warmth and closeness in conventional classrooms promises to be even more important to the success of distance education (Guerrero & Miller, 1998; Mottet, 2000).

Courtship Behavior

One commentary on nonverbal courtship behavior is found in the following excerpts from the Beatles' song "Something":

> *Something in the way she moves*
> *Attracts me like no other lover . . .*
> *Something in the way she woos me . . .*
> *Something in her smile she knows*
> *That I don't need no other lover . . .*
> *Something in her style that shows me . . .*
> *You're asking me will my love grow . . .*
> *You stick around, now*
> *It may show . . .*

As the song suggests, we know there is "something" highly influential in our non-verbal courtship behavior. We are, however, at a very early stage in quantifying these patterns of behavior. On a purely intuitive level, we know that some men and some women can exude such messages as "I'm available," "I'm knowledge-able," or "I want you" without saying a word. These messages can be expressed by the thrust of one's hips, touch gestures, extra long eye contact, carefully look-ing at the other's body, showing excitement and desire in fleeting facial expres-sions, and gaining close proximity. When subtle enough, these moves will allow both parties to deny that either had committed themselves to a courtship ritual.

Studies involving flirtation behavior between men and women in bars (sin-gles bars, hotel cocktail lounges, bars within restaurants, etc.) provide some observational data on the role of nonverbal signals in the courtship process (McCormick & Jones, 1989; Moore, 1985; Perper & Weis, 1987). Most of the early signaling seemed to be performed by women. The most frequently observed behaviors included three types of eye gaze (a room-encompassing glance; a short, darting glance at a specific person; and a fixed gaze of at least 3 seconds at a specific other); smiling at a specific other person; laughing and giggling in response to another's comments; tossing one's head, a movement sometimes accompanied by stroking of the hair; grooming, primping, and adjustment of clothes; caressing objects such as keys or a glass; a solitary dance (keeping time to the music with visible movements); and a wide variety of seemingly "acci-dental" touching of a specific other. The researchers did not specifically examine the type of clothing, nor did they examine the tone of voice used—both of which are likely to be influential flirtation behaviors. In an effort to determine whether these behaviors were more likely to occur in a context where signaling interest in and attraction to others was expected, the researchers observed the behavior of women and men in snack bars, meetings, and libraries. None of these contexts revealed anything close to the number of flirting behaviors found in bars....

Does the courtship process proceed according to a sequence of steps? Perper (1985) describes courtship's "core sequence" like this: The *approach* involves getting the two people in the same general proximity; *acknowledging and turning toward the other* is the invitation to begin talking; during *talk*, there will be an increasing amount of fleeting, *nonintimate touching and a gradually increasing intensity in eye gaze*; finally, Perper says the two will exhibit *more and more synchrony in their movements*. Obviously, either person can short-circuit the sequence at any point....

Morris (1971) also believes that heterosexual couples in Western culture go through a sequence of steps, like courtship patterns of other animals, on the road to sexual intimacy. Notice the predominant nonverbal theme:

1. Eye to body
2. Eye to eye
3. Voice to voice
4. Hand to hand
5. Arm to shoulder
6. Arm to waist
7. Mouth to mouth
8. Hand to head
9. Hand to body
10. Mouth to breast
11. Hand to genitals
12. Genitals to genitals and/or mouth to genitals

Morris ... believes these steps generally follow the same order, although he admits there are variations. Skipping steps or moving to a level of intimacy beyond what would be expected is found in socially formalized types of bodily contact, for example, a good-night kiss. It should be noted that any of the behaviors identified by ... Morris can be performed in a more or less intimate way. Mouth-to-mouth kisses, for example, may be performed with little intimacy or with a great deal of it....

Up to now, we have concentrated on the nonverbal courtship behavior of unmarried men and women. The use of specific types of gazing, touching, and other actions studied in heterosexual courtship patterns is also an important part of homosexual courtship (Delph, 1978).

SUMMARY

The term *nonverbal* is commonly used to describe all human communication events that transcend spoken or written words. At the same time, we should realize that these nonverbal events and behaviors can be interpreted through verbal symbols. We also found that any classification scheme that separates things into two discrete categories (e.g., verbal/nonverbal, left/right brain, vocal/nonvocal, etc.) will not be able to account for factors that do not seem to fit either category. We might more appropriately think of behaviors as existing on a continuum with some behaviors overlapping two continua....

The theoretical writings and research on nonverbal communication can be broken down into the following three areas:

1. The communication environment (physical and spatial)
2. The communicator's physical characteristics
3. Body movement and position (gestures, posture, touching, facial expressions, eye behavior, and vocal behavior)

Nonverbal communication should not be studied as an isolated phenomenon but as an inseparable part of the total communication process. The interrelationships between verbal and nonverbal behavior were illustrated in our discussion of how nonverbal behavior functions in repeating, conflicting with, substituting for, complementing, accenting/moderating, and regulating verbal communication. Nonverbal communication is important because of its role in the total communication system, the tremendous quantity of informational cues it gives in any particular situation, and its use in fundamental areas of our daily life....

REVIEW QUESTIONS

1. Define *nonverbal communication* in a way that does not depend on the "non" and that acknowledges the virtual impossibility of separating verbal and nonverbal cues.
2. What are "traces of action," and how have they affected your communicating?
3. Define *proxemics, territoriality, artifacts, adaptors,* and *gaze.*
4. Give an example of how nonverbal cues communicate immediacy. Do the same with status and responsiveness.
5. Describe three important nonverbal facets of a funeral and three different important nonverbal facets of a church service.
6. How is nonverbal communicating important in a job interview?
7. How do you think a judge's nonverbal behavior in the courtroom can affect the outcome of a trial?
8. Describe three obvious ways nonverbal communication functions in the interpersonal communication class that you are currently taking.

PROBES

1. What happens to your understanding when everyday human behavior is categorized into "spatial environment," "gestures," "eye behavior," "touching behavior" and the other categories used by nonverbal researchers?
2. Some research—and everyday experience—indicates that, when a person's verbal and nonverbal cues contradict each other, people tend to

believe what's being communicated nonverbally. Do you agree or disagree? Explain.

3. In your opinion, what is more important in dating contexts: eye gaze, vocal behavior, or touch? Explain.
4. From your dating experience, what are the two most important nonverbal elements of successful dating behavior?
5. Some people complain that an emphasis on nonverbal cues in the courts, politics, and the classroom focuses on what's trivial rather than on what's important. They argue that the main meanings should be in the words, the language that's used. What is your position on this issue?

REFERENCES

Andersen, P. A., & Andersen, J. (1982). Nonverbal immediacy in instruction. In L. L. Barker (Ed.), *Communication in the classroom.* Englewood Cliffs, NJ: Prentice-Hall.

Argyle, M. (1988). *Bodily communication* (2nd ed.). London: Methuen.

Babad, E. (1992). Teacher expectancies and nonverbal behavior. In R. S. Feldman (Ed.), *Applications of nonverbal behavioral theories and research.* Hillsdale, NJ: Erlbaum.

Baringer, D. K., and McCroskey, J. C. (2000). Immediacy in the classroom: Student immediacy. *Communication Education, 49,* 178–186.

Blanck, P. D., & Rosenthal, R. (1992). Nonverbal behavior in the courtroom. In R. S. Feldman (Ed.), *Applications of nonverbal behavioral theories and research.* Hillsdale, NJ: Erlbaum.

Buller, D. B., & Street, R. L., Jr. (1992). Physician-patient relationships. In R. S. Feldman (Ed.), *Applications of nonverbal behavioral theories and research.* Hillsdale, NJ: Erlbaum.

Delph, E. W. (1978). *The silent community: Public homosexual encounters.* Beverly Hills, CA: Sage.

DePaulo, P. J. (1992). Applications of nonverbal behavior research in marketing and management. In R. S. Feldman (Ed.), *Applications of nonverbal behavioral theories and research.* Hillsdale, NJ: Erlbaum.

Givens, D. B. (1978). Contrasting nonverbal styles in mother-child interaction: Examples from a study of child abuse. *Semiotica, 24,* 33–47.

Grayson, B., & Stein, M. I. (1981). Attracting assault: Victims' nonverbal cues. *Journal of Communication, 31,* 68–75.

Guerrero, L. K., & Miller, T. A. (1998). Associations between nonverbal behaviors and initial impressions of instructor competence and course content in videotaped distance education courses. *Communication Education, 47,* 30–42.

Hecht, M., Foster, S. H., Dunn, D. J., Williams, J. K., Anderson, D. R., & Pulbratek, D. (1986). Nonverbal behavior of young abused and neglected children. *Communication Education, 35,* 134–142.

Hecker, S., & Stewart, D. W. (Eds.). (1988). *Nonverbal communication in advertising*. Lexington, MA: Lexington.

Jamieson, K. H. (1988). *Eloquence in an electronic age*. New York: Oxford University Press.

Lee, M. E., Matsumoto, D., Kobayashi, M., Krupp, D., Maniatis, E. F., & Roberts, W. (1992). Cultural influences on nonverbal behavior in applied settings. In R. S. Feldman (Ed.), *Applications of nonverbal behavioral theories and research*. Hillsdale, NJ: Erlbaum.

Masters, R. D. (1989). *The nature of politics*. New Haven, CT: Yale University Press.

McCormick, N. B., & Jones, A. J. (1989). Gender differences in nonverbal flirtation. *Journal of Sex Education & Therapy, 15*, 271–282.

McNeill, D. (1992). *Hand and mind: What gestures reveal about thought*. Chicago: University of Chicago Press.

McNeill, D. (Ed.). (2000). *Language and gesture*. New York: Cambridge University Press.

Mehrabian, A. (1970). A semantic space for nonverbal behavior. *Journal of Consulting and Clinical Psychology, 35*, 248–257.

Mehrabian, A. (1981). *Silent messages* (2nd ed.). Belmont, CA: Wadsworth.

Moore, M. M. (1985). Nonverbal courtship patterns in women: Content and consequences. *Ethology and Sociobiology, 6*, 237–247.

Morris, D. (1971). *Intimate behavior*. New York: Random House.

Mottet, T. P. (2000). Interactive television instructors' perceptions of students' nonverbal responsiveness and their influence on distance teaching. *Communication Education, 49*, 146–164.

Patterson, M. L., Churchill, M. E., Burger, G. K., & Powell, J. L. (1992). Verbal and nonverbal modality effects on impressions of political candidates: Analysis from the 1984 presidential debates. *Communication Monographs, 59*, 231–242.

Perper, T. (1985). *Sex signals: The biology of love*. Philadelphia: ISI Press.

Perper, T., & Weis, D. L. (1987). Proceptive and rejective strategies of U.S. and Canadian college women. *Journal of Sex Research, 23*, 455–480.

Philippot, P., Feldman, R. S., & McGee, G. (1992). Nonverbal behavioral skills in an educational context: Typical and atypical populations. In R. S. Feldman (Ed.), *Applications of nonverbal behavioral theories and research*. Hillsdale, NJ: Erlbaum.

Ritter, K., & Henry, D. (1990). The 1980 Reagan-Carter presidential debate. In R. V. Friedenberg (Ed.), *Rhetorical studies of national political debates: 1960–1988*. New York: Praeger.

Rosenthal, R., & Jacobson, L. (1968). *Pygmalion in the classroom*. New York: Holt, Rinehart & Winston.

Saks, M. J. (1976). Social scientists can't rig juries. *Psychology Today, 9*, 48–50, 55–57.

Sullivan, D. G., Masters, R. D., Lanzetta, J. T., McHugo, G. J., Plate, E., & Englis, B. G. (1991). Facial displays and political leadership. In G. Schubert & R. Masters (Eds.), *Primate politics*. Carbondale: University of Southern Illinois Press.

Tickle-Degnen, L., Hall, J., & Rosenthal, R. (1994). Nonverbal behavior. In V. S. Ramachandran (Ed.), *Encyclopedia of human behavior* (Vol. 3). New York: Academic Press.

Tiemens, R. K. (1978). Television's portrayal of the 1976 presidential debates: An analysis of visual content. *Communication Monographs, 45,* 362–370.

Woolfolk, A. E., & Brooks, D. M. (1983). Nonverbal communication in teaching. In E. Gordon (Ed.), *Review of Research in Education, 10.* Washington, DC: American Educational Research Association.

———

Functions of Nonverbal Behavior

Daniel J. Canary, Michael J. Cody, and Valerie L. Manusov

The readings prior to this one describe what nonverbal communication "is" and some of what it "does." In this final reading in the chapter, three communication teacher-scholars identify some of the main *functions* of nonverbal cues.

Canary, Cody, and Manusov first point out that, most of the time, no single nonverbal cue operates by itself. This is why it's dangerous to interpret a cue like folded arms as always indicating "closure" or "rejection." Instead, for example, facial cues function along with eye behavior, posture, and tone of voice to contribute to what's communicated.

One of the main functions of these nonverbal behaviors is to express emotions. The truth of this point is demonstrated every time someone says, "You say you love me, but I don't believe you," or screams, "I'm not MAD!!" In each case, the person interpreting the communication is reading emotions from the nonverbal cues, not the verbal ones. The words "I love you" express that complex emotion much less effectively than the amount of time one person spends with another, the quality of eye contact, and the amount and type of touch—all nonverbal cues. Similarly, the loud, harsh tone of voice accompanying the words "I'm not mad" reveals that the person's emotions are very different from what the words express.

The second function of nonverbal cues is to manage an individual's identity or the impression he or she leaves with others. The authors talk about the believability of "babyfaced" adults and the ways nonverbal attractiveness can lead to many other positive judgments. They note that people rely on nonverbal cues despite the potential errors in using them to assess others' identities. And they note how each of us wears certain "identity badges."

A third function is to manage conversation—to indicate whose turn it is to talk. Good conversations include the smooth exchange of speaking turns, and this is made possible mainly through nonverbal cues such as eye behavior, vocal pitch and tone, rate of speech, and gesture.

Relational messages are also sent nonverbally, and this is the fourth function discussed here. People indicate how close they feel toward others, whether power is balanced, and whether the relationship is formal or informal, for example. And they do these things, again, with eyes, voice, face, posture, gesture, and timing. People who want to change the definition of their relationship also often change nonverbal aspects of their communicating, for example, by standing closer or farther away, touching more or less, or changing the amount they smile and look the other person in the eye.

This reading and the previous one give you an overview of what nonverbal cues are and how they help people communicate.

[N] onverbal cues—whether unintended or intended, universal or culturally bound—play a significant role in our interactions with others. We might say that nonverbal cues perform a range of *communicative functions*, or tasks; they allow us to try to fulfill a number of our interpersonal goals. Such a functional approach to nonverbal behaviors makes two assumptions. First, it assumes that clusters of behaviors are used together to communicate a function; although a single behavior (e.g., gaze) may fulfill a function, it is more common for cues, including language, to work together. Second, the functional approach assumes that any one behavior can be used, alongside other cues, to communicate any of several functions. Proxemics, for example, may be a part of communicating a liking for another person or it may be an indication of the amount of power one person has over someone else.

Emotional Expression

For many people, the most obvious functions of nonverbal cues are to communicate how we feel and to reveal how others are feeling. In particular, the term "facial expression" shows the inherent connection often made between certain behaviors and their meanings. Although the previous discussion's warning against assuming an automatic, natural connection between behaviors and their meanings is important to keep in mind, nonverbal cues *are* a vital part of emotional expressions. When we are trying to understand what others are feeling, for example, we look at their face and their posture and listen to their vocal tone. When we want to communicate our feelings to others, we are inclined to do so nonverbally. But the relationship between nonverbal cues and emotional expression is complex, in large part because emotions themselves are complex.

Some researchers argue that *emotional expressions* reflect an area of universal communication that can be used and understood by all. To provide evidence for this, they point to studies that show that people from a range of cultures can recognize the emotions reflected in certain photographs (Ekman & Friesen, 1969). The similarity between the expressions used by humans and those used by other primates (e.g., showing aggression or sadness) also reflects that some expressions may have biological and evolutionary origins. However, most of the emotional expressions we actually use are modified through our culture's display rules. We learn, for example, *how* to show sadness, happiness, and anger in ways appropriate to our culture. In the United States, for example, we would likely show grief on our faces and in the quietness of our voices. We also have an idea of when our "grieving period" should be complete (i.e., a chronemic rule). In several African cultures, however, the way to show grief is through loud wailing for extended periods. The same emotion is reflected in different behaviors as dictated by the culture in which they occur.

Other work limits the extent to which emotional expressions form a simple, universal set of messages. Motley's (1993) studies revealed that most emotional expressions used in everyday conversations cannot be interpreted outside of the conversation in which they occur. Seldom do we use the kind of exaggerated expressions that led Ekman and Friesen (1969) to conclude that everyone can read emotional messages. Instead, most of the movements that our faces make in our conversations with others act as "interjections" (e.g., communicating the equivalent of "gosh," "geez," "really," or "oh, please") and make sense only when we have also heard the topic being discussed. Thus, although nonverbal behavior is an important component of emotional expression, any particular cue (e.g., a facial expression) is likely to need other behaviors (such as language or vocal cues) to be interpreted accurately.

Impression Formation/Identity Management

Not only do we look toward another's expressions, we also make assessments of his or her *expressiveness,* and this reflects our reliance on nonverbal cues for assessing what another person is like.... In this section, the focus is on showing not only how nonverbal cues work as part of person perception (*impression formation*), but also the ways in which people work to get others to see them in a certain way (*identity management*).

Many of the examples given up to this point already highlight how important nonverbal cues are for judging others. In 1988, Berry and ZebrowitzMcArthur showed not only the link between nonverbal cues and impressions, but also the important *effects* that such impressions may have. These researchers used a simulated courtroom trial to study the effects of physical attractiveness; in particular, they looked at the importance of facial maturity on perceptions and on trial outcomes. Berry and Zebrowitz-McArthur found that "babyfaced" adults are thought to be more honest than adults with more mature facial features. Because of this, the babyfaced adults in the mock trial were seen to be less likely to have intentionally committed a crime, and they subsequently received shorter criminal sentences.

Berry and Zebrowitz-McArthur's study helps show the series of links that people tend to make when judging others through nonverbal means. We see one or more behaviors or cues (e.g., little gaze or physical attractiveness) and assume that the person has certain characteristics (e.g., shyness). We may then treat that person in a particular way because we believe he or she has certain characteristics; this treatment may actually help bring around those qualities, creating a *self-fulfilling prophecy*. More likely ... we tend to *notice* those behaviors that are consistent with the beliefs we have about another and ignore those that are inconsistent. Because of this process, we come to believe that we have made the "right" judgment of another. Importantly, however, research has revealed *very few* reliable personality characteristics that are revealed through nonverbal means (Burgoon, Buller, & Woodall, 1989).

People still rely on nonverbal cues, despite the potential errors in using them to assess others. For instance, besides helping us try to figure out what another person is like, we also reflect aspects of our *own* identity (or desired identity) through nonverbal means. Others are likely to know our sex or ethnicity by observing our physical features. This ability to reflect certain aspects of ourselves to others is linked with others' ability to make judgments of us. Specifically, in her discussion of Tajfel's research, Burgoon (1994) says that,

> Manifest indications of one's cultural, social, demographic, and personal characteristics serve as "identity badges," enabling individuals to project their own identification with various personal and social categories while simultaneously enabling observers to use the same cues as an instant means of classification. Thus, not only may individuals rely on their own nonverbal behavior as affirmation or self-verification of their identities ... but others may also treat such information as outward reflections of the inner self. (p. 245)

Conversation Management

... The ways in which nonverbal cues allow for the structuring of conversation is known as *conversation management.*

Many examples show nonverbal cues' role in facilitating conversations (e.g., we gesture to make points and use high levels of gaze to show we are listening to another), but one of the most notable is how the behaviors help people take "turns" in their conversation (i.e., to know when it is our time to speak and to know when it is our conversational partner's time). According to Burgoon (1994), "[n]onverbal cues are the lubricant that keeps the conversation [turn-taking] machine well-oiled" (p. 268).

> Research has identified that speaker and listener behaviors determine whose turn it is to speak, auditor feedback cues that control speaker behavior, behaviors that mark changes in the tone and topic of interaction, the influence of interruptions and other dynamic cues on floor-holding and the flow of conversation, the role of distance and silence in maintaining engagement, and factors influencing the smoothness of interaction. (Burgoon, 1994, p. 268)

In most cases, "good" conversations include the smooth exchange of speaking turns; this is made possible largely through nonverbal cues such as eye behavior, vocal pitch and tone, rate of speech, and gestures. Cappella's work (reviewed in his 1994 chapter) refers to people's ability to *keep* the floor (i.e., to keep speaking when they want to, through both verbal and nonverbal means), and he has shown a strong link between holding the floor and others' assessments of the speaker's power and control. Those who are able to hold the floor the most tend to have more power than others have in a conversation. Not only are nonverbal cues important in how smoothly a conversation will flow, they are also vital in understanding the outcomes (e.g., perceived or actual power) of those conversations.

Relational Messages

Burgoon and Hale (1984, 1987) were some of the first researchers to discuss in depth the ways in which nonverbal cues both denote and change the relationships we have with others. For them, *relational messages* include the amount of intimacy two people share, whether the power balance is matched or not between interactants, and the degree to which one's relationship with another person is formal or informal. Overall, "relational communication addresses the processes and messages whereby people negotiate, express, and interpret their relationships with one another" (Burgoon et al., 1989, p. 289), and such messages are typically sent nonverbally.

One of the ways in which people may reflect both intimacy and equality with one another is through the degree of behavioral *synchrony* that exists. Synchrony can occur in many forms (i.e., mirroring, mimicry, or behavioral meshing), but overall it refers to the amount of coordination in peoples' behaviors (i.e., two people move in the same ways and/or their behaviors "fit" with the others). When two or more peoples' nonverbal cues are "in sync" with one another, the relational message sent is usually solidarity, agreement, support, and attraction.

Only behavior that appears to be *naturally* synchronous is likely to reflect positively on relationships. In one study, Manusov (1992) led some participants to believe that the person with whom they had interacted mirrored their behavior on purpose (the other person was actually a confederate in the study); she told others that the mirroring behavior was accidental, or she never discussed the behaviors (the control group). Those participants who were told that the behaviors were intentional judged the confederate to be less competent and attractive (and the behaviors as more disjointed and exaggerated) than he was judged when the participant was [sic] not led to think that the behaviors were purposeful, even though the confederate actually acted the same way each time. The negative evaluations were due in large part to participants' beliefs that they were being manipulated by the confederate, a common outcome of synchrony perceived to be "unnatural."

As noted, nonverbal cues can show the current state of a relationship *or* help interactants move to a different type of relationship. For example, Muehlenhard and his colleagues performed a series of studies relating specific behaviors with the intent to date (Muehlenhard, Koralewski, Andrews, & Burdick, 1986; Muehlenhard & McFall, 1981; Muehlenhard, Miller, & Burdick, 1983). Their participants watched videotapes of male-female interactions and rated the probability that the woman would accept if the man asked her for a date. Observers believed that the woman would be likely to accept a date if she maintained high levels of eye contact, smiled, leaned forward, leaned sideways, maintained a direct body orientation, moved closer to the man, touched him, and used animated speech, among other cues. Because these cues are often linked with desires to escalate a relationship, some subset of these cues is likely to help communicate that one person is ready for the relationship to change.

The process of moving from one level of relationship to another is often problematic, however, and this may be based in behavioral "mistakes" made in our quest to attain goals. Specifically, Abbey (1982) conducted a study in which male and female students engaged in a five-minute interaction while being observed from another room. After the conversation, both partners and the observers rated the extent to which the interactants were friendly, seductive, flirtatious, and promiscuous. Male and female observers saw the female interactants as friendly, but the male observers rated them as more seductive and flirtatious than did the female observers. Abbey concluded that males very often perceive a higher level of sexual intent than females do, and this could lead to different interpretations (i.e., "mistakes") for the same actions. Shotland and Craig (1988) contend, however, that there are objective distinctions between seductive behavior (e.g., long eye contact, softer speaking patterns, many short smiles, and comments that the other has been noticed before) and friendliness (e.g., more frequent brief eye contact, taking longer speaking turns, being distracted by other activities).

The idea of relational messages also connotes that nonverbal cues allow us *to relate* in a general sense to others. A recent book illustrates this idea. Cole (1998) conducted a series of interviews with people who could speak but could not rely on faces to communicate (some had Möbius syndrome, in which the face is immobile, and others were blind and therefore could not see *others'* faces). He was able to show that, unless people find another means of connecting with others (e.g., through vocal characteristics such as tone and volume), they often feel at odds with the social world. According to Cole, "without the feedback and reinforcement that facial gestures provide, there [is] little relatedness and engagement" (p. 10). This discussion shows just how profound social relationship to others is and highlights the importance of nonverbal cues in the process of engagement.

REVIEW QUESTIONS

1. Fill in the blank: "Although a single nonverbal behavior (e.g., gaze) may fulfill a function, it is more common for cues, including language, to _____."
2. How does culture affect the ways that nonverbal behaviors express emotions?
3. What is the difference between "impression formation" and "identity management"?

4. What is an "identity badge"?
5. Which nonverbal behaviors are used to manage turn taking in conversation?

PROBES

1. Are nonverbal expressions of emotion (happiness, sadness, etc.) common across most situations, or is it likely that any particular cue will need language and vocal cues to be interpreted accurately? Explain.
2. What might you do nonverbally to communicate that you are "in sync" with your conversation partner? If you choose to do this, what danger do you need to avoid?
3. Give two examples of nonverbal cues you have used to help a relationship move from one level of relationship to another higher or lower level.

REFERENCES

Abbey, A. (1982). Sex differences in attributions for friendly behavior: Do males misperceive females' friendliness? *Journal of Personality and Social Psychology, 42,* pp. 830–888.

Berry, D. S., & Zebrowitz-McArthur, L. (1988). What's in a face? Facial maturity and the attribution of legal responsibility. *Personality and Social Psychology Bulletin, 14,* pp. 24–33.

Burgoon, J. K. (1994). Nonverbal signals. In M. L. Knapp and G. R. Miller (Eds.), *Handbook of interpersonal communication* (pp. 229–285). Beverly Hills, CA: Sage.

Burgoon, J. K., & Hale, J. L. (1984). The fundamental topic of relational communication. *Communication Monographs, 51,* pp. 193–214.

Burgoon, J. K., & Hale, J. L. (1987). Validation and measurement of fundamental themes of relational communication. *Communication Monographs, 54,* pp. 19–41.

Burgoon, J. K., Buller, D. B., & Woodall, W. G. *Nonverbal communication: The unspoken dialogue.* New York: HarperCollins, 1989.

Cappella, J. N. The management of conversational interaction in adults and infants. In D. M. L. Knapp and G. R. Miller (Eds.), *Handbook of Interpersonal Communication* (2nd ed.). Thousand Oaks, CA: Sage, 1994.

Cole, J. *About face.* Cambridge, MA: Bradford/MIT Press, 1998.

Ekman, P., & Friesen, W. V. (1969). The repertoire of nonverbal behavior: Categories, origins, usage, and coding. *Semiotica, 1,* pp. 49–98.

Manusov, V. (1992). Mimicry or synchrony: The effects of intentionality attributions for nonverbal mirroring behavior. *Communication Quarterly, 40,* pp. 69–83.

Motley, M. T. (1993). Facial affect and verbal content in conversation. *Human communication research, 20,* pp. 3–40.

Muehlenhard, C. L., & McFall, R. M. (1981). Dating initiation from a woman's perspective. *Behavior Therapy, 12,* pp. 682–691.

Muehlenhard, C. L., Miller, C. L., & Burdick, C. A. (1983). Are high-frequency daters better cue readers? Men's interpretation of women's cues as a function of dating frequency and SHI scores. *Behavior Therapy, 14,* pp. 626–636.

Muehlenhard, C. L., Koralewski, M. A., Andrews, S. L., & Burdick, C. A. (1986). Verbal and nonverbal cues that convey interest in dating: Two studies. *Behavior Therapy, 17,* pp. 404–419.

Shotland, R. L., & Craig, J. M. (1988). Can men and women differentiate between friendly and sexually interested behavior? *Social Psychology Quarterly, 51,* pp. 66–73.

Making Meaning Together

"INHALING" AND "EXHALING"

As I noted in the Preface, the two chapters that make up Part Two are organized with the help of a breathing metaphor. At the most basic level, I use the terms *inhaling* and *exhaling* to begin to break down or organize the continuous, changing, multidimensional, often confusing process called "communicating." One commonsense, close-to-experience way to organize this overall process is to divide it up into what people take in (inhaling) and what they give out (exhaling).

You can figure out my second and most important reason for choosing this metaphor if you try to inhale without exhaling, or vice versa. These labels allow me to separate communication into two of its important parts while still emphasizing that the parts happen together. As I noted in Chapter 2, communicators are always receiving and sending at the same time. *While we're talking*, we're noticing how people are responding, and *while we're listening*, we're giving off mixed and primarily nonverbal cues.

No metaphor is perfect, of course, and one problem with this one is that inhaling and exhaling happen *sequentially*, while perceiving and talking take place *simultaneously*. In this sense, communication is even more dynamic than my metaphor suggests.

A third reason I'm using this metaphor is that it is organic. Breathing is a part of living for most of the organisms in the world. It's vital for humans and other animals, of course, but you can also think of the fish's intake and output of water and even the plant's intake of water and output of oxygen as forms of breathing.

The fourth reason is that this metaphor organizes breathing into a process that begins with input. If somebody asks, "What are the two parts of the breathing process?" the common answer is "inhaling and exhaling," not "exhaling and inhaling." So the metaphor allows me to focus *first* on perception and listening. This reverses the historical tendency to begin one's efforts to improve communication by focusing on what one *says*. I'm convinced that listening is the often neglected but crucially important half of the listening-speaking pair, and my metaphor makes it easier to redress some of this imbalance.

So Chapter 5 discusses how we "take in" information and impressions about others—how we perceive individuals, relationships, and social events, and how we listen. It begins with two readings about person perception, one that reviews the process and another that discusses stereotyping. Next are three readings that focus on listening. Then Chapter 6 covers what we "give out" or "exhale." Here, four readings discuss being open, expressing thoughts and feelings, practicing self-disclosure, and asking for what you want.

As you read these materials, remember that each of these chapters somewhat artificially emphasizes one part of a process that always happens as a whole—just like the inhaling and exhaling of normal breathing. It makes sense to break the process down into what's taken in and what's given out. But this isn't how we actually experience communication. As the title of Part Two indicates, people make meaning *together*, and they do it by "inhaling" and "exhaling" *together*.

CHAPTER 5

Inhaling: Perceiving and Listening

Inhaling: Perception

John Stewart, Karen E. Zediker, and Saskia Witteborn

These next pages describe the basic processes humans use to perceive anything, as well as some of the special processes we use to perceive people. It also alerts you to five practical perception problems that can distort your communicating. The reading comes from an interpersonal communication text I wrote with two colleagues.

Our first point is that people make sense out of what we encounter by engaging three fundamental perception processes: selecting, organizing, and inferring. We do not just "soak up sense data"; rather, we actively interpret everything that we encounter, and we do this with these three moves. First, we select uses to attend to or prioritize, based not only on what's available but also on past judgments, expectations, and a variety of cultural cues. Second, we organize the cues we've selected into a whole that makes sense. And finally, we go beyond the cues to infer what they mean.

Perceptual differences can occur anywhere along this line, and so can perceptual problems. Some evidence indicates that men and women select, organize, and infer differently, as do people with different native languages.

The mental patterns that help us organize what we perceive are called *cognitive schemata*. Two kinds of schemata that especially affect communication are person prototypes and scripts. The former is a generalized representation of a "type" of person—a professor, parent, physician, or priest, for example. Stereotypes are rigid person prototypes. Scripts are generalized sequences of action—how you behave in a restaurant, for example, or how you ask someone out.

The reading also explains three processes that influence our inference making, impression formation, attribution, and stereotyping. We form impressions, in part, using implicit personality theories that shape the ways we perceive people. Attributions are explanations of other people's behavior that are based on either internal or external factors. And stereotyping is a natural process, that, while unavoidable, needs to be closely monitored.

The final section briefly discusses five perception processes that can affect where your communication is on the impersonal-interpersonal scale: fast thinking, overload avoidance, the entertainment factor, snap judgments, and attributional errors. When you've finished this reading, you should have a good general understanding of how your perception processes can affect your interpersonal communicating.

PREVIEW

Remember that we're using the metaphor of inhaling and exhaling to explain the receptive and expressive parts of communication.... The first point to remember is that there's much more to inhaling than the passive reception of incoming messages. Inhaling combines the two active, interpretive processes of perceiving and listening....

People make sense out of the world through their perceptual experience, and experience is affected by culture, membership in various social groups, and in fact, by every relationship a person has. Your perceptions influence and contribute to the inhaling process in profound ways. You select sensory cues, organize them mentally, and make inferences about them. One of the reasons why people select, organize, and make inferences is that each of us lives in a complex world that we have to make sense of. Three kinds of inference-making processes that people use to make sense of the world and the people in it are stereotyping, attribution, and impression formation.

PERCEPTION: AN INTERPRETIVE PROCESS

Perception can be defined as a social and cognitive process in which people assign meaning to sensory cues. People often assume that the "truth" of things exists out there somewhere in what they are seeing, hearing, touching, tasting, and smelling. For example, you know the old saying "Seeing is believing." It is tempting to think that your eyes give you a perfect picture of what is happening in your own portion of "reality." But perception takes a picture through a lens, not through a window.

Perception is shaped by the perceiving person's experience and understanding of his or her place in the world. If perception were simply a matter of accurately processing sensory cues, you would expect everybody to perceive in a fairly similar way. However, this is not how perception works; as we said, it's an active process. When we make this point, we also mean that perception is, to a considerable extent, self-initiated and voluntary, a function of each person's response choices. You are not forced to interpret cues in a certain way; you have considerable control over your perceptual processes, especially as you become come aware of them.

Perception occurs through three basic sub-processes: selection, organization, and inference-making. But before these three can begin, a person has to receive information through the senses—touch, taste, smell, hearing, and sight. This information is received in the form of sensory data, or cues. A cue is the smallest perceivable "bit" of information. As soon as your outermost sensory neurons receive a cue, you begin selecting, organizing, and inferring from this information. It isn't possible to perceive anything without selecting, organizing, and inferring. So, from the start, perception is an *interpretive process*. The following brief exercise will show you that interpretation is a large part of perceiving things in the environment.

Selecting, Organizing, and Inferring

The three sub-processes of perception do not occur in any distinct, step-by-step sequence. They happen simultaneously as three inseparable events. Selection generally refers to how you pay attention to sensory cues. Organization describes the ways you construct and impose patterns or structure onto the stream of sensory cues you receive. Inferring is a label for the way you "go beyond" or interpret the cues that your senses select and organize.

Selecting   You first decide at some level of consciousness which cues to pay attention to. Sometimes it seems that you don't have a choice about whether or not to attend to certain cues—for example, a siren, a sudden bright light out of the dark, a loud scream, or a sharp pain. But most of the time people exercise a fair amount of choice about the cues they perceive.

Selection is operating when you're rushed for time in an airport looking for the ticket counter of your airline and you don't notice many details about the people around you. Your attention is focused on signs identifying airlines and listing arrivals or departures. Or, when looking for new shoes in a shopping mall, you selectively pay attention to store signs and window displays that relate to your task and typically ignore the bed and bath shop and the espresso stand. But if you suddenly become hungry, you shift your attention to anything that smells or looks like food. You can be at a noisy party and have trouble hearing another person standing less than two feet away, but magically overhear your name mentioned by two people gossiping at some distance. And if you are concentrating on reading this book right now, you are probably not aware of the pressure of the chair against your body or noises from the next room until reading this sentence shifts your attention to these cues.

When communicating with others, people also perceive selectively. Some research indicates that people tend to focus on whatever or whomever is easiest to attend to—the closest person, the person with the loudest voice, the person we can see most easily. For example, in a series of studies, two researchers asked subjects to observe conversations between two people and varied the seating positions of the observers (see Figure 5–1). Some observers looked directly at one of the two conversation partners but could see only the back and side of the other. When these observers were asked to rate the conversational partners on a number of scales, they found they rated the person they faced as more responsible for the topic and tone of the conversation. The observers who could see both participants equally well rated them during the same period of time as equally responsible for the tone and topics of conversation. The researchers concluded that where your attention is directed influences what you perceive. Your selective perceptions affect your judgments about the people involved (Maltz and Borker 1982).

But the process of selection is not this simple. What you attend to is not just a response to a property of some cue—the loudest, brightest, or most visually direct. You also select cues about people based on your past judgments of them. So, if you are angry with your partner, you are far more likely to perceive all sorts of little irritating habits, just as you overlook or don't see negative characteristics in someone you love. The bottom line is that you cannot perceive all the sensory cues that are available to you. Perception is selective, and what we choose to notice affects how we respond to both things and people.

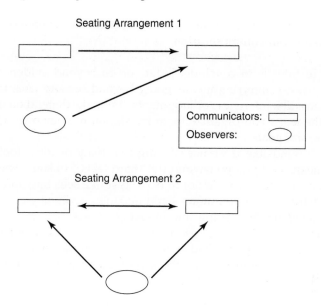

FIGURE 5–1   Diagram of Conversational Partners

Organizing   Another way people actively participate in perception is by organizing the cues they select. You literally cannot help applying structure and stability to your world of sensations. Whenever you look at something that is vague or ambiguous in shape or size or color, for example, you continue to focus on it until you recognize what it is. What you are doing is arranging and rearranging the information you have according to a series of possible patterns or forms until the information finally makes sense to you, and you have an "Oh, so that's what it is!" experience.

You can have this experience of perceiving patterns or structures whenever you listen to music, too. How do you recognize your favorite songs? Research shows that people hear something much more than note-to-note; they tend to focus on the organized *pattern* of the sounds—the melody (Fiske and Shelley 1984). If you've ever played the game Name That Tune, you have had the experience of suddenly recognizing not individual notes but the pattern that exists among the notes.

Once you apply a particular structure to your experience, you stabilize this perceptual version. For example, if you've been humming a particular tune for days, it's hard to think of how other songs sound, especially if they have somewhat similar patterns. The organization of perceptions helps you to make sense out of whatever is occurring. You can apply the patterns or structures to very small sensory events. Or you can develop patterns that characterize people you know. Later on in this [essay], we'll talk about how these more complex patterns are formed through stereotyping, the process of attribution, and impression formation. But for now, we just want to emphasize how important the way people organize cues is to the entire process of perception and the unavoidable effects this step has on your communication.

Inferring   To infer is to conclude, judge, or go beyond evidence. So in the perception process, inferring means going beyond sensory cues to your own interpretations. The inferences or judgments you make depend on the cues you select and the ways you organize them in relation to your own assumptions, expectations, and goals.

It might sound like inference making is a risky or even foolish process because it means that you go beyond the "hard facts." In some ways it is dangerous, but it's also impossible not to do it. Just like selecting and organizing, inferring is hard-wired into human sense making.... *Meaning* is a label for the outcome of selecting, organizing, and inferring.

Our interpretations of other people and events depend on our worldviews, past experiences, goals in life, and expectations, all of which differ from culture to culture. Cultures are marked by the ways they answer such basic questions as the following:

- What is the value of the individual versus the value of the group?
- How do people advance in life, by heritage or by achievement?
- How should society be organized?
- Is the nature of a human being good or evil?
- How do humans relate to each other?
- Where does meaning lie, explicitly in the language or hidden in the context? (Hall 2002; Kluckhorn and Strodtbeck 1961)

Many more elements can constitute a worldview of a culture, and the answers to each question lie on a continuum. In other words, worldviews are not simple; they are complex. You can value individualism, for example, when you want to make your own decisions about going to college. But you can value collectivism and the group when it comes to supporting your parents in their old age.

Worldviews influence responses to these questions and affect how people interpret cues. Saskia, for instance, was confused when she arrived on the West Coast of the United States and people smiled at her, greeted her in the streets, and talked with her on the bus. She was raised to be respectful and friendly to strangers but at the same time maintains her privacy and does not impose herself on people she does not know. It made her a little uncomfortable at first because she didn't know how to interpret certain cues she got from strangers. Was the man in the supermarket hitting on her when he smiled and asked how her day was going? Or was it just friendliness? When Saskia's parents came from Germany to visit her, her dad was impressed with "how many people she knew." He interpreted the greetings in the streets and the small talk of the checkers in the supermarket as meaning "They must know her, otherwise they wouldn't be talking to her." He was very surprised when he found out that they were strangers to Saskia. This example shows the impact of Saskia's family's worldview on their interpretations of communicative interactions.

But perceptual differences don't occur just between different ethnic or national groups—they are also gender specific. According to Malz and Borker (1982), women and men in North America interpret the same actions in conversation very differently. For example, men appear to perceive head nodding while listening as a way of indicating *agreement* with the speaker, whereas women tend to perceive head nodding as a way of signaling *that they are listening* to the speaker. For women, this is another way of indicating "I'm with you. Keep going." This difference may be at the root of a common complaint some women have about some men: "He never listens to me" (because he doesn't signal listening with head nodding) or "He's always so rational. Sometimes I just want emotional support." At the same time, frequent use of head nodding reinforces the stereotype some men have of women as unreliable because "You're always agreeing with me no matter what I say."

Socialization and biology play a role in how men and women communicate, especially when it comes to communicating emotions (Konner 2002). Researchers say that male and female brains differ in terms of sex differences in a frontal-lobe region that is responsible for emotional reasoning. They also found that the corpus callosum, which is a mass of fibers connecting the two halves of the brain, may be larger in women's than in men's brains. If this is so, then the larger fiber mass in women's brains might help integrate the language and emotional centers better in females brains, which means that women can verbalize feelings more than men. This does not mean that they automatically do. Socialization plays another major role in how people communicate....

Now that we have explained the basic sub-processes of perception, we want to talk more about mental guidelines, or *cognitive schemata*, that help us to organize incoming information. Then we'll talk about the processes that you engage in when you make interpretations of people or things around you.

COGNITIVE SCHEMATA

In order to recognize persons and objects around us, we need mental guidelines that help us process incoming cues. These mental guidelines are called *cognitive schemata* (in the singular it's *cognitive schema*). Schemata help us to organize incoming cues about people, animals, behaviors, and objects.

Almost 80 years ago, the originator of schema theory made the point that all remembering is constructive. Rather than storing all stimuli in memory, the brain uses schemata to provide an impression of the whole. In his experiments, Bartlett (1932) used a version of the child's game Telephone, in which a message is passed along a chain of people and the story changes with each retelling. In some experiments he asked British college students to read a story from another culture, put it aside, reproduce it, and pass it on to other students. Bartlett noticed that the stories changed in systematic ways as they were passed along. This led him to suggest that in acquiring new information, humans must assimilate the new material to existing concepts or schemas. People change new

information to fit their existing concepts by organizing it into previously existing mental structures. In this process, details are lost, and the knowledge fits the
interpretive frames of the individual (Mayer 1992, 230).

This explanation about how people organize new information makes sense.
Saskia participated in a class where the professor played the telephone game.
The students had to remember a story that included a variety of blue dragons,
monks, and story characters from Asian cultures. In the end, the monks became
"the dudes," the princess became a cheerleader, and the head monk a pharma-
cist. This does not mean that the students were careless or stupid. It means that
they adapted the information to stories they had heard before. The students also
ended their version of the story with "and they lived happily ever after," which
did not occur in the original story but which is an ending that's very common
in fairy tales that are written [in] or translated into English.

Overall, people have schemata for people, relationships, actions, and even
emotions. Let's talk a little bit more about two types of these schemata: person
prototypes and scripts.

Person Prototypes

A person prototype is a generalized representation of certain types of persons. It
is usually based on experience and repeated personal interactions with people.
Just pause and think for a moment about what *mental image* comes to your mind
when you think of student, professor, lawyer, gamer, or car salesperson. Person
prototypes contain information about traits and verbal and nonverbal behaviors
that you believe characterize a certain type of person. What are the traits and
behaviors that you associate with a professor? How about a lawyer? How about
a cheerleader? And how about a homeless person? Overall, prototypes help us
to orient ourselves in the world. They can help us to meet people who we think
we might feel comfortable with and can also help us to avoid dangerous situations. But they can also be misleading and can make us stereotype people. Why?
Because they omit specific features. If you communicate based only on your
person schemata, you will stay on the impersonal side of the communication
scale described in Chapter 2.

Scripts

Scripts, which are structures dealing with certain sequences of action, are
another type of cognitive schema. We all have a repertoire of scripts in our
heads. They are usually based on experience and help us to know what happens
next. Examples of scripts are riding the bus, greeting another person, attending
a wedding, or going to a restaurant. Consider the "restaurant script" (Abelson
1981). When people enter a restaurant, they know the different steps to go
through to accomplish the goal of satisfying their hunger, having good conversation over a good meal, or both. This knowledge of the different steps helps
us go into an almost automatic action mode so that we don't have to make

decisions every single moment. So, imagine you go to a restaurant. What do you do? We guess that you would do the following in the following order: enter, be seated, order, eat, pay, tip 10 to 20 percent of the bill, and exit.

In addition, person prototypes help you to orient yourself in your restaurant environment. Near the entrance, there will usually be a person who says, "How many?" You know that this must be a host or manager. When a person comes to your table and asks, "Are you ready to order?" wearing a certain outfit—for instance, a T-shirt with the name of the restaurant on it—you know that he or she is your server (person prototype). You also know what to expect from a server and how you are supposed to behave. You know, for instance, that the server is not supposed to yell at you, sit at your table, or spill your soda on you. The server also knows that the customer (you) is not supposed to come into the kitchen or sit on the floor when eating.

Also remember that scripts can differ in different cultures. One reason that people sometimes feel insecure when they travel is that they are not familiar with certain scripts. When Saskia is in Germany, her restaurant script looks like the following: enter the restaurant, sit down, order food and drink, eat, sit for a while after eating, call the waiter to bring the check, pay the check, leave a tip that is fair, and exit. You see that there are many similarities between the U.S. and German restaurant scripts. However, there are also differences: calling the waiter to bring the check, not leaving the money on the table, and tipping conventions. In Germany, the server will usually leave you alone for a while after you have dined, and it is considered rude to take away your plates immediately. In many European countries, clearing the table right after people have eaten and putting the check on the table is interpreted as rushing the customer. So, often you have to call the waiter or waitress to bring the check. Usually you pay directly and don't leave money on the table.

Tipping conventions in U.S. and German restaurant scripts also differ. In Germany, you round up a small bill to the next dollar or, when the bill is over 10 euros, you give 10 percent or so. In the United States the standard expectation is that the tip will be around 15 percent of the bill. Knowledge about different cultural scripts for certain situations makes you a more competent communicator and can also help you to avoid embarrassment or confusion.

Person prototypes and *scripts* influence how people *organize* sensory cues. In addition, there are three processes that influence how people make *interpretations*. These processes are *impression formation, attribution,* and *stereotyping*.

COGNITIVE PROCESSES

Impression Formation

Impression formation is the complex process of integrating or synthesizing a variety of sometimes contradictory observations into a coherent overall "picture" of a person. The impression that you form is basically a combination of traits that are similar or fit together for you. When you connect a series of related interpretations about someone's behavior, you begin to develop what's called an *implicit personality theory* about the person doing the behavior. This is simply your picture (theory) of what the person's personality "must be," based on qualities or characteristics that are implied by their behavior.

In a widely cited book about person perception, three psychologists give an excellent example of how impressions form themselves into an implicit personality theory:

> Suppose you have been watching a woman at party. A lot of other people are congregated around her and you discover that she has just had a novel published. You observe her long enough to draw some tentative conclusions about her: Some of these result from attribution work; she is smart, ambitious, but particularly hard-working—conclusions you are able to draw because few people write novels and because you discover that this is her second novel and fourth published book.... You note that she is in her early 40s and reasonably attractive; her hair is a rather unnatural shade of yellow. Furthermore, she is wearing an expensive long dress. Your snap judgment is that artificial blondes who wear expensive dresses are on the frivolous side. You note that the woman is witty, and that she giggles a great deal.... Finally, you note she is consuming drinks at a rapid pace and that she has smoked several cigarettes.

> What have you decided? Our novelist is intelligent, ambitious, hard-working, frivolous, witty, "giggly," and nervous. Now your work really begins. How, you might ask yourself, can a person be both hard-working and frivolous? Or perhaps she is trying to create a really good impression for someone so that her hairstyle does not so much indicate frivolousness as a concern to create a good impression.... But why would she be nervous? She's a hit, the star of the party. Maybe she is insecure (all those giggles); nervous people and people who try to create a good impression are nervous—or so you believe. Why is she insecure? (Schneider, Hastorf, and Ellsworth 1979)

And so on. In order to give some consistency to all these observations and inferences, people work to organize the data they perceive into some coherent, stable impression. Although this impression is continually revised, it remains a global characterization of another person in which much of the original and inconsistent details get lost. So, depending on your past experience, you may conclude, for example, that the woman is very admirable but unusually nervous, a phony who's afraid of being discovered, or book smart but socially awkward.

There is now a considerable amount of communication research showing that people differ in how effectively they perceive others. For instance, researchers have discovered that stereotyping depends upon a person's mental state. If someone has high anxiety and tries to suppress stereotypic thinking, stereotyping may actually increase (Hall and Crisp 2003). You probably have experienced this yourself. If you are traveling in a foreign country and people told you before you left to "never leave anything unattended because people steal there all the time," you may become tense and see every person around you as a potential thief.

Some people generalize and categorize more than others, and thus tend to contribute more to impersonal rather than interpersonal communication events. Their talk is *position centered* because it focuses on social roles and norms rather than the unique characteristics of individuals.

Other communicators seem better able to use the discriminatory power of perception and to note fine distinctions between one type of behavior and another. They appear to be more flexible in the perceptions they construct of others, using a higher number and more types of categories. These more sophisticated social perceivers are more likely to engage in more communication toward the right-hand end of the impersonal-interpersonal scale. These communicators are sensitive to perceptual features across a variety of different types of social situations, which makes their communication much more *person centered*. In other words, position-centered communication is nearer the left end of the continuum, and person-centered communication is nearer the right end.

Attribution

A second process of person perception is called *attribution*. When people form attributions, they devise theories or explanations about other people's behavior that provide a way of making sense out of whatever is occurring (Heider 1958; Kelley 1973). Often, this means assigning a cause or intention to the behavior (Kelley 1972). For instance, a student might come late to class and the instructor might think, "That student is lazy." In the same situation a different instructor might think, "Must have been a lot of traffic today." Each of these attributions is a way for the instructor to explain or make sense of the student's behavior. The attributions also provide the instructor with some sense that he or she can predict how the student will behave in the future. When you can devise explanations for how people behave and predictions of their future behavior, you can operate with much more certainty about what is happening in a particular situation.

Notice how one of the two causes or reasons the instructor assigned to the student's behavior is anchored in this student's personality ("lazy") and the other is anchored in external factors ("traffic"). These are the response options people commonly select from: You attribute the cause of the behavior either to a character trait, mood, or disposition (*internal factors*) or to the situation (*external factors*), or to both (Heider 1985; Rotter 1966). When your attributions emphasize internal factors, you're more likely to interpret what happened as the person's fault or responsibility. When someone else makes mistakes, people tend to attribute the behavior to internal causes. So, for instance, imagine you're giving a presentation. You have worked hard for weeks and are very nervous. A friend has promised to come and give you mental and emotional support during the presentation. You start your presentation and realize that your friend is not there. He walks in 10 minutes late, which makes you think, "I'm not worth his time. My buddy let me down." You attribute his behavior to internal causes instead of wondering whether he got stuck in traffic.

By contrast, when people make mistakes themselves, they tend to attribute their behavior to external causes. So, when you come late to class, you might automatically offer an excuse that attributes your being late to external causes, such as "The bus didn't show up" or "My roommate had a panic attack this morning and I had to drive him to the hospital." The reason why people attribute personal mistakes to external causes is to save face and keep themselves from becoming vulnerable.

If you remember what we said about fault and blame, you'll probably get a sense of why attributions can be dangerous. Although attributions about others can help guide understanding, they also often interfere with your ability to see alternative reasons for why people behave the way they do. For instance, one researcher (Manusov 1990) studied what happens when couples playing the game Trivial Pursuit have to make sense of their partner's obviously positive or negative nonverbal behavior. One member of each couple was recruited to act positively at one point in the game and to act negatively at another point. The study showed that couples who were happy with their relationship and each other tended to attribute positive behavior to internal causes in their partners. In contrast, unhappy couples made more external attributions. So, in this study, a person's overall attitude toward his or her partner significantly affected the attributions made about the partner's nonverbal behavior.

Stereotyping

A stereotype is defined in the *Oxford English Dictionary* (2003) as a "preconceived and oversimplified idea of the characteristics which typify a person, situation, etc.; an attitude based on such a preconception. Also, a person who appears to conform closely to the idea of a type." In other words, a stereotype is a category that people apply to other people, often based on their group membership. These categories can include gender, ethnic or national, religious, and vocational groups. Overall, stereotypes are a way that people make sense of the world and orient themselves to the people around them.

Two important dimensions of stereotypes are the following: (1) They can be positive or negative and (2) they can vary in intensity. Positive stereotypes are categorizations that evoke favorable associations, such as "Asians are good at math," "Chinese are polite," "African women are beautiful," or "African-Americans are athletic." Negative stereotypes are unfavorable categorizations of a whole group of people—for example, "East Coasters are rude," "Arabs are terrorists," or "football players are lazy students." In addition to direction, stereotypes can also vary in intensity—the strength with which the stereotype is maintained. Families and peer groups affect the intensity of most people's stereotypes (Tan et al. 2001). If you continually heard when you were growing up that "foreigners" are bad because they take jobs away from native-born citizens, you are likely to believe it and may even be suspicious of foreigners.

You've undoubtedly been told many times that stereotyping is dangerous and stereotypes are bad. In many ways, this is true. Racism and sexism continue, to a considerable degree, because of stereotypes. Communication based on stereotyped perceptions of people will fall on the impersonal side of the impersonal-interpersonal continuum.

On the other hand, some stereotyping is unavoidable, and in some cases it can be helpful. When you're walking alone at night in a city, it can be legitimate and helpful to stereotype the person matching your route and your pace as a threat. The natural human tendency to categorize influences all perceptions, so it is impossible to stop stereotyping completely. You just have to be careful not to let your stereotypes become too rigid. You can do that by being aware that people sometimes put other people into boxes and by trying to see the person with his or her individual characteristics behind the stereotype.

In addition, researchers have found that communication is not always influenced by stereotypes as much as it is affected by the interaction itself (Manusov and Hedge 1993; Manusov, Winchatz, and Manning 1997). For instance, researchers asked how neutral, positive, and negative stereotypes about people from other cultures affect the ways in which people communicate and the judgments they make about their conversation partners. So far, they've found that stereotype-based expectancies do affect people's evaluations of their conversation partners from other cultures, but they also found that what happens during the actual conversation is more important than the stereotype. People base their judgments of others more on facial pleasantness, fluency in conversation, relaxed posture, and similar vocal cues than on the stereotypes that they bring to the interaction (Manusov, Winchatz, and Manning 1997). This evidence indicates that even in cross-cultural conversations, where you'd think stereotypes would be most influential, these generalizations don't completely control how people respond.

PRACTICAL PERCEPTION PROBLEMS

As part of our continuing effort to blend theory and practice, we want to end this [essay] with a description of five specific difficulties that you might encounter in your perception processes. Each grows out of the complexity and culture dependence of the perception process. Each can also affect where your communication is on the impersonal-interpersonal scale.

Fast Thinking

One problem people have with the selection part of perception is that, when listening to someone, we have a great deal of spare time. In a normal conversation, native English speakers tend to speak from 115 to 130 words per minute. But normal thinking speed—if it can be quantified this way—exceeds 500 words per minute. This means that people listening to speech have a lot of extra time to get perceptually sidetracked by other cues or by their own thoughts. You might think of this perception problem as the challenge of what to do with this free time. Since it's harder to concentrate on another person's ideas than it is to focus on our own, we often take the easy way out and spend our free time thinking about our own concerns. The listening skills we describe in the next chapter clarify what else might be done with this free time.

Avoiding Overload

A second reason people sometimes tune out is to preserve some control over their environment. We are constantly bombarded with countless messages from family members, supervisors, teachers, friends, acquaintances, strangers, and the media, and if we tried to pay attention to it all, we would quickly go crazy. We can't turn off the perceptual process entirely, so we have to make decisions about the things we will attend to and the things we will let go. So sometimes we tune out to preserve our physical and emotional health. The trick is not to let the real potential of information overload force you into the habit of tuning out.

The Entertainment Factor

A third reason people sometimes fail to pay attention is that they're used to getting information in entertaining packages. Adults who grew up spending a great deal of time watching television are especially prone to expect ideas and information to come in attractive, lively, and stimulating packages with economical sound bites. If you doubt the influence of this factor, notice the way television packages the news and the way advertisers on radio, television, and in magazines present their products. Awareness of this expectation can go a long way toward reducing its impact on your perception.

In addition to these three selection problems, there are at least two types of problems that can interfere with the kind of person perception that promotes interpersonal communicating.

Snap Judgments

Snap judgments are inferences that are "usually rather immediate and do not involve complex cognitive processes" (Schneider, Hastorf, and Ellsworth 1979, 20). They are the most limited kind of stereotype people make about others. Snap judgments are usually based on the physical characteristics of the other person and a very limited set of observations of their behavior. In the earlier description of the novelist at the cocktail party, the snap judgment is that "artificial blondes who wear expensive dresses are on the frivolous side." Snap judgments result when people evaluate whether the person they're perceiving is old or young, male or female, physically able or disabled, richly or poorly dressed, from a particular culture, and under- or overweight. Occasionally a snap judgment can be useful, such as when you're aggressively approached by a telemarketer as you're sitting down for dinner. But most of the time snap judgments are liable to distort your understanding of what the person is saying.

Attributional Errors

Earlier we explained that people make attributions to help make sense out of someone else's behavior by assigning a cause or intention to their actions. These causes or reasons for behavior get associated with the other's personality (internal factors) or something in the situation (external factors). These often lead to oversimplified conclusions about fault and blame, which … interfere with our ability to see communication as a collaborative process. One form of distortion happens when people unequally balance internal and external factors and commit what's called the *fundamental attribution error* and the *ultimate attribution error*.

The fundamental attribution error is the mistaken tendency people have to attribute others' behaviors to internal, rather than external, causes. The ultimate attribution error assumes that, as we mentioned, people's negative behavior is caused by internal factors and that their positive behavior is caused by external factors. This means that there is a tendency to underestimate the impact of situational factors in producing another's behavior and to overestimate the role of personality factors (Kelley 1972).

For instance, the person evaluating her *own* tendency to drive over the speed limit or be late for an appointment would be likely to attribute her actions to the situation—she is just "keeping up with traffic" or "unavoidably delayed by traffic signals and detours." But the fundamental attribution error happens when she fails to give others the benefit of this explanation and instead accounts for *their* speeding and lateness as "irresponsibility" or "carelessness."

One example of the ultimate attribution error concerns perceptions of obesity. Researchers have concluded that many people attribute obesity in other people to internal, controllable causes. Thus, those who are significantly overweight are often regarded as having no self-control and are therefore subject to blame and ridicule (Rush 1998). Obese people are also usually viewed as unattractive, sad, depressed, and unlikable (Hiller 1981; Triplett 2003). Many people who think that obesity is the fault of the individual fall into the trap of the ultimate attribution error: They assign what is perceived to be negative behavior to internal personality characteristics. They also commit this error when they conclude that weight loss is caused by a good diet and the help of other people instead of asking themselves whether the weight loss also has something do to with the strong will of the person. It can help to avoid the fundamental attribution error by remembering that others' actions—just like our own—are responses to both internal and external factors.

SUMMARY

Our main point about perception is that the ways people select, organize, and make inferences about others affect the ways people communicate. Person perception by its very nature forms the basis of the "reality" you share with others every time you make contact with them. By becoming aware of the ways you perceive others, you can learn to generalize less, that is, to be more sensitive to the unique and distinctive features others make available to you as you communicate with them. Increasing your perceptual sensitivity is a major step in making the inhaling part of your communicating more effective.

Up until now, though, we've been treating the parts of perception that are considered cognitive or mental processes as occurring largely in your head. If we stayed with just this simple a picture, we would be seriously misrepresenting the way perception works. Why? Because, as we said before, listening is where the rubber of perception meets the road of communication. Listening is the concrete manifestation-in-communication of all the perceptual processes we have discussed in this chapter. When you communicate, your listening enables you to interpret (select, organize, and make inferences about) what your conversation partners are saying and doing. These perceptions change as you collaboratively build meaning....

REVIEW QUESTIONS

1. Explain what it means to say that perception is "a social and cognitive process."
2. How does a person's culture affect his or her perceiving?
3. Cognitive schemata are _____ _____ that help us to _____ incoming information.
4. This reading discusses two ways people organize information and three ways we make inferences. Label them.
5. What is an implicit personality theory?
6. What is the fundamental attribution error? What's the ultimate attribution error? How can such errors be avoided?

PROBES

1. How does this discussion of perception affect your definition of what it means to be "objective"?
2. Given the influence of person prototypes and scripts, how can you make your communicating responsive to the *particular*—as contrasted with the general—situation?

3. Explain the relationship between person-centered versus position-centered talk and impersonal versus interpersonal communicating.
4. "Perception" is a label for cognitive inhaling processes, and "listening" is a label for social inhaling processes. Explain.

REFERENCES

Abelson, R. P. 1981. "Psychological Status of the Script Concept." *American Psychologist*, 36: 715–729.

Bartlett, F. C. 1932! *Remembering: A Study in Experimental and Social Psychology.* London: Cambridge University Press.

Fiske, S. T., and Shelley, E. T. 1984. *Social Cognition.* New York: Random House.

Hall, B. J. 2002. *Among Cultures: The Challenge of Communication.* New York: Wadsworth.

Hall, N., and Crisp, R. 2003. "Anxiety-Induced Response Perseverance and Stereotype Change." *Current Research in Social Psychology*, 8: 242–253.

Heider, F. 1958. *The Psychology of Interpersonal Relations.* New York: Wiley.

Kelley, H. H. 1972. "Casual Schemata and the Attribution Process." In E. E. Jones, D. E. Kanouse, H. H. Kelley, R. E. Nisbett, S. Valins, and B. Weiner (eds.), *Attribution: Perceiving the Causes of Behavior.* Morristown, NJ: General Learning Press.

Kelley, H. H. 1973. "The Process of Causal Attribution." *American Psychologist*, 28: 107–128.

Kluckhorn, F. R., and Strodtbeck, F. L. 1961. *Variations in Value Orientations.* Evanston, IL: Row Peterson.

Konner, M. 2002. *The Tangled Wing: Biological Constraints on the Human Spirit.* 2nd ed. New York: Holt, Rinehart and Winston.

Maltz, D. N., and Borker, R. A. 1982. "A Cultural Approach to Male-Female Miscommunication." In J. J. Gumperz (ed.), *Language and Social Identity.* Cambridge: Cambridge University Press. Pages 196–216.

Manusov, V. 1990. "An Application of Attribution Principles to Nonverbal Behavior in Romantic Dyads." *Communication Monographs*, 57: 104–118.

Manusov, V., and Hegde, R. 1993. "Communicative Outcomes of Stereotype-Based Expectancies: An Observational Study of Cross-Cultural Dyads." *Communication Quarterly*, 41: 338–354.

Manusov, M., Winchatz, M., and Manning, L. M. 1997. "Acting Out Our Minds: Incorporating Behavior into Models of Stereotype-Based Expectancies for Cross-Cultural Interactions." *Communication Monographs*, 64: 119–139.

Mayer, R. E. 1992. *Thinking, Problem-Solving, Cognition.* 2nd ed. San Francisco: Freeman.

Rotter, J. B. 1966. "Generalized Expectancies for Internal vs. External Control of Reinforcement." *Psychological Monographs*, 80: 609.

Rush, L. L. 1998. "Affective Reactions to Multiple Social Stigmas." *Journal of Social Psychology*, 138: 421–430.

Schneider, D. J., Hastorf, A. H., and Ellsworth, P. C. 1979. *Person Perception*. 2nd ed. Reading, MA: Addison-Wesley. Pages 20–26.

It's Only Skin Deep:
Stereotyping and Totalizing Others
Julia T. Wood

Julia Wood teaches in the department of communication studies at the University of North Carolina at Chapel Hill, does research on gender and communication, and has published several interpersonal communication texts. This chapter comes from a recent book that she dedicates to enhancing its readers' understanding of "different meanings that people may attribute to what they say and do." In her book, Wood emphasizes how diversity can contribute to misunderstanding and how awareness and acceptance of diversity can help improve understanding.

As the subtitle of this selection says, this is a discussion of stereotyping, one of the most familiar and unfortunate features of the way we perceive people. As the subtitle also suggests, the key concept in this chapter is "totalizing." Wood explains that this word describes "communication that emphasizes one aspect of a person above all others." Totalizing means thinking and acting as if a single aspect of a person is the totality of that person. So calling Spike Lee a "black filmmaker" spotlights his race in a way that makes it the dominant feature that's being noticed. The same thing happens when people talk of "that short guy you dated," "a Japanese friend of mine," and "his deaf sister."

Wood makes the obvious—though important—point that totalizing has negative effects on the people who are its target. But she also describes some of the effects of totalizing on the people who do it. Basically, when we engage in totalizing, we cripple our perceiving by forcing ourselves to look through blinders. As Wood puts it, "we tend to perceive others through the labels we use to describe them."

One reason people stereotype or totalize is that it's easier to deal with a one-dimensional person than someone with many different important qualities. Another reason is that several automatic human brain processes produce classifications and generalizations. It would be impossible for us constantly to notice every detail of everything available to our senses, so our brain automatically classifies what we perceive to help keep us from going nuts.

But when we perceive people, this natural process can lead us to operate on the basis of what are called "implicit personality theories" (this same idea was discussed in the

previous reading). As both readings note, these are generalizations about groups of qualities that seem "obviously" to go together—like being overweight, happy, lazy, and undisciplined. Problems arise when we perceive one of these features—that a person is overweight,
for example—and our implicit theory about the rest of the personality fills in other features
that may or may not be parts of who the person is.

Wood discusses some of Dawn Braithwaite's research about how totalizing applies
to people with disabilities. Even that term—*disabled*—is often hurtful because it makes it
easier for others to reduce the amputee or the deaf or partly sighted person to the negative
status of being incomplete or flawed in some vital way. You can read an article on disabled
communication in Chapter 11.

Near the end of this short reading, Wood includes 10 examples of statements that often
come from well-meaning people but that are usually heard by the people they're directed to
as totalizing or stereotyping. (Compare these with the three statements Marsha Houston criticizes in the end of Chapter 12.) This list and the other ideas in this selection should help sensitize you to whatever tendencies you have to rely on stereotypes in your communication.

*I want to be known as a talented young filmmaker. That should be first. But the
reality today is that no matter how successful you are, you're black first. (p. 92)*

Those are Spike Lee's words. In an interview with Diane McDowell, reporter
for *Time* magazine, the gifted filmmaker lamented the reality that most
people see and respond to his blackness more than his other qualities and
achievements. Sometimes, awareness of Lee's blackness overrides all other
perceptions of him.

Distinguished historian John Hope Franklin made the same point in an
interview with Mark McGurl, reporter for the *New York Times*. According to
Franklin, many people assume that because he is an African American historian,
he must study African Americans. He is often introduced as the author of 12
books on black history. In reality, Franklin points out, he is *not* a historian only
of African Americans. His specialty is the history of the South and, as he notes,
that history includes both whites and blacks. In fact, several of his books have
focused primarily on whites in the South. Franklin has been elected president of
the American Historical Association, the Organization of American Historians,
and the Southern Historical Association—none of which is specifically an African American organization. Still, many people perceive his skin color above all
else and they assume his ethnicity defines his work.

The misunderstanding of identity and achievement that Spike Lee and John
Hope Franklin confront is not unique to people of minority races. Women report
that they are often asked to serve on committees. Many times the person asking
says, "We need a woman on the committee" or "We think you can provide the
woman's perspective on the issues." Like Lee and Franklin, professional women
may feel that all their accomplishments and abilities are erased by those who
ask them to be "the woman on the committee." The language in the request
communicates that all that is noticed is biological sex: She can fill the "woman
slot" on the committee.

In this [reading], we focus on communication that highlights one aspect of a person—usually race, sex, sexual orientation, disability, or economic status. We discuss common instances of such communication and explore how it fosters misunderstandings and often offense.

UNDERSTANDING THE MISUNDERSTANDING

Scholars use the term *totalize* to describe communication that emphasizes one aspect of a person above all others. When someone totalizes, he or she acts as if a single facet of an individual is the totality of that person or as if that single aspect is all that's important about the person. For example, describing Spike Lee as a *black* filmmaker spotlights his race as what is worthy of attention. Calling John Hope Franklin a *black* historian emphasizes his race and obscures his professional expertise and accomplishments. Asking a professional to provide the *woman's* perspective highlights sex as the criterion for serving on committees. Referring to a person as *gay* stresses sexual orientation and obscures all the person's other qualities. Describing people as *blue collar* or *white collar* makes their class visible and everything else about them invisible.

Totalizing affects both those who do it and those who are its targets. When we feel that someone totalizes us, we are likely to be offended and resentful. We may also be hurt that we have been reduced to a single part of our identity—perhaps not the part most important to us in a particular context. These feelings create barriers to open, healthy communication and comfortable relationships.

Less obvious but no less important is the impact of totalizing on people who engage in it. Language shapes our perceptions by calling certain things to our attention. When we use language that focuses our attention on race, class, sex, or any [other] single aspect of another person, we limit our perception of that person. In other words, we tend to perceive others through the labels we use to describe them.

Kenneth Burke, a distinguished critic of language and literature, observes that language simultaneously reflects, selects, and deflects. In his book *Language as Symbolic Action*, Burke writes: "Any given terminology is a *reflection* of reality, by its very nature as a terminology it must be a *selection* of reality; and to this extent it must function also as a *deflection* of reality" (p. 45). Burke means that the words we use to reflect our perceptions select certain aspects of what we are describing while simultaneously deflecting, or neglecting, other aspects of what we are describing. When we select *woman, black, gay,* and so forth to describe people, other aspects of those people are deflected (neglected or added as an afterthought). Consequently, we may not see in others whatever our labels deflect. Thus, we are unlikely to interact with those others in their wholeness.

Most of us wouldn't intentionally reduce another person to one aspect of who he or she is, but it happens. One motive for totalizing is the desire for reducing uncertainty. We tend to be uncomfortable when we are unsure about others and situations. To ease discomfort, we often attempt to reduce our uncertainty about others and circumstances. One way to do this is to define others as belonging to a group about which we have definite ideas (although the ideas may not be accurate). It is easier to think of Spike Lee as black than to try to perceive him as a unique individual who is—among other things—male, young, a filmmaker, educated, and African American.

In the classic book *The Nature of Prejudice*, psychologist Gordon Allport observed that stereotyping and prejudice grow out of normal—not deviant or unusual—cognitive activities. Specifically, Allport identified classification and generalization as commonplace mental activities that can foster stereotypes and prejudice. One reason we use stereotypes, then, is that they reduce our uncertainty by grouping people into broad classes that obscure individual characteristics.

A second reason we stereotype is that we rely on what psychologists call implicit personality theory. Most of us have certain unspoken and perhaps unrecognized assumptions about qualities that go together in personalities. Many people assume that attractive individuals are more extroverted, intelligent, and socially skilled than less attractive individuals. Another common implicit personality theory (one that research does not support) is that people who are overweight are also lazy, undisciplined, and happy. In both examples, we attribute to others a constellation of qualities that we associate with a particular quality we have noticed.

If we meet an individual who is overweight (in our judgment), we may assume that the person meets our implicit personality theory of overweight people and is happy, lazy, and undisciplined. Our implicit personality theories may also lead us to think that a nice-looking person must be intelligent, outgoing, and socially skilled. When we rely on our implicit personality theories, we latch onto one quality of another person—often a characteristic we can see, such as race, sex, or weight—and attribute to the person other qualities that we perceive as consistent with the quality we have identified....

One form of totalizing . . . involves defining individuals by their membership in a specific group. Years ago sociologist Louis Wirth conducted classic studies of racial prejudice. One of his more important conclusions was that when we perceive people primarily in terms of their membership in a particular racial or ethnic group, we tend to think about them and interact with them in terms of our stereotypes of race, regardless of their unique qualities, talents, and so forth. In other words, their individuality is lost, submerged in our preconceptions of the group to which we assign them.

A second form of totalizing reduces individuals to one quality or aspect of their identities. This type of totalizing is evident in some of the language used to describe persons who have disabilities. How we perceive and label people with disabilities is the research focus of Dawn Braithwaite, a communication scholar at Arizona State University West. From interviews with persons who have disabilities, Braithwaite learned that the term *disabled person* is likely to offend. The reason is that the term suggests that their personhood is disabled—that they are somehow inadequate or diminished as persons simply because they have disabilities. One of the people Braithwaite interviewed asserted, "I am a person like anyone else" (1994, p. 151). Another interviewee said, "If anyone refers to me as an amputee, that is guaranteed to get me madder than hell! I don't deny the leg amputation, but I am me. I am a whole person" (1994, p. 151).

Individuals who have disabilities have been vocal in resisting efforts to label them *disabled*. They point out that calling them disabled emphasizes their disabilities above all else. "We're people who have disabilities. People first," a deaf student explained to me. When someone with a disability is described as disabled, we highlight what they cannot do rather than all they can do....

When we think stereotypically, we expect people to conform to our perceptions of the group to which we assign them. Sometimes, however, we meet someone who doesn't fit our stereotypes of the group to which we think he or she belongs. Have you ever said or heard the phrases "woman doctor," "male nurse," or "woman lawyer"? Notice how they call attention to the sex of the doctor, nurse, or lawyer. Have you ever heard or used the phrases "man doctor," "woman nurse," or "man lawyer"? Probably not—because it is considered normal for men to be doctors and lawyers and women to be nurses. Many people perceive it as unusual for women to practice law or medicine or men to be nurses. "Woman doctor," "male nurse," and "woman lawyer" spotlight the sex of individuals as the element worthy of notice. The phrases also reflect stereotyped views of the professional groups.

When we mark an individual as an exception to his or her group, we unknowingly reveal our own stereotypes. In fact, we may reinforce them because marking an individual who doesn't conform to the stereotype as unusual leaves our perceptions of the group unchanged. All we do is remove the "exceptional individual" from the group. Consider these statements:

White manager to black manager:	"You really are exceptional at your job." [*Translation:* Black women aren't usually successful.]
Male professional to female professional:	"You don't think like a woman." [*Translation:* Most women don't think like professionals.]
Able-bodied individual to person in wheelchair:	"I'm amazed at how well you get around." [*Translation:* I assume that people who use wheelchairs don't get out much.]
Upper-class person to working-class person:	"It's remarkable that you take college classes." [*Translation:* Most working-class people aren't interested in higher education.]
White person to African American:	"I can't believe you don't like to dance." [*Translation:* I think that all blacks dance, have rhythm.]

Heterosexual to lesbian:	"I think it's great that you have some male friends."
	[*Translation:* Most lesbians hate men.]
Homeowner to maid:	"You speak so articulately."
	[*Translation:* I assume most domestic workers don't speak well and/or aren't educated.]
White man to black man:	"I never think of you as black."
	[*Translation:* You don't fit my views of blacks; you're an exception to my (negative) stereotype of blacks.]
Christian to Jew:	"I'm surprised at how generous you are."
	[*Translation:* Most Jews are tight with money.]
African American to white person:	"You're not as stuffy as most of your people."
	[*Translation:* Most whites are stuffy, or up-tight, but you're not.]

Would any of the above statements be made to a member of the speaker's group? Would a heterosexual say to a heterosexual woman, "It's great that you have some male friends"? Would a white man say to another white man, "I never think of you as white"? Would a maid say to his or her employer, "You speak so articulately"? Would a white person say to another white person, "I can't believe you don't like to dance"? In each case, it's unlikely. By changing the speakers in the statements, we see how clearly the statements reflect stereotypes of groups.

Communicating that you perceive an individual as an exception to his or her group invites two dilemmas. First, it expresses your perception that the person belongs to a group about which you have preconceptions. Understandably, this may alienate the other person or make her or him defensive. The person may feel compelled to defend or redefine the group from which you have removed that individual. An African American might, for instance, say "Lots of blacks don't enjoy dancing." A working-class person might inform an upper-class person that "education has always been a priority in my family."

A second possible response to communication that marks an individual as an exception to her or his group is the effort to deny identification with the group. A professional woman may strive not to appear feminine to avoid being judged by her colleagues' negative perceptions of women. A white person may try to "talk black" or play music by black artists to prove he or she isn't like most whites. The group stereotypes—no matter how inaccurate—are left unchallenged.

Whether individuals defend or redefine their groups or separate themselves from the groups, one result is the same: The possibilities for open communication and honest relationships are compromised.

REVIEW QUESTIONS

1. Define *totalizing* in your own words, and give an example from your own experience of how totalizing can affect communication.
2. Specifically how does totalizing affect the person who *does* it?
3. Define and give an example of *implicit personality theory*.
4. My wife, Kris, is an attorney. Use Wood's article to explain why she does not like to be called a "woman lawyer."
5. Explain the point Wood is making when she asks, "Would a white man say to another white man, 'I never think of you as white'?"

PROBES

1. On the first day of class, the instructor says in a genuinely pleased way, "It's great to have so many persons of color in the class." Explain how this can be heard as a totalizing statement.
2. Wood quotes Gordon Allport to make the point that stereotyping is a normal, natural activity. But if it's normal and natural, then how much sense does it make to encourage people not to do it?
3. Privately, if you prefer, or with a classmate, if you're willing, explore some of your own implicit personality theories. For example, if you're not thinking carefully about it, what qualities do you presume a person has who is (a) a teenage African-American male, (b) a female athlete, (c) a 20-something gay male, (d) a middle-aged female nurse?
4. If it's obviously true that a person does not have normal sight, hearing, intelligence, or mobility, what is the problem with referring to that person as "disabled"?
5. What's the connection between the main point made in this reading and the impersonal-interpersonal continuum discussed in Chapter 2?

REFERENCES

Allport, G. (1979). *The nature of prejudice*. Reading, MA: Addison-Wesley.
Braithwaite, D. (1994). Viewing persons with disabilities as a culture. In L. Samovar & R. Porter (Eds.), *Intercultural communication: A reader* (7th ed., pp. 148–154). Belmont, CA: Wadsworth.
Burke, K. (1966). *Language as symbolic action*. Berkeley, CA: University of California Press.
McDowell, D. (1989, July 17). He's got to have his way. *Time*, pp. 92–94.
McGurl, M. (1990, June 3). That's history, not black history. *The New York Times Book Review*, 13.
Wirth, L. (1945). The problem of minority groups. In R. Linton (Ed.), *The science of man* (pp. 347–372). New York: Columbia University Press.

Mindful Listening
Rebecca Z. Shafir

Rebecca Shafir, the author of this essay, reports that she has learned a great deal about communication and listening from Zen Buddhist philosophy. As you may know, Zen is an Eastern philosophy that was first imported into the United States in the 1960s. Since then, it has sometimes been stereotyped as silly, New Age thinking." But those who seriously study this philosophy know that it offers westerners insights and guidelines that can substantially improve our communicating.

One contribution from this and other Buddhist writings is the concept of "mindfulness." This is a label for a way of focusing your attention that can produce significant benefits. I have included this reading in order to clarify that "mindfulness" means and how it can improve your listening.

Initially, Shafir characterizes mindful listening as the ability to receive the spoken word accurately, retain information, sustain attention, attend to your own responsive speech, and encourage the speaker. She emphasizes the importance of a strong intent to assure a positive outcome—which means that mindfulness is not a permanent state, because no one has this strong positive intent all the time.

Mindfulness is the opposite of multitasking, which is a skill that many contemporary people value very highly. As Shafir writes, "Our environment with its constant bombardment of stimuli challenges your innate ability to relax and focus completely on one task at a time." This challenges constantly encourages mindlessness, an orientation that prevents effective listening.

Shafir's discussion of the work of one of her Buddhist mentors, Thich Nhat Hanh, emphasizes both the simplicity and the unusualness of mindfulness. Thich Nhat Hanh describes two ways to wash the dishes. "The first is to wash the dishes in order to have clean dishes and the second is to wash the dishes in order to wash the dishes." The first is mindless, because when you wash the dishes this way, your focus is not on the present but on the future—what the dish washing will accomplish. The second is mindful because your focus is on what is currently occurring, here and now. Buddhist philosophy emphasizes the importance and value of attending to the present—being mindful.

This simple example makes it clear that many Western cultural values discourage mindfulness. North Americans are praised for our abilities to "get things done," solve problems, and build impressive structures and systems. These capabilities are undeniably productive. But this cultural emphasis on constant accomplishment can divert us from important present-tense experiences: enjoying a discovery with a child, profoundly appreciating a beautiful view, taking in the aroma of a landscape, listening closely to a friend. Zen reminds us of the complementary value of these mindful experiences. One of its slogans is "Don't just do something. Sit there!"

It is important and useful, I believe, to take this advice about mindfulness into your listening. Most of us are too busy to do this all the time. But we should at least have available to us, as one of our important communication options, the ability to listen mindfully.

How tiresome it is to leave a performance review with the comment written in bold print: **"Your listening skills need work."** It is a déjà vu experience for many of us, one that we can easily recall from numerous early sources: our parents, scout leaders, coaches, and teachers. Since our youth these words of wisdom have come in various forms. For example: "Stop talking and pay attention," as if when we stop talking we somehow start paying attention, or more indirectly, "Maybe you should get your hearing checked." When we are told to listen up, what exactly does that mean? How do we know if we are really listening (and paying attention) or just acting like we are? How can we convince others, like the boss, that our listening skills are deserving of a promotion? Would we know a good listener if we met one? How far are we from being considered a good listener?

... If you were to poll various individuals and ask what it means to be a good listener, you would hear several versions. Here are some examples. Sales consultant Michael Leppo describes good listening as the ability to hear attentively. Michelle Lucas, a psychotherapist, says that good listening is a process of showing respect and validating a person's worth. The International Listening Association defines listening as "the process of receiving, constructing meaning from, and responding to spoken and/or nonverbal messages." Others say it is simply the ability to understand and remember what was said. Ralph G. Nichols, one of the founding fathers of listening studies, said, "Listening is an inside job—inside action on the part of the listener." This suggests that good listening is the ability to get into the shoes of the speaker in order to see his side of the issue.

... I will define a good listener as one who is *mindful* of the wide spectrum of listening skills. These include the ability to

- receive the spoken word accurately, interpret the whole message (the words, gestures and facial expressions) in an unbiased manner;
- retain the information for future use;
- sustain attention to the spoken word at will; listening is a process that occurs *over time;*
- attend to *your* speech and be sensitive to the accuracy of the message and the possible interpretations that could be derived from it;
- encourage a speaker to speak from his [or her] heart and expound on his or her ideas without censure. This makes your speaker feel valued and respected.

... Mindful listening is already a part of you. However, it does require a desire to listen. A desire to listen involves a curiosity for new information and a willingness to pay more respect to your speaker. If your desire is to build stronger personal and professional relationships, a degree of compassion is a basic requirement to becoming a better listener.

Mindful listening is the mind and body working together to communicate. Furthermore, it does not require two functioning ears to listen in a mindful way. Mindful listening requires you to see, hear, and feel with your whole being. To attend mindfully to the message, whether the message is spoken or signed, is to perceive as closely as possible the intent and experience of the speaker.

Mindful listening can be applied to the wide continuum of listening types:

- information processing
- information seeking
- critical or evaluative listening
- therapeutic listening
- empathetic or compassionate listening
- small-talk listening ...

MINDFULNESS: LISTENING IN THE MOMENT

Concentration is the key to performing *any* meaningful activity well. It is heartening to know that we innately possess the ability to concentrate. It does not require any special training, just frequent application. Think of an activity that requires complete, sustained attention, such as taking an important test, driving in a snowstorm, or playing chess. Your focus on these tasks is propelled by a strong intent to assure a positive outcome—to excel in school, get home safely, or choose the best move. However, the more you concentrate on the *process*, the more positive will be the outcome. Reading each test item carefully, looking for tricky wordings, and rechecking your answers increases your chance of scoring a high grade. If you were to think of nothing but getting an A, the end result would not be so positive.

On the other hand, there are activities that once required a similar level of concentration, but have now become mindless, like sweeping the floor or grocery shopping. These rote activities give the brain a chance to unwind and relax. You can think about other things and even perform other tasks simultaneously: you can eat *and* read, surf the Internet *and* listen to music. These combinations can be very enjoyable. However, you may tend to overuse this ability to multitask and misuse it when it is necessary to focus your attention on a single activity, such as listening. Our environment with its constant bombardment of stimuli challenges your innate ability to relax and focus completely on one task at a time.

Not long ago, I was in an airport with an hour wait for may plane, and I met a former high-school classmate whom I hadn't seen in more than twenty years. We decided to go across the street to a nice hotel for something to drink while we caught up on each other's lives. Outside the bar was a sign that invited us to COME IN AND RELAX. As soon as we were inside, we noticed five TVs, all tuned to different channels! In addition, there was noise from the nearby kitchen and a radio playing behind the bar. Some patrons at tables tried to maintain conversation-like activities while their eyes shifted from TV to TV. It was dizzying! It took every bit of our concentration to hear each other and even more effort to discuss anything in depth. It occurred to me that an intensely distracting environment is regarded by many people as "relaxing."

You lull yourself into a false sense of competency when you think you can make dinner, plan that sales meeting, and help your son with his homework, all at the same time. You may finish all these tasks in thirty minutes or less, but how is the quality? When you look closely, dinner was just edible, you overlooked two of the seven main points for the meeting, and your son is able to spell only six of the ten words on his vocabulary homework. Since the goal is to *finish* these tasks so that you can rush onto the next one, the results are less than satisfactory. You feel depleted and inadequate.

Such mindlessness becomes a habit and begins to creep into tasks that require your full concentration. How often do you look back at the week, the month, the year, and wonder where the time went? Many of us can't remember because most of the time we were in a fog of preoccupation with the past or planning the future. Our attention was scattered all over the place, and the quality of our actions was just good enough to get by. Substandard performance on any task results in low self-esteem and lack of fulfillment.

Eknath Easwaran, author of *Words to Live By: Inspiration for Every Day*, speaks of the dangers of mindlessness: "There is no joy in work which is hurried, which is done when we are at the mercy of pressures from outside, because such work is compulsive. All too often hurry clouds judgment. More and more, to save time, a person tends to think in terms of pat solutions and to take shortcuts and give uninspired performances."

When mindlessness teams up with personal barriers, our ability to concentrate on the message is out of reach. The antidote is to challenge those distractions and focus on the process—establishing a warm relationship with another person, seeing the other's view, and accepting it as valid whether you agree with it or not. Focus on process ensures the favorable outcome you hope for—repeat sales, cooperation from difficult people, better recall.... If, however, you still find that your barriers overpower your ability to focus, then you need to spend a bit more time thinking them through.

In my search for a practical means of improving the ability to concentrate and listen more effectively, I came across the writings of Thich Nhat Hanh, a Zen Buddhist monk. After studying his book, *The Miracle of Mindfulness,* I found that my ability to listen had become richer. The essence of Zen is to be in the present. Thich Nhat Hanh describes mindfulness as keeping your consciousness alive to the present reality. Living the present moment of any activity, paying attention to the process, lend themselves to a quality outcome.

A good way to experience mindfulness is to choose a task you typically rush through, like washing the dishes. According to Thich Nhat Hanh, "There are two ways to wash the dishes. The first is to wash the dishes in order to have clean dishes and the second is to wash the dishes in order to wash the dishes." He says that if we hurry through the dishes, thinking only about the cup of tea that awaits us, then we are not washing the dishes to wash the dishes; we are not alive during the time we are washing the dishes. In fact, we are completely incapable of realizing the miracle of life while standing at the sink. "If we can't wash the dishes," he continues, "the chances are we won't be able to drink our tea either. While drinking the cup of tea, we will only be thinking of other things, barely aware of the cup in our hands."

When you are listening to another but planning your own agenda at the same time, you are really talking to yourself and therefore not truly listening. You have escaped the present in order to be in the future. You may be physically present, but mentally you are bouncing back and forth between past events and future expectations.

Another challenge to mindful listening is that the average person speaks at a rate of 125 words per minute, yet we can process up to 500 words per minute. During that lag time, you can think about your to-do list or you can listen mindfully by using that time to summarize what the speaker has said so far or see the possibilities in what the speaker is proposing. You can also note the emphasis in his voice or the degree of concern in his gestures and facial expressions. When you are in the speaker's movie, you use your resources to be a competent, intelligent listener.

If you have difficulty putting your thoughts, judgments, and other noise aside while you are trying to get into the speaker's movie, you may need some practice staying in the present. Poor listeners have little patience for the present. Thoughts of yesterday and tomorrow are more enticing. Your barriers have little tolerance for information or ideas that are contrary or too lengthy. Impatience shows itself when you fall out of the speaker's movie or want to interrupt....

Time spent listening, consulting, teaching, or working in the present can be just as memorable as those moments is your life when time appeared to stand still. When listening mindfully, however, your perception is heightened and you experience multilevel awareness. You are able to delve into what makes the speaker tick, how well his body language matches or contradicts his spoken message, his mood, energy level, and other subtle nuances. When you are fully absorbed in the speaker's movie, you are in the present; time appears to stand still. Mindful listening is not a trance or a hypnotic state. You are aware of your surroundings, but they are not a distraction.

The first-century Buddhist philosopher Ashvagosha gives a humorous account of mindful listening:

> If we are listening to a friend, even if a parrot flies down and perches on his head, we should not get excited, point to the parrot, and burst out, "Excuse me for interrupting, but there's parrot on your head." We should be able to concentrate so hard on what our friend is saying that we can tell this urge, "Keep quiet and don't distract me. Afterwards I'll tell him about the bird."

He goes on to describe mindfulness as "one-pointedness." This means to focus the attention completely on one task at a time. By applying this approach to your daily tasks, you can complete the same number of tasks, only with better quality, and hence, better outcomes. Many of my students tell me they are better able to prioritize activities and eliminate the time wasters. When being mindful appears daunting, remember that one minute of mindfulness makes up for many minutes of mindlessness....

A similar mind-body connection was described by Mihaly Czikszentmihalyi, author of *Flow*. He defines a flow experience as the pleasant state of concentration or total absorption in a task. Those he interviewed—painters, dancers, and athletes—said that when they were in the midst of their art or hobby, their state of focused energy was like "floating" or "being carried by the flow." When you experience flow often, the quality of your life improves. The opposite of flow is mindlessness. During mindless listening, your barriers create resistance to the message; your mind is scattered....

In my listening classes, we begin to practice mindfulness in gentler doses. We begin by experiencing orange juice as I narrate. Students watch the rush of the deep orange color as the juice is poured into their cups. Together, we smell the citrus perfume and notice how our mouths begin to water. We sip and savor the tartness. We consider the work that went into producing this cup of juice and imagine the beauty of the tree from which it came. We think about the people who made it possible to get the juice to our table. This full experience endures until the last sip. As they listen and ponder the juice, it's always interesting to note that no one looks around the room; each one's gaze and mental focus are centered on the juice.

The point of the exercise is to take a simple human act, something that we typically take for granted, and make it come alive. So often we sleep through life, attributing little or no meaning to our daily activities. Imagine if you lent that same zest to sipping your coffee, conducting a meeting, or cleaning out the refrigerator; how much more satisfied would you feel at the end of the day? I can be sure my students will never again drink orange juice the old way. And if they need a mindfulness refresher, they will simply pour themselves a glass of orange juice.

Mindfulness connects us with the experience of the moment, no matter what the activity. With listening, mindfulness connects us to the listener. *Mindlessness*, on the other hand, means letting the ego-dominated self—concerns with status, past experiences, and other barriers—separate us from the listener. The mindful listener lacks this obsessive self-consciousness that interferes with the ability to concentrate. We feel happier and more positive when we are not focusing on the self....

Students ask, "Do I have to be mindful all the time? Isn't that exhausting? Doesn't it take too much time?" Ideally, to make mindfulness a habit, we should perform as many acts as possible carefully and with thought. Begin by noticing how often you act mindlessly—driving through a stoplight, leaving the house without your keys, taking down the wrong phone number. That kind of wasted energy is exhausting and time consuming. Mindfulness saves time because you think as you act. Slowing down and carrying out the task with mindfulness significantly reduces the chances of error and mishap....

Recently, a coworker who was about to leave for her vacation told me three vital points to include on an upcoming financial report. Feeling cocky (after all I was writing a book on listening!), I did not take that mindful twenty seconds to repeat what she had said or write it down. Two days later when writing the report, I was able to recall only about 90 percent of the information. To get that forgotten 10 percent, I had to spend another hour tracking down another source....

Instead of insulting yourself when mindlessness strikes, consider it a wake-up call to become mindful. Make it a point to commend yourself for the moments of mindfulness that make up your day.

Initially, it may seem like you are taking more time to carry out your tasks. You are used to doing everything in haste, so even a minute more will seem like days. Yet as your ability to concentrate improves, you will become more efficient. Tasks done mindfully are done right the first time. There is no need to recheck or redo. Mindfulness saves time.

REVIEW QUESTIONS

1. In your own words, define *mindfulness*.
2. List four specific things that you will be doing when you listen to someone mindfully. For example, describe your posture, eye behavior, and facial expression; the connection between your conversation partner's word choices and yours; and so on.
3. The average speaking rate is 125 words per minute, and we can process up to 500 words per minute. How does Shafir suggest that you use the "spare time" that is created by this difference?
4. Does Shafir believe that you should work to be mindful all the time? Explain.

PROBES

1. Do video games encourage mindfulness or mindlessness? Explain.
2. Shafir argues that "you lull yourself into a false sense of competency" when you believe that you can multitask successfully. Explain what she believes is the practical danger of multitasking. Why does she call it a "false sense of competency"?
3. Athletes and artists sometimes talk about being "in the zone" or "in the flow." What is the relationship between this experience and mindfulness?

Empathic and Dialogic Listening

John Stewart, Karen E. Zediker, and Saskia Witteborn

This reading offers a fairly extended treatment of two kinds of helpful listening. Empathic listening enables you to understand the *other* person, thoroughly and fully. Dialogic listening takes the process one step farther. Rather than focusing mainly on what the other person is thinking and feeling, dialogic listening helps the two of you—or all the people in the conversation—build meaning together. So when dialogic listening works well, everybody understands each other *and* the people involved co-create new understandings that go beyond the individuals.

Karen, Saskia, and I break emphatic listening down into three main skill sets: focusing, encouraging, and reflecting. The focusing section develops what Rebecca Shafir wrote about mindfulness—earlier in this chapter. We outline four specific ways to focus on the person you're listening to.

Encouraging skills are communication moves that "pull" more talk from the other person. They are designed to help your conversation partner(s) get more of what they're thinking and feeling on the table between you. Some encouraging skills are nonverbal, and some are verbal. We offer five ways to encourage people, and we also suggest two kinds of questions that are good to avoid.

Reflecting skills enable your conversation partner(s) to understand what you have heard and understood. This enables them to clarify their meanings, where necessary, and to correct any misunderstandings. The main reflecting skill is paraphrasing.

As we note, there are no "six easy steps" or "five sure-fire techniques" for dialogic listening. It takes a different level of understanding and practice. If you have trouble with this section of the reading, you might look over the materials in Chapter 12, "Promoting Dialogue." They reinforce what's discussed here and give some additional examples.

The primary ingredient for dialogic listening is *your willingness and ability to collaboratively co-construct meaning with your conversation partner(s)*. You can't listen dialogically until you move beyond your desire to "make sure she understands you" and "get your point across." Dialogic listening begins with the understanding that "the point" needs to be what's shared among those in the conversation, not just your ideas.

The primary metaphor for dialogic listening is "sculpting mutual meanings." We refer to the situation of two people seated on either side of a potter's wheel, with their four wet hands shaping the clay on the wheel. Taken figuratively, this is what it means to "sculpt mutual meaning."

But we don't just leave you with abstractions. We describe four specific communication moves that can help you listen dialogically: focus on "ours," paraphrase-plus, ask for a paraphrase, and run with the metaphor. We also offer an extended example conversation that illustrates these communication moves. Our goal, here and in Chapter 12, is to encourage you and empower you to work toward creating dialogic moments in more of your communicating.

EMPATHIC LISTENING

When a person is listening empathically, he or she is receptive or sensitive to the full range of characteristics shared by the other person, but responds only with his or her own impersonal characteristics. Carl Rogers, a famous counselor who pioneered the technique of empathic listening, describes it as "entering the

private perceptual world of the other and becoming thoroughly at home in it."
He continued:

> It involves being sensitive, moment by moment, to the changing felt meanings
> which flow in this other person.... To be with another in this way means that
> for the time being, you lay aside your own views and values in order to enter
> another's world without prejudice. In some sense it means that you lay aside
> yourself. (Rogers 1980, 142–143)

This kind of listening is important, for example, when you are aware that
your friend needs to vent and you are willing to listen without adding anything
beyond your friend's point of view. In fact, if you respond in these situations by
saying, "Well, if I were you..." your friend may insist, "I don't need your advice.
I want you to just *listen* to me." It can also be important to listen empathically
if you've been asked to mediate a dispute. You can't function very well as a
mediator until you fully understand each person's point of view, and empathic
listening can help you build this understanding.

Empathic listening is also an important skill for parents, teachers, and managers. Family communication research indicates, for example, that toddlers,
children, and adolescents often feel that their parents listen only from their
own point of view, rather than taking the time and effort to fully understand
the young person's thinking and feeling. Books such as *How to Talk So Kids Will
Listen and Listen So Kids Will Talk* (Faber and Mazlish 1982) also emphasize how
pity and advice can leave one feeling worse than before.

> But let someone really listen [empathically], let someone acknowledge my inner
> pain and give me a chance to talk more about what's troubling me and I begin
> to feel less upset, less confused, more able to cope with my feelings and my
> problem. (Faber and Mazlish 1982, 9)

Managers and teachers often need to listen empathically in order to understand how to help their subordinates or students, and counselors and doctors
also routinely respond this way to their clients.

In order to listen empathically, it's important to develop three sets of
competencies: focusing, encouraging, and reflecting skills (Bolton 1990). As
with any complex process, it works best to select from among the various
ways to focus, encourage, and reflect. Think of the specific skills like a salad
bar—put on your plate the ones that you're comfortable with and that fit the
situation you're in.

Focusing Skills

As with analytic listening, the first step is to orient your attention to the person
you're listening to. This begins with an internal decision about how you are going to invest your time and energy. Here it helps to recall the distinction between
spending time and *investing* it and to realize that empathic listening can often
pay the dividends of any good investment. Then you remember that listening

takes effort, and you put aside the other things you're doing to concentrate on the other person. At this point, focusing surfaces in four skills.

The first is *aiming your posture.* Turn your body so that you're facing or nearly facing the person you're listening to, and if you're seated, lean toward your conversation partner. This is a simple thing to do, and yet a variety of studies have underscored its importance. One textbook for counselors puts it this way: "Usually, the interested helper leans toward the helpee in a relaxed manner. Relaxation is important because tenseness tends to shift the focus from the helpee to the helper...." (Brammer 1979, 70). It's been demonstrated that when listeners focus their bodies this way, the people they're talking with perceive them as more "warm" and accessible and consequently they find it's easier to volunteer more information (Reece and Whiteman 1962).

A second part of focusing is making *natural and appropriate eye contact.* In Western cultures, when you look the other person in the eye, you are not only acutely aware of him or her, but you are also directly available to that person. Studies of nonverbal listening behavior in these cultures typically identify eye contact and forward body lean or movement toward the other as two of the most important indicators of attraction and contact (Clore, Wiggins, and Itkin, 1975). So, if you cannot easily make eye contact with the other person, move to a position where you can. If you're talking with children, get down on the same level by kneeling or sitting, so that they can see you looking at them.

As we've already noted, the amount and kind of eye contact that are "appropriate" depend partly on the cultural identities of the people involved. If you're talking with a person from a culture that proscribes eye contact except between intimates or from a superior to an inferior, it's important to try to honor these guidelines. If you're from one of these cultures, and your conversation partner is not, it can help to alter your own behavior in the direction of the other person's expectations as far as you comfortably can. But so long as you are operating in a generally Western communication context, it's important to work toward making eye contact 50 percent to 70 percent of the time.

In cultures that value direct eye contact, breaking it while listening can create real problems. As one of our students put it, "Based on my own experience, and that of a few others I've talked with, when a listening partner suddenly breaks eye contact to focus on something else (say a friend who's walking by and waving), it can have an almost disconfirming effect on those of us who want to express ourselves" (Adams 1996).

The third and fourth ways to focus are to *move responsively* and to *make responsive sounds.* We've known people who believed they were listening intently when they sat staring at the other person, completely immobile, and with unchanging, deadpan expressions on their faces. There are two problems with this habit. The most obvious one is that, even though you may think you're listening well, it doesn't look like you are. Unless I see some response in your body and on your face, I'm not convinced that you're really being affected by what I'm saying. The second problem is more subtle: Actually you are not fully involved in what you're hearing until your body begins to register your involvement. So even though you might think you're focused when you're immobile and silent, you are not as focused as you will be when you start moving responsively and making responsive sounds. Since everybody's mind and body are intimately connected, the kinesthetic sensations of your body's responsiveness will actually help your mind stay focused.

By moving responsively, we mean smiling, nodding or shaking your head, moving your eyebrows, shrugging your shoulders, frowning, and so on. These actions should be prompted by, in response to, and linked up with what the other person says and does. So an effective listener isn't nodding or smiling all the time; she nods or smiles when that is responsive to what the other person is saying, and she frowns or shakes her head when that's responsive.

Responsive sounds include the "Mnnhuh," "Oh?" "Yeah...," "Ahh?" "Sure!" "Really?" [and] "Awww" utterances that audibly tell the other person you're tuned in to what he or she is saying. If you doubt the importance of responsive sounds, try being completely silent the next time you're listening over the phone. After a very short time the other person will ask something like "Are you still there?" We need sounds like these to reassure us that our hearer is actually listening.

These four skills may seem overly obvious or simplistic, but it is quite clear from a number of communication studies that people differ greatly in their ability to apply these behaviors.

Encouraging Skills

The second set of empathic listening skills is designed to "pull" more talk from the other person. More talk is obviously not always a good thing. But when you want to understand as completely as possible where another person is coming from, you need to have enough verbal and nonverbal talk to make the picture clear. As a result, we want to make six specific suggestions about how to encourage.

The first is the most direct one: As a listener, respond when appropriate with "Say more," "Keep talking," "Could you elaborate on that?" or "For example?" One situation where this response can help is when someone makes a comment that sounds fuzzy or incomplete. Frequently the listener's inclination is to try to paraphrase what's been said or to act on the information even though it's uncertain whether he or she has the materials to do so. Of course, it would be pretty ridiculous to respond to "I wonder what time it is" with "Could you say more about that?" But each time you hear a new idea, a new topic, or an important point being made, we suggest you begin your empathic listening effort at that moment not by guessing what the other person means but by asking her or him to tell you. "Say more," "Keep talking," or some similar encouragement can help.

A second encouraging skill is called *mirroring*. Mirroring means repeating a key word or phrase of the other person's with a question on your face and in your voice. "Repeating?" Yes, you just pick up on one term, for example, and feed it back with a questioning inflection and raised eyebrows, and the other person will elaborate on what he has just said. "Elaborate?" Yeah—you know, he will give an example, or restate what he said in other terms, or make some such effort to clarify the point he is making. Just as we have been doing here.

A third encouraging response is the *clarifying question*. Often this takes the form "Do you mean … ?" or "When you say _____, do you mean _____?" You might ask the person to explain how he or she is defining a word or phrase, or you might ask for the implications of what is being said. In a job interview, for example, the interviewer might comment, "Our company is interested only in assertive people …" and the candidate could ask, "When you say 'assertive,' what do you mean?" Tone of voice is an important part of clarifying questions. Remember, your questions are motivated by a need to understand more clearly; they are not meant to force the other person into a corner with a demand to "define your terms!"

Open questions are a fourth way to encourage. *Closed* questions call for a yes or no, single-word, or simple-sentence answer. *Open* questions just identify a topic area and encourage the other person to talk about it. So, "Who was that person I saw you with last night?" is a closed question, and "How's your love life going?" is a more open one. Open questions often begin with "What do you think about … ?" or "How do you feel about … ?" while a closed version of a similar question might begin "Do you think … ?" "Do you like this chapter?" is a closed question; "Which parts of this chapter do you like best?" is more open. Both types of questions can be useful, but when you want to encourage, use open ones.

A fifth way to encourage is by using *attentive silence*. As we've said before, the point of empathic listening is to develop and understand the perspective of the speaker. So, stay focused and give the other person plenty of room to talk. This is frequently all a person needs to be encouraged to contribute more.

Our two final suggestions about encouraging highlight what *not* to do. Encouraging obviously involves asking questions, but not just any question. We have already explained why using open questions is generally more effective than using closed questions. But there are also two types of questions that it helps to avoid. The first are what we call *pseudoquestions*. *Pseudo* means pretended, unreal, or fake, and a pseudoquestion is a judgment or opinion pretending to be a question. "Where do you think you're going?" is not really a question, it's a pseudoquestion. In other words, if you think about how this question functions in actual conversation, you can hear how it's almost always a complaint or a judgment one person is making about the other. "Where do you think you're going?" usually says something like "Get back here!" or "I don't want you to leave." "Is it safe to drive this fast?" is another pseudoquestion; here, the hidden statement is something like "I'm scared by your driving," or "I wish you'd slow down." At times, we may use pseudoquestions to soften a more directly negative evaluation of the other person (Goodman and Esterly 1990, 760). But often such softening attempts are confusing and add more frustration than they're worth. Our point here is that if you use them in your efforts to encourage, they can backfire. Instead of pseudoquestions, try to ask only real ones, genuine requests for information or elaboration.

A second kind of question to avoid is the one that begins with the word "Why," because these questions tend to promote defensiveness. When people hear "Why?" questions, they often believe the questioner is asking them for a rationale or an excuse. "Why did you decide to bring him to this meeting?" "Why are you turning that in now?" "Why didn't you call me?" "Why did you decide to do it that way?" Do you hear the implicit demand in these questions? The problem is that "Why?" questions often put the questioned person on the spot. They seem to call for a moral or value justification. As a result, they don't work as encouragers. In their place, try asking exactly the same question but begin it with different words. For example, try "How did you decide to ... ?" or "What are your reasons for ... ?" We believe that you will find it works better.

Reflecting Skills

This third set of skills will help you directly reflect the other person's perspective in the communication process. This is the central goal of empathic listening. There are three skills in this final set. The first is called *paraphrasing. A paraphrase is a restatement of the other's meaning in your own words, followed by a verification check.* This means there are four important parts to a paraphrase: (1) It's a restatement, not a question. A paraphrase doesn't start out by asking; it starts out by telling the other what you have heard. The first words of a paraphrase might be "So you believe that ..." or "In other words, you're saying that ..."(2) It's a restatement of the other's *meaning*, not a repeat of the other's words. Meanings include both ideas and feelings, and the fullest paraphrase captures some of both. Sometimes the feeling content is very important, and sometimes it is less so. But your paraphrase ought at least to suggest the emotion that's included in what the other person said. "So you're worried that ..." or "It sounds like you are really upset because you believe that ..." are two examples of restating feelings—"worry" and "upset." (3) A paraphrase has to be in your own words.... Translating the other's meaning into your words demonstrates that you've thought about it, that it's gone through your brain cells. (4) After the restatement, you finish a paraphrase with an opportunity for the other person to verify your understanding. You can do this very simply— just by pausing and raising your eyebrows, or asking "Right?" or "Is that it?" Paraphrasing is such a powerful communication move that, if you follow these four steps periodically in your conversations, your empathic listening effectiveness will improve significantly.

The second reflective skill is *adding an example.* You can contribute to the listening process by asking the other person to respond to an example from your own experience that you believe illustrates his or her point. Remember that this is an effort to listen empathically, not to turn the conversation away from the other person's concerns and toward yours. So the example needs clearly to be one that makes his or her main point. Here is part of a conversation that illustrates what we mean.

	LAURA: I've had my share of problems with this TA position, but in some ways this job is actually rewarding.
(clarifying question)	HABIB: Since it's payday, are you talking about your check?
	LAURA: No, one of my students just wrote this note on her copy of the exam we were going over in class: "I liked the way you were willing to listen to our side and to consider giving back some points. I think it takes real confidence as a teacher to do that."
(adds example)	HABIB: That's really great. But I got a comment like that from a student once, and it turned out that he was being sarcastic. He was really ticked off about the way I graded his exam, and he even complained to the department chair. Do you think she could be setting you up?
(clarifies)	LAURA: I never thought about that. No, I don't think so. This is a returning student, and I think she appreciates it when she feels she's being treated as an adult.

Remember that understanding is very different from agreement, and that neither the paraphrase nor adding an example requires you to agree with the other person. These listening responses are designed to promote the empathic listening process, to simply help you understand the other person's perspective.

The third and final reflecting skill also takes some finesse. The skill consists of *gently pursuing verbal and nonverbal inconsistencies.* The first step is to identify when you think they've occurred. You have to be sensitive enough to recognize when the words a person is speaking don't match the way she or he is saying them. As we noted earlier, a shouted, scowling "I'm not mad!!" is an obvious example of an inconsistency between verbal and nonverbal cues. Most of the time, though, it's much more subtle. John had a friend who declared she was not going to waste any more time being angry at her boss, and then spent the next half hour complaining about the boss's most recent actions. In other situations, facial expression and tone of voice accompanying a person's "Sure," "I don't care," "Go ahead with it," or "It doesn't make any difference to me" can reveal that the words are thin masks for disappointment, concern, or hurt feelings.

As a listener you can help move beyond surface-level meanings by gently pursuing the verbal/nonverbal inconsistencies you notice. We stress the word *gently.* When you notice an inconsistency, remember that it's your interpretation of what's going on; be willing to own it as your own. Remember, too, that if the other person also sees an inconsistency, there's a reason for its being there. He or she may not be ready or willing to admit the difference between cues at one level and cues at another. So don't use this skill as a license to clobber someone with a club made out of sidewalk psychoanalysis. Instead, just describe the inconsistency you think is there and open the door for the other person to talk about it.

For example, one group of professionals John worked with were experiencing some conflict over a proposal made by their new manager. The manager decided that the group needed to be more cohesive, so she proposed that each Friday afternoon the office close down an hour early so the workers could spend some time together informally chatting over wine and cheese. Most of the people welcomed the idea, but two resisted it. They didn't like what they saw as "forced socializing," and they resented the fact that only alcoholic drinks were being served. They didn't think it was appropriate to "drink on the job." John asked the group to discuss this issue as part of their listening training. Ann, the manager, turned to Gene, one of the two persons resisting the plan, and asked what he thought about these Friday afternoon get-togethers. Gene turned slightly away in his chair, folded his arms in front of him, looked down at the floor, and said, "Well … it's a pretty … good idea …" Ann smiled and softly said, "Gene, your words tell me one thing and your body says something else." Then she was silent. After a couple of seconds, Gene relaxed his body posture, smiled, and admitted that he actually didn't like the plan very much. This began a conversation that ended up redesigning the get-togethers to respond to Gene's concerns.

The primary reason this listening response works is that nonverbal cues can "leak" implicit or hidden messages. Thus, a person's tone of voice, posture, eye behavior, and even facial expression often reveal levels of meaning that are obscured by his or her choice of words. Sensitive listeners try to respond to such inconsistencies and, as we suggest, gently pursue them.

DIALOGIC LISTENING

There is no simple recipe for dialogic listening—no "six easy steps" or "five surefire techniques." This is something that anybody who wants to can definitely do, but it requires an overall approach to communicating that's different from the stance most people ordinarily take when they listen or talk. You also need to maintain a sometimes-difficult tension or balance … between holding your own ground and being open to the person(s) you're communicating with. The best way to get a sense of this approach and this tension is to understand a little bit about the idea of *dialogue.*

Ordinarily, dialogue means just conversation between two or more people, or between the characters in a novel or play. But in two periods of recent history, the term has taken on some special meanings. First, between about 1925 and the early 1960s, the philosopher and teacher Martin Buber and some other writers used the term to talk about a special kind of communication. In his famous book *I and Thou* and in many other books and articles, Buber tried to point toward a way of communicating that he had noticed in some factories, family homes, schools, political organizations, churches, and even buses and planes, a way of communicating that accomplished genuine inter*personal* contact. Buber readily admitted that people can't and don't communicate dialogically all the time, but he maintained that we could do more of it, and if we did, we'd be better off.

For Buber, dialogue basically meant communication characterized by what we call open sensitivity. As we've noted, this definitely doesn't require agreement, but it does require alignment. It can and does sometimes happen in committee meetings, family discussions, telephone calls between friends, doctor-patient exchanges, lovers' quarrels, and even occasionally between labor-management negotiators and political enemies.

Buber's view of dialogue lost credibility in the United States when it became associated with the hippie movement of the 1960s and 1970s. But since the early 1990s, the term and the ideas surrounding it have become prominent again. Today, though, the main writer everybody's quoting is another early-twentieth-century author with the initials MB, the Russian theorist Mikhail Bakhtin (Holquist 1981).

If you're going into business, it is very likely that you will run across Bakhtin's name in discussions about the importance of dialogue in what are called "learning organizations" (Senge 1990). Management theorists from the Sloane School at M.I.T., Harvard, and other prominent business schools argue that in this age of globalization and constant rapid change, the only way a company can keep up is to be constantly learning from its successes and mis-takes. And the only way to become a learning organization is to replace tradi-tional hierarchical communication with dialogue. Beginning in the late 1990s, large organizations like Ford Motor Company and Boeing started investing thousands of hours and dollars in training designed to help their employees learn to open spaces in their organizations for dialogue.

Dialogue is also being promoted as the best way to improve the quality of public discourse in the United States (Roth, Chasin, Chason, Becker, and Herzig 1992) and Great Britain (in 1995 and 1996, British Telecommunications was engaged in a nationwide project to enhance the quality of interpersonal communication; several U.S. interpersonal communication scholars contributed to this effort). And some psychologists are arguing that the focus of the entire discipline of psychology needs to shift from the individual psyche to the dia-logic person-in-relation (Sampson 1993). The concept is also being used more and more by communication researchers and teachers (Baxter and Montgomery 1996) and Chapter 13 of this book focuses on this concept. In short, increasing numbers of influential people are recognizing that dialogue is a seriously beneficial phenomenon. The three of us believe that dialogic listening is the most direct way to promote dialogue. By "promote" we mean that dialogue can't be guaranteed, but it can be encouraged. And dialogic listening will help open up a space for the kind of person-to-person contact that Buber, Bakhtin, and all these other theorists and teachers call dialogue.

Dia-logos as Meaning-Through

One good way to open up this space is to focus on the term *dialogue* itself. This term consists of two Greek words, *dia* and *logos*. The *logos* in dia-logos is the Greek word for *meaning or understanding*. (The Greek term logos has other meanings, too. Sometimes it is translated as "logic," and at other times it comes into English as "language." But its most fundamental meaning is "meaning.") The *dia* in dia-logos means not "two" but *"through"* (Bohm 1990). So dialogue is not restricted to two-person communicating, and it is an event where meaning emerges *through* all the participants. This is another way of saying that, in dialogue, meaning or understanding is *collaboratively co-constructed*. The important implication of this idea for each participant is that, when you're listening and talking dialogically, *you are not in control of what comes out of the communicating*. This point is stated clearly by Abraham Kaplan:

> When people are in [dialogue] ... the content of what is being communicated does not exist prior to and independently of that particular context. There is no message, except in a post-hoc reconstruction, which is fixed and complete beforehand. If I am really talking with you, I have nothing to say; what I say arises as you and I genuinely relate to one another. I do not know beforehand who I will be, because I am open to you just as you are open to me. (quoted in Anderson, Cissna, and Arnett 1994)

As communication teacher Bruce Hyde points out, the main obstacle to dialogic listening is the kind of self or identity that replaces this openness to collaboration with the conviction that the ideas I utter are tightly connected with who I am. There's a big difference, Bruce notes, "between being right about something and being committed to something. Being right makes somebody else wrong; being committed has room to engage productively with other points of view." In other words, if you're committed, you might even welcome the chance to talk with someone who believes differently from the way you believe, but if you're committed to being right, there's not much room for people who don't share your position to be anything but wrong. The key difference has to do with identity. The person who's caught up in being right identifies him- or herself first as an advocate for a certain position. The person who's committed, on the other hand, identifies him- or herself first as a listener who's collaborating on, but not in control of, what comes out of the conversation. If you're going to listen dialogically, you have to be more interested in building-meaning-through than in being right. And this, Bruce writes, "in my experience is the hardest single thing you can ask of anyone." (We got this from an e-mail contribution by Hyde on August 29, 1996, to Redwood Forest Dialogue. Kimberly Pearce was crucial in sharpening what Bruce wrote.)

Communication theorist and teacher Barnett Pearce expresses basically this same idea but with a cultural slant, when he contrasts an *ethnocentric* with a *cosmopolitan* approach to communication. Recall that the term *ethnocentric* means viewing other cultures from the perspective of one's own. When I communicate from an ethnocentric attitude, I begin with the assumption that my culture's way is "normal," "natural," "preferred," and, in these important senses, "right." Barnett argues that "ethnocentric communication is the norm in contemporary American society. It is, of course, the stuff of racism, sexism, and the like. It also structures domestic political discourse" (Pearce 1989, 120). Another feature of ethnocentric communication is that it privileges *coherence*—the kind of sense that emerges when other ideas fit into a comfortable whole, in part by matching or echoing what's already there and hence what is "normal and natural." So a person who approaches communication with an ethnocentric attitude assumes that his or her ways of thinking and doing are normal and natural and that conversations ought to make the kind of sense that you get when feelings and ideas fit together into familiar patterns.

A cosmopolitan attitude, on the other hand, is one that embraces all the "politics" in the "cosmos." It is inclusive rather than exclusive. A person with a cosmopolitan attitude may be *committed* to an idea or position, but he or she does not assume that it is absolutely "right." As a result, cosmopolitan communication privileges *coordination* rather than *coherence*. There's no assumption that the only way to put ideas or people together is the "logical" way, or the way based on "what we've always believed and done." People with a cosmopolitan attitude are open to all kinds of creative syntheses of ideas, procedures, and past experiences. The main goal is to work toward alignment, even when there is little or no agreement. As psychologist Gordon Allport is reported to have said, this kind of communicator is "half-sure yet whole-hearted." *Dialogic listening begins with a cosmopolitan rather than an ethnocentric attitude.* The first step toward dialogic listening is to recognize that each communication event is a ride on a tandem bicycle, and you may or may not be in the front seat.

Sculpting Mutual Meanings

To shift from the bicycle metaphor, we've found that it helps to think and talk about the nuts and bolts of dialogic listening with the help of the image of a potter's wheel (Stewart and Thomas 1990). The sculpting mutual meanings metaphor was created by communication teacher Milt Thomas, and he uses it to suggest a concrete, graphic image of what it means to listen dialogically.

Picture yourself sitting on one side of a potter's wheel with your conversation partner across from you. As you participate (talk) together, each of you adds clay to the form on the wheel, and each uses wet fingers, thumbs, and palms to shape the finished product. Like clay, verbal and nonverbal talk is tangible and malleable; they're out there between people to hear, to record, and to shape. If I am unclear or uncertain about what I am thinking about or what I want to say, I can put something out there and you can modify its shape, ask me to add more clay, or add some of your own. Your specific shaping, which you could only have done in response to the shape I formed, may move in a direction that I would never have envisioned. The clay you add may be an idea I've thought about before—although not here or in this form—or it may be completely new to me. Sometimes these "co-sculpting" sessions will be mostly playful, with general notions tossed on the wheel and the result looking like a vaguely shaped mass. At other times, the basic shape is well defined and conversation partners spend their time on detail and refinement. Peoples' efforts, though, always produce some kind of result, and frequently it can be very gratifying. Sometimes I feel that our talk helps me understand myself better than I could have alone. At other times, we produce something that transcends anything either of us could have conceived of separately. This is because the figure we sculpt is not mine or yours but *ours,* the outcome of both of our active shapings.

So in order to enter into the sculpting process effectively, you need to remember, as we have said many times before, that the meanings that count between people are not just the ones inside somebody's head but also the ones that are constructed in conversations. With this understanding you will be willing to sit down at the potter's wheel, throw your clay on the wheel, and encourage the other person to add clay, too. Then you need to be willing to get your hands dirty, to participate in the collaborative process of molding meanings together.

As you might have guessed, in order to put this basic attitude into action, you need to practice some special kinds of focusing and encouraging.

Focus on "Ours"   We mentioned before that dialogic listening involves a crucial change from a focus on *me* or the *other* to a focus on *ours*, on what's *between* speaker(s) and listener(s). Contrast this with empathic listening, which requires you to try to experience what is "behind" another's outward communication. When you focus on ours, you don't look behind the verbal and nonverbal cues. You don't try to deduce or guess what internal state the other is experiencing. Instead, you concentrate on the meanings you and the other person are mutually creating between yourselves. Empathic listening can be helpful, as we said, but dialogic listening requires a move beyond empathy to a focus on ours.

It can make a big difference whether you are trying to identify what's going on inside the other person or whether you're focusing on building-meaning-between. When your focus is on the other's thoughts and feelings "behind" their words, you spend your time and mental energy searching for possible links between what you're seeing and hearing and what the other "must be" meaning. "Look at those crossed arms. She must be feeling angry and defensive." Or, "He said he'd 'never' pay all the money back. That means it's hopeless to try to change his mind." When you think this way, your attention is moving back and forth between what's outside, in the verbal and nonverbal talk, and what's inside the person's head. From this position, it's easy to believe that what's inside is more reliable, more important, more true, and hence more interesting than the talk on the surface.

But when you're focusing on ours, you concentrate on what's outside, not what's supposedly inside. We don't mean that you should be insensitive to the other person's feelings. In fact, you will be even more sensitive when you are focused on what's between you here and now. You concentrate on the verbal and nonverbal talk that the two (or more) of you are building together. In a sense, you take the conversation at face value; you never stop attending to *it* instead of focusing mainly on something you infer is behind it. This doesn't mean you uncritically accept everything that's said as "the whole truth and nothing but the truth." But you do realize that meaning is not just what's inside one person's head. Focusing on ours prepares you to respond and inquire in ways that make it clear that "getting to the meaning" is a mutual process.

Encouraging as Nexting   Dialogic listening also requires a special form of encouraging. Basically, instead of encouraging the other person(s) to "say more," you're encouraging him or her to respond to something you've just put on the potter's wheel in response to something he or she has just said. So your encouraging is a "nexting" move; it actively and relevantly keeps the collaborative co-construction process going.

One specific way to do this is with a *paraphrase-plus*. We've already said that a paraphrase consists of (1) a restatement, (2) of the other's meaning, (3) in your own verbal and nonverbal talk, (4) concluded with an opportunity for the other person to verify your understanding. The paraphrase-plus includes all of these elements *plus* a small but important addition.

The plus is your own response to the question "What's next?" or "Now what?" You start by remembering that the meanings you are developing are created between the two of you, and individual perspectives are only a part of that. If you stopped with just the paraphrase, you would be focusing on the *other* person exclusively instead of keeping the focus on what is happening *between* you. So, you follow your verifying or perception-checking paraphrase with whatever your good judgment tells you is your response to what the person said, and you conclude your paraphrase-plus with an invitation for the person to respond to your synthesis of his or her meaning and yours. The spirit of the paraphrase-plus is that each individual perspective is a building block for the team effort. For example, notice the three possible responses to Rita's comments.

RITA: I like having an "exclusive" relationship, and I want you to be committed to me. But I still sometimes want to go out with other people.

1. MUNEO: So even though part of you agrees with me about our plan not to date others, you're still a little uncertain about it. Right? (Paraphrase)

2. TIM: Oh, so you want me to hang around like an idiot while you go out and play social butterfly! Talk about a double standard! (Attack)

3. SCOTT: It sounds like you think there are some pluses and minuses in the kind of relationship we have now. I like it the way it is, but I don't like knowing that you aren't sure. I guess I want you to tell me some more about why you're questioning it. (Paraphrase-plus)

Muneo responds to Rita's comment with a paraphrase. This tells us that Muneo listened to Rita, but not much more. Tim makes a caricature of Rita's comment; his interpretation reflects his own uncertainty, anger, and fear. His comment is more a condemnation than a paraphrase. Scott offers a paraphrase-plus. He explains his interpretation of what Rita was saying, then he says briefly how he *responds* to her point, and then he moves the focus back between the two of them, to the middle, where both persons are present in the conversation and can work on the problem together. He does this by putting some of his own clay onto the potter's wheel. He paraphrases, but he also addresses the "What's next?" question as he interprets and responds to her comments. Then he concludes the paraphrase-plus with encouraging rather than simply verifying the accuracy of his paraphrase. When all this happens, both the paraphrase and the plus keep understanding growing between the individuals.

Another way to think about the paraphrase-plus is that you're broadening your goal beyond listening for "fidelity" or "correspondence." If you're paraphrasing for fidelity or correspondence, you're satisfied and "finished" with the task as soon as you've successfully *reproduced* "what she means." Your paraphrase is a success if it corresponds accurately to the other person's intent. We're suggesting that you go beyond correspondence to creativity, beyond reproducing to producing, to mutually constructing meanings or understandings between you.

Because paraphrasing is so potentially helpful, another sculpting skill is to *ask for a paraphrase.* Whenever you're uncertain about the extent of the other person's involvement or whether the two of you share an understanding, you can ask the person for his or her version of the point you're making. It is difficult to do this well. Often a request for a paraphrase sounds like an accusation: "Okay, stupid, why don't you try telling me what I just said." This is obviously is not going to contribute much to the co-sculpting process. The idea is to ask for a paraphrase without demanding a response and without setting up the person so you can play "Gotcha!" if she or he doesn't get it right. You can try putting it this way: "Just to make sure we're going in the same direction, could you tell me what you think we've agreed to so far?" Or you might say, "I'm not sure I've been clear—what do you hear me saying?" The point is, if it's done with an eye toward nexting, a paraphrase can promote collaborating whether it comes from your side or the other's. You can sometimes help that happen by asking for one.

Another skill you can use in the sculpting process is to *run with the metaphor.* You can build meaning into the conversation by extending whatever metaphors the other person has used to express her or his ideas, developing your own metaphors, and encouraging the other person to extend yours. As you probably know, metaphors are figures of speech that link two dissimilar objects or ideas in order to make a point. Besides "Communication is made up of inhaling and exhaling," "Conversation is a ride on a tandem bicycle," and "Dialogic listening is sculpting mutual meanings," "This place is a zoo," "My vacation was a circus," and "She's as nervous as a flea on a griddle" all contain metaphors. As these examples illustrate, metaphors don't appear only in poetry or other literature; they are a major part of most everyday conversation. In fact, it's becoming increasingly clear that virtually all language is metaphoric (Lakoff and Johnson 1980; Ricoeur 1978). In our label for this skill, "run with the metaphor," for example, the term *run* itself is metaphoric.

This skill consists of listening for both subtle and obvious metaphors and then weaving them into your responses. We have found that when other people hear their metaphor coming back to them, they can get a very quick and clear sense of how they're being heard, and they typically can develop the thought along the lines sketched by the metaphor. For example, in a workshop he was leading, John was listening to an engineer describe part of his job, which involved going before regulatory boards and municipal committees to answer questions and make arguments for various construction projects. Part of what Phil said about his job was that it was a "game." John tried to run with the metaphor by asking, "What's the name of the game?" "Winning," Phil responded. John recognized that his question had been ambiguous, so he continued: "Okay, but what kind of game is it—is it baseball, football, soccer, chess, or what?" "It's football," Phil replied. "What position do you play?" "Fullback." "And who's the offensive line?" "All the people in the office who give me the information I take to the meetings." "Who's the coach?" "We don't have one. That's the major problem." This was a telling response. In fact, from that point on, the workshop was focused on one of the major management problems that engineering firm was having.

Here's another example of how running with the metaphor can work in conversation:

TANYA: You look a lot less happy than when I saw you this morning. What's happening?

ANN: I just got out of my second two-hour class today, and I can't believe how much I have to do. I'm really feeling squashed.

TANYA: *Squashed* like you can't come up for air, or *squashed* as in you have to do what everybody else wants and you can't pursue your own ideas?

ANN: More like I can't come up for air. Every professor seems to think his or her class is the only one I'm taking.

Again, the purpose of running with the metaphor is to build the conversation between the two of you in order to produce as full as possible a response to the issues you're talking about. In addition, the metaphors themselves reframe or give a new perspective on the topic of your conversation. A project manager who sees her- or himself as a "fullback" is going to think and behave differently from one who thinks in other metaphorical terms, like "general," "Joan of Arc," "guide," or "mother hen." And the work stress that "squashes" you is different from the pressure that "keeps you jumping like a flea on a griddle." Listen for metaphors and take advantage of their power to shape and extend ideas.

Remember our point that all these specific listening skills are like dishes in a salad bar: You don't eat everything, and at different times you select different dishes. Let's look at an extended example of a conversation that illustrates some of the listening attitudes and skills we've discussed. Sally and Julio start out at opposite sides in their opinions about the class. But first Julio, and then both he and Sally dialogically listen to each other. As a result, their interpretations of the class and the teacher change; they build a meaning that neither of them had at the beginning of the conversation. At the left margins, we've labeled some of the specific empathic and dialogic listening skills they're using.

	SALLY: That class drives me up a wall.
(open question)	JULIO: I thought it was going pretty well. What happened?
	SALLY: She's so strict! We can't miss more than five hours of class, everything has to be submitted electronically, she won't take late papers. I'll bet she wouldn't even allow a makeup exam if I was in the hospital!
(say more)	JULIO: I didn't know she wouldn't take late papers. Where did you hear that?
	SALLY: Alaysha told me that on Tuesday she tried to hand in the article analysis that was due Monday and Dr. Clinton wouldn't accept it.
(clarifying question)	JULIO: Was there anything else going on? Hilary and I both turned in our journals late and she took them. I also thought the five-hour restriction and the e-mail requirement were pretty standard at this school.
(say more)	SALLY: Do you have them in other classes?
	JULIO: Yeah. My geology prof allows only two days' absence and won't accept hardly any excuses.
(say more)	SALLY: Are your other profs so stiff and formal in class?
	JULIO: Some are and some aren't. Clinton is a lot looser in her office. Have you ever talked to her there?
(paraphrase)	SALLY: No, I don't like the way she treated Alaysha.
	JULIO: So Alaysha did the assignment like she was supposed to and Clinton wouldn't take it even though it was only one day late?
	SALLY: Well, it wasn't e-mailed, but I still think it's pretty unreasonable. I haven't started the paper that's due this Friday, and I'll bet there's no way she'd accept it Monday.
(paraphrase-plus)	JULIO: I know how that feels. But if you've got a good reason, I'll bet she would. She told me last term

that most of her rules come from what other profs tell her are the standards here. This school is really into developing responsibility and treating everybody like an adult. That's why I thought they required attendance and e-mailed papers. But I think Clinton is willing to listen, and she's bent the rules for me a couple of times. You've been doing fine in class, and I'd really be surprised if she turned you down.

SALLY: I didn't know that about this school; this is my first term here.

JULIO: Well, I didn't know about Alaysha, but she probably should have printed it out.

SALLY: Yeah. Well, thanks for listening—and for the information.

Remember that we do not mean to present these skills as a guaranteed step-by-step way to instant success. They are suggestions, guidelines, examples of ways you can behaviorally work the focusing, encouraging, and sculpting processes of dialogic listening. They won't work if you apply them woodenly or mechanically; you have to use them with sensitivity to the relationship and the situation.

As you begin using these skills—and this also applies to all the skills we have discussed—you may feel awkward and even phony. This is natural. It is part of learning any new skill, whether it's skiing, tennis, aerobics, or listening. Remember that the better you get with practice, the less awkward you will feel. Try not to let any initial feelings of discomfort distract you from working on specific ways to improve.

REVIEW QUESTIONS

1. Describe the basic similarities and differences between empathic and dialogic listening.
2. Focusing skills take time. How can the distinction between "spending" and "investing" time encourage you to take the time to focus?
3. What is it important *not* to do with your eye contact, movement, and sound if you want to focus effectively?
4. What's the difference between a clarifying question and an open question?
5. What's a "pseudoquestion"? Why is it dangerous?
6. What are the four parts of a paraphrase?
7. *Dia-logos* means "meaning-through." Explain.
8. Distinguish ethnocentric from cosmopolitan communicating.
9. How is "focus on ours" different from the "focusing" that is part of empathic listening?

PROBES

1. How can people cope with the natural tendency to feel that practicing new communication skills will make their communicating sound phony and artificial?
2. What are some real-world exceptions to the authors' advice about "Why?" questions?
3. What danger accompanies the "adding an example" skill?
4. How can you "gently pursue verbal/nonverbal inconsistencies" without playing "Gotcha!"?
5. Google the word "dialogue," and identify examples of what we discuss about its importance in business and public communication.
6. Give an example from your own experience where you or your conversation partner "ran with a metaphor."

REFERENCES

Adams, J. 1996. *Journal entry in SpCmu 103, Autumn 2001.* University of Washington. Used by permission.

Anderson, R., Cissna, K. N., and Arnett, R. C. (eds.). 1994. *The Reach of Dialogue: Confirmation, Voice, and Community.* Cresskill, NJ: Hampton Press.

Baxter, L. A., and Montgomery, B. M. 1996. *Relating: Dialogue and Dialectics.* New York: Guilford.

Bohm, D. 1990. *On Dialogue.* Ojai, CA: David Bohm Seminars.

Bolton, R. 1990. "Listening Is More Than Merely Hearing." In J. Stewart (ed.), *Bridges Not Walls.* 5th ed. New York: McGraw-Hill. Pages 175–191.

Brammer, L. M. 1979. *The Helping Relationship: Process and Skills.* 2nd ed. Englewood Cliffs, NJ: Prentice-Hall.

Buber, Martin. 1970. *I and Thou.* Trans. W. Kaufmann. New York: Scribner.

Cirksena, K., and Cuklanz, L. 1992. "Male Is to Female as _____ is to _____: A Guided Tour of Five Feminist Frameworks for Communication Studies." In L. F. Rakow (ed.), *Women Making Meaning.* New York: Routledge. Page 370.

Clore, G. L., Wiggins, N. H., and Itkin, S. 1975. "Judging Attraction from Nonverbal Behavior: The Gait Phenomenon." *Journal of Counseling and Clinical Psychology,* 43: 491–497.

Faber, A., and Mazlish, E. 1982. *How to Talk So Kids Will Listen and Listen So Kids Will Talk.* New York: Avon.

Goodman, G., and Esterly, G. 1990. "Questions—The Most Popular Piece of Language." In J. Stewart (ed.), *Bridges Not Walls.* 5th ed. New York: McGraw-Hill, Page 760.

Gray, J. 1992. *Men Are from Mars, Women Are from Venus.* New York: HarperCollins.

Harding, S. 1991. *Whose Science? Whose Knowledge: Thinking from Women's Lives.* Ithaca, NY: Cornell University Press.

Holquist, M. (ed.). 1981. *Mikhail M. Bakhtin. The Dialogic Imagination*. Trans. C. Emerson and M. Holquist. Austin: University of Texas Press.

Lakoff, G., and Johnson, M. 1980. *Metaphors We Live By*. Chicago: University of Chicago Press.

Nichols, M. 1995. *The Lost Art of Listening*. New York: Guilford.

Pearce, B. 1989. *Communication and the Human Condition*. Carbondale: Southern Illinois University Press.

Rakow, L. F. 1992. *Women Making Meaning*. New York: Routledge.

Reece, M., and Whiteman, R. 1962. "Expressive Movements, Warmth and Nonverbal Reinforcement." *Journal of Abnormal and Social Psychology,* 64: 234–236.

Ricoeur, P. 1978. *The Rule of Metaphor*. Trans. R. Czerny, K. McLaughlin, and J. Costello. London: Routledge & Kegan Paul.

Rogers, C. R. 1980. *A Way of Being*. Boston: Houghton Mifflin.

Roth, S., Chasin, L., Chason, R., Becker, C., and Herzig, M. 1992. "From Debate to Dialogue: A Facilitating Role for Family Therapists in the Public Forum." *Dulwich Centre Newsletter,* 2: 41–48.

Sampson, E. E. 1993. *Celebrating the Other: A Dialogic Account of Human Nature*. Boulder, CO: Westview.

Senge, P. 1990. *The Fifth Discipline: The Art and Practice of the Learning Organization*. New York: Doubleday.

Shotter, J. 1993. *Conversational Realities: Constructing Life through Language*. London: Sage.

Stewart, J., and Thomas, M. 1990. "Dialogic Listening: Sculpting Mutual Meanings." In J. Stewart (ed.), *Bridges Not Walls*. 6th ed. New York: McGraw-Hill. Pages 184–202.

Tannen, D. 1995. *Talking from 9 to 5*. New York: William Morrow.

Weaver, R. L., II 1987. *Understanding Interpersonal Communication*. 4th ed. New York: Scott-Foresman.

Blackfeet Listening

Donal Carbaugh

This reading is meant, in part, to extend your understanding of listening to cross-cultural situations. These pages contain a prominent communication ethnographer's description of the primary listening practices of a group of people known to themselves as *nizitapi* (real people) and to others as Blackfeet, members of a tribe of Native Americans who lived in northern Montana.

"Blackfeet Listening" from *Cultures in Conversation* by Donal Carbaugh. Mahwah, NJ: Lawrence Erlbaum Associates, 2005. Reprinted by permission.

Communication teacher and scholar Donal Carbaugh describes his experiences with Two Bears, a tribal member who guided Donal on a tour of significant and sacred places and taught him about Blackfeet listening. As other Western social scientists have noted, one prominent feature of the communication of many Native Americans is silence. Especially when compared to European and African Americans, Native Americans talk less and reflect more. This kind of listening, Carbaugh argues, offers "a complex message about communication itself."

Two Bears encourages Carbaugh to use their shared periods of silence to reflect, and suggests that he may "find an answer," "talk to a tree," "hear a raven," and fruitfully "think about things." As Carbaugh explains, their specific physical location helps prompt these outcomes. Blackfeet demonstrate a keen awareness of physical and cultural places and spaces, locations where this kind of listening can especially occur. To listen in this particular Blackfeet way is "to be linked to a place and to the linked to a place this way is to live within it, at least partly, through this nonverbal form of listening." In these acts of listening, Blackfeet persons and places become inseparably connected.

The special places have three qualities: a visual scene of natural beauty, an aural tone of tranquility, and a history of valued cultural activity. These elements make the spaces sacred, and their sacred quality makes them appropriate places for listening. If this sounds abstract and strange to you, Carbaugh emphasizes that it is based in "a Blackfeet kind of realism. People, animals, rocks, and trees are *actually* co-present and co-participant with people as embodiments of the spirit(s) in the world. Attending to this 'real' world is a key motive for listening."

Like Shafir's essay about mindfulness, this one is meant to remind us that westerners do not have a lock on important knowledge about listening. We can learn a great deal about listening from cultures with different histories and priorities from our own. We can learn humility, for example—the recognition that the natural world and other people both hold mysteries that we will never completely fathom. And perhaps we can learn to adopt a stance of acceptance and receptivity, a stance that can be enormously helpful as we sit with another person and try really to listen to him or her.

In the following case, we explore a deeply significant form of "listening" used among some people known to themselves as *nizitapi* [real people], to others as Blackfeet, groups of men and women who have lived from the beginning in northern Montana, the United States. When used in a special way by Blackfeet, the term, "listening," *refers* to a form of communication that is unique to them; when *enacted* in its special way, listening connects participants intimately to a specific physical and spiritual place. Of main concern in what follows, then, is this cultural form of "listening"… in the conduct of these practices, Blackfeet people become linked intimately to physical spaces, thus providing for them a deep way of being and acting and dwelling in place.

A DISCURSIVE PRACTICE AND CULTURAL PLACES

Two Bears had agreed the day before to show me and three others around the reservation.… As we drove down Browning's Main Street, Two Bears told us: "There are about 15,000 enrolled Blackfeet tribal members. About 7,000 live on the reservation." Of these, "about four to five percent practice traditional Blackfeet ways."...

On the eastern outskirts of town, Two Bears swerved across the road, drove into a pull-off, and without any warning, continued right out into a field. Almost knocked off my seat, I realized we were following some invisible dirt path which eventually emptied right onto the plains. Rumbling along, I noticed we were situated in a bit of a small bowl, with one very slight ridge around the bowl being created a century earlier by the tracks of the Great Northern Railway. As we drove across the vast plains, Two Bears developed the idea of "sitting and listening" by describing "fasting" and other activities associated with traditional ceremonies....

Moving further out onto the open plains, we turned down a bumpy road coming to a stop on a slight rise, able to see the vast open prairie and the beauty of the plains. Two Bears turned to us and suggested something, his way of being in such a place:

> You can come out here and sit down. Just sit down and listen. In time, you might hear a raven and realize that raven is saying something to you. Or you might talk to a tree. But you have to listen. Be quiet. Be patient. The answer will come to you ... We are realists. We are part of all of this (gesturing to the plains, to the immense "backbone" of mountains to the west, trees, grass). We listen to this.

After a couple of hours and many miles of driving through several parts of the reservation's lands, we wound our way deep into an inner sanctuary, to what we learn from Two Bears is a geographic site rich with potential for contemporary living and deep with the lessons of history. Down a long dirt road, over a bridge, up on a small ridge, through two fences, again, we are no longer on a visible road, just driving across prairie grass. We stop, look over several small ridges, notice some distant cliffs of multicolored rock. Just over a close rise, a beautiful verdant valley reveals itself, a hidden emerald scene amidst a sea of golden grasses. Two Bears' thoughts turn to his contemporaries: "This would be an ideal place for those of our people having trouble with drugs or alcohol. They could come out here and think about things. It's ideal for that."

As we stand on top of a small ridge, we overlook a meandering stream punctuated with large Cottonwood trees, banks thickly covered with reeds and grasses, an oasis amid a golden brown prairie. His thoughts bring the past to the present. He explains how his ancestors ran buffalo across these ridges, guiding them through a kind of grandly orchestrated "V" of flags and stones to jump off the cliff right here. The scale of the event, covering miles, was huge and impressive. As we walk to the base of the cliff, I am amazed at the quantity of buffalo bones and teeth evident, all of which create a deep, several inch layer in the earth's surface. Signs of an immediate past lay right here. We find stones, "scrapers," used to rub buffalo flesh from hide. Twice Two Bears motions to the cliff above and the valley floor below:

> Imagine from down below here, buffalo coming over the cliff, men tending to them, drinking buffalo blood, eating the marrow, roasting and eating the back

meat, women cutting the other meat into strips and drying it in the sun. Kids excited and running around. Imagine how exciting of a time it was. Everyone was happy.

As we walk from the small valley up the hill to leave, Two Bears stops and reflects:

Just listen

> (a pause of about 1 minute reveals utter tranquility, a few birds sing, followed by a magnificent silence and stillness with no distant sound—of cars, planes, trains—to be heard)

Once I heard a mountain lion down there (gesturing to the stream).

Have you ever heard one? You'll never forget it.

This is an idea place to come....

"LISTENING" AS A FORM OF CULTURAL COMMUNICATION: A COMPLEX MESSAGE ABOUT COMMUNICATION ITSELF

How is it, as Two Bears says above, when one has "a problem" or "can't find an answer," one can go to a special place, "sit down and listen"? How can it be, if you do this, "you'll find an answer"? Or how is it that "you might hear a raven," or "talk to a tree," or listen "to a mountain lion"? Or, if you are "quiet" and "patient," "the answer will come to you"? Why is it that a remote, verdant valley is "an ideal place" for "our people having trouble with drugs or alcohol"? And how is it that this "place" is a good one in which "to think about things"? Is this largely a meta-phor as a way of saying something? Or is there a Blackfeet culture in which this form of living and these expressive practices are quite real? If so, what cultural features are active in these communicative practices? In short, what Blackfeet premises make these practices make sense?

In this day's activities and commentary by Two Bears, there appears repeatedly a prominent symbolic category, *and* a prominent form of symbolic practice, *listening*. A site of Sun Lodges, a vast prairie, a verdant valley, each demonstrates a scene in which the term, *listening*, and the practice of listening, are being used by Two Bears both to describe his life in its cultural place, and to enact a traditional way of dwelling there. Communicating through this and related terms, and conducting this and related practices provides for Two Bears and other Blackfeet people, a significant and forceful cultural form of action.

In the moments of social interaction described. Two Bears uses language that is intimately linked to and motivated by the immediate physical and cultural landscape in which he finds himself. For example, Two Bears informs us of a shared belief, "our belief that you can come out here, or to the mountains, or just about anywhere, sit down and listen." The immediate landscape is thus composed of a combination of physical and cultural qualities. Within this place, so conceived, Two Bears says, is created a cultural motive for listening. The place thus invites a cultural form of action, listening, with that form of action being attentive to the site as something to which it is worth our while to listen. His plea to us to listen, then, is aroused by the place, just as the place becomes full of significance through this cultural form. In this practice of listening, an activity and place become intimately entwined, for this cultural form and this natural site reveal themselves together.

This cultural practice by Two Bears, here, is a complex communication process. Part of the complexity involves the way a verbal message is being used to draw attention to a prominent nonverbal means of communicating. For example, in his oral utterance to us about listening, in this landscape, he is commenting about a nonoral act of listening to this landscape. This nonverbal act is itself a deeply cultural form of action in which the Blackfeet persona and the physical place become intimately linked, in a particularly Blackfeet way. To listen this way—that is, in the way Two Bears mentions, and does, here—is thus to be linked to a place and to be linked to a place this way is to live within it, at least partly, through this nonverbal form of listening. Further, Two Bears' comment, itself, "that you can come out here ... sit down and listen," follows directly from his very nonverbal act of listening in this place. The Blackfeet person and place thus become inseparably linked. As Two Bears' actions demonstrate here: One should listen to places; then one can sensibly make a linguistic reference to this listening form; with this form, in the first instance, being a nonlinguistic mode of learning from, and inhabiting places.

Some kinds of places are apparently more appropriate for this kind of Blackfeet "listening" than are others, although—according to Two Bears—"just about anywhere" might do. Examples of such places that Two Bears mentions are "here" or "out here" on the quiet plains, "this" verdant valley, the former buffalo jump as "an ideal place," or "the mountains," each being a place where "sitting and listening" can (and should) be done....

Each of these and similar places carry qualities that are conducive to certain kinds of cultural practices. The best apparently combine three, a visual scene of natural beauty, an aural tone of tranquility, and a history of valued cultural activity. For example, the Sun Lodges sit in a pleasant natural bowl, far enough from a state highway to be accessible yet generally quiet, and a known historical site of a most sacred ceremony, the Sun Dance. The buffalo jump memorializes historical activities, in a splendidly tranquil place, bountiful with nature's beauty. Ideal places for listening combine these three qualities together, a weaving of naturalistic beauty, solemnity, and historical tradition, thus transforming nature's sites into culture's sacred scenes, places that invite, can speak, and in turn be re-created through the listening form.

The link between sacredness, place, and the listening form can be a strong one. For example, those familiar with the salient cultural heritage can attend nonverbally to the remains of the Sun Lodges, and begin seeing and hearing the sacred activities, the excitement, the ways of living that have occurred there for years. The past, and all it represents, comes alive through listening in this present place....

There is another, important cultural sense in which sacredness, place, and listening are interrelated. Here, however, it is not so much that a place is already heard and known as a sacred place, as it is assumed that almost any place—"just about anywhere," according to Two Bears—might reveal sacredness to a listener. In a city watching a small child, marveling at the intricate patterns in a stone, watching a spider in the corner of the living room, all might suggest sacredness to a listener. Situated activities as these might suggest something spiritual to a listener. And one should be open to this ever-present feature in the world. "Listening," then, can be doubly placed as a cultural attentiveness to a known sacred place, and to the sacredness in just about any place. As a way of dwelling, the cultural form thus attunes to, and contributes to the creation of the sacred.

Are there specific acts that comprise listening as a cultural form of action? Two Bears mentioned several: "You can come out here ... sit down and listen ... sit and listen patiently"; "You have to listen. Be quiet. Be patient"; you can "think"; "You might hear." Listening this way can involve the listener in an intense, efficacious, and complex set of communicative acts in which one is not speaking, discussing, or disclosing, but sitting quietly, watching, and feeling the place, through all the senses. Presumed for the acts is an active co-presence with the natural and historical place in which, and to which one listens. The belief is that one can—at some times more than others—eventually "hear" and learn from it. Such acts are thus not so much internally focused on one's meditative self, but externally focused on one's place through an active attentiveness to that scene, to the highly active powers and insights it offers. In the process, one becomes a part of the scene, hearing and feeling with it.

When involved in such action, from a Blackfeet view, to what might one listen; or, what might one hear? There are many potential instruments and sources of messages being made available through this cultural form. Two Bears brings several to his commentary: "You might hear a raven and realize that raven is saying something to you"; "You might talk to a tree"; "I heard a mountain lion"; or, in short, as "realists." "We listen to [all of] this." The raven, the tree, the mountain lion, all of the animals, plants, rocks, water, trees, breeze, and so on can "speak," if one just listens. Each thus can be consulted and listened to as a source of important, inspirational, and powerful messages. The belief that the natural world is expressively active is, according to Two Bears, not a fanciful nor farcical mysticism, but a Blackfeet kind of realism. People, animals, rocks, and trees are *actually* co-present and co-participant with people as embodiments of the spirit(s) in the world. Attending to this "real" world is a key motive for listening, and renders animals and trees and places generally as spirited speakers to—and thus as potentially hearable by—us all. This is something widely accessible, if only we listen appropriately....

Yet, how does one know what a place "says"? The knowledge does not necessarily come easily. And much hinges on the listener. In fact, particular revelations may, but need not necessarily take days or years. Whatever the time frame, the objective of meditating on who and where we are, what it all means, and the means for doing so—through an active silence in place—remains the same. One listens to that immediately real, historically transmitted, spiritually infused, deeply interconnected world, to that complex arrangement in order better to understand that of which one is inevitably a small part.

The communicative process, so conceived and acted in a Blackfeet way, can also expose one as an "other" who, for whatever reasons, is somewhat deaf to these messages, doesn't quite hear them, and was caught not listening.

I was walking with Two Bears up a small trail from the valley floor to the cliff above. I was reflecting upon the hunting skills of the earlier Blackfeet community, the vibrant traditional encampments, practices that connected generations of people to each other and their places through these cultural activities. We walked slowly, quietly, sun on our backs, a refreshing breeze on our faces. Occasionally in the earth I would see a buffalo tooth, jaw, or other bone. I could hear the rustling of the wind through the short prairie grass that is unique on these northern plains. The water moved along the stream bed, adding a trickling sound to the rustling of the grass. Captured by my thoughts, I was reveling in the tranquility and solitude of the place. Two Bears turned to me and asked: "Did you get that?" My first thought was, "Get what?" I didn't hear anything. Immersed in my own reflections, I had missed something. Prompted by Two Bears' question, somehow I was able to call up from my mind's recesses an earlier and distant raven's call, "caw caw caw." Two Bears' wry smile brought to mind the immediate point of his question. Well, yes, I thought, I guess I did hear something. But the distant bird I heard was, to Two Bears, saying something worthy of comment. The raven had spoken. I wondered out loud, "What did the raven say?" Two Bears responded: "He's talkin' to ya." But what did he say, I wondered? Before I asked, I realized I had already asked this kind of question before on other occasions, several—if not too many—times. The answer was always the same. "This is for the listener to decide. The meaning will be the listener's."

I was delighted at how seamlessly listening had worked its way into Two Bears' routines, but also reminded once again of my own habitual ways, focused as they often are to hear the human over the animal, the individual person above the activities of the place, the linguistic thought over the audible nonverbal, and to Blackfeet, deeply communicative activities. Yes, indeed, Two Bears had reminded me to listen, and this meaning was mine....

To refer to listening, then, as Two Bears does, or to enact it, is to invoke a complex cultural communicative form; it is a form that derives from and helps constitute cultural and physical places; it provides a traditional, nonverbal way of being in those places; it invites various entities as spirited co-participants in this communication; it valorizes and intensely activates the nonoral communicative acts of watching, listening, and sensing nonverbally; it offers a deeply historical way of consulting the traditions and current cosmic arrangement of places as an aid to the various contingencies of contemporary life. Blackfeet listening is thus a highly reflective and revelatory mode of communication that can open one to the mysteries of unity between the physical and the spiritual, to relationships between natural and human forms, and to links between places and persons, all the while providing protection, power, and enhanced knowledge of one's small place in the world.

REVIEW QUESTIONS

1. According to Two Bears, about what percentage of Blackfeet practice traditional ways? Why do you think this is so?
2. How was the "buffalo jump" used by Two Bears' ancestors?
3. What does it mean, in Blackfeet culture, to "listen to places"?
4. Carbaugh explains that sacredness, place, and listening are interrelated in Blackfeet culture. Explain what this means.

PROBES

1. An ethnographer of communication is interested partly in the "cultural premises" that distinguish groups of people and show up in their talk. What are some of the Blackfeet premises that, as Carbaugh asks, make their listening practices make sense?
2. Developed Western cultures are not generally tied to "places," specific geographical locations. Members travel extensively, move often, and think of their time on the Internet as "visiting sites." Blackfeet people value place much more highly. What are some advantages and disadvantages of this feature of Blackfeet culture?

CHAPTER 6

Exhaling: Expressing and Disclosing

252

Being Open with and to Other People
David W. Johnson

The first half of "making meaning together" (the title of Part Two of *Bridges Not Walls*) is "inhaling," and the second half of this process involves what I'm calling "exhaling." As the metaphor indicates, this is the "output" or "sending" part of communication. The four readings in this chapter explain interpersonal openness, self-expression, choices about what to disclose, and assertiveness.

This first reading is from the 2000 edition of a book called *Reaching Out: Interpersonal Effectiveness and Self-Actualization,* by David Johnson, a teacher at the University of Minnesota. He begins with the notion that all of our relationships can be classified on a continuum from open to closed. Of course, an "open" work or school relationship is different from an "open" family or intimate relationship, but in all cases, Johnson claims, openness means both being open *with* other people (disclosing yourself to them) and openness *to* others (listening to them in an accepting way). Relationships of all sorts develop as both kinds of openness increase.

With a considerable amount of social scientific research in the background, Johnson defines self-disclosure and identifies four of its important characteristics. He notes that effective disclosure focuses on the present rather than the past, includes feelings as well as facts, has both breadth and depth, and, especially in the early stages of a relationship, needs to be reciprocal. Then Johnson outlines the impact self-disclosure has on relationships and describes some of its benefits. He argues that "if you cannot reveal yourself, you cannot become close to others, and you cannot be valued by others for who you are." Clearly, there are various ways to self-disclose and various kinds of information to share. But this author makes a strong connection between disclosure and effective interpersonal communicating.

One benefit of disclosure is that it can begin and deepen your relationships, whether at work, home, or school. It can also increase your self-awareness and your understanding of yourself. Self-disclosure can provide, as Johnson puts it, "a freeing experience" and can also help you control challenging social situations. Another benefit of self-disclosure is that it can help you manage stress and adversity.

Johnson also lists eight ways to keep self-disclosures appropriate. I think each of the eight is useful. As he notes, disclosures need to be part of an ongoing relationship, not "off the wall" or "out of nowhere." They need to be focused on the people present and sensitive to others' possible distress. Disclosure ought to be intended to improve the relationship and should move to deeper levels only gradually. Johnson also usefully notes that "there are times when you will want to hide your reactions," and he explains when and why.

In the final section of this reading, Johnson talks about the connection between self-disclosure and self-presentation. He discusses how all of us help manage others' impressions of who we are, in part with our self-disclosures. He compares and contrasts the motives of "strategic self-presentation," which means efforts to shape others' impression of us, and "self-verification," which is the desire to have others perceive us as we genuinely perceive ourselves. As he notes, "self-presentation and impression management are part of everyone's life," which is why Johnson believes that the more you know about self-disclosure, the more effective you can be at this part of your communicating.

Relationships may be classified on a continuum from open to closed. *Openness* in a relationship refers to participants' willingness to share their ideas, feelings, and reactions to the current situation. On a professional basis, relationships among collaborators who are working to achieve mutual goals tend to be quite open, while relationships among competitors who are seeking advantages over each other tend to be quite closed. On a personal level, some relationships (such as friendships) are very open, while other relationships (such as casual acquaintances) are relatively closed. The more open participants in a relationship are with each other, the more positive, constructive, and effective the relationship tends to be.

Openness has two sides. To build good relationships you must be both open *with* other people (disclosing yourself to them) and open *to* others (listening to their disclosures in an accepting way). Usually, the more that people know about you, the more likely they are to like you. Yet self-disclosure does carry a degree of risk. For just as knowing you better is likely to result in a closer relationship, sometimes it could result in people liking you less. "Familiarity breeds contempt" means that some people may learn something about you that detracts from the relationship. Because disclosing is risky, some people prefer to hide themselves from others in the belief that no reaction is better than a possible negative reaction. "Nothing ventured, nothing gained," however, means that some risk is vital to achieving any worthwhile goal. To build a meaningful relationship you have to disclose yourself to the other person and take the risk that the other person may reject rather than like you.

The other side of the coin is responding to the other person's self-disclosures. Being open to another person means showing that you are interested in how he or she feels and thinks. This does not mean prying into the intimate areas of his or her life. It means being willing to listen in an accepting way to his or her reactions to the present situation and to what you are doing and saying. Even when a person's behavior offends you, you may wish to express acceptance of the person and disagreement with the way he or she behaves.

In order for the relationship to build and develop, both individuals have to disclose and be open to other people's disclosures. Openness depends on three factors: self-awareness, self-acceptance, and trust....

OPENNESS WITH OTHER INDIVIDUALS

You are *open with* other persons when you disclose yourself to them, sharing your ideas, feelings, and reactions to the present situation, and letting other people know who you are as a person. To be open with another person you must (a) be aware of who you are, (b) accept yourself, and (c) take the risk of trusting the other person to be accepting of you. Openness thus can be described as being dependent on self-awareness (S), self-acceptance (A), and trust (T) (O = S A T). Commonly, openness is known as self-disclosure.

What Is Self-Disclosure?

Self-disclosure is revealing to another person how you perceive and are reacting to the present situation and giving any information about yourself and your past that is relevant to an understanding of your perceptions and reactions to the present. Effective self-disclosure has a number of characteristics:

1. **Self-disclosure focuses on the present, not the past.** Self-disclosure does not mean revealing intimate details of your past life. Making highly personal confessions about your past may lead to a temporary feeling of intimacy, but a relationship is built by disclosing your reactions to events you both are experiencing or to what the other person says or does. A person comes to know and understand you not through knowing your past history but through knowing how you react. Past history is helpful only if it clarifies why you are reacting in a certain way.
2. **Reactions to people and events include feelings as well as facts.** To be self-disclosing often means to share with another person how you feel about events that are occurring.
3. **Self-disclosures have two dimensions—breadth and depth.** As you get to know someone better and better, you cover more topics in your explanations (breadth) and make your explanations more personally revealing (depth).
4. **In the early stages of a relationship, self-disclosure needs to be reciprocal.** The amount of self-disclosure you engage in will influence the amount of self-disclosure the other person engages in and vice versa. The polite thing to do is to match the level of self-disclosure offered by new acquaintances, disclosing more if they do so and drawing back if their self-disclosure declines. Once a relationship is well established, strict reciprocity occurs much less frequently.

Impact of Self-Disclosure on Relationships

Healthy relationships are built on self-disclosure. A relationship grows and develops as two people become more open about themselves to each other. *If you cannot reveal yourself, you cannot become close to others, and you cannot be valued by others for who you are.* Two people who let each other know how they are reacting to situations and to each other are pulled together; two people who stay silent about their reactions and feelings stay strangers.

There are many ways in which self-disclosure initiates, builds, and maintains relationships. *First, self-disclosure enables you and other people to get to know each other.* Most relationships proceed from superficial exchanges to more intimate ones. At first, individuals disclose relatively little to another person and receive relatively little in return. When initial interactions are enjoyable or interesting, exchanges become (a) broader, involving more areas of your life, and (b) deeper, involving more important and sensitive areas. In terms of breadth, from discussing the weather and sports, as the relationship develops you may discuss a wider range of topics (such as your family, your hopes and dreams, issues at work, and so forth) and share more diverse activities (such as going to movies or plays together, going bike riding or playing tennis together, and so forth). In terms of depth, you might willingly talk with a casual acquaintance about your preferences in food and music but reserve for close friends discussions of your anxieties and personal ambitions. The longer people interact, the more topics they tend to be willing to discuss and the more personally revealing they tend to become. This does not mean that getting to know another person is a simple process of being more and more open. You do not simply disclose more and more each day. Rather, there are cycles of seeking intimacy and avoiding it. Sometimes you are candid and confiding with a friend, and other times you are restrained and distant. The development of caring and commitment in a relationship, however, results from the cumulative history of self-disclosure in the relationship.

Second, self-disclosure allows you and other individuals to identify common goals and overlapping needs, interests, activities, and values. In order to know whether a relationship with another person is desirable, you have to know what the other person wants from the relationship, what the other person is interested in, what joint activities might be available, and what the other person values. Relationships are built on common goals, interests, activities, and values. If such information is not disclosed, the relationship may end before it has a chance to begin.

Third, once common goals have been identified, self-disclosure is necessary to work together to accomplish them. Working together requires constant self-disclosure to ensure effective communication, decision making, leadership, and resolution of conflict. Joint action to achieve mutual goals can not be effective unless collaborators are quite open in their interactions with each other.

Just as relationships are built through self-disclosure, *relationships can deteriorate for lack of self-disclosure.* Sometimes people hide their reactions from others through fear of rejection, fear of a potential or ongoing conflict, or feelings of shame and guilt. Whatever the reason, if you hide how you are reacting to the other person, your concealment can hurt the relationship, and the energy you pour into hiding is an additional stress on the relationship. Hiding your perceptions and feelings dulls your awareness of your own inner experience and decreases your ability to disclose your reactions even when it is perfectly safe and appropriate to do so. The result can be the end of the relationship. Being silent is not being strong—strength is the willingness to take a risk by disclosing yourself with the intention of building a better relationship.

Benefits of Self-Disclosure

We disclose information to another person for many reasons. *First, you begin and deepen a relationship by sharing reactions, feelings, personal information, and confidences.* This topic has already been discussed.

Second, self-disclosure improves the quality of relationships. We disclose to those we like. We like those who disclose to us. We like those to whom we have disclosed. Overall, it is through self-disclosure that caring is developed among individuals and commitment to each other is built.

Third, self-disclosure allows you to validate your perception of reality. Listeners provide useful information about social reality. The events taking place around us and the meaning of other people's behavior are often ambiguous, open to many different interpretations. By seeing how a listener reacts to your self-disclosures, you get information about the correctness and appropriateness of your views. Other people may reassure you that your reactions are "perfectly normal" or suggest that you are "blowing things out of proportion." If others have similar interpretations, we consider our perceptions to be valid. Comparing your perceptions and reactions with the reactions and perceptions of others is called *consensual validation*. Without self-disclosure, consensual validation could not take place.

Fourth, self-disclosure increases your self-awareness and clarifies your understanding of yourself. In explaining your feelings in watching a sunset or why you like a certain book, you clarify aspects of yourself to yourself. In sharing your feelings and experiences with others, you may gain greater self-understanding and self-awareness. Talking to a friend about a problem, for example, can help you clarify your thoughts about a situation. Sharing your reactions with others results in feedback from others, which contributes to a more objective perspective on your experiences.

Fifth, the expression of feelings and reactions is a freeing experience. Sometimes it helps to get emotions and reactions "off your chest." After a difficult day at work, it may release pent up feelings by telling a friend how angry you are at your boss or how unappreciated you feel. Even sharing long-term feelings of insecurity with a trusted friend may free you from such feelings. Simply being able to express your emotions is a reason for self-disclosure.

Sixth, you may disclose information about yourself or not as a means of social control. You may deliberately refrain from talking about yourself to end an interaction as quickly as possible or you may emphasize topics, beliefs, or ideas that you think will make a favorable impression on the other person.

Seventh, self-disclosing is an important part of managing stress and adversity. Communicating intimately with another person, especially in times of stress, seems to be a basic human need. By discussing your fear, you free yourself from it. By sharing your anxiety, you gain insight into ways to reduce it. By describing a problem, you see ways to solve it. The more you seek out a friend in times of adversity and discuss the situation openly, the more you will be able to deal with the stress and solve your problem.

Finally, self-disclosure fulfills a human need to be known intimately and accepted. Most people want someone to know them well and accept, appreciate, respect, and like them.

Keeping Your Self-Disclosures Appropriate

You only self-disclose when it is appropriate to do so. Just as you can disclose too little, you can also be too self-disclosing. Refusing to let anyone know anything about you keeps others away. Revealing too many of your reactions too fast may scare others away. Typically, a relationship is built gradually and develops in stages. Although you should sometimes take risks in sharing your reactions with others, you should ensure that the frequency and depth of your reactions are appropriate to the situation. When you are unsure about the appropriateness of your self-disclosures, you may wish to follow these guidelines:

1. I make sure my disclosures are not a random or isolated act but rather part of an ongoing relationship.
2. I focus my disclosures on what is going on within and between persons in the present.
3. I am sensitive to the effect a disclosure will have on the other person. Some disclosures may upset or cause considerable distress. What you want to say may seem inappropriate to the other person. Most people become uncomfortable when the level of self-disclosure exceeds their expectations.
4. I only disclose when it has a reasonable chance of improving the relationship.
5. I continue only if my disclosures are reciprocated. When you share your reactions, you should expect disclosure in return. When it is apparent that self-disclosures will not be reciprocated, you should limit the disclosures you make.
6. I increase my disclosures when a crisis develops in the relationship.
7. I gradually move my disclosures to a deeper level. Self-disclosures may begin with the information acquaintances commonly disclose (such as talking about hobbies, sports, school, and current events) and gradually move to more personal information. As a friendship develops, the depth of disclosure increases as well. Disclosures about deep feelings and concerns are most appropriate in close, well-established relationships.
8. I keep my reactions and feelings to myself when the other person is competitive or untrustworthy. While relationships are built through self-disclosure, there are times when you will want to hide your reactions. If a person has been untrustworthy and if you know from past experience that the other

person will misinterpret or overreact to your self-disclosure, you may wish to keep silent....

SELF-DISCLOSURE AND SELF-PRESENTATION

The image of myself which I try to create in my own mind that I may love myself is very different from the image which I try to create in the minds of others in order that they may love me.

—*W. H. Auden*

Self-disclosure is based on self-awareness, self-acceptance, and taking the risk of revealing yourself to others. Self-disclosure takes place in an ongoing social interaction in which you choose how you wish to present yourself to others. Most people are concerned about the images they present to others. The fashion industry, the cosmetic companies, diet centers, and the search for new drugs that grow hair, remove hair, whiten teeth, freshen breath, and smooth out wrinkles, all exploit our preoccupation with physical appearance. Manners, courtesy, and etiquette are all responses to concern about the impressions our behavior makes.

In *As You Like It,* William Shakespeare wrote, "All the world's a stage, and all the men and women merely players." Erving Goffman put Shakespeare's thought into social science by arguing that life can be viewed as a play in which each of us acts out certain scripted lines. Our scripts are a reflection of the social face or social identity that we want to present to others. *Self-presentation* is the process by which we try to shape what others think of us and what we think of ourselves. It is part of *impression management*—the general process by which you behave in particular ways to create a desired social image.

In presenting yourself to others, you have to recognize that there are many complex aspects of yourself. It is as if you have a number of selves that are tied to certain situations and certain groups of people with whom you interact. The self you present to your parents is usually different from the self you present to your peers. You present yourself differently to your boss, subordinates, colleagues, customers, neighbors, same-sex friends, opposite-sex friends, and strangers. When you are playing tennis, the aspect of yourself that loves physical exercise and competition may be most evident. When you attend a concert, the aspect of yourself that responds with deep emotion to classical music may be most evident. In church, your religious side may be most evident. In a singles bar, your interest in other people may be most evident. In different situations and with different people, different aspects of yourself will be relevant.

In presenting yourself to others, you have to vary your presentation to the audience. Societal norms virtually require that you present yourself in different ways to different audiences. You are expected to address someone considerably older than you differently from the way you address your peers. You are expected to address the president of the United States differently from how you address your next-door neighbor. In formal situations you are expected to act in ways different from how you would act in informal situations. Depending on the setting, the role relationship, and your previous experience with the person, you are expected to monitor your behavior and present yourself accordingly.

In presenting yourself to others, you basically have two motives: strategic self-presentation and self-verification. *Strategic self-presentation* consists of efforts to shape others' impressions in specific ways in order to gain influence, power, sympathy, or approval. Job interviews, personal ads, political campaign promises, and a defendant's appeal to a jury are examples. Your goal may be to be perceived as likable, competent, moral, dangerous, or even helpless, depending on the situation and the relationship. You communicate who you are and what you are like through your clothes, appearance, posture, eye contact, tone of voice, manners, and gestures. There are many people who believe that you will be perceived in quite different ways depending on your style of dress, manner, and cleanliness. Clothing, they believe, transmits messages about the wearer's personality, attitudes, social status, behavior, and group allegiances. People who wear clothes associated with high status tend to have more influence than those wearing low-status clothes. Somber hues (grays, dark blues, or browns) of clothing seem to communicate ambition, a taste for moderate risks and long-range planning, and a preference for tasks that have clear criteria for success and failure. Attention to clothes, posture, eye contact, tone of voice, manners, and gestures may be especially important for first impressions.

Related to strategic self-presentation are ingratiation and self-promotion. *Ingratiation* describes acts that are motivated by the desire to get along and be liked. When people want to be liked, they put their best foot forward, smile a lot, make eye contact, nod their heads, express agreement with what is said, and give compliments and favors. *Self-promotion* describes acts that are motivated by a desire to "get ahead" and be respected for one's competence. When people want to be respected for their competence, they try to impress others by talking about themselves and immodestly showing off their knowledge, status, and exploits.

The second self-presentation motive is *self-verification*—the desire to have others perceive us as we genuinely perceive ourselves. This is sometimes known as *open self-presentation,* which consists of efforts to let others see you as you believe yourself to be. People generally are quite motivated to verify their existing self-view in the eyes of others. People, for example, often selectively elicit, recall, and accept feedback that confirms their self-conceptions. This statement does not mean that they wish to fool others about who they are. People often work hard to correct others whose impressions of them are mistaken. They may want to make a good impression, but they also want others (especially their friends) to have an accurate impression, one that is consistent with their own self-concept.

Self-presentation and impression management are part of everyone's life. Some people do these things more consciously and successfully than others. People differ in their ability to present themselves appropriately and create the impression they want. The more self-monitoring you are, the more sensitive you tend to be to strategic self-presentation concerns, poised, ready, and able to modify your behavior as you move from one situation to another.

The self is an enduring aspect of human personality, an invisible "inner core" that is stable over time and slow to change. The struggle to "find yourself" or "be true to yourself" is based on this view. Yet at least part of the self is malleable, molded by life experiences and different from one situation to the next. In this sense, the self is multifaceted and has many different faces. Each of us has a private self consisting of our innermost thoughts and feelings, memories, and self-views. We also have an outer self, portrayed by the roles we play and the way we present ourselves in public. In fulfilling our social obligations and presenting ourselves to others, we base our presentations on the complexity of our personalities, the social norms specifying appropriate behavior, and the motives of revealing who we really are, verifying our views of ourselves, and creating strategic impressions.

REVIEW QUESTIONS

1. Explain the difference between being open *with* another person and being open *to* another person.
2. Explain O = S A T.
3. According to Johnson, what is the relationship between self-disclosure and liking?
4. List the eight possible benefits of self-disclosure.
5. Explain the relationship between self-disclosure and self-awareness.
6. Define *strategic self-presentation* and *self-verification*.

PROBES

1. Johnson argues that "in order for the relationship to build and develop, both individuals have to disclose and be open to other people's disclosures." Do you agree? Is disclosure and openness to others necessary for the development of *all* relationships? Are there any exceptions?
2. Why does self-disclosure need to be reciprocal in the early stages of a relationship? Why can it be one-sided or nonreciprocal in some later stages of a relationship?
3. Johnson notes that "there are cycles of seeking intimacy and avoiding it." Explain what he means. Why is this important to understand and practice?
4. Give an example of how self-disclosure can function as a means of social control.
5. Is there a contradiction between Johnson's preference for "openness" and his argument that self-disclosure should be "appropriate"? Doesn't appropriateness require not always being open?

6. Johnson indicates that "you have a number of selves that are tied to certain situations and certain groups of people." Do you think he believes that people also have a "core" or stable, central self? Do you?

_____

State My Path: How to Speak Persuasively, Not Abrasively

Kerry Patterson, Joseph Grenny, Ron McMillan, and Al Switzler

This selection was written by a team of business consultants who have worked extensively for 25 years with managers and workers from GM, Disney, Nike, IBM, AT&T, Key Bank, and other large organizations. Two of them have also taught in the business schools at Brigham Young, the University of Kentucky, and the University of Michigan. The book that this is taken from draws on their knowledge of and experience with what they call "crucial conversations." Like Susan Scott in Chapter 1 of *Bridges Not Walls,* these authors are convinced that everyday conversations are "crucial" to the health of organizations and the success of their employees. They also show how conversation skill applies directly to your communication at home and in other, nonbusiness contexts.

In these pages, the authors offer practical and useful advice about how to "speak persuasively not abrasively." Their understanding of communication as the co-creation of a "pool of meaning," and their use of the term "dialogue" are both consistent with my explanation in Chapter 1 and all of the readings in Chapter 12. They focus here on how you can contribute "risky meaning" to a dialogue without being either "wimpy" or disrespectful.

They first describe how to maintain safety in these difficult conversations by combining confidence, humility, and communications skill. Then they develop five tools for talking about sensitive topics that can be remembered with the acronym STATE:

1. **S**hare your facts.
2. **T**ell your story.
3. **A**sk for others' paths.
4. **T**alk tentatively.
5. **E**ncourage testing.

The first step, "share your facts," reminds you to start your talk with the information on which you have based your own conclusion—for example, that your spouse is cheating on you. Facts are important because they are the least controversial, the most persuasive, and the least insulting of all the content you could begin with.

Step 2 is to put your facts into the whole picture of the situation—your "story"—that you have used the facts to help construct. One important part of this step is that it displays how you're interpreting the important facts.

"State My Path" by Kerry Patterson, Joseph Grenny, Ron McMillan, and Al Switzler from *Crucial Conversations: Tools for Talking When Stakes Are High,* pp. 119–140. NY: The McGraw-Hill Companies, 2002.

Step 3 involves asking for the other person(s) path(s). Because effective sharing is a blend of confidence and humility, you take time to discover how the other person's views differ from yours. This should make perfect sense to you after reading about listening in Chapter 5.

"Talk tentatively" is step 4. The authors explain why you want to do this, and they distinguish between being tentative and being "wimpy." They also offer the "Goldilocks test" as a way to evaluate whether your statements are too soft, too hard, or just right.

The final step is to "encourage testing." When you enter a difficult conversation with the genuine desire both to state your meaning and to hear the other's, this step can helpfully promote the kind of dialogue that leads to mutual understanding.

Although we all know that really difficult conversations do not lend themselves to simplistic, "one-two-three" solutions, the steps that these authors outline can significantly help you "exhale" your thoughts and feelings "persuasively, not abrasively."

So far we've gone to great pains to prepare ourselves for crucial conversations. Here's what we've learned. Our hearts need to be in the right place. We need to pay close attention to crucial conversations—particularly when people start feeling unsafe. And heaven forbid that we should tell ourselves clever and unhelpful stories.

So let's say that we are well prepared. We're ready to open our mouths and start sharing our pool of meaning. That's right, we're actually going to talk. Now what?

Most of the time we walk into a discussion and slide into autopilot. "Hi, how are the kids? What's going on at work?" What could be easier than talking? We know thousands of words and generally weave them into conversations that suit our needs. Most of the time.

However, when stakes rise and our emotions kick in, well, that's when we open our mouths and don't do so well. In fact, as we suggested earlier, the more important the discussion, the less likely we are to be on our best behavior. More specifically, we advocate or express our views quite poorly.

To help us improve our advocacy skills, we'll examine two challenging situations. First, we'll look at five skills for talking when what we have to say could easily make others defensive. Second, we'll explore how these same skills help us state our opinions when we believe so strongly in something that we risk shutting others down rather than opening them up to our ideas.

SHARING RISKY MEANING

Adding information to the pool of meaning can be quite difficult when the ideas we're about to dump into the collective consciousness contain delicate, unattractive, or controversial opinions.

> "I'm sorry, Marta, but people simply don't like working with you. You've been asked to leave the special-projects team."

It's one thing to argue that your company needs to shift from green to red packaging; it's quite another to tell a person that he or she is offensive or unlikable or has a controlling leadership style. When the topic turns from things to people, it's always more difficult, and to nobody's surprise, some people are better at it than others.

When it comes to sharing touchy information, the *worst* alternate between bluntly dumping their ideas into the pool and saying nothing at all. Either they start with: "You're not going to like this, but, hey, somebody has to be honest...," or they simply stay mum.

Fearful they could easily destroy a healthy relationship, those who are *good* at dialogue say some of what's on their minds but understate their views out of fear of hurting others. They talk, but they sugarcoat their message.

The *best* at dialogue speak their minds completely and do it in a way that makes it safe for others to hear what they have to say and respond to it as well. They are both totally frank and completely respectful.

MAINTAIN SAFETY

In order to speak honestly when honesty could easily offend others, we have to find a way to maintain safety. That's a bit like telling someone to smash another person in the nose, but, you know, don't hurt him. How can we speak the un-speakable and still maintain respect? Actually, it can be done if you know how to carefully blend three ingredients—confidence, humility, and skill.

Confidence. Most people simply won't hold delicate conversations—well, at least not with the right person. For instance, your colleague Brian goes home at night and tells his wife that his boss, Fernando, is micromanaging him to within an inch of his life. He says the same thing over lunch when talking with his pals. Everyone knows what Brian thinks about Fernando—except, of course, Fernando.

People who are skilled at dialogue have the confidence to say what needs to be said to the person who needs to hear it. They are confident that their opinions deserve to be placed in the pool of meaning. They are also confident that they can speak openly without brutalizing others or causing undue offense.

Humility. Confidence does not equate to arrogance or pigheadedness. Skilled people are confident that they have something to say, but also realize that others have valuable input. They are humble enough to realize that they don't have a monopoly on the truth. Their opinions provide a starting point but not the final word. They may currently believe something but realize that with new informa-tion they may change their minds. This means they're willing to both express their opinions and encourage others to do the same.

Skill. Finally, people who willingly share delicate information are good at doing it. That's why they're confident in the first place.... They speak the un-speakable, and people are grateful for their honesty.

Good Night and Good-Bye!

To see how to discuss sensitive issues, let's look at an enormously difficult problem. Bob has just walked in the door, and his wife, Carole, looks upset. He can tell from her swollen eyes that she's been crying. Only when he walks in the door, Carole doesn't turn to him for comfort. Instead, she looks at him with an expression that says "How could you?" Bob doesn't know it yet, but Carole thinks he's having an affair. He's not.

How did Carole come to this dangerous and wrong conclusion? Earlier that day she had been going over the credit card statement when she noticed a charge from the Good Night Motel—a cheap place located not more than a mile from their home. "Why would he stay in a motel so close to home?" she wonders. "And why didn't I know about it?" Then it hits her— "That unfaithful jerk!"

Now what's the worst way Carole might handle this (one that doesn't involve packing up and moving back to Wisconsin)? What's the worst way of *talking* about the problem? Most people agree that jumping in with an ugly accusation followed by a threat is a good candidate for that distinction. It's also what most people do, and Carole is no exception.

"I can't believe you're doing this to me," she says in a painful tone.

"Doing what?" Bob asks—not knowing what she's talking about but figuring that whatever it is, it can't be good.

"You know what I'm talking about," she says, continuing to keep Bob on edge.

"Do I need to apologize for missing her birthday?" Bob wonders to himself. "No, it's not even summer and her birthday is on...well, it's sweltering on her birthday."

"I'm sorry, I don't know what you're talking about," he responds, taken aback.

"You're having an affair, and I have proof right here!" Carole explains holding up a piece of crumpled paper.

"What's on that paper that says I'm having an affair?" he asks, completely befuddled because (1) he's not having and affair and (2) the paper contains not a single compromising photo.

"It's a motel bill, you jerk. You take some woman to a motel, and you put it on the credit card?! I can't believe you're doing this to me!"

Now if Carole were certain that Bob was having an affair, perhaps this kind of talk would be warranted. It may not be the best way to work through the issue, but Bob would at least understand why Carole made the accusations and hurled threats.

But, in truth, she only has a piece of paper with some numbers on it. This tangible piece of evidence has made her suspicious. How should she talk about this nasty hunch in a way that leads to dialogue?

STATE MY PATH

If Carole's goal is to have a healthy conversation about a tough topic (e.g., I think you're having an affair), her only hope is to stay in dialogue. That holds true for anybody with any crucial conversation (i.e., It feels like you micromanage me;

I fear you're using drugs). That means that despite your worst suspicions, you shouldn't violate respect. In a similar vein, you shouldn't kill safety with threats and accusations.

So what should you do? Start with Heart. Think about what you *really* want and how dialogue can help you get it. And master your story—realize that you may be jumping to a hasty Victim, Villain, or Helpless Story. The best way to find out the true story is not to *act out* the worst story you can generate. That will lead to self-destructive silence and violence games. Think about other possible explanations long enough to temper your emotions so you can get to dialogue. Besides, if it turns out you're right about your initial impression, there will be plenty of time for confrontations later on.

Once you've worked on yourself to create the right conditions for dialogue, you can then draw upon five distinct skills that can help you talk about even the most sensitive topics. These five tools can be easily remembered with the acronym STATE. It stands for:

- **S**hare your facts
- **T**ell your story
- **A**sk for others' paths
- **T**alk tentatively
- **E**ncourage testing

The first three skills describe *what* to do. The last two tell *how* to do it.

The "What" Skills

Share Your Facts   …If you retrace your Path to Action to the source, you eventually arrive at the facts. For example, Carole found the credit card invoice. That's a fact. She then told a story—Bob's having an affair. Next, she felt betrayed and horrified. Finally, she attacked Bob—"I should never have married you!" The whole interaction was fast, predictable, and very ugly.

What if Carole took a different route—one that started with facts? What if she were able to suspend the ugly story she told herself (perhaps think of an alternative story) and then start her conversation with the facts? Wouldn't that be a safer way to go? "Maybe," she muses, "there is a good reason behind all of this. Why don't I start with the suspicious bill and then go from there?"

If she started there, she'd be right. The best way to share your view is to follow your Path to Action from beginning to end—the same way you traveled it. Unfortunately, when we're drunk on adrenaline, our tendency is to do precisely the opposite. Since we're obsessing on our emotions and stories, that's what we start with. Of course, this is the most controversial, least influential, and most insulting way we could begin.

To make matters worse, this strategy creates still another self-fulfilling prophecy. We're so anxious to blurt out our ugly stories that we say things in extremely ineffective ways. Then, when we get bad results (and we *are* going to get bad results), we tell ourselves that we just can't share risky views without creating problems. So the next time we've got something sticky to say, we're even more reluctant to say it. We hold it inside where the story builds up steam, and when we do eventually share our horrific story, we do so with a vengeance. The cycle starts all over again.

Facts are the least controversial. Facts provide a safe beginning. By their very nature, facts aren't controversial. That's why we call them facts. For example, consider the statement: "Yesterday you arrived at work twenty minutes late." No dispute there. Conclusions, on the other hand, are highly controversial. For example: "You can't be trusted." That's hardly a fact. Actually, it's more like an insult, and it can certainly be disputed. Eventually we may want to share our conclusions, but we certainly don't want to open up with a controversy.

Facts are the most persuasive. In addition to being less controversial, facts are also more persuasive than subjective conclusions. Facts form the foundation of belief. So if you want to persuade others, don't start with your stories. Start with your observations. For example, which of the following do you find more persuasive?

"I want you to stop sexually harassing me!"

or

"When you talk to me, your eyes move up and down rather than look at my face. And sometimes you put your hand on my shoulder."

While we're speaking here about being persuasive, let's add that our goal is not to persuade others that we are *right*. We aren't trying to "win" the dialogue. We just want our meaning to get a fair hearing. We're trying to help others see how a reasonable, rational, and decent person could end up with the story we're carrying. That's all.

When we start with shocking or offensive conclusions ("Quit groping me with your eyes!" or "I think we should declare bankruptcy"), we actually encourage others to tell Villain Stories about us. Since we've given them no facts to support our conclusion, they make up reasons we're saying these things. They're likely to believe we're either stupid or evil.

So if your goal is to help others see how a reasonable, rational, and decent person could think what you're thinking, start with your facts.

And if you aren't sure what your facts are (your story is absolutely filling your brain), take the time to think them through *before* you enter the crucial conversation. Take the time to sort out facts from conclusions. Gathering the facts is the homework required for crucial conversations.

Facts are the least insulting. If you do want to share your story, don't start with it. Your story (particularly if it has led to a rather ugly conclusion) could easily surprise and insult others. It could kill safety in one rash, ill-conceived sentence.

BRIAN: I'd like to talk to you about your leadership style. You micromanage me, and it's starting to drive me nuts.

FERNANDO: What? I ask you if you're going to be done on time and you lay into me with....

If you start with your story (and in so doing, kill safety), you may never actually get to the facts.

Begin your path with facts. In order to talk about your stories, you need to lead the others involved down your Path to Action. Let them experience your path from the beginning to the end, and not from the end to—well, to wherever it takes you. Let others see your experience from your point of view—starting with your facts. This way, when you do talk about what you're starting to conclude, they'll understand why. First the facts, then the story—and then make sure that as you explain your story, you tell it as a possible story, not as concrete fact.

BRIAN: Since I started work here, you've asked to meet with me twice a day. That's more than with anyone else. You have also asked me to pass all of my ideas by you before I include them in a project. [*The facts*]

FERNANDO: What's your point?

BRIAN: I'm not sure that you're intending to send this message, but I'm beginning to wonder if you don't trust me. Maybe you think I'm not up to the job or that I'll get you into trouble. Is that what's going on? [*The* possible *story*]

FERNANDO: Really, I was merely trying to give you a chance to get my input before you got too far down the path on a project. The last guy I worked with was constantly taking his project to near completion only to learn that he'd left out a key element. I'm trying to avoid surprises.

Earn the right to share your story by starting with your facts. Facts lay the groundwork for all delicate conversations.

Tell Your Story   Sharing your story can be tricky. Even if you've started with your facts, the other person can still become defensive when you move from facts to stories. After all, you're sharing potentially unflattering conclusions and judgments.

Why share your story in the first place? Because the facts alone are rarely worth mentioning. It's the facts plus the conclusion that call for a face-to-face discussion. In addition, if you simply mention the facts, the other person may not understand the severity of the implications. For example:

> "I noticed that you had company software in your briefcase."
> "Yep, that's the beauty of software. It's portable."
> "That particular software is proprietary."
> "It ought to be! Our future depends on it."
> "My understanding is that it's not supposed to go home."
> "Of course not. That's how people steal it."

(*Sounds like it's time for a conclusion.*) "I was wondering what the software is doing in your briefcase. If look like you're taking it home. Is that what's going on here?"

It takes confidence. To be honest, it can be difficult to share negative conclusions and unattractive judgments (e.g., "I'm wondering if you're a thief"). It takes confidence to share such a potentially inflammatory story. However, if you've done your homework by thinking through the facts behind your story you'll realize that you *are* drawing a reasonable, rational, and decent conclusion. One that deserves hearing. And by starting with the facts, you've laid the groundwork. By thinking through the facts and then leading with them, you're much more likely to have the confidence you need to add controversial and vitally important meaning to the shared pool....

Ask for Others' Paths   We mentioned that the key to sharing sensitive ideas is a blend of confidence and humility. We express our confidence by sharing our facts and stories clearly. We demonstrate our humility by then asking others to share their views.

So once you've shared your point of view—facts and stories alike—invite others to do the same. If your goal is to learn rather than to be right, to make the best decision rather than to get your way, then you'll be willing to hear other views. By being open to learning we are demonstrating humility at its best.

For example, ask yourself: "What does the schoolteacher think?" "Is your boss really intending to micromanage you?" "Is your spouse really having an affair?"

To find out others' views on the matter, encourage them to express their facts, stories, and feelings. Then carefully listen to what they have to say. Equally important, be willing to abandon or reshape your story as more information pours into the Pool of Shared Meaning.

The "How" Skills

Talk Tentatively   If you look back at the vignettes we've shared so far, you'll note that we were careful to describe both facts and stories in a tentative way. For example, "I was wondering why..."

Talking tentatively simply means that we tell our story as a story rather than disguising it as a fact. "Perhaps you were unaware..." suggests that you're not absolutely certain. "In my opinion..." says you're sharing an opinion and no more.

When sharing a story, strike a blend between confidence and humility. Share in a way that expresses appropriate confidence in your conclusions while demonstrating that, if appropriate, you want your conclusions challenged. To do so, change "The fact is" to "In my opinion." Swap "Everyone knows that" for "I've talked to three of our suppliers who think that." Soften "It's clear to me" to "I'm beginning to wonder if."

Why soften the message? Because we're trying to add meaning to the pool, not force it down other people's throats. If we're too forceful, the information won't make it into the pool. Besides, with both facts and stories, we're *not* absolutely certain they're true. Our observations could be faulty. Our stories—well, they're only educated guesses.

In addition, when we use tentative language, not only does it accurately portray our uncertain view, but it also helps reduce defensiveness and makes it safe for others to offer differing opinions. One of the ironies of dialogue is that when we're sharing controversial ideas with potentially resistant people, the more forceful we are, the less persuasive we are. In short, talking tentatively can actually increase our influence.

Tentative, not wimpy. Some people are so worried about being too forceful or pushy that they err in the other direction.... They figure that the only safe way to share touchy data is to act as if it's not important.

"I know this is probably not true..." or "Call me crazy but..."

When you begin with a complete disclaimer and do it in a tone that suggests you're consumed with doubt, you do the message a disservice. It's one thing to be humble and open. It's quite another to be clinically uncertain. Use language that says you're sharing an opinion, not language that says you're a nervous wreck.

A "Good" Story—The Goldilocks Test   To get a feel for how to best share your story, making sure that you're neither too hard nor too soft, consider the following examples:

Too soft: "This is probably stupid, but..."
Too hard: "How come you ripped us off?"
Just right: "It's starting to look like you're taking this home for your own use. Is that right?"

Too soft: "I'm ashamed to even mention this, but..."
Too hard: "Just when did you start using hard drugs?"
Just right: "It's leading me to conclude that you're starting to use drugs. Do you have another explanation that I'm missing here?"

Too soft: "It's probably my fault, but..."
Too hard: "You wouldn't trust your own mother to make a one-minute egg!"
Just right: "I'm starting to feel like you don't trust me. Is that what's going on here? If so, I'd like to know what I did to lose your trust."

Too soft: "Maybe I'm just oversexed or something, but..."
Too hard: "If you don't find a way to pick up the frequency, I'm walking."
Just right: "I don't think you're intending this, but I'm beginning to feel rejected."

Encourage Testing   When you ask others to share their paths, how you phrase your invitation makes a big difference. Not only should you invite others to talk, but you have to do so in a way that makes it clear that no matter how controversial their ideas are, you want to hear them. Others need to feel safe sharing their observations and stories—even if they differ. Otherwise, they don't speak up and you can't test the accuracy and relevance of your views.

This becomes particularly important when you're having a crucial conversation with people who might move to silence. Some people make Sucker's Choices in these circumstances. They worry that if they share their true opinions, others will clam up. So they choose between speaking their minds and hearing others out. But the *best* at dialogue don't choose. They do both. They understand that the only limit to how strongly you can express your opinion is your willingness to be equally vigorous in encouraging others to challenge it.

Invite opposing views. So if you think others may be hesitant, make it clear that you want to hear their views—no matter their opinion. If they disagree, so much the better. If what they have to say is controversial or even touchy, respect them for finding the courage to express what they're thinking. If they have different facts or stories, you need to hear them to help complete the picture. Make sure they have the opportunity to share by actively inviting them to do so: "Does anyone see it differently?" "What am I missing here?" "I'd really like to hear the other side of this story."

Mean it. Sometimes people offer an invitation that sounds more like a threat than a legitimate call for opinions. "Well, that's how I see it. Nobody disagrees, do they?" Invite people with both words and tone that say "I really want to hear from you." For instance: "I know people have been reluctant to speak up about this, but I would really love to hear from everyone." Or: "I know there are at least two sides to this story. Could we hear differing views now? What problems could this decision cause us?"

Play devil's advocate. Occasionally you can tell that others are not buying into your facts or story, but they're not speaking up either. You've sincerely invited them, even encouraged differing views, but nobody says anything. To help grease the skids, play devil's advocate. Model disagreeing by disagreeing with your own view. "Maybe I'm wrong here. What if the opposite is true? What if the reason sales have dropped is because…"

BACK TO THE MOTEL

To see how all of the STATE skills fit together in a touchy conversation, let's return to the motel bill. Only this time, Carole does a far better job of bringing up a delicate issue.

BOB: Hi honey, how was your day?

CAROLE: Not so good.

BOB: Why's that?

CAROLE: I was checking our credit card bill, and I noticed a charge of forty-eight dollars for the Good Night Motel down the street. [*Shares facts*]

BOB: Boy, that sounds wrong.

CAROLE: It sure does.

BOB: Well, don't worry. I'll check into it one day when I'm going by.

CAROLE: I'd feel better if we checked right now.

BOB: Really? It's less than fifty bucks. It can wait.

CAROLE: It's not the money that has me worried.

BOB: You're worried?

CAROLE: It's a motel down the street. You know that's how my sister found out that Phil was having an affair. She found a suspicious hotel bill. [*Shares story—tentatively*] I don't have anything to worry about do I? What do you think is going on with this bill? [*Asks for other's path*]

BOB: I don't know, but you certainly don't have to worry about me.

CAROLE: I know that you've given me no reason to question your fidelity. I don't really believe that you're having an affair. [*Contrasting*] It's just that it might help put my mind to rest if we were to check on this right now. Would that bother you? [*Encourages testing*]

BOB: Not at all. Let's give them a call and find out what's going on.

When this conversation actually did take place, it sounded exactly like the one portrayed above. The suspicious spouse avoided nasty accusations and ugly stories, shared facts, and then tentatively shared a possible conclusion. As it turns out, the couple had gone out to a Chinese restaurant earlier that month. The owner of the restaurant also owned the motel and used the same credit card imprinting machine at both establishments. Oops.

By tentatively sharing a story rather than attacking, name-calling, and threatening, the worried spouse averted a huge battle, and the couple's relationship was strengthened at a time when it could easily have been damaged....

SUMMARY—STATE MY PATH

When you have a tough message to share, or when you are so convinced of your own rightness that you may push too hard, remember to STATE your path:

- *Share your facts.* Start with the least controversial, most persuasive elements from your Path to Action.
- *Tell your story.* Explain what you're beginning to conclude.
- *Ask for others' paths.* Encourage others to share both their facts and their stories.
- *Talk tentatively.* State your story as a story—don't disguise it as a fact.
- *Encourage testing.* Make it safe for others to express differing or even opposing views.

REVIEW QUESTIONS

1. What are the three ingredients of "maintaining safety" in a difficult conversation? How can you communicate each?
2. What do the authors mean by your "Path to Action"?
3. The authors emphasize that, when they talk about being "persuasive," they do not mean that their goal is to persuade others that they are *right*. What do they mean?
4. What's the difference, for these authors, between being tentative and being "wimpy"?
5. Explain the Goldilocks test.

PROBES

1. Explain the connections and overlaps between the ideas in this reading and the main points of (a) my essay in Chapter 2 and (b) Susan Scott's essay in Chapter 2.
2. Facts become meaningful when they are arranged into, and used to give credibility to, a *story*. Explain some of the dangers of moving from facts to story.
3. Explain the relationship between the authors' point about humility and their point in the "Mean it" paragraph near the end of this reading.
4. Give an example from your own communication experience of a conversation where you either (a) applied most of the STATE suggestions or (b) should have done so.

I Want …

Susan Campbell

This next reading in the "Exhaling" chapter focuses on a communication skill that is simple to understand but can often be difficult to do: expressing a desire. The author's background in psychology leads her to believe that many of us learn in childhood not to express what we want, because we are often disappointed. But whatever the psychological cause, the communication cure is to learn to helpfully and appropriately express what you want without demands, threats, or manipulations.

First, Campbell reminds her readers that one of the appropriate purposes of close interpersonal relationships is for the partners to get and give what each other wants. This is one of the main reasons why people date, hook up, partner, and marry. But wants are almost impossible to fulfill if they are generic or global. Like Rebecca Shafir in Chapter 5, Campbell encourages her readers to focus on the present. As she writes, "a here-and-now want is something you might actually be able to receive or not receive. An announcement about some generic want, such as 'I want you to trust me more,' is too general. It is not a request that can be met in this moment."

On the other hand, "putting your request in very specific terms lets the other know what type of help and nurturance work for you." This reduces the likelihood that the other person will be confused by your request or that he or she will feel defensive because it appears that you're trying to control him or her.

Timing, Campbell writes, is critical. You should express a want when it is possible and likely to happen. But if a communication partner distorts this insight about timing to consistently postpone asking, pressure gets built up behind the want. Then, when the want is expressed, the pressure emerges, again, as an effort to control, and your partner is not as likely to respond positively and may well feel forced or manipulated.

One key idea in this reading is that your expressions of want need to grow out of trust, so that they do not come with the requirement that they be met. Campbell emphasizes that it is profoundly risky to express a genuine desire, and in a healthy relationship, there is always the real possibility that the other may not desire, or be able to respond to the "I want..." message. Near the end of this reading, Campbell outlines a way to express a want that is combined with, first, "And I want you to know that no is an okay answer," and second, if the answer is "No," a candid expression of disappointment. Why is all this communication maneuvering important? "If you cannot handle hearing no, then you also are not a very good prospect for a successful long-term relationship."

Sections of this reading address several common mistaken beliefs that get in the way of clean expressions of want. One is the belief that "If you love me, you should know what I want; I shouldn't have to ask." Another is the assumption that expressing wants puts you in a one-down position. A third is the indignation that results when something is asked of you—blaming the requester for being weak or dependent.

Like much of the advice in self-help books, what's presented here reflects patterns that are most common in middle- and upper-middle-class white cultures. But there are communication principles in this reading that can be adapted to relationships in any culture and across cultures. Staying in the present and being clear are two features of successful communication in many long-term relationships. I encourage you to take as much from this essay as you can.

I want to hear your feelings about what I'm saying.
I want to have a talk with you about something I've had on my mind.
I want to feel your arms around me.
I want you to come with me to the store.
I want you to just listen and not say anything until I'm finished.

A want is a special type of feeling. You can usually feel a want in your body, and it often has an emotional tone to it. If you'd like more intimacy in your life, it's good to express your wants frequently and shamelessly.

Partnership is a place for giving and receiving attention, help, touch, and emotional nurturance. But because most of us did not get enough high-quality attention and nurturance as children, it's often difficult to stay in present time about our current wants. Based on early life experiences, we may have learned that expressing wants (or just *feeling* our wants) brings disappointment. So we carry the expectation into our present life that feeling and expressing wants leads to pain. Having this unconscious negative expectation is one way to protect ourselves.

When you have unfinished emotional business from your past, it's hard to be open to the real possibilities of the present moment. Most of us recall a number of painful experiences where we asked for what we wanted and felt frustrated at the lack of response. This experience can lead to a pattern where you either overcommunicate or undercommunicate your wants. Either you go over the top with demands, threats, or manipulations, or you minimize your wants by hinting, being indirect, accommodating, or giving up too soon. Does either of these patterns sound familiar to you? Can you see either of these tendencies in someone close to you?

THE TIME FOR WANTS IS NOW

The key phrase "I want..." coupled with a very specific statement of what it is you need, brings you into the here and now as you make a request. The aim of this phrase is to help you express a want that you are feeling in this very moment. It helps to interrupt any tendency you may have to make "announcements" about things that you need in general or forevermore. This is an important distinction: a here-and-now want is something you might actually be able to receive or not receive. An announcement about some generic want, such as "I want you to trust me more," is too general. It is not a request that can be met in this moment.

To be in present time with your wants, you would tell your partner, "I want you to look into my eyes," not "I want you to look at me *whenever* I'm speaking to you." In addition to the fact that the whenever phrase is less palpable, the word *whenever* also makes the whole statement sound more like a directive than a request. A directive is controlling. You're not making yourself vulnerable to receiving or not receiving in this moment. It is a general, once-and-for-all notification of a want. You're "putting the other person on notice" that from now on this is how he should treat you. The statement "I want you to look into my eyes" is specific to this moment. It comes from an actual *feeling* of wanting. The statement "I want you to look at me *whenever* I'm speaking" is not relational. It has a controlling flavor to it because it does not come from a present felt experience. It is more from the mind than from the heart—so the feeling tone is much different.

In recommending that you speak your in-the-moment wants, I am not saying that you should never make generic requests or directives. But the generic request is not so present and does not support stepping into the unknown with your partner. Real intimacy requires stepping into the unknown with someone—asking for what you want without trying to control the outcome.

A generic once-and-for-all request is usually a way to play it safe. You're trying to make sure your future needs will be met without your having to ask. When you are playing it safe, you are in a controlling stance. The once-and-for-all style of requesting is actually a control pattern. Remember, a control pattern is anything you do to avoid the anxiety of facing the unknown, the ambiguous, or the uncontrollable. Relating is present-time—allowing the future to be what it will be. The future is always unknown and uncontrollable. The best practice for learning to get comfortable with this fact of life is to feel any anxiety you may have about this rather than masking your anxiety with a control pattern. Anxiety about the unknown is normal. When you let go of trying to control things (including your own anxiety) and feel what you feel in the present, then your anxiety will diminish.

BE SPECIFIC

Putting your requests in very specific terms lets the other know what type of help and nurturance work for you. A big mistake that many people make when asking for what they want is asking in a way that is so vague and general that the other person has no idea how to fulfill their request. They say, "I want you to be more reassuring." This is too general. Instead, I suggest saying, "I want you to tell me you're happy to see me." Likewise, instead of saying, "I want you to be more affectionate," tell your partner, "I like it when you come over and hug me when we're around the house together. I'd love a hug right now." Being specific is like painting a word picture that shows precisely what you want and how you want it. There is enough detail to help the other feel cared about and involved. The picture you paint shows you and your partner together, doing something satisfying or pleasurable. When you ask for what you want using specific language, it's more of a risk than when you ask for something using general terms. You're taking a risk on behalf of your relationship. You're putting yourself on the line. The other person will feel this and appreciate it.

Consider these additional examples of how to express your wants in specific terms:

- "I want you to find out what's playing at the movie theater and pick the film you most want to see and surprise me."
- "I love it when you hold my head in your hands and pull me toward you. Will you do that for me now?"
- "I want you to lie with me on the couch and put your arms around me."

Being specific brings both people into their bodies. It gives you a chance to kinesthetically try on having what you want. Making yourself present kinesthetically is a way of affirming your freedom to ask for whatever you are asking for.

TIMING IS CRITICAL

Besides being too vague or general, another mistake people make when expressing a want is asking for it at a time when it is unlikely to happen. Don't ask him to help you prepare dinner when he's studying for a final exam. Don't ask her to listen to the story of your frustrating day when she is about to receive an important phone call. If you have had a long-standing want and just can't seem to get it satisfied, notice your timing. Are you asking for it at a time when you are actually feeling it? Or do you deliver a directive, as in, "I want more sex"? As I've demonstrated, generic requests do not have the same impact as asking for something at the very time you want it. "I'd like to make love with you this afternoon" has more impact than the generic, once-and-for-all "I want more sex."

The main reason a timely request has more impact is that your request is being made in present time. You are actually feeling your want, your vulnerability, and your openness to receive in this moment. There is an energetic connection between the two of you that your partner can feel. There is a real need occurring in you right now and a real possibility right now for your partner to act on your request (or not). You are taking a bigger risk. This gives your request more weight....

POSTPONING ASKING—NOT A GOOD IDEA!

Some people don't like to appear pushy, demanding, or needy, so they try to be very patient about their wants. As a result they wait to ask for what they want until there is a lot of pressure built up behind the want. In postponing their requests, they are trying to be nice or perhaps trying to appear "low maintenance." This strategy usually backfires because when you ask only infrequently, you are more likely to have expectations that the other should give you what you're asking for. (After all, you've been so accommodating!) Any time you have a lot of internal pressure behind a want, there will be a demanding or controlling tone to your request. Thus, what might have been an act of transparent vulnerability turns into an expectation or a "should." (You've held off a long time on this need...haven't been asking for much...so the least your partner can do is grant this one tiny request!) The other person is likely to pick up your urgency and perhaps feel pressured or manipulated. The moral of this story is it's better to ask whenever you feel a want rather than saving up and asking only for the really important things.

ASKING WITHOUT EXPECTATIONS

Expressing your in-the-moment wants, simply and directly, is a profound act of trust. As such, it helps you learn self-trust. Here's how that works: You are making a commitment to this moment, stepping into the unknown without knowing how the other will respond. You recognize that you may get what you want and you may not. By asking from an open-to-hearing-yes-or-no frame of mind, you are affirming both your right to ask and the other's right to refuse. And you are affirming that however things go, you will deal with it. It is very important that you do not unconsciously assume that you must have your want satisfied. This would be affirming the opposite—that you won't be okay unless the other says yes to your request.

Can you see how staying open, rather than being controlling, helps build your self-trust? When you allow for the possibility of not getting what you want, you are trusting yourself to deal with whatever happens. If your request does *not* feel like a step into the unknown, then maybe you have a belief that you should always get what you ask for. Check to see if your request contains the embedded message: "You'd better give me what I want, or there'll be trouble!" If you do believe that you must get what you ask for, do some self-inquiry about where this belief originated and what pain you're trying to avoid. For example, ask yourself when in the past you experienced so much pain about not getting what you wanted that you thought you might never recover. This would be the pain you are still trying to avoid.

WHY DIRECTIVES LEAD TO DISAPPOINTMENT

Here's another reason to be here now. Whenever you announce in advance a want that you expect the other to remember from this point forward, you are setting yourself up for disappointment. When Sheira tells Carlos, "I want you to help around the house more," she is giving a directive that she expects him to remember. If he's like most people, Carlos is not going to be thinking of his wife's need for help with housework on a daily basis. He'd do better if he heard her want at a time when she's feeling it and when he is free to say yes if he chooses to.

I have mentioned several reasons why generic directives do not work: the timing of the request is too distant from when the help might actually occur and so his experience of her need is not as palpable and has less impact. Even more significant than these reasons is the fact that putting someone on notice comes across as controlling. It's like giving someone marching orders rather than communicating a heartfelt need. Most people resist being controlled.

If people could say what they want more often, instead of making generic requests and holding secret expectations that the other is expected to divine, there would be less frustration and anger in the world. Much of our anger comes from suppressing our assertion—so we walk through life with unexpressed, and therefore unrequited, wants. Frustrated people are angry people. Let's help reduce the overall frustration level in the world by creating more favorable conditions for our wants to be heard and received.

WHY WE DON'T SAY WHAT WE WANT

Some people are uncomfortable expressing wants because they imagine they'll appear demanding or controlling. ("What if I ask for what I want, and he sees me as a nag?") But...expressing wants can be an act of transparency or vulnerability. It really depends on the intent. Are you asking in a way that *reveals* what you want? Or does your manner of asking *imply a threat* that if you don't get what you're asking for, there's going to be trouble? Asking in a way that reveals your self is an act of love. This is an example of the intent to *relate*. Asking in a way that implies a threat is aggressive and fear-inducing. This would be an example of the intent to *control*.

But even if you do get good at revealing your wants, it is still possible that the other might feel controlled—even though this was not your intent. Consider Vera's story. Vera has been dating Howie for six months. Howie has told her that he often felt overcontrolled as a child, and is therefore vigilant about others' attempts to control him. Through trial and error, Vera has discovered a good way to bring both herself and Howie more present. After stating a want, she checks in with Howie to find our how her request has come across.

Here's an example of how I have used Vera's discovery in my life. I call my partner at work to ask him to come home on time tonight so we can have a long, intimate evening together. While my aim is to be open and noncontrolling in my request, I can't help but recall times in the past when my partner has disclosed that my asking something like this resulted in his feeling controlled and choosing to stay at the office even later "just to assert my freedom." So now, as I consider making this request again, I feel some trepidation. In an effort to be transparent and vulnerable, I tell him, "I want you to come home on time tonight, and I also feel some fear about asking for this." Then I ask how he is feeling receiving my request—does it seem controlling? Does he feel resistance? Then I am silent as I listen to this response.

I SHOULDN'T HAVE TO ASK

Many people inhibit asking for what they want because they believe "If he really loved me, he'd know what I like." They assume that the person should care enough and know them well enough to know what they want, without their having to ask for it. For people like this, asking is seen as equivalent to admitting to themselves that the other doesn't care very much. They think, "If I have to ask for it, it's less valuable" or "If he sincerely wanted to please me, he'd do it without my having to ask." Holding this attitude is another patterned way to avoid taking the risk of asking for what you want. When you operate as if this were true, you don't ask for very much, so you don't have to hear no very often. The problem is, by using this self-protection strategy, you miss the chance to develop the resilience and confidence that come from asking without knowing how the other person will respond. Obviously you can never know in advance how the other is going to receive your request—so asking is always a bit of a risk. But if the person cares about you, it is an intelligent risk. You will survive even if you hear a no, and either way, by opening yourself up to the unknown, you'll deepen your self-trust and begin to heal any outdated view you may have of yourself as too fragile.

I DON'T WANT TO FEEL INDEBTED

Yet another reason people give for not expressing wants is they assume that asking for something puts them in a one-down position. They may say, "Asking for attention or help puts me in a dependent relationship to the other person. I'm admitting that I can't do something. Feeling needy feels unattractive or uncomfortable" or "If I ask for and receive what I want, this means I'm beholden or indebted to the other."

If either of these sentiments is familiar to you, perhaps you harbor the unconscious belief that it's not okay or not safe to be needy or to depend on others....

It may have been true in the past that some specific important person in your life was not dependable, but be careful about the mind's tendency to assume that the present will be a repeat of your past.... This prevents you from learning two very important and real lessons: (1) that this present person is not the same person as the one who hurt you; and (2) even if the present situation does lead to pain or disappointment, you are bigger and more resourceful now, so you'll probably be able to cope. You will not be as devastated now (as an adult) when a loved one says, "I don't have time for you," as when you were a child. If you have trouble asking for help or attention, you may be stuck in a self-protective pattern stemming from a belief learned long ago. It's probably time to update your beliefs. Let the key phrase "I want..." be part of your self-healing program....

BLAMING THE REQUESTER

Some people have a control pattern of getting indignant when a request is made of them, as in, "How could you ask that of me?" They'll criticize you for asking in order to avoid feeling the anxiety, fear, or internal pressure that your want creates. Perhaps they want to say no to your request, but they are afraid of your reaction, so they avoid feeling their fear by acting self-righteous.

Sandra and Dan's relationship exhibited this pattern. Whenever she would ask, "I'm wondering if you have any plans for this weekend," he would react, "Plans! Why do you always need to know my plans?! Why can't you just relax and go with the flow?" Dan could have just as easily responded with, "I haven't thought about that," or "I'm not into making plans for the weekend. I want to let things flow along." But he had an unconscious belief that "if a woman asks for plans, you have to give her plans!" In his story, you do not have the freedom to say, "I have no plans," or even "I don't want to talk about it now." We could speculate as to where this belief came from. It's likely that he is bringing an outdated assumption from his childhood into this present situation.

If you recognize yourself or someone you know in this example, take another look at what is actually being asked for, here and now. Ask yourself, What "surplus meaning" am I giving to the request, based on my past conditioning? Am I perhaps seeing the other's request as a demand or as a bid for control? Then notice that voice inside your own head that puts pressure on you—pressure that is coming from your own mind, not from the other person.

ALLOWING YOURSELF TO FEEL DISAPPOINTED

It's true that some people can't stand to disappoint anyone. The consequence of this fear of being a disappointment is that they're likely to feel controlled by almost any request. They do not give themselves permission to say no, but they project this lack of permission onto the other and imagine that she is being controlling and that it is not safe to say no to her.

If you are with someone who blames you when you make a request, how might you deliver your request in order to minimize this sort of misunderstanding? How can you get it across to him that you *can* take no for an answer, even as you ask for what you want? In my experience with this type of partner, I've found it helpful to state my want openly and simply and then to add, "And I want you to know that no is an okay answer." Then, if I ever do get a no, it's important to respond by sharing my feelings of disappointment, or whatever I feel, while at the same time appreciating him for being honest. Don't hide your disappointment if you feel it. Here's an example of saying what's real when I hear a no from this other person: "I'm really disappointed to hear that you don't want to spend the evening together, and at the same time, I so appreciate that you're saying how you really feel."

I believe that by letting my partner hear about my disappointment, I am helping him learn to tolerate the normal discomfort of "disappointing a woman." By not shielding him from my pain, I am helping him get used to feeling a type of discomfort that every healthy relationship needs to make room for. If he cannot allow me to feel unhappy with him sometimes, he's not a good prospect for a successful long-term relationship.

You can help a partner like this heal from his past conditioning by showing him that you can handle hearing no and feeling disappointed without freaking out. And while you're at it, notice your own attitude about being disappointed. If you cannot handle hearing no, then you also are not a very good prospect for a successful long-term relationship. Two people are not always going to want the same thing at the same time. To create a healthy, mature relationship, both people need to feel free to refuse a request without fear of punishment. And they need to be willing to feel unhappy or disappointed with each other at times. . . .

HOW ASKING FOR WHAT YOU WANT HELPS

I have mentioned a number of ways that this key phrase fosters emotional healing: it teaches you that *asking* is much more important than *getting* everything you ask for—thus teaching you to focus on what you can control (asking) instead of on what you cannot (whether you get it); it prompts you to speak about wants that you actually feel in the here and now, thus enhancing your capacity for present-centered contact; it prompts you to be specific about your wants, another way to enhance your personal presence; and it gives you permission to ask for anything and everything you desire rather than caretaking or protecting others from your wants. This helps you unhook from the notion that wants should be reasonable and that you need to protect others from your wants. Allowing yourself to want whatever you really want is an excellent way to affirm how innocent and noncontrolling the state of wanting really is. Wanting is making yourself vulnerable. It is not controlling.

REVIEW QUESTIONS

1. List the kinds of messages that Campbell contrasts with an effective expression of a want. One is the generic announcement "I want you to trust me more" or "I want more sex." What are others?
2. Campbell claims that "the once-and-for-all style of requesting is actually a control pattern." Explain her point.
3. What connection does Campbell make between expressing wants and anger/frustration?
4. Paraphrase the following: "Asking in a way that reveals your self is an act of love. This is an example of the intent to *relate*. Asking in a way that implies a threat is aggressive and fear-inducing. This would be an example of the intent to *control*."
5. What does Campbell mean by "blaming the requester"?

PROBES

1. Like the reading "Mindful Listening" in Chapter 5, this one emphasizes the importance of keeping your communication in the present. In this reading, Campbell mentions the importance of staying in the here-and-now several times. Explain why she emphasizes this point.
2. How can you put together Campbell's advice not to postpone the expression of a want and her reminder that you have to time such an expression appropriately?
3. Explain the relationship Campbell asserts between asking for what you want and trusting.
4. What are, for you, the most difficult parts of following Campbell's advice?

What to Tell: Deciding When, How, and What to Self-Disclose

Lawrence B. Rosenfeld and Jack M. Richman

This reading about engaging others is a case study rather than an analytical or theoretical discussion. The senior author, Lawrence Rosenfeld, is one of the field's foremost self-disclosure scholars, but this is not a report of his research. It's a story about how a new university student manages the challenges of what to disclose about herself, to whom, and when.

Katherine, the new student, misses an opportunity to talk with her dad about this important time in her life, encounters a new roommate, considers how to present herself to the rest of the people in the dorm, and meets some interesting men. She also has to figure out how to respond to Russ, a man she's interested in, when he puts down people with learning disabilities, especially because Katherine herself has attention deficit disorder (ADD). She gets some guidance from her mom and from a counselor at the learning disabilities center.

Katherine learns that when it comes to self-disclosure, every relationship is different, but some guidelines can help. The counselor at the center discusses them with Katherine and helps her decide what to tell her roommate and what to say to Russ. This story doesn't wrap up everything into a neat bundle, but it does show how one person you might be able to relate to copes with the practical applications of some of the principles and concepts that have been discussed in earlier readings in this chapter.

T he summer went by too quickly. All the plans for the trip to college had to fall into place *now*.

"Katy-Leigh, hurry up and get your bags down here so we can pack the car!" Katherine's mother shouts, even though the house is small enough that shouting isn't necessary.

Katherine's father comes into her room and helps move her bags out to the hallway. He stops by the door, turns, and tells Katherine, "I remember when I went off to college...the first day...getting ready. I was excited and scared, happy and downhearted.... Yes, I was a bit bewildered! So, I was wondering how you were feeling."

Katherine looks at her father, confused, thinking, *I thought Mom would be talking to me about this? What's Dad up to?* "Well, yeah," she tells him, "I'm feeling pretty okay about all this."

"Okay, let's get these bags into the car," Katherine's Dad tells her. "I guess we can talk later, if you want."

Three hours and a hundred and forty miles later, they arrive at Western State University. As Katherine looks at the long set of stairs leading up the hill to her dormitory, all she can think about is getting her stuff into her room, meeting her roommate, and getting started on her first year of college. She grabs the smallest, lightest bag and hustles up to her dorm room so she can get to see her roommate before her parents embarrass her!

"Hi, my name's Katherine."

"Great to meet you. I'm Kim. I guess we're going to be spending the year together."

"Yeah, I see you've got your stuff in the closets already. I guess you want that side of the room." Katherine thinks, *Maybe I wanted that side of the room*, but says, "No problem, I'll take this side. I need to warn you: my parents will be up here in a minute, and there's no telling what they'll ask you. Just nod a lot. My folks are really great...most of the time."

"No problem! My mom just left—and if you had been here she would have grilled you about anything and everything. She has to be sure her daughter isn't living with a lunatic!"

Katherine's parents enter loaded down with boxes and suitcases, and the process begins—of moving in, meeting Kim, and making jokes that cover the tension everyone feels. Within a few hours everything is put away, the beds are made, and Katherine and her parents, with Kim, go out for dinner.

Later, Katherine and Kim collapse on their beds and wonder what's next. The answer appears in the doorway in the shape of the Resident Advisor, "Sarah-the-RA" (which seems to be her full name), telling them about the dorm meeting scheduled for 8:00 P.M. Living in a co-ed dorm means meeting the other women and men.

"Kim?" Katherine asks without posing a question. "Do you realize that we have a rare opportunity here? I mean, in an hour we'll be meeting lots of people, but right now they don't know us. We can be whoever and whatever we want to be! I'm not sure whether I want to be 'Katherine' or 'Kathy,' or even 'Katy-Leigh,' my parents' nickname for me."

"I can be 'Kim' or 'Kimberly,' or even 'Kimmy,' but I never liked that nickname. My brother uses that when he wants to be really obnoxious."

"I'm not sure what kind of impression I should make. Should I be 'sophisticated Katherine'? Or should I be 'easy-to-get-to-know Kathy'? "

"I think we're going to be whoever we are, whatever we call ourselves. But I agree with you, we're probably all feeling a little insecure and flustered. When we get back here, you can let me know how I came across, and I'll let you know. But we have to be honest with each other!"

The meeting is in the lounge on the first floor, between the elevators and the Coke machines. A hundred people scatter on the chairs and floor, and lean against the walls. Sarah-the-RA calls the meeting to order, and what follows is a lengthy speech about rules and regulations, quiet hours, and planned social events. Ears perk up at the mention of social events. Then Sarah-the-RA offers soft drinks and cookies to encourage the residents to hang around.

"Kathy?" a voice calls out to her. "Kathy? It's me, Russ. I was a year ahead of you in high school—remember? We went out once. I've been here a year, but I still like living in the dorms."

"Oh, yeah, Russ...sure...high school. You were friends with those kids on the basketball team." Katherine thinks, *I really liked you...and wanted to get to know you better...I don't know why you never called me again after we went out.*

After a moment of awkward silence, Katherine asks, "How do you like Western? I'm registering for classes tomorrow. Any suggestions?"

They talk about Western, classes, the weather, majors, "do-ya-know-so-and-so" questions, and other topics that are safe and usual. They agree to meet the next day for lunch after registration. Kim walks up, nudges Katherine, and clears her throat loudly.

"Russ, this is Kim. She's my roommate. Kim, this is Russ...he's a sophomore here...and he went to my high school."

"Hi, Russ! Sorry to interrupt, but I just wanted to tell Katherine...or is it Kathy?...or is it Katy-Leigh—have you decided? Well, I just wanted to tell you that I'm meeting some friends from Smith Hall. There's a guy there I know from high school. See ya!" Without waiting for a response, Kim is gone.

"What's up with Kim? Doesn't she know your name?" Russ asks.

"Oh, it's nothing. She was just kidding."

Later that night, lying on her bed, Katherine stares at the ceiling and goes over the day in her head. *I never did get to have that conversation Dad wanted.... I can't believe I'm in college, in a dorm room, away from home!...What would I be doing at 10:00 P.M. at home on a Sunday night—probably not much less than this!...Am I boring? What is this place really, really like? I think Kim is already having a better social life than I am.... I wish she asked me to go with her! Why did she mention that "name thing" to Russ? How embarrassing!*

Katherine's thoughts come to an abrupt halt when she hears a key in the door. Kim comes in and says, "How was your night? Russ is cute!"

"Oh, we just talked for a few minutes. I'm meeting him tomorrow after registration. A lunch thing."

"Do you like him?"

Katherine hesitates. *I'd like to tell Kim that Russ and I went out once, and about my feelings for him, whatever they are. I want to talk to Kim and sort out my feelings— about Russ, being away for the first time, college. But...I'm not ready. I mean, should I trust her? What if I say something really stupid? What if she thinks I'm an immature jerk?* She says, "He's OK. What did you do?"

"It was weird! I went over to meet Mike, and the first thing I notice is he's cut all his hair off! I'm not sure I like that! I really liked him in high school, but I don't know if I want to jump into a relationship—not with all these other guys around! You see...I was in a relationship for two years, and while it was good in a lot of ways, it felt a little like prison...a nice prison, but a prison anyway. You know what I mean?"

"I've had some boyfriends, but nothing as serious as two years. What was it like?"

Katherine and Kim talk about high school and the pros and cons of dating someone for a long time, and Katherine wonders, *Maybe I can tell her how I felt being left at the meeting, and about her mentioning the Katherine-Kathy-Katy-Leigh thing to Russ. After all, she's told me so much about herself.* "When I was talking to Russ, and you left…and I came up here by myself. It was…well…a little scary. I mean, it dawned on me, I really am alone here."

"How terrible! I didn't mean to leave you! I know how that feels. You know? I've felt the same way. I grew up in a single-parent family, and had a lot of responsibility, and I used to think that I was alone, having to figure out everything for myself. I'm sorry."

Katherine thinks, *I'm lucky! Kim really seems to understand me…and she's a great listener!* "It's OK, I'm probably a little hyper today. First day. Our relationship isn't going to be a 'prison,' even if we're roomies for four years!"

Lunch the next day comes at the perfect moment: Katherine is closed out of several classes, registers for a class in Botany that meets a science requirement but isn't something she's particularly interested in taking, and finds herself with a schedule that requires being on campus from 8:00 Ḃ. until 5:00 l Ḃ. five days a week. Frustrated, she meets Russ and plunks her books on the table. Russ tells her, "You look terrible!"

"Thanks. You would too if you had to work so hard to get the awful schedule I'm stuck with! I couldn't get Dr. Rawlings for English, like you told me to, so I had to sign up for Dr. Spencer. I hear she requires a lot of reading!"

"Well, welcome to college! Only the learning disabled *really* have trouble keeping up!"

Katherine is surprised: *He said "learning disabled" like it was a horrible disease, and he doesn't know that I "have it"! I wonder what he would think if he knew I was ADD? A lot of reading is a real challenge for me. I have to stick with it for a long time. I've worked so hard to overcome my disability…why does it have to be a problem?*

The rest of the conversation follows the first-lunch rules: Say nothing too deep, ask nothing too personal, and keep yourself looking good. And it ends with plans to meet again on the weekend. But later that day, Katherine recognizes old feelings: *How can I tell Russ about my ADD? I never even heard of attention deficit disorder, much less "ADD," which is what everyone calls it, until I found out I had it. And why should I have to explain myself to him in the first place? What will he think about me? He seems to think that anyone with a learning disability is less than a real student? I like him, but can I have a relationship with him?*

Katherine needs some advice. She calls her mother and tells her about the problems with registration and with Russ. "What can I do?" she asks her mother.

"Look, Katy-Leigh, one reason we selected Western was because they're supposed to have a great Learning Disabilities Center. Remember, when we met Dr. O'Neill, he said to come by any time. So why not call him? I'm sure you're not alone in having to tell people about your ADD."

"I know I'm not alone, but I sure feel alone."

Following her mother's advice, Katherine calls the Learning Disabilities Center and makes an appointment for the next day with Dr. O'Neill.

"What's up, Katherine? I'm glad to see you chose Western. What can I do for you?"

"Well, for starters, you can give me a magic pill that'll get rid of my ADD!"

"You sound frustrated. How is your ADD a problem? Classes don't begin until next week."

Katherine recounts her conversation with Russ, and about needing some advice. "How can I tell him about my ADD, which I have to if I want any kind of relationship with him that's more than superficial? I'm afraid he'll not want any relationship at all if I tell him."

"OK, you're feeling conflict over being honest with him and with risking the potential for a close relationship."

"That's it! So what do I do?"

"First, you need to decide if being open with Russ is what you want to do. There are no hard-and-fast rules about when and what to tell someone about yourself. Don't panic; you're in control here. Now, is this about Russ thinking bad things about you, or is it about your own fears about college and how well you'll do?"

"It's not the ADD. I know my problem with organizing, about having to concentrate when I listen in class, about not getting distracted, about following through on assignments. I've learned ways to sustain my concentration and mental effort when I'm doing my school work. I know all that. I've been taught how to use structure in my life, use time-outs when I get really frustrated, and to keep a sense of humor about the whole thing."

"So what's the problem?"

"The problem is how do I tell Russ, and my roommate, Kim, and anybody else at Western—without feeling exposed, unprotected, and maybe unworthy of being here."

"OK, I get the point. You need some guidelines. Well, every relationship is different, and it's not safe to make generalizations, but that's never stopped me before! Really, here are some things to think about. First of all, you need to think about how important Russ or Kim or anyone else is to you. Is the person you want to tell a big risk or a small risk? I mean, how much can you trust the person to treat what you say confidentially and with respect? Holding back with people you don't feel comfortable with may not be a bad idea! Second, you have to think about whether what you want to say about yourself is an appropriate topic to talk about. Your ADD may be something important to tell your teachers, but not just any student in one of your classes. See what I mean?"

"I see. But it seems relevant to tell Russ because he obviously has negative feelings about people with a learning disability. And if we're going to have any friendship at all—of any kind—this has got to get cleared up. I guess I just decided it's worth the risk!"

"Seems like it! Also, think about *when* you're going to tell Russ. You need a space that's comfortable and that allows for privacy. You don't want Russ to feel as if he *has* to be polite and say the 'right thing.' And here's a last consideration. You need to think about the possible outcomes and be prepared for whatever might be said. Why don't we do a few role plays. I'll play you and you can be Russ, then you can be yourself and I'll play Russ. This way you're sure to be clear and understandable if you decide to be open with him."

Katherine and Dr. O'Neill practice what Katherine might say to Russ, and she leaves his office feeling more confident in her ability to interact with Russ successfully and deal with whatever his response might be. Walking up the stairs to her dorm room, she thinks: *If Kim asks me where I've been, I'll tell her about meeting Dr. O'Neill and see how she reacts. I think it's worth the risk with Kim. We're going to be living together, and she seems to be understanding.*

As if on cue, Kim asks her, "So what's going on?"

"I'm just getting back from the Learning Disabilities Center."

"Getting a tutoring job?"

"Not really—I may be one of those who needs tutoring!"

"I don't understand."

"I saw Dr. O'Neill, the Center's Director. I wanted to talk to him about how to tell people about my learning disability."

"Great, so tell me."

"I have ADD—that's Attention Deficit Disorder. And Russ made some insensitive put-down of people with learning disabilities. So Dr. O'Neill and I decided how best to deal with all this. Am I clear? I can hear myself sounding scattered—shifting topics. Welcome to my ADD! This is what happens when I get nervous."

"OK, so you have ADD. What's the problem? You must be doing something right if you got into Western."

"The problem is I need to work harder than most people just keeping myself on task, on organizing my work. And sometimes I think I don't belong here ... and I'm afraid the other students are going to judge me. That's why I feel so alone sometimes!"

"I don't know much about ADD, but if it helps, it looks to me like you're pretty task oriented and you seem organized. Is there anything I can do?"

"No, just listening to me helps. It feels good just to have someone know and be supportive. It would be great if you could learn to sleep with the light on while I'm taking the extra time I need to study. Just kidding!"

"So what's the issue with Russ? He doesn't seem like a jerk, except maybe for his remark about learning disabilities."

"That's the point. I don't know."

"Well, if you talk to him, you can clarify how you feel and how he feels. I'm sure he'll tell you if you tell him! And then you'll get it off your chest. You know, he may even think you're brave to tell him. I think you're brave! It takes guts to be up front with someone.... Anyway, it'll give him a chance to understand how his remark hurt you and to apologize, or let you know he's not worth having a relationship with."

"That makes sense. But if he says more insensitive stuff, I'll probably be so frustrated and angry that I'll want to hit him!"

"Yeah, being rejected, even if it's by a jerk, still hurts. But, it's either tell him, or plan on nothing more than nodding hello when you pass him on campus."

"I'm meeting him this weekend. I'll take the risk."

That Saturday night, sitting across from each other at a local pizza parlor, Katherine looks Russ in the eyes and says, "You said something when we were having lunch a few days ago, and I need to talk to you about it."

REVIEW QUESTIONS

1. Is the relationship portrayed here between Katherine and her roommate, Kim, a realistic one? Explain.
2. Who do you think is more open in this story, Kim or Katherine?
3. Katherine believes that Russ's comment "Only the learning disabled *really* have trouble keeping up" accurately reflects part of his view of people with ADD. Do you agree? Explain.

PROBES

1. Before they go to the dorm meeting, Katherine tells Kim, "We can be whoever and whatever we want to be" when they meet the other women and men. Do you agree? When you're new, do you have relatively complete freedom to present whatever self you want to others? Or are you strongly limited by your appearance, culture, and habits?
2. The readings in Chapter 2 emphasize that communication happens *between* people; it's not something one person does "to" another. In this story, Russ says, "Only the learning disabled *really* have trouble keeping up," and Katherine interprets this as a threat to her possible future with Russ. "The communication" emerges *between* them. Which parts of "the communication" are Russ's and which are Katherine's?
3. Write out the rest of the conversation between Katherine and Russ that Katherine begins at the end of the story.

REFERENCES

Cline, R. J. W. (1989). The politics of intimacy: Costs and benefits determining disclosure intimacy in male-female dyads. *Journal of Social and Personal Relationships, 6,* 5–20.

Derlega, V. J., Metts, S., Petronio, S., & Margulis, S. T. (1993). *Self-disclosure.* Newbury Park, CA: Sage.

Foubert, J. D., & Sholley, B. K. (1996). Effects of gender, gender role, and individualized trust on self-disclosure. *Journal of Social Behavior and Personality, 11*(5), 277–288.

Laurenceau, J. P., Barrett, L. F., & Pietromonaco, P. R. (1998). Intimacy as an interpersonal process: The importance of self-disclosure, partner disclosure, and perceived partner responsiveness in interpersonal exchanges. *Journal of Personality and Social Psychology, 74,* 1238–1251.

Petronio, S., Martin, J., & Littlefield, R. (1984). Prerequisite conditions for self-disclosing: A gender issue. *Communication Monographs, 51,* 268–273.

Rosenfeld, L. B. (2001). Overview of the ways privacy, secrecy, and disclosure are balanced in today's society. In S. Petronio (Ed.), *Balancing the secrets of private disclosures.* Mahwah, NJ: Lawrence Erlbaum.

Rosenfeld, L. B. (1979). Self-disclosure avoidance: Why I am afraid to tell you who I am. *Communication Monographs, 46,* 63–74.

Rosenfeld, L. B., & Kendrick, W. L. (1987). Choosing to be open: Subjective reasons for self-disclosing. *Western Journal of Speech Communication, 48,* 326–343.

Toukmanian, S. G., & Brouwers, M. C. (1998). Cultural aspects of self-disclosure and psychotherapy. In S. S. Kazarian & D. R. Evans (Eds.), *Cultural clinical psychology: Theory, research, and practice* (pp. 106–124). New York: Oxford University Press.

Wintrob, H. L. (1987). Self-disclosure as a marketable commodity. *Journal of Social Behavior and Personality, 2,* 77–88.

Relationships

One of the ways to understand the organization of *Bridges Not Walls* is to think about Part Three of the book as the place where we move from theory to practice. The four chapters in Part One defined communication and interpersonal communication, showed how selves get built and changed communicatively, and surveyed the two basic ways we make contact—verbally and nonverbally. Then the two chapters in Part Two analyzed and illustrated how people make meaning together by taking in cues via perception and listening— "inhaling"—and giving off cues via self-expression and self-disclosure—"exhaling." Now we turn to the main arenas or contexts where this communicating happens: family, friends, and intimate partners.

But if you've read the earlier chapters, you know that this way of understanding them doesn't quite work, because they aren't all theory. Practice and theory have been woven together from the beginning, and this is an important part of studying interpersonal communication. The theories that scholars have developed are systematic descriptions of practice. In this part of the communication discipline, there are no abstract theoretical generalizations that are totally disconnected from people's lived experiences. Every theoretical principle—for example, that culture is part of all communicating, that selves are built in verbal/nonverbal talk, and that all perception involves interpretation—grows out of and can significantly affect actual practice.

So the readings in Part Three continue the marriage between theory and practice that characterizes all the materials in *Bridges Not Walls*.

CHAPTER 7

Communicating with Family and Friends

What's a Family, Anyway?

Julia T. Wood

I chose this selection because it offers a realistic description of what "family" now means, especially in the United States. These realities are different from the cultural ideal of the past *and* from what some Christian and Jewish people believe is the model prescribed in the Bible. So you may or may not believe that some contemporary forms of "family" are appropriate or desirable. There's room for a wide variety of opinions on this issue. But it's very likely that as you move through your life, you will encounter people in many different kinds of families, and Wood's comments can help your communication with these people go more smoothly.

Wood begins by contrasting the actual status of U.S. families with the myth of the traditional nuclear family—children living with a married mother and father. As she points out, the traditional picture excludes the *majority* of people living in the United States and much of the rest of the world.

Wood describes, for example, how the notion of "immediate family" is more expanded for many African Americans than for many whites. She also describes how lesbian and gay families are frequently misunderstood. She discusses some of the communication challenges faced by interracial families. And she outlines some ways members of divorced and blended families are often stereotyped.

As a member of a childless couple, Wood also talks briefly about misunderstandings that occur around families without children. She often has to field the question "Why don't you have a family?" responding with something like, "I *do* have a family—I have a husband, a sister, three nephews, and a niece." The final section in this part of the reading talks about families of choice. These are the family circles created by many gay, lesbian, bisexual, and other persons "bound together by commitment, regardless of whether there are biological or legal ties."

The second major part of this reading directly addresses the discomfort some people have about discussions of family diversity because, for example, "My church says that homosexuality is immoral [and] I can't approve of that," or "It's wrong for members of one race to adopt children of a different race." Wood argues that you can respect a family form as a legitimate choice for others without embracing the choice for yourself. She also describes how family forms change over time in any culture, and she underscores the reality of family diversity today. Wood concludes by suggesting that you can learn from observing and interacting with families different from your own. She gives an example of her own experience of learning about the relative lack of playfulness in her relationship with her partner by experiencing a family with young children.

Some of Wood's ideas are provocative. You may find yourself or some classmates resisting what she says. I hope that the group you're in will be able to discuss these responses as openly and productively as possible. I believe that the perspective on families that is offered here can provide a starting place for some fruitful thinking and talking about family communication.

DIFFERENT VIEWS OF WHAT FAMILY MEANS

…One of the students I advise is an African American man who is preparing for a career in marketing. Franklin is an ideal student—smart, curious about ideas, responsible in getting his work done, and serious about his studies. Not long ago, Franklin came to me visibly upset, so I invited him to sit down and tell me what was bothering him.

"My grandmother had to go in the hospital for heart surgery, so I went home to be with her." I nodded. "I missed an exam in my history class. When I got back to school, I went to see Dr. Raymond to schedule a make-up and he says he won't excuse my absence."

"Why not?" I asked. "Did he want some assurance that your grandmother really was in the hospital?"

Franklin shook his head. "No, I brought a copy of her admission form as proof. That's not the problem. He says he only excuses absences for medical problems in the student's *immediate* family."

Dr. Don Raymond, like many middle-class white people, thought of family as a mother, father (or stepmother or stepfather), and children. After all, when he was growing up, Don lived with his parents and two sisters. His other relatives did not live nearby and he saw them only once or twice a year, if that often. Now 48 years old, Don lives with his second wife and their two children, ages 12 and 15. He seldom sees his sisters and visits with his parents and in-laws only over Christmas. Aunts, uncles, and grandparents are not part of the immediate family that Don Raymond knows.

It wasn't difficult to resolve Franklin's situation. I simply called Don Raymond and talked with him about some of the typical differences between white and black family structures, and I emphasized that many African American families are more extended than those of most European Americans. Large, extended families are also common among second-generation Americans of many ethnic origins. Once Don understood that grandparents were immediate family to Franklin, he was more than willing to schedule a make-up examination.

There was nothing mean spirited or intentionally discriminatory in Don's initial refusal to schedule a make-up exam for Franklin. The problem was that he assumed—without even knowing he was making an assumption—that his definition of family was everyone's definition of family. He simply didn't understand that Franklin considered his grandmother immediate family. After all, she had raised him for the first seven years of his life, a situation not uncommon in African American families. She was more like a mother (in white terms) than a grandmother to him.

Lesbian and Gay Families

Lesbian and gay families are also frequently misunderstood. Not long ago I was having lunch with Jean and Arlene, who have been in a committed relationship for 15 years. With us were their two children, Michael and Arthur, age 6 and 8, respectively. A colleague of mine saw us in the restaurant and came over to our table to engage in small talk for a few minutes.

I offered the standard introduction: "Chuck Morris, I'd like you to meet Jean Thompson and Arlene Ross. And these are their sons, Michael and Arthur."

"Good to meet you," Chuck said. "Do you live here?"

"Yes, our home is just off Lystra Road," Arlene said. "And what about you?" Chuck asked Jean.

"Same place. The four of us are a family," she replied.

Chuck had made the mistake of assuming that the two women and the two sons constituted separate families. Once Jean clarified the relationship, Chuck understood and was not taken aback by the fact that Jean and Arlene were lesbians. Yet he was confused about the boys. "So how old were they when you got them?" he asked, assuming the boys were adopted.

"Depends on whether you count the gestation period," Jean said with a smile. She had run into this assumption before. "I carried Michael and Arlene carried Arthur." ·

"Oh, so they're your biological children?" he asked.

Arlene and Jean nodded.

Chuck made the mistake of assuming that lesbians (and gay men, too) can't be biological parents. Obviously they can, because sexual orientation has no bearing on a man's ability to produce viable sperm or a woman's ability to produce fertile eggs and carry a child in her womb. When we assume gay men and lesbians cannot have biological children, we conflate sexual orientation with reproductive ability.

Interracial Families

Misunderstandings also surround many interracial families. Matt and Vicky had been married for six years when they realized they weren't able to have biological children. They decided to adopt, first, James, and three years later, Sheryl. They love their son and daughter and consider themselves a close family. But, whenever they go out as a family, others subject them to stares and sometimes thoughtless comments.

"Are you baby-sitting?"

"Whose children are these?"

If you guessed that James and Sheryl are not the same race as Matt and Vicky, you're correct. The children are African American, and Matt and Vicky are European American. In recent years, two of my white friends have adopted children of other races—a young girl from China for one and a Native American girl for another. Like Matt and Vicky, they are hurt when people assume their children are not their children. Comments such as "Are you baby-sitting?" deny the families they have created.

Divorced and Blended Families

You have probably read the statistic that half of first marriages end in divorce. In addition, even more than half of second and subsequent marriages end in divorce. Divorce may end a marriage, but it doesn't end family. Instead, it changes the character and dynamics of family life.

If the former spouses had children, they are still parents, but how they parent changes. In some cases, one parent has sole custody of children and the other parent may have visiting rights. In other cases, parents agree to joint custody with each parent providing a home to children part of the time. Children experience two homes and two sets of rules, which may be inconsistent. One parent may have rigid requirements about dating, curfews, and household chores while the other parent is more relaxed.

If one or both parents remarry, families combine to create what are called blended families. Years ago *The Brady Bunch* was a popular television situation comedy. In it, two parents, each with several children, married and became a blended family. Among the Bradys, liking and comfort seemed effortless. Unlike the Bradys, many blended families find it difficult to reorganize into a functional, comfortable unit. Children may have to accommodate other children, from both former marriages and the current one, so jealousy and conflict often surface. New household rules may cause confusion, resentment, and resistance. Parents may have to accept the children's other parents and grandparents. And people outside the family may have to recognize multiple parents of children and both former and current spouses of parents.

Some children in blended families call their stepparent mother or father; other children reject that term. Similarly, some children in blended families consider their step-siblings and half-siblings brothers and sisters whereas other children don't accept those labels. When communicating with people who belong to divorced or blended families, we should be sensitive to how they perceive and name their family ties.

Families without Children

My partner and I have been married for 23 years, and we have no children. We are a family without children. I am annoyed and hurt when people ask me, as they frequently do, "Why don't you have a family?" Sometimes I reply with a question: "What do *you* mean by family?" On other occasions, I respond by saying, "I *do* have a family—I have a husband, a sister, three nephews, and a niece." I consider all six of these people my immediate family. Like other people who don't have children, I resent it when others assume that I don't have a family just because Robbie and I don't have children.

What's a Family, Anyway?

Yet another kind of family was introduced by Kathy Weston in her book, *Families We Choose*. Weston describes close friendship circles of gays and lesbians as the families they choose. For Weston, families are people who are bound together by commitment, regardless of whether there are biological or legal ties. Some biologically related people may have no commitment to each other and may refuse to interact. Siblings sometimes feel such animosity toward each other that they decide not to visit, write, call, or otherwise have contact. Some parents and children are estranged, and in extreme cases parents sometimes disown children. Biology, then, doesn't guarantee commitment.

Legal and religious procedures are also insufficient to ensure the level of commitment and caring most of us consider the crux of what a good family is. As noted earlier, current statistics indicate that approximately one-half of marriages in the United States will end in divorce. Laws that define marriage can be negated by laws that grant divorce. In a 1993 poll of the baby boom generation, only 58% of respondents said they considered it likely they would stay married to the same person for life. Pledging "until death do us part" before a magistrate or member of the clergy may create a legal marriage. It does not, however, guarantee that the people making the pledge will, in fact, be able or willing to stay together for life. These statistics show that the nature of family is neither as fixed nor as uniform as Dan Quayle suggested.

Thus, concludes Weston, it's reasonable to define family as people who elect to commit to each other in a sustained way—to have a family we choose. Their commitments may or may not be recognized by current laws or religious practices; but they are families, if by family we mean people who care about one another, organize their lives together, take care of one another, and intend to continue being together and caring for one another. This enlarged view of family pivots on the idea that people can commit to casting their fates together.

IMPROVING COMMUNICATION

When I teach about family diversity at my university, some of my students are uncomfortable. "I understand what you're saying," they often tell me, "but my church says that homosexuality is immoral. I can't approve of that." Others say, "It's wrong for members of one race to adopt children of a different race. The children will never understand their ethnic heritage. I just can't agree with interracial adoptions."

Distinguish between Personal Choice and Respect for Others' Choices

What I try to show my students is that they don't have to embrace various family forms for themselves in order to respect them as legitimate choices for other people. In other words, there's a big difference between deciding what you personally want in a family (or career or spiritual practice or education or home life) and deciding to honor the choices that others make.

We already recognize and respect varied choices in many aspects of family life. For example, some parents believe that physically punishing children is wrong; other parents believe that if you spare the rod, you spoil the child. Some parents bring up children within strong religious traditions; other parents don't introduce children to any religious or spiritual path. In some families, children have to do chores and sometimes take on jobs outside the home to earn money; children in other families get automatic allowances. Few of us would label any of these choices wrong, deviant, or antifamily. Yet we sometimes find it difficult to accept other variations among families.

Recognize That Views of Family Change

Recently I collaborated with Steve Duck, who conducts research on communication and personal relationships, to co-edit a book. It includes chapters on different kinds of families, such as cohabiting couples, long-distance relationships, gay and lesbian commitments, and African American and Hispanic families. The chapters in this book document the diversity of family forms in the United States today.

Family historian Stephanie Coontz points out that during the 300 years since Columbus landed in this hemisphere, families in the United States have taken many forms. The Iroquois lived with extended and matriarchal families, whereas the more nomadic Indian groups had small families. African American slaves saw their nuclear families wrenched apart, so they developed extended communal networks, routinely engaged in co-parenting, and took orphaned children into their homes and raised them as their own, usually without formally adopting them.

The family form idealized by Dan Quayle came late in U.S. history and sustained its status as the dominant family form for only a short period. According to Coontz, only beginning in the 1920s did the majority of working-class white people in the United States live in families that had male breadwinners and female homemakers. Today, by contrast, the majority of women work outside the home, and approximately one-half of wives who work outside the home have salaries equal to or greater than those of their husbands. The male breadwinner/female homemaker model simply doesn't describe the majority of U.S. families today.

Intact families, also part of Quayle's model, are more the exception than the rule in this country.... Nearly half of first marriages (and an even greater percentage of second marriages) end in divorce. Only 50% of children live with both their biological parents, and nearly one-quarter live with single parents, usually their mothers.

The Census Bureau's 1996 survey of 60,000 U.S. households noted several trends in families. The greatest shift is in the number of single-parent households. Between 1990 and 1995, the number of single-parent families rose by a scant 3%. In the single year 1995–1996, families headed by single mothers rose 12% as did families headed by single fathers. Some single-parent households, such as Murphy Brown's, represent choices. In other cases, single parenting is not desired or anticipated, but it becomes the only or the most acceptable option.

Recognize Diversity in Family Forms

Demographic trends in the United States clearly challenge the accuracy of any singular view of what a family is. Effective participation in current society requires us to understand that people have diverse ideas about what counts as a family and they have equally diverse ways of structuring family life. As one gay man said to me, "I don't care if straights like me and my partner or not, but I do care that they recognize I have rights to love a person and have a family just like they do." Understanding this point can help us interact effectively in two ways.

First, when we recognize the normal diversity of family forms, we can communicate more respectfully with people who have varying family structures. No longer is there a universal definition of family. Dan Quayle says single mothers are an affront to family values, but single mothers are no more or less successful in parenting than married women. Just like mothers who are married, some single mothers are devoted and effective parents, and some are not. Just like married mothers, single mothers' effectiveness depends on a variety of factors including support networks, income, education, and employment.

Most states do not recognize gay and lesbian commitments, yet the evidence suggests they can be as healthy, stable, and enduring as heterosexual unions. Even if gay and lesbian families do break up, that doesn't mean they weren't families at one time. After all, if a heterosexual couple divorces, we don't assume they were never married. Like heterosexuals, gays and lesbians can pledge a lifetime of love and loyalty; like some heterosexuals, some gays and lesbians will not realize that promise.

And what about the children of lesbian and gay parents? Child development specialist Charlotte Patterson reports that there are currently between 1 million and 5 million lesbian mothers and 1 million and 3 million gay fathers in the United States and between 6 million and 14 million children who have a gay or lesbian parent. Many states don't allow gay or lesbian partners to be legal parents, even if one partner is the biological parent. These states argue that lesbians and gays cannot raise healthy children, but this argument isn't justified, according to *New York Times* columnist Jane Gross. Based on reviewing 35 studies of children who have gay or lesbian parents, Gross concluded that these children are as well adjusted as children of heterosexual parents and that they are no more or less likely to become gay or lesbian than the children of heterosexual parents. In a separate review of research, Charlotte Patterson found that children of gay and lesbian parents and children of heterosexual parents are no different in terms of intelligence, self-concept, and moral judgment. Existing evidence shows that both heterosexuals and gays and lesbians can raise children who are healthy and happy—and both can raise poorly adjusted children who have low self-concepts.

Learn from Differences

Diverse family forms also offer an opportunity for us to consider how we form our own families and live in them. Martha Barrett interviewed same-sex couples and concluded that they tend to relate to each other on equal terms more than do heterosexual couples. Barrett suggests that gays and lesbians have something to teach the heterosexual community about equality in rights and responsibilities in intimate relationships. Similarly, interracial families may discourage us from overemphasizing race in our thinking about personal identity and family. And families in which there are children may learn from child-free families about ways to keep couple communication alive and intimate.

We can learn about others and ourselves if we are open to differences in how people form and live in families. As long as we interact only with people whose families are like ours, it's hard for us to see some of the patterns and choices we've made in our own relationships. The particular ways that we charter our families remain invisible, unseen and unseeable because they seem "normal," "the only way to be a family." Yet when we consider some of the contrasts provided by interacting with people who have families different from ours, what was invisible and taken for granted in our own relationships becomes more visible. This realization allows us to reflect on the way we've created our families. In turn, this knowledge enables us to make more informed, more thoughtful choices about the kind of family we want to have.

In other words, heterosexuals don't have to change their sexual orientation to gain insight into their own relationships by observing gay and lesbian families. A heterosexual friend of mine once told me that only through her friendship with a lesbian couple had she realized how fully she centered her life around her male partner. She chose to stay married, but she and her husband communicated about ways they could be less centered on each other and enlarge their circle of friends.

A child-free family doesn't need to have children to learn something about their own relationship from interacting with families in which children are present, I've learned a lot about my relationship with Robbie by spending time with my sister Carolyn and her husband, Leigh, and their children, Michelle and Daniel. One of the insights I've gained from visiting them is that Robbie and I didn't include much play and frolic in our relationship.

Notice I used the past tense (didn't). Watching Carolyn and Leigh play with Michelle and Daniel and then blend into playfulness with each other allowed Robbie and me to notice that the playful dimension of relating was largely missing in our interaction. When Robbie and I played with Michelle and Daniel and then with them and their parents, we revived our dormant sense of how to be playful. Since learning this, Robbie and I have become more playful, even silly at times, with each other, and this enriches our marriage. Opening ourselves to various ways of being a family allows us to enlarge our personal identities and our relationships, including our own families.

REVIEW QUESTIONS

1. What is a nuclear family? How many nuclear families do you contact regularly? How many nonnuclear families do you contact regularly?
2. Who would you say makes up your immediate family?
3. What is a blended family?
4. Given all the different kinds of family forms Wood discusses, how do you believe she would define *family?* How do you define it? What does it take, in your opinion, to have a family?
5. Fill in the blanks and discuss the significance: Between 1990 and 1995, the number of single-parent families rose by _____ percent. In the single year 1995–1996, the number of single-parent families rose by _____ percent.
6. What does the initial research indicate about children raised by gay or lesbian parents?

PROBES

1. If you feel accepting of gay and lesbian couples being parents, what do you believe are the two or three strongest arguments against or challenges to those family configurations? If you have trouble accepting gay and lesbian couples being parents, what do you believe are the two or three strongest arguments in support of those family configurations?
2. A great deal of contemporary evidence indicates that globalization is a fact of life in business, music, banking, and academia. How is globalization related to interracial families?
3. What makes stepparenting such a difficult role to perform satisfactorily?
4. Wood argues that since we already respect considerable diversity in parenting styles, it should be possible to extend this respect to nontraditional family forms. How do you respond to this argument?
5. How diverse is your experience of other families? What is one way you might be able to increase the diversity of this part of your communication experience?

REFERENCES

Barrett, M. B. (1989). *Invisible lives: The truth about millions of women-loving women.* New York: Morrow.

Card, C. (1995). *Lesbian choices.* New York: Columbia University Press.

Changes in families reach plateau, study says. (1996, November 27). *Raleigh News and Observer,* pp. 1A and 10A.

Coontz, S. (1992). *The way we never were: American families and the nostalgia trap.* New York: Basic Books.

Coontz, S. (1996, May–June). Where are the good old days? *Modern Maturity,* pp. 36–43.

Ferrante, J. (1995). *Sociology: A global perspective* (2nd ed.). Belmont, CA:
　　Wadsworth.

Goodman, E. (1997, January 17). Adopting across racial lines. *Raleigh News
　　and Observer*, p. 13A.

Gross, J. (1991, February 11). New challenge of youth growing up in a gay
　　home. *New York Times*, pp. 2B, 6B.

Guttmann, J. (1993). *Divorce in psychosocial perspective: Theory and research.*
　　Hillsdale, NJ: Lawrence Erlbaum.

Indulgent "boomers" bring an unraveling of society. (1993, October 17).
　　Raleigh News and Observer, p. 6E.

Marciano, T., & Sussman, M. B. (Eds.). (1991). *Wider families.* New York:
　　Haworth Press.

Patterson, C. (1992). Children of lesbian and gay parents. *Child Development,*
　　63, 83–96.

Salter, S. (1996, April 7). With this ring I thee wed, or whatever. *San Francisco
　　Examiner*, p. B11.

Singer, B. L., & Deschamps, D. (Eds.). (1994). *Gay and lesbian stats: A pocket,
　　guide of facts and figures.* New York: The New Press.

Weston, K. (1991). *Families we choose.* New York: Columbia University Press.

Wood, J. T., & Duck, S. (Eds.). (1995). *Understanding relationship processes, 6:
　　Understudied relationships: Off the beaten track.* Thousand Oaks, CA: Sage.

Separating Messages from Metamessages in Family Talk

Deborah Tannen

The writer of this selection is a Distinguished Professor of Linguistics at Georgetown University and the author of several best-selling books. Her work combines scholarship and readability, academic rigor and straightforward explanation. These pages come from the first chapter of a book that discusses many aspects of family communicating, including family secrets, "fighting for love," gender patterns in family talk, mothers and adult children, sibling communication, and communication among "in-laws and other strangers."

The most important point Tannen makes in this selection is the distinction between messages and metamessages. As she explains, "The *message* is the meaning of the words and sentences spoken, what anyone with a dictionary and a grammar book could figure out.... The *metamessage* is the meaning that is not said—at least not in so many words—but that we glean from every aspect of context: the way something is said, who is saying it, or the fact that it is said at all." Just about any two people in a situation can agree on the message. But metamessages are much more difficult to decipher and, much of the time, to interpret.

For example, in one short example of conversation that Tannen provides, a daughter asks her mother, "Am I too critical of people?" That's the message. But the mother hears the metamessage that her daughter is criticizing *her*. Metamessages are especially significant in family communication, because they often grow out of the history of the relationship, and they almost always have to do with the ways conversation partners are defining themselves and each other—for example, "I'm innocent," "Remember I'm in charge here," "You probably won't agree with this," or "If you love me, you'll say yes."

In family communication, metamessages are often negative. Speakers embed criticism in seemingly straightforward comments and questions like "Are you serving french bread?" which can mean, "Why didn't you bake dinner rolls?" Another example is "Please start your shower at seven, not seven-thirty," which can easily be interpreted as yet another complaint about the person's always being late. A paradox of family communicating is that we depend on those closest to us to see our best side, but because they are close, they also see our worst. And what they intend to be caring communication often gets expressed or interpreted as criticism.

One antidote to the problems that metamessages create is to *metacommunicate*—to talk about your ways of talking. If a family member expresses concern because he feels that his every suggestion or comment is heard as criticism, other family members are in a better position to work on this problem. He might learn to preface his comment with such metacommunicative statements as "I'm not criticizing the French bread" or, to be more direct, "I would really like it if you would make those delicious dinner rolls."

Tannen also clarifies how family communication is constantly challenged by the members' simultaneous but conflicting desires for connection and for control. Both are at the heart of a family. And ways of talking create both. "Younger siblings or children can make life wonderful or miserable for older siblings or parents by what they say—or refuse to say." If you keep in mind this simultaneous and conflicting desire, you can clarify comments and questions that might otherwise create problems. For example, "Don't start eating yet" can be heard as a control maneuver and as a connection move—and importantly, such a statement is usually both.

In a section called "Small Spark, Big Explosion," Tannen makes the point we've all experienced—what seem to be ridiculously trivial comments leading to major family disagreements. And she illustrates how metacommunication and the awareness of the twin motivations of connection and control can help.

There is more to family communication than Tannen explains here. But this reading can alert us to some troublesome elements of listening and talking with family members, and it suggests some ways to help family communication run more smoothly.

D o you really need another piece of cake?" Donna asks George.
"You bet I do," he replies, with that edge to his voice that implies, "If I wasn't sure I needed it before, I am darned sure now."

Donna feels hamstrung. She knows that George is going to say later that he wished he hadn't had that second piece of cake.

"Why are you always watching what I eat?" George asks.

"I was just watching out for you," Donna replies. "I only say it because I love you."

Elizabeth, in her late twenties, is happy to be making Thanksgiving dinner for her extended family in her own home. Her mother, who is visiting, is helping out in the kitchen. As Elizabeth prepares the stuffing for the turkey, her mother remarks, "Oh, you put onions in the stuffing?"

Feeling suddenly as if she were sixteen years old again, Elizabeth turns on her mother and says, "*I'm* making the stuffing, Mom. Why do you have to criticize everything I do?"

"I didn't criticize," her mother replies. "I just asked a question. What's got into you? I can't even open my mouth."

The allure of family—which is, at heart, the allure of love—is to have someone who knows you so well that you don't have to explain yourself. It is the promise of someone who cares enough about you to protect you against the world of strangers who do not wish you well. Yet, by an odd and cruel twist, it is the family itself that often causes pain. Those we love are looking at us so close-up that they see all our blemishes—see them as if through a magnifying glass. Family members have innumerable opportunities to witness our faults and feel they have a right to point them out. Often their intention is to help us improve. They feel, as Donna did, "I only say it because I love you."

Family members also have a long shared history, so everything we say in a conversation today echoes with meanings from the past. If you have a tendency to be late, your parent, sibling, or spouse may say, "We have to leave at eight"—and then add, "It's really important. Don't be late. Please start your shower at seven, not seven-thirty!" These extra injunctions are demeaning and interfering, but they are based on experience. At the same time, having experienced negative judgments in the past, we develop a sixth sense to sniff out criticism in almost anything a loved one says—even an innocent question about ingredients in the stuffing. That's why Elizabeth's mother ends up feeling as if she can't even open her mouth—and Elizabeth ends up feeling criticized.

When we are children our family constitutes the world. When we grow up family members—not only our spouses but also our grown-up children and adult sisters and brothers—keep this larger-than-life aura. We overreact to their judgments because it feels as if they were handed down by the Supreme Court and are unassailable assessments of our value as human beings. We bristle because these judgments seem unjust; or because we sense a kernel of truth we would rather not face; or because we fear that if someone who knows us so well judges us harshly we must really be guilty, so we risk losing not only that person's love but everyone else's, too. Along with this heavy load of implications comes a dark resentment that a loved one is judging us at all—and has such power to wound.

… No matter what age we've reached, no matter whether our parents are alive or dead, whether we were close to them or not, there are times when theirs are the eyes through which we view ourselves, theirs the standards against which we measure ourselves when we wonder whether we have measured up. The criticism of parents carries extra weight, even when children are adults.

I CARE, THEREFORE I CRITICIZE

Some family members feel they have not only a right but an obligation to tell you when they think you're doing something wrong. A woman from Thailand recalls that when she was in her late teens and early twenties, her mother frequently had talks with her in which she tried to set her daughter straight. "At the end of each lecture," the woman says, "my mother would always tell me, 'I have to complain about you because I am your mother and I love you. Nobody else will talk to you the way I do because they don't care.'"

It sometimes seems that family members operate under the tenet "I care, therefore I criticize." To the one who is being told to do things differently, what comes through loudest and clearest is the criticism. But the one offering suggestions and judgments is usually focused on the caring. A mother, for example, was expressing concern about her daughter's boyfriend: He didn't have a serious job, he didn't seem to want one, and she didn't think he was a good prospect for marriage. The daughter protested that her mother disapproved of everyone she dated. Her mother responded indignantly, "Would you rather I didn't care?"

As family members we wonder why our parents, children, siblings, and spouses are so critical of us. But as family members we also feel frustrated because comments we make in the spirit of caring are taken as criticizing.

Both sentiments are explained by the double meaning of giving advice: a loving sign of caring, a hurtful sign of criticizing. It's impossible to say which is right; both meanings are there. Sorting out the ambiguous meanings of caring and criticizing is difficult because language works on two levels: the message and the metamessage. Separating these levels—and being aware of both—is crucial to improving communication in the family.

THE INTIMATE CRITIC: WHEN METAMESSAGES HURT

Because those closest to us have front-row seats to view our faults, we quickly react—sometimes overreact—to any hint of criticism. The result can be downright comic, as in Phyllis Richman's novel *Who's Afraid of Virginia Ham?* One scene, a conversation between the narrator and her adult daughter, Lily, shows how criticism can be the metronome providing the beat for the family theme song. The dialogue goes like this:

LILY: Am I too critical of people?
MOTHER: What people? Me?

LILY: Mamma, don't be so self-centered.

MOTHER: Lily, don't be so critical.

LILY: I knew it. You do think I'm critical. Mamma, why do you always have to
find something wrong with me?

The mother then protests that it was Lily who asked if she was too critical, and
now she's criticizing her mother for answering. Lily responds, "I can't follow
this. Sometimes you're impossibly hard to talk to."

It turns out that Lily is upset because her boyfriend, Brian, told her she is too
critical of him. She made a great effort to stop criticizing, but now she's having
a hard time keeping her resolve. He gave her a sexy outfit for her birthday—it's
expensive and beautiful—but the generous gift made her angry because she
took it as criticism of the way she usually dresses.

In this brief exchange Richman captures the layers of meaning that can make
the most well-intentioned comment or action a source of conflict and hurt among
family members. Key to understanding why Lily finds the conversation so hard
to follow—and her mother so hard to talk to—is separating messages from
metamessages. The *message* is the meaning of the words and sentences spoken,
what anyone with a dictionary and a grammar book could figure out. Two
people in a conversation usually agree on what the message is. The *metamessage*
is meaning that is not said—at least not in so many words—but that we glean
from every aspect of context: the way something is said, who is saying it, or the
fact that it is said at all.

Because they do not reside in the words themselves, metamessages are
hard to deal with. Yet they are often the source of both comfort and hurt. The
message (as I've said) is the word meaning while the metamessage is the heart
meaning—the meaning that we react to most strongly, that triggers emotion.

When Lily asked her mother if she was too critical of people, the message
was a question about Lily's own personality. But her mother responded to what
she perceived as the metamessage: that Lily was feeling critical of *her*. This was
probably based on experience: Her daughter had been critical of her in the past.
If Lily had responded to the message alone, she would have answered, "No, not
you. I was thinking of Brian." But she, too, is reacting to a metamessage—that
her mother had made herself the point of a comment that was not about her
mother at all. Perhaps Lily's resentment was also triggered because her mother
still looms so large in her life.

The mixing up of message and metamessage also explains Lily's confused
response to the gift of sexy clothing from her boyfriend. The message is the gift.
But what made Lily angry was what she thought the gift implied: that Brian
finds the way she usually dresses not sexy enough—and unattractive. This implication is the metamessage, and it is what made Lily critical of the gift, of
Brian, and of herself. Metamessages speak louder than messages, so this is what
Lily reacted to most strongly.

It's impossible to know whether Brian intended this metamessage. It's possible that he wishes Lily would dress differently; it's also possible that he likes

the way she dresses just fine but simply thought this particular outfit would look good on her. That's what makes metamessages so difficult to pinpoint and talk about: They're implicit, not explicit.

When we talk about messages, we are talking about the meanings of words. But when we talk about metamessages, we are talking about relationships. And when family members react to each other's comments, it's metamessages they are usually responding to. Richman's dialogue is funny because it shows how we all get confused between messages and metamessages when we talk to those we are close to. But when it happens in the context of a relationship we care about, our reactions often lead to hurt rather than to humor.

… A key to improving relationships within the family is distinguishing the message from the metamessage, and being clear about which one you are reacting to. One way you can do this is *metacommunicating*—talking about communication.

"WHAT'S WRONG WITH FRENCH BREAD?" TRY METACOMMUNICATING

The movie *Divorce American Style* begins with Debbie Reynolds and Dick Van Dyke preparing for dinner guests—and arguing. She lodges a complaint: that all he does is criticize. He protests that he doesn't. She says she can't discuss it right then because she has to take the French bread out of the oven. He asks, "French bread?"

A simple question, right? Not even a question, just an observation. But on hearing it Debbie Reynolds turns on him, hands on hips, ready for battle: "What's wrong with French bread?" she asks, her voice full of challenge.

"Nothing," he says, all innocence. "It's just that I really like those little dinner rolls you usually make." This is like the bell that sets in motion a boxing match, which is stopped by another bell—the one at the front door announcing their guests have arrived.

Did he criticize or didn't he? On the message level, no. He simply asked a question to confirm what type of bread she was preparing. But on the metamessage level, yes. If he were satisfied with her choice of bread, he would not comment, except perhaps to compliment. Still, you might ask, So what? So what if he prefers the dinner rolls she usually makes to French bread? Why is it such a big deal? The big deal is explained by her original complaint: She feels that he is *always* criticizing—always telling her to do things differently than she chose to do them.

The big deal, in a larger sense, is a paradox of family: We depend on those closest to us to see our best side, and often they do. But because they are so close, they also see our worst side. You want the one you love to be an intimate ally who reassures you that you're doing things right, but sometimes you find instead an intimate critic who implies, time and again, that you're doing things wrong. It's the cumulative effect of minor, innocent suggestions that creates major problems. You will never work things out if you continue to talk about the message—about French bread versus dinner rolls—rather than the metamessage—the implication that your partner is dissatisfied with everything you do. (*Divorce American Style* was made in 1967; that it still rings true today is evidence of how common—and how recalcitrant—such conversational quagmires are.)

One way to approach a dilemma like this is to *metacommunicate*—to talk about ways of talking. He might *say* that he feels he can't open his mouth to make a suggestion or comment because she takes everything as criticism. She might *say* that she feels he's always dissatisfied with what she does, rather than turn on him in a challenging way. Once they both understand this dynamic, they will come up with their own ideas about how to address it. For example, he might decide to preface his question with a disclaimer: "I'm not criticizing the French bread." Or maybe he *does* want to make a request—a direct one—that she please make dinner rolls because he likes them. They might also set a limit on how many actions of hers he can question in a day. The important thing is to talk about the metamessage she is reacting to: that having too many of her actions questioned makes her feel that her partner in life has changed into an in-house inspection agent, on the lookout for wrong moves....

GIVE ME CONNECTION, GIVE ME CONTROL

There is another dimension to this argument—another aspect of communication that complicates everything we say to each other but that is especially powerful in families. That is our simultaneous but conflicting desires for connection and for control....

Both connection and control are at the heart of family. There is no relationship as close—and none as deeply hierarchical—as the relationship between parent and child, or between older and younger sibling. To understand what goes on when family members talk to each other, you have to understand how the forces of connection and control reflect both closeness and hierarchy in a family.

"He's like family," my mother says of someone she likes. Underlying this remark is the assumption that *family* connotes closeness, being connected to each other. We all seek connection: It makes us feel safe; it makes us feel loved. But being close means you care about what those you are close to think. Whatever you do has an impact on them, so you have to take their needs and preferences into account. This gives them power to control your actions, limiting your independence and making you feel hemmed in.

Parents and older siblings have power over children and younger siblings as a result of their age and their roles in the family. At the same time, *ways of talking create power*. Younger siblings or children can make life wonderful or miserable for older siblings or parents by what they say—or refuse to say. Some family members increase their chances of getting their way by frequently speaking up, or by speaking more loudly and more forcefully. Some increase their influence by holding their tongues, so others become more and more concerned about winning them over.

"Don't tell me what to do. Don't try to control me" are frequent protests within families. It is automatic for many of us to think in terms of power relations and to see others' incursions on our freedom as control maneuvers. We are less likely to think of them as connection maneuvers, but they often are that, too. At every moment we're struggling not only for control but also for love, approval, and involvement. What's tough is that the *same* actions and comments can be either control maneuvers or connection maneuvers—or, as in most cases, both at once.

CONTROL MANEUVER OR CONNECTION MANEUVER?

"Don't start eating yet," Louis says to Claudia as he walks out of the kitchen. "I'll be right there."

Famished, Claudia eyes the pizza before her. The aroma of tomato sauce and melted cheese is so sweet, her mouth thinks she has taken a bite. But Louis, always slow-moving, does not return, and the pizza is cooling. Claudia feels a bit like their dog Muffin when she was being trained: "Wait!" the instructor told Muffin, as the hungry dog poised pitifully beside her bowl of food. After pausing long enough to be convinced Muffin would wait forever, the trainer would say, "Okay!" Only then would Muffin fall into the food.

Was Louis intentionally taking his time in order to prove he could make Claudia wait no matter how hungry she was? Or was he just eager for them to sit down to dinner together? In other words, when he said, "Don't start eating yet," was it a control maneuver, to make her adjust to his pace and timing, or a connection maneuver, to preserve their evening ritual of sharing food? The answer is, it was both. Eating together is one of the most evocative rituals that bond individuals as a family. At the same time, the requirement that they sit down to dinner together gave Louis the power to make Claudia wait. So the need for connection entailed control, and controlling each other is in itself a kind of connection.

Control and connection are intertwined, often conflicting forces that thread through everything said in a family. These dual forces explain the double meaning of caring and criticizing. Giving advice, suggesting changes, and making observations are signs of caring when looked at through the lens of connection. But looked at through the lens of control, they are put-downs, interfering with our desire to manage our own lives and actions, telling us to do things differently than we choose to do them. That's why caring and criticizing are tied up like a knot.

The drives toward connection and toward control are the forces that underlie our reactions to metamessages. So the second step in improving communication in the family—after distinguishing between message and metamessage—is understanding the double meaning of control and connection. Once these multiple layers are sorted out and brought into focus, talking about ways of talking—metacommunicating—can help solve family problems rather than making them worse.

SMALL SPARK, BIG EXPLOSION

Given the intricacies of messages and metamessages, and of connection and control, the tiniest suggestion or correction can spark an explosion fueled by the stored energy of a history of criticism. One day, for example, Vivian was washing dishes. She tried to fix the drain cup in an open position so it would catch debris and still allow water to drain, but it kept falling into the closed position. With a mental shrug of her shoulders, she decided to leave it, since she didn't have many dishes to wash and the amount of water that would fill the sink wouldn't be that great. But a moment later her husband, Mel, happened by and glanced at the sink. "You should leave the drain open," he said, "so the water can drain."

This sounds innocent enough in the telling. Vivian could have said, "I tried, but it kept slipping in, so I figured it didn't matter that much." Or she could have said, "It's irritating to feel that you're looking over my shoulder all the time, telling me to do things differently from the way I'm doing them." This was, in fact, what she was feeling—and why she experienced, in reaction to Mel's suggestion, a small eruption of anger that she had to expend effort to suppress.

Vivian was surprised at what she did say. She made up a reason and implied she had acted on purpose: "I figured it would be easier to clean the strainer if I let it drain all at once." This thought *had* occurred to her when she decided not to struggle any longer to balance the drain cup in an open position, though it wasn't true that she did it on purpose for that reason. But by justifying her actions, Vivian gave Mel the opening to argue for his method, which he did.

"The whole sink gets dirty if you let it fill up with water," Mel said. Vivian decided to let it drop and remained silent. Had she spoken up, the result would probably have been an argument.

Throughout this interchange Vivian and Mel focused on the message: When you wash the dishes, should the drain cup be open or closed? Just laying out the dilemma in these terms shows how ridiculous it is to argue about. Wars are being fought; people are dying; accident or illness could throw this family into turmoil at any moment. The position of the drain cup in the sink is not a major factor in their lives. But the conversation wasn't really about the message—the drain cup—at least not for Vivian.

Mel probably thought he was just making a suggestion about the drain cup, and in the immediate context he was. But messages always bring metamessages in tow: In the context of the history of their relationship, Mel's comment was not so much about a drain cup as it was about Vivian's ability to do things right and Mel's role as judge of her actions.

This was clear to Vivian, which is why she bristled at his comment, but it was less clear to Mel. Our field of vision is different depending on whether we're criticizing or being criticized. The critic tends to focus on the message: "I just made a suggestion. Why are you so touchy?" The one who feels criticized, however, is responding to the metamessage, which is harder to explain. If Vivian had complained, "You're always telling me how to do things," Mel would surely have felt, and might well have said, "I can't even open my mouth."

At the same time, connection and control are in play. Mel's assumption that he and Vivian are on the same team makes him feel comfortable giving her pointers. Furthermore, if a problem develops with the sink's drainage, he's the one who will have to fix it. Their lives are intertwined; that's where the connection lies. But if Vivian feels she can't even wash dishes without Mel telling her to do it differently, then it seems to her that he is trying to control her. It's as if she has a boss to answer to in her own kitchen.

Vivian might explain her reaction in terms of metamessages. Understanding and respecting her perspective, Mel might decide to limit his suggestions and corrections. Or Vivian might decide that she is overinterpreting the metamessage and make an effort to focus more on the message, taking some of Mel's suggestions and ignoring others. Once they both understand the metamessages as well as the messages they are communicating and reacting to, they can metacommunicate: talk about each other's ways of talking and how they might talk differently to avoid hurt and recriminations. . . .

THE PARADOX OF FAMILY

When I was a child I walked to elementary school along Coney Island Avenue in Brooklyn, praying that if a war came I'd be home with my family when it happened. During my childhood in the 1950s my teachers periodically surprised the class by calling out, "Take cover!" At that cry we all ducked under our desks and curled up in the way we had been taught: elbows and knees tucked in, heads down, hands clasped over our necks. With the possibility of a nuclear attack made vivid by these exercises, I walked to school in dread—not of war but of the possibility that it might strike when I was away from my family.

But there is another side to family, the one I have been exploring in this chapter. My nephew Joshua Marx, at thirteen, pointed out this paradox: "If you live with someone for too long, you notice things about them," he said. "That's the reason you don't like your parents, your brother. There's a kid I know who said about his friend, 'Wouldn't it be cool if we were brothers?' and I said, 'Then you'd hate him.'"

We look to communication as a way through the minefield of this paradox. And often talking helps. But communication itself is a minefield because of the complex workings of message and metamessage. Distinguishing messages from metamessages, and taking into account the underlying needs for connection and control, provides a basis for metacommunicating. With these insights as foundation, we can delve further into the intricacies of family talk. Given our shared and individual histories of talk in relationships, and the enormous promise of love, understanding, and listening that family holds out, it's worth the struggle to continue juggling—and talking.

REVIEW QUESTIONS

1. What's a metamessage?
2. What's metacommunication? How can metacommunication help solve problems created by metamessages?
3. "When we talk about messages, we are talking about the _____ of _____ . But when we talk about metamessages, we are talking about _____ ."
4. Explain what it means for Tannen to say "ways of talking create power."

PROBES

1. Tannen explains that one huge value of being a member of a family is that someone always "has your back"—someone who knows you so well that you don't always have to explain yourself. Yet paradoxically, family members can and do often cause pain. How can your family communication help work with this paradox?
2. Although Tannen does not make this point, other family communication writers have noted that many, if not most, metamessages are nonverbal. They are communicated by tone of voice, timing, facial expression, or touch. Review how Tannen defines metamessages. Do you think they are primarily nonverbal, primarily verbal, or both?
3. Give an example from your own experience of a piece of family communication that includes both the desire for connection and the desire for control. Explain how it might be misunderstood.

————

Our Friends, Ourselves

Steve Duck

Steve Duck, an interpersonal communication professor at the University of Iowa, has written a number of books about how to understand and improve personal relationships. He begins this reading by explaining how "relationshipping" is a skill that each of us is taught—more or less effectively—and that we can learn to do better. He doesn't believe that building friendships is *nothing but* a mechanical process of applying certain skills, but he is convinced that skills are part of this process, just like they're part of the process of painting the *Mona Lisa*. As he suggests, the main advantage of treating relationshipping this way is that it can give you confidence in your ability to improve the ways you make and keep friends.

Duck talks about the general features that people expect friends to have and the friend-ship rules that people generally expect to be observed. Then he dedicates the bulk of this reading to a discussion of what he calls the "provisions" of friendships, that is, what they "provide" or do for us. He explains six reasons why we need friends: belonging and sense of reliable alliance; emotional integration and stability; opportunities for communication about ourselves; assistance and physical support; reassurance of our worth and value and opportunity to help others; and personality support.

His discussion helps me understand important features of the friendships I enjoy. For example, a family friend sometimes picks Lincoln up from school—a clear example of her giving us "assistance and physical support." During the times Kris and I are around this friend, our friendship with her gives both of us opportunities for communication about our-selves as we discuss how we share or differ with her priorities and values. Our friendship with her also gives us opportunities to help, which feel good because they provide reassur-ance of our worth and value. I can further sense some of what our friendship provides her, how we might change things to make our relationships even better. It's clear from just this brief example that the ideas in this reading can help you understand your friendships and even improve them.

• • •   "Relationshipping" is actually a very complicated and prolonged process with many pitfalls and challenges. Relationships do not just happen; they have to be made—made to start, made to work, made to develop, kept in good working order and preserved from going sour. To do all this we need to be active, thoughtful and skilled. To suggest that one simply starts a friendship, courtship, romantic partnership or marriage and "off it goes" is simple-minded. It is like believing that one can drive down the street merely by turning the ignition key, sitting back and letting the car take care of itself.

On the contrary, to develop a close personal relationship (with someone who was, after all, at first a stranger to us) careful adjustment and continuous moni-toring are required, along with several very sophisticated skills. Some of these are: assessing the other person's needs accurately; adopting appropriate styles of communication; indicating liking and interest by means of minute bodily activi-ties, like eye movements and postural shifts; finding out how to satisfy mutual personality needs; adjusting our behaviour to the relationship "tango" with the other person; selecting and revealing the right sorts of information or opinion in an inviting, encouraging way in the appropriate style and circumstances; build-ing up trust, making suitable demands; and building up commitment. In short, one must perform many complex behaviours. These necessitate proficiency in presenting ourselves efficiently, attending to the right features of the other per-son at the right time, and pacing the friendship properly.

Rather as learning to drive a car does, learning to steer a relationship in-volves a range of different abilities and these must be coordinated. Just as when, even after we have learned to drive, we need to concentrate harder each time we get into a new model, drive in an unfamiliar country or travel through unknown streets, so when entering unfamiliar relationships we have to relearn, modify or re-concentrate on the things that we do. All of us have pet stories about the strain, embarrassment and awkwardness that occurred in a first meeting with a new neighbour or a "friend of a friend": some clumsy silence, an ill-judged phrase, a difficult situation. It is in such situations that the skills of friendship are bared and tested to the limits, and where intuition is so clearly not enough.

Because it is a skill, relationshipping—even in these novel situations—is something that can be improved, refined, polished (even coached and practised) like any other skill, trained like any other, and made more fluent. It can be taken right up to the level of expertise where it all flows so skillfully and automatically that we can metaphorically focus away from the position of the relational brakes or accelerator and devise ways to drive (the relationship) courteously, skillfully, carefully, or enjoyably, so that the others in it can have a smoother ride!

Since we are not usually disposed to think of friendship and close relation-ships in this new kind of way, people sometimes feel irrationally resistant to doing so. "How can you represent a close personal relationship as a simple mechanical skill?" they ask. "Isn't it more mystical, more magical, more moral, less manipulative than you make it sound?" Such people seem happy to see relationships merely as pleasant, passive states: relationships just happen to us and we don't have to do anything particular—let alone do anything properly.

My answer is clear: I am not saying that friendship is all mechanical, any more than making a beautiful piece of furniture or playing an enchanting piano rhapsody or winning a sports championship is simply a mechanical exercise. But each of these activities has some mechanical elements that must be mastered before the higher-level aspects of skill can be attempted. You can't paint the *Mona Lisa* until you know something about painting figures, using a canvas, holding a brush, mixing paints, and so on. Furthermore, research backs this up. Scholars now regard "relationship work" as a process that continues right through the life of the relationship, with a constant and perpetual need for the right actions and activities at the right time to keep it all alive (for example, Baxter and Dindia, 1990)....

There are many advantages to this way of looking at relationships. It leads to a direct and useful form of practical advice for people who are unhappy with one or more of their relationships, or who are lonely or frustrated. It focuses on the things that one can do to improve relationships. It also runs counter to the common, but rather simplistic, assumption that relationships are based only on the matching of two individuals' personalities. This pervasive myth says that there is a Mr. or a Ms. Right for everyone or that friends can be defined in advance. If this were true, then we could all list the characteristics of our perfect partner—looking for a partner or being attractive to one would be like shopping for or making a checklist of things we liked. By contrast, the new approach adopted here will focus on performance, on behaviour, on the simple mistakes that people make at the various stages of friendship development.

Is it such a strange and unacceptable idea that people can be trained to adopt more satisfactory styles in relationships? Not really. Therapists, social workers, doctors and dentists nowadays receive instruction on the ways to establish rapport with patients and how to develop a reassuring and constructive "bedside manner." We know also that insurance or car sales staff are trained in how to relate to possible customers, that airline cabin crew and the police alike receive instruction on relating to the public, and that managers are now encouraged to spend time building up good personal relationships with employees. Such emphasis on skills takes us beyond the trite commonsense advice for lonely persons to "go out and meet more people." It focuses us on the fact that relationship problems derive in part, if not on the whole, from people "doing relationships" wrongly rather than simply not getting enough opportunities to be in them.

The evidence suggests that all of us are probably missing out and not maximizing our potential for relationships. American research (Reisman, 1981) shows that people claim to have about fifteen "friends" on average, although the numbers change with age (17-year olds claim about nineteen, while 28-year olds have only twelve; 45-year olds have acquired sixteen, while people in their sixties enjoy an average of fifteen). When people are asked to focus only on the relationships that are most satisfying, intimate and close, however, the number drops dramatically to around six (5.6 to be precise)....

THE NATURE OF FRIENDSHIP

A friend of mine once defined a "friend" as someone who, seeing you drunk and about to stand up on a table and sing, would quietly take you aside to prevent you[r] doing it. This definition actually embodies quite a few of the important aspects of friendship: caring, support, loyalty and putting high priority on the other person's interests. We shall see later in the [reading] why these are important. However, when researchers have taken a more precise look at the meaning of friendship, they have focused on two specific things: the general *features* that humans expect friends to have and the *rules* of friendship that humans expect to be observed.

There are certain features that we find particularly desirable in friends and certain characteristics that everyone believes that being a friend demands. K. E. Davis and Todd (1985) found that we regularly expect a friend to be someone who is honest and open, shows affection, tells us his or her secrets and problems, gives us help when we need it, trusts us and is also trustworthy, shares time and activities with us, treats us with respect and obviously values us, and is prepared to work through disagreements. These are things that people *expect* a friend to do for them and expect to do for the friend in return. These features constitute a quite complex picture. However, when one looks at the *rules* of friendship that people actually adhere to, then the strongest ones are rather simple (Argyle & Henderson, 1985): hold conversations; do not disclose confidences to other people; refrain from public criticism; repay debts and favours. These researchers also demonstrate that emotional support, trust and confiding are among the rules that distinguish high-quality friendships from less close ones.

In ideal circumstances, then, a friend is an open, affectionate, trusting, help-ful, reliable companion who respects our privacy, carries out interactions with all due respect to the norms of behaviour and ourselves, does not criticize us in public, and both does us favours and returns those that we do. In the real world, friendship is unlikely to live up to this ideal and we all have some range of toler-ance. However, it is a *voluntary* bond between two people and the above ideals can be seen as part of an unwritten contract between them, whose violation can become the grounds for the dissolution of the relationship (Wiseman, 1986).

Another important view of friendship has been offered by Wright (1984). He too stresses the "voluntary interdependence" of friendship: it is important that people freely choose to be intertwined together in the relationship. He also places emphasis on the "person qua person" element, or the extent to which we enjoy the person for his or her own sake, rather than for the things that he or she does for us. More recent research on this idea (Lea, 1989) finds indeed that "self-referent rewards," or the way the other person makes us feel about ourselves, are just as important as these other things. The way in which the relationship helps us to feel about ourselves, and its voluntary nature, are crucial to the nature of friendship. There are good reasons why this is the case.

THE "PROVISIONS" OF FRIENDSHIP

There are several ways to start answering the large question: "Why do we need friends?" We could just decide that everyone needs intimacy, possibly as a result of dependency needs formed in childhood, just as the psychoanalysts tell us. There may be something to this, as we shall see, but there is more to the need for friendships than a need for intimacy—and there is more to the need for intimacy than we may suppose, anyway. For instance, we might want to ask how inti-macy develops, how it is expressed, what else changes when it grows, and so on. We might also note the curious finding (Wheeler et al., 1983; R. B. Hays, 1989) that both men and women prefer intimate partners who are women! Indeed, Arkin and Grove (1990) show that shy men prefer to talk to women even when they are not in an intimate encounter. Not only this, but those people who talk to more women during the day have better health than those who talk to fewer women (Reis, 1986). Clearly the nature of needs for intimacy and friendship is rather intriguing and may be mediated by gender and other social contexts....

Belonging and a Sense of Reliable Alliance

In writing about loneliness and the "provisions" of relationships—what it is that they do for us—Weiss (1974) proposed that a major consequence of being in relationships is a sense of belonging and of "reliable alliance." He is touching on something very important about human experience. We all like to belong or to be accepted; even those who choose solitude want it to be the result of their own choice, not someone else's. No one wants to be an outcast, a pariah or a social reject. Indeed, the powerful effects of being made *not* to belong were long recognized as a severe punishment in Ancient Greece, where people could be ostracized and formally exiled or banished. The modern equivalent is found in the British trade union practice of "sending someone to Coventry" when they break the union rules: the person's workmates, colleagues, neighbours and associates are instructed to refuse to speak to the person about anything.... .

By contrast, relationships give us a sense of inclusion, a sense of being a member of a group—and, as the advertisers keep emphasizing, membership has its privileges. One of these privileges is "reliable alliance"; that is to say, the existence of a bond that can be trusted to be there for you when you need it. To [quote] a phrase, "A friend in need is a friend indeed"—or in our terms, the existence of a friendship creates a reliable alliance: one of the signs that someone is a true friend is when they help you in times of trouble.

Emotional Integration and Stability

Importantly, communities of friends provide a lot more than just a sense of belonging and reliable alliance (Weiss, 1974). They also provide necessary anchor points for opinions, beliefs, and emotional responses. Friends are benchmarks that tell us how we should react appropriately, and they correct or guide our attitudes and beliefs in both obvious and subtle ways. As an example, consider how different cultures express grief differently. In some countries it is acceptable to fall to the ground, cover oneself with dust and wail loudly; in other cultures it is completely unacceptable to show such emotion, and the emphasis falls on dignified public composure. Imagine the reaction in Britain if the Queen were to roll on the ground as a way of demonstrating grief, or in the United States if the President and First Lady attended military funerals with their faces blacked and tearing their clothes. Humans have available many different ways of demonstrating grief but they typically cope with this strong emotion in a way particularly acceptable to their own culture.

Like cultures, friends and intimates develop their own sets of shared concerns, common interests and collective problems, as well as shared meanings, common responses to life and communal emotions. Friends are often appreciated exactly because they share private understandings, private jokes, or private language. Indeed, communication researchers (Hopper et al., 1981; Bell et al., 1987) have shown that friends and lovers develop their own "personal idioms" or ways of talking about such things as feelings, sex and bodily parts, so that they are obscure to third parties. By using a phrase with secret meaning, couples can communicate in public places about things that are private. Good examples are to be found in newspaper columns on St. Valentine's Day. What, for example, are we to make of a message I found in the local student newspaper: "Dinglet, All my dinkery forever, Love, Scrunnett"? Presumably it meant something both to the person who placed the advertisement and to the person who was the intended object of it. Be alert: the couple who announce that "We are going home to make some pancakes" may in fact be planning to have a night of passion!

Such language is just a localized version of the fact that different cultures use different dialects or languages. Equally, friends have routines of behaving or beliefs that are not shared by everyone in a particular country or culture, but for that reason they are more important in daily life. Loneliness is, and isolation can be, wretched precisely because it deprives people of such psychological benchmarks and anchor points. Lonely people lose the stability provided by the chance to compare their own reactions to life with the reactions of other people that they know, like and respect....

So loneliness and isolation are disruptive because they deprive the person of the opportunity for comfortable comparison of opinions and attitudes with other people—of close friends. People who are parted from friends become anxious, disoriented, unhappy and even severely destabilized emotionally; they may become still more anxious just because they feel themselves behaving erratically, or they may experience unusual mood swings. They often report sudden changes of temper and loss of control, sometimes resulting in violent outbursts; but in any case their judgment becomes erratic and unreliable, and they may become unusually vigilant, suspicious or jumpy in the presence of other unfamiliar people.

Another function of friendship, then, a reason why we need friends, is to keep us emotionally stable and to help us see where we stand vis-à-vis other people and whether we are "doing OK." It is particularly noticeable in times of stress and crisis. I remember an occasion when all the lights [went out] in a student residence block where I was a [residence advisor]. The rational thing to do was to find a flashlight and await the restoration of power. What we all actually did was to stumble down to the common-room and chatter amongst ourselves: the need to compare our reactions to the emergency was so powerful and so universal that even the warden, a medical researcher who had doctoral degrees from both Oxford and Cambridge, did the same. Such behaviour often happens after any kind of stress or crisis, from the crowd of people who gather to swap stories after a fire or a car accident, to the nervous chatter that schoolchildren perform when the doctor comes to inject them against measles or TB....

Opportunities for Communication about Ourselves

There is a third reason why we need friends (Weiss, 1974). A centrally important need is for communication. This particular wheel was strikingly reinvented by the Quaker prison reformers several generations ago, who attempted to cut down communication between criminals in prison in order to stop them [from] educating one another about ways of committing crime. Accordingly, one of their proposals was that prisoners should be isolated from one another. What occurred was very instructive: the prisoners spent much of their time tapping out coded messages on walls and pipes, devising means of passing information to one another, and working out other clever ways of communicating. Evidently, people who are involuntarily isolated feel a need to communicate. One additional function that healthy friendships provide, then, is a place for such communication to occur—communication about anything, not just important events but also trivial stuff as well as personal, intimate details about oneself. In a study at the University of Iowa, I and my students (S. W. Duck et al., 1991) have found that most conversations with friends last very short periods of time (about three minutes on average) and deal with trivialities. They are nonetheless rated as extremely significant. They revitalize the relationship, reaffirm it and celebrate its existence, through the medium of conversation.

A mild form of this overwhelming need to communicate is to be found on railway trains, planes and long-distance buses. Here many lonely people strike up conversations—but usually monologues—which allow them to communicate to someone or to tell someone about themselves and their opinions. A striking thing about this is the intimacy of the stories that are often told. Perfect strangers can often be regaled with the life history, family details, and personal opinions of someone they have not seen before and will probably never see again. Indeed, that is probably a key part of it, for the listener who will not be seen again cannot divulge the "confession" to friends or colleagues and so damage the confessor's reputation. (In cases where it is known that the listener and confessor will meet again, as in the case of doctors and patients, priests and parishioners, counsellors and clients, or lawyers and consultants, the listeners are bound by strict professional ethical codes not to reveal what they have been told. On the train, the "ethics" are simply left to statistical chance, and the extreme improbability of the two strangers meeting one another's friends is a comfort in itself.) . . .

Provision of Assistance and Physical Support

Another "provision" of relationships is simply that they offer us support, whether physical, psychological or emotional (Hobfoll and Stokes, 1988). This section focuses on physical support and assistance, which are often as significant to us as is any other sort of support.

For example, when people lose a friend or a spouse through bereavement, they report a lack of support—they are cut off from someone who has helped them to cope with life and to adjust to its problems, tasks, and changing uncertainties. This can take one of two forms: physical support (such as help with day-to-day tasks) and psychological support (such as when someone shows that we are appreciated, or lets us know that our opinions are valued). Human beings need both of these types of support, but the types are significantly different.

This is very simply illustrated. When your friend gives you a birthday present you are supposed to accept it in a way that indicates your own unworthiness to receive it and also the kindness of the friend ("Oh you shouldn't have bothered. It really is very good of you"). In short, you repay your friend by accepting the gift as a token of friendship and by praising the friend. You "exchange" the gift for love and respect, as it were. Imagine what would happen if you repaid by giving the friend the exact value of the gift in money. The friend would certainly be insulted by the ineptness: you would have altered the nature of the social exchange and also, in so doing, the nature of the relationship, by focusing on money rather than the gift as a symbol for friendship. Indeed, Cheal (1986) has shown that gift-giving as a one-way donation is rare and gift *reciprocity* is the norm, indicating that it serves an important relational function. Gift exchange serves the symbolic function of cementing and celebrating the relationship.

There are other clear examples of this point—that the nature of the exchange or support helps to define the degree and type of relationship. For instance, many elderly people get resentful of the fact that they gradually become more and more physically dependent on other people for help in conducting the daily business of their lives. The elderly cannot reach things so easily, cannot look after themselves and are more dependent physically, while at the same time they are less able to repay their friends by doing services in return. This, then, is one reason why many people dislike or feel uneasy with old age: they resent the feeling of helpless dependency coupled with the feeling of perpetual indebtedness that can never be paid off. For many elderly people, then, the mending of a piece of furniture, the making of a fruit pie, or the knitting of a sweater can be traded off against dependency: elderly people *need to be allowed* to do things for other people as a way of demonstrating to themselves and to everyone else that they are valuable to others and can still make useful contributions to the world....

Reassurance of Our Worth and Value, and Opportunity to Help Others

People who are lonely characteristically say that no one cares about them, that they are useless, uninteresting, of low value and good for nothing. Studies of the conversation of severely depressed people invariably reveal indications that they have lost their self-respect or self-esteem (Gotlib and Hooley, 1988). In other words, they have come to see themselves as valueless, worthless and insignificant, often because that is how they feel that everyone else sees them. Furthermore, analysis of suicide notes shows that many suicide attempts are carried out as a way of forcing some particular friend to re-evaluate the person, or to shock the friend into realizing just how much he or she really does esteem the person making the attempt. For this reason, Alfred Adler (1929) has claimed, with characteristic insight, that every suicide is always a reproach or a revenge.

One reason, then, that we appreciate friends is because of their contribution to our self-evaluation and self-esteem. Friends can do this both directly and indirectly: they may compliment us or tell us about other people's good opinions of us. Dale Carnegie's multimillion-seller book on *How to Win Friends and Influence People* stressed the positive consequences of doing this. Friends can also increase our self-esteem in other ways: by attending to what we do, listening, asking our advice, and generally acting in ways that indicate the value that they place on our opinions. However, there are less obvious and more indirect ways in which they can communicate this estimation of our value. For one thing, the fact that they choose to spend time with us rather than with someone else must show that they value our company more than the alternatives.

There is a subtler version of these points too. Just as we look to friends to provide us with all of these things, so we can get from friendship one other key benefit. Because friends trust us and depend on us, they give us the chance to help them. That gives us the opportunity to take responsibility for them, to see ourselves helping them with their lives, to give them our measured advice and consequently to feel good. Friends provide us with these possibilities of taking responsibility and nurturing other people.

Undoubtedly, these things are important in the conduct of relationships and in making them satisfactory for both partners, and it is critical that we learn to evince them effectively. However, one important point to note is that those people who are poor at doing this (e.g., people who are poor at indicating interest, or who seem to have little time for other people, or never let them help or let them give advice) will find that other people are unattracted to relationships with them. All people need indications of their estimability and need chances to nurture just as we do, and if we do not adequately provide such signs then these people will reject us—just as we would do in their position....

Personality Support

Yet there is something even more fundamental to close relationships than this. Recent research indicates that each feature mentioned above—sense of community, emotional stability, communication, provision of help, maintenance of self-esteem—in its own way serves to support and integrate the person's personality (S. W. Duck and Lea, 1982). Each of us is characterized by many thoughts, doubts, beliefs, attitudes, questions, hopes, expectations and opinions about recurrent patterns in life. Our personalities are composed not only of our behavioural style (for example, our introversion or extraversion) but also of our thoughts, doubts and beliefs. It is a place full of symbols, a space where we are ourselves, a system of interlocking thoughts, experiences, interpretations, expectancies and personal meanings. Our personality would be useless to us if all of these opinions and meanings were not, by and large, supported. We would simply stop behaving if we had no trust in our thoughts or beliefs about why we should behave or how we should behave, just as we stop doing other things that we are convinced are wrong. Some schizophrenics and depressives actually do stop behaving when their thought-world falls apart: they just sit and stare.

Each of us needs to be assured regularly that our thought-worlds or symbolic spaces are sound and reliable. A friend can help us to see that we are wrong and how we can change, or that we are right about some part of our thinking. We may have vigorous discussions about different attitudes that we hold—but our friends are likely to be very similar to us in many of our attitudes and interests, so that these discussions are more probably supportive than destructive. However, we all know the anger and pain that follow a really serious disagreement with a close friend—much more unpleasant than a disagreement with an enemy. What we should deduce from all this is that we seek out as friends those people who help to support our thought-world-personality, and we feel chastened, sapped or undermined when they do not provide this support.

What sort of person best gives us the kind of personality support that I have described here? In the first instance, it is provided by people who share our way of thinking. The more of these "thought-ways" that we share with someone, the easier it is to communicate with that person: we can assume that our words and presumptions will be understood more easily by someone who is "our type" than by someone who is not—we shall not have the repetitious discomfort of perpetually explaining ourselves, our meanings and our jokes.

Yet there is much more to it than this, although it has taken researchers a long time to sort out the confusing detail of the picture. For one thing, the type of similarity that we need to share with someone in order to communicate effectively depends on the stage that the relationship has reached. At early stages it is quite enough that acquaintances are broadly similar, but at later stages the similarity must be more intricate, precise, refined, and detailed. One of the skills of friend-making is to know what sorts of similarity to look for at which times as the relationship proceeds. General similarity of attitudes is fine at the early to middle/stages, but matters much less later if the partners do not work at discovering similarities at the deeper level of the ways in which they view other people and understand their characters. Very close friends must share the same specific sorts of framework for understanding the actions, dispositions and characters of other people in general, and in specific instances of mutual acquaintance. Such similarity is rare and prized. For that reason, if for no other, it is painful and extremely significant to lose the persons who offer it.

Loss or absence of particular intimates or friends deprives us of some measure of support for our personality, and it is essential to our psychological health that we have the skill to avoid this. Losing an intimate partner or friend not only makes us die a little, it leaves floating in the air those bits of our personality that the person used to support, and can make people fall apart psychologically. Of course, this will depend on how much our personality has been supported by that partner, which particular parts are involved, how readily these parts are supported by others, how much time we have had to anticipate and adjust to the loss, and so on. But essentially the loss or absence of friends and of close, satisfying relationships does not merely cause anxiety, grief or depression; it can cause other, more severe, forms of psychological disintegration or deterioration, often with the physical and mental side-effects noted earlier. Many of the well-known psychosomatic illnesses and hysterical states are actually caused by relationship problems, although this has not been realized by as many doctors as one might expect (see Lynch, 1977). For too long the accepted medical folklore has assumed that the person's inner mental state is a given, and that it causes psychosomatic effects when it gets out of balance. It is now quite clear that the surest way to upset people's mental balance is to disturb their close relationships (Gerstein and Tesser, 1987). We need friends to keep us healthy both physically and mentally: therefore it is doubly important that we perfect the ways of gaining and keeping friends. An important first step is to recognize the different needs that each relationship can fulfill for us, and the means by which this can be achieved.

REVIEW QUESTIONS

1. Define *relationshipping*.
2. How many "satisfying, intimate, and close" relationships does the research say that people of your age typically have?
3. Duck lists four main rules that characterize friendship, according to the research. What are they?
4. Fill in the blank, explain, and tell whether you agree or disagree, and why: "Both men and women prefer intimate partners who are _____ ."
5. What does it mean to have "a sense of reliable alliance"?
6. Paraphrase and give an example from your own experience of the reality-checking function of friendships.
7. Explain what Duck means when he says that sometimes elderly people need to be allowed to do things for others.
8. According to Duck, what is the relationship between friendship networks and personal mental health? Do you agree or disagree with this claim?

PROBES

1. In what ways does Duck's example of learning to drive a car fit your experience of learning how to "do" relationships? In what ways does it not fit?
2. Test Duck's claim about the average number of "friends" reported by people of your age and the average number of "satisfying, intimate, and close" relationships. Do you find any differences among the people you know?
3. What is the function in intimate relationships of private language and personal idioms? What does the presence of these private modes of expression suggest about the similarities between friendships and cultures?
4. What explanation does Duck give for the "stranger on the train (bus, plane)" phenomenon, where your seatmate, whom you don't know, tells you intimate details of his or her life? Why does this happen?
5. How do you respond to Duck's claim that, in some important ways, birthdays are times when many people give *gifts in exchange for* respect and love?
6. Paraphrase and respond to Duck's explanation of the role of similarities in friendship relationships.

REFERENCES

Adler, A. (1929). *What Your Life Should Mean to You*. New York: Bantam.
Argyle, M., & Henderson, M. (1985). *The Anatomy of Relationships*. London: Methuen.
Arkin, R., & Grove, T. (1990). Shyness, sociability and patterns of everyday affiliation. *Journal of Social and Personal Relationships* (7), 273–81.
Baxter, L. A., & Dindia, K. (1990). Marital partners' perceptions of marital maintenance strategies. *Journal of Social and Personal Relationships* (7), 187–208.

Bell, R. A., Buerkel-Rothfuss, N., & Gore, K. (1987). "Did you bring the yarmulke for the cabbage patch kid?": The idiomatic communication of young lovers. *Human Communication Research* (14), 47–67.

Cheal, D. J. (1986). The social dimensions of gift behaviour. *Journal of Social and Personal Relationships* (3), 423–39.

Davis, K. E., & Todd, M. (1985). Assessing friendship: Prototypes, paradigm cases, and relationship description, in S. W. Duck & D. Perlman (eds.), *Understanding Personal Relationships*. London: Sage.

Duck, W., & Lea, M. (1982). Breakdown of relationships as a threat to personal identity, in G. Breakwell (ed.), *Threatened Identities*. Chichester: Wiley.

Duck, S. W., Rutt, D. J., Hurst, M., & Strejc, H. (1991). Some evident truths about communication in everyday relationships: All communication is not created equal. *Human Communication Research* (18), 114–29.

Gerstein, I. H., & Tesser, A. (1987). Antecedents and responses associated with loneliness. *Journal of Social and Personal Relationships* (4), 329–63.

Gotlib, I. H., & Hooley, J. M. (1988). Depression and marital distress: Current and future directions, in S. W. Duck (ed.) with D. F. Hay, S. E. Hobfoll, W. Ickes, & B. Montgomery, *Handbook of Personal Relationships*. Chichester: Wiley.

Hays, R. B. (1989). The day-to-day functioning of close versus casual friendship. *Journal of Social and Personal Relationships* (1), 75–98.

Hobfoll, S. E., & Stokes, J. P. (1988). The process and mechanics of social support, in S. W. Duck (ed.) with D. F. Hay, S. E. Hobfoll, W. Ickes, & B. Montgomery, *Handbook of Personal Relationships*. Chichester: Wiley.

Hopper, R., Knapp, M. L., & Scott, L. (1981). Couples' personal idioms: Exploring intimate talk. *Journal of Communication* (31), 23–33.

Lea, M. (1989). Factors underlying friendship: An analysis of responses on the acquaintance description form in relation to Wright's friendship model. *Journal of Social and Personal Relationships* (6), 275–92.

Lynch, J. J. (1977). *The Broken Heart: The Medical Consequences of Loneliness*. New York: Basic Books.

Reis, H. T. (1986). Gender effects in social participation: Intimacy, loneliness, and the conduct of social interaction, in R. Gilmour & S. W. Duck (eds.), *The Emerging Field of Personal Relationships*. Hillsdale, NJ: Lawrence Erlbaum.

Reisman, J. (1981). Adult friendships, in S. W. Duck & R. Gilmour (eds.), *Personal Relationships 2: Developing Personal Relationships*. London: Academic Press.

Weiss, R. S. (1974). The provisions of social relationships, in Z. Rubin (ed.), *Doing unto Others*. Englewood Cliffs, NJ: Prentice-Hall.

Wheeler, L., Reis, H. T., & Nezelek, J. (1983). Loneliness, social interaction and sex roles. *Journal of Personality and Social Psychology* (35), 742–54.

Wiseman, J. P. (1986). Friendship: Bonds and binds in a voluntary relationship. *Journal of Social and Personal Relationships* (3), 191–211.

Wright, P. H. (1984). Self referent motivation and the intrinsic quality of friendship. *Journal of Social and Personal Relationships* (1), 114–30.

Mother-Daughter E-Mail and IM Communication

Deborah Tannen

This description of online communicating between mothers and daughters is from a book written by the best-selling author and Distinguished University Professor of Linguistics at Georgetown University. The descriptions and conclusions are based on her analysis of tape-recorded conversations of U.S. mother-daughter dyads from a variety of age and ethnic groups.

This research has led Tannen to describe family communication generally as a dance between the two motives or purposes of *connection* and *control*—a point she made in the "messages and metamessages" reading earlier in this chapter. In this reading, Tannen clarifies how "electronic communication transforms the balance of connection and control." In face-to-face communicating, both parties immediately experience elements of connection and control. A telephone call makes a connection, but "it is also an intrusion, and the control is lopsided." On the other hand, e-mail balances control more evenly; because one person sends a message but it doesn't intrude on the other person's life until she retrieves it. And instant messaging (IM) is a hybrid; the receiver can disengage, but not without violating the sender's expectations. "Daughters and mothers can use all these communication technologies to create and negotiate the interplay of connection and control that constitutes their relationship."

In many cases, when mothers and daughters are separated by the daughter's college attendance, for example, their relationship blossoms via telephone calls, e-mail, and IM. I have watched this phenomenon occur with Marcia, my older daughter, and my granddaughter Jamie, after Marcia moved 2000 miles away from Jamie to complete her education degree at the college where I work. This was the first time this mother-daughter pair was geographically separated, and I've been surprised to discover that they talk on the telephone at least twice a day and IM frequently. Electronic media are obviously facilitating the continuation and blossoming of the relationship that this mother and daughter enjoyed when they were living in the same house.

Tannen's research shows that e-mail can create closeness by reinforcing similarities between mother and daughter. Earlier generations used letters for some of these same purposes. It also illustrates how electronic media provide even access to all children. Quiet siblings may lose out in a face-to-face group encounter, but e-mail and IM equalize the opportunities for contact. In addition, the connection/control dynamic can be affected by the fact that daughters are usually more familiar with e-mail and IM communicating than their mothers are. This gives them advantages in the exchanges. The resulting power equalization can contribute to the resolution of conflicts.

In the final section of the reading, Tannen mentions some potential liabilities of e-mail and IM communicating. The relative lack of nonverbal cues increases the risk of misunderstanding—which is why many e-mails contain emoticons. Feedback delay is another liability, as is the speed of the media. As Tannen notes, "Once you press SEND, you can't change your mind, as you could decide not to mail a letter."

Even if you're not a mother or a daughter, you can learn from these pages to notice how your electronic communicating affects your relationships.

E ven two seemingly similar modes of communication can have vastly different capabilities and resulting implications for relationships. I'll focus on two types of electronic communication, e-mail and Instant Messaging (IM), because these are the ones most often heard about when I talked to women about communication with their mothers and daughters, though many also mentioned other media, such as cellphones and text messages that appear on handheld devices such as BlackBerries, Treos, or cellphones.

… Electronic communication transforms the balance of connection and control. A telephone call makes a connection, but it is also an intrusion, and the control is lopsided. The caller initiates contact; the person called can answer the phone or not, but in either case, she is reacting. E-mail apportions control more evenly: One person initiates a message, but it does not intrude into the other person's life until the recipient decides to get it. The words we use to talk about e-mail capture this difference. A person to whom an e-mail is sent does not *receive* it—a passive act—but rather *retrieves* it, an act of volition that she controls. Even if her computer announces intrusively "you've got mail" when a message arrives, it does so only because she set it to function in this way; the volition still resides with her.

We don't give up familiar means of communicating when we discover new ones; we choose among all the available media to suit the context and what we want to say. Imagine a daughter who uses her cellphone to call her mother while traveling to work, leaves a spoken message on her voice mail, sends an e-mail when she gets to work, and in the evening either talks to her mother on the telephone or exchanges real-time written messages using IM. She could write and send a letter on paper, but she probably wouldn't. One young woman, in explaining—on e-mail—why she uses that medium to communicate with her mother, ended by saying, "I suppose these things could have been done through snail mail also, but it would be ridiculous to write her paper letters!" The very term "snail mail," which was coined and has meaning in contrast to e-mail, makes clear why paper letters strike this young woman as ridiculous: They move too slowly. Daughters and mothers can use all these communication technologies to create and negotiate the interplay of connection and control that constitutes their relationship.

Let's look at how some actual daughters and mothers do this with e-mail and IM.

I LOVE YOU—SEND

Though many mothers and daughters who have excellent relationships use only the telephone to communicate, and others use e-mail infrequently, I encountered many daughters and mothers who send each other e-mails daily, or many times a day, just keeping in touch, letting the other know what she is up to. For some this provides another medium for exchanging the same information they could exchange in person or over the phone. But for others it is a type of communication—and a type of closeness—that did not exist before e-mail made it possible.

A woman in her fifties, replying to my (e-mailed) query, wrote,

> The relationship with my daughter has blossomed like I never thought possible. When she was in high school she hardly talked to me. When she went off to college the change started. She would call at least twice a day. Now, it's constant e-mails about sweet little nothings.... and I don't disrupt the baby's nap, or when she's busy.

I particularly like this woman's choice of the verb "blossom" to describe how her relationship with her daughter developed thanks to e-mail. The change in communication with her daughter began when the girl went away to college, and the physical distance between them made it necessary to create the connection that was a given when they lived in the same house. Grandchildren introduce new possibilities for connection and caring (though also for criticism), as the daughter and mother (now grandmother) share love and concern for the children. E-mail becomes fertile earth in which this seed of shared love and concern can grow and blossom, because it apportions control evenly: the mother is free to send messages as often as she likes because her daughter can control when she retrieves them, and the daughter, too, can send messages—and baby pictures—throughout the day, knowing that her mother will retrieve them when it's convenient for her. (No doubt the frequency with which this daughter and mother exchange e-mails is increased because neither works outside her home.)

The way e-mail provides connection between a college student and her mother was explained to me by Julie Dougherty, a Georgetown student. Answering my question about the role that electronic communication plays between mothers and daughter, Julie wrote, "My mom sends me an email every day while I'm at school, just to say hi. She knows that I love getting emails and getting an email from her guarantees that I'll always have at least one real letter in my inbox." By "real letter," Julie clearly means a communication that conveys personal information, providing the connection side of the mother-daughter relationship that has to be reinforced when the daughter attends college in a distant city. Julie's description shows how e-mail can be an electronic extension of the "How was your day?" intimacy that many women cherish:

> My mom and I are very close and talking about my day with her, and vice versa, has always been important. If we are unable to talk much during the day (which is the case when I'm at school or work), email is great because I can just

write out some insignificant part of my day before I forget to tell her about it and she'll do the same. We both have a general idea about what's going on.... We both love it for quick little notes, jokes, and random things we feel the other needs to know about.

Every reminder that the other is interested in the insignificant details of her life lets Julie and her mother know that they are not alone as each goes through her day, even though they are in different cities and inhabiting very different lives.

E-mail can also create closeness between mother and daughter by reinforcing the impression of their similarity, another element that many women mention when they define closeness. Julie wrote, "Email made me realize how similar my mom and I are. We write in the same way and our sense of humor is identical. Our jokes are obvious to the two of us and I can always tell when she's writing something in jest." The reminder that they share a sense of humor is particularly eloquent given the cryptic nature of e-mail communication, so the metamessage of intimacy and rapport that is created when a listener gets a joke is enhanced when the joke was conveyed by e-mail. This may be, moreover, why such a large percentage of e-mail that people send around consists of jokes. Several women I spoke to told me that most of their communication with their mothers takes place on the phone but that they use e-mail to send each other jokes.

There is another way that e-mail is particularly suited to enhance connection to their mothers when daughters are away at college, and that is its one-way nature. Earlier generations discovered this advantage in writing letters. One woman recalls that she became closer to her mother when she went to college. This might seem surprising; how can going farther away make you closer? The answer was, letters. By exchanging weekly letters, each got to know the other in ways she had not, perhaps could not, when they communicated face-to-face. The one-way nature of letters was crucial. In a letter, each could say at length what was on her mind, and the other had to "listen." How many mothers in their busy lives regularly schedule time just to sit and listen to their daughters tell, at length and at leisure, what's happening in their lives? Writing letters allowed each to show herself and view the other in new ways. The same function can be served now by e-mail.

Another advantage of e-mail is that it gives every child in a family equal access, whereas with face-to-face communication, more talkative children tend to fill the conversational space before the quieter ones can get the floor. Providing a way into the conversation can be especially precious to daughters who were previously overshadowed by brothers. (One woman commented that when her son went off to college, she discovered her daughter could talk.)

With e-mail, mothers and daughters can extend their rapport long after the daughter graduates from college. Perhaps the most dramatic example of this I encountered in interviewing women for this book was the experience of a deaf woman, Amanda, whose mother is hearing. At the time that Amanda was born and grew up, experts in education for the deaf believed that deaf children could and should be taught to read lips and speak. (It has since become clear that this is impossible for all but a very few deaf children.) These experts advised parents not to learn sign language, the medium that would make it possible for them to communicate with their deaf children, because, the experts cautioned, that would impede the children's learning to talk. Amanda's mother followed this advice. As a result, Amanda had been unable to communicate with her mother throughout her childhood. When she went to college, she began exchanging letters with her mother. Only then did she get to know her, and feel close to her. Now, like many other mothers and daughters, they continue this exchange through e-mail. It gives them, literally, a language in which to communicate....

BRB: A BRIDGE OVER THE GENERATION GAP

When daughters in college communicate with their mothers through e-mail and IM, the daughters are almost always more comfortable with and skilled in using these new media than their mothers are. Indeed, it's often the daughter who, like Julie Dougherty in the earlier example, taught her mother to use them. Electronic communication is an integral part of most young people's lives, and has been as far back as they can remember; their parents began using it, if they use it at all, in middle age, when it's harder to learn new things and their habits for managing relationships are already set. Exchanging messages by e-mail and IM is in itself a way of bridging the divide between generations, but the difference in familiarity with the media constitutes a reminder of the generations' differing perspectives and life experience.

Just as a mother has to teach a small child the proper way of answering the phone, young adult children need to teach their parents the conventions of IM. So when Kathryn typed the IM message "oh mom ... brb," her mother had to ask, "brb what does that mean?" Nine minutes later (IM messages are preceded by the exact time at which they were sent) Kathryn wrote, "ok I'm back ... see that didn't even take ten minutes. brb = be right back."

Since speed and casualness are the defining characteristics of IM, the young people for whom it is a second language have developed standardized acronyms; others include LOL for "laugh out loud," TTYL for "talk to you later," ic for "I see," and j/k for "just kidding." (Novelist and writing teacher Robert Bausch calls this style of writing "license-plate sentences." He doesn't like it.) The fact that Kathryn has to teach her mother these conventions in itself equalizes the balance of power between them. This is one arena in which the mother's greater age and life experience do not give her more expertise as compared to her daughter; on the contrary, they give her less.

It is not merely the conventions of IM and e-mail that separate the generations. The different technologies represent different worlds that are referenced by the conventions, and each world comes with contrasting assumptions about what's appropriate once the references are understood. One young woman, Alexandra, was caught in a misunderstanding that arose out of such differences.

Many people attach a "signature" to their e-mails, a message or quotation that automatically gets appended to every message they send. Alexandra's mother was upset by her daughter's signature, which read, "When you're there I sleep lengthwise, when you're gone I sleep diagonal across the bed." She sent her daughter an e-mail telling her to change the signature because she regarded it as improper. Alexandra switched media to resolve this conflict. She used IM to ask her mother what the problem was. After a few exchanges, it became clear that her mother thought Alexandra had composed the signature lines herself, announcing to the world details of a personal relationship. In fact the lines are the lyrics—and the only lyrics—to a song by the group called Phish; the song consists of repeating these lines over and over. Alexandra used them in her signature simply to reference the song that she and her friends like. The source of the lines and the reason for attaching them to her signature would be obvious to Alexandra's friends but was opaque to her mother. Alexandra thought that once she had cleared up the misunderstanding, the signature could stay. But even though her mother was relieved to learn the lines were song lyrics, she still considered them inappropriate, since others could make the same mistake she had. Alexandra heeded her mother's caution and changed her signature.

The conflict between Alexandra and her mother arose from and was settled through electronic communication. Sometimes e-mail can be a useful tool to settle disagreements regardless of the medium in which they occurred. ... [One] woman, Leah, repeatedly asked her daughter Erin to help her mother out by accompanying her grandmother, Leah's mother, from Florida to a family reunion in Milwaukee. Although Leah had said explicitly, "I don't want to make you feel guilty; I'm just asking," Erin had protested, "Obviously I do feel guilty when you keep asking me." E-mail played a role in resolving this conflict. Leah sent Erin an e-mail message in which she apologized, admitting she had been wrong to ask three times (though also mentioning that she had forgotten how many times she'd asked, and that maybe her forgetting was related to her own aging—the same reason she was reluctant to fly between Milwaukee and Florida four times in three days). In response, Erin sent a message thanking her mother for apologizing and not being defensive, though she lamented, with irony, "Now I can't chew you out." Leah, sufficiently chastened, replied, "Sure, chew me out if you want to." The episode ended with Erin's generous reply, "Now I don't want to."

Leah and Erin could have had this interchange either face-to-face or on the telephone, but it seems not entirely by chance that the resolution took place in an e-mail exchange. I suspect it was easier for Leah to apologize, admit fault, and invite a "chewing out" when she was not directly facing her daughter or hearing her voice in real time on the phone. For one thing, many people are likely to snap and get defensive when first accused. They are more likely to see the other's point of view after recovering from the initial surprise and hurt. And many also find it hard to apologize, because admitting they were at fault feels like a public humiliation; e-mail reduces that aspect of the apology: When you are sitting alone at your computer, the embarrassment of apologizing feels less public. Moreover, since e-mail is one-way communication, the writer has time to organize her thoughts and present them in a way that she feels fully expresses—and therefore helps justify—her point of view.

In all these examples, mothers and daughters used new electronic media to communicate. There are many, though, who communicate mostly, or exclusively, by an older technology: the telephone. Some mothers and daughters prefer to talk by phone instead of, or in addition to, online, but in some cases one or the other (usually the parent) prefers the phone, or simply assumes that this is the main or even the only appropriate means of communication. Differing habits regarding use of these media can result in cross-cultural (in the sense of cross-generational) misunderstanding....

INTO THE FUTURE

Every medium offers unique opportunities for human communication and relationships, as well as unique risks. New technologies entail new ways of staying in touch, reinforcing closeness, and resolving conflicts. But they also provide new ways of expressing anger, hurting feelings, and risking misunderstandings. Electronic media such as e-mail and IM facilitate more frequent communication without entailing more intrusiveness in the form of unannounced visits and jangling phones. E-mail also provides the extra time (of which daughters and mothers may or may not take advantage) to recover from the initial flash of emotion that a remark or request might spark.

But electronic communication also entails liabilities. First, there is an added risk of misinterpretation because, as with any written medium, metamessages cannot be clarified by tone of voice and facial expression. To make up for this failing, e-mailers can use "emoticons": representations of facial expressions created by combinations of punctuation marks and parentheses, such as ":)" for a smile and ":(" for a frown. (If you don't immediately see a facial expression in these markings, rotate the image in your mind ninety degrees, so the colon becomes two dots for eyes and the parentheses become an upturned mouth for a smile or a downturned mouth for a frown.) Emoticons help signal how a statement is meant, but they can do only so much :(.

E-mail is also heir to the liability of any one-way communication. As with written memos, letters, and spoken voice mail, senders lack feedback, so they cannot know when their words are being taken badly. If you know that something you said has inadvertently offended the person you're talking to, you can move quickly to correct the misunderstanding. You are far more likely to get immediate evidence of such a response when a person is facing you or responding in real time on the phone. Without that feedback, you may dig yourself deeper into a hole, oblivious of the effect you're having. Another risk of one-way communication is that many people become more vituperative, working themselves up into greater expressions of anger or hostility, than they would if the object of their anger were looking right at them or listening at the other end of a telephone line.

A risk unique to electronic communication is also a function of its greatest asset: the speed and ease of sending messages and of copying and forwarding them. Speed can be wonderful, but it can also be dangerous. Once you press SEND, you can't change your mind, as you could decide not to mail a letter. And speed means that when you don't have much time, you may express yourself in an e-mail too cryptically and send it too precipitously.

Even riskier is the ease of copying and forwarding messages. A message forwarded is a message transformed. Every utterance gets meaning not only from the words spoken but from the context, so if the context is changed, the meaning is changed as well. Reading a message that was written to someone else can be like overhearing a conversation not intended for you. You may listen with interest, but you may also be offended by tones or implications that would not have been there had the message been sculpted with you in mind. Disastrously, e-mails often come trailing a long history of correspondence. A person forwarding a current message or sending a copy of a reply to a third party may forget what was written several messages back, where a bit of information or a nuance may be hurtful—or worse—to the recipient who becomes an overhearer to an earlier exchange, one not intended for her ears.

New communication technologies are being introduced at an ever-quickening pace. It is too early to understand fully how e-mail, IM, and other electronic means of communicating such as text messaging will transform relationships between daughters and mothers. We do know, and have seen, that they expand all the possibilities of face-to-face conversation: the precious connection that comes of keeping in frequent touch and of exchanging small details of daily life, the chance to seek and provide comfort, to express love and caring. But they also amplify the possibilities of misunderstandings and hurt feelings, and of creating problems by forwarding or copying messages to people who were not addressees. E-mail provides rich opportunities for going back over troublesome conversations, figuring out what caused trouble, and offering explanations and apologies. But sometimes it will be more efficient and effective to pick up the phone to resolve a problem, or wait to discuss it face-to-face. Understanding the benefits and risks of each communication technology makes it easier to take advantage of the opportunities and minimize the liabilities that come with each medium.

REVIEW QUESTIONS

1. Family communication continuously negotiates a balance between _____ and _____ .
2. Electronic communication can emphasize the similarities between mother and daughter. Explain.
3. Two defining characteristics of IM and e-mail are _____ and _____ .

PROBES

1. The phenomenon of daily (or more) cell phone or e-mail contact happens between mothers and daughters but not between mothers and sons or fathers and sons. What do you know about gender and communication that explains this difference?
2. How important to the "control" element of family communicating is the fact that e-mail, cell phone calls, and IM give equal parental access to all siblings? How important is the fact that daughters generally have to teach their mothers how to manage e-mail and IM?
3. Give an example from your own experience of the use of e-mail and/or IM to manage a family conflict.
4. How do you manage the risk of your e-mail being misinterpreted? How do you manage the risk of others copying and forwarding your e-mail?

CHAPTER 8

Communicating with Intimate Partners

Gendering the Conversation
Robert Hopper

Robert Hopper was a gifted and loved professor of communication at the University of Texas at Austin who died in 1998 after a courageous struggle with cancer. Because he was such an effective teacher over so many years in a prominent and productive institution, he influenced many students who continue to shed light on how communication works, especially in everyday conversations. This reading comes from the first pages of his book that is dedicated to showing how people "perform" gender at every turn in their lives. One of the marks of Hopper's work was that he resisted oversimplified popular concepts that reinforce cultural stereotypes; another was that he argued, as one of his students put it, "for a more humanely, justly gendered society."

Hopper's first point—highlighted by his title—is that gender creeps into talk consistently and pervasively. One of his goals is to enhance our awareness of where and how this is happening. The title also points to the fact that, not only do we gender clothing, room décor, career paths, household chores, and sexuality, we also consistently gender talk—the verbal/nonverbal contact that fills much of our lives.

For example, he asks, why do we say "*opposite* sex"? What are the historical precursors of that utterance, and more importantly, how does it affect the conversations in which it is used? One of the first questions asked about an unborn child, for example, is "What is it?" which means, is it a boy or a girl? The belief in sex differences, he notes, is a "mythology" that must be taken "as a central social fact."

And yet, Hopper reports, "as a social scientist, I have slowly and grudgingly become convinced that men and women are more alike than different and that our experience of male-female differences is an artful, cultural construction, a trick of the ear, something we all believe in, regardless of the facts." This conclusion is startlingly different from the popular messages about "Mars versus Venus" and "report versus rapport talk." One main point of this essay is to encourage you to reflect on Hopper's argument and to test his conviction against your own experience.

Another main point is that, despite what he sees as similarities between male and female talk, Hopper also keenly notices how consistently and how often our talk is gendered. Naming practices, terms for intimate relationships, and especially understandings of sexual intimacy are thoroughly gendered. Even our understandings of communication itself, he argues, are gendered. Monologue and its public expressions in persuasion is interpreted as male, and dialogue, team building, and collaboration as female. The two notions of monologue and dialogue, Hopper insists, "must be repeatedly sharpened on each other. Neither notion by itself explains human speech."

I begin this chapter with Hopper's words in order to encourage you both to pay close attention to how often and how importantly gender considerations enter into interpersonal communication and to encourage you not to yield to the simplistic distinctions found in the

"Gendering the Conversation" by Robert Hopper from *Gendering Talk*, pp. 1–7 and 9–10. Michigan State University Press, 2003.

popular press. The next reading, by Malcolm Parks, makes this same point from the perspective of a social scientist.

Conversation is Henri Matisse's title for a painting completed about 1909, in the fortieth year of the artist's long life. Matisse wrote that this work is a study in the color blue, but it is also a study in gendering talk.

The pictured figures face one another: The artist himself stands in pajamas, and a woman, presumably his wife, sits across a window from him. The interior of their room is monochrome dark blue, a deep, rich, depressed color that contrasts with the bright colors visible through the window. Matisse frequently included colorful windows in his paintings. In this painting the bright window separates the deadpan spouses.

This is a picture of a prosperous midlife marriage. This woman and man remain in their sleeping clothes when the riot of color in the window between them suggests that the sun is well up in the sky. Yet these partners do not look out the window. They look straight, unblinkingly, at one another, opposing each other across the window. The man stands upright in straight, stark stripes of blue and white. The seated woman appears as rounded dark curves. Her eyes and forehead bear a dark smudge. Her right hand is visible; his is in his pocket.

The figures face each other eyeball to eyeball across the bright window. Perhaps the window grillwork connecting the estranged bodies of husband and wife spells the French word *non*, but probably that is a forced interpretation. Still, the painting does reflect opposition, a contest of wills such as occurs with an accusation or an unwelcome announcement. At such a problematic moment partners seek explanations for their stiff, careful discomfort: "Here we go again."

At couple crises, gender is particularly available to explain problems. How and why we gender the talk in our lives, a topic in Matisse's painting, is also the subject of [this essay].

Matisse sold *Conversation* to a rich Russian ninety years ago. My parents were babies then, cars and radios were novelties. The wiring of telephones and electronic lights was in its first generation. That time may now be seen as the cradle of modern consciousness, yet the painting was created before two world wars, the Holocaust, television, the Soviet Union, rock music, the baby boom, LSD, or the silicon chip. Still somehow this painting continues to ring true today. It points to our implicitly gendered conversation performances. We are still going about gendering talk.

Gendering talk is a phrase with two meanings. It refers to certain features in talk that are strongly saturated with gender, for example, my use of the word "woman" to describe a character in Matisse's painting. The sense that some talk seems more gendered than other talk is communicated by emphasis on my title's first word—*gendering* talk. To use the word "woman" is to infuse gender into the human conversation. Such gendering action may be implicit or subliminal. To say "woman" is not necessarily to think about gender. Gendering talk creates social problems because there are so many ways that gender creeps into talk, and we employ them so often.

A second sense of this phrase, pronounced gendering *talk,* refers to the on-going, taken-for-granted project to gender the world of social experience. Talk is not the only thing we gender: We also gender clothing, jewelry, room decor, career paths, public restrooms, household chores, and above all, sexuality. Yet gendering talk binds together our many disparate social senses of sex difference, sexuality, and stereotype. The consequence is a world in which the difference between men and women is taken for granted, as is sexual pair-bonding, as is a mythical battle between the sexes which from time to time propels us into these stymied conversations with a member of the opposite sex.

Why do we say *opposite* sex? Well, it is argued, men and women are quite different from one another, and this difference leads women and men to com-municate differently—to speak different languages—and hence to misunder-stand each other. Men and women face each other numbly and grimly before the world's colorful window. "You just don't understand," each of us rails at the opposite other. The prototype case, the person who understands us least, is a spouse at midlife. How can this be? Did God Almighty invent marriage to introduce me to one person completely different from me?

I wrote *Gendering Talk* after many years of married conversation with Kay. At certain problematic moments, Kay has seemed to represent much that differs from me. The marriage conversation manufactures a special kind of social lens, a fun house mirror that stretches the notion of sex differences. Writers of self-help books about male-female differences concentrate on examples of conversations between members of midlife married couples. Many of these authors, John Gray and Deborah Tannen, for instance, write at length of their own frustrations in married midlife—the age of Dante when he became lost in the woods, the age of Matisse when he painted *Conversation.* Midlife marriage makes a prototype case that men and women act differently. Even Matisse's title, *Conversation,* suggests that the painting takes up a topic more general than a certain conversational moment at midlife marriage. The title suggests that experiences in marriage can be taken as indicators of communicative problems—gender troubles that evolve out of gender differences.

Marriage partners affect not only each other but also their societies. Parents teach to children their own special preoccupation with sex differences, mostly by example. This social preoccupation is present to some degree at every age of the life cycle. This week (in early 1998) Kay and I eagerly await sonogram evidence of the sex of our unborn first grandchild. Of any expected or recently born child we ask, "What is it?" which means, "Is it is a boy or a girl?" Friends and relatives ask this question to know what color gift to buy and how to greet the child. To a boy child I may say, "Hey slugger," delivered deadpan from deep in the throat and accompa-nied by a tummy tickle. To a girl child it is more likely I will say, "Hello sweetheart" in a high pitch and accompanied by a gentle knuckle dimpling the cheek.

The belief in sex differences is elaborated and buttressed by myths of romantic love between a man and a woman—myths that frame many adolescent struggles.

Any understanding of gendering talk must take this mythology as a central social fact. I discovered the importance of talk during adolescence by noticing my conversational failures at early courtship. This discovery of conversation led quite directly (if accidentally) to my life's vocation: thirty years as a college teacher of speech communication. I have taught more than fifty semester courses about speech and gender to students at the University of Texas at Austin. During this time, I have launched a dozen scholarly attempts to describe the communicative differences between men and women. Each of these attempts has failed.

As a social scientist I have slowly and grudgingly become convinced that men and women are more alike than different and that our experience of male-female differences is an artful, cultural construction, a trick of the ear, something we all believe in, regardless of the facts. As a member of our culture I believe in sex differences, too. However, in comparative studies I have failed to unearth substantial male-female speech differences. I conclude that women and men do not actually talk so differently from one another. Rather, men and women listen and talk similarly: We all listen to women differently than we listen to men. Sometimes we talk differently to a woman than to a man. We all talk differently about men than about women. We all talk differently to a sexual partner than to anyone else (whatever our sexual preference). We make gender in the social world by practices of gendering talk.

Many writers suggest that gender troubles result only from male-female differences. John Gray has sold millions of books claiming that men and women are so different from one another as to hail from different planets. Others suggest that patriarchal traditions divide males and females, as well as members of different races and social classes. Yet such generalizations do not help us much unless we describe, in detail, how ordinary people communicate to make gender salient to any particular moment.

Men and women are not from separate planets; instead, we are co-performers of gender in the social planet we all inhabit. Let us listen carefully to each other, with that special attention we might lavish upon poetry being read aloud. Let us not be so sure what the problem is. The problem has many parts and a long history.

• • •

Gender hangs around us like a communicative albatross. We slouch toward possible male-female political equality, while at the same time we fear that communication between the sexes is biased and troublesome. We struggle to communicate with intimate others. Sometimes we believe the problems stem from communicating with a differently gendered other. We worry about sex discrimination in employment and discrimination against those of unpopular sexual orientation. We worry about sexual harassment and sexual violence. Sometimes we fret about the political correctness of gendered language.

Whatever our politics on matters of gender—feminist, traditionalist, or gay rights activist—each of us routinely encounters gender in everyday social interaction. Naming practices illustrate how often gender is marked in talk. We gender the names for occupations from priest to president. We gender most of our personal given names (Tom, Sallie). We gender our terms for intimate relationships (mother, son, girlfriend).

Most humans believe that males and females are pretty different, but our theories about gender remain a patchwork of partially contradictory folklore and inconclusive research. In our confusion we follow different standards of sexual politics within different settings. In matters of public professions, Western laws and customs increasingly ask us to turn a blind eye to sex and gender. However, in matters of sociality and intimacy, *vive la différence!* Many of us attempt to enact egalitarian scripts in our careers, yet abandon notions of sexual equality or similarity when we pair up to dance, flirt, or start a family.

We may momentarily forget gender, only to find that it crops up unexpectedly, like a neighborhood dice game, to affect a plan or to transform a social setting. "We have been engendered," writes social historian Donna Haraway. This wording suggests that being infused with gender is something that has happened *to* us. Yet who are the actors in this gendering? Gendered scenes and actions always happen here and now. However, gendering talk unfolds so obviously, so smoothly, that we seldom even notice our own actions.

Even our understandings of communication itself are gendered. We hold two partial understandings of how communication works: monologue and dialogue. We associate those notions with myths about masculine and feminine talk.

In a monologue view, communication is the travel of information from a source to a recipient. The monologue view, which grows from the study of writing, characterizes precise achievements of command and control, grammar, computer programming, and scientific reports. Effective monologue is accurate (high-fidelity) communication, in which an information source expresses a clear meaning that a recipient understands as accurately as possible. Communication problems occur when message flow is distorted or stopped or when sender and receiver differ in code.

Monologue is associated with masculine gender, getting the right answer, and dominance. Monologue is the primary understanding most educated people hold about communication. In this view gender troubles are consequences of male-female speech differences.

A dialogue understanding of interpersonal communication is difficult to formulate in (monologic) writing. Effective dialogue occurs over time, through interaction of more than one participant, in listening with care, in keeping the conversation going, in opening possibilities, in letting more than one speaker contribute to the direction of events, and in building community.

Consider the first moments of a telephone conversation: "Hello," "Hi Pat," "How are you," and the like. These utterances show modest content but are saturated with the dialogic demands of relationship and culture. The telephone opening sets implicit ground rules for more content-laden talk that follows. Therefore, the telephone opening is a very important phase of an encounter, even though it has little content. Dialogue carries the stream of consciousness; dialogue works the amorphous gel of both cultures and human relationships.

The concept of social interaction as dialogue within a network of relationships is associated with feminine gender.

Monologue views of gender trouble in talk emphasize male-female differences that distort clarity; dialogue hearings emphasize that men and women are all in the same boat, trying to solve problems. In monologue each individual speaker should be assertive and clear in each speaking turn. Effective dialogue entails each speaker listening carefully and responding appropriately within evolving goals and outcomes.

In a monologue view, men's and women's different language patterns create puzzles akin to intercultural communication. The sexes are doomed to gendered separateness unless we become facile translators or unless men's and women's languages converge. In a dialogue hearing, we may be unable to calculate either the extent of male-female language differences or their importance. We can, however, engage optimistically in the communicative tasks of mutual understanding, support, intimacy, and politics.

These two notions, monologue and dialogue, must be repeatedly sharpened on each other. Neither notion by itself explains human speech. An effective communicator must be able to operate in both monologue and dialogue modes. I lean toward dialogic explanation, in part to balance the dominance of monologue in the history of thought. Yet I also question the gendered stereotyping of monologue and dialogue and try to uncouple this dichotomy of communication forms from oversimplified assignment to gendered categories.

... We perform gender in talk. We make, in everyday interaction, the differences that seem to gender our lives. In addition to this, men and women may also speak differently. Evidence remains sketchy on this point, and I cannot firmly deny this possibility. Even if this is so, however, our task is to understand the interactive gendering talk that misleads us into thinking that difference is our *only* problem. If we learn to understand the range and variety of gendering talk, we might yet discover that women and men inhabit a single, slowly improving planet.

REVIEW QUESTIONS

1. What are the two meanings of the title of this selection?
2. What point is Hopper making when he writes that "gender hangs around us like a communicative albatross"?
3. Explain how, in Hopper's writing, monologue and dialogue are gendered (see Chapter 12).

PROBES

1. What point about culture and communication is Hopper making with his "Hey slugger" and "Hello sweetheart" examples?

2. Hopper writes, "Men and women are not from separate planets; instead, we are co-performers of gender in the social planet we all inhabit." Discuss.
3. Hopper believed that the first moments of telephone conversations are "saturated with the dialogic demands of relationship and culture." Is this also true with e-mail and IM communication? Explain.
4. I often share hugs with other men. Some students who have observed this behavior have concluded that I am gay. How has your gender identity been constructed, in part, by others?

Gender and Ethnic Similarities and Differences in Relational Development

Malcolm R. Parks

This reading may challenge you in a couple of ways, and, if it does, you will definitely profit from meeting the challenge. Malcolm Parks is a communication teacher and researcher who uses social scientific methods to study personal networks—the webs of family members, friends, co-workers, and others among and with whom we live our lives. Because he is a social scientist, his writing is more dense than several of the other essays in *Bridges Not Walls*. This is one challenge; you will probably have to read this selection slowly and maybe more than once.

A second challenge comes from the findings and conclusions he reports. Parks' and his colleagues' work demonstrates how much we can learn about personal relationships when we progress from studying individuals or pairs to examining interpersonal networks. This reading uses the findings of network research to seriously question two popular beliefs, one about gender differences in personal relationships ("Men are from Mars and women are from Venus") and the other about the connection between ethnicity and culture ("Blacks tend to... whereas Latinos and Asians are more..."). Parks demonstrates with ample research citations that both beliefs are oversimplified, inaccurate, and damaging.

The first section of the reading focuses on the role of gender in the development of personal relationships. Parks outlines several problems with studies that have ignored the impact of personal networks. First, he reviews some of the work that has led to oversimplified conclusions about gender differences, and then he reports some studies that challenge those findings.

Throughout the book that this reading was taken from, Parks cites six "core studies" that included sophisticated network measures. In this selection, he uses this research and other

"Gender and Ethnic Similarities and Differences in Relational Development" by Malcolm R. Parks from *Personal Relationships and Personal Networks*, pp. 146–150, 154–158, and 165–168. Mahwah, NJ: Lawrence Erlbaum Associates, 2007. Reprinted by permission.

publications to probe several simplistic conclusions. He reports, for example, that "contrary to stereotype, men were just as committed to their personal relationships as women. This was true in both same-sex friendships and romantic relationships." In addition, "There was no difference in the level of support for the relationship that men and women perceived from members of their friends, their partner's friends, or their own family."

Parks wraps up this section on gender differences with these words: "In summary, significant sex differences were found on only 6 of the 21 measures.... Comparisons of women and men in relational development and social network involvement can be summarized rather simply. There are a lot more similarities than differences."

The next section of the reading debunks oversimplified beliefs about the impact of ethnic differences in personal relationships. To get a sense of the complexity of the perspective that Parks and his colleagues bring to their work, notice that the studies on ethnicity that he cites measure not only depth or intimacy of relational development but also "commitment, perceived interactive synchrony, personalized communication, predictability and understanding, and the amount of communication with the partner." In addition, the research measures five network factors: "amount of overlap between the partner's networks, the number of people the subject had met in the partner's network, how often he or she communicated with them, the amount of contact between members of the two networks, and measures of support from the subject's own network as well as the partner's network." It seems fairly clear to me that, if this research can gather valid and reliable data about all these factors, and if the data are interpreted carefully, we should be able to trust the findings more completely than we can trust the findings from research that gathers data only about individual and global factors such as satisfaction, supportiveness, or communication topic.

Parks' conclusion from his review of the ethnicity and personal relationships research is similar to his conclusion about gender and personal relationships: Humans are a whole lot more similar than different. There are some differences in some aspects of relational development and interpersonal behavior. But, as he puts it, "Why do both lay observers and professional researchers persist in believing that gender and ethnicity will explain behavior in personal relationships when the evidence plainly suggests that they do not?"

The answer is that we are thinking too superficially, he suggests. Gender and ethnicity are visible and simple differences, and it takes considerable effort to move beyond them. "Put simply, we pay more attention to obvious factors than to more subtle factors that may take more effort to recognize." There are also readily available anecdotes about gender and ethnic stereotyping to support the oversimplified claims. "Unfortunately, ease and simplicity do not always breed accuracy."

The book that this reading is taken from, along with the specific findings cited in this excerpt, clearly demonstrate the value of considering personal network factors when trying to understand interpersonal relationships. I hope that you will carry forward what you learn in this reading to your understanding of the other materials in *Bridges Not Walls*.

Those wishing to understand the role of gender in the development of personal relationships immediately encounter three problems with the previous literature. First, researchers have looked for sex or gender differences in only a few of the characteristics of personal relationships and their networks that change over time. Second, researchers have focused far more on whether males and females differ on select characteristics such as supportiveness than on the question of whether various characteristics are associated in different ways for males than for females. Finding that women typically express verbal support more often than males does not, for instance, imply that verbal support functions any differently for males and females. We must compare patterns of association and not merely average differences if we are to determine whether theoretic predictions about the process of relationship development hold equally for men and women. Finally, the terms *sex* and *gender* are often conflated. By convention, writers generally use the [first] term, sex, to refer to biologically based character-istics and the [second] term, gender, to refer to characteristics and behaviors that are acquired through cultural socialization. I have used *sex* when referring to specific, direct comparisons of male and female subjects and *gender* when refer-ring to differences or similarities more generally. We should recognize, however, that nearly any distinction is arbitrary and misleading. As we come to under-stand more about the interplay of physiology and social experience, it becomes apparent that the biological and social can no longer be separated in a meaning-ful way. We know, for example, that differences in interaction with the physical and social environment lead to differences in the way genes are expressed, even in identical twins (Fraga et al., 2005).

Intimacy and supportiveness have been the dominant topics in research on sex in personal relationships. The most common conclusion reached in the studies and commentary on these topics is that women are more intimate, caring, and emotionally supportive than men (e.g., Bank & Hansford, 2000; Bascow & Rubenfeld, 2003; Fehr, 2004; Wood, 2000). It is also commonly argued that men and women specialize in different ways of expressing closeness or caring. Men, for example, tend toward doing favors, offering assistance, sharing activities, and other forms of behavioral or instrumental assistance as expressions of close-ness; whereas women are more likely to judge how close a relationship is by its emotional expressiveness and level of personal disclosure (e.g., Maltz & Borker, 1982; Wood & Inman, 1993).

The emphasis on expressiveness and personal disclosure also emerges in studies of women's friendships (e.g., Aries & Johnson, 1983; Walker, 1994). Goodman and O'Brien (2000) gave this homage to talk when describing their longtime friendship: "We were friends; we had to talk. It was the single most important—and most obvious—connection. Talk is at the very heart of women's friendships, the core of the way women connect. It's the given, the absolute assumption of friendship" (pp. 34–35).

Whereas women's relationships emphasize closeness in talk, men's rela-tionships emphasize "closeness in the doing" (Swain, 1989). Men express affec-tion to their same-sex friends, but are likely to do it in more indirect ways (Floyd, 1995). The lower levels of intimacy and supportiveness assumed to characterize male relationships are usually viewed as the result of males being socialized to value emotional restraint and avoid behavior that might be viewed as a sign of homosexuality (Bank & Hansford, 2000).

The belief that men are less intimate or emotionally supportive than women has, however, come under intense criticism. Many of the most extreme claims in the popular press have been debunked (Goldsmith & Fulfs, 1999). The conclusions of several well-cited academic studies purporting to show sex differences have also been called into question (e.g., Kyratzis, 2001; MacGeorge et al., 2004). For example, common beliefs asserting that males are less supportive or that they express less concern for others have not withstood careful empirical test. Moreover, it appears that men and women have similar ideas of what being close is and that they rate the intimacy of a given interaction in similar ways (Parks & Floyd, 1996b; Reis, Senchak, & Solomon, 1985). Differences in intimacy, closeness, support, and a variety of other personal relationship characteristics tend to be inconsistent and, when they appear at all, tend to be relatively small (Aries, 1996; Canary et al., 1997; Goldsmith & Dun, 1997; MacGeorge et al., 2004; P. H. Wright, 1982).

We are therefore left without a clear set of hypotheses about the role of gender in the social contextual model. The situation is made even difficult by the fact that there is almost no research on gender differences in the social network factors associated with relational development. We know that we need to look at gender differences and similarities, but we do not know how to place our bets.

Gender and sex differences in personal relationships may take two general forms. One is a difference between groups or means. Females may report, for example, [that] they love their partners or interact with network members more or less, on average, than males. Gender differences could also appear in how these factors are correlated; that is, feelings of closeness and frequency of interaction with the partner's network might be much more strongly correlated for women than for men. These and other possibilities are examined in the sections that follow.

Sex Differences in Relational and Network Factors

… Closeness, the amount of communication with the partner, and the level [of] commitment were assessed with 11 different measures across the core studies. Six of these contributed to closeness. Of these, significant sex differences were observed on only two. Women reported greater satisfaction with their interactions than did men. Women also reported somewhat higher levels of interpersonal solidarity. Neither of these effects was particularly large, but the effect for communication satisfaction was the larger of the two…. There were no interaction effects, so these differences applied equally to same-sex friendships and romantic relationships as well as to adolescents and young adults. No other significant differences were observed among the remaining indicators of closeness. Women and men did not differ in how much they loved their partners [or] liked their partners, how similar they felt to their partners, or how uncertain they were about the relationship. Nor did any of these indicators interact with age or relational type. That is, men and women were similar across all groups.

Two measures were used to determine the amount of interaction between relational partners. One asked respondents to indicate how many days in the previous 2 weeks they had communicated with their partners, whereas the other asked respondents to estimate the percentage of their free time they had spent with the relational partner in the previous 2 weeks. There was no sex difference in the first of these. Women, however, reported spending 11% more of their free time (48% vs. 37%) with their partners than men reported spending with theirs.

The final set of relational indicators assessed commitment to the relationship. No significant differences were found in any of the three indicators. There were no significant interactions with age or relational type. Contrary to stereotype, men were just as committed to their personal relationships as women. This was true in both same-sex friendships and romantic relationships.

. . . Most researchers have been concerned with the support that network members provide for individuals. Here our concern is with whether the individual perceives that friends and family in the surrounding network approve [of] or oppose the relationship. Individuals obviously cannot know for sure what network members really think. They may misjudge others' approval or opposition as well. Whatever the basis of the judgment, however, the women and men in our studies tended to report similar levels of support from network members. There was no difference in the level of support for the relationship that men and women perceived from members of their friends, their partner's friends, or their own family. Similar findings emerged in another study, although the men in that study reported that family members were more approving of their dating relationship (Sprecher & Felmlee, 2000). Interestingly, in our studies, women tended to believe that their partner's family members were somewhat more supportive. This was, however, a small difference. In general, men and women perceived similar levels of support across the network of friends and family. This was true for both adolescents and young adults and in both romantic relationships and same-sex friendships.

The next set of network factors dealt with how much contact people had with members of their partner's network. Once again, there were few sex differences. Men and women reported that they had met similar numbers of their partner's family and communicated with those whom they had met with equal regularity. Although women reported that they had met a slightly greater number of their partner's friends (5.0 vs. 4.2), there was no difference in how often they communicated with the ones they had met. These findings were consistent with previous investigations showing that men and women are equally likely to meet each other's networks, although women are somewhat more likely than men to tell friends or family about a date (Rose & Frieze, 1989, 1993). National survey data indicates that 70% to 80% of all adolescents in romantic relationships report having met their partner's parents. Females were slightly more likely to meet the partner's parents, to tell others that they were a couple, and to go out together as a couple in a group. Nonetheless, the majority of males and females engaged in these behaviors and the sex difference in the percentage of people doing each of these things is small, generally less than 10% (Carver et al., 2003).

The final pair of measures assessed the extent to which people liked the members of the partner's network. There was no difference in how much women and men liked the partner's family members. There was, however, a small difference in liking for the partner's friends. Women tended to like their partner's friends somewhat more. Although their study was limited to dating relationships, Sprecher and Felmlee (2000) also found that women expressed somewhat greater liking for their boyfriend's friends than men expressed for their girlfriend's friends.

In summary, significant sex differences were found on only 6 of the 21 measures of relational development and network involvement. Although women reported higher values on all six, the magnitude of differences was rather small.... Moreover, there were no significant interactions with age or type of relationship observed in any of the analyses. Thus, both adolèscent and young adult women and men reported similar levels of relational development and social network involvement in their same-sex friendships and romantic relationships....

Summary of Sex Similarities and Differences

Comparisons of women and men in relational development and social network involvement can be summarized rather simply. There are a lot more similarities than differences. Men and women differed significantly on less than one third of the measures. The few differences that were observed did not fall into a pattern, but were scattered across several different factors. Aside from the women's generally higher level of satisfaction with their interactions, the differences tended to be quite small, typically accounting for only 2% to 3% of the variance. It also appears that men and women go about developing personal relationships in much the same way. For both men and women, closeness, commitment, and the amount of communication with the partner are all positively linked to each other and to the level of support and interaction with network members. When it comes to judging how close and committed the relationship is, women appear to put somewhat more weight on meeting people in the partner's network and on the amount of interaction they have with their partners. These differences were most apparent in same-sex friendships, but even here they were relatively small. Men also placed weight on the same factors.

EXPLORING INTERETHNIC RELATIONSHIPS

The growing prevalence in relationships between people of different ethnic or racial groups affords another opportunity to test the generality of the social contextual perspective. The number of interracial marriages in the United States grew by over 1,000% between 1960 and 2002 (Bureau of the Census, 2002). Although the absolute number of interracial marriages is still small, more than one half of adults in the United States report having a family member or close friend who is involved in an interracial romantic relationship and, depending on the particular ethnic/racial combination, between one third and one half say they have dated outside their ethnic group themselves (Kaiser Family Foundation, 2001; Tucker & Mitchell-Kernan, 1995). Reliable figures are not available, but the proportion of people with interethnic friendships or workplace relationships is probably far higher.

In spite of their increasing prevalence, the mainstream literature on personal relationships has paid little attention to issues of multiethnic relationships, or to issues of culture and ethnicity in personal relationships more generally (Berscheid, 1999; Felmlee & Sprecher, 2000; Gaines & Liu, 2000). Researchers have traditionally focused on general attitudes toward interethnic relationships rather than on the relationships themselves (e.g., Fang, Sidanius, & Pratto, 1998; Todd, Mckinney, Harris, Chadderton, & Small, 1992). The literature at this writing contains only a handful of studies of relationship development between people of differing ethnicity or cultural background (e.g., Gaines et al., 1999; Gurung & Duong, 1999; Shibazaki & Brennan, 1998).

To overcome this limitation, I return to the study of dating relationships.... Compared to our other studies, this study was intended to address a more detailed set of relational and network indicators and, most importantly, to draw a more diverse sample of young adult respondents. Just over half (51.4%) came from ethnic groups other than European American. Not counting European Americans, 11 different ethnic or racial groups were represented in the sample. Chinese/Chinese Americans, Filipinos, Korean/Korean Americans, Vietnamese/Vietnamese Americans, African Americans, and "Other" were the most common designations, each accounting for 5% or more of the sample.

Subjects who reported different ethnic backgrounds from their partners were classified as having an interethnic dating relationship. Subjects whose ethnic identification matched the ethnic identification obtained from the partner were classified as having a dating relationship within their ethnic group (intra-ethnic). A total of 82 relationships (38%) were classified as interethnic, while the remaining 136 relationships (62%) were classified as intraethnic. These groups were then compared, first in terms of mean differences on various indicators of relational development and network involvement, and then in terms of the associations between relational development and network factors.

Interethnic Versus Intraethnic Differences in Relational and Network Factors

The data set used for these comparisons contained 26 different measures.... The six relational development factors included depth (intimacy), commitment, perceived interactive synchrony, personalized communication, predictability and understanding, and the amount of communication with the partner. The five network factors included the amount of overlap between the partner's networks, the number of people the subject had met in the partner's network, how often he or she communicated with them, the amount of contact between members of the two networks, and measures of support from the subject's own network as well as the partner's network. Differences that did not account for at least 2% of the variance... are excluded from the discussion to follow.

Differences and Similarities in Measures of Relational Development   Expectations for intimacy or depth of interaction in personal relationships vary considerably across cultural groups (Argyle, Henderson, Bond, Izuka, & Contarello, 1986; Gudykunst & Nishida, 1986; Ting-Toomey, 1991). Although love may be a cultural universal, its expression in specific relationships is nonetheless subject to substantial ethnic and cultural variation (S. Hendrick & C. Hendrick, 2000; Minatoya, 1988). Although these considerations suggest that depth and intimacy might be harder to obtain in interethnic relationships, we found no differences on our measures. Similar levels of self-disclosure, closeness, and love were reported in both types of relationships.

Those involved in interethnic and intraethnic relationships also displayed similar levels of commitment. Those in interethnic relationships rated the probability (0% to 100%) of their relationship lasting in the short term (3 months) somewhat lower than those dating members of their own ethnic group (79% vs. 88%). Otherwise, there were no significant differences between the groups. Interethnic and intraethnic daters attributed similar importance to the relationship, expressed equal willingness to work to maintain it, and thought they were equally likely to get married at some point in the future. At least one other study has also failed to find differences in commitment in interethnic and intraethnic romantic relationships (Gurung & Duong, 1999).

Differences in ethnic background should make it more difficult for relational partners to understand and anticipate each others' responses. This belief has been supported in studies of interethnic acquaintance and friendship (Gudykunst, 1986; Gudykunst, Sodetani, & Sonoda, 1987). Studies of interethnic communication also point to differences in [the] way that interaction is structured, regulated, and contextualized (Gumperz, 1982; Philips, 1983). These differences should make it more difficult for participants in interethnic relationships to coordinate or synchronize their interactions. When these ideas were put to the test, however, the results were mixed. Interethnic romantic partners expressed slightly more uncertainty about their relationship on a scale developed by Parks and Adelman (1983), but the two groups did not differ on a scale of attributional confidence developed by Gudykunst and Nishida (1986). The results for the measures of interactive synchrony were also mixed. Significant differences were found on two of the four items used to assess this dimension of interdependence. Interethnic relationships were characterized by more frequent awkward silences and the perception that it was not as easy to talk to the dating partner. On the other hand, participants in interethnic and intraethnic relationships did not differ with regard to perceptions of how smoothly conversation flowed or how much effort was needed to communicate.

There were no significant differences in the remaining measures of relational development. Those involved in a romantic relationship with a person from a different ethnic group spent an almost identical proportion of their free time with their partners as those involved in a romantic relationship with someone from their own ethnic group (59% vs. 61%). Those involved in interethnic and intraethnic relationships also felt that their communication was personalized to the same degree. Participants in both types of relationships were equally likely to assign "special meanings" to words, to use distinctive nicknames or terms of endearment, to employ special looks or gestures, and to be able to communicate without having to be verbally explicit.

Differences and Similarities in Measures of Network Involvement   Previous research provides little guidance to those embarking on a relationship outside their ethnic group regarding how others might react. It is commonly assumed that interethnic couples will encounter hostile reactions from some, if not most, members of their social networks. To be sure, it depends on whether one is perceived as "dating up" or "dating down" in terms of social status. Nonetheless, multiracial couples often report that they are the recipient of racist comments or behaviors (Rosenblatt, Karis, & Powell, 1995). Most observers believe that social network members place enormous stress on interethnic couples. The higher divorce rate among interracial marriages is sometimes attributed in part to lack of support from network members (Gaines & Brennan, 2001). Even when network members are supportive, geographic and social segregation may make it more difficult for network members to come into contact with the partners or to provide support (Abrahamson, 1996; Tucker & Mitchell-Kernan, 1995).

Although these views might lead one [to] think that social network involvement would differ greatly for interethnic and intraethnic couples, we found little evidence that interethnic couples' social networks are structured differently or provide different levels of support. In purely structural terms, there were few differences in the level of network overlap, cross-network contact, or cross-network density. A significant difference was observed on only one of the seven measures of these dimensions. On average, participants in interethnic relationships had met about one fewer member in their partner's network of 12 frequent contacts. Interestingly, there was no difference in the number of people the partner had met in the subject's network. Generally, interethnic couples named a similar number of people as common members met a greater number of people in each other's network.... Both of these correlations differed significantly from the corresponding correlations in interethnic relationships, where the amount of communication between the partners was not significantly related to either network overlap or the number of people met in the partner's networks.

GENDER AND ETHNICITY IN PERSPECTIVE

Gender and the degree of ethnic similarity appear to have relatively little impact on how personal relationships develop, on how relational partners relate to each other's social networks, or on how network factors are associated with the developmental pathways of romance and friendship. The young men and women we studied reported generally similar levels of intimacy, commitment, communication, contact with network members, and support from network members in their personal relationships. Support and communication with network members was related to perceptions of intimacy, commitment, and communication within the relationship in comparable ways for men and women. Similarly, within the limits of our sample, relationships between people of different ethnic groups were experienced in much the same way as relationships between people of the same ethnic group. There were few differences in measures of relational development, the structure of relational partners' social networks, or in the level of support they reported from network members.

This is not to say that there may not be important gender differences in other aspects of relational development or interpersonal behavior. However, rather than reinforcing the idea of difference by dwelling on the relatively minor differences, it may be more useful to ask why assumptions about gender and ethnicity play such a prominent role in the popular and academic literature on personal relationships. That is, why are we so eager to conclude that men and women experience relational life in dramatically different ways when the research shows that there are actually few differences of any magnitude? And if relationships between people of different ethnic groups develop and are experienced in much the same way as relationships between people of the same ethnic group, why do we place so much weight on ethnicity in personal relationships? Why do both lay observers and professional researchers persist in believing that gender and ethnicity will explain behavior in personal relationships when the evidence plainly suggests that they do not?

Part of the appeal of gender and ethnicity as explanations for interpersonal behavior is their visibility and simplicity. Except in rare cases, biological sex is readily discerned and almost instantly triggers a gender-based interpretative framework. Ethnic and racial differences are perhaps not so obvious, but are nonetheless more easily discerned than any number of other differences in socioeconomic background, personality, and communicative style. Because so little effort is needed to recognize these differences, we are likely to be biased in favor [of] using them as a basis for explaining behavior. Put simply, we pay more attention to obvious factors than to more subtle factors that may take more effort to recognize (Zipf, 1949). This bias is reinforced by the fact that most people can readily identify examples that appear to confirm stereotyped differences. If one is looking for evidence, for example, that men are less committed than women to personal relationships, it is usually rather easy to think of a given male who is less committed than a given female within one's own circle of acquaintance. The fact that the overall distribution of commitment levels is generally very similar for males and females does not prevent people from selecting examples of less committed men and more committed women. Armed with an example that appears to confirm their initial stereotype, most people do not search their memories further for counterexamples or engage in more sophisticated cognitive evaluations.

Explanations based on gender and ethnicity are also appealing because of their simplicity. They each draw on straightforward binaries (female vs. male; same vs. different) that draw us into uncomplicated generalizations about human nature and human groups. They take advantage of the well-documented bias toward explaining others' behavior in terms of relatively stable characteristics and dispositions rather than in terms of less enduring, but often more relevant, interactive and situational factors (e.g., Ross & Nisbett, 1991). Once relational behavior is attributed to the actor's sex or ethnicity, it is no longer necessary to consider more complex situational or relational factors. Thus people frequently rely on gender and ethnicity to explain behavior because it is easy and simple to do so.

Unfortunately ease and simplicity do not always breed accuracy. The characteristics of the situation and the unfolding structure of the interaction itself are often more informative. Moreover, it may be misleading to attribute differences to sex or ethnicity even when they appear to make a difference. Differences that are assumed to be the result of sex, for example, have often been shown to be the result of underlying power differences (e.g., Molm, 1985; Scudder & Andrews, 1995).

In many parts of the world gender is still a critical feature in the organization and experience of personal relationships. In contemporary industrialized democracies like the United States, however, sex differences are becoming less pronounced. Ironically, this may be part of the reason we are so sensitive to them. As large differences disappear, small differences take on a greater perceptual importance. Thought about in this way, scholarly debate regarding whether *sex* or *gender* is the most appropriate term is in fact evidence that sex differences are attenuating. If biological sex differences were broadly predictive, it is doubtful that we would have as much need for the concept of *gender* in personal relations. Gender is, after all, an attempt to explain what cannot be explained by biological sex alone.

This is not to say that sex differences in personal relationships no longer exist or are unimportant. Important sex differences may exist in areas beyond those examined here. Some research, for example, suggests that young women may be more likely than men to attempt to alter their parents' views of their romantic partner or relationship (Leslie, Huston, & Johnson, 1986). This sort of finding begs additional research. Are women also more likely to try to influence their friends' views? Are they generally more successful at influencing network members? Are women and men equally able to ignore contrary views of network members?

Although ethnicity remains important, often to the point of bloodshed, in many parts of the world, ethnic differences are diminishing in many other areas. The young adults who participated in our research, for example, were all associated with a university in a rather diverse coastal North American city. They were therefore part of an institution that is more or less explicitly designed to bring differing ideas and people into amicable contact as well as residents of a city with numerous opportunities and mechanisms for bringing diverse people together. Moreover, young adults of diverse backgrounds often share elements of a common popular culture. Culturally diverse forms of music are, for instance, readily incorporated into popular music that is shared with an increasingly global audience.

This notion of shared culture is underscored by the fact that most (75%) of the participants in our study on ethnic differences had been born in the United States. One might argue that some shared version of "American culture" masked differences in ethnic background. A more complete examination of this hypothesis, as well as more detailed comparison of specific ethnic or racial groups, is beyond the scope of the present work. We did, however, compare subjects who were born in the United States to those who had not been born in the United States and found no consistent pattern of difference.

The similarities between relationships between people of the same and different ethnic groups also challenge our traditional conceptions of ethnicity and culture. The traditional approach to the concept of culture is to view it as a higher order social category that summarizes and controls all aspects of a more or less defined group of people. This is the view of culture as a shared set of beliefs, values, and ways of behaving. Within this perspective, any given behavior is explained by referring it to the common corpus of which it was a part. This is still a popular approach to understanding culture, including cultures of ethnicity and gender. Unfortunately, as the results in this [essay] illustrate, it does not do a very good job of accounting for either the variation within cultural groups or the similarities across cultural groups. Nor is it the only way to view culture. By the 1970s, this traditional conceptualization of culture gave way, first, to views of culture as a historically transmitted symbol system by which people develop and express meanings for social life (e.g., Geertz, 1973), and then, to views of culture as a set of repertoires, tools, or resources that people draw on to make sense and solve the problems of daily life (Philipsen, 1992; Swidler, 2001). In the latter perspective, culture is not so much something one has as something one uses. It describes individual choices in interaction rather than consistent patterns of group difference. In sum, whether one looks to the growing cross-fertilization of cultural influences or follows recent trends in scholarly thought, it is apparent that differences in ethnicity and gender are diminishing.

In spite of this, explanations based on cultural stereotypes persist. They do so not only because they are easy, simple, and perhaps made more visible even as they grow smaller, but also because speculation about ethnic and gender differences frequently serve [a] broader social agenda. Those wishing to advance the interests of minorities, for example, often take the position that members of the group speak "in a different voice" (Gilligan, 1982). The rhetoric of difference provides a basis for a common group identity and buttresses claims for enhanced status and more just treatment. In other cases the agenda is not so much political as it is commercial. Publishers and broadcasters find a ready and lucrative market for materials that play up differences in ethnicity and gender in personal relationships. These books and movies appear to offer some insight, but all too often simply recycle and reinforce existing stereotypes. They are successful, not because they challenge our existing views, but precisely because they give us comfort, making us feel that we understood all along.

The ultimate result of these discourses of difference is to encourage us to see large differences where there are small differences and to overlook underlying similarities in personal relationships across groups. In this [essay] we have explored differences in age, relationship type, gender, and ethnic composition in personal relationships. Much remains to be done to test the generality of the theory, but it does appear that the social contextual approach can help us understand several different types of personal relationships. Although the results demonstrate that social network factors and relational factors are linked in similar ways across a variety of personal relationships, they have not adequately illuminated the more specific processes by which network and relational factors interact. The broad associations between network and relational factors examined thus far undoubtedly reflect the more particular ways in which people manage information and relationships from day to day and utterance to utterance....

REVIEW QUESTIONS

1. Parks acknowledges research that has found gender differences in intimacy, supportiveness, and expressiveness but also cites studies that "debunk" these findings. How are they "debunked"?
2. What has been the basic finding about men's and women's commitment to their personal relationships?
3. What did Parks' research reveal about differences in the level of difficulty in coordinating the actions of intraethnic versus interethnic relationships? Is it more difficult for people in an interethnic relationship to coordinate their actions?
4. Parks' discussion of interethnic relationships includes the terms "dating up" and "dating down." Explain what these terms mean.
5. One of the conclusions we can draw from Parks' discussion of interethnic relationships is that ethnicity does not equal culture. Explain what this means.

PROBES

1. Parks says that one problem with earlier gender research is that the researchers focused far more on whether males and females differed than on whether various characteristics were associated in different ways for males than for females. Explain what he means.
2. Parks reports on research about intimacy, supportiveness, expressiveness, amount of communication with one's partner, interpersonal solidarity, commitment to the relationship, support network members provide for the

relationship, contacts with members of partners' networks, and liking of network members. Which of these variables do you believe gives the best picture of a relationship?

3. What practical advice emerges from Parks' review of research about inter-ethnic relationships? What does this research indicate that people in these relationships should do or not do?

4. Parks speculates that one of the reasons people may focus on gender and ethnic differences rather than similarities is that gender and ethnic markers are so visible and simple. Explain what he means.

5. There are some very important political ramifications that flow from Parks' conclusions about interethnic similarities and differences. Describe them.

REFERENCES

Abrahamson, M. (1996). *Urban enclaves: Identity and place in America.* New York: St. Martin's Press.

Argyle, M., Henderson, M., Bond, M., Izuka, Y., & Contarello, A. (1986). Cross-cultural variations in relationship rules. *International Journal of Psychology, 21,* 287–315.

Aries, E. J. (1996). *Men and women in interaction. Reconsidering the differences.* New York: Oxford University Press.

Aries, E. J., & Johnson, F. L. (1983). Close friendship in adulthood: Conversational content between same-sex friends. *Sex Roles, 9,* 1183–1196.

Bank, B. J., & Hansford, S. L. (2000). Gender and friendship: Why are men's best same-sex friendships less intimate and supportive? *Personal Relationships, 7,* 63–78.

Bascow, S. A., & Rubenfeld, K. (2003). "Troubles talk": Effects of gender and gender-typing. *Sex Roles, 48,* 183–187.

Berscheid, E. (1999). The greening of relationship science. *American Psychologist, 54,* 260–266.

Bureau of the Census. (2002). *Interracial married couples.* Retrieved January 25, 2003, from http://landview.census.gov/population/socdemo/ms-la/tabms-3.txt and http://landview.census.gov/population/socdemo/hh-fam/tabMS-3.txt

Canary, D. J., Emmers-Sommer, T. M., & Faulkner, S. (199). *Sex and gender differences in personal relationships.* New York: Guilford Press.

Carver, K., Joyner, K., & Udry, J. R. (2003). National estimates of adolescent romantic relationships. In P. Florsheim (Ed.), *Adolescent romantic relations and sexual behavior: Theory, research, and practical implications* (pp. 23–56). Mahwah, NJ: Lawrence Erlbaum Associates.

Fang, C. Y., Sidanius, J., & Pratto, F. (1998). Romance across the social status continuum: Interracial marriage and the ideological asymmetry effect. *Journal of Cross-Cultural Psychology, 29,* 290–305.

Fehr, B. A. (2004). A prototype model of intimacy interactions in same-sex friendships. In D. J. Mashek & A. Aron (Eds.), *Handbook of closeness and intimacy* (pp. 9–26). Mahwah, NJ: Lawrence Erlbaum Associates.

Floyd, K. (1995). Gender and closeness among friends and siblings. *Journal of Psychology: Interdisciplinary and Applied, 129,* 193–202.

Fraga, M. F., Ballestar, E., Paz, M. F., Ropero, S., Setien, F., Ballestar, M. L., et al. (2005). Epigenetic differences arise during the lifetime of monozygotic twins. *Proceedings of the National Academy of Sciences, 102,* 10604–10609.

Gaines, S. O., Jr., Granrose, C. S., Rios, D. I., Garcia, B. F., Youn, M. S. P., Farris, K. R., et al. (1999). Patterns of attachment and responses to accommodative dilemmas among interethnic/interracial couples. *Journal of Social and Personal Relationships, 16*(2), 275–285.

Gaines, S. O., Jr., & Liu, J. H. (2000). Multicultural/multiracial relationships. In C. Hendrick & S. Hendrick (Eds.), *Close relationships: A sourcebook* (pp. 97–108). Thousand Oaks, CA: Sage.

Goldsmith, D. J., & Dun, S. A. (1997). Sex differences and similarities in the communication of social support. *Journal of Social and Personal Relationships, 14,* 317–337.

Goldsmith, D. J., & Fulfs, P. A. (1999). "You just don't have the evidence": An Analysis of claims and evidence in Deborah Tannen's *You Just Don't Understand.* In M. E. Roloff (Ed.), *Communication yearbook 22* (pp. 1–49). Thousand Oaks, CA: Sage.

Goodman, E., & O'Brien, P. (2000). *I know just what you mean: The power of friendship in women's lives.* New York: Simon & Schuster.

Gudykunst, W. B., & Nishida, T. (1986). The influence of cultural variability on perceptions of communication behavior associated with relationship terms. *Human Communication Research, 13,* 147–166.

Gumperz, J. J. (1982). *Discourse strategies.* Cambridge, England: Cambridge University Press.

Gurung, R. A. R., & Duong, T. (1999). Mixing and matching: Assessing the concomitants of mixed-ethnic relationships. *Journal of Social and Personal Relationships, 16,* 639–657.

Hendrick, S., & Hendrick, C. (2000). Romantic love. In C. Hendrick & S. Hendrick (Eds.), *Close relationships: A sourcebook* (pp. 203–215). Thousand Oaks, CA: Sage.

Kaiser Family Foundation. (2001). *Race and ethnicity in 2001: Attitudes, perceptions and experiences.* Retrieved January 25, 2003, from http://www.kff.org/content/2001/3143/

Kyratzis, A. (2001). Children's gender indexing in language: From the separate worlds hypothesis to considerations of culture, context, and power. *Research on Language and Social Interactions, 34,* 1–13.

MacGeorge, E. L., Graves, A. R., Feng, B., Gillihan, S. J., & Burleson, B. R. (2004). The myth of gender cultures: Similarities outweigh differences in men's and women's provision of and responses to supportive communication. *Sex Roles, 50,* 143–175.

Maltz, D. N., & Borker, R. A. (1982). A cultural approach to male-female miscommunication. In J. J. Gumperz (Ed.), *Language and social identity* (pp. 196–216). Cambridge, England: Cambridge University Press.

Minatoya, L. Y. (1988). Women's attitudes and behaviors in American, Japanese, and cross-national marriages. *Journal of Multicultural Counseling and Development, 16*, 45–62.

Parks, M. R., & Adelman, M. B. (1983). Communication networks and the development of romantic relationships: An expansion of uncertainty reduction theory. *Human Communication Research, 10*, 55–79.

Parks, M. R., & Floyd, K. (1996b). Meanings for closeness and intimacy in friendship. *Journal of Social and Personal Relationships, 13*, 85–107.

Philips, S. U. (1983). *The invisible culture: Communication in classroom and community on the Warm Springs Indian Reservation.* New York: Longman.

Reis, H. T., Senchak, M., & Solomon, B. (1985). Sex differences in the intimacy of social interaction: Further examination of the potential explanations. *Journal of Personality and Social Psychology, 48*, 1204–1217.

Rosenblatt, P. C., Karis, T. A., & Powell, R. D. (1995). *Multiracial couples: Black and White voices.* Thousand Oaks, CA: Sage.

Shibazaki, K., & Brennan, K. A. (1998). When birds of different feathers flock together: A preliminary comparison of intra-ethnic and inter-ethnic dating relationships. *Journal of Social and Personal Relationships, 15*, 248–256.

Sprecher, S., & Felmlee, D. (2000). Romantic partners' perceptions of social network attributes with the passage of time and relationship transitions. *Personal Relationships, 7*, 325–340.

Swain, S. (1989). Covert intimacy: Closeness in men's friendships. In B. J. Risman & P. Schwartz (Eds.), *Gender in intimate relationships* (pp. 71–86). Belmont, CA: Wadsworth.

Ting-Toomey, S. (1991). Intimacy expressions in three cultures: France, Japan, and the United States. *International Journal of Intercultural Relations, 15*, 29–46.

Todd, J., Mckinney, J. L., Harris, R., Chadderton, R., & Small, L. (1992). Attitudes toward interracial dating: Effects of age, sex, and race. *Journal of Multicultural Counseling and Development, 20*, 202–208.

Tucker, M. B., & Mitchell-Kernan, C. (1995). Social structural and psychological correlates of interethnic dating. *Journal of Social and Personal Relationships, 12*, 341–361.

Walker, K. (1994). Men, women, and friendship: What they say, what they do. *Gender and Society, 8*, 246–265.

Wood, J. T. (2000). Gender and personal relationships. In C. Hendrick & S. Hendrick (Eds.), *Close relationships: A sourcebook* (pp. 301–313). Thousand Oaks, CA: Sage.

Wood, J. T., & Inman, C. (1993). In a different mode: Recognizing male modes of closeness. *Journal of Applied Communication Research, 21*, 279–295.

Wright, P. H. (1982). Men's friendships, women's friendships and the alleged inferiority of the latter. *Sex Roles, 8*, 1–20.

Gendered Standpoints on Personal Relationships

Julia T. Wood

Without repeating the extreme generalizations of the "Mars/Venus" popular books, communication teacher and scholar Julia Wood reviews some basic feminine and masculine standpoints on personal relationships. Wood acknowledges that "not all women operate from feminine standpoints and not all men act from masculine ones." But there are patterns and tendencies, she argues, and it is helpful to understand them.

These patterns arise mainly because of the different ways girls and boys are socialized. The speech communities we grow up in are gendered, Wood argues, and we learn how to be masculine or feminine there.

The two main principles that girls and women learn is that intimacy is a continuous process and that personal communication is the primary way to build relationships. So even when commitment is secure, women "tend to see partners and relationships as continuously evolving," which means that they continue to focus on and work with these relationships. Generally, the research indicates, women's communication is more emotionally expressive than men's.

The two main principles that boys and men learn is that intimacy is "an event that is resolved at some point" and that relationships are built by activities more than by talk. As a result, many men feel that, after a commitment is made, no continuous work on the relationship is necessary. We also prefer to *do* things together to build a relationship, rather than *talking* about the relationship.

Differences between these standpoints suggest why misunderstandings between men and women often occur, and Wood briefly outlines how this can happen. She does not provide the magic remedy for all gender difficulties here, but she does offer some ways to understand the problems all of us have experienced with our cross-sex conversation partners. You can use this understanding combined with insights from Parks' essay to troubleshoot the difficulties you have.

Writing in 1992, Sharon Brehm observed that "probably the most powerful individual difference that affects how we experience love is that of gender.... [M]ales and females construct their realities of love in very different terms" (p. 110). Research studies on topics ranging from emotional expressiveness (Christensen & Heavey, 1990), to love styles (Hendrick & Hendrick, 1988), to conflict styles (Gottman, 1994a; Jones & Gallois, 1989) report general differences between women and men. So significant are differences between the sexes' approaches to intimacy that a 1993 popular magazine (*Utne*, January) carried this cover headline: "Men and Women: Can We Get Along? Should We Even Try?" Although most of us seem to think it's worth the effort to get along, doing so is sometimes very frustrating and confusing. Much of the misunderstanding that plagues communication between women and men results from the fact that they are typically socialized in discrete speech communities. [According to] standpoint theory, social structures and processes in Western society foster gender-distinctive perspectives on relationships and equally distinctive communication and perceptions within relationships.

Gendered speech communities teach most men and women to understand, interpret, and communicate in ways consistent with society's views of femininity and masculinity. Through gender-differentiated contexts, activities, and instruction, a majority of boys and girls internalize views of relationships and how to interact that reflect their respective genders. Pragmatically, this implies that women and men, in general, may have somewhat different views of what closeness is and how to create, express, and sustain it (Inman, 1996; Wood & Inman, 1993). Numerous studies and reviews of research demonstrate that distinct gender cultures exist and that they differ systematically in some important respects (Aries, 1987; Beck, 1988; Coates & Cameron, 1989; Gottman & Carrère, 1994; Johnson, 1989; Kramarae, 1981; Maltz & Borker, 1982; Wood, 1993, 1994a, b, c, 1995, 1996, 1999). Although not all women operate from feminine standpoints and not all men act from masculine ones, research indicates that many women and men do adopt the standpoints of their respective speech communities.

FEMININE STANDPOINTS ON PERSONAL RELATIONSHIPS

Perhaps the two most basic principles of a feminine standpoint on relationships are that intimacy is understood as a continuous process and that personal communication is regarded as the primary dynamic that sustains connections with others (Riessman, 1990; Wood, 1986, 1993, 1996, 1999). Because women are generally taught to build and nurture relationships, they typically understand close connections as fluid processes. Thus, even when commitment is secure, women tend to see partners and relationships as continuously evolving in large and small ways (Gilligan, 1982; Schaef, 1981; Wood, 1986, 1993). From this standpoint, intimacy is never finished, never resolved in a final form. There is always more to be learned about each other, new layers of understanding and experience to be added to a relationship. Because women, more than men, are socialized to prioritize relationships, intimacy is a central and continuing focus of thought, interest, and investment (Acitelli, 1988, 1993; Gilligan, 1982; Wood, 1986, 1993b, 1999). A formal commitment such as marriage does not settle intimacy but is only one moment in an ongoing process.

Perhaps because feminine socialization emphasizes building and refining connections with others, women generally regard communication as a primary way to create, express, enlarge, and celebrate closeness with others. From her study of troubled marriages, Catherine Riessman (1990) concluded that women see talking deeply and closely as "the centerpiece of relationships" (p. 24). In general, women's communication is more emotionally expressive than men's (Christensen & Heavey, 1990; Roberts & Krokoff, 1990); it is also more verbally responsive to others than men's (Beck, 1988; Burleson, 1982; Miller, Berg, & Archer, 1983).

Expressive communication is especially prominent in some lesbian relationships. Lesbian partners, more than heterosexuals or gay men, rely on communication to provide emotional support and responsiveness (Eldridge & Gilbert, 1990; Kurdek & Schmitt, 1986; Wood, 1994b). Women are also more likely than men to find talking about a relationship rewarding, even when there are no major issues or problems (Acitelli, 1988; Wood, 1998b). Thus, spending an evening discussing a relationship may enrich a woman's sense of connection to a partner more than doing something together.

But what is meant by communicating? Substantial research indicates that women tend to place high priority on daily talk and the process of engaging others, whether or not the topics of discussion are important (Riessman, 1990; Wood, 1993, 1998b, 1999). Thus, most women find pleasure and significance in talking about unremarkable, daily issues with partners and see this as important to continually enriching personal relationships and keeping lives interwoven (Aries, 1987; Tannen, 1990). To capture how women typically create closeness, women's friendships are described as "an evolving dialogue" (Becker, 1987). Within a feminine perspective on relationships, talk is not just a means to other objectives such as resolving problems or coordinating activities. In addition, talk is a primary goal in its own right—the process of engaging is the *raison d'être* of communicating.

MASCULINE STANDPOINTS ON PERSONAL RELATIONSHIPS

Two linchpins of a masculine orientation toward close relationships are a view of intimacy as an event that is resolved at some point and a focus on activities as the heart of closeness. Unlike women in general, many men tend to see intimacy as something that is established at one time and then stays more or less in place (Rubin, 1985; Schaef, 1981). Thus, when a commitment is made, some men regard it as a given that does not need ongoing comment or attention. This diverges from a feminine view of relationships as ongoing processes that call for and are enriched by continuous attention and talk.

Because masculine socialization emphasizes accomplishments, an instrumental view of communication tends to be endorsed by most men (Block, 1973; Brehm, 1992). Thus, more than women, men tend to use communication as a way to achieve particular objectives—to settle a problem, express an idea, arrange a plan, and so forth. In other words, it should serve some purpose, should accomplish something (Maltz & Borker, 1982; Riessman, 1990; Wood, 1993c). From this perspective, small talk may seem pointless, and conversation about a relationship itself may seem unnecessary unless there are specific problems that need attention (Acitelli, 1988; Wood, 1993, 1998b). Masculine communication, both verbal and nonverbal, also tends to be relatively unexpressive verbally, because its focus is not feelings, but content, and because men, more than women, are socialized to control emotions (Christensen & Heavey, 1990; Fletcher & Fitness, 1990; Roberts & Krokoff, 1990). Gay partners, both of whom usually are socialized in masculine speech communities, tend to be the least emotionally attentive and expressive of all types of couples (Blumstein & Schwartz, 1983; Eldridge & Gilbert, 1990; Kurdek & Schmit, 1986; Wood, 1994d).

In place of communication, activities tend to occupy center stage in how men generally create and express closeness. Dubbing this "closeness in the doing," Scott Swain (1989) found that men's friendships typically grow out of shared activities. Swain interpreted the focus on doing not as a substitute for intimacy but as an alternate path to closeness, as well as an alternative form. Research by other scholars (Paul & White, 1990; Sherrod, 1989; Tavris, 1992; Wood & Inman, 1993; Wright, 1988) supports Swain's findings and his interpretations that activities are a means to closeness, one that differs from but is just as legitimate as closeness through dialogue. Doing things with and for partners also seems to characterize many men's orientations toward heterosexual romantic relationships (Cancian, 1987, 1989; Inman, 1996; Riessman, 1990; Wood, 1993, 1998b). Thus, a man might wash his partner's car to express affection and might consider going out to a ball game a good way to celebrate an anniversary.

TENSIONS BETWEEN GENDERED VIEWS
OF RELATIONSHIPS

Differences between masculine and feminine standpoints suggest why misunderstandings can—and often do—occur. For example, a woman may perceive a man's lack of interest in talking about a relationship as evidence he cares less about it than she does. Yet from his perspective, as long as the relationship is solid there's no need to focus on it. Similarly, men sometimes feel women's talk about small issues is trivial, and they regard women's interest in discussing a relationship that is in good shape as pointless. This interpretation, however, is based on only the content level of meaning, and it ignores the relationship level at which the point of talking is to connect with each other.

Another frequent frustration is what linguist Deborah Tannen (1990) calls "troubles talk." For example, a woman might tell her partner about a problem with a co-worker in the hope that he will sympathize with her and support her feelings. Instead, he may offer advice on how to solve the problem. To her, this may seem cold, because advice fails to acknowledge her feelings. Yet his intention was to support her by fixing the problem. He is communicating at the content level of meaning, she is communicating at the relationship level, and neither understands the other. Similarly, when men want to do things instead of talking, women sometimes feel the men are rejecting intimacy. Conversely, men generally experience closeness through activities, so they may not experience closeness in dialogue (Riessman, 1990; Wood & Inman, 1993). Problems arise not because either style of relating is bad but because partners don't understand each other's ways of expressing and creating closeness.

Lenny

> Ever since I started having relationships with girls, it seems I've had problems. I did not understand why they obsessed on talking about a relationship when nothing was wrong, or why they would get bent out of shape if I suggested we watch a game or go to a movie instead of talking. Now I understand a lot more about what things mean to girls. Also, I'm now able to explain to my girlfriend what I mean. Like the last time I suggested we go out to a game, I explained to her that I felt close to her when we did things together. She mulled that one over a bit and agreed to go. We've been having some pretty interesting conversations about different ways we see things in our relationship.

In sum, gendered standpoints are one of many influences on how partners view a relationship and how they interpret each other's actions. As we've seen, socialization is generally sex segregated to a large degree, so many women and men learn different ways of communicating and develop distinctive understandings of how intimacy operates. The differences themselves are not necessarily troublesome, but how we interpret or misinterpret each other can be toxic. Perhaps the soundest course of action is to avoid interpreting others through our own perspectives and to try, instead, to understand them on their own terms. Learning to do this requires partners to communicate openness to each other's ways of experiencing and expressing closeness.

REVIEW QUESTIONS

1. Explain what Wood means when she says that women and men are "typically socialized into discrete speech communities." What does "socialized" mean? What is a "speech community"?
2. Explain the two basic principles of a feminine standpoint on relationships and the two basic principles of a masculine standpoint on relationships.
3. Sometimes a woman will be frustrated by a man's unwillingness or disinterest in maintaining a relationship, especially if he doesn't want to *talk* about the relationship. From a masculine point of view, why does this unwillingness or disinterest make sense? From a woman's point of view, what's frustrating about it?
4. Small talk can seem pointless to men and important to women. Explain why.
5. Often when a woman tells a man about a problem, the man tries to fix or solve it. But in many situations, this is *not* what the woman wants. Why? What's happening here?

PROBES

1. Given the different ways they are socialized, how might women and men define communication differently? What could be the practical impact of this difference?
2. What do you believe is Wood's response to the argument made by Parks in the previous reading?
3. Reflect on your own experience with communication and gender. Do you agree more with Wood or with Parks? What do you find most insightful or helpful in the article you agree with *least?*

REFERENCES

Acitelli, L. (1988). When spouses talk to each other about their relationship. *Journal of Social and Personal Relationships, 5,* 185–199.

Acitelli, L. (1993). You, me, and us: Perspectives on relationship awareness. In S. W. Duck (Ed.), *Understanding relationship processes, 1: Individuals in relationships* (pp. 144–174). Newbury Park, CA: Sage.

Aries, E. (1987). Gender and communication. In P. Shaver (Ed.), *Sex and gender* (pp. 149–176). Newbury Park, CA: Sage.

Beck, A. (1988). *Love is never enough.* New York: Harper & Row.

Becker, C. S. (1987). Friendship between women: A phenomenological study of best friends. *Journal of Phenomenological Psychology, 18,* 59–72.

Block, J. H. (1973). Conceptions of sex role: Some cross-cultural and longitudinal perspectives. *American Psychologist, 28,* 512–526.

Blumenstein, P., & Schwartz, P. (1983). *American couples: Money, work, and sex.* New York: Morrow.

Brehm, S. (1992). *Intimate relationships.* New York: McGraw-Hill.

Burleson, B. R. (1982). The development of comforting communication skills in childhood and adolescence. *Child Development, 53,* 1578–1588.

Christensen, A., & Heavey, C. (1990). Gender and social structure in the demand/withdraw pattern in marital conflict. *Journal of Personality and Social Psychology, 59,* 73–81.

Coates, J., & Cameron, D. (Eds.). (1989). *Women and their speech communities.* New York: Longman.

Eldridge, N. S., & Gilbert, L. A. (1990). Correlates of relationship satisfaction in lesbian couples. *Psychology of Women Quarterly, 14,* 43–62.

Fletcher, G. J., & Fitness, J. (1990). Occurrent social cognition in close relationship interaction: The role of proximal and distal variables. *Journal of Personality and Social Psychology, 59,* 464–474.

Gilligan, C. (1982). *In a different voice: Psychological theory and women's development.* Cambridge, MA: Harvard University Press.

Gottman, J. (1994). *What predicts divorce? The relationship between marital processes and marital outcomes.* Hillsdale, NJ: Erlbaum.

Gottman, J., & Carrère, S. (1994). Why can't men and women get along? Developmental roots and marital inequities. In D. Canary & L. Stafford (Eds.), *Communication and relational maintenance* (pp. 203–229). New York: Academic Press.

Hendrick, C., & Hendrick, S. S. (1988). Lovers wear rose-colored glasses. *Journal of Social and Personal Relationships, 5*, 161–184.

Inman, C. C. (1996). Friendships among men: Closeness in the doing. In J. T. Wood (Ed.), *Gendered relationships* (pp. 95–110). Mountain View, CA: Mayfield.

Johnson, F. (1989). Women's culture and communication: An analytic perspective. In C. M. Lont & S. A. Friedley (Eds.), *Beyond boundaries: Sex and gender diversity in communication.* Fairfax, VA: George Mason University Press.

Jones, E., & Gallois, C. (1989). Spouses' impressions of rules for communication in public and private marital conflicts. *Journal of Marriage and the Family, 51*, 957–967.

Kramarae, C. (1981). *Women and men speaking: Frameworks for analysis.* Rowley, MA: Newbury House.

Kurdek, L. A., & Schmitt, J. P. (1986). Relationship quality of partners in heterosexual married, heterosexual cohabiting, and gay and lesbian relationships. *Journal of Personality and Social Psychology, 51*, 711–720.

Maltz, D. N., & Borker, R. (1982). A cultural approach to male-female miscommunication. In J. J. Gumpertz (Ed.), *Language and social identity* (pp. 196–216). Cambridge, England: Cambridge University Press.

Miller, L., Berg, J., & Archer, R. (1983). Openers: Individuals who elicit intimate self-disclosure. *Journal of Personality and Social Psychology, 44*, 1234–1244.

Paul, E., & White, K. (1990). The development of intimate relationships in late adolescence. *Adolescence, 25*, 375–400.

Riessman, C. (1990). *Divorce talk: Women and men make sense of personal relationships.* New Brunswick, NJ: Rutgers University Press.

Roberts, L. J., & Krokoff, L. L. (1990). A time-series analysis of withdrawal, hostility, and displeasure in satisfied and dissatisfied marriages. *Journal of Marriage and the Family, 52*, 95–105.

Rubin, L. (1985). *Just friends: The role of friendship in our lives.* New York: Harper & Row.

Schaef, A. W. (1981). *Women's reality.* St. Paul, MN: West.

Sherrod, D. (1989). The influence of gender on same-sex friendships. In C. Hendrick (Ed.), *Close relationships* (pp. 164–186). Newbury Park, CA: Sage.

Swain, S. (1989). Covert intimacy: Closeness in men's friendships. In B. J. Risman & P. Schwartz (Eds.), *Gender in intimate relationships* (pp. 71–86). Belmont, CA: Wadsworth.

Tannen, D. (1990). *You just don't understand: Women and men in conversation.* New York: Simon & Schuster.

Tavris, C. (1992). *The mismeasure of woman.* New York: Simon & Schuster.

Wood, J. T. (1986). Different voices in relationship crises: An extension of Gilligan's theory. *American Behavioral Scientist, 29*, 273–301.

Wood, J. T. (1993). Engendered relations: Interaction, caring, power, and responsibility in intimacy. In S. W. Duck (Ed.), *Understanding relationship processes 1: Individuals in relationships.* Newbury Park, CA: Sage.

Wood, J. T. (1994a). Engendered identities: Shaping voice and mind through gender. In D. Vocate (Ed.), *Interpersonal communication: Different voices, different minds* (pp. 145–167). Hillsdale, NJ: Erlbaum.

Wood, J. T. (1994b). Gender and relationship crises: Contrasting reasons, responses, and relational orientations. In J. Ringer (Ed.), *Queer words, queer images: The construction of homosexuality* (pp. 238–264). New York: New York University Press.

Wood, J. T. (1994c). Gender, communication, and culture. In L. Samovar & R. Porter (Eds.), *Intercultural communication: A reader* (7th ed.) (pp. 155–164). Belmont, CA: Wadsworth.

Wood, J. T. (1994d). *Who cares? Women, care and culture.* Carbondale: Southern Illinois University Press.

Wood, J. T. (1995). Feminist scholarship and research on personal relationships. *Journal of Social and Personal Relationships, 12,* 103–120.

Wood, J. T. (Ed.). (1996). *Gendered relationships.* Mountain View, CA: Mayfield.

Wood, J. T. (1999). *Gendered lives: Communication, gender, and culture* (3rd ed.). Belmont, CA: Wadsworth.

Wood, J. T., & Inman, C. C. (1993). In a different mode: Masculine styles of communicating closeness. *Journal of Applied Communication Research, 21,* 279–295.

Wright, P. H. (1988). Interpreting research on gender differences in friendship: A case for moderation and a plea for caution. *Journal of Social and Personal Relationships, 5,* 367–373.

Romance in Cyberspace: Understanding Online Attraction

Alvin Cooper and Leda Sportolari

When the Internet first created possibilities for people to meet and converse in cyberspace, the prevailing belief was that all online relationships would necessarily be superficial. Now we have had enough experience with chat rooms, listservs, distance education, and e-mail to understand that the online environment affords opportunities for interpersonal communication that, for a long time, were considered to be highly unlikely, if not impossible. Students in online project teams develop strong working relationships, family members and dating partners maintain intimate connections, and strangers even develop unusually trusting, high-stakes commercial relationships via eBay. This reading explains some of what's been learned about romance in cyberspace.

The first sentence announces that the topic is "the healthy development of romantic relationships, which may indeed carry over into 'real life.'" The authors cite research that substantiates the notion that CMR (computer-mediated relating) can become as personal as FTF (face-to-face) relating. Some computer users even rated e-mail and computer conferencing as rich as FTF and telephone conversations, or richer.

One important and, many would say, desirable feature of CMR is that physical attractiveness does not influence relationship initiation as it does in FTF contexts. It is well known that people overgeneralize from physical appearance when they meet someone face-to-face, whereas online, people meet many to whom they might not be attracted, were they face-to-face. As one researcher summarizes, in an FTF situation, we meet someone and then get to know him or her, and online, the processes are reversed. First, we get to know someone, and this may or may not lead to meeting him or her. If two people meet after having connected online, they may well have already developed some intimate bonds that serve as the context or frame for whatever impressions they may generate based on physical appearance.

Attraction is highest when the partner is perceived as being both physically attractive and attitudinally similar, and people who have difficulty connecting with others in FTF interactions have a better chance of meeting an attitudinally similar person online. Self-disclosure can also be facilitated in CMR because it is less risky than FTF disclosure. Each partner has more control over what is disclosed and how, and the resulting increase in confidence can be attractive to the relational partner. The more oral sense of online written messages maintains a sense of presence, even though each partner has time to reflect and compose, at least in asynchronous contexts.

Erotic connections can even be enhanced by the point already made—that emotional involvement rather than lustful attraction is the foundation of the relationship. As one scholar puts it, "Psychological intimacy ... is an intangible, subtle, powerful motivator of our sexual expression." The interpersonal space that characterizes CMR can also minimize the impact of stereotyped gender roles on the development of intimacy. For example, women do not have to be primarily concerned about saying "no" online. Both men and women can experiment with their communication in ways that are impossible FTF.

This reading does not tell you how to develop a dating—or other kind of—relationship online, but it does provide a wealth of insights that can guide your own experiences with interpersonal communication in cyberspace.

This article presents and discusses ways in which the structure and process of online relating facilitates positive, warm interpersonal connections, including the healthy development of romantic relationships, which may indeed carry over into "real life." While recognizing that the Net can be used in sexually compulsive or deviant ways, we consider how sexual intensity may develop in positive ways within these relationships. By applying psychosocial theories of relationship formation as well as describing qualities of the interpersonal space that's created online, we account for the richness and depth relationships may take on via this seemingly impersonal medium.

A priori assumptions about Internet relating tend to be that it is less involving, less rich, and less personal than face-to-face (FTF) communication due to the lack of facial and body language cues, the lack of the "felt presence" of the other, the lack of a "shared social context" between the communicators, and the "lean" bandwidth of the medium (i.e., written text alone without visual, auditory, olfactory, and other nonverbal impressions of the other available) (Walther, 1994).

While some experimental research seemed to substantiate the notion that computer mediated communication (CMC) was less personally engaging and more task oriented than FTF communication, field research showed contrary results. CMC relationships were found to take longer to develop than FTF relationships because of the slowness of the communication exchange and the limited bandwidth (it takes longer to form impressions of the other), but over time they did become as personal as FTF relationships, along dimensions such as affection, immediacy, receptivity, trust, and depth (Walther and Burgoon, 1992). Asynchronous CMC was even found to allow for more personal relating than FTF when groups were involved in task completion, because the sender did not have to worry about slowing the whole group down by interjecting personal comments or asking personal questions, since receivers could individually read the comments addressed to the group at their own leisure (Walther and Burgoon, 1992). Indeed, some experienced computer users rated e-mail and computer conferencing as "rich" [as] or "richer" than FTF and telephone conversations (Jaffe, Lee, Huang, and Oshagan, 1995).

ONLINE RELATIONSHIP DEVELOPMENT

To make sense of these research findings as well as the many popular press reports of online love affairs, both of which point to the personally involving, even captivating, nature of electronic relating—we turn to theories of interpersonal attraction and early relationship formation, which were conceptualized with FTF relating in mind, and apply them to this new high-tech forum. Many "real world" relationships begin with attraction based on external attributes, such as physical appearance. If the relationship progresses, the attraction then evolves into an attachment based on similarity of values and beliefs. The development of rapport, mutual self-disclosure, and the empathic understanding of the other (Brehm, 1992, p. 156) are involved in a deepening of the connection, which moves the relationship to a more intimate stage. The relationship may become sexualized at any point, either initially as a spark from physical attraction or later based on a sense of being intimately connected emotionally. Certainly, each relationship online as well as offline is unique and its evolution defies simple categorizing.

PHYSICAL ATTRACTIVENESS

Clearly, as the technology stands now, CMR [computer mediated relating] does not start off or develop due to attraction based on physical attributes. In a culture that emphasizes physical appearance, the Internet affords a different way of developing initial attraction. This may change if video cameras become standard equipment; for many people video imaging will likely be experienced as a loss of the freedom to not care about how they look when communicating. However, even with a videocam image, the physical press of the interaction will not be as powerful as it is in FTF interaction; it will be less salient, relegated to one aspect of the overall online presentation, rather than the overwhelmingly dominant one.

Initial impressions online are based on how someone describes and expresses him/herself. Online, one's physical presence—attractiveness, age, race, ethnicity, gender, and mannerisms—is not evident except through what is conveyed by a name unless users choose to describe these aspects of themselves. People can present themselves and be "seen" free from some of the conscious and unconscious stereotypic notions that affect FTF relating from the outset. Self-presentation is more under one's control online; people can make decisions about when and how to disclose negative information about themselves. Sometimes it is better (in terms of advancing the relationship) to reveal such information about oneself early on; under other conditions, it may be best to wait (Hendrick and Hendrick, 1983).

In FTF interaction, people make quick judgments based on physical attributes, and good-looking individuals have a distinct social advantage. People over-generalize from appearance, assuming that those who are attractive on the outside are also nicer on the inside and have better future prospects; this well known phenomenon has been termed the "what-is-beautiful-is-good stereotype" (Brehm, 1992, p. 65). People who may in FTF encounters unwittingly keep themselves from intimate relationships by being overly focused upon or critical of their or others' physical appearance are freed up online to develop connections. Electronic relating offers a different basis for interaction than that of the "meat market" of the singles scene: "Concepts of physical beauty on the Net don't apply. We are all just bits and bytes blowing in the phosphorous stream" (Deuel, 1996, p. 143).

On the Net, the vast array of people to whom we are not physically drawn, yet with whom we might connect quite well if given the opportunity, becomes available to us. As one online participant commented, "You meet everyone you pass on the street without speaking to... you learn to look at people differently" (Turkle, 1995, p. 224). The compelling but often risky appeal of chemistry or "love at first sight" is reduced. The experience of being swept away upon first contact often involves a combination of raw physical attraction and tangled up projections, and for many people would better serve as a red flag than a basis for jumping right in (Hendrix, 1988).

Rheingold reflects,

> The way you meet people in cyberspace puts a different spin on affiliation: In traditional kinds of communities, we are accustomed to meeting people, then getting to know them; in virtual communities we get to know someone and then choose to meet them. (Rheingold, 1993, pp. 26–27)

By the time people meet each other in person, an intimate bond can already be formed. The felt intensity and meaning of any unappealing physical traits are then more likely to be mitigated by the overall attraction that exists. Certainly, the subjective experience of knowing and liking someone can profoundly influence how attractive s/he *seems:* Perceived beauty correlates more strongly than objective beauty to interest in dating (Brehm, 1992).

Attraction is also known to be fostered through proximity and familiarity. There is some evidence that mere frequency of exposure can create a degree of attraction between people (Hendrick and Hendrick, 1983). Electronic communication

> creates a feeling of greater propinquity [spatial proximity] with others, regardless of their actual geographic dispersion. This "electronic propinquity" might be expected to foster friendships, as actual propinquity is known to do. (Walther, 1992)

Rapport can develop easily and casually online. Frequent contact with others is possible with little inconvenience or cost, from the comfort and safety of one's own home or workplace. One can access synchronous groups anytime for immediate interaction and can e-mail others whenever desired without being concerned about intruding, since they can retrieve messages at their convenience.

SIMILARITY

Studies point to attraction being highest when the partner is perceived as being both physically attractive and attitudinally similar to oneself (Brehm, 1992). The Net increases one's chances of connecting with like-minded people due to the computer's ability to rapidly sort along many dimensions simultaneously.

People who have difficulty connecting with others in FTF interactions have a better chance of meeting a compatible person online. For instance, an obese woman who feels insecure approaching new people in FTF interactions because of her weight may interact online with a variety of people who share her interests. She may then

> put [her weight] out to 40 different potential partners and eventually one of them will say "Your weight doesn't bother me." Emotionally speaking, it's much harder to say that to 40 different people in person. But on the Internet, it feels a lot less painful. (Williams, 1996, p. 11)

SELF-DISCLOSURE

Mutual self-disclosure is a key ingredient in developing intimacy between two people. Partners who self-disclose more to each other report greater emotional involvement in dating relationships and greater satisfaction in marriage (Brehm, 1992). A person who discloses intimate information about him/herself is generally better liked than one who is superficial. New acquaintances tend to match each other's level of self-disclosure, each disclosing more if the other person does so and holding back if the other person withdraws (Hendrick and Hendrick, 1983).

CMR provides sufficient distance to make it safer for people who may be restrained in FTF encounters to reveal more than they normally would. A woman who married a man she met online states,

> Had we met each other in person, I think we would have talked, but I don't think we would have given each other the opportunity to know each other.... It's pretty easy to talk about feelings and hopes and hurts when you don't see the person and think you're never going to meet. (Puzzanghera, 1996, p. 1A)

People who are shy have an opportunity to relate online, developing social skills and increasing their confidence as they go. A shy so-called computer "nerd" may connect better online because he is more confident: ". . . being able to type fast and write well is equivalent to having great legs or a tight butt in the real world" (Branwyn, 1993, p. 784). He may be able to carry the confidence and the social skills acquired online with him into FTF encounters; if not, with the ease of meeting people online he may meet a compatible person who will accept him with all his social awkwardness off as well as online.

> Some people, many people, don't do well in spontaneous spoken interaction, but turn out to have valuable contributions to make in a conversation in which they might have time to think about what they say. These people, who might constitute a significant proportion of the population, can find written communication more authentic than the FTF kind. (Rheingold, 1993, p. 23)

For people who may normally stay clear of intimate relationships due to concerns about feeling trapped or burdened or losing themselves in some way, online relating makes it easier to feel in control and therefore to get involved. Net relating tends toward frequent small, casual interactions, as compared to a long talk that can induce a sense of pressure and so be avoided or put off. People are freer to engage and disengage when they want to, to modulate the intensity of their interactions.

> The computer is sort of practice to get into closer relationships with people in real life. If something is bothering me, you don't have to let the person know or you can let the person know. (Turkle, 1995, p. 203)

Or you can log off.

Because of its informality, online written text resembles oral communication more than most other forms of writing. At the same time, certain qualities distinctive to writing and unavailable in spoken interactions can heighten the experience of being intimately understood: Writing offers time for reflection and revision, so that what is communicated may be complete and intentional, with the author neither forgetting important points nor saying too much. Due to the diminished interpersonal press, the weakened link between sender and receiver in CMR, the receiver is able to offer focused attention while staying centered within him/herself. S/he can access the message when s/he has the time and inclination to fully attend to it. Because words can be saved, they can be reread by the receiver, their importance not lost in a quickly spoken phrase, their meaning not denied in an anxious moment. There's [a] quality of putting oneself on the line in writing, of being more vulnerable and exposed to the other, a confessional quality: "As high tech as it is, there's something very old-fashioned about it. The writing and the feelings... [sic]" (Puzzanghera, 1996).

EROTIC CONNECTION

All psychological intimacy has the potential to provoke an eroticization of the person with whom it is shared (Levine, 1992), a desire to physically express the intimate connection. Online relating has some features that may promote and heighten such an erotic connection in positive ways. By minimizing an initial attraction based on physical attributes and facilitating intimate, less inhibited sharing, the Net allows erotic interests to develop out of emotional involvement rather than lustful attraction. "Psychological intimacy... is an intangible, subtle, powerful motivator of our sexual expression" (Levine, cited in Lobitz and Lobitz, 1996, p. 71). Desire is strongest and most enduring when both partners value sexuality as a means of expressing intimacy.

Communication is a key to maintaining robust erotic connections. Failing to communicate intimately can spill over and impair sexual relationships (Chesney, Blackeney, Cole, and Chen, 1981). Online, partners have to verbally communicate; they can't fall back on unstated romantic scripts and nonverbal cues: "It's not like you can go to the movie together and not say anything" (Anning, 1996, p. 1A). Turn taking is built in so both people need to put themselves forward and cannot interrupt each other or speak at the same time.

All too often, psychological intimacy and sexuality are disconnected rather than integrated, with gender strongly influencing how people hold these two dimensions of relating. The interpersonal space the Net provides, reducing the emotional and physical press of FTF dating, may facilitate men's and women's freedom to deviate from constricting gender roles related to sexuality that are often automatically activated in FTF encounters.

Internet relating can be conducive to the way many females in our culture experience sexuality, linking sexual desire to the overall relationship context and the degree of emotional intimacy. Online relating also frees women from the concern that if they or their partner reveal too much too soon, the relationship will get too intimate, too sexual too quickly: Women don't have to be primarily concerned about saying "no" online. In the anonymity and safety of Net-space, women may feel free to be more directly and explicitly sexual, to take charge of their desire, without fear of potential real life consequences (e.g., pregnancy, forced sex, or STDs) or the need to deal with the male's more powerful physical presence.

A woman who feels inhibited about presenting herself as sexual yet desires to be sexually attractive to men can experiment with being more flirtatious. She may find a way to describe herself online as attractive and sexually appealing, affording her the chance to incorporate this view into her self-image, off as well as online. Physical attractiveness is not merely a question of endowment; how one comes across has much to do with projecting confidence, knowing how to accent one's strengths and minimize one's flaws, appreciating and presenting oneself as uniquely beautiful even when one's looks don't fit society's standard images of attractiveness.

Conversely, men, who often feel pressure to move a developing relationship along by being appropriately assertive and "getting somewhere," may feel less responsible for setting the pace of the relationship, including pushing for its sexual development; men can relax and let relationships develop in a more organic way, with sexuality springing from an emotional connection rather than vice versa.

SUMMARY

While many people think that electronic relating promotes emotionally dis-connected or superficially erotic contacts, the structure and process of online relating can facilitate positive interpersonal connections, including the healthy development of romantic relationships. Computer mediated relating (CMR) reduces the role that physical attributes play in the development of attraction, and enhances other factors such as propinquity, rapport, similarity, and mutual self-disclosure, thus promoting erotic connections that stem from emotional intimacy rather than lustful attraction. The Net is a model of intimate, yet separate, relating. It allows adult (and teen) men and women more freedom to deviate from typically constraining gender roles that are often automatically activated in face-to-face interactions.

REVIEW QUESTIONS

1. What makes online relating as rich as or richer than face-to-face relating for some people?
2. Explain what these authors refer to as the "what-is-beautiful-is-good stereo-type."
3. Face-to-face, you meet someone and then, perhaps, get to know him or her. Online you first get to know someone and then, perhaps, meet him or her. Describe the benefits of each.

4. How does the relative distance of CMR make self-disclosure easier? Are there problems with this dynamic?
5. What are some of the benefits of the enhanced control that individuals have when they are relating online?
6. Explain two ways that women and men can escape gender stereotypes in their CMR experiences.

PROBES

1. Consider how your physical appearance affects how you develop relationships face-to-face. What would be some benefits, for you specifically, of developing a relationship online, where the other person would not be responding to your physical appearance?
2. When you're communicating online, you miss the immediate, real-time, subtle facial expressions and posture changes that tell you how your conversation partner is responding to what you're saying. Isn't this vitally important information? How can CMR be as fulfilling, honest, and trustworthy as FTF relating if all this "presentness" is missing?
3. Isn't the discussion of erotic connection in this reading a little far-fetched? Can you imagine—or have you experienced—examples of CMR that actually generate erotic connections between people? Explain.

REFERENCES

Anning, V. (1996). Doctors analyze effect of Internet on relationships. *Stanford Daily*, October 15.

Branwyn, G. (1993). Compu-sex: Erotica for cybernauts. *South Atlantic Quarterly, 92*(4), 779–791.

Brehm, S. (1992). *Intimate relationships*. New York: McGraw-Hill.

Chesney, A. P., Blackeney, P. E., Cole, C. M., and Chen, F. (1981). A comparison of couples who have sought sex therapy with couples who have not. *Journal of Sex and Marital Therapy, 7*, 131–140.

Deuel, N. (1996). Our passionate response to virtual reality. In S. Herring (Ed.), *Computer-mediated communication: Linguistic, social and cross-cultural perspectives*. Philadelphia: John Benjamin.

Hendrick, C., and Hendrick, S. (1983). *Liking, loving and relating*. Monterey: Brooks/Cole.

Hendrix, H. (1988). *Getting the love you want: A guide for couples*. New York: Henry Holt.

Jaffe, J. M., Lee, Y., Huang, L., and Oshagan, H. (1995). *Gender, pseudonyms and CMC: Masking identities and baring souls*. [Online]. Available: <http://www.iworld.net/~yesunny/genderps.html>

Levine, S. B. (1992). *Sexual life: A clinician's guide*. New York: Plenum Press.

Lobitz, W. C., and Lobitz, G. K. (1996). Resolving the sexual intimacy paradoxes: A developmental model for the treatment of sexual desire disorder. *Journal of Sex and Marital Therapy, 22*(2), 71–84.

Puzzanghera, J. (1996). Double click on love. *San Jose Mercury News,* April 27, 1A.

Rheingold, H. (1993). *The virtual community: Homesteading on the electronic frontier.* Reading: Addison-Wesley.

Turkle, S. (1995). *Life on the screen.* New York: Simon and Schuster.

Walther, J. B. (1992). Interpersonal effects in computer-mediated interaction: A relational perspective. *Human Communication Research, 20*(4), 473–501.

———. (1994). Anticipated ongoing interaction versus channel effects on relational communication in computer mediated interaction. *Human Communication Research, 20*(4), 473–501.

Walther, J. B., and Burgoon, J. K. (1992). Relational communication in computer mediated interaction. *Human Communication Research, 19,* 50–88.

Williams, M. (1996). Intimacy and the Internet. *Contemporary Sexuality, 30*(9), 1–11.

Bridges Not Walls

The first three parts of this book are designed to help you understand the foundations of interpersonal communication (Part One), the ways in which people make meaning together (Part Two), and the relationships people inhabit (Part Three). Part Four focuses on interpersonal problems that people experience and how communication can help them cope with these problems.

The first chapter of Part Four describes a variety of painful communication walls—deception, betrayal, aggression, hurtful messages, defensiveness, the manipulative use of power, and bullying. Then Chapter 10 focuses on the general communication wall called conflict, offering both understandings and skills for managing conflict effectively. Next, Chapter 11 discusses how to bridge cultural differences, and Chapter 12 explains how dialogue can bring people together. The materials on dialogue bring much of the book into a full circle by returning to the approach to interpersonal communication that I outlined in Chapter 2 and showing how dialogue can work in many different settings.

As a whole, Part Four translates the practical theory and principles of the first three parts of the book into strategies for helping you cope with many of the communication difficulties that most of us experience every day.

CHAPTER 9

Coping with Communication Walls

Deception, Betrayal, and Aggression

John Stewart, Karen E. Zediker, and Saskia Witteborn

This reading discusses three of the more difficult elements of interpersonal communicating: lying, betrayal, and aggression. The reading combines insights from recent research into these phenomena with some practical suggestions about how to cope with them.

Karen, Saskia, and I begin by reviewing some research and some suggestions about deception or lying. We make the point that, like all forms of communication, lying is a joint action. Some people make it relatively easy for others to lie to them, and others make it desirable. This is not to "blame the victim" of deception, but only to remind communicators that it takes more than one person to lie. It is also important to realize that lying can be both intentional and unintentional. Especially when people are paying attention to social expectations and rules—which is just about all the time—it can be almost impossible to "tell the whole truth and nothing but the truth."

Next we discuss six motives for lying that emerge from some recent research, three of which the researchers call "positive," and three "negative," because of their likely impact on receivers. We also describe some of the most common consequences of deception. We note that the collaborative nature of deception becomes clearest when the deceived person decides to expose his or her relational partner's lies or to ignore or suppress them.

Then we summarize the viewpoint of another researcher who argues that there are no "positive" motives for lying. We ask you to consider which of these views makes most sense to you—that deception is inevitable and is sometimes a good thing, or that lying always objectifies and dehumanizes the receiver, and should be avoided whenever possible.

The second section of the reading focuses on betrayal, communication that violates trust and the expectations on which the relationship is based. We note that a very high percentage of relational and dating partners report that they have experienced betrayal, which is more common than you might think. We discuss five features of betrayal that may empower you to understand it more effectively the next time it happens to you and that may also remind you how to reduce the number of times you betray others.

The final section discusses hurtful messages, aggression, and violence. The first part pulls highlights from the next reading in this chapter, by Anita Vangelisti. Dr. Vangelisti's research identified 10 types of hurtful messages that people experience in relationships with partners, friends, and family members. In the next reading, she describes the outcomes of her research in more detail than we do here.

The section of the reading on verbal aggression defines the phenomenon and describes how it takes some of its various forms. We also offer some suggestions for dealing with the verbal aggression you experience.

The final paragraphs of this reading briefly treat psychological abuse and physical violence. These brief paragraphs certainly do not do justice to these important topics, but we hope enough is said here to empower those who suffer abuse or violence to begin to

The mental effort expended to make sense of hurtful messages varies, as you might expect, with the closeness of the relationship. Few people invest much effort in a hurtful message from a store clerk, but a comment from one's spouse might provoke considerable work. There are exceptions to this rule, however, including the son who excuses his father's put-downs with "I guess that's what fathers are supposed to do" and the abused wife who minimizes the negative messages received from her husband.

The final section of this reading focuses on how hurtful messages affect relationships. When the message is perceived to be unintentional, the impact on the relationship tends to be negligible. When the hurt is perceived to be intentional, there is a greater impact, but this tendency is balanced by the tendency to excuse intimates. In both family and dating relationships, hurtful messages are often forgiven.

Anita's research clearly demonstrates the inaccuracy of the old adage "Sticks and stones can break my bones, but names can never hurt me." Hurt is a relational phenomenon that depends not only on what is said but when, by whom, to whom, and how seriously. But the potential of destructive words is clearly great. "Names" and other hurtful messages can cut deep.

After my parents got divorced, my father sat down and had a long talk with me. He told me a lot of things that my mom did to hurt him and tried to explain his side of the story. I already knew most of what he said, but there was one thing that really surprised me. He said, "Your mother never really loved you as much as she did your brother or sister.... It was obvious from the start. You looked like me and she couldn't hide her feelings." He probably didn't mean this the way I took it, but it has bothered me ever since. I wish now he wouldn't have said it. I'm not sure why he did. I guess he was just expressing his anger.

Although most of us have used the old adage "sticks and stones may break my bones,"[1] few who study communication would argue that the impact of words on people and relationships is less than that of physical objects—whether those objects be sticks, stones, bats, or fists. Words not only "do" things when uttered (Austin, 1975), but they have the ability to hurt or harm in every bit as real a way as physical objects. A few ill-spoken words (e.g., "You're worthless," "You'll never amount to anything," "I don't love you anymore") can strongly affect individuals, interactions, and relationships.

Feeling hurt, by its nature, is a social phenomenon. Except in relatively rare circumstances, people feel hurt as a result of some interpersonal event—something they perceive was said or done by another individual. The hurtful utterance may be spoken with the best of intentions or it may be overtly aggressive. It may occur as a one-time event or it may be embedded in a long history of verbal abuse. It may be spoken by a complete stranger or by a life-long friend. Regardless of intentionality, context, or source, feelings of hurt are evoked by and expressed through communication. Although theorists of emotion and of communication have acknowledged the potential association between social interaction and the elicitation of emotions such as hurt, theoretical work has only recently begun to explain the processes that link communication and emotion (Averill, 1980; Bowers, Metts, & Duncanson, 1985; de Rivera & Grinkis, 1986; Shimanoff, 1985, 1987; Weiner, 1986).

Weiner (1986) suggested that emotions are determined, in part, by attributions. He and his colleagues have found, for example, that the attributions people make about interpersonal events distinguish whether individuals feel anger, guilt, or pity (Weiner, Graham, & Chandler, 1982). Given this, when people feel hurt, their attributions concerning the messages that initially evoked their feelings should distinguish those (hurt) feelings from other similarly "negative" emotions. Although researchers have begun to study the association between attribution and emotion, they have largely neglected the relationship between communication and attribution. Because attributions are based, in part, on individuals' observations of interpersonal events, the messages that people believe evoked their feelings of hurt are central to understanding how hurt is elicited.

The purpose of this reading is to begin to describe the social interactions that people define as hurtful....

EXAMINING MESSAGES THAT HURT

To begin to describe hurtful messages, data collected from two groups of undergraduate students were examined. The first set of data was collected from students (N = 179) enrolled in a large, introductory communication course. The second data set was collected approximately 1 year later and consisted of responses from individuals (N = 183) enrolled in one of several introductory communication courses.

Respondents were instructed to recall a situation in which someone said something to them that hurt their feelings. Then they were asked to write a "script" of the interaction as they remembered it. They were told to include what was said before the hurtful comment was made, what the comment was, and how they reacted to the comment.[2] After completing their script, participants were asked to look back on the conversation they described and to rate how hurtful it was (a high score indicated that it was "Extremely Hurtful" and a low score that it was "Not At All Hurtful").[3]

Inductive analysis (Bulmer, 1979) was used to develop a category scheme to describe the acts of speech that characterize hurtful messages.[4] With the exception of the data from five respondents (who could not recall any particularly hurtful messages), over 96% of the messages were codable into the typology. Definitions and examples of the categories are provided in Table 1.... The most commonly perceived hurtful messages across both data sets were accusations, evaluations, and informative messages, whereas the least common were lies and threats.

TABLE 1 Typology of Hurtful Message Speech Acts

Definition	Examples
Accusation: A charge of fault or offense.	"You are a liar." "You're such a hypocrite."
Evaluation: A description of value, worth, or quality.	"Well, if I met him and liked him, I would have remembered him." "Going out with you was the biggest mistake of my life."
Directive: An order, set of directions, or a command.	"Just get off my back." "Just leave me alone, why don't you!"
Advice: A suggestion for a course of action.	"Break up with her so you can have some fun." "I think we should see other people."
Expression of Desire: A statement of preference.	"I don't want him to be like you." "I don't ever want to have anything to do with you."
Information: A disclosure of information.	"You aren't a priority in my life." "Well, I'm really attracted to Julie."
Question: An inquiry or interrogation.	"Why aren't you over this [a family death] yet?"
Threat: An expression of intention to inflict some sort of punishment under certain conditions.	"If I find out you are ever with that person, *never* come home again."
Joke: A witticism or prank.	"The statement was really an ethnic joke against my ethnicity."
Lie: An untrue, deceptive statement or question.	"The worst part was when he lied about something …"

A brief perusal of these data suggested that the messages varied in terms of how hurtful they were to respondents. Interactions ranged from a former coach telling a respondent, "My, you seem to have put on a few pounds" to a physical education teacher exclaiming, "You are the worse [*sic*] player I've ever seen in my life!" In one case, a peer asked a respondent who was mourning her father's death, "When are you going to get over this?" In another, a respondent's stepmother told her, "You caused your grandmother's death. She died of a broken heart because you didn't show her how much you loved her." Although all of these examples were rated above the midpoint in terms of how hurtful they were to respondents, some were rated as more hurtful than others....

The topics addressed by hurtful messages were coded using a procedure identical to the one outlined for the coding of message type. Initial categories were generated, the data were coded, the categories were refined, and the data were recoded. Table 2 provides a list of topic categories as well as examples of each topic. Over 93% of the messages reported were codable into the typology....

TABLE 2 Examples of Hurtful Topics

Topic	Example
Romantic Relations	"He never liked you anyway. He just used you to get back at me."
Nonromantic Relations	"You're trying too hard to be popular … you're ignoring your 'real' friends."
Sexual Behavior	"Why? Do you still want to sleep around?"
Physical Appearance	"God almighty you're fat!"
Abilities/Intelligence	"I guess it's hard for you teenage illiterates to write that stuff."
Personality Traits	"Well, I think you're selfish and spoiled!"
Self-Worth	"I don't need you anymore."
Time	"We don't do things together like we used to."
Ethnicity/Religion	"You're a stupid Jew!"

WHY SOME MESSAGES HURT MORE THAN OTHERS

Of the hurtful messages described, informative statements were the only speech acts that were rated extremely hurtful more often than they were rated low in hurtfulness. Informative statements, in short, were most typically seen as highly hurtful messages. Although potential explanations for this finding vary, the ability of recipients to "repair" or offer alternatives to the content of the message seems a particularly likely contributor. Whereas listeners are less likely than speakers to initiate repair (Schegloff, Jefferson, & Sacks, 1977), when accused or evaluated, recipients have the control to either overtly or covertly "defend" themselves against hurt. If the speaker does not initiate repair, the recipient may do so by offering alternatives to the accusation (e.g., accounts, excuses, justifications) and even verifying those alternatives with examples from his or her own experiences.[5] On the other hand, when informed of something, there are few such arguments available. The opportunities for recipients to repair any damage to their own face are severely limited. If, for example, a person is accused of being selfish and inconsiderate, that person can point out instances in which that has not been the case. However, if the same person is informed by a lover that the lover is "seeing someone else," there is little the person can say to counter the statement.

Like informative statements, hurtful messages (in the second data set) centering on romantic relationships were, more often than not, perceived as extremely hurtful (although this difference was significant only for the second data set, messages in the first data set were similarly distributed). Given that over 54.5% of the informative messages concerned romantic relationships (i.e., "I don't love you anymore," "I've been sleeping with someone else," "I decided we can only be friends"), this finding is not surprising. It is interesting, however, that participants tended to rate these relational hurts as more hurtful, whereas they tended to rate some personal or individual hurts (i.e., statements regarding self-worth) as less hurtful. One explanation for this contrast involves the potential recency of the messages concerning romantic relationships. Because the sample for this study was college students, events centering on romantic relationships may have been more recent and therefore more salient in the minds of respondents. However, this was not the case.... Furthermore, participants' ratings of hurtfulness were positively correlated with the amount of time that had passed since the hurtful event....

A second explanation is that hurtful messages focusing on relational issues, like those comprised of informative statements, may be more difficult for recipients to repair than messages that emphasize nonrelational issues. This explanation is supported by the finding (in the first data set) that hurtful messages concerning nonromantic relationships were seen as extremely hurtful more often than not. (In the second data set this difference was not significant, but the data were distributed in a similar pattern.) Because relationships involve two people, they are at once controllable and uncontrollable. Each individual has the power to influence, but neither has complete reign. In contrast, many nonrelational issues such as time management are more controllable. Recipients may repair by excusing, justifying, or apologizing for their behavior or choices (McLaughlin, 1984). Further, because recipients have access to a great deal of information concerning their own behavior (e.g., the situational parameters they face), they may be able to rationalize their limitations by adjusting their own criteria for evaluating the behavior. Other nonrelational issues such as physical appearance and intelligence are relatively uncontrollable. Recipients therefore need not take responsibility for evaluative remarks or questions from others.

In comparison to nonrelational issues, relational issues present both recipients and speakers with a unique situation. Neither has complete control or responsibility for relational outcomes. As a result, when one partner evaluates ("You aren't going to make a very good husband") or makes an accusation ("You don't care about our friendship at all") concerning the relationship, the other is faced with a dilemma. He or she must seek a repair strategy that addresses the (relational) issue at hand without threatening the face of either partner. In many cases, these two goals are incompatible. The difficulties of dealing with such incompatible goals are reflected by the findings of a pilot study that suggest that recipients tend to react to extremely hurtful messages by withdrawing—either by crying or verbally acquiescing to their conversational partner (Vangelisti, 1989).

In addition to presenting participants with potentially difficult behavioral choices, extremely hurtful messages may also create some difficult cognitive tasks. When a loved one says something that hurts, participants may make one of at least two attributional choices. First, they may reason that the person did not intend to hurt their feelings. If this choice is made, the message may evoke feelings of hurt, but might not have a major effect on the relationship ("After all, she didn't *mean* to hurt my feelings"). Second, participants may believe that the message was intentionally hurtful. If so, they will likely have more difficulty discounting the impact of the message on the relationship ("How could anyone say something like that *on purpose?*"). In some cases, people may examine the available data to determine whether or not a message was intended to hurt. In others, the need or

desire to maintain a close relationship may encourage participants to make attributions that minimize the intentionality they attach to hurtful messages.

The cognitive "effort" that individuals expend to make sense of hurtful
messages should depend, in part, on the individuals' relationship with the person who uttered the message. For example, if a clerk in a department store hurts
a person's feelings, that person is probably less likely to spend time contemplat-
ing the clerk's motives than if the same person was treated badly by a friend,
parent, or spouse. Why? In part because people expect to be treated by intimate
relational partners in relatively positive ways.

Obviously, there are exceptions to this rule. For instance, when explaining
why his father said something hurtful to him, one respondent noted, "I don't
understand why he always puts me down. I guess that's what fathers are supposed to do." Clearly this respondent did not expect positive feedback from his
father. The rather bewildered account of his father's behavior suggests that the
hurtful message described by the respondent may have been one of many—
that it was contextualized in an ongoing stream of verbal abuse (Leffler, 1988;
Vissing, Straus, Gelles, & Harrop, 1991; Yelsma, 1992) and/or intentional verbal
aggression (Infante, Riddle, Horvath, & Tumlin, 1992; Martin & Horvath, 1992).
Another example would be a physically abused wife who comes to expect negative behavior from her spouse. Even in such extreme cases, however, researchers
have found that both the abused and the abuser use cognitive strategies to
minimize the control and intentionality associated with abusive acts (Andrews,
1992; Herbert, Silver, & Ellard, 1991; Holtzworth-Munroe, 1992). In the context of
close relationships, acts of violence are often interpreted as representing "love"
rather than more obvious emotions such as anger or rage (Cate, Henton, Koval,
Christopher, & Lloyd, 1982; Henton, Cate, Koval, Lloyd, & Christopher, 1983;
Roscoe & Kelsey, 1986). In short, relational intimacy, the type of relationship people have with those who utter hurtful messages, and the intentionality attributed
to the message should affect the impact of hurtful messages on relationships....

DISCUSSING THE IMPACT OF HURTFUL
MESSAGES ON RELATIONSHIPS

Although the vast majority (64.8%) of hurtful messages were perceived to be
unintentional, those that were seen as intentional had a significantly greater distancing effect on the relationship. Recipients' remarks regarding intentionality
reflected their willingness to make allowances for a variety of speaker difficulties.
When asked whether the speaker intended to hurt them, recipients often made
comments such as "she was mad at someone else," "he just doesn't know how to
fight," "he has a personal problem with alcohol," or "he said it because he loves
me." If speakers seemed to regret the hurtful message (Knapp et al., 1986), or if
the message was offered for the good of the recipient (Weber & Vangelisti, 1991),
the message did not have as strong an effect on the relationship. In contrast,
when recipients perceived that the message was intentionally hurtful, their

remarks frequently focused on stable personality traits of the speaker: "She's just that sort of person," "he is very cruel and unforgiving," "he doesn't care about anyone except himself."...

The impact of hurtful messages on relational intimacy was also affected by ratings of relational closeness at the time the message was uttered. Ratings of relational closeness were negatively associated with the distancing effect of hurtful messages. Because there was not a similarly negative association between closeness and message hurtfulness, the apparent lack of distancing in more intimate relationships was not due to the fact that the messages hurt less. Instead, those who were involved in intimate relationships may be more willing to offer interpretations of the hurtful messages that are less harmful to the relationship. It is also possible that intimates have developed idiosyncratic patterns to deal with hurtful events (Montgomery, 1988), or that they have developed enough of a positive regard for one another that a single hurtful message does not affect relational intimacy (Knapp, 1984).

Similar explanations may be offered for the findings concerning family relationships. Although intimacy did not significantly differentiate between family and nonfamily relationships, results indicated that hurtful messages occurring in the context of the family had less of an effect on the relationship than did those occurring in nonfamily contexts. In contrast to intimate nonfamily relationships, family associations may encourage people to deal with hurtful messages by relying on the assumption that the relationships are involuntary and therefore virtually impossible to dissolve. One respondent noted in the margin of his questionnaire that "It seems if something happens with your family ... [you are] a lot more apt to forgive them." Because family members are, for all practical purposes, irreplaceable, recipients of hurtful messages may feel more obligated to absorb the blow of a hurtful message without allowing it to impact the family relationship. In addition, the variety of circumstances family members have experienced together may create a sort of "immunity" to the impact of hurtful messages. Family members' experience with other negative interpersonal events may better prepare them for the feelings of hurt that can be elicited by other members....

In sum, the findings of this research suggest that the old adage concerning "sticks and stones" requires, at the very least, a lengthy addendum. Hurt is a socially elicited emotion (de Rivera, 1977)—people feel hurt because of the interpersonal behavior of others. Because feelings of hurt are elicited through social interaction, words can "hurt"—both individuals and relationships.

REVIEW QUESTIONS

1. Paraphrase the relationship between attributions and hurtfulness that Anita outlines in the third paragraph of this reading.
2. What is the main characteristic of a hurtful message that informs?

3. Why does Anita believe that informative hurtful messages are so painful?
4. What is Anita's theoretical explanation for the finding that recipients tend to react to extremely hurtful messages by withdrawing?
5. How does the desire to maintain a close relationship sometimes affect attributions about a hurtful message?
6. What do you make out of the finding that almost 65 percent of hurtful messages were perceived to be unintentional?

PROBES

1. If you were a participant in Anita's first study, what two examples of hurtful messages would you first recall? Label them using the categories in Table 1. Then identify the topics of these messages, as in Table 2.
2. What is the frequency of hurtful messages in your life by topic type? Which topic in Table 2 do you hear the most hurtful messages about? What is ranked second and third?
3. "Time heals all wounds," the saying goes. Yet Anita found that "participants' ratings of hurtfulness were positively correlated with the amount of time that had passed since the hurtful event." Comment on this finding.
4. Explain how, in the context of close relationships, "acts of violence are often interpreted as representing love.'"
5. Anita found in her research that the distancing effects of hurtful messages in intimate relationships were less than she expected. How does she explain this finding?

NOTES

1. Steve Duck has informed me of a German proverb that provides a more accurate representation of the association between words and feelings of hurt: "Böse Disteln stechen sehr, böse Zungen stechen mehr." A colleague from Germany, Jurgen Streeck, confirmed the translation: "Nasty thistles hurt/stick a great deal, but nasty words hurt/stick more."
2. Respondents participating in the second data collection session were also asked to indicate how long ago the hurtful message occurred.
3. To reduce demand characteristics, participants were also informed that some people may not have experienced (or may not be able to remember) the type of conversations called for by the questionnaire and that part of the research project was to assess the percentage of people who could and could not do so. Subjects were further reminded that they would receive extra credit regardless of whether or not they completed the questionnaire (see Planalp & Honeycutt, 1985).
4. Because the data were collected approximately 1 year apart, the analyses were conducted separately (also approximately 1 year apart). The initial

category scheme, therefore, was primarily developed using the first data set. The second set of data was collected, in part, to demonstrate the applicability of the category scheme and to replicate the frequencies found using the first data set.

5. Work on accounts, blaming, excuses, and attributions (e.g., Cody & McLaughlin, 1988; Fincham, Beach, & Nelson, 1987; Fincham & Jaspers, 1980; Harvey, Weber, & Orbuch, 1990; Hilton, 1990; McLaughlin, Cody, & French, 1990; Weber & Vangelisti, 1991; Weiner, Amirkhan, Folkes, & Verette, 1987) certainly supports the notion that people generate such alternatives to explain unexpected social circumstances, potentially negative behavior, or broken social contracts.

REFERENCES

Andrews, B. (1992). Attribution processes in victims of marital violence: Who do women blame and why? In J. H. Harvey, T. L. Orbuch, & A. L. Weber (Eds.), *Attributions, accounts, and close relationships* (pp. 176–193). New York: Springer-Verlag.

Austin, J. L. (1975). *How to do things with words* (2nd ed., J. O. Urmson & M. Sbisa, Eds.). Cambridge, MA: Harvard University Press.

Averill, J. R. (1980). A constructivist view of emotion. In R. Plutchik & K. Kellerman (Eds.), *Theories of emotion* (Vol. 1, pp. 305–339). New York: Academic Press.

Bowers, J. W., Metts, S. M., & Duncanson, W. T. (1985). Emotion and interpersonal communication. In M. L. Knapp & G. R. Miller (Eds.), *Handbook of interpersonal communication* (pp. 500–550). Beverly Hills, CA: Sage.

Bulmer, M. (1979). Concepts in the analysis of qualitative data. *Sociological Review, 27*, 651–677.

Cate, R. M., Henton, J. M., Koval, J., Christopher, F. S., & Lloyd, S. (1982). Premarital abuse: A social psychological perspective. *Journal of Family Issues, 3*, 79–90.

Cody, M. J., & McLaughlin, M. L. (1988). Accounts on trial: Oral arguments in traffic court. In C. Antake (Ed.), *Analyzing everyday explanation: A casebook of methods* (pp. 113–126). London: Sage.

de Rivera, J. (1977). *A structural theory of the emotions.* New York: International Universities Press.

de Rivera, J., & Grinkis, C. (1986). Emotions in social relationships. *Motivation and Emotion, 10*, 351–369.

Fincham, F. D., Beach, S., & Nelson, G. (1987). Attribution processes in distressed and nondistressed couples: III. Casual and responsibility attributions for spouse behavior. *Cognitive Therapy and Research, 11*, 77–86.

Fincham, F. D., & Jaspers, J. M. (1980). Attribution of responsibility: From man the scientist to man as lawyer. In L. Berkowitz (Ed.), *Advances in experimental social psychology* (Vol. 13, pp. 82–139). New York: Academic Press.

Harvery, J. H., Weber, A. L., & Orbuch, T. L. (1990). *Interpersonal accounts.* Oxford: Blackwell.

Henton, J. M., Cate, R. M., Koval, J., Lloyd, S., & Christopher, F. S. (1983). Romance and violence in dating relationships. *Journal of Family Issues, 4,* 467–482.

Herbert, T. B., Silver, R. C., & Ellard, J. H. (1991). Coping with an abusive relationship: I. How and why do women stay? *Journal of Marriage and the Family, 53,* 311–325.

Hilton, D. J. (1990). Conversational processes and causal explanation. *Psychological Bulletin, 107,* 65–81.

Holtzworth-Munroe, A. (1992). Attributions and maritally violent men: The role of cognitions in marital violence. In J. H. Harvery, T. L. Orbuch, & A. L. Weber (Eds.), *Attributions, accounts, and close relationships* (pp. 165–175). New York: Springer-Verlag.

Infante, D. A., Riddle, B. L., Horvath, C. L., & Tumlin, S. A. (1992). Verbal aggressiveness: Messages and reasons. *Communication Quarterly, 40,* 116–126.

Knapp, M. L. (1984). *Interpersonal communication and human relationships.* Boston: Allyn & Bacon.

Knapp, M. L., Stafford, L., & Daly, J. A. (1986). Regrettable messages: Things people wish they hadn't said. *Journal of Communication, 36,* 40–58.

Leffler, A. (1988). *Verbal abuse and psychological unavailability scales and relationship to self-esteem.* Paper presented at the annual meeting of the American Psychological Association, Atlanta, GA.

Martin, M. M., & Horvath, C. L. (1992, November). *Messages that hurt: What people think and feel about verbally aggressive messages.* Paper presented at the annual meeting of the Speech Communication Association, Chicago, IL.

McLaughlin, M. L. (1984). *Conversation: How talk is organized.* Beverly Hills, CA: Sage.

McLaughlin, M. L., Cody, M. J., & French, K. (1990). Account-giving and the attribution of responsibility: Impressions of traffic offenders. In M. J. Cody & M. L. McLaughlin (Eds.), *The psychology of tactical communication* (pp. 244–267). Clevedon, England: Multilingual Matters.

Montgomery, B. M. (1988). Quality communication in personal relationships. In S. W. Duck (Ed.), *Handbook of personal relationships* (pp. 343–359). New York: Wiley.

Planalp, S., & Honeycutt, J. M. (1985). Events that increase uncertainty in personal relationships. *Human Communication Research, 11,* 593–604.

Schegloff, E. A., Jefferson, G., & Sacks, H. (1977). The preference for self-correction in the organization of repair in conversation. *Language, 53,* 361–382.

Shimanoff, S. B. (1985). Rules governing the verbal expression of emotion between married couples. *Western Journal of Speech Communication, 49,* 147–165.

Shimanoff, S. B. (1987). Types of emotional disclosures and request compliance between spouses. *Communication Monographs, 54,* 85–100.

Vangelisti, A. L. (1989, November). *Messages that hurt: Perceptions of and reactions to hurtful messages in relationships.* Paper presented at the meeting of the Speech Communication Association, San Francisco, CA.

Vissing, Y. M., Straus, M. A., Gelles, R. J., & Harrop, J. W. (1991). Verbal aggression by parents and psychosocial problems of children. *Child Abuse and Neglect, 15,* 223–238.

Weber, D. J., & Vangelisti, A. L. (1991). "Because I love you": The use of tactical attributions in conversation. *Human Communication Research, 17,* 606–624.

Weiner, B. (1986). *An attributional theory of motivation and emotion.* New York: Springer-Verlag.

Weiner, B., Amirkhan, J., Folkes, V. S., & Verette, J. A. (1987). An attributional analysis of excuse giving: Studies of a naïve theory of emotion. *Journal of Personality and Social Psychology, 52,* 316–324.

Weiner, B., Graham, S., & Chandler, C. C. (1982). Pity, anger, and guilt: An attributional analysis. *Personality and Social Psychology Bulletin, 8,* 225–232.

Yelsma, P. (1992, July). *Affective orientations associated with couples' verbal abusiveness.* Paper presented at the bi-annual meeting of the International Society for the Study of Personal Relationships, Orono, ME.

Defensive Communication

Jack R. Gibb

The next selection, a classic article by communication consultant Jack Gibb, describes how defensiveness happens and what you can do to build a supportive rather than a defensive communication climate. Although it is old, this essay contains an elegant description of a very important and prevalent communication "wall."

As Gibb points out, when you anticipate or perceive that you are threatened by a person or a situation, you will usually react defensively, and so will the other persons involved. When any combination of the six "defensiveness-producing" elements is present, a spiral usually begins, a spiral that starts with a little discomfort and often escalates into all-out conflict.

But, Gibb notes, you can also start a spiral in the other direction. The more supportive you can be, the less other people are likely to read into the situation distorted reactions created by their own defensiveness. So when you can manifest any combination of the six alternative attitudes and skills, you can help reduce the defensiveness that's present. You

"Defensive Communications" by Jack Gibb from *Journal of Communication,* September 1961, Vol. 11, No. 13, pp. 141–148. Reprinted by permission of Blackwell Publishing Ltd.

don't have to give up or give in. You just have to stop trying so hard to demean, control, and impose your hard-and-fast superiority on the others.

Most of the people I work with find this article very useful. They discover that they can apply Gibb's analysis of the six characteristics of defensive and supportive communication climates to their own experience. They also find that Gibb is right when he says that most people are much more aware of being manipulated or deceived than the manipulators or deceivers think and that such awareness creates defensiveness. They are usually able to perceive quite accurately another's communication strategy or gimmicks. When they learn that sometimes it's their own transparently manipulative behavior that creates defensiveness in others, they get one step closer to communicating interpersonally.

This essay was written before authors understood that it's inappropriate to refer to people in general as "he" and "him." I hope you'll be able to read beyond this feature of the language for Gibb's excellent ideas. Defensiveness is a common communication "wall," and there are some helpful actions you can take to bridge it.

One way to understand communication is to view it as a people process rather than as a language process. If one is to make fundamental improvement in communication, he must make changes in interpersonal relationships. One possible type of alteration—and the one with which this paper is concerned—is that of reducing the degree of defensiveness.

DEFINITION AND SIGNIFICANCE

Defensive behavior is defined as that behavior which occurs when an individual perceives threat or anticipates threat in the group. The person who behaves defensively, even though he also gives some attention to the common task, devotes an appreciable portion of his energy to defending himself. Besides talking about the topic, he thinks about how he appears to others, how he may be seen more favorably, how he may win, dominate, impress, or escape punishment, and/or how he may avoid or mitigate a perceived or an anticipated attack.

Such inner feelings and outward acts tend to create similarly defensive postures in others; and, if unchecked, the ensuing circular response becomes increasingly destructive. Defensive behavior, in short, engenders defensive listening, and this in turn produces postural, facial, and verbal cues which raise the defense level of the original communicator.

Defense arousal prevents the listener from concentrating upon the message. Not only do defensive communicators send off multiple value, motive, and affect cues, but also defensive recipients distort what they receive. As a person becomes more and more defensive, he becomes less and less able to perceive accurately the motives, the values, and the emotions of the sender. The writer's analyses of tape recorded discussions revealed that increases in defensive behavior were correlated positively with losses in efficiency in communication.[1] Specifically, distortions became greater when defensive states existed in the groups.

TABLE 1 Categories of Behavior Characteristic of Supportive and Defensive Climates in Small Groups

Defensive Climates	Supportive Climates
1. Evaluation	1. Description
2. Control	2. Problem orientation
3. Strategy	3. Spontaneity
4. Neutrality	4. Empathy
5. Superiority	5. Equality
6. Certainty	6. Provisionalism

The converse, moreover, also is true. The more "supportive" or defense reductive the climate the less the receiver reads into the communication distorted loadings which arise from projections of his own anxieties, motives, and concerns. As defenses are reduced, the receivers become better able to concentrate upon the structure, the content, and the cognitive meanings of the message.

CATEGORIES OF DEFENSIVE AND SUPPORTIVE COMMUNICATION

In working over an eight-year period with recordings of discussions occurring in varied settings, the writer developed the six pairs of defensive and supportive categories presented in Table 1. Behavior which a listener perceives as possessing any of the characteristics listed in the left-hand column arouses defensiveness, whereas that which he interprets as having any of the qualities designated as supportive reduces defensive feelings. The degree to which these reactions occur depends upon the personal level of defensiveness and upon the general climate in the group at the time.[2]

Evaluation and Description

Speech or other behavior which appears evaluative increases defensiveness. If by expression, manner of speech, tone of voice, or verbal content the sender seems to be evaluating or judging the listener, then the receiver goes on guard. Of course, other factors may inhibit the reaction. If the listener thought that the speaker regarded him as an equal and was being open and spontaneous, for example, the evaluativeness in a message would be neutralized and perhaps not even perceived. This same principle applies equally to the other five categories of potentially defense-producing climates. The six sets are interactive.

Because our attitudes toward other persons are frequently, and often necessarily, evaluative, expressions which the defensive person will regard as nonjudgmental are hard to frame. Even the simplest question usually conveys the answer that the sender wishes or implies the response that would fit into his value system. A mother, for example, immediately following an earth tremor that shook the house, sought for her small son with the question: "Bobby, where are you?" The timid and plaintive "Mommy, I didn't do it" indicated how Bobby's chronic mild defensiveness predisposed him to react with a projection of his own guilt and in the context of his chronic assumption that questions are full of accusation.

Anyone who has attempted to train professionals to use information-seeking speech with neutral affect appreciates how difficult it is to teach a person to say even the simple "who did that?" without being seen as accusing. Speech is so frequently judgmental that there is a reality base for the defensive interpretations which are so common.

When insecure, group members are particularly likely to place blame, to see others as fitting into categories of good or bad, to make moral judgments of their colleagues, and to question the value, motive, and affect loadings of the speech which they hear. Since value loadings imply a judgment of others, a belief that the standards of the speaker differ from his own causes the listener to become defensive.

Descriptive speech, in contrast to that which is evaluative, tends to arouse a minimum of uneasiness. Speech acts which the listener perceives as genuine requests for information or as material with neutral loadings is descriptive. Specifically, presentations of feelings, events, perceptions, or processes which do not ask or imply that the receiver change behavior or attitude are minimally defense producing. The difficulty in avoiding overtone is illustrated by the problems of news reporters in writing stories about unions, communists, Blacks, and religious activities without tipping off the "party" line of the newspaper. One can often tell from the opening words in a news article which side the newspaper's editorial policy favors.

Control and Problem Orientation

Speech which is used to control the listener evokes resistance. In most of our social intercourse someone is trying to do something to someone else—to change an attitude, to influence behavior, or to restrict the field of activity. The degree to which attempts to control produce defensiveness depends upon the openness of the effort, for a suspicion that hidden motives exist heightens resistance. For this reason attempts of nondirective therapists and progressive educators to refrain from imposing a set of values, a point of view, or a problem solution upon the receivers meet with many barriers. Since the norm is control, noncontrollers must earn the perceptions that their efforts have no hidden motives. A bombardment of persuasive "messages" in the fields of politics, education, special causes, advertising, religion, medicine, industrial relations, and guidance has bred cynical and paranoidal responses in listeners.

Implicit in all attempts to alter another person is the assumption by the change agent that the person to be altered is inadequate. That the speaker secretly views the listener as ignorant, unable to make his own decisions, uninformed, immature, unwise, or possessed of wrong or inadequate attitudes is a subconscious perception which gives the latter a valid base for defensive reactions.

Methods of control are many and varied. Legalistic insistence on detail, restrictive regulations and policies, conformity norms, and all laws are among the methods. Gestures, facial expressions, other forms of nonverbal communication, and even such simple acts as holding a door open in a particular manner are means of imposing one's will upon another and hence are potential sources of resistance.

Problem orientation, on the other hand, is the antithesis of persuasion. When the sender communicates a desire to collaborate in defining a mutual problem and in seeking its solution, he tends to create the same problem orientation in the listener; and, of greater importance, he implies that he has no predetermined solution, attitude, or method to impose. Such behavior is permissive in that it allows the receiver to set his own goals, make his own decisions, and evaluate his own progress—or to share with the sender in doing so. The exact methods of attaining permissiveness are not known, but they must involve a constellation of cues and they certainly go beyond mere verbal assurances that the communicator has no hidden desires to exercise control.

Strategy and Spontaneity

When the sender is perceived as engaged in a stratagem involving ambiguous and multiple motivations, the receiver becomes defensive. No one wishes to be a guinea pig, a role player, or an impressed actor, and no one likes to be the victim of some hidden motivation. That which is concealed, also, may appear larger than it really is with the degree of defensiveness of the listener determining the perceived size of the suppressed element. The intense reaction of the reading audience to the material in *Hidden Persuaders* indicates the prevalence of defensive reactions to multiple motivations behind strategy. Group members who are seen as "taking a role," as feigning emotion, as toying with their colleagues, as withholding information, or as having special sources of data are especially resented. One participant once complained that another was "using a listening technique" on him!

A large part of the adverse reaction to much of the so-called human relations training is a feeling against what are perceived as gimmicks and tricks to fool or to "involve" people, to make a person think he is making his own decision, or to make the listener feel that the sender is genuinely interested in him as a person. Particularly violent reactions occur when it appears that someone is trying to make a stratagem appear spontaneous. One person has reported a boss who incurred resentment by habitually using the gimmick of "spontaneously" looking at his watch and saying, "My gosh, look at the time—I must run to an appointment." The belief was that the boss would create less irritation by honestly asking to be excused.

Similarly, the deliberate assumption of guilelessness and natural simplicity is especially resented. Monitoring the tapes of feedback and evaluation sessions in training groups indicates the surprising extent to which members perceive the strategies of their colleagues. This perceptual clarity may be quite shocking to the strategist, who usually feels that he had cleverly hidden the motivational aura around the "gimmick."

This aversion to deceit may account for one's resistance to politicians who are suspected of behind-the-scenes planning to get his vote, to psychologists whose listening apparently is motivated by more than the manifest or content-level interest in his behavior, or to the sophisticated, smooth, or clever person whose "oneupmanship" is marked with guile. In training groups the role-flexible person frequently is resented because his changes in behavior are perceived as strategic maneuvers.

In contrast, behavior which appears to be spontaneous and free of deception is defense reductive. If the communicator is seen as having a clean id, as having uncomplicated motivations, as being straightforward and honest, and as behaving spontaneously in response to the situation, he is likely to arouse minimal defense.

Neutrality and Empathy

When neutrality in speech appears to the listener to indicate a lack of concern for his welfare, he becomes defensive. Group members usually desire to be perceived as valued persons, as individuals of special worth, and as objects of concern and affection. The clinical, detached, person-is-an-object-of-study attitude on the part of many psychologist-trainers is resented by group members. Speech with low affect that communicates little warmth or caring is in such contrast with the affect-laden speech in social situations that it sometimes communicates rejection.

Communication that conveys empathy for the feelings and respect for the worth of the listener, however, is particularly supportive and defense reductive. Reassurance results when a message indicates that the speaker identifies himself with the listener's problems, shares his feelings, and accepts his emotional reactions at face value. Abortive efforts to deny the legitimacy of the receiver's emotions by assuring the receiver that he need not feel bad, that he should not feel rejected, or that he is overly anxious, though often intended as support giving, may impress the listener as lack of acceptance. The combination of understanding and empathizing with the other person's emotions with no accompanying effort to change him apparently is supportive at a high level.

The importance of gestural behavioral cues in communicating empathy should be mentioned. Apparently spontaneous facial and bodily evidences of concern are often interpreted as especially valid evidence of deep-level acceptance.

Superiority and Equality

When a person communicates to another that he feels superior in position, power, wealth, intellectual ability, physical characteristics, or other ways, he arouses defensiveness. Here, as with the other sources of disturbance, whatever arouses feelings of inadequacy causes the listener to center upon the affect loading of the statement rather than upon the cognitive elements. The receiver then reacts by not hearing the message, by forgetting it, by competing with the sender, or by becoming jealous of him.

The person who is perceived as feeling superior communicates that he is not willing to enter into a shared problem-solving relationship, that he probably does not desire feedback, that he does not require help, and/or that he will be likely to try to reduce the power, the status, or the worth of the receiver.

Many ways exist for creating the atmosphere that the sender feels himself equal to the listener. Defenses are reduced when one perceives the sender as being willing to enter into participative planning with mutual trust and respect. Differences in talent, ability, worth, appearance, status, and power often exist, but the low defense communicator seems to attach little importance to these distinctions.

Certainty and Provisionalism

The effects of dogmatism in producing defensiveness are well known. Those who seem to know the answers, to require no additional data, and to regard themselves as teachers rather than as co-workers tend to put others on guard. Moreover, in the writer's experiment, listeners often perceived manifest expressions of certainty as connoting inward feelings of inferiority. They saw the dogmatic individual as needing to be right, as wanting to win an argument rather than solve a problem, and as seeing his ideas as truths to be defended. This kind of behavior often was associated with acts which others regarded as attempts to exercise control. People who were right seemed to have low tolerance for members who were "wrong"—i.e., who did not agree with the sender.

One reduces the defensiveness of the listener when he communicates that he is willing to experiment with his own behavior, attitudes, and ideas. The person who appears to be taking provisional attitudes, to be investigating issues rather than taking sides on them, to be problem solving rather than debating, and to be willing to experiment and explore tends to communicate that the listener may have some control over the shared quest or the investigation of the ideas. If a person is genuinely searching for information and data, he does not resent help or company along the way.

CONCLUSION

The implications of the above material for the parent, the teacher, the manager, the administrator, or the therapist are fairly obvious. Arousing defensiveness interferes with communication and thus makes it difficult—and sometimes impossible—for anyone to convey ideas clearly and to move effectively toward the solution of therapeutic, educational, or managerial problems.

REVIEW QUESTIONS

1. How does Gibb define *defensiveness?*
2. What does defensiveness defend? What does supportiveness support?
3. How can description accomplish the same purpose as evaluation?
4. Based on what you've already read about empathy in Chapter 5, how is neutrality the opposite of empathy?

PROBES

1. Does Gibb see defensiveness as a relational thing—something that's created *between* persons—or does he see it as something one person or group creates and forces on another person or group?
2. Gibb cautions us about the negative effects of evaluation. But is it possible actually to be non-evaluative? Or is that what Gibb is asking us to do?
3. Although most of Gibb's examples use verbal cues, each of the categories of defensiveness and supportiveness is also communicated nonverbally. Can you identify how you nonverbally communicate evaluation? Control? Strategy? Superiority? Spontaneity? Empathy? Equality?
4. Self-disclosing is one way to communicate spontaneity. Can you identify communication behaviors that help create the other kinds of supportive climate?
5. Which categories of defensive behavior are most present in your relationship with your lover or spouse? Your employer? Your parents? Which categories of supportive behavior characterize those relationships?

NOTES

1. J. R. Gibb, "Defense Level and Influence Potential in Small Groups," *Leadership and Interpersonal Behavior,* ed. L. Petrullo and B. M. Bass (New York: Holt, Rinehart and Winston, 1961), pp. 66–81.
2. J. R. Gibb, "Sociopsychological Processes of Group Instruction," *The Dynamics of Instructional Groups,* ed. N. B. Henry (Fifty-ninth Yearbook of the National Society of the Study of Education, Part II, 1960), pp. 115–135.

Power: The Structure of Conflict
William W. Wilmot and Joyce L. Hocker

This excerpt from the book called *Interpersonal Conflict* explains how power works in conflict situations and how you can manage it. The authors have years of practical experience helping individuals and groups deal with conflict, and *Interpersonal Conflict* has been one of the most trusted conflict texts for years.

After defining power, Wilmot and Hocker explain two different orientations toward power, one that increases difficulties and another that can help resolve conflicts. The first is an "either/or" orientation to power that is common in news stories and the understandings of the person-on-the-street. From this orientation, power is force that pushes people around against their will. Almost no one thinks that he or she has enough of this kind of power, and we all think that others have more than we do. In what the authors call a "distressed system," power concerns outrank concerns about rights and interests. In an effective system, by contrast, interests are primary, rights are important, and power plays a smaller role.

An effective and ethical system for exercising power is found in the second "both/and" way. This means that parties understand that everyone involved has some power and that, if the focus stays on harmony and cooperation, power relationships can be worked out. This both/and orientation is common in Japanese and Javanese cultures, and it is often the first choice of women in Western cultures. Another term for this orientation is "relational," and in the next section of the reading Wilmot and Hocker develop a relational theory of power.

The starting point of this theory is that power happens between people. One person does not "have" power on his or her own; he or she has power only *in relation to* other people, certain topics, particular times, certain contexts, and so on. As one author puts it, "power is always interpersonal"; power dynamics are fluid, changing, and dependent on the specific situation.

From this relational perspective, individuals possess various power currencies, and Wilmot and Hocker discuss four of them that spell the word RICE. *R* is for resource control, which is the power to control rewards or punishments. *I* stands for interpersonal linkages, the power to connect people to accomplish goals. A third currency is *C*ommunication skills—persuasive ability, listening skills, leadership skills, and the ability to communicate caring and warmth. All these skills generate power in various contexts. The fourth power currency is *E*xpertise—special knowledge, skills, and talents that are useful for certain tasks. It's easy to understand how all these "RICE" elements are relational when you realize, for example, that expertise is powerful only if it's relevant. If a project or a problem involves sports, the expertise of a space scientist may be worthless. But if the project or problem has to do with physics or space travel, the scientist will have abundant power. As Wilmot and Hocker summarize, it helps to understand the power currencies available to you and other parties in a conflict because all can move from believing that they have no choice but to respond in a given way to understanding that everyone has some power.

Next, Wilmot and Hocker discuss how calm persistence can help lower-power people deal with powerful institutions or authorities. They offer four specific ways that lower-power people can cope with conflict situations.

The final section of the reading focuses on metacommunication, which basically means communication about communication. By talking explicitly about the importance and value of the relationship or by deciding in advance how the parties will handle their conflicts, power difficulties can be avoided. Metacommunication focuses the parties on the process of their communication with each other and can engage them in a joint effort to improve the situation.

Wilmot and Hocker conclude by explaining what they call the "paradox of power." To be effective, people need to take advantage of opportunities and use resources at their disposal, but within an ongoing relationship, maximizing individual power is counterproductive for everyone involved. So the paradox is that each of us needs some power, but if we have too much, communication will be difficult. Each conflict partner's goal should be to balance the power that exists between or among the parties so that power facilitates rather than prevents interpersonal communication.

WHAT IS POWER?

In interpersonal and all other conflicts, perceptions of power are at the heart of any analysis. Hundreds of definitions of power tend to fall into three camps. Power is seen as (1) *distributive* (either/or), (2) *integrative* (both/and), or (3) *designated* (power to a certain relationship). *Distributive* definitions of power stress that "with force, control, pressure or aggression, one individual is able to carry his or her objective over the resistance of another and thus gain power" (Dahl 1957, 3). Distributive approaches focus on power over or power against the other party.

Integrative definitions of power highlight power *with* the other. Integrative views stress "joining forces with someone else to achieve mutually acceptable goals" (Lilly 1989, 281). Integrative definitions focus on "both/and"—both parties have to achieve something in the relationship. As we shall see, it is not what outsiders say about power, but the views the conflict parties have that determine the outcomes of their conflicts.

Designated power "gives" power to a certain relationship, rather than power being held by individuals or even teams. In designated power, people confer power on a marriage, a work group, a family, or a group of friends with whom one is in relationship....

ORIENTATIONS TO POWER

When a dispute occurs between two people, they often talk about power, and their perspectives on how it operates will predispose them to engage in certain communicative moves. People feel passionately about power—who has it, who ought to have more or less, how people misuse power, and how justified they feel in trying to gain more power for themselves. This orientation toward power seems to be true for many reasons.

We each need enough power to live the life we want. We want to influence events that matter to us. We want to have our voices heard, and make a difference. We want to protect ourselves against perceived harm. We want to hold in high esteem ourselves and those we care about. We do not want to be victimized, misused, or demeaned. No one can escape feeling the effects of power—whether we have too much or too little, or someone else has too much or too little.

When people struggle with each other, they almost never agree on anything having to do with power. For example, if you are a student intern in a real estate firm and you feel that brokers have all the power, you are likely to keep silent even when you disagree—giving the impression that you agree when you don't. If, on the other hand, you feel that both you and the brokers have sources of power, you will be more likely to engage in discussion to work through issues. As an intern, you may have sources of power such as a different set of acquaintances, free time on weekends when the brokers are involved with their families but need to work, or a fresh outlook and a desire to learn. If you think of yourself, however, as "just a lowly intern," you may miss many opportunities to be a team member because you have assessed your power incorrectly.... .

Either/Or Power

When you examine typical newspaper stories about power, you read about the either/or (distributive) notions of power. In fact, it is difficult to even find examples of any other orientation toward power in the popular press. Many people think that power is only "force"—pushing others around against their will. When you examine nations using military might against other nations, you see either/or power in operation.

Once a relationship begins to go downhill, concerns with power increase. As any relationship deteriorates, the parties shift to a more overt focus on power—and this shift is reflected in their discourse (Beck 1988). In fact, a characteristic of destructive power is that parties start thinking and talking about power. Almost no one thinks that he or she has more power than the other power, at least when emotions run very high. We think the other has more power, which then justifies dirty tricks and our own attempt to gain more power. We often see ourselves as blameless victims of the other's abuse of power. When partners are caught in this destructive cycle of either/or power, their communicative interactions show a lot of "one up" responses, or attempts to demonstrate conversational power over each other (Sabourin and Stamp 1995). Partners might say, "She is just trying to control me," or "I'm not going to let him push me around." People, whether married couples or work colleagues, try to "keep score"—watching the "points" they have vis-à-vis the other party (Ross and Holmberg 1992). When partners develop an overt concern with power, their struggles over power are directly related to relationship satisfaction (Kurdek 1994). Figure 1 demonstrates how concerns rank in a distressed relationship.

FIGURE 1 Power emphasized in a distressed system.
Source: From William Ury, Jeanne M. Brett, and Stephen B. Goldberg, Getting Disputes Resolved: Designing Systems to Cut the Costs of Conflict. *Copyright © 1988 Jossey-Bass Inc., Publishers, San Francisco, California. Reprinted by permission.*

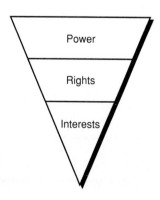

As Ury, Brett, and Goldberg (1988) so aptly note, the focus for a dispute becomes power—who has the right to move the other. The teenager who says, "You can't boss me around," the spouse who shouts, "Just who do you think you are?" and the co-worker who states, "Well, we'll see who the boss is around here!" are all highlighting power and giving it center stage in the dispute. These struggles often escalate. Dissatisfied couples are more than three times as likely to escalate episodes and focus on power than satisfied couples (Alberts and Driscoll 1992).... We are not suggesting that power shouldn't be an issue. Rather, we suggest that when power itself becomes the main focus of thinking and discussion, parties are likely to be involved in an escalating power struggle, and may well have temporarily lost sight of interests and solutions.

Notice in Figure 1 that disputes also involve "rights" and "interests." Rights, similar to our idea of core concerns, include not being discriminated against, being free from physical harm, and other constitutional and legal guarantees we have as citizens. Sometimes it is more appropriate that disputes get settled on the basis of rights rather than power or interests. For example, if the famous *Brown* v. *Board of Education* case in 1954 outlawing segregation in public schools had been settled on the basis of power, it would have resulted in a struggle in the streets. If, on the other hand, it had been settled on the basis of interests, Brown might have negotiated her way into school, but the country's social policy would not have changed. When we solve a dispute based on interests, the goals and desires of the parties are the key elements. For instance, if you don't want your teenage son to use the car, you can (1) tell him it is not OK as long as you pay the bills in the house (power); (2) let him know that you own the car and have all the rights to its use (rights); or (3) let him know that you are dissatisfied with how he drives, and until you are convinced he will be safe, you will not lend the car (interests). Thus, disputes can occur on any one of the three levels. When power becomes the only personal goal, the dispute is harder to resolve.

Figure 2 illustrates an effective system in which the emphasis is on interests with rights and power playing smaller but still important roles. As you can see by comparing Figure 1 with Figure 2, an overemphasis on power is symptomatic of a distressed system.

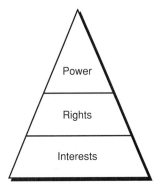

FIGURE 2 Power de-emphasized in an effective system.
Source: From William Ury, Jeanne M. Brett, and Stephen B. Goldberg, Getting Disputes Resolved: Designing Systems to Cut the Costs of Conflict. *Copyright © 1988 Jossey-Bass Inc., Publishers, San Francisco, California. Reprinted by permission.*

Both/And Power

Two alternatives to viewing disputes as power struggles can help us out of the distributive power dilemma. Boulding (1989) notes that "the great fallacy, especially of political thinking in regard to power, is to elevate threat power to the position of dominance" (10). Interpersonal relationships reflect the same fallacy—many people just can't envision power in terms other than "either/or," or "win/lose." Yet a study of the dynamics of successful disputes and ongoing relationships reveals that power functions on a broader basis than either/or thinking. Disputes become power struggles if the parties allow them to be defined as such. If we think of power "merely in terms of threat, we will get nowhere" (250). Conceptually, the alternative to framing disputes as power struggles is to place power in a position subordinate to rights and needs.

To help us understand the cultural basis of our assumptions, Augsburger (1992) details the lack of verbal fighting in some other cultures. In these cultures, power is activated as both/and or designated power, discussed in the next section. In Japanese and Javanese cultures, for instance, to name two obvious examples, harmony and cooperation are basic values, and verbal contradiction is not the automatic first choice in conflict. A more accepted process is to affirm the strengths of each other's position, let them stand without attack, and then join in exploring other options. Both parties search for superior options (59).

Both/and power is often the first choice of women in our culture. Researchers at the Stone Center at Wellesley have spent two decades explicating "relational theory" in an attempt to balance the traditional male orientation that permeates United States culture. In their view, relational theory is a belief system that describes how growth and effectiveness occur (Fletcher 1999). Masculine theories, which until the last 20 years or so have been accepted as the only psychologically sound theories, often assumed that maturity and competence depend on autonomy, or separation from constraints, other people, and group identity. Boys, for instance, learn to relate to power through games and competition more than girls do. Boys learn to be comfortable with the hierarchy of teams, captains, coaches, and bosses. Girls learn to play with less focus on hierarchy. Many girls' games are cooperative in nature, with girls taking roles to play out, after discussing together what to do. As Heim (1993) notes, "There's no boss in dolls." For boys, conflict means competition, which often enhances relationships. For girls, competition is often painful and damages relationships. Girls often prefer to look for a win/win situation (Heim 1993, 27).

Relational theory and practice offer the idea that maturity and competence depend on growth-in-connection and mutuality. The ability to develop relationally depends on mutual empathy, mutual empowerment, responsibility to both oneself and others, and the ability to experience and express emotion, to experience and learn from vulnerability, to participate in the development of another, and to enhance each other's efforts (Fletcher 1999; Jordan et al. 1991). This approach does not need to be seen strictly as a female approach. Many effective forms of conflict resolution depend on a relational approach. Some situations in which power is heavily unbalanced also require a level of competition and assertiveness that does not come naturally for many women. If competition remains the dominant approach, however, constructive conflict resolution is unlikely to occur, except temporarily....

A RELATIONAL THEORY OF POWER

A common perception is that power is an attribute of a person. If you say, "Lynn is a powerful person," you may, if she is your friend, be referring to such attributes as verbal facility, intelligence, compassion, warmth, and understanding. Or you may refer to a politician as powerful, alluding to her ability to make deals, call in favors, remember names and faces, and understand complex economic issues. In interpersonal relationships, however, excluding situations of unequal physical power and use of violence, power is a property of the social relationship rather than a quality of the individual. Lynn, for instance, has power with her friends because she has qualities they value. When she suggests something to do, like going on an annual women's backpacking trip, her friends try to clear their calendars because they like her, have fun with her, and feel understood by her. Lynn has a way of making a group feel cohesive and at ease. But if an acquaintance hated backpacking, did not like some of the other people going on the trip, and was irritated at Lynn because of a misunderstanding that had not yet been cleared up, Lynn's power with the irritated acquaintance would lessen considerably.

Similarly, if a politician did not show any interest in a bill that a human rights group was trying to get on the table in their state legislature and, furthermore, if the politician were a congresswoman representing another state, the congresswoman would have little power with the human rights group. Would she still be "a powerful person"? She would be to her constituents but not to the interest group in question.

Power is not owned by an individual but is a product of the social relationship in which certain qualities become important and valuable to others (King 1987; Rogers 1974; Harsanyi 1962a; Deutsch 1958; Dahl 1957; Soloman 1960). Deutsch (1973) states the case well: "Power is a relational concept; it does not reside in the individual but rather in the relationship of the person to his environment. Thus, the power of an agent in a given situation is determined by the characteristics of the situation" (15). Rather than residing in people, "power is always interpersonal" (May 1972, 23). In the strictest sense, except when violence and physical coercion are used, power is given from one party to another in a conflict. Power can be taken away when the situation changes. Power dynamics are fluid, changing, and dependent on the specific situation. Each person in a conflict has some degree of power, though one party may have more compared to the other, and the power can shift during a conflict....

INDIVIDUAL POWER CURRENCIES

You may have had the experience of traveling in a foreign country and trying to adapt to the use of different currencies. Drachmas, used in Greece, are worthless in India, where rupees are used to buy items of value. A pocketful of rupees is worthless in France unless you exchange it for the local currency. Just as money depends on the context in which it is to be spent (the country), your power currencies depend on how much your particular resources are valued by the other persons in your relationships (Rodman 1967, 1972). You may have a vast amount of expertise in the rules of basketball, but if your fraternity needs an intramural football coach, you will not be valued as much as you would be if they needed a basketball coach. Power depends on having currencies that other people need. In the same manner, if other people possess currencies you value, such as the ability to edit a term paper or the possession of a car, they potentially maintain some degree of power over you in your relationships with them. Conflict is often confusing because people try to spend currency that is not valued in a particular relationship....

R

Resource control: Often comes with one's formal position in an organization or group. An example is the controlling of rewards or punishments such as salary, number of hours worked, or firing. Parents control resources such as money, freedom, cars, and privacy for teenagers.

I

Interpersonal linkages: Your position in the larger system, such as being central to communication exchange. If you are a liaison person between two factions, serve as a bridge between two groups that would otherwise not have information about each other, or have a network of friends who like each other, you have linkage currencies.

C

Communication skills: Conversational skills, persuasive ability, listening skills, group leadership skills, the ability to communicate caring and warmth, and the ability to form close bonds with others all contribute to interpersonal power. All people need to be related to others, to matter to others, and to be understood by others. Those who communicate well gain value and thus interpersonal power.

E

Expertise: Special knowledge, skills, and talents that are useful for the task at hand. Being an expert in a content area such as budget analysis, a process area such as decision-making methods, or a relational area such as decoding nonverbal cues may give you power when others need your expertise.

Resource control often results from attaining a formal position that brings resources to you. The president of the United States, regardless of personal qualities, will always have some resources that go along with the job. Leadership and position, by their very nature, place a person in a situation in which others are dependent upon him or her, thus bringing ready-made power. Whatever your position—secretary, boss, chairperson, teacher, manager, or volunteer—you will be in a position to control resources that others desire. Many resources are economic in nature, such as money, gifts, and material possessions (Warner, Lee, and Lee 1986). Many people try to be close and supportive to those around them by buying gifts. They trade on economic currencies in order to obtain intimacy currencies from others. Their gifts are not always valued enough to bring them what they want, however. Not surprisingly, people who give gifts to each other often try to work out an agreement, probably implicitly, about the amount of money that can be spent to keep the dependence (and power) equal. If an inordinate amount of money is spent by one person, then typically the other person feels overly indebted. As Blau (1964) writes, "A person who gives others valuable gifts or renders them important services makes a claim for superior status by obligating them to himself" (108). People with little money usually have limited access to these forms of power. College graduates who cannot find jobs must remain financially dependent on parents, thus limiting independence on both sides. Elderly people whose savings shrink due to inflation lose power; mothers with children and no means of support lose most of their choices about independence, thus losing most of their potential power. Economic currencies are not the only important type of power currency, but they operate in small, personal conflicts as well as in larger social conflicts.

Another cluster of power currencies comes from one's *interpersonal linkages,* a set of currencies that depend on your interpersonal contacts and network of friends and supporters. People often obtain power based on whom they know and with whom they associate. For instance, if you have a good friend who has a mountain cabin you can share with others, then you have attained some power (if your family or friends want to go to the cabin) because of your ability to obtain things through other people. Young children try to trade on their linkage currencies when they say such things as "My Uncle Ben is a park ranger, and he will give us a tour of the park."

Interpersonal linkages help one attain power through coalition formation. Whenever you band together with another (such as a good friend) to gain some sense of strength, this coalition can be a form of power (Van de Vliert 1981). The small boy who says, "You better not hit me, because if you do, my big sister will beat you up" understands the potential value of coalitions.... Interpersonal linkages are a source of power when people check out their network for what classes to take, where jobs might be available, where rentals might be found, and other kinds of information. "Who you know" is often a source of power.

One's *communication skills* also serve as potential power currencies. If you can lead a group in a decision-making process, speak persuasively, write a news release for your organization, serve as an informal mediator between people who are angry with each other, or use tact in asking for what you want, you will gain power because of your communication skills. Many times, students who have developed their communication skills are employed upon graduation because of their skills. Employers are willing to teach technical and specialized skills later. Conversationally, your skills make a considerable difference, too. As Millar and Rogers (1988) demonstrated, when others allow us to dominate the conversation we have attained a source of power. Likewise, if you can facilitate the social process of a group, serve as the fun-loving joker in the family, or get conversations started at work, others typically will value you. It is not only the qualities, per se, that bring power but that these currencies are valued by others.

Communication skills also include the ability to form bonds with others through love, sex, caring, nurturing, understanding, empathic listening, warmth, attention, and other characteristics of intimate relationships. If a father provides genuine warmth and understanding to his teenage daughter who is going through a tough time at school, his support is a currency for him in their father-daughter relationship....

Expertise currencies are involved when a person has some special skill or knowledge that someone else values. The worker who is the only one who can operate the boiler at a large lumber mill has power because the expertise is badly needed. The medical doctor who specializes in a particular area has expertise power because her information and skills are needed by others. Almost all professions develop specialized expertise valued by others, which serves as a basis of power for people in the profession. Family members develop expertise in certain areas that others within the family come to depend on, such as cooking, repairing the car, or babysitting.

We limit our own power by developing some currencies at the expense of others. For example, women have traditionally been most comfortable using power to bond with others (Miller 1991), providing more warmth and affection than men do (Johnson 1976). If this particular communication skill is developed at the expense of the ability to clarify a group discussion, a woman unnecessarily limits her power potential. The person who trades on currencies of interpersonal linkages, such as access to the boss, may neglect the development of expertise. The person who gains power by controlling resources, such as money or sex, may neglect the development of communication skills, resulting in a relationship based on coercive instead of shared power; withdrawing warmth in intimate relationships too often substitutes for good communication skills. A worker who focuses on the development of expertise in computer programming and systems analysis may ignore the power that can be developed through interpersonal linkages, thus furthering a tendency toward isolation in the organization. The most effective conflict participant develops several forms of power currencies and knows when to activate the different forms of power. A repertoire of currencies is a better base for sharing power than exclusive reliance on one form of power, which too often leads to misuse of that power.

Clarifying the currencies available to you and the other parties in a conflict helps in the conflict analysis. People are often unaware of their own sources of productive power, just as they do not understand their own dependence on others. Desperation and low-power tactics often arise from the feeling that one has no choice, that no power is available. Analyze your power currencies when you find yourself saying, "I have no choice." Usually, you are overlooking potential sources of power....

The Power of Calm Persistence

Lower-power people in a conflict often can gain more equal power by persisting in their requests. Substantive change, when power is unequal, seldom comes about through intense, angry confrontation. Rather, change results from careful thinking and from planning for small, manageable moves based on a solid understanding of the problem (Lerner 1989, 15). When intensity is high, people react rather than observe and think. We overfocus on the other instead of an analysis of the problem, and we move toward polarization. Lower-power parties cannot afford to blow up. One source of power the lower-power person has, however, is careful, calm analysis that directs attention to the problem. If lower-power people have patience and avoid giving up out of frustration, they gain "nuisance value," and the higher-power person or group often listens and collaborates just to get them to go away. Persuasive skills become crucial. The low-power person must analyze the rhetorical situation well, taking into account what will be judged appropriate, effective, credible, and practical....

Some suggestions for dealing with large, impersonal institutions are as follows:

- Identify the individuals on the phone by name and ask for them when you call back.
- Stay pleasant and calm. State clearly what you want, and ask for help in solving the problem.
- Follow the rules even if you think they are ridiculous. If they want five copies of a form, typed and folded a certain way, give it to them. Then point out that you have followed the rules and expect results.
- Write simple, clear memos summarizing what you want, what you have done, and when you expect a response.
- Tell them all the steps you took to try to get a response from them.
- Avoid taking out your frustration on low-power individuals in the organization. They may respond with "I'm just following the rules," avoiding personal responsibility—and who could blame them? Instead, be courteous and ask for help. Humor always helps if it is not at someone else's expense....

Rather than remaining in self-defeating spirals, Lerner (1989, 35) suggests that people in low-power positions adopt the following moves:

- *Speak up and present a balanced picture of strengths as well as weaknesses.* One might say, "It's true that I am afraid to ask my boss for a raise, even though you want me to. But I earn a steady paycheck and budget and plan well for our family. I want some credit for what I do already contribute."
- *Make clear what one's beliefs, values, and priorities are, and then keep one's behavior congruent with these.* An entry-level accountant in a large firm was asked by the comptroller to falsify taxable deductions, hiding some of the benefits given to employees. The accountant, just out of school and a single parent, said, "When you hired me I said I was committed to doing good work and being an honest accountant. What you are asking me to do is against the code of ethics and could result in my losing my license. I can't afford to take that risk. I'm sure you'll understand my position."
- *Stay emotionally connected to significant others even when things get intense.* It takes courage for a low-power person to let another person affect him or her. One teenage son was furious and hurt when his father decided to remarry, since the son did not like the wife-to-be at all and felt disloyal to his mother. After some tough thinking, he decided to tell his father honestly how he felt, what he did not like, and what he feared about the new marriage instead of taking another way out, such as angrily leaving his father's house to live with his mother in another state. This conversation balanced the power between father and son in an entirely new way.
- *State differences, and allow others to do the same.* The easiest, but often not the best, way for a low-power person to manage conflict is to avoid engagement. Again, courage is required to bring up differences when a power imbalance is in place. Brad, a college freshman, worked at a fast-food place during school. He was unhappy because the manager kept hiring unqualified people (without checking their references) and then expected Brad to train them and provide supervision, even though Brad was barely making more than minimum wage. Finally Brad told the manager, "I have a different way of looking at whom you should hire. I try to do a good job for you, but I have to try to work with people who have no experience and maybe don't have the personality to pitch in and work hard as part of the team. Would you consider letting me sit in on interviews and look over applications?" The manager was pleased with Brad's initiative and said yes.

Empowerment of Low-Power People by High-Power People

Sometimes it is clearly to the advantage of higher-power groups or individuals to purposely enhance the power of lower-power groups or individuals. Without this restructuring of power, working or intimate relationships may end or rigidify into bitter, silent, passive aggressive, and unsatisfactory entanglements. Currencies valued by higher-power people can be developed by lower-power people if they are allowed more training, more decision-making power, or more freedom. For instance, in one social service agency, Sharon was not doing well at directing a grant-funded program on finding housing for homeless people. Jan, the director of the agency, realized that Sharon was a good fund-raiser but not a good program director. By switching Sharon's job description, the agency gained a good employee instead of continuing a series of negative job evaluations that would have resulted in Sharon's eventual termination....

Metacommunication

Another way to balance power is to transcend the win/lose structure by jointly working to preserve the relationship during conflict. By metacommunicating during or before conflicts (talking about the relationship or about how the parties will handle their conflicts), the parties can agree about behaviors that will not be allowed (such as leaving during a fight).

Metacommunication focuses the parties on the process of their communication with each other. They talk about their communication, and if that fails, they can agree to bring in outside mediators or counselors. They can agree that whenever a serious imbalance occurs, the high-power party will work actively with the low-power party to alter the balance in a meaningful way. Usually romantic partners, friends, family members, and work partners can accomplish such joint moves if they agree that the maximization of individual power, left unrestrained, will destroy the relationship. They see that individual power is based relationally, that dependence begets power, and that successful relationships necessitate a balancing of dependencies and therefore of power. The lack of a balanced arrangement is a signal to reinvest in the relationship rather than a clue that the relationship is over. The person temporarily weaker in the relationship can draw on the relationship currencies, as if the relationship were a bank and the currencies were savings. The weaker party can claim extra time, space, money, training, empathy, or other special considerations until the power is brought back into an approximation of balance....

Most of us are caught in a paradox of power. To be effective people, we need to maximize our abilities, take advantage of opportunities, and use resources at our disposal so we can lead the kind of lives we desire. Yet within the confines of an ongoing relationship, *maximization of individual power is counterproductive* for both the higher-power and lower-power parties. The unrestrained maximization of individual power leads to damaged relations, destructive moves, more destructive countermoves, and the eventual ending of the relationship. Since people are going to take steps to balance power—destructively if no other means are available—we can better manage conflict by working to balance power in productive and creative ways. Equity in power reduces violence and enables all participants to continue working for the good of all parties, even in conflict.

REVIEW QUESTIONS

1. Distinguish among *distributive, integrative,* and *designated* power. Give an example of each.
2. If people are talking about how little power they have in a conflict, this can be a sign that the system they're in is what Wilmot and Hocker call "distressed." Explain.
3. What does it mean to say that both/and power is often the first choice of women in Western cultures?
4. "Power is not owned by an individual but is a product of the social relationship in which certain qualities become important and valuable to others." Explain.
5. Define resource control, interpersonal linkages, communication skills, and expertise as aspects of a person's power.
6. Paraphrase Wilmot and Hocker's advice to the low-power person in a conflict.
7. Define *metacommunication.*
8. Explain the "paradox of power."

PROBES

1. Wilmot and Hocker's idea of both/and power sounds good, but it may be naïve. If you are in a conflict with someone who sees power only as either/or, how can you change his or her orientation?
2. Recall a specific conflict that you have experienced in the past few weeks. Analyze your power in this conflict in R-I-C-E terms. What resource control did you have? What interpersonal linkages were important? What communication skills gave you power in this situation? What expertise did you have? How are the outcomes of that event related to the power that you had?
3. Give an example of how metacommunication can help balance power in an interpersonal conflict.

REFERENCES

Alberts, J., and G. Driscoll. (1992). Containment versus escalation: The trajectory of couples' conversational complaints. *Western Journal of Communication* 56: 394–412.

Augsburger, D. W. (1992). *Conflict mediation across cultures: Pathways and patterns.* Louisville, Ky.: Westminster/John Knox Press.

Beck, A. T. (1988). *Love is never enough.* New York: Harper & Row.

Blau, P. M. (1964). *Exchange and power in social life.* New York: John Wiley & Sons.

Boulding, K. (1989). *Three faces of power.* Newbury Park, Calif.: Sage Publications.

Dahl, R. A. (1957). The concept of power. *Behavioral Science* 2: 201–215.

Deutsch, M. (1949). A theory of competition and cooperation. *Human Relations* 2: 129–151.

———. (1958). Trust and suspicion. *Journal of Conflict Resolution* 2: 265–279.

———. (1973). Conflicts: Productive and destructive. In *Conflict resolution through communication*, edited by F. E. Jandt. New York: Harper & Row.

Fletcher, J. (1999). *Disappearing acts: Gender, power, and relational practice at work*. Cambridge, Mass.: MIT Press.

Heim, P., and S. K. Galant. (1993). *Smashing the glass ceiling: Tactics for women who want to win in business*. New York: Simon & Schuster.

Johnson, P. (1976). Women and power: Toward a theory of effectiveness. *Journal of Social Issues* 32: 99–110.

Jordan, J., S. Kaplan, J. Miller, I. Stiver, and J. Surrey. (1991). *Women's growth in connection*. New York: Guilford Press.

King, A. (1987). *Power and communication*. Prospect Heights, Ill.: Waveland Press.

Kurdek, L. A. (1994). Areas of conflict for gay, lesbian, and heterosexual couples: What couples argue about influences relationship satisfaction. *Journal of Marriage and the Family* 56: 923–935.

Lerner, H. G. (1989). *The dance of intimacy*. New York: Harper & Row.

Lilly, E. R. (1989). The determinants of organizational power styles. *Educational Review* 41: 281–293.

May, R. (1972). *Power and innocence: A search for the sources of violence*. New York: Dell Publishing.

Millar, F. E., and L. E. Rogers. (1987). Relational dimensions of interpersonal dynamics. In *Interpersonal processes: New directions in communication research*, edited by M. E. Roloff and G. R. Miller, 117–139. Vol. 14 of *Sage Annual Reviews of Communication Research*. Newbury Park, Calif.: Sage Publications.

———. (1988). Power dynamics in marital relationships. In *Perspectives on marital interaction*, edited by O. Noller and M. A. Fitzpatrick, 78–97. Clevedon, UK: Multilingual Matters.

Miller, J. B. (1986). What do we mean by relationships? In *Work in progress*. Stone Center Working Paper Series, no. 22. Wellesley, Mass.: Stone Center, Wellesley College.

———. (1991). Women's and men's scripts for interpersonal conflict. *Psychology of Women Quarterly* 15: 15–29.

Rodman, H. (1967). Marital power in France, Greece, Yugoslavia, and the United States: A cross-national discussion. *Journal of Marriage and the Family* 29: 320–325.

———. (1972). Marital power and the theory of resources in cultural context. *Journal of Comparative Family Studies* 3: 50–69.

Rogers, M. F. (1974). Instrumental and infra-resources: The bases of power. *American Journal of Sociology* 79: 1418–1433.

Ross, M., and D. Holmberg. (1992). Are wives' memories for events in relationships more vivid than their husbands' memories? *Journal of Social and Personal Relationships* 9: 585–604.

Sabourin, T. C., and G. H. Stamp. (1995). Communication and the experience of dialectical tensions in family life: An examination of abusive and nonabusive families. *Communication Monographs* 62: 213–242.

Soloman, L. (1960). The influence of some types of power relationships and game strategies upon the development of interpersonal trust. *Journal of Abnormal and Social Psychology* 61: 223–230.

Ury, W., J. Brett, and S. Goldberg. (1988). *Getting disputes resolved.* San Francisco, Calif.: Jossey-Bass.

Van de Vliert, E. (1981). Siding and other reactions to a conflict. *Journal of Conflict Resolution* 25, no. 3: 495–520.

Warner, R. L., G. R. Lee, and J. Lee. (1986). Social organization, spousal resources, and marital power: A cross-cultural study. *Journal of Marriage and the Family* 48: 121–128.

Bullying: Correlates of Verbally Aggressive Communication in Adolescents

Charles K. Atkin, Sandi W. Smith, Anthony J. Roberto, Thomas Fediuk, and Thomas Wagner

This is an edited version of an essay that appeared in 2002 in *The Journal of Applied Communication Research.* This journal publishes communication studies that have obvious and direct practical application. The five authors put together reviews of research done by others and their own survey of 2,300 male and female adolescents between the ages of 13 and 15 to determine the extent of bullying or verbal aggression, its relation to physical aggression, its demographic correlates, and relationships between bullying and music and music video preferences.

The key feature of bullying communication is that one "attacks the self-concept of the person in order to hurt the other person psychologically." Bullying used to be viewed as an unfortunate but normal part of growing up, but it is now seen as potentially dangerous. One estimate is that up to 30 percent of U.S. elementary and junior high school students endure bullying at school, and another study found that 81 percent of urban middle school students had engaged in at least one act of bullying in the month prior to the study. One of the authors' research questions was focused on verifying how widespread these events are.

The authors also wanted to test the hypothesis that there is a positive relationship between being bullied and bullying others. In addition, they tested for a relationship between verbal aggression and physical aggression, asked whether boys bully more than girls, checked whether students bully more in the eighth grade than the seventh, and tested for the relationship between bullying and grade point average. One of the most interesting parts of this research is that the authors also tested for the impact of exposure to violent television programming, verbally aggressive talk shows, and verbally aggressive music and music videos on bullying. Their final questions had to do with the effects of observing peer verbal aggression, legal deviancy, and substance abuse.

As you will read, they found that bullying is widespread and that verbal attacks often escalate to physical ones. Bullies are likely to be performing poorly in school and abusing some substance. Media have a modest impact on verbal aggression, with the exception of violently oriented music.

The authors draw several conclusions from this study. First, because bullying is as widespread as it is, "prevention of verbally aggressive communication behavior merits a greater investment of resources." There is some evidence that a zero-tolerance policy helps. This article also makes some specific suggestions about how to educate students to reduce bullying. It's important to adapt education to specific male or female audiences and to clarify differences between constructive arguments and bullying. Parents are also alerted to steps they can take.

I include this article in *Bridges Not Walls* to increase your awareness of how widespread and potentially hurtful bullying can be. As each of us has learned in our communication lives, the slogan "Sticks and stones can break my bones but names can never hurt me" has never been true and is not true today. Those of you who work at parks, recreation centers, swimming pools, and other adolescent gathering places need to be alert to verbal aggression. Teachers at every level need to help keep classrooms and recreation venues safe. And when you are a parent, you will have even a greater responsibility. Bullying is a kind of communication that can hurt, and you can help do something about it.

Bullies shove their way into the nation's schools. (Peterson, 1999a)
Bullies, victims grow into roles that can last a lifetime. (Peterson, 1999b)

Headlines similar to the above often appear in the national press, and indicate that verbal and physical aggression are a fact of life for many school children in the United States. One large survey conducted by the Parents' Resource Institute for Drug Education (Gleaton, 2001) questioned over 114,000 students in 28 states and found that almost 40 percent of those surveyed had threatened physical violence against another student between sixth and twelfth grade. Approximately one-fourth reported that they were afraid another student would hit them, and almost as many reported that they had actually been the victim of physical violence in that they had been hit, slapped, or kicked. Other research indicates that percentages of bullying and victimization are dramatically higher when verbal aggression is included (e.g., name-calling, mean and nasty personal comments, swearing, etc.). Many severe and negative outcomes are associated with either being a perpetrator or a victim of bullying, including conduct, academic, physical, social, and emotional problems (Nansel, Overpeck, Pilla, & Ruan, 2001; Spivak & Prothrow-Spivak, 2001). For example, Olweus (1992) reported that former bullies were four times more likely to engage in criminal behavior by their mid-twenties, and that former victims were more likely to be depressed and to have poor self-esteem when they reached their mid-twenties.

Clearly, both verbal and physical aggression are pervasive problems for many adolescents in our society. Spivak and Prothrow-Stith (2001) note that "violence prevention, including bullying as a component, must be a priority for all who are concerned about the health of children and youth" (p. 2131). This investigation seeks to identify the correlates of verbally aggressive communication, including physical aggression, to heed this call. Further, since the majority of research on bullying has been conducted in Europe and Australia (Nansel et al., 2001), it is important to examine a United States sample to see if previous findings are generalizable to this culture.

[THE RESEARCH]

Verbal Aggression

Verbal aggression has been defined as "an exchange of messages between two people where at least one person in the dyad attacks the self-concept of the other person in order to hurt the other person psychologically" (Infante & Wigley, 1986, p. 67). Common types of verbally aggressive messages include character attacks, competence attacks, background attacks, physical appearance attacks, teasing, ridicule, threats, profanity, and nonverbal emblems (Infante, 1987)....

While verbal aggression was once viewed as a normal part of childhood and adolescence, chronic teasing is now being viewed as a potentially dangerous social act. Recent studies reported by Shear and Salmon (1999, May 2) estimate that up to 30 percent of children, or an estimated five million U.S. elementary and junior high school students, endure verbal harassment in school. By the time they are in junior and senior high school, 8 percent of urban students report that they miss at least one day of school each month because they are afraid to attend due to the threat of verbal and physical aggression (Shear & Salmon, 1999). Another study found that 81 percent of urban middle students had engaged in at least one act of bullying behavior in the month previous to the study (Bosworth, Espelage, & Simon, 1999). The first research question concerns the relative frequencies of the different categories of bullying in this sample:

RQ$_1$: How widespread are different forms of verbal aggression in the lives of adolescents between 13 and 15 years of age in terms of being a witness, victim, of perpetrator of such aggression?

The Reciprocal Nature of Verbal Aggression

Recent research suggests that victims of verbal aggression are often likely to engage in verbal aggression themselves (Haynie, Nansel, Eitel, & Crump, 2001). Singer, Miller, Guo, Flannery, Frierson, and Slovack (1999) found that witnessing or being the target of physical aggression correlated strongly with children behaving violently toward others. Infante, Sabourin, Rudd, and Shannon (1990) and Sabourin, Infante, and Rudd (1993) reported a reciprocal relationship between verbally aggressive behavior of husbands and wives. Infante et al. (1990) conclude that "a norm of reciprocity operates for verbal aggression (i.e., verbal aggression begets the same)" (p. 364). Apparently, an attack by one person instigates a response, thus perpetuating a pattern over time where the interactants share the roles of perpetrator and victim. Evidence from these studies suggests that there is a reciprocal relationship between experiencing and committing verbal aggression in adult populations. Therefore, it is expected that adolescent victims of verbal aggression are likely to engage in verbal aggression themselves, although this association is untested. Thus, the first hypothesis is:

H_1: There will be a positive relationship between experiencing and engaging in verbal aggression.

The Relationship between Verbal and Physical Aggression

Infante and his colleagues (Infante & Wigley, 1986; Infante, Chandler, & Rudd, 1989; Infante et al., 1990; Sabourin et al., 1993) argue that verbal aggression can lead to physical aggression when people do not have the skills, such as argumentativeness, for dealing with normal frustrations and conflicts. The Argumentative Skills Deficiency Model (ASDM) posits that people who are both frustrated and low in argumentativeness will turn first to verbal aggression and next to physical violence as their only alternatives. More specifically, this model claims that individuals low in argumentativeness *and* high in verbal aggressiveness are more likely to resort to physical aggression than individuals with other combinations of these predispositions. . . .

Consistent with the ASDM, Roberto (1999) predicted that adolescent boys low in argumentativeness and high in verbal aggressiveness would be more likely to get suspended from school for fighting (assessed using school suspension records) than boys with other combinations of these predispositions. Similarly, Roberto and Wilson (1996) predicted adolescent boys low in argumentativeness and high in verbal aggressiveness would demonstrate a greater "propensity towards violence" (measured by self-report responses to three hypothetical situations) than boys with other combinations of these predispositions. In both cases, high verbal aggressiveness, but not argumentativeness, was found to predict the physically aggressive behavior under investigation. Thus, this line of research finds support for the prediction that physical aggression among adolescents is a consequence of high verbal aggression, but not for the interaction effect between low argumentativeness and high verbal aggression. Thus, the following hypothesis is advanced:

H_2: There will be a positive relationship between the frequency of engaging in verbal aggression and frequency of engaging in physical aggression.

Demographic Correlates

Gender   Roberto and Finucane (1997) found that seventh and eighth grade boys were significantly more argumentative and more verbally aggressive than girls. These findings are consistent with those of other researchers studying adult subjects (Infante, 1985; Infante et al., 1984; Infante et al., 1990). Nansel et al. (2001) reported that boys most often identified themselves as both bullies and victims. Thus, to confirm these patterns in this sample the third hypothesis is:

H_3: Boys will report being significantly more verbally aggressive than will girls.

Age   Roberto and Finucane (1997) found that eighth-graders are significantly more argumentative than seventh-graders, and significantly more verbally aggressive than seventh-graders. Rancer et al. (1997, 2000) offer further support for these findings. Their research shows that while adolescents can be taught higher levels of argumentativeness, and that these higher levels of argumentativeness can be sustained for at least one year, verbal aggressiveness still increased significantly between the seventh and eighth grade. Therefore, the following hypothesis is advanced:

H_4: There will be a positive relationship between verbal aggression and age level among adolescents.

School Performance   Grades in school can be both a predictor and a consequence of verbal aggression. Those with lower grades may perform more verbally aggressive behavior because they are less intelligent, less skilled in resolving conflict, or more frustrated by their school experience. Bronston (1999) reports that victims of teasing and bullying tend to have poorer academic performance in school. She reports that 22 percent of fourth- through eighth-graders have had academic difficulties because of peer abuse. Nansel et al. (2001), however, found that persons who bullied others had poorer academic achievement. These findings lead to the following research questions:

RQ_2: Do victims of verbal aggression have lower grades in school than those who are not victims of verbal aggression?

RQ_3: Do those who have lower grades in school perform more verbally aggressive behavior than those who have higher grades?

Media Correlates

Television Viewing   Television provides people with access to a wide range of observational learning experiences. Individuals can observe how a vast array of other people behave in a response to a variety of situations (Heusmann, 1982). Verbal aggression is portrayed on television more often than physical aggression because it is a response that is more normative in our society (Worting & Greenberg, 1973). Certain genres of television content prominently feature verbal aggression, particularly confrontational daytime talk shows and music videos by "gangsta rap" or heavy metal performers. Although Infante et al. (1984) claimed that social learning may be an important source of verbal aggressiveness, Whaley (1982) did not find exposure to verbal aggression on television to lead to increased verbal aggressiveness. However, Martin, Anderson, and Cos (1993) found that viewers high in verbal aggression who did not report being hurt by verbally aggressive messages and who watched a verbally aggressive television show were more likely to express affinity for the show and the main character. Viewers who reported being psychologically hurt from receiving verbally aggressive messages in their lives showed less affinity. Thus, it appears that verbally aggressive persons may believe that verbal aggression is more socially appropriate and beneficial in achieving goals, and this might have a reinforcing effect on those viewers.

In contrast to verbal aggression portrayals, physical aggression on television has been shown to impact verbal aggressiveness in viewers (Sebastian, Parke, Berkowitz, & West, 1978). Many studies have demonstrated that viewing of violence contributes to physical aggression (Paik & Comstock, 1994), and some of the same processes of vicarious learning, disinhibition, arousal, and instigation may produce a similar impact on verbal aggression. Increased toleration of real-life aggression may result from changing beliefs and attitudes toward violence following exposure to television aggression. Exposure to televised violence in the context of dramatic programs may suggest to viewers that aggressive behavior is both commonplace and an appropriate method of conflict resolution. Exposure to televised violence results in increased acceptance of aggression on the part of viewers as being both normative and morally correct in conflict situations, and it may lead to decrease in the likelihood of intervention by witnesses to others' aggression (Thomas & Drabman, 1978). Again, certain television influence processes that shape desensitization may be extrapolated from physical aggression to verbal aggression.

The portrayal of rewards and punishments is probably the most important of all contextual factors for viewers as they interpret the meaning of what they see on television. Kunkel, Wilson, Linz, Potter, Donnerstein, Smith, Blumenthal, and Gray (1995) note that "viewers who would otherwise think of a class of behaviors such as violence as bad, over time will learn that those behaviors are good (e.g., useful, successful, or desirable) if they are repeatedly and consistently portrayed as rewarded or unpunished." They note that 73 percent of the incidents of television violence do not show the perpetrator being punished for committing violence, and 51 percent of violence presented is plausible or possible in real life. These portrayals of verbal aggression are likely to be even more acceptable and realistic. Based upon the foregoing discussion of media and verbal aggressiveness, the following hypothesis and research question are advanced:

H_5: There will be a positive relationship between exposure to violent television programming and verbal aggression.

RQ_4: Is there a relationship between exposure to verbally aggressive talk shows and verbal aggression?

Music and Music Video Preferences   Music is a large part of youth culture. Music can be heard on the radio, [on] television, on streets, in shopping malls, in movie theaters, and now over the Internet. With the prevalence of music in the life of an adolescent, as with television and other mass media, it is not surprising that music and music videos may play a role in verbal and physical aggression as they grow up. Where much focus has been given to television and its effects on adolescence, the picture is just beginning to emerge with regard to music and music video effects on adolescents. The answer to the research question posed below will provide evidence as to whether or not the connection between violent music and verbal aggression exists.

There are claims that consumption of music and music videos has substantial impact on the lives of adolescents, and there are counter-arguments to this position as well. Christensen and DeBenedittis (1986) argued that more attention needs to be given to youth consumption of radio. They pointed out that 52 percent have radios in their rooms and 69 percent report having a favorite station. Listening to the radio is more likely to be done alone, parents are much less likely to listen to radio with their children than they are likely to watch television with them, and parents are not as concerned about the impact of popular music....

In a review of the literature, Abelman and Atkin (1999) concluded that viewers more heavily exposed to violent rap videos were more likely to express greater acceptance of the use of violence. They also reported a higher probability that these viewers would engage in violent acts themselves. Viewers of aggressive music videos tend to be more antagonistic toward women and are more likely to condone violence in themselves (Roberts, 1997). Due to the conflicting claims and findings of previous research on the impact of music and music videos on aggressive behavior, the following research question is advanced:

> RQ₅: Is there a relationship between preference for verbally aggressive music and music videos and performance of verbally aggressive behavior?

Social Correlates

Peer Experiences and Verbal Aggressiveness   A considerable amount of recent research (Huesmann & Guerra, 1997; Henry, Guerra, Huesmann, Tolan, VanAcker, & Eron, 2000) indicates that normative beliefs concerning aggression correlate highly with aggressive behavior. Friends may display certain behaviors that have direct or indirect implications for acting aggressively. Peers who behave in an unhealthy or deviant manner serve as role models or instigators, and set normative standards that may influence verbal aggression and increase the probability of victimization. Observation of verbal aggression may lead to greater frequency of performing verbal aggression. Two other potentially influential peer behavior patterns are substance use (i.e., drinking, smoking, drug use) and legal deviancy (i.e., getting in trouble with police). Thus, the following hypothesis and research questions are advanced:

H₆: A positive relationship will exist between observing peer verbal aggression and engaging in verbal aggression.

RQ₆: Is there a relationship between verbal aggressiveness and substance abuse by friends?

RQ₇: Is there a relationship between verbal aggressiveness and legal deviancy by friends?

METHOD

This study used a mail survey to gather information from a representative sample of 2,300 male ($n = 1{,}110$) and female ($n = 1{,}190$) adolescents between the ages of 13 and 15 ($M = 14.03$, $SD = .85$)....

DISCUSSION

These descriptive findings clearly demonstrate that verbal aggression is widespread among young adolescents, indicating a need for improved programs on conflict resolution. It appears that committing and experiencing verbal aggression are reciprocal, such that disputes and verbal attacks escalate and perpetuate themselves over time. Verbal aggression is closely related to the more serious behaviors of physical aggression, so prevention of verbally aggressive behavior may help reduce the harmful consequences associated with other violent incidents.

Frequency of Verbal Aggression

There are surprisingly small differences in verbal aggression according to gender, age, family income, race, and size of school; none account for more than 1 percent of the variance in committing verbal aggression. This is a further indication of the pervasiveness of verbally aggressive behavior, which saturates all demographic segments of the adolescent culture. The factor most substantially related to verbal aggression is poor performance in school, which is also associated with a variety of problematic behaviors in adolescence.

Social influences from peers seem to play a major role in contributing to verbal aggression. In particular, peer substance abuse was the strongest single correlate in the regression analysis. It accounted for more variance in verbal aggression than did the full set of demographic variables. Those who interact with friends who display deviant behavior tend to display greater aggression and are more often victims of verbal abuse. This underscores the need to devise interventions focused on everyday informal interpersonal contexts in and out of school, and to target the subset of adolescents who are involved with a friendship network that uses drugs and runs afoul of the law.

Finally, the impact of media on verbal aggression appears to be relatively modest. There are fairly small correlations between verbal aggression and viewing of television, violent programming, and talk shows. Although television programming portrays a substantial amount of verbal aggression, the degree of learning or disinhibition is apparently quite limited; thus, reducing exposure levels or restricting content will not produce a significant improvement in verbally aggressive responses by television viewers. The main exception is found for violently oriented music appearing in music videos as well as on the radio and compact disc players. This index correlates moderately with verbal aggression, and the relationship remains when other variables are controlled. Despite the conflicting claims and findings of previous research, a positive relationship between preference for violently oriented music and verbal aggression was found here. The more intense verbally aggressive language and the hostile expressions of the performers may provide an influential novel input to adolescents. Attempts to minimize access to this form of entertainment may achieve a larger payoff than efforts to control television programming.

Practical Implications

First, the survey evidence showing the high prevalence of verbal aggression and the close relationship to physical aggression indicates that this form of anti-social behavior should receive greater attention from school principals and teachers, youth program leaders, parents, government officials, and media executives. Prevention of verbally aggressive communication behavior merits a greater investment of resources relative to higher-profile problems involving adolescents in our society.

The school system seems the most promising venue for prevention activities. Schools might consider adopting a "zero tolerance" policy for verbal aggression, as many schools have already done for physical aggression. The reduction of verbal aggression can be readily incorporated into ongoing violence prevention and intervention programs. The potential for targeting verbal aggression in this context is highlighted by Meyer, Roberto, Boster, and Story (2001), who evaluated a 12-lesson violence prevention curriculum for seventh-graders. Compared to a control school, students experiencing the intervention reported significantly less verbally aggressive acts, more negative attitude toward verbal aggression, and stronger beliefs that verbal aggression would get them into trouble.

The findings from the present study provide insights into the possible content for school-based interventions. For example, the conventional male-oriented violence prevention curriculum should be adapted specifically to the target audience of females who verbally aggress on other females. The curriculum should include media literacy modules focusing on violent musical genres and television talk shows.

Additional curriculum content should feature adolescent-oriented material adapted from Infante's (1995) collegiate verbal aggression training, which focuses on enhancing students' understanding of verbal aggression and helping students to develop and internalize strategies for controlling verbal aggression.

His key approaches include distinguishing between constructive argumentativeness vs. destructive verbal aggressiveness, identifying various types of verbally aggressive messages such as character attacks and competency attacks, and discussing the detrimental effects of verbal aggression. They seem particularly appropriate to children and youth (Rancer et al., 1997, 2000; Roberto, 1999; Roberto & Wilson, 1996).

There are several implications for parents, who should be made more aware of the need to address the problem of verbal aggression. Because the two strongest correlates of verbal aggression are peer substance use and violent music enjoyment, parents have another reason for discouraging their children from associating with the "wrong crowd" and from consuming rap and heavy metal musical entertainment at a young age. Indeed, parental efforts to promote studying and improved school performance may produce a bonus payoff in terms of lower verbal aggression. Parents can also attempt to directly teach their children how to avoid initiating and escalating verbal attacks on peers.

Because it appears that television and radio programming contribute to the problem of verbal aggression among youth, these institutions are responsible for devoting some public service time to prevention messages. Certain PSAs can be targeted to parents, alerting them to the importance of verbally aggressive communication patterns and suggesting how they can try to prevent it. Other broadcast spots should be aimed at adolescents to supplement the school-based training. These messages might be patterned after violence prevention campaigns, using simple messages recommending that youth break the reciprocal spiral of attack and counterattack.

It should be noted that television violence, a widely blamed culprit for other youth problems, does not seem to produce verbal aggression. Thus, regulating the content or controlling the exposure to violent characters and programs is not a priority in this case. Similarly, the conventional strategy of cutting down on the total amount of television viewed by adolescents is not likely to reduce the problem.

Finally, the findings of this study suggest several implications for demographic emphases of prevention efforts. Because age, sex, race, family income, and school size are not highly related to overall prevalence of verbal aggression, all segments of the youth population need to be reached rather than targeting the usual trouble-maker profiles. With respect to the focal issue of aggression against adolescent females, prevention programs must focus on female-to-female situations as well as dealing with the problem of male perpetrators.

REVIEW QUESTIONS

1. Give a brief example of each of the kinds of bullying that are listed: character attacks, competence attacks, background attacks, physical appearance attacks, teasing, ridicule, threats, profanity, and nonverbal emblems.
2. Explain the difference between highly argumentative communication and verbally aggressive communication.

3. Why do you think there is a correlation between bullying and performance in school? Why do bullies tend to have lower grade point averages?
4. What was done in your junior high and high school to combat bullying?
5. What do the authors suggest that parents can do to reduce bullying?

PROBES

1. These authors obviously believe that verbal aggression is dangerous. But do you agree? How do you respond to the person who says that young people need to develop thick skins in order to prepare for the "real world" and that bullying seldom hurts anyone seriously?
2. These authors did not find strong correlations between bullying and violent television programming or verbally aggressive talk shows. How can you explain this finding?
3. These authors found very little relationship between verbal aggression and gender, age, family income, race, or size of school. "None account for more than 1 percent of the variance in committing verbal aggression." Boys bully as much as girls, low-income students as much as high-income, blacks and whites as much as browns, and so on. Why do you think this is the case?

REFERENCES

Abelman, R., & Atkin, D. (1999). *Contemporary music and violence: A literature review and critique.* Report for the Recording Industry Association of America.

Ballard, M. E., & Coates, S. (1995). The immediate effects of homicidal, suicidal, and nonviolent heavy metal and rap songs on the moods of college students. *Youth and Society, 27,* 148–168.

Bosworth, K., Espelage, D. L., & Simon, T. R. (1999). Factors associated with bullying behavior in middle school students. *The Journal of Early Adolescence, 19,* 341–362.

Bronston, B. (1999, August 23). Bully proofing: Teach a child what to do about peer abuse. *The Times Picayune,* p. C1.

Christensen, P. G., & DeBenedittis, P. (1986). "Eavesdropping" on the FM band: Children's use of radio. *Journal of Communication, 36,* 27–38.

Gleaton, T. J. (2001). Safe and drug free schools. (On-Line), Available at www.pridesurveys.com.

Greeson, L. E., & Williams, R. A. (1986). Social implications of music videos for youth: An analysis of the content and effects of MTV. *Youth and Society, 18,* 177–189.

Hansen, C. H., & Hansen, R. D. (1990). The influence of sex and violence on the appeal of rock music videos. *Communication Research, 17,* 212–234.

Haynie, D. L., Nansel, T., Eitel, P., & Crump, A. D. (2001). Bullies, victims, and bully/victims: Distinct groups of at-risk youth. *The Journal of Early Adolescence, 21,* 29–49.

Henry, D., Guerra, N., Huesmann, L. R., Tolan, P., VanAcker, R., & Eron, L. (2000). Normative influences on aggression in urban elementary school classrooms. *American Journal of Community Psychology, 28*, 59–81.

Heusmann, L. R. (1982). Television violence and aggressive behavior. In D. Pearl, L. Bouthilet, & J. Lazar (Eds.), *Television and behavior* (pp. 126–137). Rockville, MD: National Institute of Mental Health.

Huesmann, L. R., & Guerra, N. G. (1997). Children's normative beliefs about aggression and aggressive behavior. *Journal of Personality and Social Psychology, 72*, 408–419.

Infante, D. A. (1985). Inducing women to be more argumentative: Source credibility effects. *Journal of Applied Communication Research, 13*, 33–44.

Infante, D. A. (1987). Aggressiveness. In J. C. McCroskey & J. A. Daly, (Eds.). *Personality and interpersonal communication* (pp. 157–192). Newbury Park, CA: Sage.

Infante, D. A. (1995). Teaching students to understand and control verbal aggression. *Communication Education, 44*, 51–63.

Infante, D. A., Chandler, T. A., & Rudd, J. E. (1989). Test of an argumentative skill deficiency model of interspousal violence. *Communication Monographs, 56*, 163–177.

Infante, D. A., & Rancer, A. S. (1982). A conceptualization and measure of argumentativeness. *Journal of Personality Assessment, 46*, 72–80.

Infante, D. A., Sabourin, T. C., Rudd, J. E., & Shannon, E. A. (1990). Verbal aggression in violent and nonviolent marital disputes. *Communication Quarterly, 38*, 361–371.

Infante, D. A., Trebing, J. D., Shepherd, P. E., & Seeds, D. E. (1984). The relationship of argumentativeness to verbal aggression. *Southern Speech Communication Journal, 50*, 67–77.

Infante, D. A., & Wigley, C. J. (1986). Verbal aggressiveness: An interpersonal model and measure. *Communication Monographs, 53*, 61–69.

Johnson, J. D., Jackson, L. A., & Gatto, L. (1995). Violent attitudes and deferred academic aspirations: Deleterious effects of exposure to rap music. *Basic and Applied Social Psychology, 16*, 27–41.

Kunkel, D., Wilson, B. J., Linz, D., Potter, J., Donnerstein, E., Smith, S., Blumenthal, E., & Gray, T. (1995). Violence in television programming overall: University of California, Santa Barbara Study. *National Television Violence Study, 1994–1995*. Studio City, CA: Mediascope, Inc.

Martin, M. M., Anderson, C. M., & Cos, G. C. (1993). Verbal Aggression: A study of the relationship between communication traits and feelings about a verbally aggressive television show. *Communication Research Reports, 14*, 195–202.

Martin, G., Clarke, M., & Pearce, C. (1993). Adolescent suicide: Music preferences as an indicator of vulnerability. *Journal of the Academy of Child and Adolescent Psychiatry, 32*, 530–535.

Meyer, G., Roberto, A. J., Boster, F. J., & Story, H. L. (2001, November). *Get real about violence®:An outcome evaluation of a youth violence prevention curriculum.* Manuscript presented to the Applied Communication Division of the National Communication Association, Atlanta, GA.

Nansel, T. R., Overpeck, M., Pilla, R. S., & Ruan, W. J. (2001). Bullying behaviors among US youth: Prevalence and association with psychosocial adjustment. *Journal of the American Medical Assciation, 16,* 2094–2100.

Olweus, D. (1992). Bullying among schoolchildren: Intervention and prevention. In R. D. Peters, F. J. McMahon, & V. L. Quinsey (Eds.), *Aggression and violence throughout the lifespan* (pp. 100–125). London: Sage.

Paik, H., & Comstock, G. (1994). The effects of television violence on antisocial behavior: A meta-analysis. *Communication Research, 21,* 516–546.

Peterson, K. S. (1999a, September 7). Bullies shove their way into the nation's schools. *USA Today,* p. 1D.

Peterson, K. S. (1999b, September 8). Bullies, victims grow into roles that can last a lifetime. *USA Today,* p. 7D.

Prinsky, L. E., & Rosenbaum, J. L. (1987). Leer-ics or lyrics: Teenage impressions of rock 'n' roll. *Youth and Society, 18,* 384–397.

Rancer, A. S., Avtgis, T. A., Kosberg, R. L., & Whitecap, V. G. (2000). A longitudinal assessment of trait argumentativeness and verbal aggressiveness between seventh and eighth grades. *Communication Education, 49,* 114–119.

Rancer, A. S., Whitecap, V. G., Kosberg, R. L., & Avtgis, T. A. (1997). Testing the efficacy of a communication training program to increase argumentativeness and argumentative behavior in adolescents. *Communication Education, 46,* 273–286.

Roberto, A. J. (1999). Applying the argumentative skills deficiency model of interpersonal violence to adolescent boys. *Communication Research Reports, 16,* 325–332.

Roberto, A. J., & Finucane, M. E. (1997). The assessment of argumentativeness and verbal aggressiveness in adolescent populations. *Communication Quarterly, 45,* 21–36.

Roberto, A. J., & Wilson, S. R. (1996). *The effects of argumentativeness, verbal aggressiveness, and situation on perception of intent and propensity towards violence in adolescent boys.* Paper presented to the Interpersonal Communication Division of the International Communication Association. Chicago, IL.

Roberts, D. F. (1997). *Research on adolescent uses and of responses to heavy metal and rap music.* Testimony prepared for Senate Hearings on "The Social Impact of Music Violence," Washington DC, November 6, 1997.

Sabourin, T. C., Infante, D. A., & Rudd, J. E. (1993). Verbal aggression in marriages: A comparison of violent, distressed but nonviolent, and nondistressed couples. *Human Communication Research, 20,* 245–267.

Sebastian, R. J., Parke, R. D., Berkowitz, L., & West, S. G. (1978). Film violence and verbal aggression: A naturalistic study. *Journal of Communication, 28,* 164–171.

Shear, M. D., & Salmon, J. L. (1999, May 2). An education in taunting: Schools learning dangers of letting bullies go unchecked. *The Washington Post,* p. C1.

Singer, M. I., Miller, D. B., Guo, S., Flannery, D. J., Frierson, T., & Slovack, K. (1999). Contributors to violent behavior among elementary and middle school children. *Pediatrics, 104,* 878–884.

Smith, B. S. (1995). The effects of exposure to violent lyric music and consumption of alcohol on aggressiveness. *Dissertation Abstracts International: Section B: The Sciences and Engineering, 56,* 3487.

Spivak, H., & Prothrow-Stith, D. (2001). The need to address bullying—an important component of violence prevention. *Journal of the American Medical Association, 16,* 2131–2132.

Thomas, M. H., & Drabman, R. S. (1978). Effects of television violence on expectations of other's aggression. *Personality and Social Psychology Bulletin, 4,* 73–76.

Walker, J. R, (1987). How viewing of MTV relates to exposure to other media violence. *Journalism Quarterly, 64,* 756–762.

Wanamaker, C. E., & Reznikoff, M. (1989). Effects of aggressive and nonaggressive rock songs on projective and structured tests. *Journal of Psychology, 123,* 561–570.

Whaley, A. B. (1982). Televised violence and related variables as predictors of self reported verbal aggression. *Central States Speech Journal, 33,* 490–497.

Worting, C. E., & Greenberg, B. S. (1973). Experiments in televised violence and verbal aggression: Two exploratory studies. *Journal of Communication, 23,* 446–460.

CHAPTER 10

Conflict: Turning Walls into Bridges

Conflict and Interaction

Joseph P. Folger, Marshall Scott Poole, and Randall K. Stutman

One of the places where it is most challenging and most important to turn communication walls into bridges is in conflict. Although conflict is a natural and normal part of every work, family, roommate, and dating relationship, few people enjoy it, and even fewer believe that they manage it well. This chapter collects some of the best advice from eight people who can help each of us "do" conflict better.

The first reading comes from a conflict management textbook written by three communication teachers. It lays out some of the basic ideas that I think are important to understand if you're going to approach conflict constructively and effectively.

The authors begin with a "textbook case" that illustrates both the bad side and the potentially good side of conflict. Although they don't emphasize this point, the case shows how your view of conflict can strongly affect the ways you deal with it. For example, many people view conflict as always painful. From this point of view, unless you enjoy being blamed, put down, and shouted at, it's hard to be positive about conflicts. So if you see conflict as something entirely negative, you'll behave accordingly and will probably help create a self-fulfilling prophecy—the more you believe it's awful, the worse it will get. But as the case study shows, there are actually some benefits to conflict. Feelings get out in the open where they can be dealt with, and often people discover creative solutions to problems that had stumped them. So the first step toward handling conflict effectively is to be open to the positive values of conflict so you can, as these authors suggest, analyze "both the specific behaviors and interaction patterns involved in conflict and the forces that influence these patterns."

Folger, Poole, and Stutman define *conflict* as "the interaction of interdependent people who perceive incompatible goals and interference from each other in achieving those goals." This means that struggles inside one person's head are not "conflict" as it's defined here. Conflict always involves communication. The definition also emphasizes that conflict doesn't happen unless the people involved are interdependent. It only happens when one person's beliefs or actions have some impact on the other's. Otherwise the parties could just ignore each other.

The central section of this [reading] distinguishes productive from destructive conflict interaction. One difference is that productive conflicts are *realistic,* which means that they focus on substantive problems the parties can potentially solve, while *nonrealistic* conflicts are mainly expressions of aggression designed to defeat or hurt the other. Productive conflict attitudes and behaviors are also *flexible,* while destructive ones are *inflexible.* In addition, productive conflict management is grounded in the belief that all parties can realize at least some of their goals, while destructive conflict is thoroughly win/lose. Finally, productive conflict happens when the parties are committed to working through their differences, rather than either avoiding them or simply favoring one position over the other.

In the final section, the authors develop the idea that every move made in a conflict affects the other parties and that this is why conflicts often degenerate into destructive cycles or patterns. These cycles can only be understood as unified wholes, and they can often be self-reinforcing. This means that, if you want to manage conflict effectively, you have to (1) look for the cycles, and (2) be willing and able to take unilateral action to break the destructive pattern. Subsequent readings in this chapter suggest what you can do *after* this to handle conflicts more effectively.

THE POTENTIAL OF CONFLICT INTERACTION

It is often said that conflict can be beneficial. Trainers, counselors, consultants, and authors of conflict textbooks point to the potential positive functions of conflict: conflicts allow important issues to be aired; they produce new and creative ideas; they release built-up tension; they can strengthen relationships; they can cause groups and organizations to reevaluate and clarify goals and missions; and they can also stimulate social change to eliminate inequities and injustice. These advantages, and others, are raised to justify conflict as a normal, healthy occurrence and to stress the importance of understanding and handling it properly.

But why must such an argument be made? Everyone has been in conflicts, and almost everyone would readily acknowledge at least some benefits. Why then do social scientists, popular authors, and consultants persist in attempting to persuade us of something we already know? Perhaps the answer can be found by studying an actual conflict. The twists and turns of a specific case often reveal why negative views of conflict persist. Consider the fairly typical case study of a conflict in a small work group in Case 1.A.

Case 1.A   The Women's Hotline Case

Imagine yourself as a staff member in this organization:
   How would you react as this conflict unfolded?
   What is it about this particular conflict that makes it seem difficult to face—let alone solve?

Women's Hotline is a rape and domestic crisis center in a medium-sized city; the center employs seven full- and part-time workers. The workers, all women, formed a cohesive unit and made all important decisions as a group; there were no formal supervisors. The hotline had started as a voluntary organization and had grown by capturing local and federal funds. The group remained proud of its roots in a democratic, feminist tradition.

The atmosphere at the hotline was rather informal. The staff saw each other as friends, but there was an implicit understanding that people should not have to take responsibility for each other's cases. Since the hotline's work was draining, having to handle each other's worries could create an unbearable strain. This norm encouraged workers to work on their own and keep problems to themselves.

The conflict arose when Diane, a new counselor who had only six months' experience, was involved in a very disturbing incident. One of her clients was killed by a man who had previously raped her. Diane had trouble dealing with this incident. She felt guilty about it; she questioned her own ability and asked herself whether she might have been able to prevent this tragedy. In the months following, Diane had increasing difficulty in coping with her feelings and began to feel that her co-workers were not giving her the support she needed. Diane had no supervisor to turn to, and, although her friends outside the hotline were helpful, she did not believe they could understand the pressure as well as her co-workers.

Since the murder, Diane had not been able to work to full capacity, and she began to notice some resentment from the other counselors. She felt the other staff were more concerned about whether she was adding to their workloads than whether she was recovering from the traumatic incident. Although Diane did not realize it at the time, most of the staff felt she had been slow to take on responsibilities even before her client was killed. They thought Diane had generally asked for more help than other staff members and that these requests were adding to their own responsibilities. No one was willing to tell Diane about these feelings after the incident, because they realized she was very disturbed. After six months, Diane believed she could no longer continue to work effectively. She felt pressure from the others at the center, and she was still shaken by the tragedy. She requested two weeks off with pay to get away from the work situation for a while, to reduce the stress she felt, and to come back with renewed energy. The staff, feeling that Diane was slacking off, denied this request. They responded by outlining, in writing, what they saw as the responsibilities of a full-time staff worker. Diane was angry when she realized her request had been denied, and she decided to file a formal work grievance.

Diane and the staff felt bad about having to resort to such a formal, adversarial procedure. No staff member had ever filed a work grievance, and the group was embarrassed by its inability to deal with the problem on a more informal basis. These feelings created additional tension between Diane and the staff.

Discussion Questions

- *Can you foresee any benefits to this conflict?*
- *Is it possible to foresee whether a conflict will move in a constructive or destructive direction?*
- *What cues would lead you to believe that conflict is going to be productive?*

The situation at the Women's Hotline has several features in common with destructive conflicts, and might easily turn in a destructive direction. **First, the situation is tense and threatening.** The weeks during which the incident evolved were an extremely difficult time for the workers. Even for "old hands" at negotiation, conflicts are often unpleasant and frightening. **Second, participants are experiencing a great deal of uncertainty.** They are unable to understand many aspects of the conflict and how their behavior affects it. Conflicts are confusing; actions can have consequences quite different from those intended because the situation is more complicated than assumed. Diane did not know her co-workers thought she was slacking even before the tragedy. When she asked for time off, she was therefore surprised at their refusal, and her own angry reaction nearly started a major battle. **Third, the situation is extremely fragile.** The conflict may evolve in very different ways depending on the behavior of just a single worker. If, for example, the staff chooses to fire Diane, the conflict might be squelched, or it might fester and undermine relationships among the remaining members. If, on the other hand, Diane wins allies, the staff might split over the issue and ultimately dissolve the hotline. As the case continues below, observe staff members' behavior and their method of dealing with this tense and unfamiliar situation.

Case 1.B   The Women's Hotline Case, Continued

Imagine yourself in the midst of this conflict:
   What would you recommend this group do to promote a constructive outcome to this conflict?

The staff committee who received Diane's grievance suggested that they could handle the problem in a less formal way if both Diane and the staff agreed to accept a neutral third-party mediator. Everyone agreed that this suggestion had promise, and a third party was invited to a meeting where the entire staff would address the issue.

At this meeting, the group faced a difficult task. Each member offered reactions they had been unwilling to express previously. The staff made several pointed criticisms of Diane's overall performance. Diane expressed doubts about the staff's willingness to help new workers or to give support when it was requested. Although this discussion was often tense, it was well directed. At the outset of the meeting, Diane withdrew her formal complaint. This action changed the definition of the problem from the immediate work grievance to the question of what levels of support were required for various people to work effectively in this difficult and emotionally draining setting. Staff members shared doubts and fears about their own inadequacies as counselors and agreed that something less than perfection was acceptable. The group recognized that a collective inertia had developed and that they had consistently avoided giving others the support needed to deal with difficult rape cases. They acknowledged, however, the constraints on each woman's time; each worker could handle only a limited amount of stress. The group recognized that some level of mutual support was essential and felt they had fallen below that level over the past year and a half. One member suggested that any staff person should be able to ask for a "debriefing contract" whenever they felt they needed help or support. These contracts would allow someone to ask for ten minutes of another person's time to hear about a particularly disturbing issue or case. The group members adopted this suggestion because they saw it could allow members to seek help without overburdening each other. The person who was asked to listen could assist and give needed support without feeling that she had to "fix" another worker's problem. Diane continued to work at the center and found that her abilities and confidence increased as the group provided the support she needed.

Discussion Questions

- *In what ways did the parties in this conflict show "good faith"?*
- *Is "good faith" participation a necessary prerequisite to constructive conflict resolution?*

This is a "textbook" case in effective conflict management because it resulted in a solution that all parties accepted. The members of this group walked a tightrope throughout the conflict, yet they managed to avoid a fall. The tension, unpleasantness, uncertainty, and fragility of conflict situations make them hard to face. Because these problems make it difficult to deal with issues in a constructive way, conflicts are often terminated by force, by uncomfortable suppression of the issues, or by exhaustion after a prolonged fight—all outcomes that leave at least one party dissatisfied. Entering a conflict is often like making a bet against the odds: you can win big if it turns out well, but so many things can go wrong that few people are willing to chance it. It is no wonder that many writers feel a need to reassure us. They feel compelled to remind us of the positive outcomes of conflict because all too often the destructive results are all that people remember.

The key to working through conflict is not to minimize its disadvantages, or even to emphasize its positive functions, but to accept both and to try to understand how conflicts move in destructive or productive directions. Such an understanding requires a conception of conflict that calls for a careful **analysis of both the specific behaviors and interaction patterns involved in conflict and the forces that influence these patterns.** Moreover, we can only grasp the fragility of conflicts and the effects that tension and misunderstandings have in their development if we work at the level at which conflicts unfold—specific interactions among the parties.

DEFINITION OF CONFLICT

Conflict is the interaction of interdependent people who perceive incompatible goals and interference from each other in achieving those goals (Hocker and Wilmot 1985). This definition has the advantage of providing a much clearer focus than definitions that view conflict simply as disagreement, as competition, or as the presence of incompatible interests (Fink 1968). **The most important feature of conflict is that it is based in interaction.** Conflicts are constituted and sustained by the behaviors of the parties involved and their reactions to one another. Conflict interaction takes many forms, and each form presents special problems and requires special handling. The most familiar type of conflict interaction is marked by shouting matches or open competition in which each party tries to defeat the other. But conflicts can also be more subtle. Often people react to conflict by suppressing it. They interact in ways that allow them to avoid confrontation, either because they are afraid of possible changes the conflict may bring about or because the issue "isn't worth fighting over." This response is as much a part of the conflict process as the open struggles commonly associated with conflict. This book deals with the whole range of responses to conflict and how those responses affect the development of conflicts. Conflicts can best be understood and managed by concentrating on specific behavioral patterns and the forces shaping them.

People in conflict perceive that they have incompatible goals or interests and that others are a source of interference in achieving their goals. The key word here is "perceive." Regardless of whether goals are actually incompatible or if the parties believe them to be incompatible, conditions are ripe for conflict. Regardless of whether an employee really stands in the way of a co-worker or whether the co-worker interprets the employee's behavior as interference, the co-worker may move against the employee or feel compelled to skirt certain issues. Thus, the parties' interpretations and beliefs play a key role in conflicts. This does not mean that goals are always conscious as conflict develops. People can act without a clear sense of what their goals or interests are (Coser 1961). Sometimes people find themselves in strained interactions but are unsure how they got there. They realize afterward what their implicit goals were and how their goals were incompatible with those held by others (Hawes and Smith 1973). Communication looms large because of its importance in shaping and maintaining the perceptions that guide conflict behavior.

Indeed, communication problems are sometimes the cause of conflicts. Tension or irritation can result from misunderstandings that occur when people interact with very different communication styles (Tannen 1986, Grimshaw 1990). One person's inquisitive style may be perceived by someone else as intrusive and rude. One person's attempt to avoid stepping on another's toes may be perceived by someone else as distant and cold. Style differences create difficult problems that are often related to differences in cultural backgrounds (Kochman 1981, Dubinskas 1992). However, the old adage "most conflicts are actually communication problems" is not always true. The vast majority of conflicts would not exist without some real difference of interest. This difference may be hard to uncover, it may be redefined over time, and occasionally it may be trivial, but it is there nonetheless. Communication processes can cause conflicts and can easily exacerbate them, but they are rarely the sole source of the difficulty.

Conflict interaction is colored by the interdependence of the parties. For a conflict to arise, the behavior of one or both parties must have consequences for the other. Therefore, by definition, the parties involved in conflict are interdependent. The conflict at the hotline would not have occurred if Diane's behavior had not irritated the other workers and if their response had not threatened Diane's position. Furthermore, any action taken in response to the conflict affects both sides. The decision to institute a "debriefing contract" required considerable change by everyone. If Diane had been fired, that too would have affected the other workers; they would have had to "cover" Diane's cases and come to terms with themselves as co-workers who could be accused of being unresponsive or insensitive.

But interdependence implies more than this: when parties are interdependent they can potentially aid or interfere with each other. **For this reason, conflicts are always characterized by a mixture of incentives to cooperate and to compete.** Any comment during conflict interaction can be seen either as an attempt to advance the speaker's own interest or as an attempt to promote a good outcome for all involved. A party may believe that having their own point accepted is more important, at least for the moment, than proposing a mutually beneficial outcome. When Diane asked for two weeks off, she was probably thinking not of the group's best interest but of her own needs. In other cases, a participant may advance a proposal designed to benefit everyone, as when the staff member suggested the "debriefing contract." In still other instances, a participant may offer a comment with a cooperative intent, but others may interpret it as one that advances individual interests. Regardless of whether the competitive motive is intended by the speaker or assigned by other members, the interaction unfolds from that point under the assumption that the speaker may value only his or her own interests. Subsequent interaction is further likely to undermine incentives to cooperate and is also likely to weaken members' recognition of their own interdependence. The balance of incentives to compete or cooperate is important in determining the direction the conflict interaction takes.

ARENAS OF CONFLICT INTERACTION

Conflict occurs in almost all social settings. Most people learn at a very young age that conflicts arise in families, playgrounds, classrooms, Little League fields, ballet centers, scout troops, and cheerleading teams. Even as relationships become more complex and people become involved in more diverse and public settings, conflicts remain remarkably similar to those experienced in childhood. (Indeed, some argue that early experiences shape involvement in conflict throughout our lives.) Adults encounter conflict in casual work relationships and emotionally intense, intimate relationships as well as in close friendships or in political rivalries. Conflict is encountered in decision-making groups, small businesses, large corporations, church organizations, and doctors' offices. Given the diversity of conflicts typically encountered, what often is of most concern is how much is at stake in any conflict. Conflicts are assessed as pedestrian or profound, trivial or tremendous, or as major or minor maelstroms. The estimate of the significance of any conflict often influences the time and effort invested in strategizing or in developing safeguards or fallbacks....

Forms of interaction are patterns of actions and reactions or moves and countermoves that parties engage in during a conflict. Violent exchanges are a form of interaction that can occur in interpersonal, intragroup, or intergroup conflicts. Similarly, negotiation is a form of interaction in which parties engage in any of these settings. Negotiation, sometimes referred to as bargaining, occurs when parties agree to explicit or implicit rules for exchanging proposals or concessions to reach a mutual agreement (Pruitt 1981, Putnam and Poole 1987). People often think of negotiation as a separate arena because labor-management negotiations are the most prominent example of negotiations in most people's minds. However, negotiations can occur in any of the arenas. Husbands and wives can negotiate their divorce agreements, a professor and student can negotiate a grade, environmental groups can negotiate a land-use policy, or neighborhood groups can negotiate historical preservation standards.

There are other insights, besides those centering on forms of interaction, that apply to all the arenas of conflict covered in this book. For example, most conflicts are concerned with power because power is integral to all forms of interdependence among people. How conflict influences relationships and how climate is central to the way conflict unfolds will also be examined.

PRODUCTIVE AND DESTRUCTIVE CONFLICT INTERACTION

As previously noted, people often associate conflict with negative outcomes. However, there are times when conflicts must be addressed regardless of the apprehension they create. When differences exist and the issues are important, suppression of conflict is often more dangerous than facing it. The psychologist Irving Janis points to a number of famous political disasters, such as the Bay of Pigs invasion and the failure to anticipate the Japanese attack on Pearl Harbor, where poor decisions can be traced to the repression of conflict by key decision-making groups (Janis 1972). The critical question is: what forms of conflict interaction will yield the obvious benefits without tearing a relationship, a group, or an organization apart?

Years ago the sociologist Lewis Coser (1956) distinguished realistic from nonrealistic conflicts. **Realistic conflicts are conflicts based in disagreements over the means to an end or over the ends themselves.** In realistic conflicts, the interaction focuses on the substantive issues the participants must address to resolve their underlying incompatibilities. **Nonrealistic conflicts are expressions of aggression in which the sole end is to defeat or hurt the other.** Participants in nonrealistic conflicts serve their own interests by undercutting those of the other party. Coser argues that because nonrealistic conflicts are oriented toward the expression of aggression, force and coercion are the means for resolving these disputes. Realistic conflicts, on the other hand, foster a wide range of resolution techniques—force, negotiation, persuasion, even voting—because they are oriented toward the resolution of some substantive problem. Although Coser's analysis is somewhat of an oversimplification, it is insightful and suggests important contrasts between productive and destructive conflict interaction (Deutsch 1973). What criteria could be used to evaluate whether a conflict is productive? **In large part, productive conflict interaction depends on flexibility.** In constructive conflicts, members engage in a wide variety of behaviors ranging from coercion and threat to negotiation, joking, and relaxation to reach an acceptable solution. **In contrast, parties in destructive conflicts are likely to be much less flexible because their goal is more narrowly defined: they are trying to defeat each other.** Destructive conflict interaction is likely to have protracted, uncontrolled escalation cycles or prolonged attempts to avoid issues. In productive conflict, on the other hand, the interaction in the group will change direction often. Short cycles of escalation, de-escalation, avoidance, and constructive work on the issue are likely to occur as the participants attempt to manage the conflict.

Consider the hotline case. The group exhibited a wide range of interaction styles, from the threat of a grievance to the cooperative attempt to reach a mutually satisfactory solution. Even though Diane and the members engaged in hostile or threatening interaction, they did not persist in this mode, and when the conflict threatened to escalate, they called in a third party. The conflict showed all the hallmarks of productive interaction. In a destructive conflict the members might have responded to Diane's grievance by suspending her, and Diane might have retaliated by suing or by attempting to discredit the center in the local newspaper. Her retaliation would have hardened others' positions and they might have fired her, leading to further retaliation. Alternatively, the hotline conflict might have ended in destructive avoidance. Diane might have hidden her problem, and the other members might have consciously or unconsciously abetted her by changing the subject when the murder came up or by avoiding talking to her at all. Diane's problem would probably have grown worse, and she might have had to quit. The center would then revert back to "normal" until the same problem surfaced again. While the damage done by destructive avoidance is much less serious in this case than that done by destructive escalation, it is still considerable: the hotline loses a good worker, and the seeds of future losses remain. In both cases, it is not the behaviors themselves that are destructive—neither avoidance nor hostile arguments are harmful in themselves—but rather the inflexibility of the parties that locks them into escalation or avoidance cycles.

In productive conflicts, interaction is guided by the belief that all factions can attain important goals (Deutsch 1973). The interaction reflects a sustained effort to bridge the apparent incompatibility of positions. This effort is in marked contrast to destructive conflicts where the interaction is premised on participants' belief that one side must win and the other must lose. **Productive conflict interaction results in a solution satisfactory to all and produces a general feeling that the parties have gained something** (for example, a new idea, greater clarity of others' positions, or a stronger sense of solidarity). In some cases, the win-lose orientation of destructive conflict stems from fear of losing. People attempt to defeat alternative proposals because they believe that if their positions are not accepted they will lose resources, self-esteem, or the respect of others. In other cases, win-lose interaction is sparked, not by competitive motives, but by the parties' fear of working through a difficult conflict. Groups that rely on voting to reach decisions often call for a vote when discussion becomes heated and the members do not see any other immediate way out of a hostile and threatening situation. Any further attempt to discuss the alternatives or to pursue the reasons behind people's positions seems risky. A vote can put a quick end to threatening interaction, but it also induces a win-lose orientation that can easily trigger destructive cycles. Members whose proposal is rejected must resist a natural tendency to be less committed to the chosen solution and may try to "even the score" in future conflicts. **Productive conflict interaction is sometimes competitive; both parties must stand up for their own positions and strive for perceived understanding if a representative outcome is to be attained** (Cahn 1990). A great deal of tension and hostility may result as people struggle with the conflict. Although parties in productive conflicts hold strongly to their positions, they are also open to movement when convinced that such movement will result in the best decision. The need to preserve power, save face, or make the opponent look bad does not stand in the way of change. In destructive conflict, parties often become polarized, and the defense of a non-negotiable position becomes more important than working out a viable solution. This description of productive and destructive conflict interaction is obviously an idealization. It is rare that a conflict exhibits all the constructive or destructive qualities just mentioned; indeed, many conflicts exhibit both productive and destructive interaction. However, better conflict management will result if parties can sustain productive conflict interaction patterns.

CONFLICT AS INTERACTIVE BEHAVIOR

Conflict is, by nature, interactive. It is never wholly under one person's control (Kriesberg 1973). The other party's reactions and the person's anticipation of the other's response are extremely important. **Any comment made during a conflict is made with some awareness or prediction about the likely response it will elicit.** This predictive basis for any move in interaction creates a strong tendency for conflict interaction to become cyclic or repetitive. Suppose Robert criticizes Susan, an employee under his supervision, for her decreasing productivity. Susan may accept the criticism and explain why her production is down, thus reducing the conflict and moving toward a solution. Susan may also shout back and sulk, inviting escalation, or she may choose to say nothing and avoid the conflict, resulting in no improvement in the situation. Once Robert has spoken to Susan and she has responded, the situation is no longer totally under Robert's control: his next behavior will be a response to Susan's reaction. Robert's behavior, and its subsequent meaning to Susan, is dependent on the interchange between them. **A behavioral cycle of initiation-response—counterresponse results from the conflict interchange. This cycle cannot be understood by breaking it into its parts, into the individual behaviors of Robert and Susan.** It is more complex than the individual behaviors and, in a real sense, has a "life" of its own. The cycle can be self-reinforcing, if, for example, Susan shouts back at Robert, Robert tries to discipline her, Susan becomes more recalcitrant, and so on, in an escalating spiral. The cycle could also limit itself if Robert responds to Susan's shouting with an attempt to calm her and listen to her side of the story. Conflict interaction cycles acquire a momentum of their own. They tend in a definite direction—toward escalation, toward avoidance and suppression, or toward productive work on the conflict. The situation becomes even more complex when we remember that Robert formulated his criticism on the basis of his previous experience with Susan. That is, Robert's move is based on his perception of Susan's likely response. In the same way, Susan's response is based not only on Robert's criticism, but on her estimate of Robert's likely reaction to her response. Usually such estimations are "intuitive"—that is, they are not conscious—but sometimes parties do plot them out ("If I shout at Robert, he'll back down and maybe I won't have to deal with this"). They are always based on the parties' perceptions of each other, on whatever theories or beliefs each holds about the other's reactions. Because these estimates are only intuitive predictions, they may be wrong to some extent. The estimates will be revised as the conflict unfolds, and this revision will largely determine what direction the conflict takes. The most striking thing about this predictive process is the extraordinary difficulties it poses for attempts to understand the parties' thinking. When Susan responds to Robert on the basis of her prediction of Robert's answer, from the outside we see Susan making an estimate of Robert's estimate of what she means by her response. If Robert reflects on Susan's intention before answering, we observe Robert's estimate of Susan's estimate of his estimate of what Susan meant. This string of estimates can increase without bounds if one tries to pin down the originating point, and after a while the prospect is just as dizzying as a hall of mirrors.

Several studies of arms races (Richardson 1960, North, Brody, and Holsti 1963) and of marital relations (Watzlawick, Beavin, and Jackson 1967; Rubin 1983; Scarf 1987) and employee-supervisor interactions (Brown 1983) have shown how this spiral of predictions poses a critical problem in conflicts. If the parties do not take the spiral into account, they run the risk of miscalculation. However, it is impossible to calculate all the possibilities. At best, people have extremely limited knowledge of the implications their actions hold for others, and their ability to manage conflicts is therefore severely curtailed. Not only are parties' behaviors inherently interwoven in conflicts, but their thinking and anticipations are as well. The key question ... is: **how does conflict interaction develop destructive patterns—radical escalation, prolonged or inappropriate avoidance of conflict issues, inflexibility—rather than constructive patterns leading to productive conflict management?**

REVIEW QUESTIONS

1. Describe what the authors mean when they say that the case study about Diane and her co-workers shows how conflict situations are tense and threatening, uncertain and fragile.
2. Explain what is significant about each of the following terms in the authors' definition of conflict: *interaction, interdependent, incompatible goals, interference.*
3. Why do the authors disagree with the old adage "Most conflicts are actually communication problems"?
4. Distinguish between realistic and nonrealistic conflict.

PROBES

1. As you read the case study about Diane and her co-workers, what single feature of the situation strikes you as the most important positive move that was made? In other words, what one thing most helped resolve this conflict productively?
2. Give an example from your own experience of the difference between a realistic and a nonrealistic conflict.
3. At one point the authors argue about the wisdom of resolving a conflict by voting. (a) What is their rationale for discouraging voting? (b) How do you respond; that is, do you agree or disagree, and why?
4. The authors end this excerpt with "the key question" of how conflicts develop destructive patterns. After you've read the other four readings in this chapter, what is your response to this key question?

REFERENCES

Brown, L. D. (1983). *Managing conflict at organizational interfaces.* Reading, MA: Addison-Wesley.

Cahn, D. 1990. *Intimates in conflict: A communication perspective.* Hillsdale, NJ: Lawrence Erlbaum.

Coser, L. (1956). *The functions of social conflict.* New York: Free Press.

Coser, L. (1961). The termination of conflict. *Journal of Conflict Resolution, 5:* 347–353.

Deutsch, M. (1973). *The resolution of conflict.* New Haven, CT: Yale University Press.

Dubinskas, F. (1992). Culture and conflict: The cultural roots of discord. In D. M. Kolb and J. M. Bartunek, Eds., *Hidden conflict in organizations:* 187–208. Newbury Park, CA: Sage.

Fink, C. F. (1968). Some conceptual difficulties in the theory of social conflict. *Journal of Conflict Resolution, 12:* 412–460.

Grimshaw, A. D., Ed. (1990). *Conflict talk: Sociolinguistic investigations of arguments in conversations.* Cambridge: Cambridge University Press.

Hawes, L., and Smith, D. H. (1973). A critique of assumptions underlying the study of communication in conflict. *Quarterly Journal of Speech, 59:* 423–435.

Hocker, J. L., and Wilmot, W. W. (1985). *Interpersonal conflict.* Dubuque, IA: Wm. C Brown.

Janis, I. (1972). *Victims of groupthink.* Boston: Houghton Mifflin.

Kochman, T. (1981). *Black and white styles in conflict.* Chicago: University of Chicago Press.

Kriesberg, L. (1973). *The sociology of social conflicts.* Englewood Cliffs, NJ: Prentice-Hall.

North, R. C., Brody, R. A., and Holsti, O. (1963). Some empirical data on the conflict spiral. *Peace Research Society: Papers I.* Chicago Conference: 1–14.

Pruitt, D. G. (1981). *Negotiating behavior.* New York: Academic Press.

Putnam, L., and Poole, M. S. (1987). Conflict and negotiation. In F. Jablin, L. Putnam, K. Roberts, and L. Porter, Eds., *Handbook of organizational communication:* 549–599. Beverly Hills, CA: Sage.

Richardson, L. F. (1960). *Arms and insecurity.* Pittsburgh: Boxwood Press.

Roloff, M. E. (1987). Communication and conflict. In C. Berger and S. H. Chaffee, Eds., *Handbook of communication science:* 484–534. Beverly Hills, CA: Sage.

Rubin, L. (1983). *Intimate strangers.* New York: Harper and Row.

Scarf, M. (1987). *Intimate partners: Patterns in love and marriage.* New York: Ballantine.

Tannen, D. (1986). *That's not what I meant.* New York: William Morrow.

Watzlawick, P., Beavin, J. H., and Jackson, D. D. (1967). *Pragmatics of human communication.* New York: Norton.

Communication Spirals, Paradoxes, and Conundrums

William W. Wilmot

Bill Wilmot is an interpersonal communication and conflict management teacher and a mediator who helps people in conflict all over North America. As these excerpts from his book *Relational Communication* illustrate, he has an unusually sharp sense of the complexities of interpersonal relationships. This reading combines Bill's discussion of communication spirals and his ideas about paradoxes and conundrums (relationship puzzles). It offers some helpful advice about how to turn these particular communication walls into bridges.

"Communication Spirals, Paradoxes and Conundrums" by William Wilmot from *Relational Communication,* 4th Edition. Reprinted by permission of William Wilmot.

The first section begins by explaining that a "communication spiral" happens when "the actions of each person in a relationship magnify those of the other." Wilmot gives several examples of both positive and negative spirals that can happen in family, work, and dating relationships. He emphasizes that spirals can be powerful because they pick up a momentum that feeds back on itself. This means that closeness and harmony can create more of the same, and that bitterness and hostility can operate the same way. He lists seven features of a communication spiral and then goes into some detail about generative and degenerative spirals.

An example of a generative spiral is the teacher who searches for the positive in a student and rewards it appropriately. As Wilmot summarizes it, "the more genuinely the teacher relates to the student, the better the student performs; the higher the quality of his or her performance, the more positive the teacher becomes."

Degenerative spirals are the mirror images of generative ones. Discord leads to more discord, and the spiral intensifies. So, for example, if a person is hesitant to relate to others, he or she shuns contacts, which in turn makes it more difficult to overcome the hesitancy. Some research that Wilmot cites shows that one of the most common degenerative spirals in a marriage occurs when the husband withdraws emotionally, the wife expresses dissatisfaction to her husband, and the husband then withdraws even more.

Wilmot follows this analysis of spirals with five concrete suggestions about how to alter degenerative ones. The first is deceptively simple sounding: "Do what comes unnaturally." Spirals are relational phenomena, which is to say that they are fed by both (or all) the parties in a relationship. Change is impossible so long as things continue as they have. At least one party has to "do what comes unnaturally."

A second suggestion is to use third parties—friends, counselors, relatives, clergy, or others whom you trust. A specific suggestion for breaking the toxic pattern can often come from an informed but not intimately involved outsider. A third suggestion is to reaffirm your relational goals. It can often help for people in a spiral to remind themselves and each other about the commitment they have to the relationship. This is a form of suggestion number four, "metacommunicating." This just means that you communicate about your communicating. You talk about the relationship and whatever has led to the degenerating series of actions.

The final two suggestions are that you try spending less time with the person and consider changing the external situation. Sometimes these moves will also break troublesome patterns.

The section of this reading on paradoxes and conundrums consists of brief discussions of 12 two-directional pulls that many people experience in their relationships. It can be reassuring to read that others feel some of the same tensions you do, and Wilmot also includes some suggestions about how to cope with these relational puzzles.

The first is that people want contradictory things in relationships: freedom and closeness, stability and excitement. It can be helpful to recognize that this is normal, and not necessarily problematic. A second is that both "objective" third-person observations and "subjective" insider observations about a relationship are fraught with errors. It's important to get both perspectives and not to believe that either provides "the Truth" about the relationship.

Paradox 3 is that if you leave relationships completely alone, they'll probably dissolve, and if you try to force them to happen, you can destroy them. It works best to stay in the middle of this tension. Number four is the tension between expecting a relationship to generate happiness when its purpose may be the sense of wholeness that comes from the inherently unstable dialectical encounter between two people. The fifth paradox is that we get the most pleasure *and* the most pain from our closest relationships.

Wilmot also discusses some paradoxes about the connection between "the self" and "the relationship" and the fact that "relationships can serve as springboards for growth or just toss you higher so you land harder." Number nine reminds us how changes in any part or level of a relationship reverberate to other levels. The tenth sketches the power inherent in and the problems created by relationship labels. And the last two emphasize the ever-changing, emergent quality of relationships.

By the time you complete this reading, you should have an appreciation for the sometimes startling complexity of the relationships you are a part of.

A communication spiral occurs when the actions of each person in a relationship magnify those of the other. Communication spirals are evident almost everywhere, happening between humans, between us and other species, and among other species as well. A human-animal illustration should clarify the essential nature of spirals. My son Jason at age 3 saw a sleek, shiny cat. With the reckless abandonment of a child his age, he rushed at the cat to pet it. The wise cat, seeing potential death, moved out of Jason's reach. Not to be outdone, Jason tried harder. The cat moved farther away. Jason started running after the cat. The cat, no dummy about life, ran too. In a short 10 seconds from the initial lunge at the cat, Jason and the cat were running at full tilt. Luckily, the cat was faster and survived to run another day. Similarly, spirals occur in many contexts:

- A child disobeys the parent, the parent acts more punitively and harshly, and the child becomes even more unruly.
- A parent and 22-year-old son embark on a foreign adventure for 2 months—just the two of them. As the trip draws to a close, they both note on the plane ride home how close they feel to one another, and how easy their communication has become.
- An employee may be quiet and not forthcoming to the supervisor, the supervisor puts pressure on him to talk, and he becomes even more silent.
- Two guys are sitting in a bar; one accidentally touches the other, the first pushes him, an insult is uttered, and within a minute the two are fighting in the street.
- A supervisor is dissatisfied with an employee's performance but doesn't tell the employee. The employee is complaining to others about the supervisor. Both the employee and supervisor keep doing more of the same—the employee withdrawing and talking to others, the supervisor getting more annoyed and not telling the employee. Then 6 months later during the performance appraisal, the supervisor says, "We are reorganizing the office, and you won't be needed anymore."

- Two close friends buy a cabin midway between their two towns. Each time they go to the cabin, their relationship is reinforced, and not only do they ski better, they enjoy one another's company more.
- Two romantic partners feel that the other is pulling away. So each shares less, harbors grudges, and spends less time with the other, until there is a fight during which they end the relationship.
- Two opposite-sex friends spend a lot of time with one another. As they spend more time, they exclude others and feel closer and closer. It gets to the point that they don't want to begin other friendships because this one is so fulfilling.

All spirals, whether building in a positive or negative direction, tend to pick up a momentum that feeds back on itself—closeness and harmony build more closeness and harmony; misunderstanding and dissatisfaction create more misunderstanding and dissatisfaction. The responses produce a lock-step effect in relationships (Leary, 1955; Kurdek, 1991). Quality relationships, like close friendships, develop an "end in themselves"—quality—and become self-sustaining (Rose & Serafica, 1986).

Communication spirals, whether they head in positive or negative directions, are characterized by these elements:

1. The participants' meanings intertwine in such a way that each person's behavior accelerates the dynamism of the relationship. The relational synergy builds upon itself in a continuously accelerating manner.
2. *Each* person's actions contribute to the overall dynamic. Whether you talk, retreat, engage, reinvest, or disinvest in the relationship, your communication (or lack of communication) directly impacts the other person, and vice versa. Each person reacts to the other (Kurdek, 1991).
3. Bateson (1972, 1979) noted long ago that spirals manifest either (1) *symmetrical* communication moves or (2) *complementary* communication moves. In symmetrical spirals, as Person One does "more of the same" Person Two also does "more of the same"—for example, two people shouting at each other. In complementary spirals, as Person One does "more of the same" Person Two does "more of the opposite"—Person A shouts and Person B withdraws in silence (Wilden, 1980).
4. At any given period of time, a spiral is contributing to the relationship in either generative or degenerative ways. Generative spirals promote positive feelings about the relationship and more closeness; degenerative spirals induce negative feelings about the relationship and more distance.
5. Both generative and degenerative spirals tend to continue accelerating until the participants check the movement by some action.
6. Spirals can be changed, their pace quickened or slowed, or the direction reversed by the participants' actions.
7. Based on the communication spirals that unfold, relationships expand, wither, and repeat patterns of close-far.

FIGURE 1   A communication
spiral.

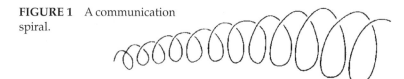

A diagram of the nature of spirals in Figure 1 shows how the dynamics of the communication for both persons tend to increase over time. Notice how the cycles get larger and larger across time—which is the nature of all communication spirals.

Generative Spirals

When communicative behaviors interlock to produce more positive feelings about the relationship, the participants are in a *generative spiral.* For instance, the teacher who can be open and accepting of students often experiences such spirals. Searching for the positive in a student and rewarding him or her appropriately can open a student up for teacher influence. The more genuinely the teacher relates to the student, the better the student performs; the higher the quality of his or her performance, the more positive the teacher becomes.

Generative spirals are obviously not limited to teacher-student relationships. A highly motivated worker illustrates the same ever-widening nature of spirals. As one improves working conditions, the worker's motivation increases, which cycles back and makes for an even better climate, which increases …

In generative spirals, the perceptions of the partners become more productive and their mutual adjustments continue to build. In romantic couples, "love generates more love, growth more growth, and knowledge more knowledge" (O'Neill & O'Neill, 1972). The favorableness builds upon itself. Trust and understanding cycle back to create more trust and understanding. The relationship is precisely like a spiral—ever-widening.

We all experience generative spirals. The student who begins doing work of a high caliber earns better grades, becomes self-motivated, and enters a generative spiral. Each piece of work brings a reward (good grades or praise) that further encourages him or her to feats of excellence. And if conditions are favorable, the spiral can continue. Teachers who retrain and become more knowledgeable discover that they have more to offer students. The excited students, in turn, reinforce the teachers' desire to work hard so they can feel even better about their profession. In generative spirals, the actions of each individual [supply] a multiplier effect in reinforcement. The better you do, the more worthwhile you feel; the more worthwhile you feel, the better you do. The effects of a simple action reverberate throughout the system. An unexpected tenderness from your loved one, for instance, will not stop there. It will recycle back to you and probably come from you again in increased dosage. A good relationship with your supervisor promotes you to want to please more, and the supervisor, seeing your increased involvement, gives even more recognition to you.

Degenerative Spirals

Degenerative spirals are mirror images of generative spirals; the process is identical, but the results are opposite. In a degenerative spiral misunderstanding and discord create more and more relationship damage. As with generative spirals, degenerative spirals take many forms.

The inability to reach out and develop meaningful relationships is often compounded. The person who has reduced interest in others and does not form effective relationships suffers a lower self-esteem (because self-esteem is socially derived), which in turn cycles back and produces less interest in others. "The process is cyclical and degenerative" (Ziller, 1973). Or if one is afraid to love others, he or she shuns people, which in turn makes it more difficult to love. Also, such degenerative spirals often happen to people with regard to their sense of worth concerning work. People who have not established themselves in their profession but have been in the profession for a number of years may get caught in a spiral. They may spend time trying to appear busy, talking about others, or using various techniques to establish some sense of worth. Behavior that can change the spiral—working hard or retraining—are those least likely to occur. It is a self-fulfilling prophecy with a boost—it gets worse and worse. With each new gamut or ploy perfected (acquiring a new hobby, joining numerous social gatherings, etc.), the performance issues become further submerged.

A simple example of a degenerative spiral is the case of a lonely person. Lonely people tend to be less involved, less expressive, and less motivated in interactions. As a result, their partners in the conversation see the lonely person as uninvolved and less competent, and are less likely to initiate and maintain conversations with them. As a result, lonely people become further isolated from the social networks needed to break the cycle (Spitzberg & Canary, 1985).

Degenerative cycles are readily apparent when a relationship begins disintegrating. When distrust feeds distrust, defensiveness soars and the relationship worsens, and such "runaway relationships" become destructive for all concerned. In a "gruesome twosome," for instance, the two participants maintain a close, negative relationship. Each person receives fewer gratifications from the relationship, yet they maintain the attachment by mutual exploitation (Scheflen, 1960). When the relationship prevents one or both partners from gratifying normal needs, but the relationship is maintained, the twosome is caught in a degenerative spiral. Recent marital research demonstrates that, as love declines, negative conflict increases—a clear degenerative spiral (Lloyd & Cate, 1985).

Degenerative spirals, like generative spirals, occur in a variety of forms. A typical case involves the breakup of a significant relationship such as marriage. During a quarreling session one evening the husband says to the wife, "If you had not gone and gotten involved in an outside relationship with another man, our marriage could have made it. You just drained too much energy from us for our marriage to work." The wife responds by saying, "Yes, and had you given me the attention and care I longed for, I wouldn't have had an outside relationship." The infinite regress continues, each of them finding fault with why the other caused the termination of the marriage. The spiraling nature is clear. The more the wife retreats to an outside relationship, the less chance she has of having her needs met in the marriage. And the more the husband avoids giving her what she wants in the relationship, the more she will be influenced to seek outside relationships. One of the most common negative spirals between wives and husbands occurs when (1) the husband withdraws emotionally and (2) the wife expresses dissatisfaction to the husband (Segrin & Fitzpatrick, 1992).

Degenerative spirals are not limited to romantic relationships—they occur in all types. Parents and children often get caught up in spirals that create a dysfunctional system. The more dependent the child is on the parent, the more responsible and overburdened the parent is. And the more the parent takes responsibility for the child, the more this promotes dependence on the part of the child. It works like this: "One's actions toward other people generally effect a mirror duplication or a counter-measure from the other. This in turn tends to strengthen one's original action" (Leary, 1955)....

Altering Degenerative Spirals

Spirals, obviously, do change, with people going in and out of generative and degenerative spirals over the course of a relationship. And, as a relationship participant, you can have [an] impact on the nature of the spirals—even altering degenerative spirals once they start. There are specific choices you can make that can alter the direction a relationship is flowing.

First, alter your usual response—do what comes unnaturally. For example, if you are in a relationship where you and the other tend to escalate, [and] call each other names, you can stop the spiral by simply not allowing yourself to use negative language. Or, you can say, "This will just lead to a shouting match. I'm going to take a walk and talk with you when I come back," then exit from the normally hostile situation. Or say you have a roommate who is not very talkative and over the past 2 months you have tried to draw him out. You see that the more you talk, the more he retreats and the less he talks. Doing "more of the same" does not work, so do "less of the same." Don't act on the natural inclination to talk when he is silent; in fact, talk less and outwait him. Similarly, if you are often quiet in a group of four friends, people adapt to that by sometimes leaving you out of the decisions. Then, for the first time, begin to tell them what you would like to do. Change the patterns, and you change the spiral.

Wilmot and Stevens (1994) interviewed over 100 people who had "gone through a period of decline," and then improved their romantic, friendship, and family relationships—basically pulling out of a degenerative spiral. When asked what they did to "turn it around," it was found that a potent way of altering the patterns was to change behavior. The changes of behavior, of course, took many forms, given the particular type of relationship spiral that had occurred. Some people became more independent, some gave more "space" to the other, others changed locations or moved, and still others sacrificed for the partner or spent more time together. But the basic principle is the same—when in a degenerating or escalating set of communication patterns, change!

One last anecdote about changing patterns. I know one parent whose 11-year-old daughter was getting low grades in school. The parent had been a superb student, and the daughter, in the past, had done well. But, in the middle of the school year, the daughter started getting lower and lower grades. As the grades went down, the parent's criticism went up. Pretty soon, both the girl's grades and the mother-daughter relationship were in the cellar! After some help from an outsider, the mother took a vow to *not* talk anymore about grades, regardless of what happened. It was very difficult, for each evening the two had been arguing about grades; grades had become the focal point of the entire relationship. It only took 2 weeks, and the daughter's grades made dramatic jumps. The mother, who found "giving up" very difficult, had taken her negative part out of the communication system—and it changed.

One final note on changing your behavior. The people in the Wilmot and Stevens (1994) study noted that "persistence" was one important key to bringing about a change in the relationship. If the parent above had only stopped her criticism for one night, as soon as she resumed it, off the spiral would have gone again. The other person will be suspicious of your change at first, probably question[ing] your motives and [having] other negative interpretations. But if you are persistent in bringing the change, it will have effects on the other person, for his or her communication patterns are interlocked with yours.

Second, you can use third parties constructively. Friends, counselors, relatives, clergy, and others can sometimes provide a different perspective for you to begin to open up a degenerative system for change. Third parties can often make specific suggestions that will break the pattern of interlocking, mutually destructive behaviors that keep adding fuel to the degenerating relationship. In one case, a husband and wife went to a marriage counselor because they had come to a standoff. He was tired of her demands to always talk to her and pay attention. She was tired of his demands for more frequent sexual activity. As a result, they became entrapped in a degenerative spiral—he talked less, and she avoided situations of physical intimacy. Upon seeing the counselor, they both realized that they were getting nowhere fast. Each was trying to get the other to change first. With the help of the counselor, they renegotiated their relationship, and each began giving a little bit. Over a period of a few days they found themselves coming out of the degenerating patterns.

Third, you can reaffirm your relational goals. Often when people get stuck in negative patterns of interaction, the other automatically assumes you want to "jump ship." If you are in a downward spiral, whether with your parents, boss, lover, child, or friend, reaffirming what you each have to gain from the relationship can promote efforts to get it back. The couple who saw the counselor found that they both had an important goal to stay together—for if either one had "won" the fight and lost the relationship, neither would have gotten what he or she wanted. Relational reaffirmation can help you focus on all the things you can do to get the relationship back to a more positive phase. Good relationships

take energy to sustain; similarly, making a commitment to the relationship obvious to the other will help pull you out of the debilitating negative patterns.

Fourth, you can alter a spiral by metacommunicating. Wilmot and Stevens' (1994) respondents reported having a "Big Relationship Talk"—talking
about the relationship and what had led to the degenerating series of actions.
When you comment on what you see happening, it can open up the spiral
itself for discussion. One can say, "Our relationship seems to be slipping—I
find myself criticizing you, and you seem to be avoiding me, and it looks
like it is getting worse. What can we do to turn it around?" Such metacommunication, whether pointed to the conversational episodes or the overall
relationship patterns, can set the stage for productive conflict management
and give participants a sense of a control over the relationship dynamics.
Metacommunication, especially when coupled with a reaffirmation of your
relational goals ("I don't want us to be unhappy, I want us to both like being
together, but we seem to ... "), can alter the destructive forces in a relationship.
And, of course, you can use metacommunication in any type of relationship,
such as on the job. J. P., for example, says, "Sally, it seems to me like our work
enthusiasm is slipping away. What might we do to get that sense of fun back
like we had about 6 months ago?"

Fifth, try to spend more or less time with the person. If you are on the
"outs" with your co-workers, you could begin to spend more time with
them—go to lunch, have coffee, take short strolls together. It is amazing what
kinds of large changes can be purchased with just a small amount of time.
Likewise, relationships often suffer because the people spend more time
together than they can productively handle. So Tom always goes on a 3-day
fishing trip with me in the summer as a way to both get more distance and
independence in his marriage (and, coincidentally, to reaffirm our relationship
with one another). Getting more distance and independence can bring you
back refreshed and ready to relate again. Interestingly, Wilmot and Stevens
(1994) found such "independence" moves an important way to alter a degenerating spiral.

Finally, we all recognize that changing an external situation can alter a
degenerating relationship. One parent has a son who got into an ongoing battle
with the principal of the junior high school. The feud went on for months, with
the principal (according to the mother) tormenting her boy and the boy retaliat-
ing by being mischievous. The mutually destructive actions were arrested only
when the boy switched schools. He (and the principal) had a chance to start
over, not contaminated by the previous interlocking patterns.

Another way to change the external situation is to stay in the presence of
the other person but move to a new environment. Many married couples have
gone for extended vacations in order to give themselves time to work out new
solutions to relationship problems. If the relationship is important to you and
you want to preserve it, effort expended to help the relationship reach productive periods is time well spent. Retreats, for business partners, romantic
partners, and friends, can allow an infusion of fresh energy into a declining

relationship. Because once the degenerative phases are reached, the behaviors of each person tend to be mutually reinforcing and damaging. Each person can blame the other and claim his or her own innocence, but that will not alter the degeneration. It sometimes takes long, hard work to alter a negative spiral, and it may be successful if both put in some effort. But as every counselor knows from experience, one person alone can usually not change the relationship. If that person makes changes, and the other reciprocates, you have a chance to turn the spiral around.

Woody Allen captured the essence of relational change when he said, "Relationships are like a shark. They either move forward, or they die." Our relationships are dynamic, always moving and changing either toward or away from improvement. Participants' behaviors interlock so that each one's behavior influences the others, and the mutually conjoined behaviors intensify the other's reactions.

People look at their relationships using different time frames. Some people tend to only look at the macro perspective, charting the changes in yearly units such as "do I feel as good about my job today as I did a year ago." A relationship may not look any different today than it did yesterday, but over a year's time, you can see either overall improvement or disintegration. The long-term spirals are identified by comparing the relationship to a much earlier state.

Other times one may process and categorize a relationship on an hour-by-hour basis. For example, when Jan's romantic partner announced that she wanted to "call it off," Jan spent the next 2 weeks thinking about the relationship, talking to her partner, and doing endless processing of all the changes coming her way. Rapid relational change, especially if it is unexpected, can cause intense processing of the relationship, sometimes to the point of overload. Those who suffer from an unexpected firing, termination of a romance, or disinheritance from the family find themselves processing at a depth they didn't think possible.

What is important, is to begin to sensitize yourself to the ebbs and flows inherent in all relationships, so you can make informed choices. Becoming attuned to the nature of communication spirals can increase your understanding of these processes.

TANGLES IN THE WEB: PARADOXES AND CONUNDRUMS

As you go through life, whether you are 18 or 80, the experience and understanding of your relationships is not a linear, step-by-step process. Like relationships themselves, our understanding is imperfect, and it is easy to overestimate how much we know. Relationships are elusive.

There are some relational paradoxes (statements that are both true but contradict one another) (Wilmot, 1987) and conundrums—puzzlements and elements that are inherently unsolvable. Here are a few of them.

1. We want contradictory things in relationships: freedom and closeness, openness to talk yet protection, stability and excitement. These dialectic tensions seem to be present in all relationships.

In many romantic relationships we want both freedom and connection, excitement and stability. In the family context we often want the others to accept who we are, yet we spend inordinate amounts of time centering on how we can change them. We talk openly about the importance of "communication" in relationships, but it appears to be more of a cultural belief than an actual fact (Wilmot & Stevens, 1994; Parks, 1982). Maybe we can begin to celebrate the tension inherent in all relationships rather than trying to solve the contradictory needs, flowing with the needs as they change back and forth.

2. Both insider and outsider views of relationships are fraught with errors.

Outsiders to relationships can more accurately observe our actual communication behavior but are less accurate than we are at specifying the *meaning* of those behaviors within this particular relationship. When you, as an outsider, look at someone else's relationship, your judgments can be a good projective test for what you personally believe is the "key" to success. Think of a marriage you know that you would describe as high quality. To what would you attribute it?

- hard work
- good match on background characteristics
- being raised in nondysfunctional families
- luck
- how well they communicate with one another
- a fine match on introversion/extroversion
- similar religious affiliations
- the support of their networks of family and friends
- both being raised in the same part of the country
- the length of time they have been together
- their ability to raise children successfully
- their mutual respect and compassion
- their intelligence
- their warmth and expressiveness
- their similar life struggles
- their commitment to one another
- their clarity about how to perform their roles
- their overriding love of one another
- their supportive friends
- similar hobbies and pastimes
- being at the same level of attractiveness

Outsiders, looking at someone else's relationship, tend to rely on external or situational factors in making their guesses (Burgoon & Newton, 1991). And we tend to evaluate others a bit more harshly than they do themselves, with us seeing the limitations of one or both of the partners: "I can't believe she stays married to him—he is so boring in public." When looking at someone's communication behavior, outsiders judge conversations less favorably than do those on the inside (Street, Mulac, & Wiemann, 1988). Outsiders generate faulty hypotheses about the intentions of the communicators—"she did that because she wants to control him" (Stafford, Waldron, & Infield, 1989). When we observe others' communication, we compensate for lack of information about their internal states by using our own personal theories—our "implicit personality theories" (Stafford, Waldron, & Infield, 1989). As an outsider, our observations are fraught with errors and overinterpretations, sort of "what we get is what we see," with most of it coming from us.

As insiders, our views aren't any less biased; we just tend to focus on different aspects (Dillard, 1987; Sillars & Scott, 1983). For example, insiders to marital relationships tend to overestimate their similarity and act with confidence on their views of the other. Yet the perceptions are not objectively accurate. Therefore, *all* views of relationships are inherently distorted—outsiders and insiders alike. Researchers and book writers (including this one) are themselves influenced by their own needs and perspectives, often looking for some order in the midst of considerable chaos.

3. Relationships are problematic—if we don't do anything about their natural dynamic, they may atrophy. If we try to force them, to "make them happen," we may destroy their essential nature.

The natural forces on relationships, marriage partners having to earn a living and nurture children, friends moving away from one another, tend to move most in the direction of decreased quality over time. In a sense, it is as if there is an energy in relationships that, if you don't continually reinvest in it, will cause the relationship to atrophy. Yet, on the other hand, we need to not try to "force" relationships. It is a rare individual in this culture who can command himself or herself to "love" someone else. The question of how to enhance a long-term relationship—whether family, romantic, or friend—looms large for all of us.... It is clear that, so far, there are no guarantees in relationships.

4. Committed relationships, such as marriage, may bring us much unhappiness because we think their purpose is happiness generation. Maybe their purpose is wholeness, grounded in the dialectical encounter between mates (Guggenbuhl-Craig, 1977).

In North America and most western cultures, people choose marriage partners and friends for what they do for us—make us happy, excite us sexually, provide a sense of fun and connection. Yet ..., maybe this "what does it do for me" sets us up for disappointment and failure. From a spiritual perspective, one could say that our relationships, while started to "make us happy," have a more difficult and nobler purpose—to allow us to be challenged, to grow, and to change. Lifetime friends, for example, may serve the function of helping us correct ourselves when we get out of line in public. Romantic partners will set the stage for our unresolved issues of life and eccentricity to flourish, and see their downside. Family members will test our commitment, resilience and love, and if we move through that test we can emerge on a higher plane of relatedness.

5. The more intimacy and closeness we want, the more risk we face in the relationship. The greatest pleasure *and* pain come from those to whom we are the closest. Relationships bring both joy and suffering.

The very relationships people spend so much time processing—romantic, family, and friendship—are the ones to bring both the extremes of joy and pain. The less close relationships, while they can bring stability and meaning into life, may not address some of our deepest needs. Risk and reward seem to be opposite sides of the same coin.

6. We often see the "self" as concrete and findable. Yet relationships are no less "real" than an individual self is.

In our culture, we take, as has been noted many times, the "self" as individual, disconnected, separate, and findable. We put the locus of most things into the self—discussing "self-esteem" and "personality" as if they were real things and not abstract concepts. Relationships are neither more nor less figments of our concepts than are our selves—but we don't tend to see it that way in this culture. It is important to note that our selves do have a conventional reality—there is a person standing there. Yet upon close examination, the "self" cannot be found. Is your brain your self? Your torso? Your legs? Your emotions? We impose the concept of "self" onto the physical and emotional aspects and stop our analysis. Relationships, while not physically represented, are no less real than are our selves. We talk about relationships, and their "reality," upon examination, is just as findable (and no less so) [as] that of the self.

7. Self is produced in relationship to others; relationships are produced from two selves.

... It has been argued that we originate and live in-relation; we co-create our selves in relation to one another. And relationships are produced from the two persons who have a communication connection. Self and other produce, and are produced by, relationship. And self is more fruitfully viewed as "with the ecological system" rather than as the center of one's world (Broome, 1991, p. 375).

8. The greatest individual growth, and the greatest derailment of individual growth, comes from the hurt and disappointment of relationships gone awry. Relationships can serve as springboards for growth or just toss you higher so you land harder.

When we face the natural traumas of life, our response determines the outcome. Trauma can bring transformation or derailment. Some people are broken when a relationship terminates, for example, or when an important person dies. Others, through grieving and slowly transforming themselves, reopen to relationships and life, reconnecting anew and building better relationships in the future.

9. We can solve problems in relationships by (1) internal, personal change; and (2) changing the external, communication connection between the two. Change at any one level reverberates to the other level, for both us and the other person.

Like the chicken and the egg, which comes first—you or relationship? And if you have difficulties, do you "get your stuff together" and then reenter other relationships, or do you begin other relationships so you can become stronger? Both routes are used, and both can work. If you undergo change, it will reverberate in all your relationships: the boundaries are permeable. If your relationship changes, it will alter you; the influence always flows both ways.

10. We can't fully understand our relationships without concepts, and as soon as we use an abstract notion we impose its limitations on what we are seeing. Labels are essential and limiting, and cannot capture an ever-changing reality. As Wilden says, "all theories of relationship require a certain artificial closure" (Wilden, 1980, p. 114).

We can't really proceed with understanding without labels, and when you introduce your "boyfriend" to your family, it gives them a clue about the relationship. Yet when you use the label, it restricts both your and the other's views of that relationship. Each relationship contains many complex and contradictory elements, and it cannot be accurately captured by "boyfriend." Further, there is always "label lag"—the relationship changes, and the label stays the same. A "married couple" of 6 months will be very different than that very same couple at 6 years or 6 decades, yet they are still referred to as married. All concepts and labels are limiting and constricting—and essential.

11. General conclusions about gender, culture, and relationships may not apply at all to your particular relationships.

One of the problems in talking about "gender" or "cultural" effects is that we are always talking about groupings that help us "understand" on an abstract level. But your particular relationship may not reflect the general norms at all. Just like a theory of gravity cannot tell you about when a particular apple will fall from a tree, studying relational dynamics will not tell you about what will happen in your relationship. When studies on gender, for example, show that females are more expressive than males, what do you do if the woman in a cross-sex romantic relationship is the less expressive of the two? It is probably better to focus on the central issue—expressiveness, and the match or mismatch between the partners—rather than trying to reflect the general norm. Similarly, the finding that gay males have more partners than lesbians or heterosexuals does not mean that a gay man cannot live a life of commitment to another.

12. Learning about relationships occurs before, during, and after the relationship is a findable event.

Our perspectives on our relationships do not end—they only change. Just think for a moment about how you interpret events that happened to you in your childhood. As you move through time you will reinterpret them many times, focusing on different aspects, and seeing them in a different light. Likewise, the friendship that you used to see as a barometer of yourself may be later seen as not helping you at all at a stage of life. A devastating romantic termination may be seen later as the "best thing that ever happened to me." While many of us do not seek difficulties, most of us say, in retrospect, that it is what produced the learning so essential to the next stage of our life. I was once talking to a fellow on a flight from Helsinki, Finland, to Boston. He was in a long-distance relationship with a Finnish woman, and he lived in Boston, and here is what he said. "I did fatherhood and marriage, so I guess I'm doing this for awhile"—making retrospective sense of his relationship that was allowing him to collect considerable frequent flyer miles!

REVIEW QUESTIONS

1. Define *communication spiral*.
2. According to this reading, what is necessary in order to stop a spiral?
3. What's the difference between a generative and a degenerative spiral?
4. What does Wilmot and Stevens's research indicate about the role of persistence in altering a degenerative spiral?
5. What is metacommunicating?
6. What is a dialectic tension in a relationship?
7. What are the specific problems Wilmot identifies with both insider and outsider views of a relationship?

PROBES

1. Explain what Wilmot means when he says that, in a spiral, "each person's behavior accelerates the dynamism of the relationship." Give an example that includes a positive dynamism and one that includes a negative dynamism.
2. Could a spiral that appears to be generative to some member(s) of a relationship appear to be degenerative to others? Explain.
3. What is one generative spiral in your communication experience that you could *enhance*? What is one degenerative spiral in your communication experience that you could *break*?
4. Wilmot suggests that one of the ways you can "do what comes unnaturally" is to stop trying to make things better. Explain why this might work.
5. Wilmot suggests that you might change an external situation in order to alter a degenerating spiral. This could include changing locations—your home, work, or school. But some people also emphasize that "Wherever you go, there you are," which is to say that you need to change your attitude or approach, not your location. What do you think works best?

6. Do you believe that the main purpose of a long-term relationship like a marriage is happiness generation, or what Wilmot calls "wholeness, grounded in the dialectical encounter between mates"?
7. What is the relationship between Wilmot's brief discussion of the self in paradoxes 6 and 7 and Stewart, Zediker, and Witteborn's discussion of the self in Chapter 3?
8. Identify one general conclusion about gender, culture, and relationships that does *not* apply to one of your relationships.

REFERENCES

Bateson, G. (1972). *Steps to an Ecology of Mind.* New York: Ballantine Books.

Bateson, G. (1979). *Mind and Nature: A Necessary Unity.* New York: Bantam Books.

Broome, B. J. (1991). Building shared meaning: Implications of a relational approach to empathy for teaching intercultural communication. *Communication Education, 40,* 235–249.

Burgoon, J. K., & Newton, D. A. (1991). Applying a social meaning model to relational message interpretations of conversational involvement: Comparing observer and participant perspectives. *The Southern Communication Journal, 56,* 96–113.

Dillard, J. P. (1987). Close relationships at work: Perceptions of the motives and performance of relational participants. *Journal of Social and Personal Relationships, 4,* 179–193.

Guggenbuhl-Craig, A. (1977). *Marriage Dead or Alive.* Murray Stein (trans.). Dallas, TX: Spring Publications.

Kurdek, L. A. (1991). Marital stability and changes in marital quality in newlywed couples: A test of the contextual model. *Journal of Social and Personal Relationships, 5,* 201–221.

Leary, T. (1955). The theory and measurement methodology of interpersonal communication. *Psychiatry, 18,* 147–161.

Lloyd, S. A., & Cate, R. M. (1985). The developmental course of conflict in dissolution of premarital relationships. *Journal of Social and Personal Relationships, 2,* 179–194.

O'Neill, N., & O'Neill, G. (1972). *Open Marriage.* New York: M. Evans.

Parks, M. R. (1982). Ideology in interpersonal communication: Off the couch and into the world. In Burgoon, M. (Ed.), *Communication Yearbook 5.* New Brunswick, NJ: International Communication Association/Transaction Books, pp. 79–107.

Rose, S., & Serafica, F. C. (1986). Keeping and ending casual, close and best friendships. *Journal of Social and Personal Relationships, 3,* 275–288.

Scheflen, A. (1960). Communication and regulation in psychotherapy. *Psychiatry, 26,* 126–136.

Segrin, C., & Fitzpatrick, M. A. (1992). Depression and verbal aggressiveness in different marital types. *Communication Studies, 43,* 79–91.

Sillars, A. L., & Scott, M. D. (1983). Interpersonal perception between intimates: An integrative review. *Human Communication Research, 10,* 153–176.

Spitzberg, B. H., & Canary, D. J. (1985). Loneliness and relationally competent communication. *Journal of Social and Personal Relationships, 2,* 387–402.

Stafford, L., Waldron, V. R., & Infield, L. L. (1989). Actor-observer differences in conversational memory. *Human Communication Research, 15,* 590–611.

Street, R. L., Jr., Mulac, A., & Wiemann, J. M. (1988). Speech evaluation differences as a function of perspective (participant versus observer) and presentational medium. *Human Communication Research, 14,* 333–363.

Wilden, A. (1980). *System and Structure: Essays on Communication and Exchange,* 2nd ed. London: Tavistock Publications.

Wilmot, W. W. (1987). *Dyadic Communication.* New York: Random House.

Wilmot, W. W., & Stevens, D. C. (1994). Relationship rejuvenation: Arresting decline in personal relationships. In Conville, R. (Ed.), *Communication and Structure.* Philadelphia, PA: Ablex, pp. 103–124.

Ziller, R. C. (1973). *The Social Self.* New York: Pergamon Press.

Handling the Break-Up of Relationships

Steve Duck

Like the previous reading by Wilmot, this one analyzes how relationships get into trouble and how they might be rescued. Steve Duck is a Brit, which is why you'll find the word "whilst" and the spelling "behaviour" here. For a number of years, he's been a distinguished interpersonal communication teacher and researcher at the University of Iowa. This excerpt from his book *Human Relationships* provides a way to understand how personal relationships come apart and how they can sometimes be put back together.

Duck explains the four typical phases that people go through when breaking up. The first is "intrapsychic" or internal, and consists of at least one member of the relationship brooding about his or her partner. The second phase is called "dyadic" because it's the time when the two partners (the dyad) talk with each other about breaking up. This leads, usually rapidly, to the third step, a "social" phase when they tell other people and seek their support. The final phase is called "grave-dressing," because it consists of communication that tries to "bury the relationship good and proper." During this phase, the people involved create an account of the relationship's history and demise. This account gives the partners and others a way to make sense out of what happened.

One benefit of this model is that it suggests what relational partners might do if they want to "put the relationship right" or rebuild it. You obviously can't just reverse the steps of the breakup, because memories of the old relationship and its demise are necessarily going to be involved in any new relationship that's developed. But the model does identify what people can do at the different stages or phases of dissolution. So, for example, Duck notes that if the relationship is at the intrapsychic phase of dissolution, then "repair should aim to reestablish liking for the partner rather than to correct behavioural faults in ourselves or our nonverbal behaviour." Other strategies are appropriate at other phases of a breakup. As Duck concludes, "Different parts of the story need to be addressed at different phases of breakdown."

B y far the most common experience of negative things in relationships is the management of minor irritations and trivial hassles that arise day to day in relationships of all kinds (Duck and Wood, 1995). The rosy picture of relational progress is thus only part of the truth (and Cupach and Spitzberg, 1994, devote a whole book to the dark side). For instance, why have researchers just focused on love and overlooked needling, bitching, boredom, complaints, harassment and enemyships (Duck, 1994b)? Why do we know more about romantic relationships than we do about troublesome relationships (Levitt et al., 1996)? Things often go wrong in relationships in all sorts of ways and cause a lot of pain when they do, some of it intentionally hurtful (Vangelisti, 1994). Sometimes it is Big Stuff and leads to break-up of the relationship, but most of the time it is relatively trivial and leads to nothing except hurt feelings and the conflicts involved in *managing* the occurrence. How does it happen?

WHEN THINGS GO WRONG

There are several parts to acquaintance, and so we should expect there to be several parts to the undoing of acquaintance during relational dissolution. This is partly because relationships exist in time and usually take time to fall apart, so that at different times different processes are taking a role in the dissolution. It is also because, like a motor car, a relationship can have accidents for many reasons, whether the 'driver's' fault, mechanical failure or the actions of other road users. Thus, in a relationship, one or both partners might be hopeless at relating; or the structure and mechanics of the relationship may be wrong, even though both partners are socially competent in other settings; or outside influences can upset it. All of these possibilities have been explored (Baxter, 1984; Duck, 1982a; Orbuch, 1992). However, I am going to focus on my own approach to these issues and refer you elsewhere for details of the other work....

The essence of my approach to relational dissolution is that there are several different phases, each with a characteristic style and concern (Duck, 1982a). Thus, as shown in Figure 1, the first phase is a breakdown phase where partners

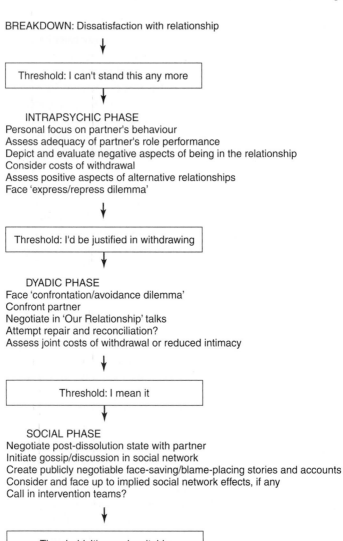

BREAKDOWN: Dissatisfaction with relationship

Threshold: I can't stand this any more

INTRAPSYCHIC PHASE
Personal focus on partner's behaviour
Assess adequacy of partner's role performance
Depict and evaluate negative aspects of being in the relationship
Consider costs of withdrawal
Assess positive aspects of alternative relationships
Face 'express/repress dilemma'

Threshold: I'd be justified in withdrawing

DYADIC PHASE
Face 'confrontation/avoidance dilemma'
Confront partner
Negotiate in 'Our Relationship' talks
Attempt repair and reconciliation?
Assess joint costs of withdrawal or reduced intimacy

Threshold: I mean it

SOCIAL PHASE
Negotiate post-dissolution state with partner
Initiate gossip/discussion in social network
Create publicly negotiable face-saving/blame-placing stories and accounts
Consider and face up to implied social network effects, if any
Call in intervention teams?

Threshold: It's now inevitable

GRAVE DRESSING PHASE
'Getting over' activity
Retrospection; reformulative post-mortem attribution
Public distribution of own version of break-up story

FIGURE 1   A sketch of the main phases of dissolving personal relationships.
Source: Reprinted from Duck (1982a; 16) 'A topography of relationship disengagement of dissolution', in S. W. Duck (ed.), Personal Relationships 4: Dissolving Personal Relationships. *London: Academic Press. Reproduced by permission.*

(or one partner only) become(s) distressed at the way the relationship is conducted. This generates an *intrapsychic phase* characterized by a brooding focus on the relationship and on the partner. Nothing is said to the partner at this point: the agony is either private or shared only with a diary or with relatively anonymous other persons (bar servers, hairdressers, passengers on the bus) who will not tell the partner about the complaint. Just before exit from this phase, people move up the scale of confidants so that they start to complain to their close friends, but do not yet present their partner with the full extent of their distress or doubts about the future of the relationship.

Once we decide to do something about a relational problem we have to deal with the difficulties of facing up to the partner. Implicit—and probably wrongly implicit—in my 1982 model was the belief that partners would tell one another about their feelings and try to do something about them. Both Lee (1984) and Baxter (1984) show that people often leave relationships without telling their partner, or else by fudging their exits. For instance, they may say: 'I'll call you' and then not do it; or 'Let's keep in touch' and never contact the partner; or 'Let's not be lovers but stay as friends' and then have hardly any contact in the future (Metts et al., 1989). Given that my assumption is partly wrong, it nevertheless assumes that partners in formal relationships like marriage will have to face up to their partner, whilst partners in other relationships may or may not do so. The *dyadic phase* is the phase when partners try to confront and talk through their feelings about the relationship and decide how to sort out the future. Assuming that they decide to break up (and even my 1982 model was quite clear that they may decide *not* to do that), they then move rapidly to a *social phase* when they have to tell other people about their decision and enlist some social support for their side of the debate. It is no good just leaving a relationship: we seek other people to agree with our decision or to prop us up and support what we have done. Other people can support us in ways such as being sympathetic and generally understanding. More important, they can side with our version of events and our version of the partner's and the relationship's faults ('I always thought he/she was no good', 'I could never understand how you two could get along—you never seemed right for each other'). This is the *grave-dressing* phase: once the relationship is dead we have to bury it 'good and proper'—with a tombstone saying how it was born, what it was like and why it died. We have to create an account of the relationship's history and, as it were, put that somewhere so that other people can see it and, we hope, accept it. In this phase, people may strategically reinterpret their view of their partner, for example by shifting from the view of the person as 'exciting' to being 'dangerously unpredictable' or from being 'attractively reliable' to being 'boring'—exactly the same features of the person are observed, but they are given different *labels* more suited to one's present feelings about the person (Felmlee, 1995).

In breakdown of relationships as elsewhere in life, gossip plays a key role. Here it works in the social and grave-dressing phases and in a dissolving relationship we actively seek the support of members of our social networks and do so by gossiping about our partners (La Gaipa, 1982). In some instances, we look for 'arbitrators' who will help to bring us back together with our partner. In other cases, we just want someone to back up and spread around our own version of the break-up and its causes. A crucial point made by La Gaipa (1982) is that every person who leaves a relationship has to leave with 'social credit' intact for future use: that is, we cannot just get out of a relationship but we have to leave in such a way that we are not disgraced and debarred from future relationships. We must leave with a reputation for having been let down or faced with unreasonable odds or an unreasonable partner. It is socially acceptable to say 'I left because we tried hard to make it work but it wouldn't.' It is not socially acceptable to leave a relationship with the cheery but unpalatable admission: 'Well basically I'm a jilt and I got bored dangling my partner on a string so I just broke the whole thing off when it suited me.' That statement could destroy one's future credit for new relationships.

Accounts often serve the purpose of beginning the 'getting over' activity that is essential to complete the dissolution (Weber, 1983). A large part of this involves selecting an account of dissolution that refers to a fault in the partner or relationship that pre-existed the split or was even present all along (Weber, 1983). This is the 'I always thought she/he was a bit of a risk to get involved with, but I did it anyway, more fool me' story that we have all used from time to time.

However, accounts also serve another purpose: the creation of a publicly acceptable story is essential to getting over the loss of a relationship (McCall, 1982). It is insufficient having a story that we alone accept: others must also endorse it. As McCall (1982) astutely observed, part of the success of good counsellors consists in their ability to construct such stories for persons in distress about relational loss.

PUTTING IT RIGHT

If two people wanted to put a relationship right, then they could decide to try and make it 'redevelop'; that is, they could assume that repairing a relationship is just like acquaintance, and go through the same processes in order to regain the previous level of intimacy. This means that we have to assume that break-up of relationships is the reverse of acquaintance, and that to repair it, all we have to do is 'rewind' it. This makes some sense: developing relationships grow in intimacy whereas breaking ones decline in intimacy so perhaps we should just try to rewind the intimacy level.

However, in other ways this idea does not work. For instance, in acquaintance we get to know more about a person but in breakdown we cannot get to know less, we must just reinterpret what we already know and put it into a different framework, model, or interpretation ('Yes, he's always been kind, but then he was always after something').

I think that we need to base our ideas about repair not on our model of acquaintance but on a broader model of breakdown of relationships that takes account of principles governing formation of relationships in general. Research on relationships has begun to help us understand what precisely happens when things go wrong. By emphasizing processes of breakdown of relationships and processes of acquaintance, we have the chance now to see that there are also processes of repair. These processes do, however, address different aspects of relationships in trouble. This, I believe, also gives us the chance to be more helpful in putting things right. Bear in mind the model just covered, as you look at Figure 2, and you will see that it is based on proposals made earlier. There are phases to repair of relationships, and some styles work at some times and not at others (Duck, 1984a).

If the relationship is at the intrapsychic phase of dissolution, for instance, then repair should aim to reestablish liking for the partner rather than to correct behavioural faults in ourselves or our nonverbal behaviour, for instance. These latter may be more suitable if persons are in the breakdown phase instead. Liking for the partner can be reestablished or aided by means such as keeping a record, mental or physical, of the positive or pleasing behaviour of our partner rather than listing the negatives and dwelling on them in isolation (Bandura, 1977). Other methods involve redirection of attributions, that is, attempting to use more varied, and perhaps more favourable, explanations for the partner's behaviour—in brief, to make greater efforts to understand the reasons that our partner may give for what is happening in the relationship.

At other phases of dissolution, different strategies of repair are appropriate, according to this model. For instance, at the social phase, persons outside the relationship have to decide whether it is better to try to patch everything up or whether it may serve everyone's best interests to help the partners to get out of the relationship. Figure 2 thus indicates that the choice of strategies is between pressing the partners to stay together or helping them to save face by backing up their separate versions of the break-up. An extra possibility would be to create a story that is acceptable to both of them, such as 'It was an unworkable relationship ... and that is nobody's fault.'

Essentially, this model proposes only three things: relationships are made up of many parts and processes, some of which 'clock in' at some points in the relationship's life and some at others; relationships can go wrong in a variety of ways; repairing of disrupted relationships will be most effective when it addresses the concerns that are most important to us at the phase of dissolution of relationships which we have reached.

The ways we change our 'stories' about a relationship provide important psychological data, and they indicate the dynamic nature of the help that outsiders have to give to relationships in trouble. Different parts of the story need to be addressed at different phases of breakdown. Is one and the same kind of intervention appropriate at all stages of a relationship's decline? Probably not. It makes more sense to look for the relative appropriateness of different intervention techniques as those dynamics unfold. There are few 'scripts' for handling break-up of relationships and many intriguing research questions surround the actual processes by which people extricate themselves (or can be helped to

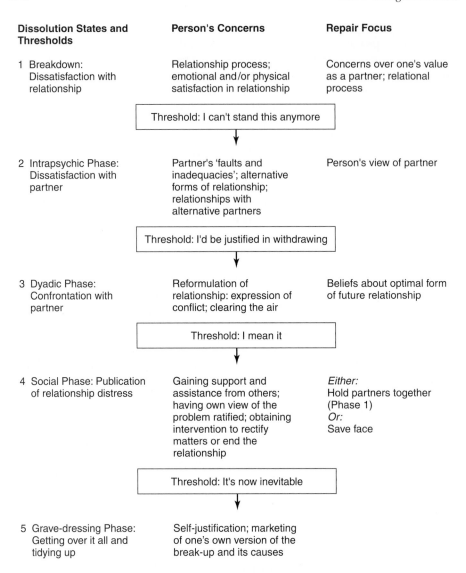

Dissolution States and Thresholds	Person's Concerns	Repair Focus
1 Breakdown: Dissatisfaction with relationship	Relationship process; emotional and/or physical satisfaction in relationship	Concerns over one's value as a partner; relational process

Threshold: I can't stand this anymore

2 Intrapsychic Phase: Dissatisfaction with partner	Partner's 'faults and inadequacies'; alternative forms of relationship; relationships with alternative partners	Person's view of partner

Threshold: I'd be justified in withdrawing

3 Dyadic Phase: Confrontation with partner	Reformulation of relationship: expression of conflict; clearing the air	Beliefs about optimal form of future relationship

Threshold: I mean it

4 Social Phase: Publication of relationship distress	Gaining support and assistance from others; having own view of the problem ratified; obtaining intervention to rectify matters or end the relationship	*Either:* Hold partners together (Phase 1) *Or:* Save face

Threshold: It's now inevitable

5 Grave-dressing Phase: Getting over it all and tidying up	Self-justification; marketing of one's own version of the break-up and its causes	

FIGURE 2   A sketch of the main concerns at different phases of dissolution.
Source: Reprinted from Duck (1984: 169) 'A perspective on the repair of relationships: repair of what when?', in Duck, S. W. (ed.), Personal Relationships 5: Repairing Personal Relationships. *London: Academic Press. Reproduced by permission.*

extricate themselves) from unwanted relationships. For example, Miller and Parks (1982) look at relationship dissolution as an influence process and show that different strategies for changing attitudes can help in dissolution. It is now a major aim in the personal relationships field to explain dissolution and repair of relationships.

REVIEW QUESTIONS

1. Define *intrapsychic, dyadic, social,* and *grave-dressing.*
2. According to Duck, what role does gossip have in the breaking-up process?
3. What are "accounts," and how do they function in the breaking-up process?
4. Why isn't the rebuilding process just the reverse of the breaking-up process?

PROBES

1. Sometimes romantic partners—especially if they're married—do try to work through their serious problems, but often the problems are so painful that they move directly from brooding to themselves to discussing with friends. How prevalent and how important do you think Duck's "dyadic" phase actually is?
2. Duck doesn't discuss the "threshold" parts of the two figures in this reading. What are they, and what is their significance?
3. Sometimes break-ups happen because of poor communication. Do you believe that a relationship ever ends because of *good* communication? Explain.

REFERENCES

Bandura, A. (1977). *Social Learning Theory.* Englewood Cliffs, NJ: Prentice-Hall.

Baxter, L. A. (1984). Trajectories of relationship disengagement, *Journal of Social and Personal Relationships, 1:* 29–48.

Cupach, W. R., & Spitzberg, B. Y. (1994). *The Darkside of Interpersonal Communication.* Hillsdale, NJ: Erlbaum.

Duck, S. (1982). A topography of relationship disengagement and dissolution, in S. W. Duck (Ed.), *Personal Relationships 4: Dissolving Personal Relationships.* London: Academic Press.

Duck, S. W. (1984). A perspective on the repair of personal relationships: Repair of what, when? In S. W. Duck (Ed.), *Personal Relationships 5: Repairing Personal Relationships.* London: Academic Press.

Duck, S. W. (1994). Stratagems, spoils, and a serpent's tooth: On the delights and dilemmas of personal relationships. In W. Cupach and B. H. Spitzberg (Eds.), *The Darkside of Interpersonal Relationships.* Hillsdale, NJ: Erlbaum.

Duck, S. W., & Wood, J. T. (Eds.) (1995). *Confronting Relationship Challenges, Vol. 5. Understanding Relationship Processes.* Thousand Oaks, CA: Sage.

Felmlee, D. H. (1995). Fatal attractions: Affection and disaffection in intimate relationships, *Journal of Social and Personal Relationships, 12,* 295–311.

La Gaipa, J. J. (1982). Rituals of disengagement. In S. W. Duck (Ed.), *Personal Relationships 4: Dissolving Personal Relationships.* London: Academic Press.

Lee, L. (1984). Sequences in separation: A framework for investigating the endings of personal (romantic) relationships, *Journal of Social and Personal Relationships, 1*: 49–74.

McCall, G. J. (1982). Becoming unrelated: The management of bond dissolution, in S. W. Duck (Ed.), *Personal Relationships 4: Dissolving Personal Relationships*. London: Academic Press.

Metts, S., Cupach, W., & Bejlovec, R. A. (1989). "I love you too much to ever start liking you": Redefining romantic relationships, *Journal of Social and Personal Relationships, 6*: 259–274.

Miller, G. R., & Parks, M. R., (1982). Communication in dissolving relationships. In S. W. Duck (Ed.), *Personal Relationships 4: Dissolving Personal Relationships*. London: Academic Press.

Orbuch, T. L. (Ed.) (1992). *Relationship Loss*. New York: Springer-Verlag.

Vangelisti, A. (1994). Messages that hurt. In W. R. Cupach and B. H. Spitzberg (Eds.), *The Darkside of Interpersonal Communication*. New York: Guilford, pp. 53–82.

Weber, A. (1983). The breakdown of relationships. Paper presented to Conference on Social Interaction and Relationships, Nags Head, North Carolina, May.

I Hear You, and I Have a Different Perspective

Susan M. Campbell

This reading offers a simple but powerful suggestion for helping to turn a communication wall into a bridge. For some readers, it might have been enough simply to bullet this statement—"I hear you, and I have a different perspective"—and leave it up to you to apply it. But as Campbell unpacks the statement, I think you'll get a sense of why it works, and how.

Like most self-help materials, this is filled with examples taken from the author's experience with students and clients. I hope these give you a concrete sense of why this statement can help get a conflict unstuck.

One reason is that the statement doesn't put any conflict party "in the wrong." It embodies the fact that two people have different perspectives, without fault finding or blaming. It also helps build trust by putting beliefs and conclusions on the table, where both parties can reflect on them. In addition, you can enhance your trust in yourself because you move beyond assuming that "you'll lose yourself if you become open to the other's views." As Campbell emphasizes, "If you cannot get to the point where you can sincerely speak [these] words ... you will never be a very good negotiator." Holding differences is an advanced communication skill, and an important one.

Another communication skill that this statement evidences is what Campbell calls "the ability to shift into a bigger mind." Especially when two people have a problem, each often brings a perspective that is anchored in her or his own preferences, expectations, assumptions, and style. There is nothing inherently wrong with this—in Chapter 12 Karen Zediker and I call this "holding your own ground." But as we also indicate there, if conflict is to be managed, this perspective needs to be broadened to include the other parties. As Campbell puts it, "Using the phrase 'I hear you, and ...' affirms the reality and validity of both views, while at the same time giving partners a structure for containing the pain that the difference causes." This is an important point. The broader perspective that this statement offers can function to acknowledge both the difference and the pain, and it does so in a way that allows both parties to continue the conversation.

This one statement is not a panacea; it won't eliminate or manage all the conflict in your life. But it can help enhance your conflict communicating.

> *I hear that you want to spend the weekend with your parents, and I'd prefer that we spend a romantic weekend alone.*
> *I hear you saying you want to get a new truck, and I'm afraid we won't be able to make the payments.*
> *I hear that you want to start being sexually open to other lovers, and I still want to be monogamous.*
> *I hear you saying you think we should forbid Suzie from going out with boys until she is sixteen, and I'm afraid she'll just do it behind our backs.*

It can be scary when someone you care about disagrees with you. Most of us prefer harmony to conflict. But if you've ever been in an emotionally engaging relationship, you probably realize that life without conflict is an impossible dream. No two people are going to want exactly the same thing at all times.

The good news is that it is possible to embrace your differences in a way that doesn't threaten your connection and in fact deepens it. Using the key phrase "I hear you, and I have a different perspective" will help you learn to honor both people's values, needs, or positions simultaneously.

Ron felt panicky every time his wife Rose stated an opinion that differed from his. As CEO of a very successful midsize company, he wasn't used to feeling intimidated by disagreement, but with Rose it felt different. In his work life, he was used to telling people what he wanted and having them agree. Noting the discrepancy between how he felt at home and at work he couldn't help but wonder, "Have I always been afraid of conflict? Is that why I made sure I got to the top of the corporate ladder?" With this question in mind, he sought the help of a Getting Real coach, hoping to learn more about practicing the truth skill "Holding Differences."

During coaching sessions he found that he had always operated on the assumption that in a conflict situation, you have basically two choices: you get others to agree with you or you give in. It never occurred to him that he might hold in mind two seemingly opposing views—that he could listen openly to someone who disagreed with him without this threatening his own viewpoint. To help him get a felt experience of this new insight, I asked him to invite Rose into a session with us.

At the time of our session, he and Rose were in disagreement about how to handle the fact that their twenty-five-year-old son, Peter, was still living at home, didn't have a job, and didn't seem motivated to live independently from his parents. Rose thought they should tell Peter that he could no longer live with them; they would let him stay one more month, and then he was out. Ron felt worried that Peter would wind up on the streets selling drugs. As their coach, it was not my intent to solve the problem about Peter so much as to give them tools to resolve this conflict as well as future conflicts.

I asked Rose to state her position and then asked Ron to respond using the phrase "I hear you, and I have a different perspective." Here's how that went:

ROSE: I am not willing to have Peter around anymore. I'm ready to tell him he has to leave our home.
RON: I hear you saying that you're ready to ask Peter to leave, and I have a different feeling about this.

Ron's words sounded strained and unconvincing, but it was a good start. I asked Rose to state another opinion so Ron could get more practice holding differences:

ROSE: I think he'll get a job if he has to. I don't think he'll wind up living out of a shopping cart.
RON: I hear that you think he'll get himself a job if he has to, and I have a different prediction.

After a few more such practice rounds, I asked Ron to elaborate on his disagreement with Rose's position. So in addition to using the one-sentence "I hear you, and I have a different perspective," he was encouraged to expand on his initial statement, as in, "I'm afraid he'll resort to selling drugs. That's even worse than the shopping cart scenario."

He found it much less stressful to do this now that he had the idea that it was really okay to have a different view. He told us that using this key phrase was helping him feel less threatened by the fact that he and Rose disagreed. It showed him that their differences were not about one person being right and one being wrong. And the biggest insight of all was his discovery that as his fear of conflict lessened, his ability to be present with Rose increased. He was no longer defensive and guarded around her. Rose felt the shift and told him it helped her trust him more: "Now I'm not so worried that you're just trying to avoid a confrontation with Peter by taking the position you have taken. Before we learned this communication skill, I couldn't trust what you said about anything if it involved disagreeing with me. Now, I trust that you'll let me know how you really feel."

HOLDING DIFFERENCES SUPPORTS MUTUAL TRUST

The ability to be present to yourself and to another at the same time builds trust: it builds self-trust because you're no longer assuming that you'll lose yourself if you become open to the other's views; and it helps others trust you because they can sense that while you're really showing up for yourself, you care about their views as well.

If you cannot get to the point where you can sincerely speak the words "I hear you, and . . . ," you will never be a very good negotiator. All relationships require frequent negotiations of one sort or another. People see things differently and want different things. It's a fact of life. And if you want your relationships to work, people need to feel that you are not just out for yourself, but that you care about their needs and views. Of course, you cannot allow yourself to be truly open to another's view if you're in fear of losing touch with your own. That's why this key phrase is so important. Holding differences is a rather advanced communication skill. But it is one that is going to become more and more useful as the world becomes more diverse, interconnected, and complex. . . .

SHE WANTS TO TALK NOW AND
HE WANTS TO DO IT LATER

Here's a tough situation that many couples experience: One of you wants to talk about the argument you just had right away so you can get it resolved. The other needs time to cool down or collect himself. If you're the one who wants to do it now, you probably feel a fair degree of urgency. Can you imagine putting out your request, hearing the other say, "Not now," and responding with, "I hear you say you don't want to talk about it now, and I feel strongly that I want to do it right away"? Can you imagine how that might shift your consciousness from pain over your own frustration to holding a larger perspective—the pain of feeling this difference between you?

The ability to shift into a bigger mind is a very advanced relationship skill. You are not in any way abandoning your own needs. What you are doing is including *more* in your point of view. Holding a more expanded point of view fosters a deeper sense of connection with others. It also supports a higher level of creative problem solving—because it promotes cooperation instead of competitiveness. When two people have a problem, the best, most lasting and viable solution is the one that grows out of both people's participation. Using the phrase "I hear you, and . . ." affirms the reality and validity of both views, while at the same time giving partners a structure for containing the pain that the difference causes. When you use this statement, it shows your partner that you are feeling pain over the discrepancy between his wants and your own. It connects you with his pain about that very same discrepancy. So, in essence, it is a shared experience of pain. Shared pain about something significant can bring partners closer together—even as they mourn the fact of their differences.

This statement also helps partners feel seen and heard. When partners feel seen, heard, and moved by the other, new creative energy gets released that had been tied up in the conflict. Using this key statement affirms that there is space for two points of view, not just one, in this relationship. This makes the relationship feel more spacious.

HOW THIS STATEMENT FOSTERS PRESENCE

Any time you are attached to getting your own way, you're probably in a state of fear. When your mind is on some feared future outcome, you're not present. This key phrase helps you get present by embracing the reality that you and your partner have differing perceptions or needs. It helps you consider and attend to more of the total reality of your current situation. The ability to see and feel more, without shutting down around the things you wish were not so, brings you more present. It's like affirming that you have the capacity to hold a view of your differences that is inclusive of both partners' needs.

REVIEW QUESTIONS

1. Explain what Campbell means when she says that this phrase is a way to "embrace your differences" without "threatening your connection."
2. Explain how this key phrase can move a conversation from "either/or" to "both/and."
3. Describe how this phrase can help build self-trust and trust between conflict partners.
4. Explain what Campbell means when she writes that this phrase "fosters presence."

PROBES

1. Campbell argues that this phrase can permit the kind of elaboration Ron made when he said, "I'm afraid he'll resort to selling drugs." What's the connection between this statement and the communication move that Ron made next?
2. Why is the "presence" that Campbell discusses at the end of this reading important?

How to Resolve Issues Unmemorably

Hugh and Gayle Prather

This reading offers a fairly complete outline of how to think about and prepare for a productive, rather than a destructive, conflict with a loved one. The authors have a long connection with *Bridges Not Walls.* When I was working on the first edition of this book in 1973, I wrote Hugh Prather asking for permission to reprint excerpts from his book *Notes to Myself.* I was struck by how his brief, journal-like notations captured several of the central points I wanted this book to make. He generously agreed to let me use some of his material, and his selections have appeared prominently in this book ever since. Now Hugh and his wife Gayle have written *A Book for Couples,* and I believe their discussion of conflict is among the best I've read.

They begin with an example of a typical everyday conflict that reveals how many issues are often buried in an argument between friends or intimates. It starts as an argument about the cat window and lasts only a couple of minutes, but the Prathers identify 17 separate issues that get raised. No wonder arguments like this create more problems than they solve!

The next important point that's made in this reading is that discussions like the one about the cat window "create the relationship's terrain." In other words, the way these discussions are carried out defines the quality of the couple's relationship. This means that *process* is vital. *How* an argument happens is more important than the outcome that emerges. Process is literally more important than product.

With their tongues firmly planted in their cheeks, the Prathers then offer seven "magic rules for ruining any discussion." You can probably recognize some of your favorite fighting moves in this list—I know I do. The point of the list is to contrast the main features of productive and destructive conflict.

Then the authors explicitly highlight the point about process that they introduced earlier. They urge you to recognize that when you are in a conflict with a person you're close to, "to agree is not the purpose." Rather, "the only allowable purpose" for this kind of discussion "is to bring you and your partner closer." This, it seems to me, is a profoundly simple but important idea. It challenges one primary assumption most of us carry into our conflicts with people we care about: that the point is to get my way, be sure the other knows how I feel, or make the other feel bad. What might happen if couples could actually internalize this idea: that the real point of our argument is to get closer?

The rest of this reading builds on this foundation. The Prathers offer five steps for preparing to argue. All of these guidelines make good sense and, taken together, as I mentioned earlier, they provide a fairly comprehensive outline of how to prepare to "do" conflict well. I won't repeat what they say here, but I do want to highlight some points.

Preparation step 2 is to "try to let go" of the issue you're thinking of raising. Although I don't think it's good to suppress genuinely felt emotions, I do believe that couples could frequently profit from applying this suggestion. I've found that it can frequently be relaxing, freeing, and empowering simply to let an irritation go.

Preparation steps 4 and 5 operationalize the Prathers' point about the only allowable purpose for a conflict. It's revealing to ask about a conflict whether "communication is your aim" rather than winning or venting. It is also helpful for me to try to be clear that "the problem is the relationship's and not your partner's."

As I read some sections of their essay, I am a little frustrated by what can sound like oversimplification and naïveté. The really tough arguments are much more intense and difficult than these two authors seem to realize. But when I look again at their advice, I recognize that they understand well enough how gut-wrenching a fight with a loved one can be. They are simply convinced, as have been a great many wise people over the ages, that returning anger for anger doesn't help. Ultimately, love, which in this case means the often unromantic commitment to a relationship, is stronger than defensiveness and bitterness.

UNFINISHED ARGUMENTS ACCUMULATE

It's not that issues don't get resolved. Indeed they are settled but settled like ketchup settles into a carpet. An uncleaned carpet can triple in weight within five years, and most relationships get so laden with undigested arguments that they collapse into a dull, angry stupor and cease to move toward their original goal.

"Albert, you've just got to install the cat window. I woke up again at 3 A.M. with Runnymede standing on my chest staring at me. I'm not getting enough alpha sleep."

"Sorry about that, Paula. I'll get to it this weekend."

"But Albert, you've been saying that for a month."

"Well, you know, honey, we could just put the cat out at night like every-one else."

"Oh, sure, and then what if he needed to get in? What if something was after him? What then?"

"What difference will the cat window make? He can still stay out all night if he wants to."

"Yes, Albert, but he can *also* get in if he *needs* to. You know, if you're not going to be a responsible pet owner, you shouldn't have a pet."

"Now there's a thought."

"I see. And I guess you don't mind breaking Gigi's heart."

"That's another thing, Paula, her name is Virginia, not Gigi. Why do we have to have a cat named Runnymede and a daughter named Gigi? Besides, I'll buy her a nice stuffed Garfield after the cat is comfortably settled in at the animal shelter."

"You know, Albert, this conversation is opening my eyes to something I've felt for a very long time."

"What's that, Paula?"

"You only care about mixed soccer. Since joining that team with the silly name you haven't been playing horsey with Gigi and you haven't been scratching Runnymede under the chin where he can't lick. You certainly pretended to like Runnymede well enough when we were dating."

"You were the one who insisted I join the team. You were the one who said it would be good for me to 'get out of the house for a change.' I like the cat. I love my daughter. But I don't want to spend my Saturdays ruining a window with a perfectly good view."

"I guess you don't really care about me either, Albert. And you can stand there calmly peeling your Snickers while wanting Runnymede to be gassed. If I didn't know how much emotion you devote to *mixed* soccer I would say you have become psychotically insensitive and unfeeling. Perhaps you should seek help."

Here Albert, proving that he is neither insensitive nor unfeeling, flings his Snickers at the window in question, grabs his soccer gear, and storms from the house, where in an afternoon match playing goalie for the Yuma Yuccas he fractures the middle three phalanges in his right hand, thus ending the question of installing anything.

EACH NEW ISSUE RESURRECTS THE OLD

We wish we could say that this dialogue was a transcript but it is a composite. If we reprinted verbatim some of the typical arguments we have heard during counseling, they would be dismissed as overwrought fiction. The large number of digressions seen here is actually commonplace and illustrates the typical residue of unsettled questions found in most long-term relationships. The difference between this and the average disagreement is that some of these words might have been thought but left unspoken. Yet the feeling of estrangement by the end of the argument would have been the same.

On this Saturday morning Paula is upset because her sleep continues to be interrupted by the cat asking to be put out. That is the sum of the issue. If the couple had sat down together instead of using the problem as a means of separating still further, they could easily have solved this one difficulty in any of a hundred different mutually acceptable ways. But a hive of older discord lies just beneath their awareness, and therefore settling just one problem in peace is harder than it would seem.

The cry of unresolved issues is strong and persistent. Any couple will feel their failure to have joined. They yearn to bridge the old gaps and fear the potential of further separation more than they welcome the opportunity to reverse the process. To bring up former differences during a discussion is not blameworthy, it is in fact a call for help, but it is mistimed.

Without realizing it—because most arguments are conducted with no deep awareness—Albert and Paula allude to seventeen other issues, none of which had to be brought up to solve *this* problem. In the order they appear, here are the questions they have left unanswered in the past, a small fraction of the total residue if you consider all the others that will be mentioned in future arguments: (1) Why has Albert's promise gone unfulfilled for a month? (2) Should the cat be left out overnight? (3) Is Albert irresponsible? (4) Should the family continue having this pet? (5) Is Albert insensitive to his daughter? (6) Should Paula continue calling Virginia "Gigi"? (7) Should the cat be renamed? (8) Would a stuffed animal sufficiently compensate? (9) Is mixed soccer affecting Albert's attitude toward his daughter and pet? (10) Does the team have a silly name? (11) Is Albert being sufficiently attentive to Paula or has he changed in some fundamental way? (12) Does Paula want Albert around the house? (13) How important is the window view to Albert's happiness? (14) Does Albert still love Paula? (15) Should Albert eat Snickers? (16) Is Albert's contact with other women on Saturdays the root cause of his, in Paula's view, wavering commitment to his family? (17) Does Albert have serious psychological problems?

As can be seen here, it is not easy for most couples to concentrate on a single issue. Nevertheless it is certainly possible and, in itself, to practice doing so will begin giving them a new kind of evidence: that within this relationship there are still grounds for unity and happiness. If one of the partners deviates from this guideline, the other should not make still another issue of this or get caught up in the irrelevant point raised, but should see instead the real desire behind the digression and treat it gently and answer it with love.

DISCUSSIONS CREATE THE RELATIONSHIP'S TERRAIN

… To resolve issues in the usual way is as damaging to a relationship as not resolving them at all, because the gap is not truly bridged and the unsuccessful attempt merely adds more weight to the couple's doubts about each other. In the argument over the cat window, Paula's concern about the health of her marriage surfaces, a question of far greater importance to her than how she will manage to get more sleep, and yet without fully realizing it she exacerbates this larger problem and works against her own interests. By arguing in the manner they did, this couple, as do most, merely manufactured new issues between them. Albert probably did not mean to take that hard a stand on getting rid of the cat—he may actually have wanted to keep it. And Paula did not have real doubts about Albert's mental health.

The past that drives so many relationships into the ground is built piece by piece, smallness fitted to smallness, selfishness answered with selfishness. Yet the process is largely unconscious. Each couple quickly settles into a few sad methods of conducting arguments, but seldom is the means they use thought through or the results closely examined. One person nags, the other relents. One person reasons, the other becomes silent. One person flares, the other backs down. One person cajoles, the other gives in. But where are the joy and grandeur, where is the friendship that was supposed to flourish, the companionship that through the years was to fuse an invulnerable bond, a solace and a blessing at the close of life? Instead there is a bitter and widening wedge between the two, and even the briefest of discussions contains a hundred dark echoes from the past.

No matter how entrenched are our patterns of problem solving, they can be stepped away from easily once we see that they do not serve our interests. The only interest served in most discussions is to be right. But, truly, how deep is this? Do we actually want to make our partner wrong, to defeat a friend, and slowly to defeat a friendship? It certainly may feel that way. Caught up once again in the emotions of a disagreement, we stride doggedly toward our usual means of concluding every argument: adamant silence, crushing logic, patronizing practicality, collapsed crying, quelling anger, martyred acquiescence, loveless humor, sulking retreat.

These postures and a thousand more are attempts to prove a point other than love, and as with all endeavors to show up one's partner, the friendship itself is the victim, because the friendship becomes a mere tool, a means of making the other person feel guilty. The love our partner has for us is now seen as leverage, and in our quiet or noisy way we set about making the relationship a shambles, not realizing that we ourselves are part of the wreckage.

THE MAGIC RULES FOR RUINING ANY DISCUSSION

… The dialogue with which we began this [reading] incorporates a few of but not all the rules for disastrous communication—yet only one or two are needed to neutralize the best of intentions. Follow these guidelines, even a little sloppily, and you are guaranteed a miserable time:

1. *Bring the matter up when at least one of you is angry.*
   Variations: Bring it up when nothing can be done about it (in the middle of the night; right before guests are due; when one of you is in the shower). Bring it up when concentration is impossible (while driving to a meeting with the IRS; while watching the one TV program you both agree on; while your spouse is balancing the checkbook).
2. *Be as personal as possible when setting forth the problem.*
   Variations: Know the answer before you ask the question. While describing the issue, use an accusatory tone. Begin by implying who, as usual, is to blame.
3. *Concentrate on getting what you want.*
   Variations: Overwhelm your partner's position before he or she can muster a defense (be very emotional; call in past favors; be impeccably reasonable). Impress on your partner what you need and what he or she must do without. If you begin losing ground, jockey for position.
4. *Instead of listening, think only of what you will say next.*
   Variations: Do other things while your partner is talking. Forget where your partner left off. In other words, listen with all the interest you would give a bathroom exhaust fan.
5. *Correct anything your partner says about you.*
   Variations: Each time your partner gives an example of your behavior, cite a worse example of his or hers. Repeat "That's not what I said" often. Do not

accept anything your partner says at face value (point out exceptions; point out inaccuracies in facts and in grammar).

6. *Mention anything from the past that has a chance of making your partner defensive.*
Variations: Make allusions to your partner's sexual performance. Remind your husband of his mother's faults. Compare what your wife does to what other women do, and after she complains, say, "I didn't mean it that way."

7. *End by saying something that will never be forgotten.*
Variations: Do something that proves you are a madman. Let your parting display proclaim that no exposure of your partner could be amply revealing, no characterization too profane, no consequence sufficiently wretched. At least leave the impression you are a little put out.

TO AGREE IS NOT THE PURPOSE

All couples believe they know how to hold a discussion, and yet it is not an exaggeration to say that in most long-term relationships there has rarely been one wholly successful argument. Obviously they are filled with disagreements that end in agreements, but when these are examined, it can be seen that at least a small patch of reservation had to be overlooked in order for accord to be reached.

We believe this is simply how differences are settled, and so even though we sense that our partner is still in conflict, we barge ahead with our newly won concession, thinking the bad moment will pass. Later it becomes painfully clear that it has not and we judge our partner irresolute. Or if we are the one who complied, we count our little sacrifice dear and wait for reparation—which never comes or is never quite adequate, and we cannot understand why our partner feels such little gratitude.

The aim of most arguments is to reach outward agreement. Until that is replaced with a desire for friendship, varying degrees of alienation will be the only lasting outcome. Couples quickly develop a sense of helplessness over the pattern that their discussions have fallen into. They believe they are sincerely attempting to break out of it and are simply failing. They try different responses, going from shouting to silence, from interminable talking to walking out of the room, from considering each point raised to sticking tenaciously to one point, but nothing they do seems to alter the usual unhappy ending.

There is no behavioral formula to reversing the habitual course of an argument. It requires a shift in attitude, not in actions, even though actions will modify in the process. No more is needed than one partner's absolute clarity about the purpose of the argument. This is not easy but it is simple. Therefore let us look again at what the aim should be....

The only allowable purpose for a discussion is to bring you and your partner closer. Minds must come together to decide instead of backing away in order to apply pressure. How is this possible, given the fact that you and your partner are deeply selfish? Fortunately, the selfishness is compartmentalized and your hearts remain unaffected. You need not eliminate it; merely bypass it because you recognize that it is not in your interests to be selfish. To the ego, this concept is insane because it sees no value in love. But love is in your interests because you *are* love, or at least part of you is, and thus each discussion is a way of moving into your real self.

A little time is obviously needed to see one's true interests. If you rush into a discussion you will operate from your insensitivity by habit and aim for a prize your heart cares nothing about. Do not kid yourself. You *do* know whether the discussion is ending with the two of you feeling closer. The selfish part of your mind will tell you that the little sadness and sense of distance you may now feel was a small price to pay for the concession you won or the point you made. Or it will argue that it was all unavoidable. This may happen many times before you begin reversing your ordinary way of participating. This transition is an important stage of growth and entails looking more and more carefully at selfish impulses and their aftermath. Is how you feel really worth it? Was the way it went truly unavoidable?

Thus you will come to see the result you want, and this deeper recognition will begin to eclipse your pettiness in the midst of an argument. Gradually you will catch the mistakes sooner, and eventually you will learn to avoid them from the start. For you *do* want these times of deciding to warm your hearts and lighten your steps. So persist in the guidelines we will give, and these little defeats to your relationship will slowly give way to friendship.

We are so used to thinking of a discussion as a symbol of separation that it can often be helpful to change its form enough that something new will appear to be happening and thus the old mind set is undercut. To take the usual process, break it into steps and put them in order is usually all that is needed to accomplish this.

An issue could be said to pass through five stages in reaching resolution. First, it must be thought of by at least one of the partners as an issue. Second, a moment is chosen to bring the matter up. Third, a decision is made as to the manner in which it will be presented. Fourth, there is an exchange of thoughts and feelings. And fifth, the discussion is concluded.

Most couples give very little thought to the first three stages. They simply find themselves in the thick of a so-called spontaneous argument and no one is certain at what point it began. Obviously you must become more conscious of the subjects you bring up so carelessly. Any sign of fear over what you are about to say is a very useful indicator. If you see you have a question about whether to say it, let this be your cue to break these preliminary choices into conscious steps. Do not begrudge the time; remember instead how strongly you want to begin building a real friendship.

FIVE STEPS IN PREPARING TO ARGUE

First, you might ask yourself if the issue you are thinking of is actually a present issue or merely one you have been reminded of. In other words, be certain this is currently a problem and not one the relationship may already be on its way to solving. Many people habitually rake over their marriage for signs of imperfection and naturally they find a great many, but it can be far more disrupting to friendship to be constantly questioning and comparing than to wait to see if the problem continues in any severe way. Meanwhile, enjoy what is already between you without telling yourself what this is....

If the issue is unquestionably a present one, the second step you might try is to let go of it. Letting go is not "better," but it is an option that current values tend to underrate. However, it must be accomplished thoroughly and honestly or the issue will grow like mold in a dark unseen place. If it is done consciously dismissal is not denial. Essentially it entails examining in detail what you do not like and then making a deliberate effort to identify with another part of you that never "takes issue" with any living thing, that is still and at ease, that acts only from peace....

If a couple espouses world energy consciousness or is on a tight budget, for one of the partners to habitually leave the hot water running, not turn off lights, or keep the refrigerator door open may be grating or even shocking to the other partner. Yet the spectacle of someone wasting energy and money is *not* grating or shocking. The interpretation we assign it, and not the act itself, determines the emotions we feel. Jordan, age two, is "shockingly irresponsible." He has even been known (yesterday, in fact) to flush a toilet five times in a row and then run to tell his big brother about the accomplishment. "John, I flush, I flush!" "That's nice." said John, blatantly contributing to the delinquency of a minor. The reason Jordan didn't tell his father (who is the family's conscience in these matters) was that he was the very one who kept showing him how it was done, thereby encouraging him to waste over fifteen gallons of water (plus six more his father used researching that figure)....

So here we have four reactions issuing from four interpretations: pride from the father, support from the seven-year-old, excitement from the two-year-old and, having no originality, curiosity from the cat. Clearly no uniform effect was produced by an external and unreachable cause. How then might you let go of your reaction to your spouse's wasteful habits in lieu of bringing it up one more time? Certainly you would not try dishonestly to convince yourself that the practice was not costing money or energy. Or that it did not really matter to you. Neither would you attempt to assign some motive to your partner's acts that you did not believe, such as not knowing any better or really trying hard but being unable to stop. Dishonesty does not end an unhappy line of thought. That is why reinterpretation is generally not effective....

If in your moment of consideration you are able to see these facts deeply enough, you may open your eyes to your partner's innocence and no longer feel compelled to understand why he or she does these things. But if after making the attempt to free your mind you see that you have not let the issue go, then perhaps to bring it up would be the preferable course, for undoubtedly that is better than storing anger or fear....

The third step is to consider if this is the time. If you feel an urge to bring it up quickly, be very alert to anger. Your heart is willing to wait but your ego is not, especially if it senses an opportunity to strike back. The ego is merely our love of misery, of withdrawal and loneliness, and it can feel like our own deep impulse even though it exists on the most superficial level of the mind.

For too long now our relationships have been jerked around by our own lack of awareness. There is more to your mind than selfishness. So be still a moment and let peace arise from you. Is this the time? A simple question. There need not be great soul-searching and hand-wringing over it. If your partner has just done something and this is the issue, clearly he or she is likely to be more defensive if instantly called on it. If your partner is not in a particularly happy frame of mind, is hostile, worried or depressed, a more receptive state will surely come and nothing is lost by waiting. Is this the time? Merely look and know the answer. The urge to attack when you are angry is very strong, but if you will allow yourself time to reflect on your genuine feelings, this will do more to relieve your frustration.

The fourth step is to be certain that communication is your aim. Trying to get someone to change is not communication because you have already decided what change is needed. Your partner is therefore left with nothing to say and will definitely feel your unwillingness to consider, to listen, to appreciate. So before you speak take time to hear your heart.

You are not two advocates arguing a case. You are interested in joining, not in prevailing. You are like the directors of a business you both love coming together to help it over a difficult situation. You don't care from whose lips the solution comes. You welcome the *answer.* To this end what are you willing to do if your partner becomes defensive? Are you prepared, and have you prepared, to carry through your love of the relationship?...

The final point to consider is whether you are clear that the problem is the relationship's and not your partner's. In our example the problem was not Paula's, because her lack of sleep was affecting Albert also. One person's jealousy, appetite, hypersensitivity, frigidity, phobia or any other characteristic that has become an issue cannot successfully be viewed as more one's responsibility than the other's because friendship is always a mutual sharing of all burdens....

You must understand that unless you make a specific effort to see through the fallacy, you *will* go into a discussion thinking one of you is more to blame than the other, and this will make it very hard to listen and be open. Learn to treat every issue as an impersonal and neutral enemy and to close ranks against it. An addiction, for example, can be viewed as you would a hurricane or a deluge—you need each other's help to survive the storm. Our dog, Sunny Sunshine Pumpkin Prather (whose very name is a masterpiece of family compromise), gets sprayed by a skunk about once a month and the smell is everyone's problem. What good would it do to blame the dog? And yet we have seen other families get angry at their dog "for being so stupid."...

These preliminary steps, which should only take an instant or two to complete, will at least make it possible for a discussion to begin with some chance of success. Now you are ready for a *real* argument, one in which your minds can join rather than separate.

REVIEW QUESTIONS

1. What point are the Prathers making by listing 17 issues that were brought up in the argument between Albert and Paula?
2. What do the authors mean when they say that discussions "create the relationship's terrain"?
3. Paraphrase this statement: "The only allowable purpose for a discussion is to bring you and your partner closer." Do you agree or disagree with it? Explain.
4. What do the authors mean when they say that you should "learn to treat every issue as an impersonal and neutral enemy and to close ranks against it"?
5. What keeps the "protect your gains" step from being selfish?

PROBES

1. What alternative do the authors offer to "being right" in a conflict?
2. What general principle or principles are violated by the seven "magic rules for ruining any discussion"? In other words, what general attitudes make these moves destructive?
3. Which of the five steps for preparing to argue do you *least* often follow? What does that fact tell you about your way of "doing" conflict?
4. A fundamental, perhaps even a radically different, perspective or point of view is behind just about everything the Prathers say about "resolving issues unmemorably." By "different," I mean different from the attitude we normally carry into a conflict. How would you describe this alternative point of view or perspective?

CHAPTER 11

Bridging Cultural Differences

Building Relationships with Diverse Others
David W. Johnson

Cultural differences have created human problems since recorded history began. Sometimes it seems as if the strongest tendency we humans have inherited from our nonhuman animal forebears is fear and hatred of anybody different from us. So it's definitely a challenge to bridge cultural differences.

The five readings in this chapter approach this problem generally and specifically. The first two readings analyze general cultural differences and show how it's possible to connect with people, even when they're not all "like us." The last three readings are specific discussions of some of the most difficult cultural differences to bridge: religion, race or ethnicity, and disability. One of these is written by a female African American communication teacher and scholar about contacts with white women, one by a Muslim committed to dialogue, and the third by two communication professionals who work with and for disabled people.

For more than 25 years, educational psychologist David Johnson has been helping teachers and schools in North America, Central America, Europe, Africa, Asia, the Middle East, and the Pacific Rim take advantage of the benefits of collaborative and cooperative learning. One of the fruits of his labor is his book *Reaching Out: Interpersonal Effectiveness and Self-Actualization*, from which I've taken the next reading. This is a basic introduction to the attitudes and skills of connecting with people who are different from you.

Johnson begins with the point that although globalization is making diversity among acquaintances, classmates, co-workers, and neighbors increasingly inevitable, it is in some ways not "natural" for humans to want to get along with diverse others. For 200,000 years, as he puts it, humans lived in small hunting-and-gathering groups, interacting infrequently with others. But today we are regularly thrown together with cultural strangers. Both men and women in what have traditionally been single-sex jobs (firefighter, nurse, mail carrier, parking checker) are having to team with opposite-sex colleagues. Older and younger workers are forced to collaborate, and blacks, Latinos, Asians, whites, Arabs, Pacific Islanders, and members of other ethnic groups are thrown together with those with different, and sometimes competing, identities.

The chapter this reading was taken from explains six steps for building relationships with diverse peers, and this excerpt discusses four of the six: Accept yourself, lower barriers, recognize that diversity is a valuable resource, and work to clarify misunderstandings. The first step echoes some of what is in the readings about self-awareness in Chapter 3. Johnson encourages you to reflect on your own identity, which can be subdivided into your self-schema, gender identity, and ethnic identity, as a first step toward connecting with people different from you.

Then he offers some suggestions about lowering three barriers: prejudice, the tendency to blame the victim, and cultural conflict. Prejudice—manifested in ethnocentrism, stereotyping, or discrimination—can be a major hurdle, and Johnson explains four specific ways to overcome it. Blaming the victim occurs when people "attribute the cause of discrimination or misfortune to the personal characteristics and actions of the victim." In this section, Johnson reviews some of the information about external and internal attributions that is discussed in the first reading in Chapter 5, and shows how careful attributions can enhance your experience. Culture clash is the third barrier Johnson explains.

The next section of the reading explains some specific ways in which diversity can be openly recognized and genuinely valued. Johnson suggests four steps that can help lead toward profitable collaboration among diverse people.

The final section of this reading highlights the importance of clarifying miscommunications. Johnson could have said a great deal more here than he does, but this section does remind us of how language sensitivity and a developed awareness of stylistic differences among diverse communicators can help people deal effectively with those who are different from themselves. Johnson ends this section with seven specific suggestions; the first is "Use all the communication skills discussed in this book." Even though "this book" he was talking about was *Reaching Out,* you can interpret it as a reference to *Bridges Not Walls.* As Johnson recognizes, the skills developed in all 12 chapters of *this* book can be brought to bear on the project of improving relationships among diverse people.

You may have already thought through the ideas that Johnson discusses here. But if you haven't (or if you have and would still appreciate a reminder), this is an excellent introduction to the frame of mind and some specific skills needed to bridge differences between you and people you might initially think of as "strangers."

INTRODUCTION

We live in one world. The problems that face each person, each community, each country cannot be solved without global cooperation and joint action. Economically, for example, there has been a globalization of business reflected in the increase in multinational companies, coproduction agreements, and offshore operations. As globalization becomes the norm, more and more companies must translate their local and national perspectives into a world view. Companies that are staffed by individuals skilled in building relationships with diverse peers have an advantage in the global market.

Interacting effectively with peers from different cultures, ethnic groups, social classes, and historical backgrounds does not come naturally. For 200,000 years humans lived in small hunting and gathering groups, interacting only infrequently with other nearby small groups. Today we are required to communicate effectively with people cross-culturally, through the generations, among races, between genders, and across those subtle but pervasive barriers of class. No wonder this feels uncomfortable—we have never been required to do it before!

Diversity among your acquaintances, classmates, co-workers, neighbors, and friends is increasingly inevitable. North America, Europe, and many other parts of the world are becoming more and more diverse in terms of culture, ethnicity, religion, age, physical qualities, and gender. You will be expected to interact effectively with people with a wide variety of characteristics and from a wide variety of backgrounds. In order to build relationships with diverse peers, you must

1. Accept yourself.
2. Lower the barriers to building relationships with diverse peers.
3. Recognize that diversity exists and is a valuable resource....
4. Clarify misunderstandings.

ACCEPTING YOURSELF

If I am not for myself, who will be for me? But if I am only for myself, what am I?

—The Talmud

Two basic human needs are to

1. Join with others in a cooperative effort to achieve something great.
2. Be a unique and separate individual who is valued and respected in one's own right.

In order to meet this second need, you must accept yourself as you are and build a distinct image of yourself as a certain kind of person who has an identity differentiated and discernible from others. The greater your self-acceptance, the more stable and integrated your personal identity. Building a coherent, stable, and integrated identity that summarizes who you are as a separate, autonomous, and unique individual is the first step in building constructive relationships with diverse peers.

The Person You Think You Are

What kind of person are you? How would you describe yourself to someone who does not know you? Would your description be disjointed and contradictory, or would it be organized and consistent? Would it change from day to day, or would it stay the same over a period of years? Do you like yourself, or do you feel a basic sense of shame and contempt when you think of yourself? We all need a strong and integrated sense of personal identity that serves as an anchor in life.

Early philosophers advised us to "know thyself" and poets have told us, "To thine own self be true." We have taken their advice. Hundreds of books have been written dealing with how to get to know yourself and the *Oxford English Dictionary* lists more than 100 words that focus on the self, from *self-abasement* to *self-wisdom*. When you form a conception of who you are as a person you have an identity.

Your *identity* is a consistent set of attitudes that defines who you are. It is a subjective self-image that is a type of cognitive structure called a self-schema. A *self-schema* is a generalization about the self, derived from past experience, that organizes and guides your understanding of the information you learn about yourself from interacting with others. You have multiple schemas, multiple identities, and multiple selves. They include your view of your physical characteristics (height, weight, sex, hair and eye color, general appearance), your social roles (student or teacher, child or parent, employee or employer), the activities you engage in (playing the piano, dancing, reading), your abilities (skills, achievements), your attitudes and interests (liking rock and roll, favoring equal rights for females), and your general personality traits (extrovert or introvert, impulsive or reflective, sensible or scatterbrained). Your *gender identity* is your fundamental sense of your maleness or femaleness. Your *ethnic identity* is your sense of belonging to one particular ethnic group. Your identity consists not only of various self-schemas that you currently possess but of selves that you would like to be or that you imagine you might be. These potential selves include ideals that you would like to attain and standards that you feel you should meet (the "ought" self). They can originate from your own thoughts or from the messages of others.

Each of your self-schemas is viewed as being positive or negative. You generally look at yourself in an evaluative way, approving or disapproving of your behavior and characteristics. Your self-schemas are arranged in a hierarchy. The more important an identity is, or the higher it stands in the hierarchy, the more likely it is to influence your choices and your behavior.

To cope with stress you need more than one self. The diversity and complexity of the identity reduces the stress you experience. Self-complexity provides a buffer against stressful events. If you have only one or two major self-schemas, any negative event is going to have an impact on most aspects of your identity. The woman who sees herself primarily as a wife, for example, is likely to be devastated if her husband says he wants an immediate divorce. In contrast, the individual who has a more complex representation of self may be more protected from negative events that primarily involve only one or two of several roles. The woman who sees herself not only as wife, but also as a mother, lawyer, friend, and tennis player will have other roles to fall back on when impending divorce threatens her role of spouse. People with more complex identities are less prone to depression and illness; they also experience less severe mood swings following success or failure in one particular area of performance....

Some of the Benefits of Self-Acceptance

There is a common saying that goes, "I can't be right for someone else if I'm not right for me!" *Self-acceptance* is a high regard for yourself or, conversely, a lack of cynicism about yourself. There are a number of benefits to accepting yourself as you are, and a relationship exists among self-acceptance, self-disclosure, and being accepted by others. The more self-accepting you are, the greater your self-disclosure tends to be. The greater your self-disclosure, the more others accept you. And the more others accept you, the more you accept yourself. A high level of self-acceptance, furthermore, is reflected in psychological health. Psychologically healthy people see themselves as being liked, capable, worthy, and acceptable to other peoples. All of these perceptions are based on self-acceptance. Considerable evidence abounds that self-acceptance and acceptance of others are related. If you think well of yourself you tend to think well of others. You also tend to assume that others will like you, an expectation that often becomes a self-fulfilling prophecy.

DIFFICULTIES WITH DIVERSITY

Once you are accepting of yourself, you are in a position to be accepting of others. There are, however, a number of barriers to accepting diverse peers. They include prejudice, the tendency to blame the victim, and cultural conflict.

Prejudice

To know one's self is wisdom, but to know one's neighbor is genius.

—*Minna Antrim (author)*

Building relationships with diverse peers is not easy. The first barrier is prejudice. Prejudice, stereotyping, and discrimination begin with categorizing. In order to understand other people and yourself, categories must be used. *Categorizing* is a basic human cognitive process of conceptualizing objects and people as members of groups. We categorize people on the basis of *inherited traits* (culture, sex, ethnic membership, physical features) or *acquired traits* (education, occupation, lifestyle, customs). Categorizing and generalizing are often helpful in processing information and making decisions. At times, however, they malfunction and result in stereotyping and prejudice.

    To be prejudiced means to prejudge. *Prejudice* can be defined as an unjustified negative attitude toward a person based solely on that individual's membership in a particular group. Prejudices are judgments made about others that establish a superiority/inferiority belief system. If one person dislikes another simply because that other person is a member of an ethnic group, sex, or religion, that is prejudice.

    One common form of prejudice is ethnocentrism. *Ethnocentrism* is the tendency to regard our own ethnic group, culture, or nation as better or more correct than others. The word is derived from *ethnic,* meaning a group united by similar customs, characteristics, race, or other common factors, and *center.* When ethnocentrism is present, the standards and values of our culture are used as a yardstick to measure the worth of other ethnic groups. Ethnocentrism is often perpetuated by *cultural conditioning.* As children we are raised to fit into a particular culture. We are conditioned to respond to various situations as we see others in our culture react.

Prejudices are often associated with stereotypes. A *stereotype* is a set of beliefs about the characteristics of the people in a group that is applied to almost all members of that group. Typically, stereotypes are widely held beliefs within a group and focus on what other cultural and ethnic groups, or socioeconomic classes are "really like." Women have been stereotyped as more emotional than men. Men have been stereotyped as more competitive than women. Tall, dark, and handsome men have been stereotyped as mysterious. Stereotypes distort and exaggerate in ways that support an underlying prejudice or fundamental bias against members of other groups. Stereotypes are resistant to change because people believe information that confirms their stereotypes more readily than evidence that challenges them. Stereotypes almost always have a detrimental effect on those targeted, interfering with the victim's ability to be productive and live a high quality life.

Stereotypes reflect an *illusionary correlation* between two unrelated factors, such as being poor and lazy. Negative traits are easy to acquire and hard to lose. When you meet one poor person who is lazy you may tend to see all poor people as lazy. From then on, any poor person who is not hard at work the moment you notice him or her may be perceived to be lazy. Our prejudiced stereotype of poor people being lazy is protected in three ways. Our prejudice makes us notice the negative traits we ascribe to the groups we are prejudiced against. We tend to have a *false consensus bias* by believing that most other people share our stereotypes (i.e., see poor people as being lazy). We tend to see our own behavior and judgments as quite common and appropriate, and to view alternative responses as uncommon and often inappropriate. Finally, we often develop a rationale and explanation to justify our stereotypes and prejudices.

When prejudice is put into action, it is discrimination. *Discrimination* is an action taken to harm a group or any of its members. It is a negative, often aggressive action aimed at the target of prejudice. Discrimination is aimed at denying members of the targeted groups treatment and opportunities equal to those afforded to the dominant group. When discrimination is based on race or sex, it is referred to as racism or sexism.

Diversity among people can either be a valued resource generating energy, vitality, and creativity, or it can be a source of prejudice, stereotyping, and discrimination. To reduce your prejudices and use of stereotypes, these steps may be helpful:

1. Admit that you have prejudices (everyone does, you are no exception) and commit yourself to reducing them.
2. Identify the stereotypes that reflect your prejudices and modify them.
3. Identify the actions that reflect your prejudices and modify them.
4. Seek feedback from diverse friends and colleagues about how well you are communicating respect for and valuing of diversity.

Blaming the Victim

It is commonly believed that the world is a just place where people generally get what they deserve. If we win the lottery, it must be because we are nice people who deserve some good luck. If we are robbed, it must be because we are careless and want to be punished for past misdeeds. Any person who is mugged in a dark alley while carrying a great deal of cash may be seen as asking to be robbed. Most people tend to believe that they deserve what happens to them. Most people also believe that others also get what they deserve in the world. It is all too easy to forget that victims do not have the benefit of hindsight to guide their actions.

When someone is a victim of prejudice, stereotyping, and discrimination, all too often they are seen as doing *something* wrong. *Blaming the victim* occurs when we attribute the cause of discrimination or misfortune to the personal characteristics and actions of the victim. The situation is examined for potential causes that will enable us to maintain our belief in a just world. If the victim can be blamed for causing the discrimination, then we can believe that the future is predictable and controllable because we will get what we deserve.

Blaming the victim occurs as we try to attribute a cause to events. We constantly interpret the meaning of our behavior and events that occur in our lives. Many times we want to figure out *why* we acted in a particular way or why a certain outcome occurred. If we get angry when someone infers we are stupid, but we could care less when someone calls us clumsy, we want to know why we are so sensitive about our intelligence. When we are standing on a street corner after a rainstorm and a car splashes us with water, we want to know whether it was caused by our carelessness, the driver's meanness, or just bad luck. This process of explaining or inferring the causes of events has been termed *causal attribution.* An attribution is an inference drawn about the causes of a behavior or event....

In trying to understand why a behavior or event occurred, we generally choose to attribute causes either to

1. Internal, personal factors (such as effort and ability)
2. External, situational factors (such as luck or the behavior/personality of other people)

For example, if you do well on a test, you can attribute it to your hard work and great intelligence (an internal attribution) or to the fact that the test was incredibly easy (an external attribution). When a friend drops out of school, you can attribute it to a lack of motivation (an internal attribution) or lack of money (an external attribution).

People make causal attributions to explain their successes and failures. These are *self-serving* attributions, designed to permit us to take credit for positive outcomes and to avoid blame for negative ones. We have a systematic tendency to claim our successes are due to our ability and efforts while our failures are due to bad luck, evil people, or a lack of effort. We also have a systematic tendency to claim responsibility for the success of group efforts ("It was all my idea in the first place and I did most of the work") and avoid responsibility for group failures ("If the other members had tried harder, this would not have happened")....

Attributing the causes of others' failure and misfortune to their actions rather than to prejudice and discrimination can be a barrier to building constructive relationships with diverse peers. Bad things do happen to good people. Racism does exist. Innocent bystanders do get shot. It is usually a good idea to suspend any tendency to blame the victim when interacting with diverse peers.

Culture Clash

Another common barrier to building relationships with diverse peers is cultural clashes. A *culture clash* is a conflict over basic values that occurs among individuals from different cultures. The most common form is members of minority groups' questioning the values of the majority. Common reactions by majority group members when their values are being questioned are feeling:

1. *Threatened:* Their responses include avoidance, denial, and defensiveness.
2. *Confused:* Their responses include seeking more information in an attempt to redefine the problem.
3. *Enhanced:* Their responses include heightened anticipation, awareness, and positive actions that lead to solving the problem.

Many cultural clashes develop from threatening, to confusing, to enhancing. Once they are enhancing, they are no longer a barrier.

As prejudice, stereotyping, and discrimination are reduced, the tendency to blame the victim is avoided, and cultural clashes become enhancing, the stage is set for recognizing and valuing diversity.

RECOGNIZING AND VALUING DIVERSITY

In order to actualize the positive potential of diversity, you must recognize that diversity exists and then learn to value and respect fundamental differences among people. This is especially true in countries in which widely diverse groups of people live. The United States, for example, is a nation of many cultures, races, languages, and religions. In the last eight years alone, over 7.8 million people journeying from over 150 different countries and speaking dozens of different languages made the United States their new home. America's pluralism and diversity has many positive values, such as being a source of energy and creativity that increases the vitality of American society. Diversity among collaborators has been found to contribute to achievement and productivity, creative problem solving, growth in cognitive and moral reasoning, perspective-taking ability, and general sophistication in interacting and working with peers from a variety of cultural and ethnic backgrounds (Johnson & Johnson, 1989).

Within a relationship, a community, an organization, a society, or a world, the goal is not to assimilate all groups so that everyone is alike. The goal is to work together to achieve mutual goals while recognizing cultural diversity and learning to value and respect fundamental differences while working together to achieve mutual goals. Creating a *unum* from *pluribus* is done in basically four steps. *First, you develop an appreciation for your own religious, ethnic, or cultural background.* Your identification with the culture and homeland of your ancestors must be recognized and valued. The assumption is that respect for your cultural heritage will translate into self-respect.

Second, you develop an appreciation and respect for the religious, ethnic, and cultural backgrounds of others. A critical aspect of developing an ethnic and cultural identity is whether ethnocentricity is inherent in your definition of yourself. An in-group identity must be developed in a way that does not lead to rejection of out-groups. There are many examples where being a member of one group requires the rejection of other groups. There are also many examples where being a member of one group requires the valuing and respect for other groups. Outgroups need to be seen as collaborators and resources rather than competitors and threats. Express respect for diverse backgrounds and value them as a resource that increases the quality of your life and adds to the viability of your society. The degree to which your in-group identity leads to respect for and valuing of out-groups depends on developing a superordinate identity that includes both your own and all other groups.

Third, you develop a strong superordinate identity that transcends the differences between your own and all other groups. Being an American, for example, is creedal rather than racial or ancestral. The United States is a nation that unites as one people the descendants of many cultures, races, religions, and ethnic groups through an identification with America and democracy. And America has grown increasingly diverse in social and cultural composition. Each cultural group is part of the whole and members of each new immigrant group, while modifying and enriching our national identity, learn they are first and foremost Americans. America is one of the few successful examples of a pluralistic society where different groups clashed but ultimately learned to live together through achieving a sense of common nationhood. In our diversity, there has always been a broad recognition that we are one people. Whatever our origins, we are all Americans.

Fourth, you adopt a pluralistic set of values concerning democracy, freedom, liberty, equality, justice, the rights of individuals, and the responsibilities of citizenship. It is these values that form the American creed. We respect basic human rights, listen to dissenters instead of jailing them, and have a multiparty political system, a free press, free speech, freedom of religion, and freedom of assembly. These values were shaped by millions of people from many different backgrounds. Americans are a multicultural people knitted together by a common set of political and moral values.

Diverse individuals from different cultural, ethnic, social class, and language backgrounds come together primarily in school, career, and community settings. Sometimes the results are positive and individuals get to know each other, appreciate and value the vitality of diversity, learn how to use diversity for creative problem solving and enhanced productivity, and internalize a common superordinate identity that binds them together. If diversity is to be a source of creativity and energy, individuals must value and seek out diversity rather than fear and reject it. Doing so will eventually result in cross-cultural friendships....

CLARIFYING MISCOMMUNICATIONS

Imagine that you and several friends went to hear a speaker. Although the content was good, and the delivery entertaining, two of your friends walked out in protest. When you asked them why, they called your attention to the facts that the speaker continually said "you guys" even though half the audience was women, used only sports and military examples, only quoted males, and joked about senility and old age. Your friends were insulted.

Communication is actually one of the most complex aspects of managing relationships with diverse peers. To communicate effectively with people from a different cultural, ethnic, social class, or historical background than yours you must increase your

1. *Language sensitivity:* knowledge of words and expressions that are appropriate and inappropriate in communicating with diverse groups. The use of language can play a powerful role in reinforcing stereotypes and garbling communication. To avoid this, individuals need to heighten their sensitivity and avoid using terms and expressions that ignore or devalue others.
2. *Awareness of stylistic elements of communication:* knowledge of the key elements of communication style and how diverse cultures use these elements to communicate. Without awareness of nuances in language and differences in style, the potential for garbled communication is enormous when interacting with diverse peers.

Your ability to communicate with credibility to diverse peers is closely linked to your use of language. You must be sophisticated enough to anticipate how your messages will be interpreted by the listener. If you are unaware of nuances and innuendoes contained in your message, then you will be more likely to miscommunicate. The words you choose often tell other people more about your values, attitudes, and socialization than you intend to reveal. Receivers will react to the subtleties conveyed and interpret the implied messages behind our words. The first step in establishing relationships with diverse peers, therefore, is to understand how language reinforces stereotypes and to adjust our usage accordingly.

You can never predict with certainty how every person will react to what you say. You can, however, minimize the possibility of miscommunicating by following some basic guidelines:

1. Use all the communication skills discussed in this book.
2. Negotiate for meaning whenever you think the other persons you are talking with misinterpreted what you said.

3. Use words that are inclusive rather than exclusive such as women, men, participants.
4. Avoid adjectives that spotlight specific groups and imply the individual is an exception, such as black doctor, woman pilot, older teacher, blind lawyer.
5. Use quotes, references, metaphors, and analogies that reflect diversity and are from diverse sources, for example, from Asian and African sources as well as from European and American.
6. Avoid terms that define, demean, or devalue others, such as cripple, girl, boy, agitator.
7. Be aware of the genealogy of words viewed as inappropriate by others. It is the connotations the receiver places on the words that are important, not your connotations. These connotations change over time so continual clarification is needed. There are loaded words that seem neutral to you but highly judgmental to people of diverse backgrounds. The word lady, for example, was a compliment even a few years ago, but today it fails to take into account women's independence and equal status in society and, therefore, is offensive to many women. Words such as girls or gals are just as offensive.

SUMMARY

In a global village highly diverse individuals interact daily, study and work together, and live in the same community. Diversity among your acquaintances, classmates, co-workers, neighbors, and friends is inevitable. You will be expected to interact effectively with people with a wide variety of characteristics and from a wide variety of backgrounds. In order to gain the sophistication and skills needed to do so you must accept yourself, lower the barriers to building relationships with diverse peers, recognize that diversity exists and is a valuable resource, ... and clarify misunderstandings.

All people need to believe that they are unique and separate individuals who are valued and respected in their own right. In order to do so, you must accept yourself as you are and build a coherent, stable, and integrated identity. Your identity helps you cope with stress, it provides stability and consistency to your life, and it directs what information is attended to, how it is organized, and how it is remembered. Your identity is built through your current relationships and identifications with real, historical, and fictional people. Actually, you have many interrelated identities. You have a family identity, a gender identity, and a country identity. An important aspect of your identity is your identification with your cultural, ethnic, historical, and religious background.

The more accepting you are of yourself, the more able you are to be accepting of others. But there are barriers to building positive relationships with diverse peers. The most notable barriers are prejudice, blaming the victim, and culture clash. Minimizing these barriers makes it easier to recognize that diversity exists and fundamental differences among people are to be both respected and valued. To do so you must respect your own heritage, respect the heritages of others, develop a superordinate identity that transcends the differences, and [adopt] a pluralistic set of values.

Accepting yourself, minimizing the barriers, and respecting and valuing diversity set the stage for actually gaining cross-cultural sophistication. Being able to relate effectively to people from a variety of cultures depends on seeking opportunities to interact cross-culturally, building trust, so that enough candor exists that you can learn what is and what is not disrespectful and hurtful to them. It is only through building friendships with diverse peers that the insights required to understand how to interact appropriately with people from a wide variety of backgrounds can be obtained. Two requirements for developing such friendships are highlighting cooperative efforts to achieve mutual goals and clarifying miscommunications that arise while working together.

REVIEW QUESTIONS

1. Explain what Johnson means—as specifically as you can—when he says that globalization has made diversity increasingly inevitable.
2. What is a self-schema? Give an example of one of your own self-schemas (see Chapter 3).
3. Explain the connection Johnson makes between prejudice and discrimination.
4. Explain how blaming the victim can contribute to stereotyping.
5. What does Johnson mean by "a strong superordinate identity that transcends the differences between your own and all other groups"?
6. What is a pluralistic set of values?
7. Give an example of how (a) language sensitivity and (b) awareness of stylistic elements of communication could enhance relationships with diverse others.

PROBES

1. People who belong to such organizations as a militia, skinhead, or Ku Klux Klan group often argue for the importance of ethnic purity and exclusivity. Members of men-only and women-only groups make similar arguments about gender exclusivity. Johnson's basic assumption in this reading is that these arguments for exclusivity are naïve, because diversity is a fact of the contemporary world. What specific examples can you cite to support Johnson's assumption? Where do you notice the concrete evidence of increasing diversity?
2. *Why* does Johnson say that the first step toward successfully interacting with diverse others is to learn to accept yourself?

3. Cognitive scientists pretty much agree that categorization is a basic human mental function. Our brains naturally and constantly categorize almost everything we perceive. If this is true, then we automatically categorize the people we perceive. How, then, can a person possibly avoid prejudice?
4. As Johnson defines *culture clash*, it is inevitable. Various cultures will naturally have conflicts over basic values. Tell how he suggests we respond to this inevitability.
5. Which of the previous readings in this book do you think could contribute most directly to your efforts to bridge differences with diverse others?

REFERENCE

Johnson, D. W. & Johnson, R. (1989). *Cooperation and competition: Theory and research.* Edina, MN: Interaction Book Company.

The Same and Different: Crossing Boundaries of Color, Culture, Sexual Preference, Disability, and Age
Letty Cottin Pogrebin

Letty Cottin Pogrebin published an exhaustive book on friendship based on two very thorough friendship surveys, many additional published research reports, and interviews with almost 150 people ranging in age from early adolescence to 82 years and representing most of the spectrum of cultures and subcultures in the United States. The following reading consists of excerpts from Chapter 11 of her 16-chapter book. As the title indicates, the chapter deals with friendship across a variety of cultural boundaries, including color, culture, sexual preference, disability, and age. As with other readings, I chose this one because it blends sound research and straightforward writing, credible theory, and solid practice.

This rigorous but accessible flavor of Pogrebin's work emerges in the section right after the introduction. She begins with the obvious but important point that if you're going to cross a boundary, you'll find yourself doing a lot of explaining—to yourself, to each other, and to your respective communities. Then she takes a couple of pages to elaborate on what that "explaining" will probably consist of.

The next major section develops another potentially profound theme: Intercultural relationships consistently have to deal with the reality that the two persons might be "the same" but that they're also "never quite the same." She illustrates the point with examples from black/redneck white, Jewish/Irish-Catholic, Puerto Rican/white, and Spanish/Jewish relationships. Pogrebin's discussion of "moving in one another's world" extends the notion of "the same but never quite the same" to include challenges introduced by second and third languages and fundamental cultural values. She also discusses several "hazards of crossing" that emerge when fundamental differences in cultural values meet.

Under the heading "The Problem with 'Them' Is 'Us,'" Pogrebin discusses gay/straight, disabled/nondisabled, and young/aged relationships. All three topics became current only in recent decades as the minority rights movement spread to include gays and lesbians, the disabled, and "senior citizens," and government regulations made these groups increasingly visible. As the author notes, these groups warrant separate discussions, in part because "to a large degree, our society still wants to keep them out of sight—gays and lesbians for 'flaunting their alternative lifestyles,' the disabled for not 'getting better,' and the old for reminding us of our eventual fate."

Pogrebin's outline of the kinds of explaining one has to do about his or her gay/straight relationships accurately captures the last 10 years or so of my experience communicating with some gay and lesbian people. The strong relationship Kris and I have with our friends Bill and John Paul is one example of some of the problems and much of the potential Pogrebin discusses. I also appreciate her summary of the contrasts between gay and straight views on homophobia, AIDS, lesbian politics, and acceptance.

Until recently, disabled persons in the United States made up perhaps an even more invisible subculture. Thanks in part to major changes in building codes affecting all public construction, wheelchair-bound, deaf, and blind persons are becoming increasingly visible. Pogrebin explains some of the unique problems the nondisabled can have establishing and maintaining relationships with these persons. As one quadriplegic succinctly puts it, "We need friends who won't treat us as weirdo asexual second-class children or expect us to be 'Supercrips'—miracle cripples who work like crazy to make themselves whole again. . . . We want to be accepted the way we are." Some nondisabled persons are guilty of exactly these charges and can be shocked to hear them expressed so bluntly. Dawn and Charles Braithwaite develop some of these ideas in the final reading of this chapter.

In the final section of this reading, Pogrebin discusses cross-age friendships. She cites some studies that indicate that three-year-olds already have developed "ageist" perceptions of the elderly—believing that old people are sick, tired, and ugly. Other studies reveal the stereotypes older people have of children and teenagers. She discusses some of the typical reasons for cross-age miscommunication and then suggests some reasons why age can be immaterial to developing friendships. As the average age of the U.S. populace continues to increase, Pogrebin's comments will become more and more applicable and important.

I appreciate the breadth of application in this reading. Pogrebin is writing about some cutting-edge aspects of interpersonal communication, and her ideas are going to become increasingly important.

On August 21, 1985, as they had done several times before, twenty-one men from a work unit at a factory in Mount Vernon, New York, each chipped in a dollar, signed a handwritten contract agreeing to "share the money equally & fairly to [sic] each other," and bought a ticket in the New York State Lottery. The next day, their ticket was picked as one of three winners of the largest jackpot in history: $41 million.

The story of the Mount Vernon 21 captivated millions not just because of the size of the pot of gold but because of the rainbow of people who won it. Black, white, yellow, and brown had scribbled their names on that contract—Mariano Martinez, Chi Wah Tse, Jaroslaw Siwy, and Peter Lee—all immigrants from countries ranging from Paraguay to Poland, from Trinidad to Thailand.

"We're like a big family here," said Peter Lee. "We thought by pooling our efforts we would increase our luck—and we were right."[1]

The men's good fortune is a metaphor for the possibility that friendships across ethnic and racial boundaries may be the winning ticket for everyone. This is not to say that crossing boundaries is a snap. It isn't. There are checkpoints along the way where psychic border guards put up a fuss and credentials must be reviewed. We look at a prospective friend and ask, "Do they want something from me?" Is this someone who sees personal advantage in having a friend of another race at his school, in her company, at this moment in history? Is it Brotherhood Week? Does this person understand that "crossing friendships" require more care and feeding than in-group friendship, that it takes extra work?

EXPLAINING

Most of the extra work can be summed up in one word: *explaining*. Whatever the boundary being crossed—race, ethnicity, or any other social category—both partners in a crossing friendship usually find they have to do a lot of explaining—to themselves, to each other, and to their respective communities.

Explaining to Yourself

One way or another, you ask yourself, "What is the meaning of my being friends with someone not like me?"

In his classic study, *The Nature of Prejudice*, Gordon Allport distinguishes between the in-group, which is the group to which you factually belong, and the reference group, which is the group to which you relate or aspire.[2] Allport gives the example of Blacks who so wish to partake of white skin privilege that they seek only white friends, disdain their own group, and become self-hating. One could as easily cite Jews who assume a WASP identity or "Anglicized Chicanos" who gain education and facility in English and then sever their ties of kinship and friendship with other Mexican-Americans.[3]

When you have a friend from another racial or ethnic group, you ask yourself whether you are sincerely fond of this person or might be using him or her as an entrée into a group that is your unconscious reference group. The explaining you do to yourself helps you understand your own motivations. It helps you ascertain whether the friend complements or denies your identity, and whether your crossing friendships are in reasonable balance with your in-group relationships.

Explaining to Each Other

Ongoing mutual clarification is one of the healthiest characteristics of crossing friendships. The Black friend explains why your saying "going ape" offends him, and the Jewish friend reminds you she can't eat your famous barbecued pork. Both of you try to be honest about your cultural sore points and to forgive the other person's initial ignorance or insensitivities. You give one another the benefit of the doubt. Step by step, you discover which aspects of the other person's "in-groupness" you can share and where you must accept exclusion with grace.

David Osborne, a white, describes his close and treasured friendship with an American Indian from Montana: "Steve was tall and athletic—the classic image of the noble full-blooded Indian chief. We were in the same dorm in my freshman year at Stanford at a time when there were only one or two other Native Americans in the whole university. He had no choice but to live in a white world. Our friendship began when our English professor gave an assignment to write about race. Steve and I got together to talk about it. We explored stuff people don't usually discuss openly. After that, we started spending a lot of time together. We played intramural sports. We were amazingly honest with each other, but we were also comfortable being silent.

"When I drove him home for spring vacation, we stopped off at a battlefield that had seen a major war between Chief Joseph's tribe and the U.S. Cavalry. Suddenly it hit me that, had we lived then, Steve and I would have been fighting on opposite sides, and we talked about the past. Another time, an owl flew onto our windowsill and Steve was very frightened. He told me the owl was a symbol of bad luck to Indians. I took it very seriously. We were so in touch, so in sync, that I felt the plausibility of his superstitions. I was open to his mysticism."

Mutual respect, acceptance, tolerance for the faux pas and the occasional closed door, open discussion and patient mutual education, all this gives crossing friendships—when they work at all—a special kind of depth.

Explaining to Your Community of Origin

Accountability to one's own group can present the most difficult challenge to the maintenance of crossing friendships. In 1950 the authors of *The Lonely Crowd* said that interracial contact runs risks not only from whites but from Blacks who may "interpret friendliness as Uncle Tomism."[4] The intervening years have not eliminated such group censure.

In her article "Friendship in Black and White," Bebe Moore Campbell wrote: "For whites, the phrase 'nigger lover' and for Blacks, the accusation of 'trying to be white' are the pressure the group applies to discourage social interaction."[5] Even without overt attacks, people's worry about group reaction inspires self-censorship. Henry, a Black man with a fair complexion, told me he dropped a white friendship that became a touchy subject during the Black Power years. "We'd just come out of a period when many light-skinned Negroes tried to pass for white and I wasn't about to be mistaken for one of them," he explains. "My racial identity mattered more to me than any white friend."

Black-white friendships are "conducted underground," says Campbell, quoting a Black social worker, who chooses to limit her intimacy with whites rather than fight the system. "I'd feel comfortable at my white friend's parties because everybody there would be a liberal, but I'd never invite her to mine because I have some friends who just don't like white people and I didn't want anybody to be embarrassed."

If a white friend of mine said she hated Blacks, I would not just keep my Black friends away from her, I would find it impossible to maintain the friendship. However, the converse is not comparable. Most Blacks have at some point been wounded by racism, while whites have not been victimized from the other direction. Understanding the experiences *behind* the reaction allows decent Black people to remain friends with anti-white Blacks. That these Blacks may have reason to hate certain whites does not excuse their hating all whites, but it does explain it.…

Historically, of course, the biggest enemies of boundary-crossing friendships have not been Blacks or ethnic minorities but majority whites. Because whites gain the most from social inequality, they have the most to lose from crossing friendships, which, by their existence, deny the relevance of ethnic and racial hierarchies. More important, the empowered whites can put muscle behind their disapproval by restricting access to clubs, schools, and businesses.

If you sense that your community of origin condemns one of your crossing friendships, the amount of explaining or justifying you do will depend on how conformist you are and whether you feel entitled to a happiness of your own making.…

THE SAME BUT NEVER QUITE THE SAME

"I go coon hunting with Tobe Spencer," said former police officer L. C. Albritton about his Black friend in Camden, Alabama. "We're good friends. We stay in town during the day for all the hullabaloo and at night we go home and load up the truck with three dogs and go way down into the swamps. We let the dogs go and sit on a log, take out our knives and a big chew of tobacco … and just let the rest of the world go by."

Looking at a picture of himself and Spencer taken in 1966, Albritton mused: "It's funny that a police officer like me is standing up there smiling and talking to a nigger because we were having marches and trouble at that time.… Old Tobe Spencer—ain't nothing wrong with that nigger. He's always neat and clean as a pin. He'll help you too. Call him at midnight and he'll come running just like that."[6]

Two friends with the same leisure-time pleasures, two men at ease together in the lonely night of the swamps. Yet race makes a difference. Not only does the white man use the derogatory "nigger," but he differentiates his friend Tobe from the rest of "them" who, presumably, are not neat and clean and helpful. The *same but never quite the same.*

Leonard Fein, the editor of *Moment,* a magazine of progressive Jewish opinion, gave me "the controlling vignette" of his cross-ethnic friendships: "An Irish-Catholic couple was among our dearest friends, but on that morning in 1967 when we first heard that Israel was being bombed, my wife said, 'Who can we huddle with tonight to get through this ordeal?' and we picked three Jewish couples. Our Irish friends were deeply offended. 'Don't you think we would have felt for you?' they asked. 'Yes,' we said, 'but it wasn't sympathy we wanted, it was people with whom, if necessary, we could have mourned the death of Israel—and that could only be other Jews.'

"The following week, when the war was over, my wife and I went to Israel. The people who came to live in our house and take care of our children were our Irish friends. They had understood they were our closest friends yet they could never be exactly like us." ...

For Raoul, a phenomenally successful advertising man, crossing friendships have been just about the only game in town. He reminisced with me about growing up in a Puerto Rican family in a Manhattan neighborhood populated mostly by Irish, Italians, and Jews:

"In the fifties I hung out with all kinds of guys. I sang on street corners—do-wopping in the night—played kick the can, and belonged to six different basketball clubs, from the Police Athletic League to the YMCA. My high school had 6000 kids in it—street kids who hung out in gangs like The Beacons, The Fanwoods, The Guinea Dukes, The Irish Lords, and The Diablos from Spanish Harlem and Jewish kids who never hung out because they were home studying. The gang members were bullies and punks who protected their own two-block area. They wore leather jackets and some of them carried zip guns and knives. I managed to be acceptable to all of them just because I was good at sports. I was the best athlete in the school and president of the class. So I was protected by the gangs and admired by the Jewish kids and I had a lot of friends."

Raoul's athletic prowess won him a scholarship to a large midwestern university where he was the first Puerto Rican to be encountered by some people. "They wanted me to sing the whole sound track of *West Side Story.* They asked to see my switchblade. And I was as amazed by the midwesterners as they were by me. My first hayride was a real shock. Same with hearing people saying 'Good morning' to each other. Every one of my friends—my roommate, teammates, and fraternity brothers, Blacks from Chicago and Detroit and whites from the farms—they were all gentle and nice. And gigantic and strong. Boy, if one of them had moved into my neighborhood back home, he'd have owned the block.

"After graduation, a college friend went to work in a New York City ad agency that played in a Central Park league and needed a softball pitcher. He had me brought in for an interview. Even though I knew nothing about advertising, I was a helluva pitcher, and the owner of the agency took sports seriously. So he hired me. I always say I had the only athletic scholarship in the history of advertising. I pitched for the agency, I played basketball with the owner, and I learned the business. So I found my friends and my career through sports. Even though I may have been a Spic to most everyone, sports opened all the doors."

The same but never quite the same....

"At the beginning, because of difficulties of adaptation, we immigrants protect ourselves by getting together with people from the same culture who speak the same language," says Luis Marcos, a psychiatrist, who came to the United States from Seville, Spain. "Next, when we feel more comfortable, we reach out to people who do the same work we do, mostly those who help us or those we help in some way. Then we have a basis for friendship. My mentor, the director of psychiatry at Bellevue, is a native-born American and a Jew. He helped me in my area of research and now he's one of my best friends. I also began to teach and to make friends with my medical students as they grew and advanced."

That Marcos and his friends have the health profession in common has not prevented misunderstandings. "When we first went out for meals together, my impulse was to pay for both of us," he says of another doctor, a Black woman who taught him not to leave his own behavior unexamined. "It wasn't that I thought she couldn't afford to pay; we were equally able to pick up the check. It was just that the cultural habit of paying for a woman was ingrained in my personality. But she misconstrued it. She felt I was trying to take care of her and put her down as a Black, a professional, and a woman. In order for our friendship to survive, she had to explain how she experiences things that I don't even think about."

MOVING IN ONE ANOTHER'S WORLD

Ethnotherapist Judith Klein revels in her crossing friendships. "My interest in people who are different from me may be explained by the fact that I'm a twin. Many people look to be mirrored in friendship; I've had mirroring through my sister, so I can use friendship for other things. One thing I use it for is to extend my own life. People who aren't exactly like me enhance my knowledge and experience. They let me be a vicarious voyager in their world."

As much as friends try to explain one another's world, certain differences remain particular barriers to intimacy.

Luis Marcos mentions the language barrier. "No matter how well I speak, I can never overcome my accent," he says. "And some people mistake the way I talk for lack of comprehension. They are afraid I won't understand an American joke, or if I choose to use aggressive words, they don't think I mean it, they blame my 'language problem.'"

While many Americans assume people with an accent are ignorant, many ethnics assume, just as incorrectly, that someone *without* an accent is smart. Some Americans have a habit of blaming the other person for doing or saying whatever is not understandable to Americans. Ethnics also have been known to blame their own culture—to use their "foreignness" as an excuse for behavior for which an American would have to take personal responsibility. "I can't help it if we Latins are hot-tempered" is a way of generalizing one's culpability.

Of course, the strongest barrier to friendship is outright resistance. After two years of off-and-on living in Tokyo, Angie Smith came to terms with the fact that "the Japanese do not socialize the way we do." She found, as many have, that in Japan friendship is considered an obligation more than a pleasure and is almost always associated with business.[7]

"Three times I invited two couples for dinner—the men were my husband's business associates—and three times the men came and the women didn't," Smith recalls. "They sent charming little notes with flowers, but they would not have been comfortable in our house for an evening of social conversation. Yet these same Japanese women would go out to lunch with me and tell me more intimate things than they tell each other. While we were in Japan, I just had to get used to sex-divided socializing and not having any couple friendships."

When people's differences are grounded in racism rather than alien styles of socializing, it can be especially painful to move in the other person's world.

"I felt myself a slave and the idea of speaking to white people weighed me down," wrote Frederick Douglass a century ago.[8] Today, most Blacks refuse to be weighed down by whites. They do not "need" white friends. Some doubt that true friendship is possible between the races until institutional racism is destroyed. Feminists of every shade have debated the question "Is Sisterhood Possible?" Despite the issues that affect *all* women, such as sexual violence, many Black women resist working together for social change or organizing with white women because they believe most whites don't care enough about welfare reform, housing, teen pregnancies, or school dropouts—issues that are of primary concern to Blacks.

A writer and a professor of Afro-American studies named bell hooks wrote: "All too frequently in the women's movement it was assumed one could be free of sexist thinking by simply adopting the appropriate feminist rhetoric; it was further assumed that identifying oneself as oppressed freed one from being an oppressor. To a very great extent, such thinking prevented white feminists from understanding and overcoming their own sexist-racist attitudes toward black women. They could pay lip service to the idea of sisterhood and solidarity between women but at the same time dismiss black women."[9]

Phyllis Marynick Palmer, a historian, says white women are confounded by Black women's strong family role and work experience, which challenge the white stereotype of female incapacity. White women also criticize Black women for making solidarity with their brothers a priority rather than confronting Black men's sexism. In turn, Black women get angry at white women who ignore "their own history of racism and the benefits that white women have gained at the expense of black women."[10] With all this, how could sisterhood be possible? How can friendship be possible?

"I would argue for the abandonment of the concept of sisterhood as a global construct based on unexamined assumptions about our similarities," answers Dill, "and I would substitute a more pluralistic approach that recognizes and accepts the objective differences between women."

Again the word "pluralistic" is associated with friendship. An emphasis on double consciousness, not a denial of differences. The importance of feeling both the same and different, of acknowledging "the essence of me," of understanding that friends need not *transcend* race or ethnicity but can embrace differences and be enriched by them. The people who have managed to incorporate these precepts say that they are pretty reliable guidelines for good crossing friendships. But sometimes it's harder than it looks. Sometimes, the "vicarious voyage" into another world can be a bad trip.

The Hazards of Crossing

"Anglo wannabes" are a particular peeve of David Hayes Bautista. "These are Anglos who wanna be so at home with us that they try too hard to go native. For instance, Mexicans have a certain way that we yell along with the music of a mariachi band. When someone brought along an Anglo friend and yelled 'Yahoo, Yahoo' all night, every Chicano in the place squirmed."

Maxine Baca Zinn gives the reverse perspective: of a Chicano in an Anglo environment. "Once, when I was to speak at the University of California, a Chicana friend who was there told me that the minute I walked into that white academic world my spine straightened up. I carried myself differently. I talked differently around them and I didn't even know it." Was Zinn just nervous about giving her speech or did she tighten up in anticipation of the tensions Chicanos feel in non-Hispanic settings? She's not certain.

When Charlie Chin, a bartender, started work in a new place, a white co-worker quipped, "One thing you have to watch out for, Charlie, are all the Chinks around here." I winced when Chin said this, but he told me, "I just smiled at the guy. I'm used to those jokes. That's the way whites break the ice with Asians. That's the American idea of being friendly." ...

For another pair of friends, having different sensitivities did not destroy the relationship but did create a temporary misunderstanding. Yvonne, a Black woman, was offended when her white friend, Fran, came to visit, took off her shoes, and put her feet up on the couch. "I felt it showed her disregard for me and I blamed it on race," says Yvonne. "Black people believe the way you behave in someone's home indicates the respect you have for that person. Also, furniture means a lot to us because we buy it with such hard-won wages." Weeks later, Yvonne saw one of Fran's white friends do the same thing while sitting on Fran's couch. Yvonne realized that the behavior had nothing to do with lack of respect for Blacks. "For all I know millions of whites all over America put their feet up when they relax—I'd just never seen that part of their world before."

What Bill Tatum discovered about a couple of his white friends was not so easy to explain away. When the couple asked Tatum to take some food to Helen, their Black housekeeper who was sick, he asked her name and address. They knew her only as "Helen" but were able to get her address from their 6-year-old who had spent a week at her apartment when they had been on vacation.

"I arrived to find a filthy, urine-smelling building, with addicts hanging out on the front stoop. Rags were stuffed in the broken windows in Helen's apartment. She was wearing a bag of asafetida around her neck, a concoction made by southern Blacks to ward off bad luck and colds. She was old, sick, and feverish. She said she'd never been sick before and her employers—my friends—had provided her with no health insurance. Obviously, they'd never imagined where or how this poor woman might live—or else they wouldn't have left their little girl with her. They treated their Black housekeeper with none of the respect and concern they showed me, their Black *friend* and a member of their economic class."

Until that experience, if anyone had ever accused the couple of racism, Tatum says he'd have gone to the mat defending them. Now he has to square what he's seen with his old love for them and he is finding it very, very difficult.

He makes another point about moving in the world of white friends. "Some whites make me feel completely comfortable because they say exactly what they think even if it contradicts whatever I've said. But other whites never disagree with me on anything. They act as if Blacks can't defend their positions, or they're afraid it would look like a put-down to challenge what I say even though they would challenge a white person's opinion in a minute."

While Tatum resents whites' misguided protectiveness, he also finds fault with "many Blacks who are climbing socially and are too damned careful of what *they* say. They won't advance an opinion until they have a sense of what the white friend is thinking." Not only is that not good conversation, he says, "that's not good friendship."

THE PROBLEM WITH "THEM" IS "US"

If you're a young, heterosexual, nondisabled person and you do not have one friend who is either gay, old, or disabled, there might be something wrong with *you*. If you're gay, old, or disabled and all your friends are just like you, it may not be because you prefer it that way.

Gay people, the elderly, and disabled people get the same pleasure from companionship and intimacy and have the same problems with friendship as does anyone else. They merit a separate discussion in this book for the same reason that class, race, and ethnicity required special discussion: because on top of the usual friendship concerns, they experience additional barriers.

In essence, the barriers exist because we don't *know* each other. Many people—some of whom are homophobic (have a fear of homosexuality)—reach adulthood without ever to their knowledge meeting a homosexual or a lesbian. Many have neither known someone who is blind or deaf or who uses a wheelchair nor spent time with an old person other than their grandparents. That there are such things as Gay Pride marches, disability rights organizations, and the Gray Panthers does not mean that these groups have achieved equal treatment under the law or full humanity in the eyes of the world. To a large degree, our society still wants to keep them out of sight—the gays for "flaunting their alternative lifestyles," the disabled for not "getting better," and the old for reminding us of our eventual fate.

As a result of our hang-ups, these populations may be even more segregated than racial or ethnic minorities. When these groups are segregated, "we" don't have to think about "them." Out of sight, out of mind, out of friendship. People told me they had no gay, elderly, or disabled friends because "we live in two different worlds" or because "they" are so different—meaning threatening, unsettling, or strange. Closer analysis reveals, however, that we *keep* them different by making this world so hard for them to live in and by defining human norms so narrowly. It is our world—the homophobic, youth-worshipping, disability-fearing world—that is threatening, unsettling, and strange to them. In other words, their biggest problem is us.

To make friends, we have to cross our self-made boundaries and grant to other people the right to be both distinctive and equal.

Gay-Straight Friendship

Forming relationships across gay-straight boundaries can be as challenging as crossing racial and ethnic lines because it too requires the extra work of "explaining":

- Explaining to yourself why, if you're gay, you need this straight friend ("Am I unconsciously trying to keep my heterosexual credentials in order?"), or why, if you're straight, you need this gay friend ("Am I a latent homosexual?")
- Explaining to each other what your lives are like—telling the straight friend what's behind the words "heavy leather" or explaining to the gay friend just why he *cannot* bring his transvestite lover to a Bar Mitzvah
- Explaining to your respective communities why you have such a close relationship with one of "them"

Gay-straight friendship is a challenge not only because the heterosexual world stigmatizes gays but because homosexual society is a culture unto itself. Straights who relate comfortably with their gay friends say they get along so well because they respect the distinctive qualities of gay culture—almost as if it were an ethnic group. Interestingly enough, a Toronto sociologist has determined that gay men have the same institutions, "sense of peoplehood," and friendship networks as an ethnic community; all that gays lack is the emphasis on family.[11] And in places where lesbians congregate, such as San Francisco, there are women's bars, music, bookstores, publications, folklore, and dress styles—an elaborate self-contained culture.[12]

Since gay men and lesbians have to function in a straight world during most of their lives, it's not too much to ask a straight friend to occasionally accommodate to an environment defined by homosexuals. But even when both friends accommodate, gay-straight relations can be strained by disagreements over provocative issues.

Gay-Straight Debate

The Gay's View	The Straight's View
On Homophobia	
You're not relaxed with me. You think gayness rubs off or friendship might lead to sex. You act like every gay person wants to seduce you. You fear others will think you're gay. You are repulsed by gay sex though you try to hide it. You bear some responsibility for the discrimination against gays and if you're my friend, you'll fight it with me.	I am the product of a traditional upbringing. I cannot help being afraid or ignorant of homosexuality. My religion taught me that homosexuality is a sin. I'm trying to overcome these biases and still be honest with you about my feelings. I support gay rights, but I cannot be responsible for everyone else's homophobia.
On AIDS	
Ever since the AIDS epidemic, you have not touched me or drunk from a glass in my house. I resent your paranoia. I shouldn't have to watch my gay friends die and at the same time feel that my straight friends are treating me like a leper. If I did get AIDS, I'm afraid you would blame the victim and abandon me. Can I trust a friend like that?	I *am* afraid. I don't know how contagious the AIDS virus is or how it's transmitted. From what I read, no one does. All I know is that AIDS is fatal, homosexuals are the primary victims, and you are a homosexual. I'm caught between my affection for you and my terror of the disease. I don't know what's right and you're in no position to tell me.
On Lesbian Politics	
Lesbianism is not just sexual, it's political. Every woman should call herself a lesbian, become woman-identified, and reject everything masculinist. Women who love men and live in the nuclear family contribute to the entrenchment of patriarchal power and the oppression of women. Authentic female friendship can only exist in lesbian communities. If you don't accept "lesbian" as a positive identity, it will be used to condemn all women who are not dependent on men.	I support lesbian rights and even lesbian separatism if lesbians choose it. I believe lesbian mothers must be permitted to keep their children. I oppose all discrimination and defamation of lesbians. I believe that lesbian feminists and straight women can work together and be friends, *but* I resent lesbian coercion and political strong-arming. I also resent your more-radical-than-thou attitude toward heterosexuals. Like you, what I do with my body is my business.
On Acceptance	
You want me to act straight whenever having a gay friend might embarrass you. I'm not going to tone down my speech or dress to please your friends or family. I do not enjoy being treated as a second-class couple when my lover and I go out with you and your spouse. If you can kiss and hold hands, we should be able to show affection in public. If straights ask each other how they met or how long they have been married, they should ask us how we met and how long we've been together.	You refuse to understand how difficult it is to explain gay lifestyles to a child or an 80-year-old. You make me feel like a square in comparison with your flashy gay friends. You treat married people like Mr. and Mrs. Tepid, as if the only true passion is gay passion. Your friends make me feel unwanted on gay turf and at political events when I'm there to support gay rights. You put down all straights before you know them. It's hard to be your friend if I can't introduce you to other people without your feeling hostile or judging their every word....

Disabled and Nondisabled Friendship

About 36 million Americans have a disabling limitation in their hearing, seeing, speaking, walking, moving, or thinking. Few nondisabled people are as sensitive to the experiences of this population as are those with close friends who are disabled.

"Last week," recalls Barbara Spring, "I went to have a drink at a midtown hotel with a friend who uses a wheelchair. Obviously it's not important to this hotel to have disabled patrons because we had to wait for the so-called accessible elevator for thirty minutes. Anyone who waits with the disabled is amazed at how long the disabled have to wait for everything."

"In graduate school, one of my friends was a young man with cerebral palsy," says Rena Gropper. "Because he articulated slowly and with great difficulty, everyone thought he was dumb and always interrupted him, but if you let him finish, you heard how bright and original his thinking was."

Terry Keegan, an interpreter for the deaf, has become friends with many deaf people and roomed for two years with a co-worker who is deaf. "If they don't understand what we're saying it's not because they're stupid but because we aren't speaking front face or we can't sign." Keegan believes all hearing people should learn 100 basic words in Ameslan, American Sign Language. "Historically, this wonderful language has been suppressed. Deaf people were forced to use speech, lipreading, and hearing aids so they would not look handicapped and would 'fit in' with the rest of us. Their hands were slapped when they tried to sign. This deprived them of a superior communication method. Deafness is not a pathology, it's a difference. When we deny deaf people their deafness, we deny them their identity."

Many nondisabled people have become sensitized to idioms that sound like racial epithets to the disabled, such as "the blind leading the blind" or "that's a lame excuse." Some find "handicapped" demeaning because it derives from "cap in hand." A man who wears leg braces says the issue is accuracy. "*I'm* not handicapped, people's attitudes about me handicap me." Merle Froschl, a nondisabled member of the Women and Disability Awareness Project, points out that the opposite of "disabled" is "*not* disabled"; thus, "nondisabled" is the most neutral term. Disabled people are infuriated by being contrasted with "normal" people—it implies that the disabled are "abnormal" and everyone else is perfect. And the term "able-bodied" inspires the question, Able to do what: Run a marathon? See without glasses? Isn't it all relative?

"Differently abled" and "physically challenged" had a brief vogue, but, says Harilyn Rousso, those terms "made me feel I really had something to hide." Rousso, a psychotherapist who has cerebral palsy, emphasizes, "Friends who care the most sometimes think they're doing you a favor by using euphemisms or saying 'I never think of you as disabled.' The reason they don't want to acknowledge my disability is that they think it's so negative. Meanwhile, I'm trying to recognize it as a valid part of me. I'm more complex than my disability and I don't want my friends to be obsessed by it. But it's clearly there, like my eye color, and I want my friends to appreciate and accept me with it."

The point is not that there is a "right way" to talk to people who are disabled but that friendship carries with it the obligation to *know thy friends,* their sore points and their preferences. That includes knowing what words hurt their feelings as well as when and how to help them do what they cannot do for themselves.

"Each disabled person sends out messages about what they need," says Froschl. "One friend who is blind makes me feel comfortable about taking her arm crossing the street, another dislikes physical contact and wants to negotiate by cane. I've learned not to automatically do things for disabled people since they often experience help as patronizing.

"I need someone to pour cream in my coffee, but in this culture, it's not acceptable to ask for help," say Rousso, adding that women's ordinary problems with dependence are intensified by disability. "I have to feel very comfortable with my friends before I can explain my needs openly and trust that their reaction will not humiliate both of us. For some people it raises too many anxieties."

Anxieties that surround the unknown are dissipated by familiarity. Maybe that explains why so many disabled-nondisabled friendships are composed of classmates or co-workers who spend a lot of time together.

"There are those who can deal with disability and those who can't," says Phil Draper, a quadriplegic whose spinal cord was injured in a car accident. "If they can't—if they get quiet or talk nervously or avoid our eyes—the work of the relationship falls entirely on us. We need friends who won't treat us as weirdo asexual second-class children or expect us to be 'Supercrips'—miracle cripples who work like crazy to make themselves whole again. Ninety-nine percent of us aren't going to be whole no matter what we do. We want to be accepted the way we are."

To accept friends like Phil Draper, the nondisabled have to confront their unconscious fears of vulnerability and death. In one study, 80 percent of nondisabled people said they would be comfortable having someone in a wheelchair as their friend. But "being in a wheelchair" came immediately after "blind" and "deaf-mute" as the affliction they themselves would least want to have.[13] If we fear being what our friend is, that feeling is somewhere in the friendship.

Nondisabled people also have to disavow the cult of perfectability. Disabled people are not going to "get better" because they are not "sick"; they are generally healthy people who are not allowed to function fully in this society—as friends or as anything else.

"Friendship is based on people's ability to communicate," says Judy Heumann, the first postpolio person to get a teacher's license in New York City and now a leader of the disability rights movement. "But barriers such as inaccessible homes make it hard for disabled people to just drop in. Spontaneity is something disabled people enjoy infrequently and the nondisabled take for granted.

"While more public places have ramps and bathrooms that accommodate wheelchairs, many parties still occur in inaccessible spaces. If I have to be carried upstairs or if I can't have a drink because I know I won't be able to use the bathroom later, I'll probably decide not to go at all. One way I measure my friends is by whether they have put in the effort and money to make their houses wheelchair-accessible. It shows their sensitivity to me as a person.

"Good friends are conscious of the fact that a movie theater or concert hall has to be accessible before I can join them; they share my anger and frustration if it's not. They understand why I'm not crazy about big parties where all the non-disabled are standing up and I'm at ass-level. It makes me able to function more as an equal within the group if people sit down to talk to me. I can't pretend I'm part of things if I can't hear anyone. I don't want to *not* be invited to large parties—I just want people to be sensitive to my needs....

"I always need help cooking, cleaning, driving, going to the bathroom, getting dressed. I pay an attendant to do most of those things for me but sometimes I have to ask a friend for help, which presents a lot of opportunities for rejection. Often, the friends who come through best are other disabled people whose disabilities complement mine. I can help a blind woman with her reading, child care, and traveling around town; she can do the physical things I need. And we don't have to appreciate each other's help, we can just accept it." ...

Cross-Age Friendship

I am now 46, my husband is 51. Among our good friends are two couples who are old enough to be our parents. One woman, a poet, can be counted on for the latest word on political protests and promising writers. She and I once spent a month together at a writer's colony. The other woman—as energetic and as well-read as anyone I know—is also involved in progressive causes. Although the men of both couples have each had a life-threatening illness, the one with a heart condition is a brilliant civil liberties lawyer and the one who had a stroke is a prize-winning novelist with stunning imaginative powers. The lawyer taught our son to play chess when he was 5. The novelist has encouraged our daughters to write stories ever since they could read. The men have been fine surrogate grandfathers.

When I described these couples to someone my own age, he said, "Ah, it's easy to be friends with *interesting* old people, but what about the dull ones?" The answer is, I am not friends with dull young or middle-aged people so why should I want to be friends with dull old people? And why does he immediately think in terms of old people *not* being interesting? Perhaps the crux of the problem with cross-generational friendship is this *double* double standard. First, to think we "ought" to be friends with the elderly—as a class—denies old people the dignity of individuality and devalues their friendship through condescension. But second, to assume that those who are young or in mid-life will necessarily be more interesting and attractive than those over 65 maintains a double standard of expectation that cheats younger people of friends like ours.

Ageism hurts all ages. And it begins early: Studies show that 3-year-olds already see old people as sick, tired, and ugly and don't want to associate with them.[14] Older people also have their biases about youthful behavior. Some

70-year-olds think children are undependable [and] unappreciative, ask too many questions, and must be told what to do. They believe teenagers are callow, impatient, and unseasoned.[15]

The authors of *Grandparents/Grandchildren* write, "We shouldn't blame adolescents for not being adults. To become adults, the young need to be around adults."[16] But age segregation keeps us apart. Without benefit of mutual acquaintance, stereotypes mount, brick by brick, until there is a wall high enough to conceal the real human beings on either side.

Another big problem is miscommunication. Conversations between young and old often founder because "sensory, physical, or cognitive differences" cause "distortion, message failure, and social discomfort."[17] That's a fancy way of saying they can't understand each other. And anyone who has ever talked with a young person whose span of concentration is the length of a TV commercial or with an old person whose mind wanders to the blizzard of '48 when asked how to dress for today's weather will understand how each generation's communication style can be a problem for the other.

But stereotypes and miscommunication do not entirely account for the gulf between young and old. Homophily—the attraction to the similar self—is the missing link. Those who are going through the same thing at the same time find it comforting to have friends who mirror their problems and meet their needs, and, usually, people of similar chronological age are going through parallel experiences with wage-earning, setting up house, child-rearing, and other life-cycle events.

Age-mates also tend to have in common the same angle of vision on history and culture. Two 65-year-olds watching a film about the Depression or World War II can exchange memories and emotional responses that are unavailable to a 30-year-old who did not live through those cataclysms. And while a person of 18 and one of 75 might both love Vivaldi, their simultaneous appreciation for Bruce Springsteen is unlikely.

Claude Fischer's studies reveal that more than half of all friend-partners are fewer than five years apart. But the span is reduced to two years if their relationship dates back to their youth when age gradations matter the most and the places where youngsters meet—school, camp, military service, and entry-level jobs—are more age-segregated. Contrary to popular wisdom, elderly people, like the rest of us, prefer friends of their own age. The more old people there are in a given community the more likely it is that each one will have a preponderance of same-age friends. And, believe it or not, a majority of old people say they think it's more important for them to have age-mates than family as their intimates.

Given this overwhelming preference for homophily at every age, why am I on the bandwagon for cross-generational friendship? Because when it's good, it's very, very good—both for friends of different ages who are undergoing similar experiences at the same time and for friends of different ages who are enjoying their differences.

- A 38-year-old woman meets 22-year-olds in her contracts class at law school.

Part 4 Bridges Not Walls

- A couple in their early forties enrolled in a natural childbirth course make friends with parents-to-be who are twenty years younger.
- Three fathers commiserate about the high cost of college; two are in their forties, the third is a 60-year-old educating his second family.

Age-crossing friendships become less unusual as Americans follow more idiosyncratic schedules for marrying, having children, and making career decisions.

But there are other reasons for feeling that age is immaterial to friendship. Marie Wilson, a 45-year-old foundation executive who has five children of high school age or older, told me, "My friends are in their early thirties, and they have kids under 8. But these women are where I am in my head. We became close working together on organizing self-help for the poor. Most women my age are more involved in suburban life or planning their own career moves."

Sharing important interests can be as strong a basis for friendship as is experiencing the same life-cycle events. However, without either of those links, the age difference can sit between the young and the old like a stranger. I'm not asking that we deny that difference but that we free ourselves from what Victoria Secunda calls "the tyranny of age assumptions"[18] and that we entertain the possibility of enriching ourselves through our differences....

As we cross all these lines and meet at many points along the life cycle, people of diverse ages, like people of every class and condition, are discovering that we who are in so many ways "the same and different" can also be friends.

REVIEW QUESTIONS

1. According to the author, when we engage in a cross-cultural relationship, what do we typically need to explain about it to ourselves? To each other? To our friends?
2. What is meant by Pogrebin's label "the same but never quite the same"?
3. In the paragraph before the heading "The Hazards of Crossing," the author distinguishes *double consciousness* from a *denial of differences*. What do those two terms mean?
4. The essay includes a story about a white couple asking their black friend, Bill Tatum, to take some food to their black housekeeper who lived in Harlem and was sick. Tatum was shocked to discover the housekeeper living in a filthy slum. What was racist about the white couple's "generosity"?
5. How accurate is Pogrebin's summary of each side's views in the section titled "Gay-Straight Debate"?
6. What is the point of the author's discussion of the words we use to label disabled persons?
7. Paraphrase the following comment by Pogrebin: "If we fear being what our friend is, that feeling is somewhere in the friendship."

PROBES

1. Which of the three kinds of explaining that Pogrebin describes has been most difficult for you?
2. The author claims that "many Americans assume people with an accent are ignorant" and that "many ethnics assume, just as incorrectly, that someone *without* an accent is smart." How is this distorted value mirrored in the major television networks' choice of news anchors and reporters?
3. You may be surprised to read a discussion of gay/straight relationships here. What might justify putting a discussion of this topic in this book?
4. Do you commonly think about relationships with disabled persons as examples of "intercultural communication"? What happens when you do?
5. What problems have you encountered in your relationships with older persons? What is the most helpful thing Pogrebin says about these relationships?

NOTES

1. L. Rohter, "Immigrant Factory Workers Share Dream, Luck and a Lotto Jackpot," *New York Times*, August 23, 1985.
2. G. Allport, *The Nature of Prejudice*, Doubleday, Anchor Press, 1958.
3. J. Provinzano, "Settling Out and Settling In." Paper presented at the annual meeting of the American Anthropological Association, November 1974.
4. D. Riesman, R. Denney, and N. Glazer, *The Lonely Crowd: A Study of the Changing American Character*, Yale University Press, 1950.
5. B. M. Campbell, "Friendship in Black and White," *Ms.*, August 1983.
6. B. Adelman, *Down Home: Camden, Alabama*, Times Books, Quadrangle, 1972.
7. R. Atsumi, "Tsukiai—Obligatory Personal Relationships of Japanese White Collar Employees," *Human Organization*, vol. 38, no. 1 (1979).
8. F. Douglass, *Narrative of the Life of Frederick Douglass, an American Slave*, New American Library, Signet, 1968.
9. b. hooks, *Ain't I a Woman: Black Women and Feminism*, South End Press, 1981.
10. P. M. Palmer, "White Women/Black Women: The Dualism of Female Identity and Experience in the United States," *Feminist Studies*, Spring 1983.
11. S. O. Murray, "The Institutional Elaboration of a Quasi-Ethnic Community," *International Review of Modern Sociology*, vol. 9, no. 2 (1979).
12. J. C. Albro and C. Tully, "A Study of Lesbian Lifestyles in the Homosexual Micro-Culture and the Heterosexual Macro-Culture," *Journal of Homosexuality*, vol. 4, no. 4 (1979).
13. L. M. Shears and C. J. Jensema, "Social Acceptability of Anomalous Persons," *Exceptional Children*, October 1969.
14. R. K. Jantz et al., *Children's Attitudes toward the Elderly*, University of Maryland Press, 1976.

15. A. G. Cryns and A. Monk, "Attitudes of the Aged toward the Young," *Journal of Gerontology*, vol. 1 (1972); see also, C. Seefeld et al., "Elderly Persons' Attitude toward Children," *Educational Gerontology*, vol. 8, no. 4 (1982).

16. K. L. Woodward and A. Kornhaber, *Grandparents, Grandchildren: The Vital Connection*, Doubleday, Anchor Press, 1981, quoted in "Youth Is Maturing Later," *New York Times*, May 10, 1985.

17. L. J. Hess and R. Hess, "Inclusion, Affection, Control: The Pragmatics of Intergenerational Communication." Paper presented at the Conference on Communication and Gerontology of the Speech Communication Association, July 1981.

18. V. Secunda, *By Youth Possessed: The Denial of Age in America*, Bobbs-Merrill, 1984.

When Black Women Talk with White Women: Why Dialogues Are Difficult

Marsha Houston

Marsha Houston begins this essay by illustrating how ethnicity can "trump" gender. Even though communication between women is usually more egalitarian and mutually supportive than communication between men, when one of the women is white and the other is African American, the communication often becomes, as Houston puts it, "stressful, insensitive, and in some cases even racist." She works these difficulties into this reading by identifying specific features of black women's and white women's talk that are different and by offering some concrete communication advice to white women about what to say and what not to say.

As endnote 9 explains, Houston's conclusions come from questionnaires filled out by 135 African American women and 100 white women—professionals, undergraduates, and graduate students. So what she calls "Black women's talk" and "White women's talk" may not fit every black or white woman, but it should be fairly representative of at least many women's experiences.

Black women perceive their own talk to be strong, assertive, and reflective of black experience in a white society, and they perceive white women's talk as arrogant, weak, and submissive. White women perceive their own talk as varied, appropriate, and accent-free, and they hear black women using black dialect—saying things like "young 'uns," "wif," and "wich you." This means that white women hear themselves speaking General American

Speech and black women speaking dialect. Black women who speak both black dialect and General American Speech are often perceived to speak only Black English. Black and white speakers also notice different features of each other's language.

"However," writes Houston, "there are exceptions." The bleak picture painted by her survey ignores the successful and satisfying communication that can and often does occur between black and white women. So in the last part of this reading, Houston focuses on the communication acts that bridge this particular set of cultural differences. She explains some particularly helpful communication moves by phrasing them as suggestions to white women who want to treat black women with respect and friendship. As she puts it, "never utter: (1) 'I never even notice that you're black'; (2) 'You're different from most black people'; (3) 'I understand what you're going through as a black woman, because ...'"

If you're female and black, you can help your classmates with this material by describing the degree to which you believe Marsha Houston is right. Do your experiences resonate with hers? If you are not female and black, you can improve your ability to bridge these cultural differences not only by listening to your classmates who are but also by bringing your own cultural experience to this reading. The most important thing, I believe, is to fully understand what is problematic about the three offending phrases. Whether or not you completely agree with Houston, try simply to understand what makes these statements offensive. Use this effort to broaden your awareness of general cultural differences and to sharpen your sense of a specific group of people who are *different* from you.

My conversations with white women of equal social status involve much competition, aggression, and mutual lack of trust, intimacy, and equality. However, there are exceptions.

—A black woman graduate student

Gender and communication researchers have demonstrated that women's conversations with each other are different from their conversations with men. For example, they are more egalitarian and mutually supportive. Certainly, many conversations between African Americans[1] and white women are of this sort. Yet I, and nearly every other African American woman I know, can recall many conversations with white women that were neither egalitarian nor supportive, conversations that we would describe as stressful, insensitive, and in some cases even racist. Like the graduate student quoted above, many African American women are likely to consider such "difficult dialogues"[2] with white peers to be the rule and open, satisfying conversations the exception.

The difficulties in black and white women's interracial conversations are the focus of this essay. I do not intend to give a definitive or an exhaustive analysis of women's interracial talk, but to explore two reasons why black women so often find conversations with white women unsatisfying and to suggest three statements to avoid in interracial conversation. I write from an African American woman's perspective, from within my ethnic cultural group, but I hope this essay will spark dialogue about both the differences and commonalities between black and white women speakers....

MUTUAL NEGATIVE STEREOTYPES

A basic concept of contemporary communication theory is that a speaker does not merely respond to the manifest content of a message, but to his or her interpretation of the speaker's intention or meaning. In other words, I respond to what I *think* you *meant* by what you said. Such factors as the setting and occasion, the language variety or dialect, and the interpersonal relationship between speaker and listener influence message interpretation and response.

In addition, some understandings of talk are influenced by a speaker's gender or ethnicity. For example, researchers have found that when the same message is delivered in much the same manner by a woman or by a man, listeners interpret it quite differently, in part because they expect women and men to use different styles of talk and to have knowledge of different subjects.[3] Thomas Kochman has pointed out how the different nonverbal vocal cues that working-class African Americans and middle-class whites use to express the same emotion (e.g., sincerity or anger) can create diametrically opposed attributions regarding a speaker's intentions.[4] Each ethnic cultural group has come to expect the expression of various emotions or attitudes to sound a certain way. Thus, sincerity, when uttered in a high-keyed, dynamic, working-class black style, may sound like anger to middle-class whites. And when uttered in a low-keyed, non-dynamic, middle-class white style, it may sound like disinterest or deceit to working-class blacks. Because expectations for talk are culturally learned and seldom violated by speakers *within* a cultural group, they appear to be natural or normal to the members of that group. Misunderstanding and conflict can result when cultural expectations for how to express specific attitudes and emotions are violated.

By asking African American women to describe their communication style ("black women's talk" or "talking like a black woman") as well as that of white women ("white women's talk" or "talking like a white woman"), I endeavored to discover some of their expectations for talk.[5] Below are examples of these African American women's most frequent responses:

Black Women's Talk Is:

- standing behind what you say, not being afraid to speak your mind
- speaking with a strong sense of self-esteem
- speaking out; talking about what's on your mind
- getting down to the heart of the matter
- speaking with authority, intelligence, and common sense
- being very sure of oneself
- being very distinguished and educated
- reflecting black experience as seen by a black woman in a white patriarchal society

White Women's Talk Is:

- friendly (with an air of phoniness)
- arrogant
- know-it-all
- talking as if they think they're better than the average person
- mainly dealing with trivia
- talking proper about nothing
- weak, "air-headish"
- silly but educated
- illustrating fragility; seemingly dependent and helpless
- passive, submissive, delicate

I asked a comparable group of white women to describe their talk and that of black women. Here are their most frequent responses:

Black Women's Talk Is:

- using black dialect
- saying things like "young 'uns," "yous," "wif," and "wich you"
- using jive terms

White Women's Talk Is:

- all kinds of speech patterns
- distinct pronunciation
- using the appropriate words for the appropriate situations
- talking in a typical British-American language with no necessary accent and limited to "acceptable" middle-class women's topics

The above suggests that African American and white women hear very different things. Not only does each list contain positive descriptions of the group's own talk and negative descriptions of the other group's talk, but each focuses on different features. African American women concentrate on both their own and white women's interpersonal skills, strategies, and attributes. They see themselves as open, forthright, intelligent speakers and white women as duplicitous, arrogant, and frivolous. White women, on the other hand, concentrate their descriptions on language style—vocabulary, grammar, pronunciation—describing themselves as standard or correct and African American women as nonstandard, incorrect, or deviant.

Because they concentrated on language style, white women described only those African American women who use African-based black English as "talking like a black woman." Their descriptions suggest that black women who use General American Speech, the prestige variety of language in the U.S.,[6] are "talking white" (or talking "normally"). In contrast, African American women described themselves as speaking in "black women's talk" whenever they used particular interpersonal strategies (e.g., "standing behind what you say"; "getting down to the heart of the matter"), communication that is independent of language variety.

One reason why African American women perceived "black women's talk" as independent of language variety may be that many of us are bistylistic (able to speak two language varieties) while most white women are relatively monostylistic. College-educated, middle-class women who grew up and learned to speak in predominantly African American communities usually have a command of both Black English and General American Speech. Those of us who are bistylistic speakers switch language varieties to some extent[7] according to situations and conversational partners, but we do not feel that we shed our ethnic cultural identity when we use General American Speech. Barbara Smith describes black women's perspective on their two speaking styles in this way:

> Now, I don't think this is about acting white in a white context. It's about one, a lack of inspiration. Because the way you act with black people is because they inspire the behavior. And I *do* mean inspire … [W]hen you are in a white context, you think, 'Well, why bother? Why waste your time?' if what you're trying to do is get things across and communicate and what-have-you, *you talk in your second language.*[8]

In describing their style, African American women were able to look beneath the surface features of language choice and concentrate on underlying interpersonal skills and strategies. White women, unfamiliar with how language and interpersonal interaction work in black communities, defined only that black women's talk most different from their own in vocabulary, pronunciation, and grammar as "black."

Perhaps African American women's greater awareness of differences in language and style accounts for the final difference in the lists above. White women tended to describe their own talk as normal or universal ("all kinds of speech patterns") and African American women's talk as deviant or limited. But African American women described both their own and white women's talk as particular speaking styles.

The attention to different aspects of talk may be one reason why mutually satisfying dialogue between the two groups is often difficult. For example, researchers have noted the high value African American women place on talk that is forthright, sincere, and authentic, as did the women who responded to my questionnaire (e.g., "not being afraid to speak your mind").[9] This may sometimes conflict with the high value white women have been taught to place on politeness and propriety in speech, as several white respondents to the questionnaire indicated (e.g., "using appropriate words for the … situation").[10] Thus, white women may sound "phony" to black women because they have learned to be more concerned about being proper and polite than "getting down to the heart of the matter."

HOWEVER, THERE ARE EXCEPTIONS

The picture of black and white women's conversations painted here may seem particularly gloomy. The unequal power relationships that generally define the places of blacks and whites in the U.S. social order continue to intrude on our everyday interpersonal encounters. Our perceptions of one another as communicators are often riddled with stereotypes and misattributions. And yet open, satisfying conversations between African American and white women do occur; many black and white women are amicable colleagues and close friends.[11] As an African American woman who has been a student or professor at predominantly white universities for almost 30 years, I have many white women colleagues whose conversation I enjoy and a few friends whom I can count on for good talk. Even the graduate student whose stinging criticism of conversations with white women peers is quoted at the beginning of this essay admitted that "there are exceptions."

What is the nature of those exceptions? What communicative acts enable African American women to perceive white women's talk as authentic rather than "phony"? This is a complex question for which there may be as many answers as there are black women speakers (or as there are black and white women conversational partners). I would like to briefly suggest a response gleaned from my own interracial relationships and those of the members of my large network of African American women friends, relatives, students, and acquaintances.[12] I have chosen to phrase my response by offering three statements that a white woman who wants to treat black women with respect and friendship should never utter: (1) "I never even notice that you're black"; (2) "You're different from most black people"; (3) "I understand what you're going through as a black woman, because . . . "

(1) "I Never Even Notice . . ."

The first statement sometimes comes as "We're all the same, really—just people." It expresses what I have come to call "the myth of generically packaged people." It is based on the incorrect assumption that cultural, sexual, or generational differences do not result in different social experiences and different interpretations of shared experiences.

Although intended to be nonracist, Statement 1 actually denies the uniqueness of black women's history and contemporary experiences. It suggests that the speaker regards blackness as something negative, a problem that one "can't help" and, therefore, as something that one's white friends should overlook. It denies the possibility that blackness could be something to be valued, even celebrated. Yet many black women view our blackness as a source of pride, not only because of the many accomplished African American women and men who have overcome racism to make significant contributions, but also because of our knowledge of how our personal histories have been influenced by our blackness.

In addition, as one white woman scholar has noted, when a white woman says, "We're all alike ...," she usually means, "I can see how *you* (a black woman) are like *me* (a white woman)"; she does not mean, "I can see how *I* am like *you*."[13] In other words, "just people" means "just *white* people"—that is, people who are culturally and behaviorally similar to me, just people who share my values and beliefs, just people who do not make me aware that they are culturally or historically different and who do not insist that I honor and respect their way of being human. It is an ethnocentric statement.

Despite the nonracist intentions of the white women whom I have heard utter "I never even notice...," I interpret it as blatantly racist. It erases my ethnic cultural experience (a part of who I am), redefines it in white women's terms.

(2) "You're Different ..."

This statement is closely related to the first; I see it as an effort to subtract the blackness from the woman. Sometimes the statement precedes other negative or stereotypical statements about black people ("The black girls I went to high school with in South Georgia...," "Those black women on welfare ..."). It indicates that the speaker perceives there to be "acceptable" and "unacceptable" black women or some groups of black women whom it is okay to hate.

Although I am anxious for white women to see that there is diversity among African American women, and although some African American women desire to separate themselves from elements of our community that they (and whites) perceive as undesirable, I believe that few of us fail to see the racism lurking behind this "divide and conquer" statement. I am different from the poor black woman on welfare; I have a different personal history, more education, the ability to provide a better lifestyle and better life-chances for my son. But I am also the same as her; we share an ethnic cultural history (in Africa and the U.S.), and we share a life-long struggle with both racism and sexism. When I hear "You're different ...," I always wonder, "If I can respect and accept white women's differences from me, why can't they respect and accept my differences from them?"

(3) "I Understand Your Experience as a Black Woman Because ..."

I have heard this sentence completed in numerous, sometimes bizarre, ways, from "because sexism is just as bad as racism" to "because I watch 'The Cosby Show,'" to "because I'm also a member of a minority group. I'm Jewish ... Italian ... overweight...."

The speaker here may intend to indicate her effort to gain knowledge of my cultural group or to share her own experiences with prejudice. I would never want to thwart her efforts or to trivialize such experiences. Yet I hear in such statements examples of the arrogance perceived by the black women who described "white women's talk" in the lists above. Similar experiences should not be confused with the same experience; my experience of prejudice is erased when you identify it as "the same" as yours. In addition, there are no shortcuts to interracial relationships, no vicarious ways to learn how to relate to the people of another culture (e.g., through reading or watching television). Only actual contact with individuals over an extended period of time begins to build interracial understanding.

I believe that "I understand your experience as a black woman because …" represents white women's attempt to express solidarity with African American women, perhaps motivated by the assumption that, before we can begin a friendship, we expect them to understand our life experiences in the way they understand their own. I make no such assumption about my white women friends, and I think they make no comparable assumption about me. There is much about white women's life experiences and perspectives that I may know about, but will never fully understand. Whether my friend is black or white, I do not presume to understand all, just to respect all.

The above three statements are words I have never heard from white women whom I count among my friends. Rather than treating our ethnic cultural differences as barriers to be feared or erased before true friendship can emerge, they embrace them as features that enrich and enliven our relationships.

REVIEW QUESTIONS

1. What does "egalitarian" mean? What are the main characteristics of egalitarian communication?
2. Give a specific example of an expression of *sincerity* in a "working-class black style" that is likely to be heard as *anger* by a white listener.
3. What is General American Speech?
4. What does Houston mean when she notes that many African American women are "bistylistic"?

PROBES

1. When describing communication differences, black women in Houston's survey focused on interpersonal skills and strategies while white women concentrated on vocabulary, grammar, and pronunciation. How do you explain this difference? What cultural barriers might this difference help intensify?
2. If General American Speech is the "second language" of many black women, how might this affect their communicating?
3. What do you believe are the differences between communicating "appropriately" and communicating in a "phony" way? How might this particular cultural difference between black and white women be bridged?

4. Explain how the statement "We're all the same really—just people" can be interpreted to be insensitive or even racist.
5. How does the statement "You're different from most black people" deny African American diversity?
6. "I understand your experience as a black woman because ..." is an attempt to establish solidarity that fails, according to Houston. Why? Explain her alternative to solidarity.

NOTES

1. Gwendolyn Etter-Lewis. (1991). Standing up and speaking out: African American women's narrative legacy, *Discourse and Society, II,* pp. 426–27.
2. Essed, p. 144.
3. Barrie Thorne, Cheris Kramerae, and Nancy Henley. (1983). Language, gender, and society: Opening a second decade of research, in their *Language, Gender, and Society,* pp. 7–24. Rowley, Mass.
4. Thomas Kochman. (1981). Classroom modalities, in *Black and White: Styles in Conflict.* Urbana: University of Illinois Press.
5. One hundred thirty-five African American women (professionals, undergraduate, and graduate students) responded in writing to an open-ended questionnaire in which they freely described the talk of several social groups, including their own. A comparable group of 100 white women also responded to the questionnaire. Initial findings were reported in Marsha Houston (Stanback) and Carol Roach, "Sisters under the Skin: Southern Black and White Women's Communication," and Marsha Houston, "Listening to Ourselves: African-American Women's Perspectives on Their Communication Style," both papers presented to the Southern States Communication Association, 1987 and 1992 respectively.
6. The speaking style I refer to as "General American Speech" others sometimes call "Standard English." I prefer the former term because it connotes the way of speaking (rather than writing) English that is accorded preference and prestige in the United States; thus, "General American Speech" is both a more communicatively and culturally accurate term than "Standard English."
7. Some black women change only their intonation patterns, and not their grammar or vocabulary, when they "switch" to a more black style. See discussions of the "levels" of Black English speech in Mary R. Hoover. (1978). Community attitudes toward black English. *Language in Society,* 7, pp. 65–87.
8. Barbara Smith and Beverly Smith. (1983). Across the kitchen table: A sister to sister conversation, in *This Bridge Called My Back: Writings by Radical Women of Color,* p. 119. (eds.) Cherrie Moraga and Gloria Anzaldua. New York: Kitchen Table/Women of Color Press.

9. Anita K. Foeman and Gary Pressley. (1989). Ethnic culture and corporate culture: Using black styles in organizations, *Communication Quarterly*, 33, pp. 293–307; and Michael Hecht, Sidney Ribeau, and J. K. Alberts. (1989). An Afro-American perspective on interethnic communication, *Communication Monographs*, 56, pp. 385–410.
10. Robin Lakoff. (1975). Why women are ladies, in *Language and Woman's Place*. New York: Harper & Row.
11. Mary McCullough, Women's friendships across cultures: An ethnographic study (unpublished manuscript, Temple University, 1989).
12. I admit that I chose these three statements in an "unscientific" manner, on the basis of their high experiential validity, rather than through any statistical sample. They are the statements that the women in my large network of black women friends, relatives, students, and acquaintances most often discuss as problematic in their conversations with white women; whenever I have shared my analysis of the statements with a group of black women whom I do not know (e.g., during a public speech for professional women or guest lecture at another university) they also have indicated that they hear them often and consider them insensitive.
13. Elizabeth Spelman. (1988). *Inessential Woman: Problems of Exclusion in Feminist Thought*. Boston: Beacon Press.

Talking Can Stop Hate

Akbar Ahmed

The author of this short essay, Akbar Ahmed, is a distinguished professor of Islamic Studies and International Relations at American University in Washington, DC. He has published at least two books that discuss communication between Muslims and westerners, *Islam under Seige* (2003) and *After Terror* (with Brian Forst, 2005). This short article describes part of a trip to India Ahmed took with some of his students.

The essay begins with the kind of statement that reinforces the prejudices and fears of millions of post-9/11 westerners: "The actions of Osama bin Laden, Hezbollah, Hamas, and the Taliban, even if they kill women and children, are perfectly justified in Islam." These are not the author's words; they are spoken by one of his Indian hosts, a young Muslim named Aijaz. And, Ahmed reports, "by the time we would leave Delhi, this angry man would undergo a stunning transformation." I've included this article because this transformation came about by way of interpersonal communication.

One of this article's main points is that U.S. citizens need to understand the depth and intensity of anti-American feelings throughout the world. Whether it seems justified or not,

"Talking Can Stop Hate" by Akbar Ahmed from *AARP Magazine*, March and April 2007, pp. 32–34.

Muslims feel persecuted. They wonder why the West equates Islam with terrorism, and yet these same people often equate Americans with warmongers. As Ahmed argues, "This is why we must talk."

We can reduce stereotypes and "see into the souls of others only if we take the trouble, and the risk, to visit one another." This kind of talk is vital. When westerners take this trouble and risk, they often—but not always—find Muslims and other "enemies" to be just as afraid as they are, and just as willing to work toward mutual understanding.

There are no detailed suggestions for improving intercultural communication in this essay. But there is an important message about the powerful impact of careful communicating. After he met and talked with Professor Ahmed and his students, Aijaz, the violent young man quoted at the start of this article, changed his position fundamentally. This is the kind of change that it is actually possible for dialogue to engender.

O n a bumpy van ride to Deoband, an orthodox Islamic school a few hours from Delhi, India, our host, a young man named Aijaz, is politely discussing murder. "The actions of Osama bin Laden, Hezbollah, Hamas, and the Taliban, even if they kill women and children, are perfectly justified in Islam," he tells us. His words are startling—even frightening—but this is why we are here: to talk about our differences and, in doing so, to discover our similarities. Aijaz sits in the front seat of our van, looking back at us. Bearded and bespectacled, he's wearing white linen pants with a long coat and a small white skullcap—the traditional South Asian Muslim dress. Bumping along with me are Hailey Woldt and Frankie Martin, two of my honors students from American University in Washington, D.C., where I'm the chair of Islamic Studies. They've taken time off from their academic year to come here—paying for the trip themselves and ignoring the advice of loved ones who begged them not to go.

Hailey is dressed in impeccable Muslim clothes from Pakistan: a white, loose *shalwar kameez*, and a white scarf to cover her head in the mosque. She asks Aijaz—a Muslim scholar and the author of a book, *Jihad and Terrorism*—a series of questions, but he deflects the conversation to me. An orthodox Muslim, he is honoring Hailey's status as a woman and not looking directly at her, which would be a sign of disrespect.

He won't look at me, Hailey scribbles indignantly on a note she passes to me. She is emerging as a perceptive observer of culture and custom. We would travel to nine countries in the three major regions of Islam—the Middle East, South Asia, and Far East Asia—for two months in 2006, speaking with a wide range of people, from President Pervez Musharraf of Pakistan to students and sheiks, and visiting mosques, madrassahs, campuses, and classrooms. Our goal: to change opinions and to better understand Muslim culture—and to show a side of the United States that Muslims rarely see.

Aijaz is now talking about jihad. The Prophet Muhammad defined the "greater jihad"—the term *jihad* is derived from "to strive" in Arabic—as the struggle to elevate ourselves spiritually and morally. It has *nothing* to do with violence. The "lesser jihad" is the need to defend one's family and community. In this case, too, action is limited to defense and not aggression. But shocking as it sounds to Hailey and Frankie, Aijaz justifies attacks against Israelis and Americans as self-defense.

The popularity of Aijaz's book reflects the depth of Muslim outrage around the world. Like many Muslims, Aijaz feels his way of life and his religion are facing an onslaught, militarily and culturally. For Aijaz, bin Laden and the Taliban are the true champions of Islam. And yet, by the time we would leave Delhi, this angry man would undergo a stunning transformation.

• • •

Until you've visited the Muslim world, it's hard to grasp the intensity of anti-American feelings. Many of the people we surveyed said they would prefer Saddam Hussein, the most ruthless and vile of dictators, to the Americans in Iraq. When we visited Turkey, the nation's most popular movie was *Valley of the Wolves: Iraq,* a crudely anti-American film showing a group of Turkish Rambos on a rampage against "evil" U.S. soldiers.

The complaints we heard were the same as those in Aijaz's book: Muslims feel persecuted. They see the Iraq war as an attempt to destabilize and pull apart the Middle East. They speak angrily of Muslims imprisoned at Guantánamo Bay and tortured at Abu Ghraib. They resent U.S. support of totalitarian regimes. They feel overwhelmed by Western culture.

Muslims often asked us why the West equates Islam with terrorism, yet these same people often equate Americans with warmongers. As Frankie said, in something of a revelation after an encounter with some students in northern India, "They stereotype us just as we stereotype them."

This is why we must talk. To provide new perspectives. During our trip, Frankie and Hailey were the first Americans that many people had ever met. The effect was often startling: the stereotypes about Americans were replaced by real people. I spoke often on our trip of the friendships I enjoy with Jews, Christians, and Muslims. I spoke of how inspired I am by my friend Judea Pearl, who lost his only son, reporter Daniel Pearl, in a brutal and senseless killing in Pakistan—and who has used this tragedy as a bridge to reach out to Muslims. And yet few Americans in the Muslim world go beyond their high-security walls to meet merchants or cabdrivers. Imagine the impact if a high-profile American visited an ordinary Muslim at his home. Imagine the cultural and psychological barriers that would vanish.

Think how different the Middle East might be if the Palestinians and the Israelis attempted such understanding. Once friendship develops, everything can change.

• • •

We can see into the souls of others only if we take the trouble, and the risk, to visit one another. Only then can change occur. And we saw such change on our trip: in ourselves and in others.

In Damascus, Syria, we visited Sheik Hussam Al-Din Farfour, the head of the Fatah Institute, a well-known Islamic university, to talk with him and members of his faculty. The sheik wore a white turban, and a long black robe over his large frame; he kept a well-trimmed white beard. I asked some questions about Islam, but the conversation became another tedious diatribe against the United States. As we prepared to leave, he invited us for dinner. I tried to think of an excuse for not going—without success—so we turned up at his home the next night. Many of the professors I'd met the day before were there. The sheik seated me in the place of honor in his main living room, and Hailey, who was the only woman present, sat next to me. Soon more guests began to arrive. Many wore long black robes and white turbans signifying their high religious status. What I thought was going to be a long evening took on a different feel as the guests responded to us with such warmth and hospitality.

The sheik invited his guests into the dining room. Enjoying the company and the many Arab dishes, he began to hum, closing his eyes, swaying to the rhythm he tapped on his knees. He sang about the love, beauty, and compassion of the Prophet, and soon the others in the room had the same look of serenity on their faces. It was a side of Islam that Frankie and Hailey had rarely seen on the news back home.

After dinner the sheik escorted us to the courtyard. A chilly wind blew strong as we waited for our car. The sheik, noticing Hailey shiver, sent his son into the house. The young man reappeared with a camel-colored scarf. The sheik raised the scarf, closed his eyes, and said in Arabic: "A blessing for peace and good travels. May you be protected and live a happy life."

The day before we left Damascus, he met us in private so he could give each of us presents. He gave me one of the most beautiful Korans I have ever seen, a special edition made for President Bashar al-Assad. In it he inscribed words of beauty and encouragement. Hailey was particularly moved by the gifts. "We must approach the world," she would later write, "not from the position of fear, as I had done before this trip, but from that of love and friendship. If two Americans with their professor can make such a difference, what can a whole nation do with the power of compassion and dialogue?"

• • •

No one experienced a more radical change in thinking than Aijaz, the scholar from Deoband who had so forcefully defended Osama bin Laden.

After our initial visit, Aijaz accompanied us for the next week to many of our meetings in Delhi. He had arranged some of these himself, such as a visit to the headquarters of Jamat-i-Islami, the orthodox Islamic party of South Asia. Aijaz listened to my speeches about my American friends, both Jews and Christians. At every forum, he heard me emphasize the need for dialogue and understanding as a Koranic duty. And he would have long conversations with Hailey, Frankie, and Hadia Mubarak, a Brookings Institution research assistant who had joined us. (Although Aijaz was initially reserved about speaking directly with women, he opened up to them after a few days in the field.) These were likely the first Americans he had met, and certainly the first he had spoken with for such long periods of time. He could now put a human face on the "American barbarians." Here were Americans who listened to his opinions and discussed them. And for my students, here was a thoughtful man who was not the stereotypical "Islamic extremist."

Toward the end of our visit, Aijaz approached me and said he would like to translate my book *Islam under Siege*. This was an astonishing shift for him. The book discusses the need to create trust between societies through dialogue and understanding—a far different theme than that of Aijaz's book on jihad. He could now relate to Americans and even Israelis because they were ultimately human. His anger and ignorance were checked. And by translating the book, he will spread these ideas over a vast network of madrassahs and mosques. Instead of interpreting jihad as violence, perhaps young people will see it as a peaceful movement to create understanding.

For the United States, understanding Muslims is not a luxury. It is an imperative. There is an intense debate in the Muslim world, and it is unclear which type of Islam will prevail: the more fundamentalist, aggressive type or the more moderate, compassionate type. If the U.S. can support moderate Muslims and strengthen their position, they will eventually succeed.

I came back from my travels aware that the problem may be bigger than I had thought. Yet because of the kind and concerned individuals we met, I was also hopeful. Dialogue is the hope for the future. It will make our world a better place and a safer place.

REVIEW QUESTIONS

1. Direct eye contact is a sign of respect in many Western cultures. Describe the different understanding of eye contact mentioned in this article.
2. Explain why, according to Ahmed, Muslims feel persecuted by Americans.

PROBES

1. Much of this short article is made up of stories from the author and his students' trip. What point is made by the fact that he focuses on stories?
2. Just about everybody knows that stereotyping creates problems, and yet people continue to stereotype each other. Why does this happen? What can you do to reduce stereotyping?

———

"Which Is My Good Leg?": Cultural Communication of Persons with Disabilities

Dawn O. Braithwaite

Charles A. Braithwaite

This article reminds us that intercultural communication doesn't just happen with people who are different from us in ethnicity, gender, or age. The senior author is one of the foremost authorities on communication with disabled persons. She and her spouse use specific examples and important concepts to clarify the challenges of this kind of intercultural communicating and to suggest some very important "Dos" and "Don'ts."

The essay begins with some reports from the experiences of persons with disabilities that underscore the kinds of communication difficulties they experience. This group gained significant national attention in 1990 with the passage of the Americans with Disabilities Act (ADA). Although as many as one in five people in the United States has some type of disability, this group was nearly invisible for many years. "In the past," the Braithwaites point out, "most people with disabilities were sheltered and many were institutionalized, but today they are very much a part of the American mainstream." This is another reason why it's important to learn about communicating with persons with disabilities.

The Braithwaites explain why "the distinctive verbal and nonverbal communication used by persons with disabilities creates a sense of cultural identity that constitutes a unique social reality." They also show how this cultural view helps clarify several challenges faced by communicators who are disabled. The most significant ones are challenges to relationships, and they include uncertainties, discomfort, and embarrassment of nondisabled people. People with disabilities are regularly stereotyped as strongly as are the Muslim people discussed in the previous reading.

Most disabled people see themselves as part of a minority group or a co-culture, the Braithwaites explain. Like other minorities, they have to engage in various "balancing acts" to cope with the pressures they confront. But there are also significant differences among members of this co-culture. All disabled people are not "the same," any more than all Asians or all women are the same.

The process of redefining oneself as part of a disabled culture occurs in steps or stages. *Stigma isolation* happens when a person becomes disabled. The first tendency is to focus on rehabilitation and all of the accompanying physical changes and challenges. Stage 2 is *stigma recognition*, when the person realizes that his or her life and relationships have changed dramatically. Many disabled people resist this phase and attempt to find ways to minimize the effects of their disability. *Stigma incorporation* labels that phase at which the person with a disability begins to integrate being disabled into her or his identity, recognizing both positive and negative aspects of the disability and beginning to develop coping strategies. As Christopher Reeve, an actor who played Superman and was disabled by an accident, explains, "You move from obsessing about 'Why me?' and 'It's not fair' and move into 'Well, what is the potential?'"

The article ends with a list of five "Don'ts" and five "Dos" to guide your communicating with people with disabilities. I hope you can recognize from this article that interpersonal relationships are just as possible with these people as they are with any others.

Jonathan is an articulate, intelligent, 35-year-old professional man, who has used a wheelchair since he became paraplegic when he was 20 years old. He recalls taking a nondisabled woman out to dinner at a nice restaurant. When the waitress came to take their order, she looked only at his date and asked, in a condescending tone, "and what would *he* like to eat for dinner?" At the end of the meal, the waitress presented Jonathan's date with the check and thanked her for her patronage.[1]

Kim describes her recent experience at the airport: "A lot of people always come up and ask can they push my wheelchair. And, I can do it myself. They were invading my space, concentration, doing what I wanted to do, which I enjoy doing; doing what I was doing *on my own....* And each time I said, 'No, I'm doing fine!' People looked at me like I was strange, you know, crazy or something. One person started pushing my chair anyway. I said [in an angry tone], 'Don't touch the wheelchair.' And then she just looked at me like I'd slapped her in the face."

Jeff, a nondisabled student, was working on a group project for class that included Helen, who uses a wheelchair. He related an incident that really embarrassed him. "I wasn't thinking and I said to the group, 'Let's run over to the student union and get some coffee.' I was mortified when I looked over at Helen and remembered that she can't walk. I felt like a real jerk." Helen later described the incident with Jeff, recalling:

> At yesterday's meeting, Jeff said, "Let's run over to the union" and then he looked over at me and I thought he would die. It didn't bother me at all, in fact, I use that phrase myself. I felt bad that Jeff was so embarrassed, but I didn't know what to say. Later in the group meeting I made it a point to say, "I've got to be running along now." I hope that Jeff noticed and felt OK about what he said.

Erik Weihenmayer, the blind climber who recently scaled Mt. Everest, demonstrated another example of the regular use of nondisabled language by the disabled. During an interview with Matt Lauer on NBC's *Today Show* (June 12, 2001), he remarked that he was glad to get home so that he "could *see* his family."

Although it may seem hard for some of us to believe, these scenarios represent common experiences for people with physical disabilities and are indicative of what often happens when people with disabilities and nondisabled others communicate.

The passage of the Americans with Disabilities Act (ADA), a "bill of rights" for persons with disabilities, highlighted the fact that they are now a large, vocal, and dynamic group within the United States (Braithwaite & Labrecque, 1994; Braithwaite & Thompson, 2000). Disabled people represent one group within American culture that is growing in numbers. One in five people in the United States has some type of disability, which means that people with disabilities constitute a large segment of the American population (Cunningham & Coombs, 1997; Pardeck, 1998).

There are two reasons for increases in the numbers of persons with disabilities. First, as the American population ages and has a longer life expectancy, more people will live long enough to develop age-related disabilities. Second, advances in medical technologies now allow persons with disabilities to survive life-threatening illnesses and injuries, whereas survival was not possible in earlier times. For example, when actor Christopher Reeve became quadriplegic after a horse-riding accident in May 1995, newer advances in medical technology allowed him to survive his injuries and to live with a severe disability.

In the past, most people with disabilities were sheltered and many were institutionalized, but today they are very much a part of the American mainstream. Each of us will have contact with people who have disabilities within our families, among our friends, or within the workplace. Some of us will develop disabilities ourselves. Says Marie, a college student who became paralyzed after diving into a swimming pool:

> I knew there were disabled people around, but I never thought this would happen to me. I never even *knew* a disabled person before *I* became one. If before this happened, I saw a person in a wheelchair, I would have been uncomfortable and not known what to say.

Marie's comment highlights the fact that many nondisabled people feel extremely uncomfortable interacting with disabled people. As people with disabilities continue to live, work, and study in American culture, there is a need for both nondisabled and disabled persons to know how to communicate with one another.

DISABILITY AND CULTURAL COMMUNICATION

The goal of this chapter is to focus on communication between nondisabled persons and persons with disabilities as *intercultural communication* (Carbaugh, 1990). This claim is made because, as will be demonstrated later, persons with disabilities use a distinctive speech code that implicates specific models of personhood, society, and strategic action ... that are qualitatively different from those models used by nondisabled persons. Because persons with disabilities are treated so differently in American society, distinctive meanings, rules, and speech habits develop that act as a powerful resource for creating and reinforcing perceptions of cultural differences between persons with disabilities and nondisabled persons. The distinctive verbal and nonverbal communication used by persons with disabilities creates a sense of cultural identity that constitutes a unique social reality....

CHALLENGES FOR COMMUNICATORS WHO ARE DISABLED

When we adopt a cultural view and attempt to understand the communicative challenges faced by people with disabilities, it is useful to distinguish between "disability" and "handicap." Even though people often use these two terms interchangeably in everyday conversation, their meanings are quite different. The two terms implicate different relationships between persons with disabilities and the larger society. The term *disability* describes those limitations that a person can overcome or compensate by some means. Crewe and Athelstan (1985) identified five "key life functions" that may be affected by disability: (1) mobility, (2) employment, (3) self-care, (4) social relationships, and (5) communication. Some individuals are often able to compensate for physical challenges associated with the first three key life functions through assisting devices (e.g., using a wheelchair or cane), through training (e.g., physical therapy or training on how to take care of one's personal needs), through assistance (e.g., hiring a personal care assistant), or through occupational therapy to find suitable employment.

A disability becomes a *handicap* when the physical or social environment interacts with it to impede a person in some aspect of his or her life (Crewe & Athelstan, 1985). For example, a disabled individual with paraplegia can function well in the physical environment using a wheelchair, ramps, and curb cuts, but he or she is handicapped when buildings and/or public transportation are not accessible to wheelchair users. When a society is willing and/or able to create adaptations, disabled persons have the ability to achieve personal control and lead increasingly independent lives, which is important to their self-esteem and health (Braithwaite & Harter, 2000; Cogswell, 1977; DeLoach & Greer, 1981). For people with disabilities, personal control and independence are vitally important and "maintenance of identity and self-worth are tied to the perceived ability to control the illness, minimize its intrusiveness, and be independent" (Lyons et al., 1995, p. 134). This does not mean that people with disabilities deny their physical condition, but rather that they find ways to deal with it and lead their lives.

In fact, it is important to realize that the practical and technological accommodations that are made to adapt the physical environment for people with disabilities are useful for nondisabled people as well. Most of us are unaware of just how handicapped we would be without these physical adaptations. For example, our offices are located on the upper floors of our respective office buildings. We know that stairs take up a significant amount of space in a building. Space used for the stairwell on each level takes the place of at least one office per floor. So, the most space-efficient way to get people to the second floor would be a climbing rope, which would necessitate only a relatively small opening on each floor; however, very few of us could climb a rope to reach our offices on the second story, so we would be handicapped without stairs or elevators. When a student is walking with a heavy load of library books, automatic door openers, ramps, curb cuts, elevators, and larger doorways become important environmental adaptations that everyone can use and appreciate. Physical limitations become handicaps for all of us when the physical environment cannot be adapted to preempt our shortcomings.

Challenges to Relationships of People with Disabilities

Although it is possible to identify and to cope with physical challenges associated with mobility, self-care, and employment, the two key life functions of social relationships and communication are often much more formidable. It is less difficult to detect and correct physical barriers than it is to deal with the insidious social barriers facing people with disabilities. Coleman and DePaulo (1991) would label these social barriers as "psychological disabling," which is even more common in Western culture where "much value is placed on physical bodies and physical attractiveness" (p. 64).

When people with disabilities begin relationships with nondisabled people, the challenges associated with forming any new relationship are greater. For nondisabled people, this may be caused by a lack of experience interacting with people who are disabled. This leads to high uncertainty about how to talk with a person who is disabled. The nondisabled person feels uncertain about what to say or how to act because he or she is afraid of saying or doing the wrong thing or of hurting the feelings of the person with the disability, much like Jeff did with his group member, Helen, in the example at the beginning of this [essay]. As a result, people may feel overly self-conscious and their actions may be constrained, self-controlled, and rigid because they feel uncomfortable and uncertain (Belgrave & Mills, 1981; Braithwaite 1990; Dahnke, 1983; Higgins, 1992). The nondisabled person may try to communicate appropriately, however, "Wishing to act in a way acceptable to those with disabilities, they may unknowingly act offensively, patronizing disabled people with unwanted sympathy" (Higgins, 1992, p. 105).

Interestingly, researchers have found that the type of disability a person possesses does not change the way nondisabled persons react to them (Fichten et al., 1991). So, high levels of uncertainty can negatively affect interaction and relationship development between people. It becomes easier to avoid that person rather than deal with not knowing what to do or say. Although Uncertainty Reduction Theory can be overly simplistic, especially when applied to ongoing relationships, it can help us understand some of the initial discomfort nondisabled people may have when interacting with a stranger or early acquaintance who is disabled.

Even when a nondisabled person tries to "say the right thing," wanting to communicate acceptance to the person with the disability, his or her nonverbal behavior may communicate rejection and avoidance (Thompson, 1982). For example, people with disabilities have observed that many nondisabled persons may keep a greater physical distance, avoid eye contact, avoid mentioning the disability, or cut the conversation short (Braithwaite, 1990, 1991, 1996). In this case, a person's disability becomes a handicap in the social environment because it can block the development of a relationship with a nondisabled person, who finds the interaction too uncomfortable. In all, nondisabled people hold many stereotypes of people from the disabled culture. Coleman and DePaulo (1991) discuss some of these stereotypes concerning disabled people:

> For example they often perceive them as dependent, socially introverted, emotionally unstable, depressed, hypersensitive, and easily offended, especially with regard to their disability. In addition, disabled people are often presumed to differ from nondisabled people in moral character, social skills, and political orientation. (p. 69)

Our long experience talking with nondisabled people about interacting with persons with disabilities has shown us that many nondisabled people find the prospect of these interactions uncomfortable. They tell us they are afraid of saying or doing the wrong thing and embarrassing or hurting the person who is disabled. In addition, nondisabled persons often find themselves with conflicting advice concerning what is expected of them or how to act. On the one hand, they have been taught to "help the handicapped" and, on the other hand, they were told to treat all people equally. Americans usually conceptualize persons as "individuals" who "have rights" and "make their own choices" (Carbaugh, 1988). When nondisabled persons encounter a person with a disability, however, this model of personhood creates a serious dilemma. For example, should one help a person with a disability open a door or try to help them up if they fall? Nondisabled persons greatly fear saying the wrong thing, such as "See you later!" to a blind person or "Why don't you run by the store on your way home?" to a person using a wheelchair. In the end, it simply seems to be easier to avoid situations where one might have to interact with a disabled person rather than face feelings of discomfort and uncertainty.

It should not be surprising to learn that most people with disabilities are well aware of these feelings and fears many nondisabled persons have. In fact, in research interviews, people with disabilities reveal that they believe they "can just tell" who is uncomfortable around them or not. They are able to describe in great detail both the verbal and nonverbal signals of discomfort and avoidance nondisabled persons portray that we described previously (Braithwaite, 1990, 1996). People with disabilities report that when they meet nondisabled persons, they would hope to get the discomfort "out of the way," and they want the nondisabled person to treat them as a "person like anyone else," rather than focus solely on their disability (Braithwaite, 1991, 1996). Most often they develop ways of communicating that allow them to have their needs met and, if possible, help reduce the uncertainty and discomfort of the nondisabled person (Braithwaite & Eckstein, 2000). For example, two men who are wheelchair users described how they avoid situations where they need to ask strangers for help getting out of their van in a parking lot:

> Well, I have a mobile phone.... I will call into the store and let the store manager or whoever know, "Hey, we're in a white minivan and if you look out your window, you can see us! We're two guys in wheelchairs, can you come out and help us get out of the van?"

These men described how they plan ahead to avoid putting nondisabled strangers in potentially uncomfortable communication situations....

Redefining the Self as Part of the Disabled Culture

Most disabled people see themselves as part of a minority group or a co-culture. For some of the interviewees, this definition crosses disability lines; that is, their definition of "disabled" includes all those who have disabilities. For others, the definition is not as broad; when they think of disability they are thinking about others with the same type of disability they have. For example, some of the people with mobility-related disabilities also talked about blind and deaf people when they discussed disability, whereas others talked only about other wheelchair users. However narrowly or broadly they defined it, however, many do see themselves as part of a minority culture. For example, one of the interviewees described that being disabled "is like *West Side Story*. Tony and Maria; white and Puerto Rican. They were afraid of each other; ignorant of each others' cultures. People are people." Another man explained his view:

> First of all, I belong to a subculture (of disability) because of the way I have to deal with things, being in the medical system, welfare. There is the subculture.... I keep one foot in the nondisabled culture and one foot in my own culture. One of the reasons I do that is so that I don't go nuts.

This man's description of the "balancing act" between cultures demonstrates that membership in the disabled culture has several similarities to the experiences of other American cultural groups. Many of the interviewees have likened their own experiences to those of other cultural groups, particularly to the experiences of American people of color. Interviewees described the loss of status and power that comes from being disabled, and they expressed that they believe many people were uncomfortable with them simply because they are different.

When taking a cultural view, it is important to recognize that not everyone comes to the culture the same way. Some people are born with disabilities and others acquire them later. For those people who are not born with a disability, membership in the culture is a process that emerges over time. For some, the process is an incremental one, as in the case of a person with a degenerative disease like multiple sclerosis that develops over many years. For a person who has a sudden-onset disability, such as breaking one's neck in an accident and "waking up as quadriplegic," moving from the majority (a "normal" person) to the minority (a person who is disabled) may happen in a matter of seconds. This sudden transition into the disabled culture presents many significant challenges of redefinition and readjustment in all facets of an individual's life (Braithwaite, 1990, 1996; Goffman, 1963).

If disability is a culture, when does one become part of that culture? Even though a person is physically disabled, how they redefine themselves, from "normal" or nondisabled to disabled, is a process that develops over time. It is important to understand that becoming physically disabled does not mean that one immediately has an awareness of being part of the disabled culture (Braithwaite, 1990, 1996). In fact, for most people, adjusting to disability happens in a series of stages or phases (Braithwaite, 1990; DeLoach & Greer, 1981; Padden & Humphries, 1988). DeLoach and Greer (1981) described three phases of an individual's adjustment to disability: stigma isolation, stigma recognition, and stigma incorporation. Their model helps us understand what is occurring in the process of adjustment to disability as acculturation. During this process, persons with disabilities progress from the onset of their disability to membership in the disabled culture.

The first phase, *stigma isolation,* occurs upon becoming disabled. At this time, individuals focus on rehabilitation and all of the physical changes and challenges they are experiencing. It is likely that they have not yet noticed the changes in their social relationships and communication with nondisabled others.

The second phase, *stigma recognition,* occurs when people who are disabled realize that their life and relationships have changed dramatically and they try to find ways to minimize the effects of their disability. They may try to return to normal routines and old relationships. This can be a frustrating phase because things have often changed more than the disabled people first realize. Especially when trying to reestablish old relationships, newly disabled people may find that their old friends are no longer comfortable with them or that, without shared activities, the friendships may lapse. At this point, people who are disabled start to become aware that they are now interacting as a member of a different culture than they were before, and they begin to assimilate the new culture into their identity and behavior (Braithwaite, 1990, 1996).

This begins the third phase, what DeLoach and Greer (1981) call *stigma incorporation.* At this point, people with a disability begin to integrate being disabled into their identity, their definition of self. They can see both the positive and negative aspects of being disabled and begin to develop ways to overcome and cope with the negative aspects of disability (DeLoach & Greer, 1981). In this stage of adjustment, people with disabilities develop ways of behaving and communicating so they are able to successfully function in the nondisabled culture (Braithwaite, 1990, 1996). This is what Morse and Johnson (1991) call "regaining wellness," when newly disabled individuals begin to take back control of their own lives and relationships, to live as independently as possible, and to adapt to new ways of doing things in their lives. At this point, they are able to develop ways of communicating with nondisabled others that help them live successfully as part of the disabled and nondisabled culture simultaneously (Braithwaite, 1990, 1991, 1996; Braithwaite & Labrecque, 1994; Emry & Wiseman, 1987) or what disability researcher Susan Fox has labeled as interability, intergroup communication (see Fox et al., 2000).

In this phase, then, persons with disabilities incorporate the role of disability into their identity and into their life. One man said: "You're the same person you were. You just don't do the same things you did before." Another put it this way: "If anyone refers to me as an amputee, that is guaranteed to get me madder than hell! I don't deny the leg amputation, but I am ME. I am a whole person. ONE." During this phase, people can come to terms with both the negative and positive changes in their lives. One woman expressed:

> I find myself telling people that this has been the worst thing that has happened to me. It has also been one of the best things. It forced me to examine what I felt about myself.... my confidence is grounded in me, not in other people. As a woman, I am not as dependent on clothes, measurements, but what's inside me.

Christopher Reeve demonstrated the concept of stigma incorporation in an interview with Barbara Walters, four months after his devastating accident:

> You also gradually discover, as I'm discovering, that your body is not you. The mind and the spirit must take over. And that's the challenge as you move from obsessing about "Why me?" and "It's not fair" and move into "Well, what is the potential?" And, now, four months down the line I see opportunities and potential I wasn't capable of seeing back in Virginia in June ... genuine joy and being alive means more. Every moment is more intense than it ever was.

We can see in this example that stigma incorporation, becoming part of the disabled culture, is a process that develops over time.

REDEFINING DISABILITY WITHIN NONDISABLED CULTURE

Finally, as people with disabilities redefine themselves as members of a culture, and as they redefine what it means to have a disabling condition, they are also concerned with trying to change the view of disability within the larger culture (Braithwaite, 1990, 1996).... Most people with disabilities view themselves as public educators on disability issues. People told stories about taking the time to educate children and adults on what it means to be disabled. They are actively working to change the view of themselves as helpless, as victims, or ill and the ensuing treatment such a view brings. One wheelchair user said:

> People do not consider you, they consider the chair first. I was in a store with my purchases on my lap and money on my lap. The clerk looked at my companion and not at me and said, "Cash or charge?"

This incident with the clerk is a story heard from *every* person interviewed in some form or another, just as it happened to Jonathan and his date at the beginning of this [reading]. One woman, who had multiple sclerosis and uses a wheelchair, told of shopping for lingerie with her husband accompanying her. When they were in front of the lingerie counter, the clerk repeatedly talked only to her husband saying, "And what size does she want?" The woman told her the size and the clerk looked at the husband and said, "And what color does she want?"

Persons with disabilities recognize that nondisabled persons often see them as disabled first and as a person second (if at all). The most common theme expressed by people with disabilities in all of the interviews is that they want to be *treated as a person first*. One man explained what he thought was important to remember: "A lot of people think that handicapped people are 'less than' and I find that it's not true at all.... Abling people, giving them their power back, empowering them." The interviewees rejected those things that would not lead to being seen as persons. A man with muscular dystrophy talked about the popular Labor Day telethon:

> I do not believe in those goddamned telethons ... they're horrible, absolutely horrible. They get into the self-pity, you know, and disabled folk do not need that. Hit people in terms of their attitudes, then try to deal with and process their feelings. And the telethons just go for the heart and leave it there.

One man suggested what he thought was a more useful approach:

> What I am concerned with is anything that can do away with the "us" versus "them" distinction. Well, you and I are anatomically different, but we're two human beings! And, at the point we can sit down and communicate eyeball to eyeball, the quicker you do that, the better!

Individually and collectively, people with disabilities do identify themselves as part of a culture. They are involved in a process of redefinition of themselves, and of disability. They desire to help nondisabled people internalize a redefinition of people of the disabled culture as "persons first."

CONCLUSION

The research we have discussed highlights the usefulness of viewing disability from a cultural perspective. People with disabilities do recognize themselves as part of a culture, and viewing communication and relationships from this perspective sheds new light on the communication challenges that exist. Some time ago, Emry and Wiseman (1987) first argued for the usefulness of intercultural training about disability issues. They call for unfreezing old attitudes about disability and refreezing new ones. Clearly, the interviews indicate that people who have disabilities would seem to agree....

We hope that you will be able to understand and apply intercultural communication concepts and skills and be able to adapt that knowledge to communicating with persons in the disabled culture. Finally, we believe that people with disabilities themselves will better understand their own experience if they study intercultural communication and come to understand the cultural aspects of disability.

For nondisabled persons who communicate with persons who are disabled, we suggest that taking an intercultural perspective leads to the following proscriptions and prescriptions:

Do Not:

- *Avoid* communication with people who are disabled simply because you are uncomfortable or unsure.
- *Assume* people with disabilities cannot speak for themselves or do things for themselves.
- *Force* your help on people with disabilities.
- *Use terms* like "handicapped," "physically challenged," "crippled," "victim," and so on unless requested to do so by people with disabilities.
- *Assume* that a disability defines who a person is.

Do:

- *Remember* that people with disabilities have experienced others' discomfort before and likely understand how you might be feeling.
- *Assume* people with a disability can do something unless they communicate otherwise.
- *Let people with disabilities tell you* if they want something, what they want, and when they want it. If a person with a disability refuses your help, don't go ahead and help anyway.
- *Use terms* like "people with disabilities" rather than "disabled people." The goal is to stress the *person first,* before the disability.
- *Treat* people with disabilities as *persons first,* recognizing that you are not dealing with a disabled person but with *a person* who *has* a disability. This means actively seeking the humanity of the person you are speaking with and focusing on individual characteristics instead of superficial physical appearance. Without diminishing the significance of a person's physical disability, make a real effort to focus on the many other aspects of that person as you communicate.

REVIEW QUESTIONS

1. Describe the two reasons the Braithwaites give for the increase in the number of persons with disabilities.
2. Explain what justifies the decision to treat persons with disabilities as a *cultural* group.
3. Explain the difference between a "disability" and a "handicap."
4. What is the primary relationship challenge that is faced by people with disabilities?
5. Explain the "balancing act" that many disabled people need to maintain.
6. Describe *stigma isolation, stigma recognition,* and *stigma incorporation.*

PROBES

1. How comfortable are you when communicating with a person with an obvious disability? If you are quite comfortable, how might you help others feel that way? If you are uncomfortable, what might you do to become less so?
2. If you are a nondisabled person, you might want to "say the right thing" but still end up communicating awkwardly with a person with a disability. What might you do to address this problem?
3. Disabled people strongly desire to be treated as a person first, not primarily as a disabled person. How can you support this desire in your own communicating with people with disabilities?

NOTE

1. The quotes and anecdotes in this chapter come from in-depth interviews with people who have visible physical disabilities. The names of the participants in these interviews have been changed to protect their privacy.

REFERENCES

Belgrave, F. Z., & Mills, J. (1981). Effect upon desire for social interaction with a physically disabled person of mentioning the disability in different contexts. *Journal of Applied Social Psychology, 11,* 44–57.

Braithwaite, D. O. (1990). From majority to minority: An analysis of cultural change from nondisabled to disabled. *International Journal of Intercultural Relations, 14,* 465–483.

Braithwaite, D. O. (1991). "Just how much did that wheelchair cost?": Management of privacy boundaries by persons with disabilities. *Western Journal of Speech Communication, 55,* 254–274.

Braithwaite, D. O. (1996). "Persons first": Expanding communicative choices by persons with disabilities. In E. B. Ray (Ed.), *Communication and disenfranchisement: Social health issues and implications* (pp. 449–464). Mahwah, NJ: Lawrence Erlbaum.

Braithwaite, D. O., & Eckstein, N. (2000, November). Reconceptualizing supportive interactions: How persons with disabilities communicatively manage assistance. Presented to the National Communication Association, Seattle, WA.

Braithwaite, D. O., & Labrecque, D. (1994). Responding to the Americans with Disabilities Act: Contributions of interpersonal communication research and training. *Journal of Applied Communication, 22,* 287–294.

Braithwaite, D. O., & Harter, L. (2000). Communication and the management of dialectical tensions in the personal relationships of people with disabilities. In D. O. Braithwaite & T. L. Thompson (Eds.), *Handbook of communication and people with disabilities. Research and application* (pp. 17–36). Mahwah, NJ: Lawrence Erlbaum.

Braithwaite, D. O., & Thompson, T. L. (Eds). (2000). *Handbook of communication and people with disabilities: Research and application.* Mahwah, NJ: Lawrence Erlbaum.

Carbaugh, D. (1988). *Talking American.* Norwood, NJ: Ablex.

Carbaugh, D. (Ed.). (1990). *Cultural communication and intercultural contact.* Hillsdale, NJ: Lawrence Erlbaum.

Cogswell, Betty E. (1977). Self-socialization: Readjustments of paraplegics in the community. In R. P. Marinelli & A. E. Dell Orto (Eds.), *The psychological impact of physical disability* (pp. 151–159). New York: Springer.

Coleman, L. M., & DePaulo, B. M. (1991). Uncovering the human spirit: Moving beyond disability and "missed" communications. In N. Coupland, H. Giles, & J. M. Wiemann, (Eds.), *Miscommunication and problematic talk* (pp. 61–84). Newbury Park, CA: Sage.

Covert, A. L., & Smith, J. W. (2000). What is reasonable: workplace communication and people who are disabled. In D. O. Braithwaite & T. L. Thompson (Eds.), *Handbook of communication and people with disabilities: Research and application* (pp. 141–158). Mahwah, NJ: Lawrence Erlbaum.

Crewe, N., & Athelstan, G. (1985). *Social and psychological aspects of physical disability.* Minneapolis: University of Minnesota, Department of Independent Study and University Resources.

Cunningham, C., & Coombs, N. (1997). *Information access and adaptive technology.* Phoenix: Oryx Press.

Dahnke, G. L. (1983). Communication and handicapped and nonhandicapped persons: Toward a deductive theory. In M. Burgoon (Ed.), *Communication Yearbook 6* (pp. 92–135). Beverly Hills, CA: Sage.

DeLoach, C., & Greer, B. G. (1981). *Adjustment to severe physical disability. A metamorphosis.* New York: McGraw-Hill.

Emry, R., & Wiseman, R. L. (1987). An intercultural understanding of nondisabled and disabled persons' communication. *International Journal of Intercultural Relations, 11,* 7–27.

Fichten, C. S., Robillard, K., Tagalakis, V., & Amsel, R. (1991). Casual interaction between college students with various disabilities and their nondisabled peers: The internal dialogue. *Rehabilitation Psychology, 36,* 3–20.

Fox, S. A., Giles, H., Orbe, M., & Bourhis, R. (2000). Interability communication: Theoretical perspectives. In Braithwaite, D. O., & Thompson, T. L. (Eds). *Handbook of communication and people with disabilities: Research and application* (pp. 193–222). Mahwah, NJ: Lawrence Erlbaum.

Goffman, E. (1963). *Stigma: Notes on the management of spoiled identity.* New York: Simon & Schuster.

Herold, K. P. (2000). Communication strategies in employment interviews for applicants with disabilities. In Braithwaite, D. O., & Thompson, T. L. (Eds).

Handbook of communication and people with disabilities: Research and application (pp. 159–175). Mahwah, NJ: Lawrence Erlbaum.

Higgins, P. C. (1992). *Making disability: Exploring the social transformation of human variation.* Springfield, IL: Charles C Thomas.

Lyons, R. F., Sullivan, M. J. L., Ritvo, P. G., & Coyne, J. C. (1995). *Relationships in chronic illness and disability* Thousand Oaks, CA: Sage.

Morse, J. M., & Johnson, J. L. (1991). *The illness experience: Dimensions of suffering.* Newbury Park, CA: Sage.

Padden, C., & Humphries, T. (1988). *Deaf in America: Voices from a culture.* Cambridge, MA: Harvard University Press.

Pardeck, J. T. (1998). *Social work after the Americans with Disabilities Act: New challenges and opportunities for social service professionals.* Westport, CT: Auburn House.

Thompson, T. L. (1982). Disclosure as a disability-management strategy: A review and conclusions. *Communication Quarterly, 30,* 196–202.

Worley, D. W. (2000). Communication and students with disabilities on college campuses. In Braithwaite, D. O., & Thompson, T. L. (Eds). *Handbook of communication and people with disabilities: Research and application* (pp. 125–139). Mahwah, NJ: Lawrence Erlbaum.

CHAPTER 12

Promoting Dialogue

What Makes Dialogue Unique?

Daniel Yankelovich

Especially over the past few decades, many elected officials, teachers, trainers, managers, and community activists have been calling for more "dialogue." Of course, the term means different things to different people. Elected officials at national and local levels want better two-way communication with voters. Teachers on campuses across the country want less lecturing and more active involvement and open communication in their classrooms. Managers at Ford, Boeing, Intel, and hundreds of smaller companies want to replace the command-and-control hierarchy with collaborative work teams, shared power, and "management by wandering around and talking." Community activists in Boston; Fargo; Albuquerque; Cupertino; London; Jerusalem; Aalborg, Denmark; Canberra, Australia; Cape Town, South Africa; and dozens of other cities encourage people with diverse backgrounds and radically different beliefs to talk respectfully and candidly with each other, rather than trying to shout each other down. They also try to replace distorted media campaigns, polarizing rhetoric, and violence with facilitated and mediated conversations among political enemies. But although specific definitions vary, in every case, proponents of dialogue have in mind the kind of communication that's being championed throughout this book.

For example, how might people bridge cultural differences (Chapter 11)? With dialogue. What often works in conflict (Chapter 10)? Dialogue. What's often the best communication with intimate partners (Chapter 8)? Dialogue. What's one useful and helpful way to define interpersonal communication (Chapter 2)? As dialogue. So this chapter draws from and contributes to a significant movement that's underway in many countries around the world, and it also summarizes a great deal of the rest of this book.

This first essay clarifies what dialogue is and why it is important by anchoring it in the writings of Martin Buber (see Chapter 2), contrasting dialogue with debate and discussion, and describing three main features of dialogic communication. Its author, Daniel Yankelovich, founded the New York Times/Yankelovich public opinion poll in the 1970s and has been an influential observer of U.S. public life ever since. He serves on the board of directors of CBS, Qwest, and Brown University, and is founder of several organizations including Viewpoint Learning, which advances dialogue-based learning and leadership in the United States and Canada.

Yankelovich reports that he became a believer in the importance of dialogue as a result of his work as a social scientist studying public opinion. After more than 30 years of research, he and his colleagues discovered that a basic belief about democracy is untrue. Thomas Jefferson and others began the tradition of believing that a well-informed public is indispensable to the successful functioning of a democracy. This belief assumes that in a democracy people must gather information from news reports and other forms of expert opinion. But polls reveal that, even though the United States is clearly a functioning democracy, its public is ignorant of many basic facts. For example, huge majorities can't name the chief justice of the Supreme Court or their own senators. Yet, as Yankelovich notes, "on issues of fundamental importance to the future of our democracy, the public frequently arrives at judgments that are sound, considered, and sometimes profound." So how does the public get informed?

"The public, I have learned over the years, forms its judgments mainly through interactions with other people, through dialogue and discussion." This is why Yankelovich believes dialogue is so important. When the informal communication events that educate the public are mostly monologic, what Buber would call I-It relationships, citizens tend to be less satisfied and make poorer decisions. "But in the crunch, on the issues that really count, where the future of [an] institution is at stake... it is dialogue rather than factual analysis that engages [people]."

Yankelovich explains that the first essential feature of dialogue is "equality and the absence of coercive influences." Outside the dialogue itself, there may be huge differences between people anchored in status, amount of education, or types of experience. "But in the dialogue itself, equality must reign."

The second essential feature is "listening with empathy." In other writings, Yankelovich suggests that one way to initiate a dialogue, or to turn a debate or discussion in a dialogic direction, is to offer a gesture of empathy, a sincere and detailed paraphrase of the other person's perspective.

The third essential feature is "bringing assumptions into the open." Assumptions are the convictions or beliefs that can be found "behind" the statements that express opinions. They obviously vary among people, and one essential step toward dialogue is for the parties to identify and express these layered assumptions so they can be a topic of their conversation. This may not lead the parties to agreement. But the point of dialogue is not consensus but human contact, communication that embodies respect and civility.

In a sense, this reading and the others in this chapter summarize, for several contexts, the kind of communication that this entire book describes. Dialogue is not a panacea for all the world's troubles, but this kind of communicating, as Yankelovich and many others demonstrate, does have the power to transform many toxic human interactions.

On public television's *NewsHour with Jim Lehrer*, the last few minutes are often devoted to a segment the producers describe as "A Dialogue with David Gergen" in which Mr. Gergen interviews someone currently in the news. What distinguishes this segment from other television interviews is that Gergen's questions show that he has actually read the book or article the guest has written, thereby enabling him to make intelligent comments. This is a refreshing change from television as usual, but it is not "dialogue" in the sense that I and other practitioners use this term.

As I write these words, I have on my desk before me a number of books and articles with the word "dialogue" in their titles. In most of them the reader would be hard put to distinguish these so-called dialogues from other forms of conversation. There is nothing that sets them apart. Some feature intelligent and insightful exchanges of views, but, once again, dialogue is used as a generic term to describe two people talking with each other.

If you ask a half-dozen people at random what dialogue is, you will get a half-dozen different answers. Until recently, even specialists did not distinguish dialogue from plain-vanilla conversation, discussion, debate, or other forms of talking together. Here and there isolated practitioners such as Martin Buber and Hannah Arendt saw special qualities in dialogue when done properly, but the concept remained alien to mainstream American thought until the 1980s, when thinkers from a variety of fields began to rediscover its distinctive virtues.

Since then the topic of dialogue has gained astonishing momentum. In recent years more than two hundred independent community initiatives have brought groups normally isolated from one another together to address issues of concern to the community through dialogue. Organizations such as the Healthcare Forum have identified dialogue skills as essential to effective community leadership. At MIT, William N. Isaacs founded the Dialogue Project, dedicated to the practice of dialogue in the business community. There are dozens of similar projects and centers in the nation. Dialogue now crops up as an important subject in such diverse fields as leadership, management, philosophy, psychology, science, and religion.

UNSCRAMBLING THE FOUR Ds

When specialists use "dialogue" in a highly precise fashion at the same time when most people don't bother to differentiate it from general conversation, the result is semantic confusion. One is never quite sure how the word is being used or what dialogue is.

My guess is that the semantic confusion will not last long. As the idea of dialogue catches on (as it is now doing), the need to clarify its meaning will grow apparent and its distinctive character will become more widely recognized. This has happened with other specialized forms of conversation. Reflect for a moment on jury deliberations, diplomatic negotiations, psychotherapy, conflict resolution panels, T-groups, quality circles, organizational teaming, board meetings, workshops, and conferences. Initially, all of these forms of talk were launched with only a vague idea of the special purposes they could serve. Yet all have now been codified and formalized in varying degrees in the interest of capturing their unique capabilities.

This has not yet happened with dialogue. Most people continue to use the Four Ds—Dialogue, Debate, Discussion, and Deliberation—interchangeably. This habit of speech makes the skill requirements of dialogue needlessly complicated. The skills needed for dialogue are not esoteric or arcane. Indeed, most are obvious, such as learning to listen more attentively. The complication lies in the confusion that must be cleared away before the skills can be addressed and mastered. It is as if the task were to erect a tent in a part of a forest covered with underbrush, old roots, and stumps of trees. Putting up the tent may be less onerous than clearing a space for it.

AREAS OF CONVERGENCE

Fortunately, there is a great deal of agreement among practitioners on how to distinguish dialogue from other forms of conversation. The most revealing distinctions are those that contrast *dialogue* with *debate* and *discussion*. (Deliberation—the fourth "D"—is a form of thought and reflection that can take place in any kind of conversation.)

Debate

All practitioners of dialogue emphasize that debate is the opposite of dialogue. The purpose of debate is to win an argument, to vanquish an opponent. Dialogue has very different purposes. It would be inconceivable to say that someone "won" or "lost" a dialogue. In dialogue, all participants win or lose together. It defeats the idea of dialogue to conceive of winning or losing. Those who practice dialogue have come to see that the worst possible way to advance mutual understanding is to win debating points at the expense of others.

Visualize a small group of neighbors, some of whom are liberal in their politics and others who are conservative, having a conversation about improving standards for schools. The conversation starts civilly. All have children in school and know how important education is for the future of their children. As neighbors they share a number of communal concerns, education being among the most important. They are searching for answers to difficult and troublesome questions.

Just as they are beginning to develop a common understanding of the obstacles schools face, one of the liberals in the group attacks the conservatives' endorsement of vouchers for school choice on the grounds that it undermines the tradition of public education in the United States. One of the conservatives in the group then responds by attacking a variety of liberal school reforms that, she argues, have sacrificed quality of performance in search of an unattainable ideal of equality.

A tone of hostility has now crept into the conversation. Those who have been attacked grow defensive. They marshal their arguments to beat down the opposition. They have stopped listening for understanding; they are now listening to detect soft spots in the others' positions so that they can controvert them. It all happens so quickly and automatically that no one notices that there has been a shift from conversation to debate. One thing is certain: no dialogue can take place.

The accompanying table is adapted from the writings of Mark Gerzon, one of our most gifted practitioners of dialogue. It contrasts the differences between debate and dialogue and shows how practitioners distinguish between these two forms of conversation.

Discussion

That debate is the opposite of dialogue is clear. Where discussion fits in is less clear—and more important. For it is in the distinction between discussion and dialogue that the distinctive quality of dialogue is best revealed.

Debate Versus Dialogue

Debate	Dialogue
Assuming that there is a right answer and you have it	Assuming that many people have pieces of the answer and that together they can craft a solution
Combative: participants attempt to prove the other side wrong	Collaborative: participants work together toward common understanding
About winning	About exploring common ground
Listening to find flaws and make counterarguments	Listening to understand, find meaning and agreement
Defending assumptions as truth	Revealing assumptions for reevaluation
Critiquing the other side's position	Reexamining all positions
Defending one's own views against those of others	Admitting that others' thinking can improve on one's own
Searching for flaws and weaknesses in other positions	Searching for strengths and value in others' positions
Seeking a conclusion or vote that ratifies your position	Discovering new options, not seeking closure

It is useful to start with a *nondifference:* the erroneous assumption that serious conversation between two people is a dialogue but that if a larger group is involved it is a discussion. This artificial distinction mirrors a confusion about the literal meaning of the word "dialogue."

I recently came across a book titled *Carl Rogers: Dialogues*. It presents a series of conversations the eminent psychologist held with outstanding scholars, including Martin Buber. Since the word "dialogue" is featured in the book's title and since some of the world's most noted practitioners of dialogue are involved, one would expect to find genuine dialogues. Clearly, that was the message the editors conveyed in the title they chose for the book.

I found the conversations between Dr. Rogers and others interesting and provocative but did not initially see why they were called dialogues. They were largely interviews that Dr. Rogers conducted in the presence of an audience, with Rogers interpolating his point of view from time to time (like the interviews David Gergen conducts with his guests on the *NewsHour*). The clue to why they were called dialogues came at the end of Dr. Rogers's interview with Martin Buber. In his concluding remarks, the moderator, Professor of Philosophy Maurice Friedman, said to the audience, "We are deeply indebted to Dr. Rogers and Dr. Buber for a unique dialogue. It was unique in my experience … because you (the audience) took part in a sort of *triologue* and adding me, a *quadralogue*" (emphasis added).

Professor Friedman is making the common but mistaken assumption that dialogue literally means "two-sided." But dialogue has nothing to do with the number two. The word "dialogue" derives from two Greek words: *dia*, meaning "through" (as in the word "diaphanous," meaning "to show through") and *logos,* signifying "word" or "meaning." David Bohm, one of dialogue's most original practitioners, interprets its etymological roots as suggesting words and meanings flowing through from one participant to another. Emphatically, dialogue is not confined to conversations between two people. In fact, some writers on the subject believe that dialogue is best carried out in groups ranging from about a dozen to two dozen people. It is ironic to see the word "dialogue" incorrectly used in describing a conversation between Rogers and Buber, both eminent theorists of dialogue.

What, then, is the difference between dialogue and discussion? Three distinctive features of dialogue differentiate it from discussion. When all three are present, conversation is transformed into dialogue. When any one or more of the three features are absent, it is discussion or some other form of talk, but it is not dialogue.

1. Equality and the Absence of Coercive Influences   Practitioners agree that in dialogue all participants must be treated as equals. Outside the context of the dialogue, there may be large status differences. But in the dialogue itself, equality must reign. In genuine dialogue, there is no arm-twisting, no pulling of rank, no hint of sanctions for holding politically incorrect attitudes, no coercive influences of any sort, whether overt or indirect.

Subtle coercive influences are often present in discussion, and when they are they undermine equality and, hence, dialogue. The Rogers/Buber interview illustrates how nuances of inequality can creep into conversation. Carl Rogers claimed that he was able to engage his patients in genuine I-Thou dialogue because he empathized so totally with his patients' thoughts and feelings. But to the surprise of the audience, Buber rejected Rogers's inference. He pointed out that the relationship between Rogers and his patients is inherently unequal because patients come to Rogers looking for help but are, for their part, unable to offer comparable help to him. Under these conditions of inequality, Buber states, it is misleading to think that genuine dialogue can take place. What Buber calls dialogue between I and Thou cannot occur in the context of an unequal doctor-patient relationship. Therapy may be possible, but dialogue has nothing to do with therapy.

Mixing people of unequal status and authority does not necessarily preclude dialogue, but it makes it more difficult to achieve. Dialogue becomes possible only after trust has been built and the higher-ranking people have, for the occasion, removed their badges of authority and are participating as true equals. There must be mutual trust before participants of unequal status can open up honestly with one another. Buber did not maintain that Rogers could not engage in dialogue with people who happened to be his patients *outside* the therapeutic relationship (for example, on an issue of concern to the community); he simply said that dialogue was not possible within the constraints of the formal doctor-patient relationship.

People in positions of authority easily deceive themselves into thinking they are treating others as equals when they are not doing so. In the film *First Knight,*

King Arthur is presented as a person of truly noble character. He proudly displays his Round Table, designed so that it lacks any special place of privilege at the head of the table for himself. He presents himself as just another knight among knights. Yet each time a decision is made at the Round Table, it is in fact Arthur who makes it or influences it unduly. There is no ambiguity about who the boss is. The Round Table may symbolize equality of standing, but the reality is otherwise.

A round table is an apt symbol for dialogue because it implies that dialogue cannot take place at the table except among equals. But as the film (inadvertently) makes clear, it takes more than a piece of furniture to create the kind of equality needed for dialogue to flourish.

2. Listening with Empathy   Practitioners also agree that a second essential feature of dialogue is the ability of participants to respond with unreserved empathy to the views of others. In the example of neighbors discussing school standards, if both the liberals and the conservatives in the group were less eager to fight for their convictions and more eager to grasp the other's viewpoints, they might have been able to understand where their neighbors were coming from and why they felt the way they did.

The gift of empathy—the ability to think someone else's thoughts and feel someone else's feelings—is indispensable to dialogue. There can be discussion without participants responding empathically to one another, but then it is discussion, not dialogue. This is why discussion is more common than dialogue: people find it easy to express their opinions and to bat ideas back and forth with others, but most of the time they don't have either the motivation or the patience to respond empathically to opinions with which they may disagree or that they find uncongenial.

3. Bringing Assumptions into the Open   Theorists of dialogue also concur that, unlike discussion, dialogue must be concerned with bringing forth people's most deep-rooted assumptions. In dialogue, participants are encouraged to examine their own assumptions and those of other participants. And once these assumptions are in the open, they are not to be dismissed out of hand but considered with respect even when participants disagree with them.

For example, among African-American and white participants in discussions on subjects such as welfare, white participants sometimes make remarks that some of the African Americans regard as racist. Most of the time, the African-American participants remain silent and do not respond, assuming that it would be futile to do so. Sometimes, however, one says something like "That sounds like a racist comment to me." The white person who made the comment will either bridle silently and resentfully or heatedly deny any racist intent. Either way, an unresolved tension has entered the discussion.

A genuine dialogue on this same issue would unfold in a different manner. Someone might ask the African-American participants if they thought particular comments had racist overtones and why. Participants could then ponder the answers without defensiveness. Or, once the accusation of racism had been made, judgment would be suspended and the group would focus on what assumptions people were bringing to the dialogue and how they judged whether or not a comment was racist. Once such assumptions are made explicit, disagreement may still exist, but the level of tension will be reduced and there will be better mutual understanding.

David Bohm emphasizes that our most ingrained thought patterns, operating at the tacit level, create many of the obstacles that isolate us from one another. Bohm stresses the link between people's assumptions and their sense of self. He is, in effect, saying, "When your deepest-rooted assumptions about who you are and what you deem most important in life are attacked, you react as if you are being attacked personally."

Arguably, the most striking difference between discussion and dialogue is this process of bringing assumptions into the open while simultaneously suspending judgment. In discussion, participants usually stay away from people's innermost assumptions because to poke at them violates an unwritten rule of civility. If someone does raise them, they must expect to kick up a fuss or to tempt other participants to take offense or to close down and withdraw.

When in ordinary discussion sensitive assumptions are brought into the open, the atmosphere is likely to grow heated and uncomfortable. The discussion may or may not break down. It may later be recalled as a good or bad discussion, but—and this is the key point—it is not dialogue. The unique nature of dialogue requires that participants be uninhibited in bringing their own and other participants' assumptions into the open, where, within the safe confines of the dialogue, others can respond to them without challenging them or reacting to them judgmentally.

It takes practice and discipline to learn how to respond when touchy assumptions are brought into the open without feeling the need to rush to their defense and either swallow or ventilate the anger and anxiety we feel when others challenge our most cherished beliefs.

Think of assumptions as being "layered" (that is, assumptions exist behind assumptions behind assumptions). The more widely shared they are, the less subject they are to self-examination or to critique by others. Unexamined assumptions are a classic route to misunderstandings and errors of judgment. Dialogue is one of the very few methods of communication that permit people to bring them into the open and confront them in an effective manner.

REVIEW QUESTIONS

1. Explain the differences between debate and dialogue. How is dialogue different from discussion?
2. What is "empathy"?
3. Assume that you are in a conversation with someone about abortion. Write out one of the assumptions that helps ground your view of this topic. How might you orally express this assumption in a conversation with someone who disagrees with you on this topic?

PROBES

1. Look again at Martin Buber's essay in Chapter 2. Where does Buber talk about the specific suggestions that Yankelovich makes? For example, do you see the connection between Buber's treatment of "Being and Seeming" and Yankelovich's advice to "bring assumptions into the open"? What other connections do you see?
2. Candidate debates are an important part of U.S. political campaigns. What do you think Yankelovich is saying about the importance and even the wisdom of these debates?
3. Describe the connections between dialogue and trust. For example, how does dialogue depend on trust? How does it build trust? How does trust build dialogue?

NOTES

1. Synthesized and adapted from the work of the Public Conversations Project, National Study Circles Resources, The Common Enterprise, Educators for Social Responsibility and Choice Point Consulting. Prepared for the Bipartisan Congressional Retreat by Mark Gerzon.
2. Howard Kirshenbaum and Valerie Land Henderson, eds. (Boston: Houghton Mifflin Company, 1989).
3. Ibid., p. 64.
4. See David Bohm, *On Dialogue*, Lee Nichol, ed. (London and New York: Routledge, 1996).
5. Ibid., pp. 7–12.

Dialogue's Basic Tension

Karen E. Zediker and John Stewart

My colleague and friend Karen Zediker and I wrote this next selection specifically for *Bridges Not Walls*. The main ideas are taken from a journal article we published called "Dialogue as Tensional, Ethical Practice." We talk here about what we have become convinced is the main feature or characteristic of dialogue—a tension between letting another person "happen to you" while you hold your own ground in the conversation.

The first point we make is that for us, the term *dialogue* labels a particular kind or quality of communication. Dialogue is what happens between people who are connecting

---

"Dialogue's Basic Tension" excerpted from "Dialogue as Tensional, Ethical Practice" by Karen E. Zediker and John Stewart.

with each other *as persons,* as unique, reflective, choosing, valuing, thinking-and-feeling beings.

Next, the essay explains what a "tension" is. Our main point here is that there is a "both/and" quality to the experience of communicating dialogically. When you're in a tension, you feel pulled in two directions at once, *and* each pull is affected by what it's pulling against. Dialogue, we argue, is this kind of tensional event.

Then we label what we believe is dialogue's basic tension, and we describe each "moment," "pole," or "end" of this tension. "Letting the other happen to me" means being open to and actually affected by the ways that the other person is *different from you.* It doesn't take a rocket scientist to understand this idea, but it's a little strange in the Western world, because westerners are usually interested mainly in the other pole of this tension. It can take some courage and patience to let yourself be subject to someone else's influence.

"Holding your own ground" is the other pole, and it means what it sounds like. You do this when you assert your position or express your ideas. The most important point we make after we sketch these two poles is that when they are lived tensionally, *each transforms the other.* You don't just let somebody happen to you; you do that as a person who's holding your own ground. And you don't just assert your position; you do that as a person who's letting the other happen to you. In the final part of this reading, we give some concrete examples of how this tension works in order to clarify what's at stake here. One example is a story told by Martin Buber, an important writer, about dialogue. Other examples come from Karen's classes.

We hope that this brief description will clarify what you'll need to do when you want to help dialogue happen. You've undoubtedly figured out by now that there is no set recipe for dialogue. But if you can live with this tension, and if your conversation partner can, too, the chances are good that this quality of communication will happen between you.

INTRODUCTION

It's exciting and confirming for us to learn about all the different people who are writing about dialogue today and trying to help dialogue happen in organizations, communities, and families. Our approach to dialogue is similar to some of theirs, and different from others'. Historically, we've been most influenced by Martin Buber's writings, so we use the term "dialogue" to refer to a particular kind or quality of communication that happens when the people involved are present to each other as persons—as unique, reflective, choosing, valuing, thinking-and-feeling beings. So when one of us can perceive and listen to you as a person while being available as a person to you, and when you can do the same thing, then the communication between us can be called "dialogic" or "dialogue." When the opposite happens—when I am only focused on getting my own ideas out and you are not listening but "reloading"—only working out your response to my ideas—then the communication between us is "monologic" or "monologue."

One significant feature of dialogue as we understand it is tensionality. This means that dialogue is not a steady state, something that is stable and predictable. When people are in dialogue, they experience a dynamic, push-pull, both-and quality in their communication. There's more to dialogue than just this tensional quality, but we believe that it's important enough that we want to take the following pages to clarify what we mean when we say that dialogue is tensional and to explain and illustrate dialogue's most basic tension.

A dictionary or thesaurus provides two different images of tension—*anxiety* (associated with stress and strain) and *tautness* (associated with force, tightness and constriction). Most of us have experienced tension in both these senses. Some characterize tension as a struggle, being pulled from a variety of directions at once, somehow knowing that if one perspective has more pull, another will lose out. Others associate tension with a headache that grips both the base of your neck and the top of your eyebrows at the same time. Or the word "tension" makes some other people think of the rod that holds curtains in place in the shower by pushing in opposite directions against two walls. None of these images is exactly what we have in mind when we say that dialogue is tensional, but they do share some common features. When something is held in tension there are at least two points of contact, and there seems to be an inherent contradiction or push-pull set of forces.

Communication teachers Barbara Montgomery and Leslie Baxter (1998) highlight one important feature of tensionality when they talk about how communicators manage "the both/andness" of privacy and disclosure across the time line of a relationship. Montgomery and Baxter explain that usually privacy isn't the most important thing at one point and then open disclosure most important at another, but that at almost every moment in a relationship the people involved are experiencing some tension between *both* privacy *and* disclosure. Montgomery and Baxter say that this primary feature of dialogue "implicate[s] a kind of in-the-moment interactive multivocality, in which multiple points of view retain their integrity as they play off each other" (p. 160). Like the tension headache that hurts both at the base of your skull and your forehead at the same time, or the tension rod that pushes out against opposite walls and is held into place by the structure of the door or window frame, dialogic tensions are characterized by both/andness.

THE PRIMARY TENSION

Our own communication experiences have taught us that moments of dialogue emerge most often when the people involved maintain one primary tension—the one between *letting the other happen to me while holding my own ground*. We are aware of other tensions as well, including one between univocality and multivocality and another tension between theory and practice. But in our opinion, other dialogic tensions are dependent on this primary tension.

If you were to diagram this tension, it might look something like this:

Letting the other happen to me ←————→ Holding my own ground

In a few paragraphs, we'll highlight something misleading about this diagram. But first, let's clarify what this tension is by looking at its two ends.

Letting the Other Happen to Me

One moment in this dynamic—letting the other happen to me—consists of the concrete lived experience of what Buber and some other writers (e.g., Levinas, 1996) call experiencing the otherness of the Other. This means that you let someone happen to you when you allow who they are—especially their differences from you—to touch, connect with, and influence you. In his *Autobiographical Fragments*, Buber (1973)[1] reported that he recognized the basic quality of this moment when, as an 11-year-old, he cared for a "dapple-gray horse." When he was over 80 years old, he wrote,

> If I am to explain it now, beginning from the still very fresh memory of my hand, I must say that what I experienced in touch with the animal was the Other, the immense otherness of the Other, which, however, did not remain strange like the otherness of the ox and the ram, but rather let me draw near and touch it. When I stroked the mighty mane, sometimes marvelously smooth-combed, at other times just as astonishingly wild, and felt the life beneath my hand, it was as though the element of vitality itself bordered on my skin, something that was not I, was certainly not akin to me, palpably the other, not just another, really the Other itself; and yet it let me approach, confided itself to me, placed itself elementally in the relation of *Thou* and *Thou* with me. (p. 27)

In this fragment of his life, Buber provides a vivid example of letting the other happen to him. He realizes at a fundamental level that the horse is not an extension of himself, but something wholly other. Importantly, this lesson is one that Buber would have us learn about human beings as well. When we can experience other persons as unique individuals with opinions, beliefs, and values that are not simply extensions of our own, then we have the opportunity for genuine dialogue.

Another German writer named Hans-Georg Gadamer (1989) clarifies an important aspect of this first moment of this tension when he distinguishes between two German words for "experience," *Erlebnis* and *Erfahrung*. He explains that the first term labels experience that one "has" of something or someone. A person moves through life seeing, hearing, touching, tasting, and smelling things in order to grasp their meanings. So you might experience, in this *Erlebnis* sense, an encounter with a homeless person in which you could report where you saw her, what she said to you as you passed by, and how she smelled. *Erfahrung*, on the other hand, is the kind of experience that *happens to* one and that is the kind of experience that is consistent with Buber's notion of experiencing the otherness of the other. Gadamer describes *Erfahrung* as "experience as an event over which no one has control and which is not even determined by the particular weight of this or that observation, but in which everything is co-ordinated in a way that is ultimately incomprehensible" (p. 352). If you were to experience the homeless person in this second way, you'd experience her as a person rather than through a set of stereotypes or expectations. You might recall your eyes meeting and feeling for just that moment the sense of connection that you and she have as human beings despite the very real differences in your senses of security and community. "Experienced" people in this second sense are those who have become aware of what they have lived through, which means in part what has *happened to* them. And Gadamer notes that one form of experience as *Erfahrung* is experience of the other, "the Thou" (1989, p. 358).

Holding My Own Ground

The other moment in the primary tension of dialogue—holding my own ground—is easier for most people raised in Western traditions to understand, because of its connections with "rugged individuality." Understood as the label on one end of a continuum, holding my own ground is something that is done by an individual subject or intentional actor. You hold your own ground when you assert yourself or say exactly what's on your mind. One extreme version of this moment is present in communication teacher Barbara O'Keefe's (1997) description of the style of communication that is employed by the least developmentally sophisticated communicators she and her colleagues have studied. These people communicate in a way that O'Keefe calls "expressive." An infant communicates this way almost exclusively, but so do some adults. This way of communicating consists of

> simply thinking about the situation in relation to the self, evaluating thoughts in terms of whether they are disagreeable, repressing or misrepresenting disagreeable thoughts if uttering them might have negative consequences, but otherwise saying what comes to mind. (p. 104)

So, for example, if the baby feels bad, it cries, and if it feels good, it gurgles or smiles. What you see is what you get.

Holding my own ground presumes considerably more reflection, flexibility, and willingness to change than O'Keefe's expressive design logic, but, taken by itself, it strongly resembles what literature written in the 1970s and 1980s called "assertiveness." Assertiveness is behavior that "promotes equality in human relationships, enabling us to act in our own best interests, to stand up for ourselves without undue anxiety, to express honest feelings comfortably, to exercise personal rights without denying the rights of others" (Alberti and Emmons, 1990, p. 7). As the definition indicates, this literature encourages the assertive person to respect the "rights of others." But it emphasizes the two-step process of mental preparation and the development of behavioral skills that results in one being able to articulate and stand up for what one wants or believes.

By itself, standing my own ground can be viewed as being assertive or expressive, and letting the other happen to me can be understood as an experience that I receive or am subject to. This oppositional way of describing the tensional poles is useful, but it can also give the impression that both ends of the continuum are all about ME: what happens to me and what I make happen. Importantly, there is more to this primary tension of dialogue than the either/or of you happening to me or me happening to you.

So here's where we need to highlight what's misleading about the diagram we've provided: It makes the tension look like a connection between simple polarities, when it's not. The most important thing about poles in dialogue is that they are *in tension,* and this means that *both ends of the continuum are transformed by their interrelation.* So the other happens to me *while* and *as* I hold my own ground, and as a result, she happens to me in relation to my own position. In addition, I hold my own ground *in her presence* as she is happening to me. As a result, my own understanding of my position is fundamentally transformed by my experience of the other person. And vice versa; the other person's experiencing of me in relation to her is likely to transform her perception of her own identity and position. The constraints of language force us to talk about one end of this tension at a time, but our experience is that they are lived *together* or simultaneously.

This is an important point, so let us say it another way. When I live in this tension, my experience of the other person "happening to me" is strongly influenced by the position that I'm articulating (the ground that I'm holding), and the position that I'm expressing comes out as one that's strongly influenced by how the other is happening to me. In living communication, the two seemingly opposite moves (letting the other happen to me and holding my own ground) are *intimately interrelated.* And when lived in direct relation to one another, the two transform both the positions of the participants and their understanding of self and other.

Illustrations of the Tension

Here are two illustrations of how this works, one from Martin Buber's life and another from ours. Buber's autobiographical fragment called "Samuel and Agag" is a story of his lengthy conversation with "an observant Jew who followed the religious tradition in all the details of his life-pattern" (1973, p. 52). The two of them fell into a discussion of the section of the biblical book of Samuel in which Samuel delivered to King Saul the message that his dynastic rule would be taken from him by God because he had spared the life of Agag, the conquered prince of the Amalekites. Samuel's message to Saul was that obedience to God was more important than mercy. Buber told his conversation partner how, as a boy, he had been horrified to read how the heathen king Agag went up to Samuel with the words on his lips, "Surely the bitterness of death is past," and was butchered, "hewn to pieces" by Samuel. Buber writes that his "heart compelled me to read [this passage] over again or at least to think about the fact that this stood written in the Bible." He concluded, as he put it to his conversation partner, "I have never been able to believe that this is a message of God. I do not believe it." From one thoughtful Jew to another, it was very risky to assert that one did not believe something written in the Bible. Buber described what followed:

> With wrinkled forehead and contracted brows, the man sat opposite me and his glance flamed into my eyes. He remained silent, began to speak, became silent again. "So?" he broke forth at last. "So? You do not believe it?" "No," I answered, "I do not believe it." "So? so?" he repeated almost threateningly. "You do not believe it?" And I once again: "No." "What … what … ,"—he thrust the words before him one after the other—"what do you believe then?" "I believe," I replied without reflecting, "that Samuel has misunderstood God." And he, again slowly, but more softly than before: "So? You believe that?" And I: "Yes."
>
> Then we were both silent. But now something happened the like of which I have rarely seen before or since in this my long life. The angry countenance opposite me became transformed, as if a hand had passed over it soothing it. It lightened, cleared, was now turned toward me bright and clear. "Well," said the man with a positively gentle tender clarity. "I think so too." And again we became silent, for a good while. (pp. 52–53)

Buber and the man were both believers. The fact that Buber happened to the man is most apparent in the man's final reply: "I think so, too." But the fact that the man happened to Buber is also apparent in two things. The first is Buber's choice to include this fragment among the 20 key events of his 87-year life. The second is that in this conversation, Buber tested for the first time his previously unspoken decision, as he put it, to respond to the demand to choose between the Bible and God by choosing God (p. 53). Each also held his own ground, Buber in his disbelief and the man in his challenge. In addition, the dialogue transformed both moments for each man. Buber's experience of the man (and the man's experience of Buber) was transformed from that of a conversation partner to that of a co-conspirator in a potentially damning but personally compelling heresy. Buber's experience of his own position (and the man's experience of his) was transformed from one of lonely insistence to partnered confirmation.

There are also examples of this basic tension in our classrooms. As much as is possible, we work to foster dialogue in our classes by encouraging students to simultaneously let the other happen to them and to stand their own ground, and we attempt to do the same in relation to them. Some years ago, the primary challenge seemed to be the first moment in this tension. Students often found it difficult to listen to diverse others (let the others happen to them). Today the pole of standing one's own ground seems to be more challenging. Many students come to class with the conviction that political correctness means they have to be open to all views. Rather than engaging on issues with others who express positions they find incoherent or morally lacking, they smile, nod, and offer feedback focused on something safe like vocal delivery. When asked what they find compelling in an argument or to articulate substantive points of difference, they are often unable to do so. Superficial agreement often substitutes for engaged dialogue.

As a result, at the beginning of several of our communication courses, we attempt to enhance the potential for dialogue in two ways. Although we distribute a syllabus on the first day, almost all of the class time that day is spent exploring, not the course description, but the people in the room, beginning with us. Karen starts with a round of student responses to such questions as "What do you hope to get out of this class?" or perhaps "What do you most hope we do during this course, and what do you most hope we don't do?" Then she asks groups of two to three to form questions they would like answered about her. Often for a full class period she responds to questions about her academic background, experience teaching this course, spare-time activities, approach to teaching, test design, family history, expectations, and the degree to which she is excited about or disillusioned with contemporary students. There are also opportunities these first days to talk with, whenever possible, each person taking the course. At the end of the term, students often report that this time spent exploring *all* the people in class initiates and models a dialogic quality of contact, because both Karen and her students are put in positions where they let the others happen to them and they stand their own ground.

A second move we make is to help the class identify a limited number of topics they want to focus on throughout the term. These become topics for the speeches or discussions in public dialogue or group decision-making courses, for the research projects and case studies in a course on communication ethics, or for the series of "styles" assignments in the conflict course. This move permits sustained engagement on substantive issues, slows down some elements of the idea-pace of the course, and helps create the space for student self-reflection, enabling people taking the course to identify the beliefs and especially the values that filter their research and interpretations. This pedagogical move also helps students get beyond the stage of paraphrasing someone else's approach to an issue and into the experience of taking personal responsibility for the positions they advocate. In other words, we require assignments that offer students opportunities to stand their own ground by positioning themselves *ethically* in reference to some subject matter.

Here's one example of what sometimes happens. In a recent class of Karen's, a student we will call Jim took on the challenge of arguing in favor of sexual abstinence before marriage. He knew that his position was linked to his faith and his family's values, and he knew that his position was in the minority among his university peers. Others in the class were arguing against naïve "just say no" sex education programs, in favor of the morning-after pill and legalized prostitution. Jim knew that he had made an important choice for himself and that it would be an important choice for others to consider, but was unsure how to articulate his position in ways that enhanced dialogue. He knew that he did not want to portray himself as a preacher to his peers. He believed that quoting scripture would not be an effective way to engage his audience or persuade them to consider his position. Discussions with peers were part of the assigned preparation process, and in these discussions and e-mail conversations with Karen, Jim raised the concern that his position would be interpreted as a personal attack on or condemnation of his listeners. As he put it in an e-mail,

> The last thing that I want to do is make my audience feel as though I am preaching at them and telling them they are wrong and if they are having sex that they are all going to suffer huge consequences as a result of their actions .... All I am trying to do is make them ask questions and look inside themselves and see if what I present makes sense.

As Jim explored how to stand his ground, he realized that he did not want to give up his conviction or the opportunity to ask difficult questions simply to keep from offending anyone. One suggestion that he effectively incorporated into the first of his assigned speeches was to "steer away from being too apologetic for your position. You don't want to weaken it by worrying more about offending people than advocating for abstinence. I sense that you will get more respect than disdain."

And respect is what he gained. His listeners heard *him*—Jim—not just his position. They understood *him* and respected *him*, and this respect and understanding helped him achieve his communicative goal of getting them to ask questions and look inside themselves. Jim's ethical and moral presence helped generate the desired outcome, and the personal connection that occurred was more important than any one argument or persuasive appeal.

Importantly, Jim was also affected (transformed is only slightly too strong a word) by the communication events. As he let classmates and Karen happen to him, he was able to understand and articulate his position in ways he had not previously done. He moved from parroting the positions of his parents and the leaders of his faith community to choosing and explaining his own positions. Moments of anticipated and actual contact with others compelled Jim to reflect on his ground and to thoughtfully and assertively stand it.

The events of his preparation, presentation, and discussion of listener responses also transformed other aspects of the course. After Jim's talk, the topic of social perspectives on sex in this class was deepened beyond the superficial or selfish. Jim became a role model for standing your own ground while letting the other happen to you. Several students talked with Karen about how they too might advocate for positions they passionately and personally cared about in ways that were as direct, candid, and dialogically engaging as Jim had. They were particularly interested in prompting discussion that engaged not only arguments but also the value systems of the arguers themselves—as choice-making, ethically present persons.

CONCLUSION

In our experience, dialogue involves the negotiation of a variety of tensions, the most fundamental of which is holding my own ground and being open to the otherness of the other. To say that dialogue is tensional reminds us that (1) it is a dynamic, emergent process rather than any kind of steady state, and (2) it can be understood as happening *between* distinguishable moments or poles, each of which transforms the other. We understand that not all communication is dialogic—in fact, much of it is a series of monologues in which one end of the continuum we identify is emphasized over the other. Either the persons involved are only standing their own ground—asserting or expressing to their heart's content, almost regardless of who is present—or they are going along with what's said, regardless of their true beliefs. Dialogue, however, is made manifest when the fundamental tension between letting the other happen to me and holding my own ground is in play for all the parties involved. This tension characterizes dialogue in every context where we have experienced it—intimate contact, student advising, psychotherapy, mentoring, group decision making, public deliberation, patient-provider contact, conflict management, mediation, and superior-subordinate negotiation.

REVIEW QUESTIONS

1. How do we define *dialogue*?
2. Explain what "letting the other happen to me" means. Give an example.
3. Explain what "holding my own ground" means. Give an example.
4. Give an example from your own communication experience of holding your own ground *while* you were letting the other happen to you, and of letting the other happen to you *as* you were holding your own ground.
5. Explain how having the class identify a limited set of topics for the term can help them experience dialogue's central tension.

PROBES

1. Before you work on the tension we discuss here, think about how you negotiate both "privacy" and "disclosure" in your dating relationship(s). Notice how you work both sides of this tension at the same time. Notice how your privacy moves are affected by your disclosures, and vice versa. All this is also true about the basic tension of dialogue.
2. Identify and briefly discuss two different kinds of *experience* you've had, one that is obviously what German speakers would call *Erlebnis* and one that is obviously *Erfahrung*.
3. Some time in the next 48 hours, make a real effort to live this tension in one of your communication encounters. Immediately afterward, write down what you experienced. Bring your reflections to class, and discuss them with one to two classmates who have tried the same thing. What do you notice?

NOTE

1. We find Buber's "Autobiographical Fragments," published in 1973 as the book *Meetings*, to be a particularly fruitful source for articulating the experiential bases of his key insights and concepts. Buber collected these fragments shortly before he died, in response to the request of the editors of the *Library of Living Philosophers* to write an intellectual biography for their

volume on Buber. As Buber editor and translator Maurice Friedman notes, "These 'events and meetings' are in the fullest sense of the term 'teaching' and perhaps, in the end, the most real teaching that Martin Buber has left us .... Not only can one discover which tales 'speak to his condition,' but also the hidden teaching contained in the restraint with which Buber retells these 'legendary anecdotes' and in the order in which he has arranged them" (1973, pp. 4–5).

REFERENCES

Alberti, R. E., & Emmons, M. L. (1990). *Your perfect right: A guide to assertive living.* San Luis Obispo, CA: Impact.

Baxter, L. A., & Montgomery, B. W. (1996). *Relating: Dialogue and dialectics.* Mahwah, NJ: Lawrence Erlbaum.

Buber, M. (1970). *I and thou* (W. Kaufmann, Trans.). New York: Scribners.

Buber, M. (1973). *Meetings* (M. Friedman, Ed.). LaSalle, IL. Open Court Press.

Cissna, K. N., & Anderson, R. (1998). Theorizing about dialogic moments: The Buber-Rogers position and postmodern themes. *Communication Theory, 9,* 63–104.

Gadamer, H-G. (1989). *Truth and method* (2nd rev. ed.) (J. Weinsheimer & D. G. Marshall, Trans.) New York: Crossroads.

Levinas, E. (1996). *Emmanuel Levinas: Basic writings* (R. Bernasconi, S. Critchley, & A. Peperzak, Eds.). Bloomington: Indiana University Press.

Montgomery, B. W., & Baxter, L. A. (Eds.). (1998). *Dialectical approaches to studying personal relationships.* Mahwah, NJ: Lawrence Erlbaum.

O'Keefe, B. (1997). Variation, adaptation, and functional explanation in the study of message design. In G. Philipsen & T. L. Albrecht (Eds.), *Developing communication theories* (pp. 85–118). Albany: State University of New York Press.

———————

Fostering Dialogue Across Divides

Maggie Herzig and Laura Chasin

Martin Buber originally described "dialogue" as a kind of communication that can connect two individuals. Daniel Yankelovich, the author of the first reading in this chapter, extended this vision to public issues, and the authors of this reading join Yankelovich in this move. In fact, divisive public issues are the primary focus of the Public Conversations Project, whose directors wrote this essay. Maggie Herzig and Laura Chasin are two family therapists who, along with their colleagues, have developed an approach to public communication about difficult issues that has facilitated dialogue among people on opposite sides of such red-hot issues as abortion and gay-lesbian-bisexual-transgender rights.

The first part of this reading, taken from a publication titled *Fostering Dialogue Across Divides,* clarifies how a two-person vision of dialogue can also work in public life. This is a kind of communicating that can actually be applied to some of the most toxic public events we experience, such as polarized political diatribes, abusive labor-management conflicts, and shouting matches at school board meetings. The authors mention in the fourth paragraph the importance of the "tension" that Karen Zediker and I describe in the article before this one.

Next, this essay explains what the Public Conversations Project means by "dialogue." For them, dialogue is a conversation in which "people who have different beliefs and perspectives seek to develop mutual understanding." When people are in relationships characterized by distrust, animosity, stereotyping, and polarization, dialogue requires careful planning, communication agreements, and skilled facilitation.

The reading continues by clarifying differences between dialogue and other kinds of communicating, especially debate. Historically, debate has been a central feature of democratic governing, and all free societies are committed to "open discussion and debate." But as these authors explain, debate involves rules and produces outcomes that can make problems worse rather than better. The cartoon "Anatomy of Two Conversations" visualizes some of these differences.

The final section of this reading applies dialogue to the current problem of political polarization in the United States—the "Red-Blue divide." These pages are written for people who are motivated to reach across this divide. It provides five suggestions or steps that can be taken, each of which applies ideas that are developed in earlier parts of this reading. This section also illustrates the importance of questions. One of the insights of the Public Conversations Project is that the questions that dialogue partners ask can greatly affect the quality of their conversation. There are some excellent suggestions in this section.

I strongly encourage you to extend your understanding of dialogue by consulting the materials created by the Public Conversations Project. Their website is comprehensive and valuable—www.publicconversations.org. They are one of the most effective organizations at demonstrating the practical applicability and power of the kind of interpersonal communication called "dialogue."

1.1 THE ROLE OF DIALOGUE IN PUBLIC LIFE

The way we talk with each other makes a difference. And there is no single "best" way to talk.

Little League coaches shout simple instructions to young players.

Air traffic controllers speak in code with pilots.

"Fostering Dialogue Across Divides," 8 pages from 2 sources copyrighted by the Public Conversations Project. First 6 pages from Maggie Herzig and Laura Chasin, *Fostering Dialogue Across Divides: A Nuts and Bolts Guide from the Public Conversations Project*, Watertown, MA: Public Conversations Project, 2006, pp. 1–3, 138–140, 161, and 3 pages from a pamphlet "Reaching Out Across the Red-Blue Divide, One Person at a Time from website www.publicconversations.org/upload/red-blue. Reprinted by permission of Public Conversations Project.

Debaters cite evidence that supports their stand and counters an opposing position.

Activists proclaim short potent slogans to promote their causes.

In each case, there is a purpose to be served, and a distinctive way of talking serves that purpose. A baseball player instantly shifts his position on hearing the coach's abbreviated command. Collisions are averted through coded communication among people who speak different languages. Debaters argue for and against competing ideas. Activists' slogans energize allies and summon others to join the cause.

Dialogue is yet another way of talking that serves a distinct purpose. An effective dialogue reduces stereotyping and increases mutual understanding. Through dialogue, people who seem intractably opposed often change the way they view and relate to each other—even as they maintain the commitments that underlie their views. They often discover shared values and concerns which may lead to collaborative actions that were previously unthinkable.

Dialogue participants talk in ways that serve such purposes, communicating their views, experiences and values without attacking their opponents personally or "trashing" opposing perspectives. Dialogue participants talk about the experiences and values underlying their own views. They ask real questions. They avoid interruptions. They listen.

The need for dialogue in our public life is less well understood than the need for debate and activism. In history and civics classes in the US, debate and political activism are presented as time-honored tools in the toolbox of democracy, and rightly so. It was largely through these forms of public engagement that slavery and segregation were ended, women and African Americans got the vote, and the war in Vietnam was ended sooner rather than later.

Dialogue has a vital, if quieter, role to play in a resilient and civil democratic society. It can build bridges across divides in the body politic. It can promote healing in small communities that are struggling with a controversy. It can also reduce the likelihood of gridlock in the halls of Congress, hatred in the arena of public opinion, and potentially dangerous misrepresentations in our sound-bite saturated media.

Unbalanced by sufficient dialogue, the constructive impact of debate and activism has diminished in recent decades as public rhetoric has become riddled with polarizing assertions and demonizing stereotypes. Democratic life suffers as we increasingly gravitate to people who share our views and to media presentations that present us with the most offensive representatives of the other side. As we become selectively informed, we become selectively ignorant and increasingly unable to appreciate the extent of our ignorance.

In a polarized social and political climate, meaningful dialogue rarely happens without considerable thought and planning. In this guide we offer some of what we and our colleagues at the Public Conversations Project have come to regard as the nuts and bolts of effective dialogue design and facilitation. We hope this resource will be useful to people who are concerned about polarization and are working to bridge costly divides.

1.2 WHAT WE MEAN BY "DIALOGUE"

The word "dialogue" is used in many ways. It is sometimes used to refer to a heart-to-heart conversation between two people who care deeply about each other and who want their relationship to survive the tumult of a serious disagreement.

Some people call almost any exchange of different views a dialogue. For example, it may be used to attract an audience to an event that involves a debate between experts, followed by a Q&A session with the audience.

At PCP, we use the word "dialogue" to refer to a conversation in which people who have different beliefs and perspectives seek to develop mutual understanding. While doing so, they typically experience a softening of stereotypes and develop more trusting relationships. They often gain fresh perspectives on the costs of the conflict and begin to see new possibilities for interaction and action outside of the dialogue room.

Dialogue is very different from debate. In fact, participants in dialogue often agree explicitly to set aside argument so that they can focus on mutual understanding. Dialogue is also different from mediation, conflict resolution, and problem solving, although it may serve as a prelude to or an aspect of such processes. Finally, dialogue differs from group therapy and other conversations that have personal growth as their primary goal.

As we use the term, a dialogue can occur with little structure or planning among people whose bonds are stronger than their differences, among strangers who are genuinely interested in each others' views, and among people whose conflicts are neither intense nor long-standing. However, when people are in relationships characterized by distrust, animosity, stereotyping, and polarization, it may be very difficult to effectively pursue the goals of dialogue without

- careful, collaborative planning that ensures clarity about what the dialogue is and isn't, and also fosters alignment between the goals of the dialogue and participants' wishes.
- communication agreements that discourage counter-productive ways of talking about the issues and encourage genuine inquiry.
- meeting designs that include supportive structures for reflecting, listening, and speaking questions that invite new ways of thinking and talking about the issues.
- facilitation that is informed by careful preparation and responsive to the emerging needs and interests of the participants.

What Dialogue Is

The dialogues that PCP designs and facilitates are conversations in which the participants' primary goal is to pursue mutual understanding rather than agreement or immediate solutions. As participants pursue this goal, they sometimes decide to pursue other goals. For example, dialogue groups sometimes decide to become better informed together or to build consensus about ways that they can act on shared values.

What Dialogue Is Not

Dialogue is distinct from debate; in fact, participants in dialogue often explicitly agree to set aside persuasion and debate so that they can focus on mutual understanding. Dialogue is also different from mediation, conflict resolution, and problem solving although it may serve as a prelude to or aspect of such processes.

What Participants Do

- They listen and are listened to with care.
- They speak and are spoken to in a respectful manner.
- They share airtime so that all speakers can be heard.
- They learn about the perspectives of others.
- They reflect on their own views.

What Participants Gain

- Mutual understanding, which may stimulate new ideas for learning and action
- Communication skills that can be used in other difficult conversations

What It Takes

Dialogue is present any time people genuinely seek mutual understanding, setting aside for that time the urge to persuade or the pressure to decide. It can occur spontaneously, among friends, in classrooms, in organizations, or even among strangers. When people are experiencing polarized conflict, however, we have found that it is helpful if they

- have clarity and consensus about the purposes of the conversation.
- make communication agreements that will help them to achieve their purposes.
- have a facilitator whose sole responsibility is to help the participants honor their agreements and reach their shared purposes.

REACHING OUT ACROSS THE RED-BLUE DIVIDE, ONE PERSON AT A TIME

What This Guide Offers

This guide offers a step-by-step approach to inviting one other person—someone whose perspectives differ from your own—into a conversation in which

- you both agree to set aside the desire to persuade the other and instead focus on developing a better understanding of each other's perspectives, and the hopes, fears and values that underlie those perspectives.

Distinguishing Debate from Dialogue*

Debate	Dialogue
Premeeting communication between sponsors and participants is minimal and largely irrelevant to what follows.	Premeeting contacts and preparation of participants are essential elements of the full process.
Participants tend to be leaders known for propounding a carefully crafted position. The personas displayed in the debate are usually already familiar to the public. The behavior of the participants tends to conform to stereotypes.	Those chosen to participate are not necessarily outspoken leaders. Whoever they are, they speak as individuals whose own unique experiences differ in some respect from others on their side. Their behavior is likely to vary in some degree and along some dimensions from stereotypic images others may hold of them.
The atmosphere is threatening; attacks and interruptions are expected by participants and are usually permitted by moderators.	The atmosphere is one of safety; facilitators propose, get agreement on, and enforce clear ground rules to enhance safety and promote respectful exchange.
Participants speak as representatives of groups.	Participants speak as individuals, from their own unique experience.
Participants speak to their own constituents and, perhaps, to the undecided middle.	Participants speak to each other.
Differences within sides are denied or minimized.	Differences among participants on the same side are revealed as individual and personal foundations of beliefs and values are explored.
Participants express unswerving commitment to a point of view, approach, or idea.	Participants express uncertainties as well as deeply held beliefs.
Participants listen in order to refute the other side's data and to expose faulty logic in their arguments. Questions are asked from a position of certainty. These questions are often rhetorical challenges or disguised statements.	Participants listen to understand and gain insight into the beliefs and concerns of the others. Questions are asked from a position of curiosity.
Statements are predictable and offer little new information.	New information surfaces.
Success requires simple impassioned statements.	Success requires exploration of the complexities of the issue being discussed.
Debates operate within the constraints of the dominant public discourse. The discourse defines the problem and the options for resolution. It assumes that fundamental needs and values are already clearly understood.	Participants are encouraged to question the dominant public discourse, that is, to express fundamental needs that may or may not be reflected in the discourse and to explore various options for problem definition and resolution. Participants may discover inadequacies in the usual language and concepts used in the public debate.

*This table contrasts debate as commonly seen on television with the kind of dialogue we aim to promote in dialogue sessions conducted by the Public Conversations Project.

- you both agree to pursue understanding and to avoid the pattern of attack and defend.
- you both choose to address questions designed to open up new possibilities for moving beyond stale stereotypes and limiting assumptions.

Why Bother to Reach Across the Divide?

Many people have at least one important relationship that has been frayed by painful conversations about political differences or constrained due to fear of divisiveness. What alternatives are there? You can let media pundits and campaign strategists tell you that polarization is inevitable and hopeless. Or you can consider taking a collaborative journey with someone who is important to you, neither paralyzed with fear of the rough waters, nor unprepared for predictable strong currents. You and your conversational partner will be best prepared if you bring (1) shared hopes for the experience, (2) the intention to work as a team, and (3) a good map that has guided others on similar journeys. We hope this guide will help prepare you to speak about your passions and concerns in ways that can be heard, and to hear others' concerns and passions with new empathy and understanding—even if you continue to disagree.

Are You Ready?

Are you emotionally ready to resist the strong pull toward polarization? What's at the heart of your desire to reach out to the person you have in mind? Is pursuing mutual understanding enough, or are you likely to feel satisfied only if you can persuade them to concede certain points? What do you know about yourself and the contexts in which you are able—or not so able—to listen without interrupting and to speak with care? Are you open to the possibility—and could you gracefully accept—that the other person might decline your invitation?

Are the Conditions Right?

Do you have a conversational partner in mind who you believe will make the same kind of effort you are prepared to make? Is there something about your relationship that will motivate both of you to approach the conversation with a positive spirit? Will you have a chance to propose a dialogue in ways that don't rush or pressure the other person? Will you be able to invite him or her to thoughtfully consider not only the invitation but the specific ideas offered here—ideas that you might together modify? Can you find a time to talk that is private and free from distraction?

Anatomy of Two Conversations

If You Decide to Go Forward, Take It One Step at a Time

Extend the invitation with *clarity about its purpose* and a *spirit of collaboration*. If the invitation is declined, accept that response and talk to someone else.

> *Example*—"I've been talking to people who share my general perspective about what's happening politically. I've hesitated to talk across the red-blue divide for fear of having a fruitless and divisive battle. Would you be willing to have a conversation with me, setting aside any impulse to persuade, instead focusing on better understanding each other and being understood for what we believe?"
>
> [Pause for a response, continuing if appropriate.]
>
> "I have a conversational roadmap, some questions, and also some suggested agreements. Would you be willing to look at them, and if you're interested, we can figure out together how to proceed?"
>
> [If you decide to move forward ...]

Make some communication agreements.

> *Example*—"I hope we can bring our best selves to what could be a hard conversation. Can we agree to
>
> * *share speaking and listening time,* not interrupting each other and limiting ourselves to a preset amount of time (e.g., 4 minutes) for the opening questions?
> * *speak for ourselves* from our personal experience, not trying to represent or defend an entire political party or ideological approach?
> * *maintain the spirit of dialogue* by avoiding a critical or dismissive tone, aiming simply to understand (not to persuade)?"

Select some opening questions and take turns responding to them.

> *Example*—"Here are some suggested questions for opening the dialogue (see page 576). The suggested format is to
>
> * *read each question set*
> * *take a couple minutes to reflect* on how we want to respond, then ...
> * Each of us can *take a specified amount of time* (e.g., up to 3 or 4 minutes) for each set of questions. If one of us forgets about time, we can signal that person to wrap up. During this very structured part of the dialogue, we can jot notes to remember what we want to explore or ask about later in our conversation."

Open the conversation to each other's questions and deeper exploration.

> *Example*—"This is a less structured time, but it's still important to maintain agreements that we made. This is our chance to
>
> * *ask each other questions*—not rhetorical questions—that reflect genuine curiosity about each other's experiences and perspectives;
> * *pursue topics* that will help us further reflect on our own views, learn about each other's views, unpack the meanings we associate with certain terms, and, perhaps, identify common concerns and values.

First, let's see if we have questions for each other."

[If there are time constraints, agree to save a preset amount of time, perhaps 10 minutes, to close the conversation.]

Reflect on and close the conversation.

Example—"This is a time to say something about what this conversation was like and what we did or did not do that contributed in a positive way. We also can exchange parting words—perhaps words of appreciation, expressions of hope, or ideas about next steps."

Use Questions That Truly Open the Conversation and Avoid Narrow Debate

Some suggestions appear below. These questions are best used in the order presented here. Each question set involves one person speaking without interruption and the other listening, then the other answering the same questions, also without interruption. Take a couple minutes to reflect silently before answering questions. This is important! Thinking before speaking is a good idea, especially if you want to avoid the somewhat habitual and reactive exchanges common in polarized discussions.

Some Suggested Opening Questions:

First question set—your hopes for the dialogue and your underlying values:

- What hopes and concerns do you bring to this conversation?
- What values do you hold that lead you to want to reach across the red-blue divide?
- Where or how did you learn those values?

Second question set—sharing what's at the heart of your perspective:

- What is at the heart of your political leanings (e.g., what concerns or values underlie them) and what would you be willing to share about your life experiences that might convey what those things mean to you?

Third question set—reflecting upon complexities in your views:

- Within your general perspective on the issue(s), do you experience any dilemmas or mixed feelings, or are there gray areas in your thinking?
- In what ways have you felt out of step with the party or advocacy groups you generally support, or in what ways do those groups not fully reflect what's important to you?

Optional question set—stepping away from stereotypes:

- During divisive political debates, are there ways that your values and perspectives are stereotyped by the "other side"? If so, what is it about who you are and what you care about that makes those stereotypes especially frustrating or painful? Are there some stereotypes of your own party that you feel are somewhat deserved—even if they are not fully true—given the rhetoric used in political debates?

If you try these exercises, please let us know how it goes. Also let us know if you have invented other useful approaches or have questions that you'd like to share: e-mail **mherzig@publicconversations.org.**

REVIEW QUESTIONS

1. Describe these authors' version of the tension that Zediker and I explain in the previous reading.
2. Compare and contrast the contributions of debate and dialogue to democratic government.
3. Describe how dialogue is different from mediation and problem solving.
4. Explain how listening functions differently in debate and in dialogue.
5. Explain how questions function differently in debate and in dialogue.
6. Describe the differences in assumptions that ground debate and dialogue.

PROBES

1. Debate is widely recognized as an important feature of democracy. But as this article clarifies, it also can create problems. Describe the complementary role that dialogue can play in democratic decision making.
2. Paraphrase, and then respond to, these authors' argument for the value of reaching across the Red-Blue divide.
3. How does the form of questions affect communication?

———

Turning Enemies into Friends

Jonathan Sacks

This essay comes from a book titled *After Terror: Promoting Dialogue Among Civilizations.* Akbar Ahmed, who wrote "Talking Can Stop Hate" in Chapter 11, is this book's senior editor. The author of this particular essay, Jonathan Sacks, is chief rabbi of the United Hebrew Congregations of the Commonwealth. Sacks has been honored by many people including the Archbishop of Canterbury and has published seven books about the politics of hope.

The central idea of this essay is that a real hero is someone who uses communication to turn an enemy into a friend. In friendship, instead of fighting each other, the friends can fight the problems that confront them both, such as poverty, hunger, starvation, disease, and injustice. This might sound like a grandiose, impractical, and unrealistic idea, but Rabbi Sacks argues that it is both intensely practical and very possible.

I include this article—and Ahmed's essay in Chapter 11—because, as is obvious to anyone who observes the current world situation, the primary threat to peaceful prosperity in the world of the first half of the 21st century is the conflict among religions. As I write this, over 3000 U.S. servicemen and -women have died in wars in Afghanistan and Iraq, conflicts that are anchored in and fueled by religious hatred. Civil war between Sunni and Shiite Muslims in Iraq is killing thousands of additional people, as is civil war between Hamas and Fatah militants in Palestine. Jewish-Palestinian violence also continues, religiously based genocide rains terror in Darfur, and thousands of others are killed for their religious beliefs in Indonesia. Religion, which is supposed to be the main solution to hatred, is clearly the main problem today. Humans desperately need to reclaim the commitments to peace, justice, and love that are central to Islam, Christianity, and Judaism.

Rabbi Sacks suggests that the key is courage. Just as war demands physical courage, peace and reconciliation demand moral courage, "and that is far more rare." "In pursuit of peace, even great leaders are afraid to take the risk. The late [Egyptian president] Anwar Sadat and [Israeli prime minister] Yitzhak Rabin had the courage to take that risk, and both paid for it with their lives."

But national, regional, and local events demand this kind of courage, Sacks writes. You would think that religions would best promote forgiveness and reconciliation, but their efforts to enhance spiritual identity or an "Us" almost always also create a polarized "Them." Sacks uses an analysis of the biblical story of Cain and Abel to emphasize the necessity of dialogue to combat this division. "If hostility is not discharged through dialogue," he writes, "it will not disappear."

Sacks also argues that dialogic conversation can be considered to be "a form of prayer." "This is a radical idea," he notes, but he explains how it can be a helpful one. One insight offered by the three Abrahamic faiths of Judaism, Christianity, and Islam is that "language is holy." This is Sacks' way of saying what Stuart Sigman writes in Chapter 2 of this book: Communication is consequential. Language, or communication, or the ways people talk with one another can span "the metaphysical abyss between one center of consciousness [person] and another." This is an important idea that I hope you take from this book: *Communication matters.* How you talk and listen affects both you and others. There is a direct connection between the quality of your communication and the quality of your life (see Chapter 2).

In the final section of this article, Sacks argues that either religions will continue to be a source of long and bloody battles, which will lead people away from them to purely secular lives, or "religions will rise to the challenge." As a Jew, he understands that, for him, this means that, among other things, he must give up any vestige of hate for Germans because of their role in the Holocaust. This is an example of the kind of moral courage that is required.

The point of this article is that the huge, agonizing, and seemingly impossible problems that fill the news and define the "War on Terror" can be lessened, if not solved, with communication. It obviously is not as easy as that sentence implies, but it is actually possible for every person reading these words—for you—to do something about these problems. You can think globally and act locally. You can learn to communicate in the ways described by the writers in this book and to bring these ways into your everyday communicating.

Twenty centuries ago, Judaism's sages posed the question: Who is a hero? In most literatures until recent times, a hero was one who performed mighty deeds on the battlefield, who fought, killed, and perhaps died in a noble cause. A hero is one who defeats his enemies. The rabbis thought otherwise. *Who is a hero? One who turns an enemy into a friend.*

I find that answer profoundly wise. If I defeat you, I win and you lose. But in truth, I also lose, because by diminishing you, I diminish myself. But if, in a moment of truth, I forgive you and you forgive me, then forgiveness leads to reconciliation. Reconciliation leads to friendship. And in friendship, instead of fighting one another, we can fight together the problems we share: poverty, hunger, starvation, disease, violence, injustice, and all the other injuries that still scar the face of our world. You gain, I gain, and all those with whom we are associated gain as well. We gain economically, politically, but above all spiritually. My world has become bigger because it now includes you. Who is a hero? One who turns an enemy into a friend.

How different the world would look if that idea prevailed. In the summer of 1999 I stood in the streets of Pristina, in Kosovo, amidst the wreckage of war. The NATO operation had just come to an end. The Kosovan Albanians had returned home. But in the air there was an atmosphere of bitterness and anger. Months earlier, the Albanians were in terror of the Serbs. Now the Serbs feared reprisals from the Albanians. There was peace, but not real peace. War had ended, but reconciliation had not begun. Many of the soldiers with whom I spoke feared for the future. They thought that some day—perhaps not tomorrow, not next year, but sometime—the conflict would begin again, as it has so often in that part of the world.

It was there, surrounded by broken buildings and broken lives, that I understood how one word has the power to change the world: *forgiveness.* If we can forgive others, and act so that others can forgive us, then we can live with the past without being held prisoner by the past. But only if we forgive. Without that we condemn ourselves and our children to fight old battles again and again, with the same bloodshed, the same destruction, the same waste of the human spirit, the same devastation of God's world.

Breaking the cycle is anything but easy. War needs *physical* courage. Reconciliation demands *moral* courage, and that is far more rare. In war, ordinary people become heroes. In pursuit of peace, even great leaders are afraid to take the risk. The late Anwar Sadat and Yitzhak Rabin had the courage to take that risk, and both paid for it with their lives.

Yet if humanity is to survive the twenty-first century, there is no other way. Our capacity for destruction has grown too large. Our ability to use new communications technologies to transmit hate has grown too great. The time has passed when antagonisms were local, containable, limited in their reach. The primary beneficiary of globalization has been terror—anger felt in one place, translated into devastation in another. War is fought on a battlefield. Terror has no battlefield. It has become global. Though it can be contained by physical measures, ultimately it must be fought in the mind. In the short term, conflicts are won by weapons. In the long run, they are won by ideas.

Early in the Second World War the poet W. H. Auden said, "We must love one another or die." That may be too lofty a hope, but at the very least we must try to turn enemies into friends. We must turn the clash of civilizations into a conversation between civilizations. In this, the world's great faiths must take a lead.

IS RELIGION PRIMARILY A SOURCE OF CONFLICT?

Most religions value peace. Why, then, have they so often been a source of conflict? The word "religion" comes from the Latin root meaning "to bind." Religions bind people to one another and to God. They form a "We" greater than the "I." They create, in other words, group identity. That is precisely their power today. The twentieth century was dominated by the politics of ideology. The twenty-first century will be dominated by the politics of identity, and when it comes to identity, people turn to religion, for it contains humanity's deepest answers to the questions: Who am I? Why am I here? Of which narrative am I a part? How then shall I live?

However, the very process of creating an "Us" involves creating a "Them"—the people *not like us*, the other, the outsider, the infidel, the unredeemed, those who stand outside the circle of salvation. That is why, at the very time they are involved in creating community *within* their borders, religions can create conflict *across* those borders. That is why they both heal and harm, mend and destroy.

The Hebrew Bible contains a fateful warning at the beginning of its story of mankind. The first two human children, Cain and Abel, bring an offering to God—the first recorded act of religious worship. That led to rivalry, which led to animosity, which led to fratricide. The implication is unmistakable. Religion is like fire. It warms, but it also burns, and we are the guardians of the flame.

The original Hebrew text of the story of Cain and Abel contains an extraordinary verse which, because of its fractured syntax, is impossible to translate. Standard English versions have something like the following:

> Cain said to his brother Abel, "Let's go out to the field." And while they were in the field, Cain attacked his brother Abel and killed him. (Genesis 4:8)

However, the words, "Let's go out to the field" are not in the original text. Literally translated, the text reads:

> Cain said to his brother Abel... And while they were in the field, Cain attacked his brother Abel and killed him.

"Cain said," but we do not discover what he said. The sentence breaks off midway. Words fail. Conversation ceases. The dialogue is interrupted. The two brothers can no longer speak to one another. In this subtle but unmistakable way the Bible is signaling one of its most fundamental truths. *When words fail, violence begins.*

It is a point the Bible makes more than once. It happens in the case of Joseph, Jacob's favorite son:

> When his brothers saw that their father loved him more than any of them, they hated him and could not speak a friendly word to him. (Genesis 37:4)

Their animosity festered. At one stage, the brothers thought of murdering Joseph. Eventually they sold him into slavery.

Centuries later, King David's son Absalom discovers that his half-brother Amnon has raped his sister Tamar. At the time, he said nothing:

> Absalom did not utter a word to Amnon, either good or bad; he hated Amnon because he had violated his sister Tamar. (2 Samuel 13:22)

This was the silence not of forgiveness but of cold calculation. Two years later, Absalom took revenge.

In the case of Joseph, the biblical text contains another nuance lost in translation. The Hebrew phrase translated as "they hated him and could not speak a friendly word to him" literally means "they could not *speak him to peace.*" As in the case of Cain and Abel, syntactic awkwardness signals a powerful message. Communication is our greatest tool of conflict resolution. If hostility is not discharged through dialogue, it will not disappear. Instead, it will grow. Speech leads to peace if we can keep the conversation going, not allowing it to falter or break down under the pressure of strong emotion. Pain expressed, listened to, heeded, can be resolved. Pain unheard and unheeded, eventually explodes. In the process, lives are lost.

CONVERSATION AS PRAYER

The Babylonian Talmud (*Berakhot* 26b) contains a phrase (*Ein sichah ela tefillah*) which literally means, "Conversation is a form of prayer." This is a radical idea. In conversation I open myself up to an other. Speaking, I give voice to my hopes and fears. Listening, I hear another self and momentarily experience the world from a different perspective. Through encountering the human other, I learn what it is to encounter the Divine Other, the ultimate reality beyond the self. Prayer is an act not only of speaking but also of listening. Conversation is a form of prayer. In the give-and-take of speech lies the heart of our humanity. Genesis 2:7 states: "And the Lord God formed man from the dust of the earth and breathed into his nostrils the breath of life, and man became a living being." An ancient translation reads the last phrase as "and man became *a speaking soul.*" Speaking is what makes us human. The human body is a mix of chemicals structured by DNA, what the Bible calls "dust of the earth." It is the use of language that infuses the body with the "breath of God." The highest definition of *Homo sapiens* is "the form of life that speaks."

It is often said that the Abrahamic faiths—Judaism, Christianity, and Islam—are the three great "religions of revelation." That is the wrong way to define their distinctiveness. *All* ancient faiths believed in revelation. They believed that the gods were to be found in phenomena of nature: the wind, the rain, the sun, the sea, the storm. What made the three Abrahamic monotheisms different is not that they believed that God reveals himself, but rather that he does so in *words*. They believe that *language is holy*.

Forces of nature signify power. Words signify meaning. Nature is indifferent to mankind. Language is the unique possession of mankind. What makes Judaism, Christianity, and Islam different from other faiths is that they conceive of God as personal, and the mark of the personal is that *God speaks*. Language is the only thing that spans the metaphysical abyss between one center of consciousness and another. It redeems our solitude, affirming that in the vast echoing universe we are not alone.

Therefore, to be true to our relationship with God, Jews, Christians, and Muslims must show that speech is greater than power, conversation more compelling than the use of force. God has taught us to listen to him for a reason: to teach us to listen to the other, the human other who, though not in our image, is nonetheless in his.

FROM CONFLICT AND VIOLENCE TO RECONCILIATION AND PEACE

Beginning in the sixteenth century, Europe embarked on a long process generally known as secularization. First science, then knowledge generally, then politics and power, and finally culture, sought and gained their independence from religion. Thus were born the secular university, the secular nation-state, and secular society.

The conventional wisdom is that these things happened because people stopped believing in God. In fact, it was not so. They happened because good, thoughtful, and reasonable people came to the conclusion that *people of God could not live peaceably with one another*. It was not God who failed but those who claimed to be his representatives on earth.

The closest analogy to the new international disorder of the twenty-first century is the age—the sixteenth and seventeenth centuries—of the great European wars of religion. Two stark choices lie ahead of us. Either religions will continue to be a source of conflict, in which case, after long and bloody battles, the world will be re-secularized, or religions will rise to the challenge. I have suggested that this challenge was implicit in the Abrahamic monotheisms from the very outset. The task God set and continues to set us was not to conquer and convert the world. That is the language of imperialism, not religious faith. It is to listen to the human other as if the Divine Other were speaking to us through him or her. I do not claim that this is easy. I do claim that it is necessary.

I am a Jew, and as a Jew, I carry with me the tears and sufferings of my grandparents, and theirs, through the generations. The story of my people is the story of a thousand years of exiles and expulsions, persecutions and pogroms, beginning with the First Crusade and culminating in the murder of two-thirds of Europe's Jews. For centuries, Jews knew that they, or their children, risked being murdered simply because they were Jews. How can I let go of that pain when it is written into my very soul?

Yet, for the sake of my children I must. Will I bring one victim of the Holocaust back to life by hating Germans? Does loving God more entitle me to love other people less? If I ask God to forgive me, does he not ask me to forgive others? The duty I owe my ancestors who died because of their faith is to build a world in which people no longer die because of their faith. I honor the past by learning from it, by refusing to add pain to pain, grief to grief. That is why we must answer hatred with love, violence with peace, and conflict with reconciliation.

Today God has given us no choice. There was a time when our ancestors lived surrounded by people who were like them. They could afford to say, "We are right. The rest of the world is wrong." We are no longer in that situation. We live consciously in the presence of difference. Our lives, our safety, our environment, our very future, are bound up with countries far away and cultures unlike our own. God has brought us eyeball to eyeball with the complex interdependence of his world, and now he is asking us: Can we recognize God's image in someone who is not in our image? Can you discern my unity in your diversity?

It took the death of 6 million people to bring Jews and Christians together in mutual dignity and respect. How many more people will have to die in the Middle East, Kashmir, Northern Ireland, the Balkans, before we understand that there are many faiths but God has given us only one world in which to live together. The time has come for us to replace the clash of civilizations with a respectful conversation between civilizations, and begin the hard but sacred task of turning enemies into friends.

REVIEW QUESTIONS

1. What is a rabbi?
2. "War needs _____ courage. Reconciliation demands _____ courage."
3. What conclusion does Sacks draw from his analysis of the biblical story of Cain and Abel?
4. Everybody knows that silence can be comforting. But the silence that Sacks discusses has the opposite effect. Explain.
5. List the three "Abrahamic faiths." What does "Abrahamic" mean?

PROBES

1. Sacks writes that one main beneficiary of globalization has been terror. What does he mean? How have enhanced worldwide transportation, the

internationalization of business, the growth of global media, and the end of the Cold War all promoted terrorist activities?

2. Explain what Sacks means when he writes that "conversation is a form of prayer."

3. Explain the following quotation and paraphrase the point Sacks makes about it: "What makes Judaism, Christianity, and Islam different from other faiths is that they conceive of God as personal, and the mark of the personal is that *God speaks*."

4. What kind of listening is Sacks urging when he says we should "listen to the human other as if the Divine Other were speaking to us through him or her"?

5. Sacks writes, "As a Jew...the duty I owe my ancestors who died because of their faith is to build a world in which people no longer die because of their faith." Explain.

> *Ideas are clean. They soar in the serene supernal. I can take*
> *them out and look at them, they fit in books, they lead me*
> *down that narrow way. And in the morning they are there.*
> *Ideas are straight—*
> *But the world is round, and a*
> *messy mortal is my friend.*
> *Come walk with me in the mud....*
>
> —Hugh Prather

Photo Credits

Index

gestures and, 147–149
power of, 161–166
thought-word relationship, 138–139
written words, 137
Words to Live By: Inspiration for Every Day
(Easwaran), 222
workplace conversations, 57
worldviews and perception, 200
written words, 137

Yankelovich, Daniel, 549–557
Yarbrough, Elaine, 154

"yes, no" in communicaiton, 163–164
"you" in communication, 162
You Just Don't Understand:
Women and Men in Communication
(Tannen), 144

Zediker, Karen E., 80–91, 196–212, 225–244,
378–390, 557–567
Zen Buddhism, 219
Zinn, Maxine Baca, 510